# Macromedia®
# Flash® MX
# Professional 2004
# UNLEASHED

David Vogeleer
Matthew Pizzi

 800 East 96th Street, Indianapolis, Indiana 46240 USA

# Macromedia Flash MX Professional 2004 Unleashed

International Standard Book Number: 0-672-32606-X

Library of Congress Catalog Card Number: 2003107887

Printed in the United States of America

First Printing: January 2004

07   06   05   04        4   3   2   1

## Trademarks

## Warning and Disclaimer

## Bulk Sales

Sams Publishing offers excellent discounts on this book when ordered in quantity for bulk purchases or special sales. For more information, please contact

**U.S. Corporate and Government Sales**
**1-800-382-3419**
**corpsales@pearsontechgroup.com**

For sales outside of the United States, please contact

**International Sales**
**1-317-428-3341**
**international@pearsontechgroup.com**

**Acquisitions Editor**
Shelley Johnston

**Development Editor**
Damon Jordan

**Managing Editor**
Charlotte Clapp

**Project Editor**
Elizabeth Finney

**Copy Editors**
Margaret Berson
Kate Givens

**Indexer**
Ginny Bess

**Proofreader**
Juli Cook

**Technical Editors**
David Emberton
Steve Heckler

**Publishing Coordinator**
Vanessa Evans

**Multimedia Developer**
Dan Scherf

**Designer**
Gary Adair

# Contents at a Glance

# Table of Contents

# About the Authors

**David Vogeleer** is a Macromedia-certified Flash developer and instructor out of Richmond, Virginia. He has been working in Flash since version 4, focusing mainly on ActionScript. Currently freelancing, he also continues to speak at user groups and classes up and down the East Coast. He is also an avid poster on www.FlashMagazine.com as well as being coadministrator of www.EMLlabs.com, a Flash and dynamic content resource. And after all that, he still manages to occasionally add content to his personal site for experiments, www.evolutionar-e.com, and to go snowboarding.

**Matthew Pizzi** is the Training Director at Train Simple, a software training company specializing in multimedia products, located in Santa Monica, California. Matthew has been teaching fulltime for five years and is the author of multiple training CDs, including his "Up to Speed" series, offering computer-based training in Flash, Dreamweaver, Final Cut Pro and Photoshop. For more information on classes or training CDs, visit www.trainsimple.com.

# Dedication

*I would like to dedicate this book to my grandfathers, who have always been interested in my "computer stuff."*

—David Vogeleer

# Acknowledgments

I want to start by thanking Sams for the opportunity to take the lead role in authoring this book. Individually, and in no particular order, I would like to thank Shelley Johnston for a lot of things, but especially the Twinkies. Thanks to Damon Jordan, Elizabeth Finney, Margaret Berson, Kate Givens, Steve Heckler, David Emberton, Ginny Bess, and Juli Cook, as well as all the other people who worked on this book whom I did not have the pleasure of working with directly; their work has been invaluable. Also, big thanks to Eddie for really stepping up with EMLlabs.com while I was occupied, and to Kevin and Todd for your overwhelming support. Of course, thanks to my parents for all the support they gave, and to God for getting me through some long nights. And to all my other friends and family who have no idea what I do for a living, but support me anyway.

—David Vogeleer

# We Want to Hear from You!

As the reader of this book, *you* are our most important critic and commentator. We value your opinion and want to know what we're doing right, what we could do better, what areas you'd like to see us publish in, and any other words of wisdom you're willing to pass our way.

You can email or write me directly to let me know what you did or didn't like about this book—as well as what we can do to make our books stronger.

*Please note that I cannot help you with technical problems related to the topic of this book, and that due to the high volume of mail I receive, I might not be able to reply to every message.*

When you write, please be sure to include this book's title and author as well as your name and phone or email address. I will carefully review your comments and share them with the author and editors who worked on the book.

E-mail:      graphics@samspublishing.com

Mail:        Mark Taber
             Associate Publisher
             Sams Publishing
             800 East 96th Street
             Indianapolis, IN 46240 USA

## Reader Services

For more information about this book or others from Sams Publishing, visit our Web site at www.samspublishing.com. Type the ISBN (excluding hyphens) or the title of the book in the Search box to find the book you're looking for.

# Introduction

Macromedia Flash MX Professional 2004 is the latest in the Flash family of software. Flash was originally just a vector animation tool but is now one of the most advanced programs for creating Rich Internet applications to provide powerful user experiences. Not only is the player that plays Flash content one of the most downloaded pieces of software, surpassing both Internet Explorer and Netscape as well as nearly all media players, but the content is so small in file size that anyone can create great user experiences for dial-up users.

This new version of Flash has continued in its hard-to-follow tradition of surpassing all expectations with new features. But this time, the features are not just new types of content. Many of the improvements involve making it easier and faster for Flash developers and designers alike to create rich content. Macromedia has even built in steps for developers to extend the capabilities of the authoring environment. But don't let the new features in the authoring environment fool you: Flash MX Professional 2004 is packed with new content features such as loading images directly into text fields, streaming both audio and video directly into your Flash movies, and of course, all the new components including data components for connecting directly with XML and Web Services, the hottest thing to hit the Web since JPEGs.

Along with the newest version of Flash comes the new edition of *Flash Unleashed*. Throughout this book, you will find countless examples and explanations of some of the newest and most powerful tools Flash has to offer, including a complete overview of ActionScript 2.0, the new version of Flash's programming language. Also included in this book is a handy reference guide for ActionScript to help with faster workflow.

*Macromedia Flash MX Professional 2004 Unleashed* was created with the reader's needs in mind. Please don't hesitate to email me your experiences with this book as well as with Flash MX Professional 2004 at `missing-link@evolutionar-e.com`.

# PART I

# Getting Started

## IN THIS PART

# Flash MX Professional 2004: What's New?

Those of you who have worked in Flash MX or previous versions of Flash will find this chapter helpful as it introduces you to the new and revamped features of Flash MX 2004, as well as some of the Pro-Only features.

## The Interface

Sometimes it's hard to know how to start a chapter, but in this case Macromedia makes it easy with the first new feature of Flash MX 2004, the start page.

### The Start Page

When you first open Flash, the start page opens as shown in Figure 1.1. The choices available on this page are also available in the File menu, but they are easier to access this way. The three main selections to choose from are: Open a Recent Item, which holds many of the most recent files you have worked in; Create New, which has many new options for creating a new file (especially in Flash MX 2004 Pro); and Create from Template. You can also choose from the options in the Help panel at the bottom about getting a tour of Flash, taking built-in lessons, and updating your help system (which I recommend doing regularly). And of course, if you do not want the start page to appear every time you start Flash, you can check the Don't Show Again check box at the bottom left of the page.

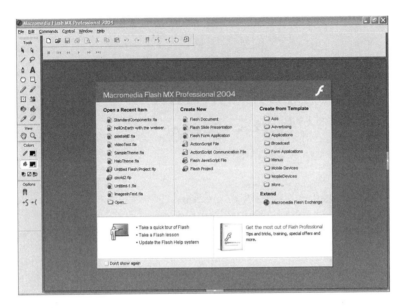

**FIGURE 1.1**    The start page.

## Tabs Tabs Everywhere

Another new feature in Flash MX 2004 is the easy-to-use tab system that is available in both the main window as well as the Actions panel (which is covered in more detail in Chapter 8, "Welcome to ActionScript 2.0").

In Flash MX, when you wanted to have multiple files open, you had to either tile the windows correctly or keep minimizing and maximizing individual files. Now with tabs you can have several files open, and when you want to go from file to file, you simply click on the file's tab, as you can see in Figure 1.2. This comes in very handy, especially with the new Flash Project file, which helps to keep track of your entire project and all of its files, including .fla, .swf, .flv, .as, and even subproject files (.flp).

Unfortunately, however, the tab system is a Windows-only feature.

## Help Panel—(F1)

Although the Help panel is not new, it has taken on a great deal more responsibility than in previous versions of Flash. It is now the central place to answer all questions, take lessons, and it also provides access to the ActionScript reference guide. And as mentioned, you can check to see if any updates are available for the Help panel. You should check this regularly because it's a free download.

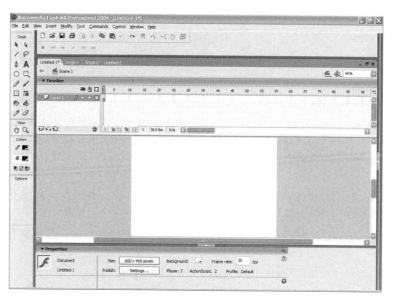

**FIGURE 1.2**    Tabbed files make it easy to go from file to file.

## The History Panel—(Alt+F10)

A new and much needed panel in Flash is the History panel. When it's open, it keeps track of every detail of what you do with your Flash document. You can go back one step at a time or several steps at once (see Figure 1.3).

But the best part about the History panel is the ability to store commands for reuse. For example, if you want to select all the objects on the stage, and then delete them all, which is a two-step process, you can do it once, and then save the step sequence as a command to reuse.

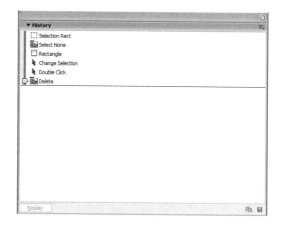

**FIGURE 1.3**    The History panel.

Here is an example of creating a rectangle, centering it, and then saving those steps as a command to reuse.

1. Start a new Flash document by going to File, New and choosing Flash Document.

2. Using the Rectangle tool (R), draw a rectangle on the stage about 100×100 with any stroke and fill color.

3. With the Arrow tool, select the rectangle by double clicking it to select the fill and the stroke, open the Align Panel (PC–Ctrl+K, Mac–Open Apple+K), and center the rectangle both horizontally and vertically making sure the "To stage" option is selected.

4. Now open the History panel, select all the steps, and click the Save button at the bottom right of the panel.

5. Name the command Draw Rectangle and Center.

Now whenever you want to draw a rectangle and center it as you did before, you can go to Commands, Draw Rectangle and Center and the command sequence will run. (Commands are discussed later in Chapter 26, "Extending the Flash Authoring Environment.")

## Save and Compact

In Flash MX and all prior versions, after you saved a file, if you undid things or deleted objects from the library, the size of the Flash file did not decrease because instead of removing the objects, Flash just appended a note to the file saying not to display those items any more. The only workaround was to save the file under a different name and then overwrite the original file.

Now, however, you can choose File, Save and Compact, which will do just that. It will completely overwrite the original file and create a brand new one without all the append notes.

## Flash Projects

A problem with using multiple Flash files and other documents is that it is hard to keep track of all of them. Now you can create these Flash project files to keep track of everything from your FLA files, external ActionScript (AS) files, image files, and any other file you would need with the project.

When you open a project file, the Project panel opens as shown in Figure 1.4. You can add files, create folders for collections of files, and test your projects. Also, with Check In, when you have multiple people working on the same project, you can always check to make sure that you have the latest file builds and that you are not overwriting someone else's work. There are even plug-ins for third-party applications such as Microsoft Visual Source Safe.

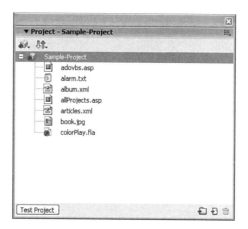

**FIGURE 1.4**   The Project panel.

Here is an example of how to work with the Project panel:

1. Start a new Flash Project by going to File, New and choosing Flash Project.

2. Name it **firstProject.flp** and save it to the desktop.

3. The Project panel should be open now, but if not go to Window, Project.

4. When the panel is open, select your project, click the Add File(s) to Project button, and start choosing files you would like to add to your project.

5. When you are done, you will see all the files you have added in a tree-like structure. If you double-click any of them, they will open in their native application.

Now whenever you come back to this Flash Project file, you will see the list of all the files included.

Another great feature of Flash MX 2004 Professional is that using the Projects panel, you can actually use FTP with your projects directly from Flash. You first have to create a site to go to.

1. Go to File, Edit Sites.

2. Choose New.

3. In the Site Definition window (see Figure 1.5), change the Connection option to FTP.

4. Put in your FTP information, and make sure that the Local Root option is the root directory of your site.

A few things to note about using FTP from Flash:

- Firewalls can sometimes cause errors when you're trying to connect, as can some proxy servers.

- Avoid using spaces and special characters in directory names.

**FIGURE 1.5**    The Site Definition window.

# Behaviors

There have been numerous additions to ActionScript in version 2.0. There have also been additions to the Actions panel (more on ActionScript in Chapter 8). But the biggest difference between Flash MX and Flash MX 2004 in the ActionScript department is the loss of normal mode in the ActionScript editor. Now all ActionScript written in the editor must be done in **expert mode**; that means you have to do straight typing or use the Actions toolbox on the side to drag blocks of code into the ActionScript editor. However, when a door closes, a window opens, and that window is behaviors.

**Behaviors** are snippets of code that you attach directly to objects on the stage, such as movie clips or buttons. Behaviors even have their own panel, as you can see in Figure 1.6. To add a behavior to an object, select the object on the stage, click the Add Behavior button in the panel, and choose which type of behavior you want and which specific one you will use. After you've done that, you can further customize the behavior by setting its event (events are covered in Chapter 14, "Events") such as onPress or onLoad.

**FIGURE 1.6**    The Behaviors panel for adding actions to objects.

Here is an example of adding a behavior to a button so that when it is clicked on, it will launch a Web page.

1. Start a new Flash document.

2. Choose Window, Other Panels, Common Libraries, Buttons. Choose your favorite button from the library and drag it out to the stage.

3. Using the Arrow tool (V), select the button and give it an instance name of myButton_btn in the Properties Inspector.

4. While the button is still selected, open the Behaviors panel (Shift+F3), click the Add Behavior button, and choose Web, Go to Web Page.

5. A pop-up window will open as shown in Figure 1.7. In the URL field, type **http://www.macromedia.com** or whichever URL you prefer. Then select "_blank" in the Open In drop-down list and click OK.

6. Now you will see the behavior in the Behaviors panel, and you want to change the event from On Release to On Press. To do that, just click under the event column on your new behavior and choose On Press.

7. You can also open up the Actions panel under Window, Development Panels, Actions (F9) and select the button to see its actions. They should look like this:

```
on (release) {
    //Goto Webpage Behavior
    //copyright Macromedia, Inc. 2003
    getURL("http://www.macromedia.com","_blank");
    //End Behavior
}
```

8. Now test the movie by choosing Control, Test Movie (PC–Ctrl+Enter, Mac–Open Apple+Return).

When you click your button, you will go to Macromedia's home page.

**FIGURE 1.7**    These are the options for the Go to Web Page behavior.

You can also create your own behaviors, which is covered later in this book in Chapter 26.

Now that we've covered a new feature that will do certain sets of code for you, we will cover a new feature that will actually do animation for you, Effects.

## Timeline Effects

Animations are what made Flash great; it's the root of its existence even now with all of its development tools. Animation is covered in Chapter 4, "Flash Animation," and Chapter 5, "Symbols and the Library," but there is a way to animate objects with built-in customizable animations called timeline effects.

Timeline effects are very easy to use. When you have an object on your stage, you can go to Insert, Timeline Effects and choose the one you want. Then a preview window will appear with options so that you can adjust and manipulate the settings until they are just right.

Here is an example of using the blur effect on a circle movie clip:

1. Start a new Flash document.

2. Draw a circle on the main stage in any color, and then select all of the circle by double-clicking it.

3. Choose Modify, Convert to Symbol (F8), name the circle `circleMC`, and make sure it is set to the Movie Clip Symbol Behavior.

4. While the circle is still selected, go to Insert, Timeline Effects, Effects, Blur and a window will open up similar to Figure 1.8.

5. You can either change the settings or leave them the way they are, but if you do change them, make sure to click the Update Preview button to see the changes before you decide.

6. When you click OK, Flash will convert the instance of your circle to another movie clip with the symbol name Blur 1. You can also find this symbol in the library as well as a folder called Effects Folder, which holds a graphic of the circle symbol.

7. Now you can make multiple copies of the circle on the stage, and they will all have the effect attached with them.

Test the movie to see how it looks.

Effects are very easy to implement as well as customizable. However, do not go overboard with multiple effects happening at the same time, as they can become quite processor-intensive.

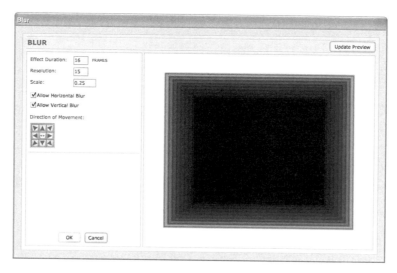

**FIGURE 1.8**   The Properties Controller of the blur effect.

Components are other good tools that do some of the work for you. They are not new to Flash but have been updated for better performance and style.

## Components—Version 2.0

First came smart clips: difficult to use, not scalable, and very heavy in file size. Then in Flash MX came components: very easy to use, easily scalable, not very pretty, and still very heavy in file size. Now come components version 2: fairly easy to use, easily scalable, slick-looking, and extremely heavy in file size.

This time around, Macromedia chose performance and style above all other factors in this version of their components. Also, they have decided to ship a lot more components with the initial software than in previous versions, and for Pro users, there are even more. Not only are there the normal user interface components, but also media components for controlling video and audio, and data components for connecting to different types of data sources as well as storing the data in an organized fashion.

Components are covered more in depth in Chapter 16, "Components," but here is a taste of the text area component and how to use it.

1. Create a new Flash document.

2. Make a second layer and select the bottom layer.

3. Drag the Text Area component out onto the stage and give it an instance name of **myText**.

4. Go to the first frame of the top layer. Open up the Actions panel (F9) and place these actions in it:

```
myText.setText("This is the text area component");
```

5. Now test the movie to see that the text is now inside the text field.

If you place more text in the text area, a scrollbar will appear. Also notice the file size, nearly 40K.

Components are good because they allow developers to focus on other parts of applications instead of having to build little elements. They are also good for designers who do not have a heavy programming background and prefer to work more on look than function.

## Streaming Media

One of the most sought-after features was the ability to put streaming video directly into a Flash movie. This was accomplished with the Flash communication server, but was difficult to implement, not to mention costly for the server software.

Thanks to Flash MX 2004, now you can stream not only video, but also audio directly into your movies, and there is even a set of components to help you do it. The video format that Flash supports is .flv, and you can also stream in MP3 as well using the same techniques.

Here is an example of streaming video directly into a Flash movie. You will need the sample.flv file from this book's companion Web site to complete this example.

1. Create a new Flash document, and save it as **movieTest.fla** on your desktop.

2. Drag a copy of sample.flv from the companion Web site onto the desktop.

3. Open up the library (F11) and in the top right corner, click on the Options menu and choose New Video.

4. Create a second layer in the main timeline and select the bottom layer.

5. Drag an instance of this new video symbol from the library onto the stage, and give it an instance name of **sample_video** in the Properties Inspector.

6. Now in the first frame of the top layer, open up the Actions panel and place these actions in it:

```
//create the net connection object
myNetConnection = new NetConnection();
mynetconnection.connect(null);
//create the net stream object
myNetStream = new NetStream(myNetConnection);
//attach the video
sample_video.attachVideo(myNetStream);
//play the video
myNetStream.play("sample.flv");
```

7. Now test the movie and you will see something similar to Figure 1.9.

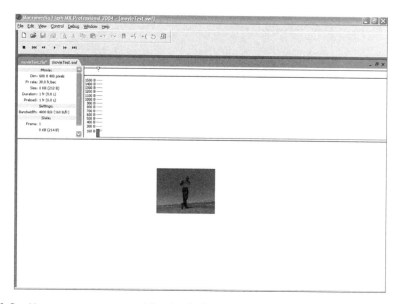

FIGURE 1.9   You can now stream video in Flash.

A plug-in is available from Macromedia that will allow any application that can export in .mov format to export into .flv format.

Another improvement in video support is the import wizard for videos, shown in Figure 1.10. You can take out small clips from the main clip imported and string them back together for a single clip. You can also set the quality for certain bandwidths.

Video is discussed further in Chapter 7, "Working with Sound and Video."

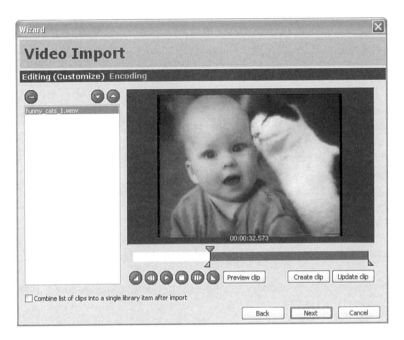

**FIGURE 1.10**    The Video Import Wizard.

## Screens: The New Timeline

Because Flash was originally a vector animation tool, you work within it in a linear time-line. For application developers in Flash, this has caused some issues because applications are not linear, but are instead structured in a more tree-like way. For all Flash Pro users, in come Screens.

Screens are a hierarchical "snapshot" of each page of a form application or slide presenta-tion. Both types of screens allow nesting of screens within screens so that one can stay visible as you navigate through the others.

The differences between the two slide types are subtle but demand attention. Slide screens are designed to build linear presentations, and by default, you can navigate through them with the arrow keys. Form Application screens, on the other hand, are designed to have multiple nested screens for a tree-structured application such as a shopping cart or a survey. By default, you must write ActionScript to navigate screens in Form Applications.

You navigate both types of screens with the Screen Layout panel, which can be found under Window, Screens. In the panel, you can expand orcollapse sections of screens including the nested screens (see Figure 1.11).

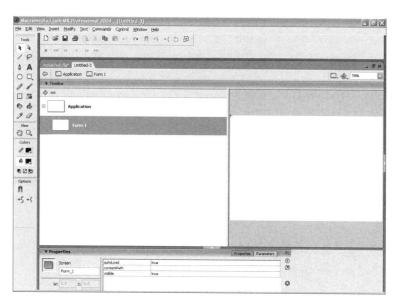

**FIGURE 1.11**   Screen Layout panel.

Also with the Screen Layout panel, when you select a screen, the appearance of the Properties Inspector changes as shown in Figure 1.12 or Figure 1.13 depending on what type of screen you are working in. Within this Properties Inspector, you have a few options for the screens, and each individual screen can have its own options. (Note: These are all the options for both Form Applications, as well as Slide Presentations, and some options are only available on one or the other.)

- autoKeyNav—This parameter tells the screens whether or not to respond to the arrow keys. It is for Slide presentations only and it has these options:
  - true—If this parameter is set to true, when you press the right arrow key (or the spacebar), the slides will move to the next screen. If you press the left arrow key, it will move back to the previous screen.
  - false—The screen will not respond to keystrokes.
  - inherit—(Default Value) If this parameter is set, the slide will look to its parent slide to see whether the inherit option is true or false. If the root slide is set to inherit, that is the same as being set to true.
- autoLoad—This option, if set to true, will load the content of the screen before it has been viewed. If set to false, it will wait until it is being viewed to load the content. This option is available to both Forms and Slides.
- contentPath—This is a link to a linkage property of a Movie clip in the library. If this parameter is set, that movie clip will load into the screen at runtime.

- overlayChildren—This parameter is used to control the visibility of child screens in Slide Presentations only; if set to true, when a user goes to each child screen, all previous child screens remain visible. If set to false, only one child screen can be shown at a time.

- playHidden—This option, if set to true (the default value) will allow movie clips on screens to play without being viewed. If it is set to false, the movie clips will not play unless viewed, and will stop when you move to another screen. This parameter is for Slide Presentations only.

- visible—This is a Form Application parameter only. When this parameter is set to true (the default value), the screen will be automatically visible at runtime. When set to false, it will be invisible at runtime until changed by ActionScript. (This will not affect the visibility of these screens during authoring.)

**FIGURE 1.12**    The Properties Inspector for Slide Presentation screens.

**FIGURE 1.13**    The Properties Inspector for Form Application screens.

> **NOTE**
>
> While you are working in a nested screen, content from parent screens remains visible, but at a more transparent level. This makes layout easy.

Here is an example of how to build a slide presentation with screens.

1. Start a new Flash Slide Presentation by going to File, New and choosing Flash Slide Presentation.

2. In the Screens panel, you will see the root screen called presentation; there you can put things you want to appear throughout the entire presentation. Using the Text Tool, create a static text field at the top of the Presentation screen and type **My First Flash Presentation** in a font size of 40.

3. Notice that, in the Screen Layout panel, the screen representing the Presentation screen now has the same text written on it.

4. There is already a child slide, but we are going to add another one by selecting the "Presentation" slide in the Screen Layout panel and then clicking the Insert Screen button; then you will see Slide 2 appear.

5. In Slide 1, use the text tool again, and put a static text field in the middle of the screen saying "Slide 1" at a font size of about 20.

6. Then select Slide 2, and repeat the preceding step, but put "Slide 2" in the text field this time.

7. Test the movie by choosing Control, Test Movie.

When you're in the test movie screen, you can use the arrow keys to move between slides, and they should look like Figures 1.14 and 1.15. Also, notice that the text you put in the root screen "Presentation" is always visible. Now it is easy to see the benefits of having child and parent screens.

> **NOTE**
>
> When you compile either the Form Application or the Slide Presentation using screens, you will notice that it takes much longer to compile than normal Flash Documents. This is because of all the coding and structure that must be included even if you are only using one slide.

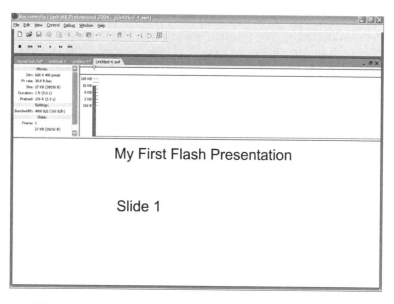

**FIGURE 1.14**   Slide 1.

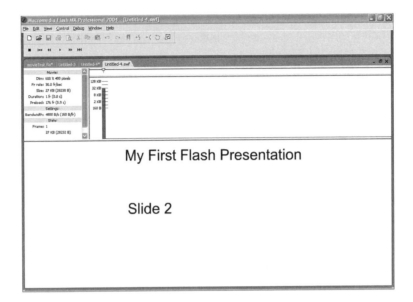

**FIGURE 1.15**    Slide 2.

## Summary

Flash MX 2004 provides many new features, especially for the Pro users, including the ability to import both Illustrator 10 files as well as PDFs. However, the entire list of new features is too large to describe in this chapter. As you work through the rest of this book, you will continue to find new features and items within different topics. Some features have received more upgrades than others (hint: text fields).

CHAPTER **2**

# Getting Started with Flash MX 2004 Professional

This chapter covers some of the basics of Flash, where it came from, what it is, and the general interface features. The first question about Flash is: What are its roots?

## Humble Beginnings— Where Flash Came From

In 1996, a small company called FutureWave software was selling a product called FutureSplash Animator. This product was designed to do vector-based drawing and animation.

---

**Vector-Based Graphics**

For those not familiar with vector-based graphics, here is an explanation:

Most graphics are **pixel-based**, which means that there are thousands of tiny blocks of color making up a picture. This becomes a problem when resizing images because for instance, if you increase the size of a JPEG, you are not redrawing it, but instead increasing the size of those tiny blocks of color, and the larger you make them, the more fuzzy and unclear the picture becomes.

**Vector-based** graphics are made with mathematical vector points so that in the case of a resize, they can redraw themselves to maintain quality. This and their generally smaller file size make them not only perfect for animation, but for the Web as well.

Figure 2.1 shows four circles; two are vector-based, and two are pixel-based JPEGs.

---

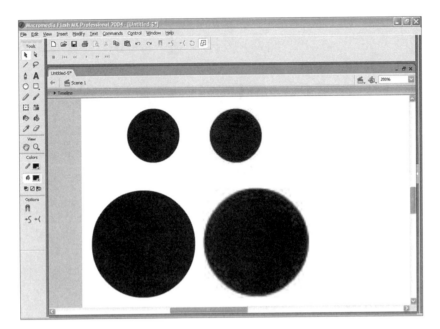

**FIGURE 2.1**    The difference between vector- and pixel-based graphics is obvious, especially in curves.

As FutureSplash Animator began to gain in popularity throughout the year, another software company began to notice, and that company was Macromedia. So in December of that same year, FutureSplash Animator was purchased by Macromedia and became Flash 1.0.

As Flash progressed, it began to transform from a simple drawing and animation tool to a multimedia tool and now into a full-blown Web application development tool. It has its own object-oriented programming language, it can tie to nearly all middleware systems, and it has one of the most downloaded pieces of software in the world as its player.

Now you know where Flash started, and where it is heading, so let's take a look at how to use it.

## The Interface

In this version of Flash, there have been many upgrades to the interface, but none so dramatic as the tabbed file system (see Figure 2.2). Unfortunately, it is only available on the PC.

The tabbed file system makes it very easy to move from file to file without ever having to minimize a window, which is a major improvement for developers and designers alike.

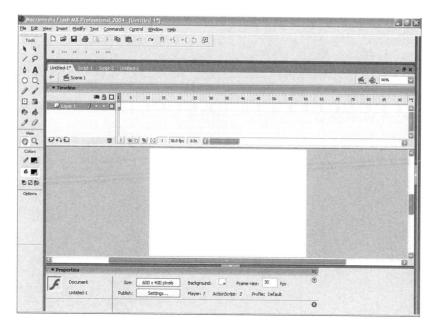

**FIGURE 2.2**   The Windows version of Flash MX 2004 Professional.

Beyond the new tab system, the first part of the interface you will notice is the large white rectangle in the middle of the screen that is called the **stage**.

## The Stage

This space represents the visible area of the file you create, and is where you will place all of your visual elements. You can see the stage in Figure 2.2 and Figure 2.3, which shows the Macintosh version of Flash.

Some default settings for the stage are as follows:

- Dimensions—550×400
- Frame Rate—12
- Player Version—7
- ActionScript version—2.0
- Background Color—#FFFFFF (White)
- Ruler Units—Pixel

You can change these settings by choosing Modify, Document (PC–Ctrl+J, Mac–Open Apple+J). This will open the Document Properties window as shown in Figure 2.4, where you can change most of the settings mentioned in the preceding list. You can also use the Properties Inspector.

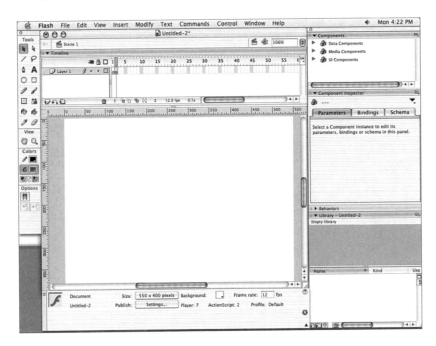

**FIGURE 2.3**     The Macintosh version of Flash MX 2004 Professional.

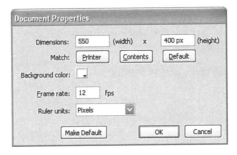

**FIGURE 2.4**     The Document Properties window for setting certain stage properties.

## The Properties Inspector Panel

This interface panel can be found by default at the bottom of the screen (but can be moved, as you will see soon) and is used for almost everything.

The Properties Inspector panel was one of the best additions to Flash MX because it changes based on what you are doing. For instance, if you use the Arrow tool, and select the stage, the Properties Inspector will look like Figure 2.5, but if you choose the Text tool, the Properties Inspector will look like Figure 2.6. And if you choose a keyframe in the timeline, the Properties Inspector will look like Figure 2.7. The Properties Inspector was designed to be the central area for changing settings and properties of all visual elements on the stage including the stage itself.

**FIGURE 2.5**   The Properties Inspector for the stage.

**FIGURE 2.6**   The Properties Inspector for the Text tool.

**FIGURE 2.7**   The Properties Inspector for a keyframe.

The Properties Inspector is just one of many dockable panels in Flash. The next section covers a few other useful ones.

## Flash Panels

In Flash, if you want to change settings such as size, rotation, or color or add ActionScript, you will have to use one of the panels. By default, most panels are on the right side of the screen. To drag and dock a panel, click and drag the top left part of the panel's title bar where it appears perforated. Then release when you see a darkened black border around the panel.

There are three basic categories of panels, and each category can be found on the Window menu. Here is a list of each group with a basic description of each panel within it.

- **Design Panels**. These panels are used mostly for visual aspects of objects:

  - **Align** (PC–Ctrl+K, Mac–Open Apple+K). This panel is used to assist in aligning objects either to the stage or to one another.

  - **Color Mixer** (Shift+F9). This panel is used to refine colors and gradients for shapes.

  - **Color Swatches** (PC–Ctrl+F9, Mac–Open Apple+F9). This panel is for choosing colors from a set of color swatches.

  - **Info** (PC–Ctrl+I, Mac–Open Apple+I). This panel is used to get information about selected objects such as size and position. It also keeps track of mouse position in the authoring environment.

  - **Scene** (Shift+F2). This panel is used to keep track of scenes as well as to add or remove scenes.

  - **Transform** (PC–Ctrl+T, Mac–Open Apple+T). This panel is used to manipulate the size, rotation, and skew of selected objects.

- **Development Panels**. These panels focus more on the functionality side of Flash.

  - **Actions** (F9). This panel is for entering and editing ActionScripts associated with frames and objects.

  - **Behaviors** (Shift+F3). This panel is for applying certain actions directly to objects, and has replaced the normal mode of the Actions panel.

  - **Components** (PC–Ctrl+F7, Mac–Open Apple+F7). This panel holds all components used in Flash; just select them and drag them directly onto the stage.

  - **Components Inspector** (Alt+F7). This panel is used to adjust certain parameters and properties of selected components.

  - **Debugger** (Shift+F4). This panel is used for debugging your application or Flash movie.

  - **Output** (F2). This panel displays errors in ActionScript or messages sent directly to it by use of the `trace` command.

  - **Web Services** (PC–Ctrl+Shift+F10, Mac–Open Apple+Shift+F10). This panel keeps track of all the Web services that you have added at any point as well as what Web methods are available in each of them.

- **Other Panels**. The name is self-explanatory; these are the panels that are left over.

  - **Accessibility** (Alt+F2). This panel is used to control the accessibility features of Flash.

  - **History** (Alt+F10). This panel keeps track of everything you do on the stage, and you can use it to create reuseable commands.

- **Movie Explorer** (Alt+F3). Use this panel to search your entire Flash document for anything including ActionScript, text, and objects.

- **Strings** (Alt+F11). This panel is used for translating Unicode text into other languages.

- **Common Libraries**. This isn't really a panel; it's a library that holds a lot of premade objects you can use in your own documents.

The great thing about these panels is that even though there are quite a few of them, they can all be docked in different sections of your screen. Not only can you dock them in place, but you can also expand and collapse them to save screen space. Figures 2.8 and 2.9 show some of the panels. To expand and collapse a panel, you just have to click on the black arrow on the panel's title bar.

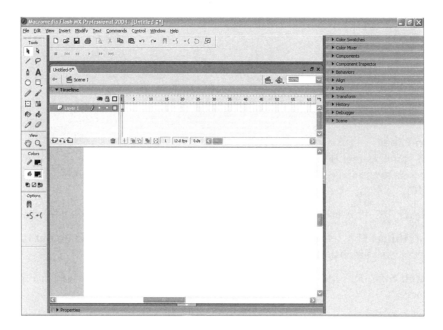

**Figure 2.8**   Several panels docked and all collapsed.

Now that you have seen how to control the panels, we are going to go over the three most commonly used panels: the Align, Transform, and Info panels.

> **NOTE**
>
> Many other panels are covered in later chapters such as Chapter 8, "Welcome to ActionScript 2.0," and Chapter 16, "Components."

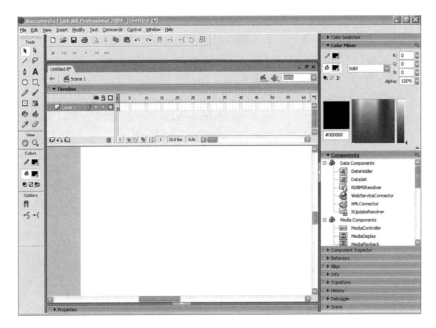

**FIGURE 2.9**    Several panels with two of them expanded.

### The Align Panel

The Align panel, as mentioned before, is used to either align and/or size objects to themselves or to the stage. It accomplishes this by means of five sets of buttons (see Figure 2.10):

- **Align**. This set is used to control the x and y coordinates of object(s) selected.

- **Distribute**. This set is used for distributing objects and spacing them out based on the objects' dimensions.

- **Match Size**. This set is used to create the same dimensions for at least two different objects.

- **Space**. This set is also for spacing out objects, but unlike the Distribute set, which spaces out items based on dimensions, Space makes sure that the items selected are evenly spaced.

- **To Stage**. This single button, when selected, will make all the other features take the stage into account.

Here is an example of how to use the Align panel:

1. Create a new Flash document.

2. Draw three separate rectangles on the stage at random spots and at different sizes.

3. Choose Edit, Select All.

4. Open the Align panel, make sure the To Stage button is selected, and choose the Align Horizontal Center button (second from the left). The rectangles should look like those in Figure 2.11.

5. While the rectangles are still selected, unselect the To Stage button and choose the Match Width and Height button from the Align panel. Now the rectangles should all be the same size and appear similar to Figure 2.12.

**FIGURE 2.10**    The Actions panel.

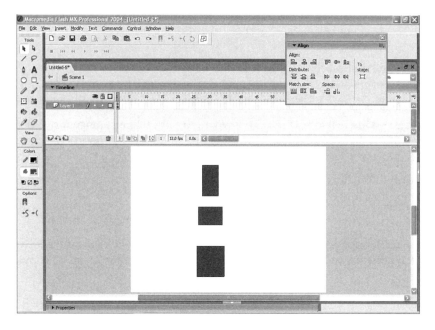

**FIGURE 2.11**    Aligning the rectangles horizontally.

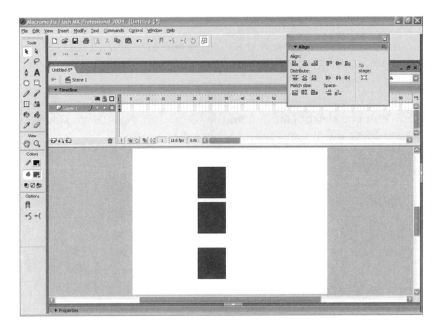

**FIGURE 2.12**    Using the Align panel, you can also match dimensions.

### The Transform Panel

The Transform panel allows users to manipulate the size, rotation, and skew of an object, as you can see in Figure 2.13. Here are the Transform panel options and their uses:

- **Sizing Options**. Two text boxes allow you to put in a percentage for vertical and horizontal sizing. If you always want them to be the same proportions, check the Constrain check box.

- **Rotate**. In the Rotate text box, put a positive or negative integer showing, in degrees, how much you want the object to rotate.

- **Skew**. There are two text boxes that accept positive or negative integers.

- **Copy and Apply Transform**. This button, the one on the left in the lower-right corner, takes the transform selected as well as the object, and creates a copy on the stage.

- **Reset**. This button, the one on the right in the lower-right corner, resets an object's transform to its original state.

### The Info Panel

The last panel we will discuss in this chapter is the Info panel. This panel can be very useful when trying to align objects in certain positions. It can also get the RGB settings of a given object as you can see in Figure 2.14.

**FIGURE 2.13**   The Transform panel.

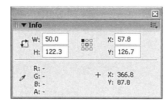

**FIGURE 2.14**   The Info panel.

## Check Your Spelling

A much-needed feature in Flash has always been the ability to spell check; text fields, code, comments, and even layer names. Well, now it has become possible using the Spell Checker window.

But before you can start checking spelling, you have to set up your spell checker first. To do that, choose Text, Spelling Setup, and the Spelling Setup window will appear as shown in Figure 2.15. You have to at least have it checking something, or it will not work at all; instead you will get a pop-up error message as shown in Figure 2.16.

When you have set the options you want, whenever you want to check spelling, just select Text, Check Spelling and the Check Spelling window will appear as shown in Figure 2.17.

Now that you have seen a lot of the interface elements and how to use them, the next step is how to customize your preferences, and the view of the stage.

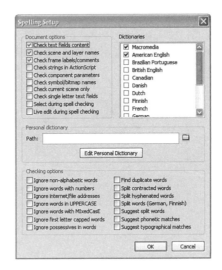

**FIGURE 2.15**    Choose what you want the spell checker to look at.

**FIGURE 2.16**    Pop-up error message if the Spelling Setup has not been completed.

**FIGURE 2.17**    The Check Spelling window.

# Preferences

One of the nice things that you can do with the authoring environment is to customize it to the way you want it. To do this, go to Preferences under the Edit menu on the PC, or under the Application menu on the Mac, and you will see one of two screens depending on your operating system, as shown in Figures 2.18 and 2.19.

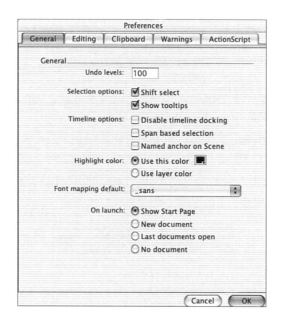

**FIGURE 2.18**   Preferences for the Mac.

The Preferences window has five tabs: General, Editing, Clipboard, Warnings, and ActionScript.

## The General Tab

This section covers the options available in the General tab as seen in Figure 2.19.

- **Undo Levels**. This number represents the number of steps that are recorded and undoable. You can increase this number all the way up to 9999, but the higher the number, the more memory it will take up.

- **Printing Options** (PC only). You can enable or disable PostScript printing; however, if it is enabled, it will slow down printing from Flash. The default value is disabled.

- **Selection Options**. The first option allows the Shift select method to be active. What this option means is that in order to select multiple objects, you must hold down the Shift key. By default, this option is already on. With the second option, you can turn off tooltips.

- **Panel Options** (PC only). This option, if disabled, makes the panels free-floating and undocking.

- **Timeline Options**. This set has several suboptions:

  - **Disable Timeline Docking**. This makes the timeline not attach while you are in Flash.

  - **Span-based Selection**. This option allows you to select frames in the timeline like a span, as opposed to frame by frame.

  - **Named Anchor on Scene**. This option makes Flash make the first frame in every Scene a named anchor.

- **Highlight Color**. This option controls the highlighting color on layers. You can either choose a color from the palette or use the layer color.

- **Font Mapping Default**. This option sets the default font if the selected font is not available on a user's computer.

- **On Launch**. This is a new preference in Flash, which allows you to select what you want to happen when Flash starts up.

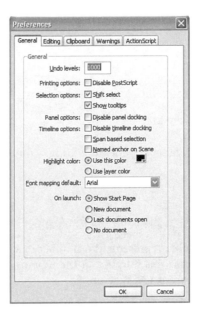

**FIGURE 2.19**    Preferences for Windows.

## The Editing Tab

This section covers the options available in the Editing tab as seen in Figure 2.20.

**FIGURE 2.20**    The Editing tab.

- **Pen Tool**. This section controls the visualizations of the pen tool as you are using it.

- **Vertical Text**. This has several suboptions:

  - **Default Text Orientation**. This option makes the default way you create text fields vertical, which is good in the case of some languages.

  - **Right to Left Text Flow**. This reverses the default way text flows.

  - **No Kerning**. This option turns off kerning for vertical text, which can help save space.

  - **Drawing Settings**. This section has several suboptions:

  - **Connect Lines**. This option connects a line to another line for you when you are in certain range of the other line and Snap to Objects is turned on.

  - **Smooth Curves**. This option sets how smooth a curve is supposed to appear.

  - **Recognize Lines**. This option sets how straight a line has to be before Flash will make it a perfectly straight line.

  - **Recognize Shapes**. This option is similar to the Recognize Lines option. It tells Flash at what level to determine if a shape is perfect.

  - **Click Accuracy**. This determines how close you have to be to an object for Flash to recognize that you are touching the object.

- **Project Settings**. These options determine whether all open project files should close when the project closes, and when the project should be saved.

36    **CHAPTER 2**    Getting Started with Flash MX 2004 Professional

## The Clipboard Tab

This section covers the options available in the Clipboard tab as seen in Figure 2.21.

**FIGURE 2.21**    The Clipboard tab on Windows.

- **Bitmaps**. This section has several suboptions.

    - **Color Depth**. The default setting is Match Screen, which means it will use enough colors to match the screen. You can increase or decrease this value.

    - **Resolution**. Setting for the Dots Per Inch (dpi) for copying a graphic.

    - **Size Limit**. This setting uses a positive integer to determine how much available space to use for copying graphics to the clipboard from Flash.

- **Gradients**. This option controls the quality of the gradient being used.

- **FreeHand Text**. This option keeps text as text when taking it over to FreeHand.

These settings are for Windows. The Mac has a slightly different-looking Clipboard tab, as you can see in Figure 2.22, and it has these options:

- **PICT Settings**. This section has several suboptions:

    - **Type**. This option allows you to choose what format to use for copying graphics to the clipboard. The Objects format is best because it maintains the vector format.

- **Resolution**. This option determines the Dots Per Inch setting when copying graphics to the clipboard. You can also keep PostScript data by checking the Include PostScript check box.

- **Gradient**. This option controls the quality of the gradient being used.

- **FreeHand Text**. This option keeps text as text when taking it over to FreeHand.

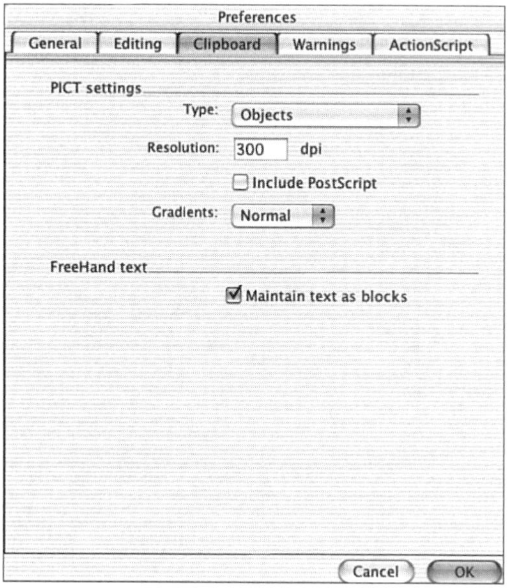

FIGURE 2.22   The Clipboard tab on OS X.

## The Warnings Tab

The Warnings tab (see Figure 2.23) just contains check boxes for when warnings should appear; they are easy to understand and follow.

## The ActionScript Tab

The ActionScript preferences tab controls the settings for the Actions panel, which is discussed further in Chapter 8. Figure 2.24 shows the tab.

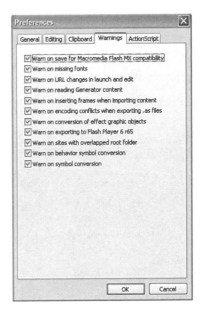

**FIGURE 2.23**    The Warnings tab.

**FIGURE 2.24**    The ActionScript tab.

# Shortcuts

When working in Flash, you will begin to notice that the abundance of tools, commands, panels, and options take up time when you have to search for them and click options in a certain order. That's why I love shortcuts. When you begin to get comfortable using them, your design and development time will begin to wither.

To see the available shortcuts, choose Edit, Keyboard Shortcuts and you will see a screen pop up as shown in Figure 2.25.

**FIGURE 2.25**  The Keyboard Shortcuts dialog box.

The options in this menu are

- **Current**. This allows you to choose which type of built-in shortcuts you prefer including Macromedia Standard, Fireworks 4, Flash 5, FreeHand 10, Illustrator 10, or Photoshop 6.

- **Commands**. This holds the groups of commands that have shortcuts including Drawing Menu Commands, Drawing Tools, Test Movie Menu Commands, Workspace Accessibility Commands, and Actions Panel Commands. In the large list box under Commands, you can see the subsets of groups.

- **Description**. Gives a description of the command when you choose one. (This is not an option that can be adjusted.)

- **Shortcuts** (+/-). Allows you to add or remove shortcuts from the selected command.

- **Press Key**. Retrieves the set of keys when you press them for the shortcut, and lets you know if they are available or not.

- **Change Button**. Sets the focus into the Press Key box.

- **Duplicate Set Button**. Duplicates the current set of shortcuts you are viewing so that you can make changes.

- **Rename Set Button**. Allows you to rename the current set of shortcuts.

- **Delete Set Button**. Allows you to delete the current set of shortcuts. (You cannot delete any of the built-in sets of shortcuts that come with Flash.)

These are the steps to creating your own custom shortcuts:

1. In the Keyboard Shortcuts dialog box, select Macromedia Standard in the Current drop-down box.

2. Click the Duplicate Set button, name the new set `mySet`, and click OK.

3. If you decide you do not like the name `mySet`, at any time, you can choose to rename the set by selecting it in the Current drop-down box and clicking the Rename Set button. Then just name it anything you want.

4. To continue to change the shortcuts, choose a set you like, such as the Drawing Tools for this example.

5. Select the Arrow selection in the list box.

6. Click the Plus sign beside Shortcuts.

7. The word <empty> will appear in the Press Key box as well as in the list box under Shortcuts.

8. Press the "D" key and then click Change.

9. Click OK. Now you can select the Arrow tool by pressing "V" or "D".

## Making a Better Workspace

Sometimes, when you're drawing graphics or working with animations, it is a lot easier to draw with rulers or grids. Well, Flash offers you both.

To turn on rulers, go to View, Rulers and your screen should now look similar to Figure 2.26.

You can also use gridlines. Gridlines are great for animation as well as application layout so that you can see exactly where to place visual objects on the stage.

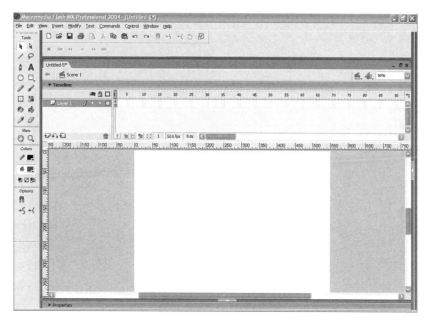

**FIGURE 2.26**   The stage with rulers turned on.

To turn gridlines on, go to View, Grid, Show Grid. And now your stage should look similar to Figure 2.27.

You can also edit the grid to better fit your needs by choosing View, Grid, Edit Grid, and the Grid Settings dialog box will appear as shown in Figure 2.28. Some of the options for the grid are as follows:

- **Color**. This is the actual color of the gridlines themselves.
- **Show Grid**. Toggles the grid visible to invisible.
- **Snap to Grid**. This option allows objects to snap to cross sections in the grid.
- **Horizontal Space**. The horizontal space between gridlines in pixels.
- **Vertical Space**. The vertical space between gridlines in pixels.
- **Snap Accuracy**. This option tells Flash how close you need to be to a cross section in the grid for the object to snap to it.

And if you want something a little more customizable, you can turn on guidelines.

Guidelines are lines you actually create yourself during authoring. To turn them on, choose View, Guides, Show Guides. In order for them to work, you must have Rulers turned on as well.

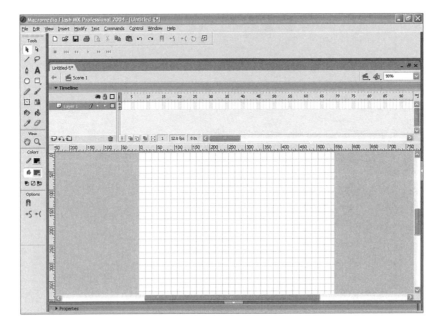

**FIGURE 2.27**    The stage with the grid turned on.

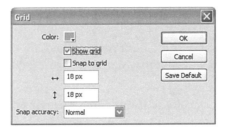

**FIGURE 2.28**    The Grid Settings dialog box.

If you have both guides and rulers turned on, you can simply click in the ruler at a set point, and drag a line out to the stage. After you release it, you can still move it by clicking on it and dragging it again. You can also lock the guides down so that you do not accidentally move them by choosing View, Guides, Lock Guides. Figure 2.29 is an example of a stage that has guides.

And you can of course customize the guidelines by choosing View, Guides, Edit Guides. The Guides Settings dialog box will pop up as shown in Figure 2.30.

The settings are the same basic settings as the grid.

Lastly, if you want to clear the guides and start over, you can select View, Guides, Clear Guides, or drag them individually back over to the rulers.

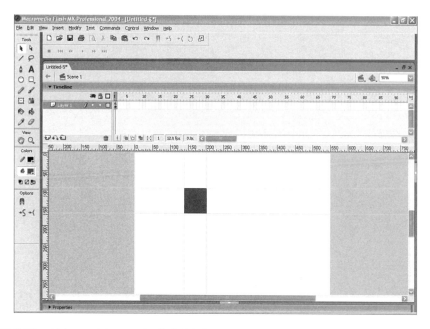

**FIGURE 2.29**   Using guides can be helpful during layout.

**FIGURE 2.30**   The Guides Settings dialog box.

# Summary

This chapter introduced you to the world of Flash and its interface. You learned how to customize it to your personal working experience as well as how to create your own keyboard shortcuts. Throughout the remainder of this book, we will continue to go in depth into the many features of Flash as well as how to expand it.

# CHAPTER **3**

# Creating Graphics in Flash

Flash has a unique drawing style associated with it. If you are familiar with other drawing applications, such as Adobe Illustrator and Macromedia FreeHand, you'll find definite similarities and some unexpected differences. Flash offers several drawing tools for creating the graphics for your Flash projects that may seem familiar to you based on some of those programs. Flash differs from those other applications by the way it handles graphics. Flash will join two items of the same color value if the two graphics intersect. The line or stroke of an item is also considered a separate element. As you will see in this chapter, these differences can be problematic, but they can also work in your favor. It's just a matter of getting used to them.

## The Tools

As just mentioned, the drawing and handling of graphics in Flash takes a little getting used to, and that's what this portion of the chapter is for. It exposes you to the tools in Flash 2004; even though they may look very similar to those in other programs, there are some differences.

All the tools will be reviewed in this chapter, so let's start taking a look at them. Figure 3.1 shows the Flash 2004 toolbar and highlights each tool found in this powerful toolset.

### The Arrow Tool
**Shortcut: PC and Mac–V**

The Arrow tool is Flash's selection tool. If you want to move an item, select and drag it with this tool. Of course, you can always use the arrow keys on your keyboard to move the item for more precise placement.

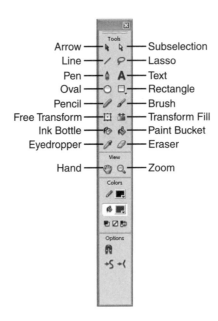

**FIGURE 3.1**   The Flash 2004 tools.

Toward the end of the chapter, when we get into actually creating artwork in Flash, you'll see how this tool can also be an aid in drawing. The Arrow tool does have one option: Snap to Objects.

Use Snap to Objects to have artwork snap to the grid. This option will also cause objects to snap to one another when you're placing the graphics, depending on how close the objects are horizontally and vertically.

## The Subselection Tool

### Shortcut: PC and Mac–A

The Arrow tool has a counterpart—the Subselection tool (also known as the **white arrow**). Remember that Flash is vector-based, so the main job of the Subselection tool is to select actual vector points of an item. This tool has no options. Again, we'll discuss this tool later in the chapter as we begin creating and working with our own artwork.

## The Line Tool

### Shortcut: PC and Mac–N

When drawing with the Line tool, you can create straight lines in any direction from the starting point. To start drawing a line, choose the Line tool in the Tools panel, click anywhere on the stage, drag the line toward the desired endpoint, and release the mouse.

The Line tool has no options. However, the size and style of the stroke will determine the appearance of the line. You can change the stroke's properties in the Properties Inspector when the Line tool is selected in the Tools panel.

You can draw several line segments to make a shape, as shown in Figure 3.2.

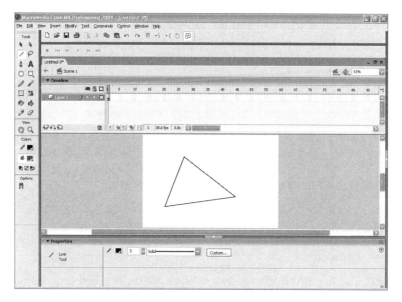

**FIGURE 3.2**    The Line tool can be used to draw a triangle by connecting three different lines. The Properties Inspector offers options for changing the line's appearance.

To change the appearance of the stroke, you can select a color and size from the Properties Inspector. You also have a choice of styles—solid, dashed, dotted, ragged, stipple, and hatched—as well as options to customize each of these styles. Simply click the Custom button in the Properties Inspector with a drawing tool selected. Here's an explanation of each style option:

> **NOTE**
>
> Flash does not offer a way to save custom style settings. Also, all units for spacing and sizing options are in points. You can access the Stroke Style dialog box by clicking the Custom button in the Properties Inspector. When you click the button, the dialog box will appear, as shown in Figure 3.3.

- **Hairline**. This stroke style draws one-pixel-wide strokes and remains one pixel, regardless of magnification or zoom. Often, when a document gets scaled, the vector lines will scale with it to preserve the proportions of the artwork. This is not an

option in the dialog box but is available through the drop-down menu in the
Properties Inspector.

- **Solid**. This option is for drawing solid lines and strokes. The only adjustable attributes are the thickness, color, and sharp corners of the stroke.

- **Dashed**. This choice generates a stroke with dashed breaks within the line. To change the length of the dash and the gap space between dashes, enter numeric values in the respective text fields in the Stroke Style dialog box. Color, thickness, and sharp corners are also adjustable attributes.

- **Dotted**. Choose the dotted style if the desired effect is to have a stroke with evenly spaced dots along the line. This style has an option for changing the distance between the dots. Color, thickness, and sharp corners are also adjustable attributes.

- **Ragged**. The ragged style creates random wavy lines with dotted separations. The Stroke Style dialog box offers options to change the pattern, wave height, and wave length. Color, thickness, and sharp corners are also adjustable attributes. Use a combination of all these styles for unlimited possibilities.

- **Stipple**. This choice creates a stroke style to resemble that of an artist's hand-stippling technique. Dot size, dot variation, and density are options for changing the appearance of the stippling effect. Color, thickness, and sharp corners are also adjustable attributes.

- **Hatched**. The hatched line style resembles an artist's hatched-line technique. The thickness attribute determines the thickness of the hatch line, which is independent of the global thickness setting. You also have options for spacing, jiggle, rotate, curve, and the length of the hatched lines. Of course, there are additional choices for global thickness, color, and sharp corners.

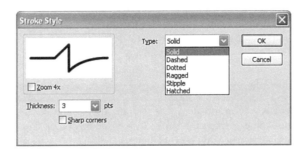

**FIGURE 3.3**   The Stroke Style dialog box.

## The Ink Bottle Tool

### Shortcut: PC and Mac–S

The Ink Bottle tool is designed to change the color, style, and thickness of strokes. If you use the Eyedropper tool to sample the stroke appearance of any art in Flash, after the sample has been made, the Eyedropper tool will automatically take on all the characteristics of the sampled stroke. The Ink Bottle does not have any options, but you can choose the color, thickness, and style of the stroke using the Properties Inspector in conjunction with one of the vector drawing tools.

## The Eyedropper Tool

### Shortcut: PC and Mac–I

Use the Eyedropper (or Dropper) tool to select color values on the screen. If you are drawing a new object and prefer for the fill or stroke color to appear the same as any other value on the screen, simply use the Eyedropper tool to sample that color value. When you click the color value, it's automatically stored in the appropriate Ink Well tool in the Tools panel. If you choose a stroke color, all attributes of that stroke (including size, color, and style) will be sampled. If you are using the Eyedropper tool from the Tools panel, you are limited to sampling within the confines of the stage. If you are using the Dropper tool built into the Swatches panel, you can sample a color from any source on the computer screen.

## The Pencil Tool

### Shortcut: PC and Mac–Y

When drawing with the Pencil tool, you'll notice it uses a stroke color opposed to a fill color. You can change its stroke appearance by choosing a stroke style in the Properties Inspector. The Pencil tool has some interesting options that can aid in the final outcome of a drawing. These options are detailed in the following list and displayed in Figure 3.4:

- **Straighten**. Choose this option if your goal is to draw a perfect circle, oval, square, rectangle, or arc. The sensitivity of how Flash determines a shape is set in the Preferences dialog box. You can access these preferences by choosing Edit, Preferences. For more information on preferences, refer to Chapter 2, "Getting Started with Flash MX 2004 Professional." Check out Figure 3.5 to see an example of drawing with Straighten turned on.

- **Smooth**. Generally this option will smooth out any curvy lines.

- **Ink**. This choice is for freehand drawing without Flash making adjustments to the lines.

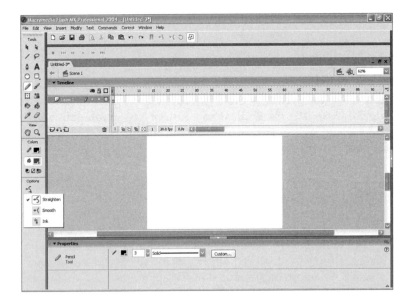

**FIGURE 3.4** Pencil tool options.

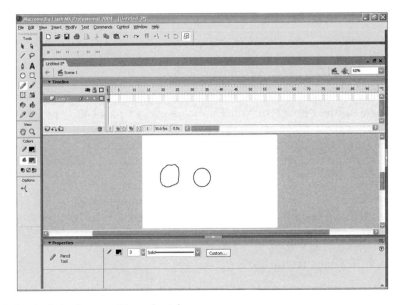

**FIGURE 3.5** A circle drawn with each style.

**TIP**

When you're drawing with the Ink option selected, it may look as if some modification is happening to your lines when the mouse is released. Flash isn't making any adjustments to the curviness or straightness of the line; rather, it's antialiasing the edges of the line.

After the line has been drawn, you may feel that it needs to be smoother or straighter. This may aid in the visual appearance of the stroke, and you might actually reduce file size by reducing the complexity of the stroke. To make a line straighter, follow these steps:

1. Click the line with the Arrow tool. The line will be selected.

2. With the line selected, in the Options portion of the toolbar, as shown in Figure 3.6, choose the Straighten button.

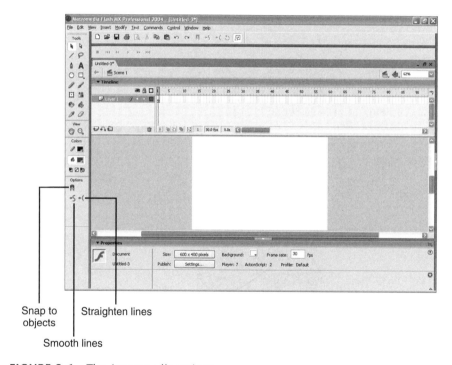

Snap to objects    Straighten lines

Smooth lines

**FIGURE 3.6**   The Arrow tool's options.

3. Click the Straighten button as many times as needed to get the desired effect.

The same method will work when smoothing a line.

## The Rectangle Tool

### Shortcut: PC and Mac–R

The Rectangle tool is used to create squares and rectangles. To create a perfect square, hold down the Shift key to constrain the drawn object's proportions to that of a square. One option the Rectangle tool has involves setting the corner radius to make rounded edges. If you click the Round Radius button in the Options section of the toolbar (or double-click the Rectangle tool in the toolbar), a dialog box will appear. In the text field, type in a numeric value between 0 and 999 that represents the corner radius.

---

**TIP**

Sometimes it is difficult to gage how much roundness you will want to put on your rectangle's corners in a numeric form, so while drawing the rectangle you can press and hold down the down-arrow key to increase the roundness, and press and hold down the up-arrow key to decrease the roundness.

---

**Drawing and Coloring Rectangle Shapes**

Here are the steps to follow to draw and color a rectangle shape:

1. Choose the Rectangle tool from the Tools panel.

2. In the Color portion of the Tools panel (or the Properties Inspector), choose a stroke color. If no stroke is desired, choose the first box in the top-right corner of the swatches, as shown in Figure 3.7.

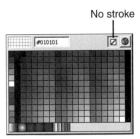

**FIGURE 3.7**    Choosing the No Stroke option.

3. If you would prefer to use a custom color, something other than a Web-safe color, click the button to the right of the No Stroke button to bring up the Color Picker. Inside the Color Picker are many different ways to view color in terms of organization.

4. Choose a fill color. All the same techniques in terms of color selection used for the stroke apply to the fill as well.

5. To create rounded edges, click the Round Rectangle Radius button in the Options section of the Tools panel.

6. Place the cursor in the stage; then click and drag until the rectangle is the desired size. If the goal is to create a perfect square, hold down the Shift key.

If you choose Snap to Objects from the options when you draw a rectangle, you'll notice it is easier to have a perfect square because your cursor will snap to a large circle around your cursor, as shown in Figure 3.8.

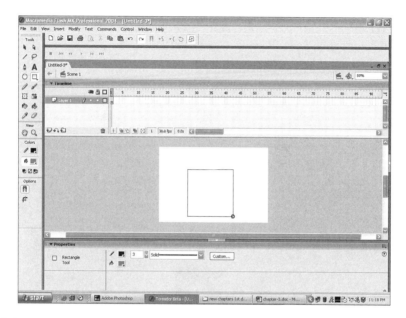

**FIGURE 3.8**    Drawing a square with Snap to Objects selected.

The higher the value entered in the Round Rectangle Radius dialog box, the more rounded the corners become. Avoid very large numbers, especially for smaller rectangles. If you do use a large number, you run the risk of turning your rectangle into a circle.

When using the Rectangle tool, you may notice some unusual behavior when it comes to moving objects. This is discussed in detail in the "Tips for Creating Graphics in Flash" section, later in this chapter.

## The Oval Tool

### Shortcut: PC and Mac–O

The Oval tool is used to create circles and ovals. To create a perfect circle, hold down the Shift key. This will constrain the drawn object's proportions to that of a circle. If Snap to Objects is selected in the options when you're drawing an oval, the shape will snap to a perfect circle when dragged at a 45-degree angle.

## The Paint Bucket Tool

### Shortcut: PC and Mac–K

The Paint Bucket is used to fill an item with a color or gradient. To choose a color or gradient, click the Fill Color tool of the fill swatch in the Tools panel or in the Properties Inspector.

After you select the fill color, move the Paint Bucket tool over an object and click it to change its fill color to the new fill color.

In the Options area of the Tools panel, notice that the Paint Bucket tool has a Gap Size option as displayed in Figure 3.9.

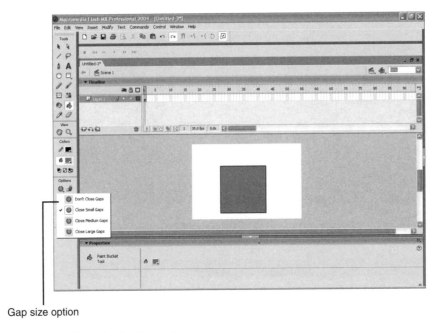

Gap size option

**FIGURE 3.9**   The Paint Bucket options.

Select the first choice, Don't Close Gaps, if there are certain areas in your artwork that shouldn't be filled.

The Close Small Gaps, Close Medium Gaps, and Close Large Gaps options all work in the same way. If you have complex drawings that need to be filled, you may want to choose one of these options. If you have Close Large Gaps selected and it doesn't seem to be working, either the gap is too large or there are too many gaps in your art.

The last option in the Tools panel is Lock Fill, which allows you to apply a gradient or bitmap fill consistently across multiple items.

**Using Lock Fill to Apply a Gradient Across Multiple Objects**

Here are the steps to follow to use Lock Fill to apply a gradient across multiple objects:

1. Draw four squares on the stage and align them using the Align panel. Space them out so that the entire stage is being used, edge to edge.

2. Choose the Paint Bucket tool in the Tools panel and be sure to choose the rainbow linear gradient in the fill swatch.

3. Click the Lock Fill button in the Options portion of the Tools panel.

4. Fill the first square, then the second, third, and fourth. You'll notice that the gradient is being applied as if the four squares are one continuous shape.

5. To see the different squares, fill each one with a gradient without the Lock Fill option selected.

   To apply a gradient across multiple items without using Lock Fill, simply choose all the items by drawing an invisible marquee with the Arrow tool or by Shift-clicking each object. Then click one of the items. You'll notice the gradient has applied color across more than one item. The effect, however, looks a bit different when compared to the Lock Fill effect.

6. If you want to fill the squares with a bitmap, choose File, Import, Import to Stage and search for the image on your computer. When the image is in Flash, highlight it and choose Modify, Break Apart. (For more information on importing bitmap graphics, see the section "Color Mixer", later in this chapter.)

## The PolyStar Tool

### Shortcut: None

New to the toolbar is the PolyStar tool. This tool is used to draw multisided polygons or multipoint stars. To select this tool, you click and hold down on the Rectangle tool in the toolbar. Then a submenu will appear as shown in Figure 3.10. Select the PolyStar tool from there. There is no shortcut key for this tool on the Mac or the PC.

When you select the PolyStar tool, there is only one option in the Options section of the toolbar, the Snap to Object button, which works very similarly here as it does with the Rectangle and Oval tool. You can change the polystar characteristics in the Properties Inspector using the Options button. This will bring up the Tool Settings dialog box (see Figure 3.11) where you can choose either polygon or star, the number of sides (or points when drawing a star), and the star point size (which only affects stars).

**NOTE**

The maximum value of sides is 32, and the minimum is 3. And the maximum value for point size is 1, with a minimum value of 0.

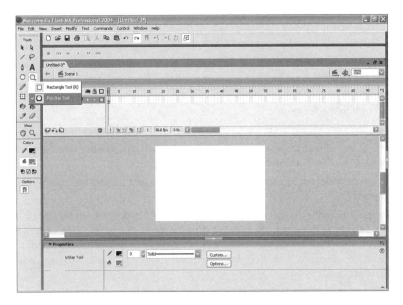

**FIGURE 3.10**    Choose the PolyStar tool to draw multisided objects as well as stars on the stage.

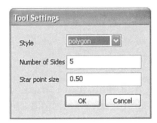

**FIGURE 3.11**    In the Tool Settings dialog box, you can choose settings for the PolyStar tool.

Drawing polystars can be a bit tricky at first because unlike the other shape drawing tools, while you are drawing the size of the shape, you can also control the rotation of the shape. Holding down the Shift key while drawing polystars will slow down the rotation and make it easier to control.

## The Fill Transform Tool

### Shortcut: PC and Mac–F

The Fill Transform tool is designed to change the appearance of an applied gradient or bitmap fill. This tool enables you to make adjustments to the direction, size, center point, and rotation of the gradient or bitmap fill.

Depending on the type of fill—radial gradient, linear gradient, or bitmap fill—the type of alterations that can be performed vary slightly. After you get some practice using the Fill Transform tool, it will be something you'll use quite often. In the next exercise, you learn how to go about modifying a radial gradient. These same principles apply to transforming a linear gradient. You'll save the bitmap fill for later in the chapter in the "Importing Bitmap Graphics" section.

### Working with the Fill Transform Tool

Here are the steps to modify a radial gradient:

1. Draw a circle using the Oval tool (remember, to draw a perfect circle, hold down the Shift key on your keyboard). When choosing a fill color for the circle, choose one of the default radial gradients.

2. With the circle on the stage, select the Fill Transform tool in the toolbar. Notice that your cursor has changed into a arrow pointer with a small gradient icon to the bottom right.

3. Click in the center of the circle. This will activate the bounding transform handles, shown in Figure 3.12.

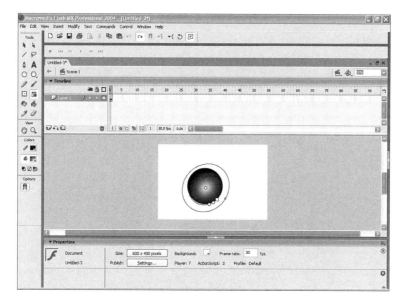

**FIGURE 3.12**    Fill Transform bounding handles.

4. The top square handle will skew the gradient. Therefore, drag the skew handle out just a few pixels.

5. The center handle will change the radius of the gradient (radial gradient only). Drag this center handle out about 40 pixels.

6. The bottom handle will change the rotation of the gradient. There is no need at this point to rotate the gradient.

7. Drag the center circle handle toward the top-left corner of your shape. This will change the center point of the gradient.

8. Click outside the gradient bounding box to deactivate it. Our circle now looks like a 3D sphere.

---

**NOTE**

Be sure to check out the instructional QuickTime movie on how to transform fills, located on this book's companion Web site, `http://www.samspublishing.com`.

---

## The Brush Tool

### Shortcut: PC and Mac–B

The Brush tool is a painting tool in Flash that offers several options for painting. It's important to note that the Brush tool uses a fill, as opposed to a stroke, like the other tools we've just looked at. The Brush tool can use solid colors, gradients, and even bitmaps to paint. The options in the Tools panel for the Brush tool are shown in Figure 3.13. The following list details these options:

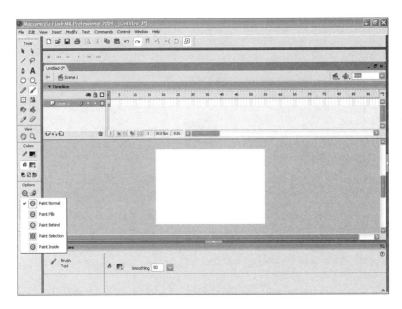

**FIGURE 3.13**    The different brush modes for the Brush tool.

- **Paint Normal**. Use this option to paint the fill color anywhere you drag the Brush tool.

- **Paint Fills**. This option allows you to paint only fill colors (although it really should be called Preserve Strokes). Paint Fills can be a bit confusing, because it will paint empty parts of the stage. However, what it won't do is alter any stroke colors.

- **Paint Behind**. Choose this option if you only want to paint an area underneath artwork already placed on the stage.

- **Paint Selection**. This option allows the Brush tool to paint only in areas that have been selected.

- **Paint Inside**. This option allows the brush to paint only in the interior section of the artwork. It will not paint or alter stroke colors. When using this option, be sure to start in the interior of the item; otherwise, the Brush tool will think the stage is the item to paint inside.

You can also change the size of the brush by using the Brush Size drop-down menu, shown in Figure 3.14. When choosing a brush size, be aware that brush sizes are always relative to the magnification of the document. For example, if you have a document magnified at 400%, and you select a certain brush size and then zoom out of the document to 100%, that same brush will appear smaller at the 100% document size than it did at 400% magnification.

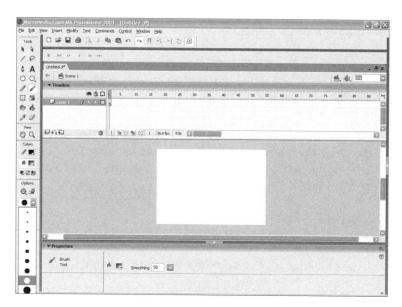

**FIGURE 3.14**    The Brush Size drop-down menu.

In the Brush Shape drop-down menu, shown in Figure 3.15, you can select a brush shape or style. It consists of squares, ovals, rectangles, and many different angle brushes. When selecting a brush shape, keep in mind that the size of the brush will also play a big role in the final appearance of the brush mark.

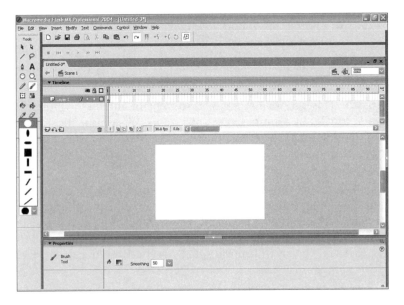

**FIGURE 3.15**   The Brush Shape drop-down menu.

The last option for the Brush tool is Lock Fill. We discussed this option in detail in the section "The Paint Bucket Tool," earlier in this chapter. This instance of Lock Fill works the same way. Of course, to get certain effects, you will need to use this option with a combination of brush modes.

Finally, note that the Brush tool offers a Pressure option when a Wacom tablet is used. See the Wacom Technology Company's Web page at www.wacom.com for more information. A Wacom tablet is a pressure-sensitive drawing pad that gives the mouse a behavior like a traditional art pad and pencil.

## The Eraser Tool
### Shortcut: PC and Mac–E

The Eraser tool, used for erasing shapes on the stage, has a few options of its own:

- **Erase Normal**. This option is the standard way of erasing content. It works exactly as you would expect: If you move the eraser over a fill or stroke color, it will be erased.

- **Erase Fills**. This option only erases the fill color of objects, without harming the stroke color.

- **Erase Lines**. Erase Lines only erases stroke colors and does not alter fills.

- **Erase Selected Fills**. This option only erases items with fills that have been selected. Any fills not selected will not be harmed.

- **Erase Inside**. Erase Inside only erases the interior color of the object in which you start erasing initially. This option will not erase anything outside the interior parameter of that object.

### The Eraser's Faucet Option

Personally, I think the Faucet tool is great. The Faucet tool literally washes the color out of a fill or stroke when you click on it.

Finally, you can choose an eraser size and shape, such as a circle or square (similar to the Brush tool).

## The Pen Tool

### Shortcut: PC and Mac–P

The Pen tool allows you to define straight lines and smooth curves. To draw with the Pen tool, move the mouse and click successively. Each new point will connect with the previous point to create a line segment. To create a curved line segment, use your mouse to drag the point in the direction you want the curve. The length of the tangent will determine the arc of the curve.

The Pen tool has some preferences that need to be set in the Preferences dialog box. To access this dialog box, choose Edit, Preferences. Inside this dialog box, select the Editing tab. Here are the options you'll find:

- **Show Pen Preview**. This option offers a preview of what the line segment will look like when an anchor is placed. If you're new to the Pen tool, this is a great option to check because it helps beginners get more comfortable with the behavior of the Pen tool.

- **Show Solid Points**. With this option selected, the selected vector points will appear hollow, and the unselected points will appear solid. By default, this option is not selected, giving the opposite appearance (solid indicates selected points and hollow refers to unselected points).

- **Show Precise**. There are two different views for the Pen tool. When using the Pen tool, you can either view the standard pen icon or choose Precise, which will display crosshairs. Checking this box will only change the default appearance of the Pen tool to Precise. This option is pretty useless, given that you can toggle between the two different views using the Caps Lock key.

The Pen tool also has several different options in terms of changing, adding, deleting, and transforming points. When these options are available, there is a slight difference in the appearance of the Pen tool's icon. The following list explains these differences:

- **Cursor 1**. This cursor icon displays a small minus sign (-). This means that if you were to click a vector point, it would be deleted.

- **Cursor 2**. This cursor icon displays a caret sign (^), which means that if you click a vector point, it will turn into a right angle.

- **Cursor 3**. This cursor icon (+) adds a vector point to the existing line segment.

- **Cursor 4**. This cursor displays a small x. This icon indicates there's no line segment present to edit. To avoid seeing this icon, be sure to have the mouse positioned directly over a line segment.

- **Cursor 5**. When the Pen tool is over the first vector point placed, you'll see the small "o" icon, indicating that this will close the path or shape.

- **Cursor 6**. When the Shift key is held down, the cursor icon changes into an arrow with a solid box. This indicates that you are moving the mouse over a line.

- **Cursor 7**. When the Shift key is held down, the cursor icon changes into an arrow with a hollow box. This indicates that you are moving the mouse over a vector point.

After drawing a path with the Pen tool, you can edit the path using any of the pen icon cursor changes just explained, or you can use the Subselection tool. The Subselection tool allows you to change selected vector points and tangent lines. Remember that tangent lines change the degrees of the arc and the direction of the curve. Figure 3.16 shows an example of tangent handles.

## The Free Transform Tool

### Shortcut: PC and Mac–Q

This tool has several options for distorting, skewing, scaling, and rotating items in Flash.

With an item selected on the stage, choose the Free Transform tool in the Tools panel. Notice the bounding box around the item. If there isn't an item selected on the stage when the Free Transform tool is chosen, you will not see this bounding box. However, if you click an item with this tool selected, the bounding box will appear around that object.

The handles on the bounding box allow you to make all sorts of modifications to the object. The handles in the corner scale down the item, and holding down the Shift key will constrain the item's proportions. Just outside the corners, you can rotate the item. Using the handles on the side will scale it horizontally and vertically. Moving the cursor between handles will allow you to skew and distort the item.

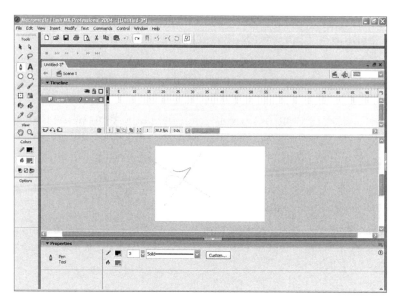

**FIGURE 3.16**    Tangent handles.

The Free Transform tool also has several options in the Tools panel (see Figure 3.17). These options are discussed in the following list:

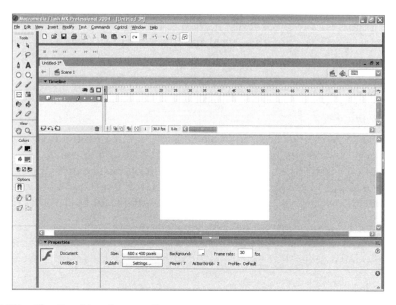

**FIGURE 3.17**    The Free Transform options.

- **Snap to Objects**. This option will assist you when you scale the item either vertically or horizontally, but want to maintain the other scaling.

- **Rotate and Skew**. This option rotates the item around the center point using the corner handles. Notice that you can move the center point to change the axis of rotation. It also allows you to skew the item using the handles on the sides.

- **Scale**. This option automatically constrains the proportions of the item when you're using the corner handles. You can also scale the object horizontally and vertically.

- **Distort**. This option moves the corner or edge points to distort the item by realigning the adjoining edges. If you drag a corner handle and hold down the Shift key on your keyboard, the edge will taper. Tapering moves the opposing corner in the opposite direction at an equal distance.

- **Envelope**. This option offers the ultimate control in transforming an item. You adjust the points, and tangent handles modify the item. This option works with one or more selected items.

> **CAUTION**
>
> The final two options of the Free Transform tool—Distort and Envelope—only work with primitive items. If the artwork is a symbol, a grouped object, a video object, or text, it will be deactivated. In order to use these options, you must break apart the artwork by choosing Modify, Break Apart.

To flip an item horizontally or vertically, it's best to use the options under the Modify menu. To flip an object, be sure it's selected and then choose Modify, Transform, Flip Horizontal or Vertical.

## The Text Tool
### Shortcut: PC and Mac–T

Using text in Flash is in some cases as simple as using text in a word processing application. In other cases, it's about as difficult to use as HTML text. Remember, in order for text to be displayed on an end user's machine, the proper font must be present on that user's system. We're going to take a look at some obstacles to using text and how to remedy any potential problems. We are also going to review the editing features Flash has to offer.

Text can be used for many different tasks in Flash—from something as basic as having a word spelled out on a page, all the way to being a container for variable information. This is why our discussion of the Text tool is broken into sections. Let's start at the editing features.

### Text Tool Editing Features

Select the Text tool in the Tools panel. The Text tool has no options. However, if you take a look at the Properties Inspector, you'll see that it's loaded with goodies for changing the appearance of your text, as shown in Figure 3.18.

**FIGURE 3.18**   Text tool's properties.

The most obvious option in the Properties Inspector is the one for changing the typeface. In the drop-down menu, you'll see a list of the available fonts installed on your system. Along with this option is the ability to change the font size. To change the font's point size, either type in a value or use the slider to increase or decrease the size. To change the color of the text, use the Text (fill) color tool to the right of the Font Size field. Of course, you also have keyboard options for making the text bold (Ctrl/Cmd+Shift+B) and italic (Ctrl/Cmd+Shift+I).

To begin typing in Flash, choose the Text tool and click where you want the text to appear on the stage. As you type, the text box will resize to accommodate all the text.

The other option, when the Text tool is first selected, is to click and drag a bounding text box on the stage. This will create a text block that will not permit any text to resize its dimensions. As you type, the text will automatically wrap and make breaks whenever and wherever necessary to fit inside the defined text box. You can always resize the text box by grabbing the handle in the top-right corner and dragging to the new desired size (see Figure 3.19).

**CAUTION**

You must use the text tool to resize the text field; if you use the Free Transform tool, it will not only resize the text field, but also stretch the text inside it.

Tracking and kerning options are also available (see Figure 3.20). What you may find tricky, however, is the fact that both options are accessed under the same slider. To adjust the tracking of the text, make sure either the entire word is highlighted in black or the text has been selected with the Arrow tool and a blue box is visible around the type.

You can type in a value, where positive numbers increase the space between the letters and negative values decrease the space. When this is done on an individual basis, such as to adjust the space between the letters *A* and *V* instead of a whole word, it's known as **kerning**.

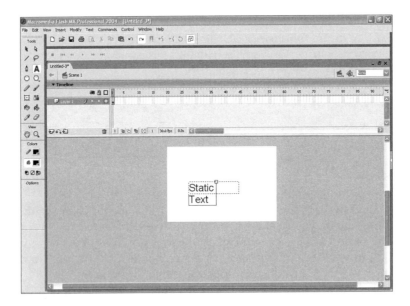

**FIGURE 3.19**    Resizing a text box.

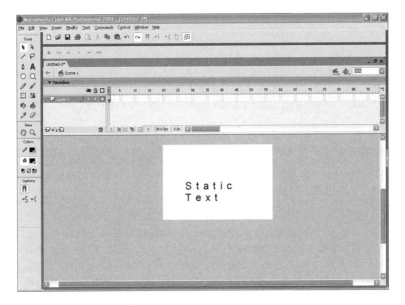

**FIGURE 3.20**    Adjusting the tracking.

To adjust the kerning between two characters, highlight both characters and use the same text box or slider to input a positive or negative value; the results are shown in Figure 3.21. Many times when you're typing this value, it is beneficial to have the Auto Kern check box selected. This gives you a good chance of returning some acceptable results—and at the very least, it offers a good starting place.

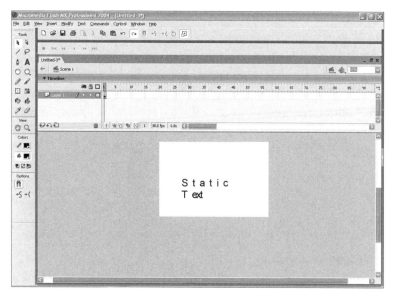

**FIGURE 3.21**    Adjusting the kerning.

Here are some important shortcuts for adjusting the kerning and/or tracking:

- **Decrease spacing by half a pixel**. Cmd+Option+left arrow (Mac) and Ctrl+Alt+left arrow (Windows)

- **Decrease spacing by two pixels**. Cmd+Shift+Option+left arrow (Mac) and Ctrl+Shift+Alt+left arrow (Windows)

- **Increase spacing by half a pixel**. Cmd+Option+right arrow (Mac) and Ctrl+Alt+right arrow (Windows)

- **Increase spacing by two pixels**. Cmd+Shift+Option+right arrow (Mac) and Ctrl+Shift+Alt+right arrow (Windows)

The Properties Inspector also has options for using subscripts and superscripts. You use subscripts to type something like "$H_2O$," where the small character is just below the baseline, and you use superscripts for something like "Macromedia®," where the small character is flush with the tops of the ascenders (like the line on a lowercase d).

### Setting Alignment and Margins
With the Text tool selected, inside the Properties Inspector, just to the right of the Italic button is another button that enables you to change the direction of the text. The three

choices are Horizontal (default left to right), Vertical Left to Right and Vertical Right to Left. Also available is the Rotate option, to rotate the text after the direction has been changed from horizontal. Depending on the direction of the text, the next four buttons provide options for justifying the text.

The alignment options include top/left justification, center, right justification, and full justification. These options predetermine the text if a justification option is chosen before the text is entered. If the text has already been entered, highlight the desired text block and then apply the desired justification.

Click the Format button for the following additional formatting options (see Figure 3.22):

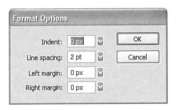

**FIGURE 3.22**    Format options.

- **Indent**. Enter a value in points to determine how much the first line of every paragraph should be indented. This option only works with predefined text blocks.

- **Line Spacing**. This option controls the space between lines in text blocks in points (this is known as **leading**). Positive numbers increase the amount of space between lines; negative numbers decrease the space.

- **Left Margin**. This option creates a margin or space on the left side of a text block in points.

- **Right Margin**. This option creates a margin or space on the right side of a text block in points.

### Device and Embedded Fonts

In Flash you can use device fonts. If you decide to use a device font, you can save a good amount of file size in your final SWF file. Included in the file when Use Device Fonts is enabled are items such as the name of the typeface, the family of the type, and some other information to help Flash Player evaluate whether the end user has the font. To enable Use Device Fonts, make sure the text field is set to Static and, in the Properties Inspector, check the Use Device Fonts box.

If the end user does not have the typeface installed on his or her system, the Flash Player will know to replace it with a serif or sans-serif typeface. Device fonts are best used with smaller text and very common typefaces. If the text is large, the best bet is to break apart the text so that it becomes a shape.

Another option at the bottom portion of the Properties Inspector includes making the text selectable and creating hyperlinks. Sometimes in Flash you may want important information on a Web site to be selectable so that the end user can copy that information. You may also want some text to be hyperlinked to additional HTML documents. You can create a hyperlink by typing in a link in the Hyperlink text box at the bottom of the Properties Inspector.

### Alias Text

A new feature for text fields in Flash MX 2004 is the Alias Text button found in the Properties Inspector when the Text tool is selected. This new feature allows text at smaller sizes to become more readable and is available in static, dynamic, and input text fields for the Flash 7 Player, but only in static text fields for earlier player versions.

This feature will affect text at all sizes, but is most effective at sizes 12 and smaller.

So far, all we have explored is static text. You'll notice a couple of other choices in the drop-down menu toward the top-right corner of the Properties Inspector. These choices—Dynamic and Input Text—are discussed in great detail in Chapter 17, "Working with Text."

## The Zoom Tool

### Shortcut: PC and Mac–Z,M

The Zoom tool allows you to zoom in to a subject as much as 2000%. This helps when you're performing precise work. When you click the Zoom tool, it always zooms in twice as much as the current magnification. To zoom out, hold down the Option (Mac) or Alt (Windows) key and click the mouse.

Double-clicking the Zoom tool will reset the magnification to 100%. Here are some keyboard shortcuts you may want to keep in mind:

- To zoom in, use Cmd (Mac) or Ctrl (Windows) with the plus key.

- To zoom out, hold down Cmd (Mac) or Ctrl (Windows) and the hyphen key (-) at the same time.

Remember, there is also the Zoom drop-down menu docked just above the timeline.

## The Hand Tool

### Shortcut: PC and Mac–H

The Hand tool is used to move around the stage. When zoomed in to a particular part of a Flash movie, you may find it difficult to navigate to different areas of the movie. This is where the Hand tool comes in, well, handy. You can literally move the stage: Just click with the Hand tool and drag until you see the desired location in which you want to work.

Also, if you double-click the Hand tool in the toolbar, the stage will size to its maximum size while still completely visible, and it will also become centered.

---
**TIP**

The spacebar acts as a toggle to turn the Hand tool on no matter what tool you are currently using.

---

## The Lasso Tool

### Shortcut: PC and Mac–L

The Lasso tool is a selection tool, and it makes the most sense to use this tool with bitmaps (which we discuss later in this chapter). Use the Lasso tool just as you would any drawing tool. To make a clean, precise selection, try to close the path the lasso makes. Otherwise, the results can be less than predictable. The Lasso tool has some options at the bottom of the Tools panel. The first is the Magic Wand tool; its settings are shown in Figure 3.23. The Magic Wand tool selects an area or value of pixels based on its set tolerance. You can set the tolerance by clicking the button to the right of the Magic Wand tool. The higher the tolerance, the more values the selection will consider to be the same.

**FIGURE 3.23**   The Magic Wand settings.

The Smoothing option is for determining how smooth the selected edge should become. Here are the choices:

- **Smooth**. Rounds the selection edges.
- **Pixels**. The selection is wrapped around the rectangular edge of similar color pixels.
- **Rough**. The selection becomes even more angular than with the Pixels option.
- **Normal**. Creates a selection that is a bit softer than Pixels but not as soft as the Smooth option.

The last option is the Polygon Lasso tool. Use this tool for angular or geometric type shapes. See Figure 3.24 for the Lasso's options.

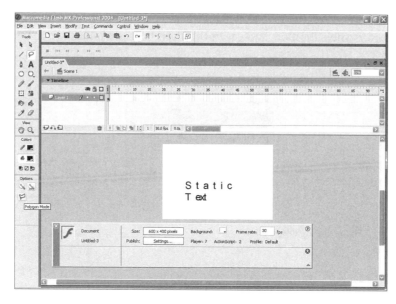

**FIGURE 3.24**   The Lasso tool's options.

# Creating Custom Colors and Gradients

Conveniently, Macromedia has incorporated the Web-safe color palette into the swatches in Flash. Often, however, you may need to use a color located on a different swatch, or you may want to create gradients using your own color choices.

Therefore, we'll take a look at a couple of panels in Flash. The first is the Color Swatches panel; the second is the Color Mixer panel. Each can be used to select different colors; however, the Mixer panel gives you precise control over certain color properties.

## Color Swatches

In the Color Swatches panel, shown in Figure 3.25, you can sort colors, load different swatch sets, and even load bitmap graphics. To import different swatch sets, click in the top-right corner of the Color Swatches panel to access the drop-down menu. Choose Add Colors, find a Flash color set file (typically located in your Flash MX program folder), and select it. This will add any additional swatch sets to the panel. However, if you choose Replace Swatches, all existing swatches will be replaced with the new loaded set.

If you've added and arranged this panel in a way that feels comfortable to you, consider making it the default. In the submenu, choose Save as Default so that every time you open Flash, these color swatches will be loaded in the panel.

However, if you feel that the swatch set you've customized is good only for certain occasions, you can simply save that swatch set as a swatch. In the submenu, choose Save

Colors, which will launch the Export Color Swatch window. Name the color set and save it in an easily accessible location, such as in the Flash program folder under \en\First Run\Color Sets.

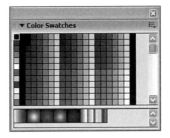

**FIGURE 3.25**    The Color Swatches panel.

## Color Mixer

The Color Mixer panel is a bit more robust in comparison to the Color Swatches panel. Notice how much the Color Mixer panel offers in Figure 3.26.

**FIGURE 3.26**    The Color Mixer panel.

The Color Swatches panel is best for accessing stored colors. The Color Mixer panel, on the other hand, is used in customizing colors and gradients. After you've created these custom colors, you can store them in the Color Swatches panel. Therefore, these two panels work well together.

At first glance, you'll see that the Color Mixer panel has a nice color ramp from which you can choose colors. As you take a closer look, you should also notice the many different ways to come up with certain colors.

By default, you can type in numbers for the red, green, and blue (RGB) values. This can be useful, especially if you're working with a graphics application such as Fireworks or Photoshop to create artwork. If you need to match a certain color element in that graphic, you can get an RGB or HSB readout in the other program and type those values into this swatch. You can easily change the RGB values to display hue, saturation, and brightness by choosing the appropriate option in the Color Mixer's submenu.

## Accessing Custom Colors Using the Color Picker

Here are the steps to follow to access custom colors using the Color Picker:

1. Open the fill swatch and choose the color wheel in the top-right corner of the palette. This will open the Color Picker dialog box. In Windows, the Color Picker dialog box looks like an overgrown Color Mixer panel. You have the color ramp, where you can select a custom color and even add that custom color to a custom swatch within the dialog box. The Mac, however, is quite different. (Notice that on the Mac, if you move the dropper away from the color swatches, you can sample any color on your computer screen.) You can see the Mac RGB Color Picker in Figure 3.27.

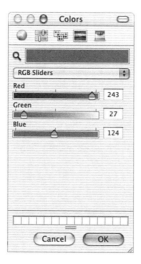

**FIGURE 3.27**    The RGB Color Picker on the Macintosh.

2. By default, the RGB Color Picker will appear. In this dialog box, you can choose a color by moving the percentage sliders from left to right. Moving them to the right will increase the amounts of the corresponding colors to higher percentages.

3. Move the Red slider to 100%.

4. Move the Green slider to 0%.

5. Move the Blue slider to 0%. Notice the color difference between the original color and the new color. The end result is a pure red. Often you'll need to refer to some numbers generated during content development so that you can match certain pieces or areas of artwork.

Figure 3.28 shows the Name Color Picker window on the Macintosh.

**FIGURE 3.28**    The Name Color Picker on the Macintosh.

6. Move the slider next to the color ramp to reveal a selection of colors.

7. Choose the desired color. Notice that all these colors have a corresponding hexadecimal value. These hexadecimal values are Web-safe colors. A Web-safe color is a color commonly shared between a Macintosh and a Windows machine if you drop them down to their lowest 256, 8-bit color display. There are only 216 Web-safe colors.

Figure 3.29 shows the HSV Color Picker window on the Macintosh.

**FIGURE 3.29**    The Hue, Saturation, and Value (HSV) Color Picker on the Macintosh.

**8.** Choose a color by clicking anywhere on the color wheel.

**9.** Use the slider on the right to adjust the brightness.

3

---

**CAUTION**

If you are new to Web development, be aware that even though 216 colors are commonly shared between the Mac and Windows operating systems, a Mac's colors are generally brighter, and the Windows colors are commonly darker. However, using Web-safe colors seems to be less and less an issue with modern-day machines displaying well over a million colors.

---

The slider underneath the color wheel will adjust the value. Moving the crosshairs around in the color wheel will adjust the hue angle as well as the percentage of the saturation.

The Crayon Color Picker allows you to choose a color with a specific name. These colors are not necessarily Web-safe colors. The Crayon Color Picker offers an assortment of nicely organized, easy-to-find colors as shown in Figure 3.30.

**FIGURE 3.30**   The Crayon Color Picker on the Macintosh.

The CMYK section is a color mixer that uses the common four-color print process of cyan, magenta, yellow, and black. As mentioned earlier, Web-safe colors are becoming less of an issue. However, you could find yourself in a situation in which your company wants a CMYK color to be used throughout its Web site. Commonly, this happens with logos. To keep in line with company standards, you may choose to use the exact colors printed in the logo. Ultimately, this will result in a consistent look throughout the Web site. Refer to Figure 3.31 for the CMYK Color Picker.

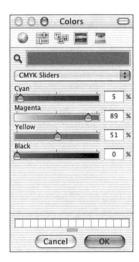

**FIGURE 3.31**    The CMYK Color Picker on the Macintosh.

## Changing a Color's Alpha

A great feature of Flash is the ability to change the alpha of a color. The Alpha setting controls how opaque or how transparent a color will be. The default is set to 100% but can be lowered all the way down to 0%. This can be useful in animations—perhaps you'd like an object to fade in or out, or you may want an item to cross over another item, in which case you may want to see the item underneath.

To change a color's alpha, choose the desired color in the fill swatch. Next, use the slider to the right of the Alpha field to lower the percentage of the alpha. You may also type in a value in the Alpha field. The lower the alpha percentage, the more transparent the color will become.

After the color has been set, you can use this new transparent color just as you would any other color. In fact, you can even save it in the swatch set.

## Saving a Color to a Swatch

It's quite simple to save any custom color you've created or selected. With the custom color in the fill or stroke swatch selected, move your cursor into the Color Swatches panel. When your cursor is in an empty area of the swatch, it turns into a Paint Bucket tool. Click an empty area and notice that the color has been added to fill the empty area with the selected fill color. You can also add a color by choosing a color in the Color Mixer panel, activating the submenu, and choosing Add Swatch.

---

**TIP**

With all these options in the Color Mixer, you may find yourself with many custom colors. After you've added these colors to the Color Swatches panel, it may be a good idea to save them as a swatch.

---

## Modifying and Creating Gradients

The Color Mixer panel is an area where you can modify existing gradient colors by changing, adding, or deleting the colors that make up any given gradient. When you have a gradient selected in the fill swatch, notice the new options in the Color Mixer panel.

In Figure 3.32, the drop-down menu contains choices for a radial gradient and a linear gradient. Also, take note of the new color ramp for the gradient. Each triangle marker in the ramp is a color that will be represented in the gradient. If you're working with a simple two-color gradient (for example, from white to black), these two colors will gradually intersect one another.

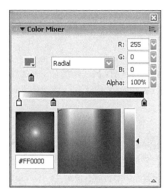

**FIGURE 3.32**    The Color Mixer panel with a gradient as the active fill.

---

**Modifying a Color Gradient**

Here are the steps to follow in order to modify a color gradient:

1. Draw a circle with no stroke and a radial gradient selected for the fill.

2. To change the gradient's colors, highlight one of the markers in the gradient ramp located in the Color Mixer panel.

3. With the triangle selected, open the Ink Well tool above the ramp in the Color Mixer panel and choose a new color. Notice that the gradient is automatically updated.

4. Select the other marker and change its color as well.

5. To edit this gradient further, you can add even more color by adding additional markers to the gradient ramp. To create a new midrange color in the gradient, simply click in an

empty area just underneath the gradient ramp. Notice the new marker with a midrange color.

6. Change the new marker's color by using the Color Picker tool in the Color Mixer panel.

7. You can add as many new markers as necessary to achieve the desired effect. To remove any unnecessary markers, click and drag them down and away from the color ramp.

8. When the gradient is complete and you feel you might use the new gradient color later down the road, you may want to save it in your Color Swatches panel. Select the submenu in the Color Mixer panel and choose Add Swatch.

**NOTE**

Be sure to check out the instructional QuickTime movie on how to create custom gradients located on this book's companion Web site, `http://www.samspublishing.com`.

## Tips for Creating Graphics in Flash

You may have noticed by now that using the drawing tools in Flash has several advantages and some disadvantages. Let's take a look at the behavior of the graphics we've created after we have them placed on the stage.

Here are the steps to  the drawing tools in Flash has several advantages and some disadvantages. Let's take a look at the behavior of the graphics we've created once we have them placed on the stage.

**Drawing and Moving Primitive Items**

Here are the steps to follow in this exercise:

1. In the Tools panel, choose the Rectangle tool. In the Options portion of the Tools panel, click the Round Rectangle Radius option.

2. In the Colors section of the Tools panel, choose a stroke color and a fill color.

3. Draw a rectangle somewhere on the stage.

4. After drawing the rectangle, choose the Arrow tool, click the center of the square, and drag the object to a new location.

5. Notice that after you move the item, a stroke is left behind. To avoid this, you must double-click the item (you'll notice the fill and stroke are both selected) and then click it one more time to move it.

Flash's primitive objects will separate strokes from fills. This, of course, can cause all sorts of problems, but there is a bright side. Although this issue can sometimes be annoying, it does provide for the ultimate control of your primitive items. For example, use the Line tool to draw a star. If you try to trace an outline of a star, it may seem rather difficult.

However, if you draw the star in the same way you'd draw it on paper without ever picking up the pencil, you can remove the interior lines to make the perfect star as shown in Figure 3.33.

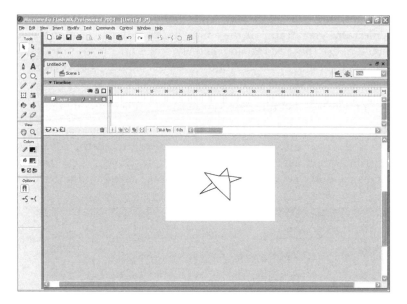

**FIGURE 3.33**    This star was drawn using the Line tool, and the interior lines being selected with the Arrow tool are to be deleted.

Flash has some additional issues we need to look at when it comes to creating graphics. Flash will also combine two items with the same fill color, or it will punch a hole in an underlying primitive object. See the next exercise for an example.

### Placing Primitive Items on Top of One Another

Here are the steps to follow for this exercise:

1. In the Tools panel, choose the Oval tool. When choosing the Oval tool, be sure to specify a fill color and a stroke color.

2. Draw an oval somewhere on the stage.

3. In the Tools panel, select the Rectangle tool. Again, be sure to select a stroke color, but this time choose a different fill color.

4. Draw a rectangle and cover a portion of the oval.

5. Click away from both objects, somewhere in the white space of the stage.

6. Notice that the rectangle looks like it is on top. This is because it was drawn after the oval.

7. Click once on the rectangle and move to another location on the stage.

8. The oval, which was located underneath the rectangle, now has a square cut out of it.

This is normal behavior for Flash. It is of the utmost importance to keep this in mind when you're developing content in the Flash environment. Small accidents can cause huge problems, and thankfully Flash has a wonderful feature called **Undo** (press Cmd+Z or Ctrl+Z or choose Edit, Undo). These drawing styles are just as much setbacks as they are features. Although this may be a different way to build artwork, it is one that can open up more possibilities. One great feature is the ability to adjust lines. If you move your cursor over a line, you'll notice that you can grab and bend that line. If your mouse cursor shows a small picture of a right angle, you can adjust the placement of that angle by clicking the angle and dragging it around.

Just keep in mind how line and fill colors can separate while changing their position.

You can avoid these problems by grouping your artwork. This may seem somewhat bizarre at first, because ultimately you are grouping an object with itself. The advantage of this is that the object is no longer a primitive and the selection style changes. Take a look at Figure 3.34 to see the differences between a grouped object and a primitive object.

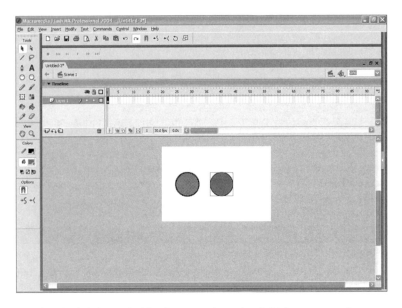

**FIGURE 3.34**    On the left is a primitive item, and on the right is a grouped one.

Notice that the grouped object has a blue bounding box as opposed to the primitive object's speckled pattern. Without the speckles, items cannot merge or punch holes in one another.

## Grouping an Item

Here are the steps to follow to group an item:

1. Choose the Rectangle tool with a stroke color and a fill color.
2. Draw a rectangle somewhere on the stage.
3. After drawing the object, choose the Arrow tool and double-click the shape you just drew. By double-clicking you are selecting not only the fill but also the stroke.
4. Choose Modify, Group (PC–Ctrl+G, Mac–Open Apple+G). This will group the object. Notice the different selection style with the bounding box.
5. Choose the Oval tool with a different fill and stroke color.
6. Draw an oval or circle on top of the grouped rectangle. You'll notice that the item you've just drawn automatically appears behind the grouped rectangle.
7. Move the grouped rectangle away from the circle. Notice that the rectangle does not punch a hole in the oval.

## Changing the Stacking Order Between Grouped Objects

Here are the steps to follow to change the stacking order between grouped objects:

1. Still working with the last file and with the Arrow tool selected, double-click the oval to select the stroke and the fill.
2. Choose Modify, Group.
3. Move the oval on top of the grouped rectangle.

Notice that the rectangle is now underneath the oval. This is because the oval was the last grouped object; therefore, it appears in front of any items grouped previously. In Flash, you have two different ways to change the stacking order of grouped objects: Either arrange them on separate layers or change their stacking order within the one layer.

## Changing the Stacking Order of Grouped Objects on One Layer

Here are the steps to follow to change the stacking order of grouped objects in one layer:

1. With the oval and rectangle grouped items already on the stage from the previous exercises, draw a new shape. Choose a different fill and stroke color for this shape.
2. Choose the Arrow tool and select the new shape by double-clicking it. After the item is selected, choose Modify, Group. Notice now that the new shape is on top.
3. With the new shape selected, choose Modify, Arrange, Send to Back. The new shape now appears below the other two grouped items.

Here are the options in the Modify, Arrange menu (you must have a grouped object selected to get these options):

- **Bring to Front**. This option moves the selected item in front of all other items.

- **Bring Forward**. This option moves the selected item in front of the item it is currently underneath. In other words, it brings the item forward one step.

- **Send Backward**. This option moves the selected item behind the item it is currently in front of. In other words, it sends the item backward one step.

- **Send to Back**. This option moves the selected item behind all other items.

You can also change the stacking order of items using layers. Each time you create a new graphic, place it on a new layer. You can create a new layer by clicking the Add Layer button in the Layers panels, as shown in Figure 3.35.

FIGURE 3.35    The Insert Layer button.

To change the stacking order of a layer, simply click and drag it either above or below the desired location of the other layers. For additional information on the Layers panel, refer to Chapter 4, "Flash Animation."

## Graphic Techniques

I'd like to point out some of the cool, but small features in Flash you can use to make your Flash graphics look a bit more interesting. Often, shadow effects are created using bitmap graphics. This largely has to do with the tonal range a raster graphic can provide. Flash, as we all know, is vector-based, and vectors cannot offer that same tonal range. Therefore, Flash has a few workarounds, but keep in mind that using them will increase the file size of your final document. Also, these effects, especially when animated, will require the end user to have a more powerful machine. The features that offer these effects can be found under the Modify, Shape menu:

- **Convert Lines to Fills**. Often, to create 3D-looking graphics, your artwork must have a large stroke and that stroke must be filled with tonal colors. To get the tonal values, a gradient must be applied. You may have noticed that there are no gradients in the stroke swatch. This is the main reason for converting the strokes into fill colors. When that adjustment has been made, you cannot fill the line color with a gradient.

- **Expand Fill**. Use this option to change the size of the fill. In the Expand Fill dialog box, choose how many pixels you'd like the fill to expand or inset. Expand will make the fill appear larger, and Inset will make the fill smaller.

- **Soften Fill Edges**. In the Soften Fill Edges dialog box, choose how many steps you'd like to take and indicate whether you'd like to expand or inset the fill. If you choose to expand the fill, it will have additional strokes applied around it in the number of steps that you have designated, and each of these strokes will gradually have less opacity. Inset works the same, but the additional strokes will cut into the size of the fill.

# Importing Bitmap Graphics

Even though Flash is a vector-based application, you can still import and work with bitmap graphics. When a graphic is inside Flash, it becomes an element that is editable. You can animate the bitmap, skew it, scale it, distort it, break it apart, and even convert it into vectors. It's very common in development to combine artwork created in Flash with artwork created in other vector programs, such as Illustrator or FreeHand, but also with images created in bitmap applications, such as Photoshop or Fireworks. And now, Flash MX 2004 supports the importing of Illustrator 10 files as well as PDF files.

### Importing a Bitmap Graphic

Here are the steps to follow to import a bitmap graphic:

1. Choose File, Import to open the Import dialog box.
2. On Windows and Mac OS X, highlight the file and click the Open button.

The bitmap will now show up on the stage. At this point, you can manipulate the graphic in any way. There are a few different things we can do with this graphic. In the next exercise, we're going to take steps to use this bitmap as a fill color, and we're also going to select portions of the image and delete them. To select these different portions, we're going to use the Lasso tool.

# Working with Bitmaps

In this section you'll learn more about using bitmapped graphics as individual elements. For instance, you can very easily use a bitmap as a fill color for another graphic.

### Breaking Apart a Bitmap and Using It As a Fill Color

Here are the steps to follow to break apart a bitmap and use it as a fill color:

1. With a bitmap graphic selected, choose Modify, Break Apart. Notice that the bitmap now looks more like a primitive object.
2. Choose the Eyedropper tool in the Tools panel, and click on the graphic.

3. Notice that the fill swatch has a small icon representing the bitmap.

4. Choose the Rectangle tool and draw a square on the stage. Notice that it's filled with the bitmap!

5. Now you have the option of transforming the fill using the Transform Fill tool.

## Trace Bitmap

Another great feature of Flash MX is the ability to turn your bitmap graphics into vectors. This can save file size, if the bitmap doesn't have a great deal of detail. It's also an advantage if you plan to animate the graphic and have it scale up. It's important not to break apart the bitmap. If you do, Flash will only recognize it as a primitive and not as a bitmap. If you have the bitmap selected on the stage, select Modify, Trace Bitmap. Here are the options you'll find in the dialog box that appears in Figure 3.36:

**FIGURE 3.36**    The Trace Bitmap dialog box.

- **Color Threshold**. This option compares adjacent pixels. If the RGB color values between the two pixels are less than the Color Threshold value, these color values will be considered the same. You can set the Color Threshold value between 1 and 500.

- **Minimum Area**. This option's value determines how many pixels to evaluate when setting the color of a pixel. You can set a value between 1 and 1000.

- **Curve Fit**. This option determines how smoothly the vector lines are drawn after the trace has been performed.

- **Corner Threshold**. In this drop-down menu, choose either Many Corners, Few Corners, or Normal. If Few Corners is chosen, corners will be smoothed out in the image. If Many Corners is selected, many of the corners in the image will be preserved. Normal is between Many and Few Corners.

If you want the graphic to look more accurate, choose Many Corners, with lower Color Threshold and Minimum Area values (see Figure 3.37). However, this will probably increase the file size and bog down animation playback. If you chose higher values, the image may be less accurate and offer a more stylized look, but it will be more functional in a Flash animation.

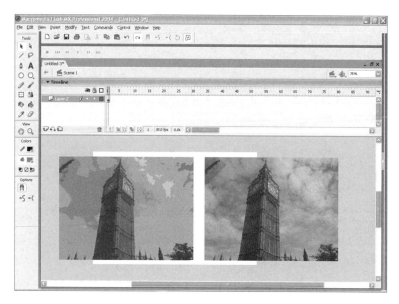

**FIGURE 3.37**    A bitmap before and after the Trace Bitmap command. Notice the stylized look on the left.

### Swap Bitmap

Swap Bitmap allows you to swap out a bitmap on the stage with any other imported bitmap in the document. With the bitmap selected on the stage, choose Modify, Swap Bitmap to launch the Swap Bitmap dialog box. In this dialog box, choose the new bitmap that will replace the existing bitmap on the stage.

## Summary

This chapter covered a lot of information from how to use all the available tools in the toolbar, to how to create custom gradients, as well as how to work with bitmap images in Flash. As we use these tools even more throughout the book, you should really begin to feel comfortable with them.

The next chapter covers how to animate these shapes as well as some good practices when working with animated graphics.

# CHAPTER **4**

# Flash Animation

In the previous chapters, we discussed the interface and drawing tools. If you are a seasoned graphic or Web designer, these topics are probably well within your comfort zone. What we've reviewed in Flash so far is similar to applications such as Illustrator, FreeHand, and Photoshop. If you haven't used an animation program before, such as After Effects or Director, the dimension and concept of time is something completely new to you. To understand how animation works, and more specifically how Flash animation works, you must understand a whole new world of terminology.

If you are familiar with After Effects or Director, consider yourself slightly ahead of the game. Fully comprehending the material in this chapter is the first step toward mastering Flash. We'll begin with deconstructing the timeline; we'll look at each of its components and how these components can speed up your productivity and enhance your animations.

## The Timeline

The timeline is a panel that contains layers, frames, and a play head. In this section, we'll dissect each component of the timeline. With all the timeline's attributes revealed and explained, we'll then start animating. Figure 4.1 shows the timeline's structure.

Do you remember those old-fashioned animation flipbooks, where you would flip the pages to see the animation play? Flash is very similar in concept. Think of a frame in the timeline as a page in an animation flipbook.

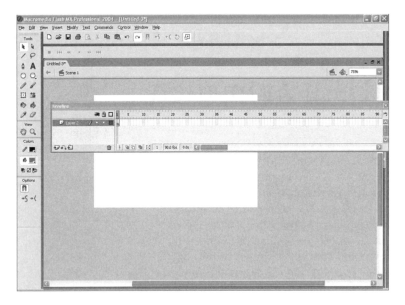

**FIGURE 4.1**    The timeline.

Here is a deconstruction of certain elements of the timeline. I'll refer to these different components throughout the book, so it's important that you're familiar with these different items, which add functionality to your animation in some way:

- **Keyframe**. A keyframe represents a major change within the animation. Referring back to the flipbook concept, a keyframe is the same as each animated page in the flipbook. To insert a keyframe, press F6–(PC) or select Insert, Timeline, Keyframe.

- **Frame**. A frame simply adds time to an animation. Usually frames don't have any sophisticated movement; they just carry over content from the previous frames. Again, referring back to the flipbook concept, if the characters in the animation have to pause for a moment, without any movement, the exact same page would need to be duplicated as many times as necessary to create the duration of the pause. In Flash, to accomplish this same effect, you would simply add a frame, which in turn adds time to the timeline. To insert a frame, press F5–(PC) or choose Insert, Timeline, Frame.

- **Blank Keyframe**. A blank keyframe does in fact represent a major change within the animation; however, the major change is that it creates a blank area on the layer. To insert a blank keyframe, press the F7–(PC) key or choose Insert, Timeline, Blank Keyframe.

- **Unpopulated Frame**. An unpopulated frame is generally the same concept as a frame, but it contains no data. Unpopulated frames are generally preceded by a blank keyframe.

- **Play Head**. The play head is the red rectangle and line that moves across the timeline, and it indicates what frame is currently being displayed on the stage. You can click and drag the play head along the timeline to view the other frames. This is called **scrubbing**. You may also use the keyboard shortcuts, which are the "<" key to move left and the ">" key to move right.

- **Insert Layer**. This button creates a new layer in the timeline. By default, the new layer will be created above the currently selected layer. To rename the layer, double-click its name to get the blinking cursor. You can also insert a new layer by choosing Insert, Timeline, Layer.

- **Add Motion Guide**. This button creates a new layer above the currently selected layer. However, this layer has a guide property, meaning that whatever is placed on it will not appear in the Flash player. If a line or stroke is drawn on this layer, symbols and grouped objects that are motion-tweened can be attached to the guide layer and can follow the stroke during the animation. You can also insert a Motion Guide by going to Insert, Timeline, Motion Guide.

- **Insert Layer Folder**. To keep all your layers organized, you can create Layer Folders within the stacking order of the layers. By moving or changing the stacking order of the layer folder, you change the stacking order of every layer within that folder.

- **Delete Layer**. This removes or deletes the selected layer, layer folder, or guide layer. Of course, if only one layer is left, you cannot delete it.

- **Show/Hide All Layers**. This turns on or off the visibility of layers. Click the eye icon to toggle between layers on and layers off. To turn on or off the visibility of just one layer, click the bullet underneath the eye icon column. To hide all layers except one, Alt+Click the bullet underneath the eye icon on the layer you want to stay visible.

- **Lock/Unlock All Layers**. This icon button and its column bullets act exactly like the Show/Hide All Layers button and its column bullets. However, this option locks the contents of the layer on the stage. This way, any unwanted editing of these items will be avoided. It's important to understand that this will only protect the artwork on the stage from being edited and will not prevent this layer's timeline from being edited.

- **Show All Layers as Outlines**. This option is also a toggle. To view artwork as outlines, click either the bullet for any given layer or the actual icon to affect all layers. This view converts all artwork on the layer to an outline view. This comes in handy for precise placement and animation tweaking.

- **Center Frame**. This option positions the timeline so that the selected or current frame will appear in the center of the timeline view.

- **Onion Skin**. This option allows you to view previous or future frames in the timeline. Onion Skin is best described as a tracing-paper feature. You can adjust the bracket that surrounds the play head to adjust how many frames are visible before and after the current frame.

- **Onion Skin Outlines**. This option allows you to see the outlines of multiple frames.

- **Edit Multiple Frames**. Even if you are viewing your animation with the Onion Skin feature, when you make a change, it will only affect the currently selected frame. Edit Multiple Frames allows you to make a change across all onion-skinned frames.

- **Modify Onion Markers**. Aside from moving the Onion Skin bracket around the play head, this drop-down menu offers other specific choices (see Figure 4.2):

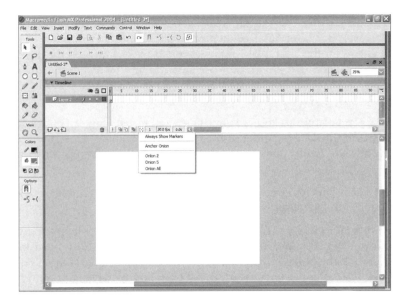

**FIGURE 4.2**    The Modify Onion Markers menu.

- **Always Show Markers**. This option is pretty self-explanatory. It always displays the Onion Skin bracket around the play head.

- **Anchor Onion**. This option leaves the Onion Skin bracket in the same place, regardless of the play head's position.

- **Onion 2**. This option will onion-skin two frames in front and two frames behind the play head.

- **Onion 5**. This option will onion-skin five frames in front and two frames behind the play head.

- **Onion All**. Choose this option to onion-skin the entire duration of the time-line.

- **Current Frame**. This is an indicator revealing what frame is currently being displayed on the stage.

- **Frame Rate**. This small box refers to the frame rate of the movie. The default frame rate is 12 fps (frames per second). To give you a point of reference, film plays at 24 fps and digital video plays at 29.97 fps. The higher the frame rate, the more realistic your animation will look. However, this animation will only play at its true frame rate if the end user's computer and Internet connection are fast enough. Therefore, keep in mind the target audience of your Web site when choosing a frame rate. To change the frame rate of your movie, choose Modify, Document or just double-click this small box.

- **Elapsed Time**. This box indicates the amount of time elapsed from the first frame to the currently selected frame, based on the frame rate of the movie.

- **Frame View Options**. This drop-down menu offers a variety of views for the timeline frames. We'll review each of these options later in this chapter, in a section titled "Changing Timeline Views," after we've worked with the timeline a bit.

## Creating Animation in Flash

You can create animation in Flash in several different ways, including the following:

- Frame-by-frame animation
- Shape tweening
- Motion tweening

We'll discuss frame-by-frame animation first. I think frame-by-frame animation is the easiest to understand because you physically create the animation yourself without any help from Flash. Keep in mind that when you create a frame-by-frame animation, every frame within the animation is a keyframe. Recall that a keyframe represents a major change within the animation, so on each keyframe your subject can be doing something different. Going back to the flipbook analogy, every page in the book is different, whether the character or whatever the subject may be is making subtle movements or more obvious ones. In order to create the effect of movement, the artwork has to be different on each page; otherwise, there would be no animation—just an object or character in the same place on each page. Think of a keyframe as a page in a flipbook. In the next exercise, we'll create a frame-by-frame animation.

### Creating A Frame-by-Frame Animation

In this exercise, we are going to create an animation of the sun with rays shooting out from its center.

Referring to Figure 4.1, click the New Layer button. You will notice a new layer named "layer 2" that appears above layer 1. Now follow these steps:

1. Double-click layer 1 to highlight the text. With the text highlighted, rename the layer "center."

2. Double-click layer 2 and rename this layer "rays."

3. Be sure to select the center layer by clicking it. Choose the Oval tool with your choice of fill and stroke colors.

4. Hold down the Shift key and in the center of the stage drag out a small circle.

   Notice that the hollow circle that once occupied the frame has turned into a solid circle, as shown in Figure 4.3. This displays the difference between a blank keyframe and a keyframe on the rays layer.

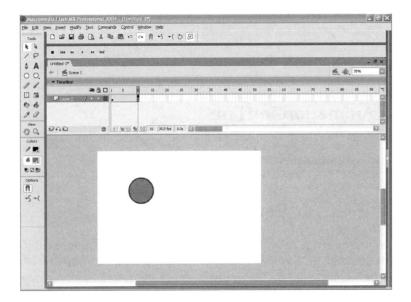

**FIGURE 4.3**    Notice the difference between a keyframe and a blank keyframe.

We want our animation to last half a second. The default frame rate is 12 fps. Simple math tells us that we need six frames in order for this animation to last half a second when the animation is playing 12 frames every second.

5. To make the animation last half a second, we need more frames on the center layer. In fact, we need five more frames to extend the time to six frames. To do this, click inside frame 6 on layer 1. Notice that frame 6 is now darker, indicating that it has been selected.

6. Choose Insert, Timeline, Frame or press F5 on your keyboard. Notice that all frames between 1 and 6 are now gray, as shown in Figure 4.3, which means they are filled with some content (in this case, a circle representing the sun).

7. Lock the center layer by clicking the black bullet under the padlock column in the Layers panel. We can no longer edit the stage for this layer.

8. Be sure to highlight the rays layer. Choose the Brush tool with any size, style, and fill color you like.

9. Draw about five small rays around the center of the sun. Notice that these rays have been placed on a new layer. To double-check this, click the black bullet under the eye column in the Layers panel. This will temporarily turn off the visibility of the layer and acts as a toggle. To turn the visibility back on, click the red × under the eye column.

We now want the animation to continue with the rays growing and bursting out over time.

10. With the play head positioned at frame 1, choose Insert, Timeline, Blank Keyframe or press F7 on your keyboard. Notice that the ray on the preceding frame is no longer on frame 2. (Remember, a blank keyframe is like a new blank page in a flip-book.)

We're now ready to draw the ray, but this time larger. Let's have the ray grow from the same location as the last ray. That's where Onion Skin comes in.

11. Click the Onion Skin button. Notice the brackets around the play head. Also notice a faded impression of the artwork on the previous frame (in this case, the first ray).

12. Draw new rays but this time extend them a bit further, as shown in Figure 4.4. You'll now have two different frames, 1 and 2, that contain two different sets of rays.

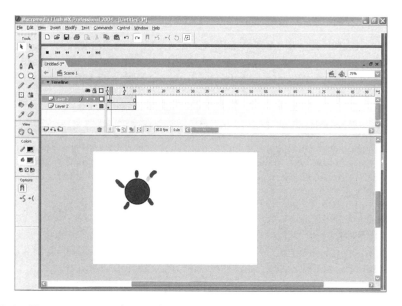

**FIGURE 4.4**    The new rays are being drawn and their locations are based on Onion Skin.

13. Now that we have another set of rays on frame 2, we're ready to draw frames on frame 3, extending our animation. With the play head on frame 2 and the rays layer

selected, press F7 on the keyboard or choose Insert, Timeline, Frame. This will insert a blank keyframe on frame 3.

14. Notice that the Onion Skin markers move with the play head. Extend out the rays by drawing a new set on frame 3.

15. Repeat steps 13 and 14 so that the animation will have the rays growing and bursting out over time.

    Toward the end of the animation, we want the rays to look as if they are burning out. The next step will trick our eyes into thinking that the rays are actually growing over time and then suddenly burn out.

16. Insert a blank keyframe for frame 5 by pressing F7 on your keyboard. In frame 5, draw a small dot at the end of each ray. This will make the rays look as if they are running out of steam.

17. Insert a blank keyframe on the sixth and final frame. By leaving this frame blank, it will appear in the animation that the rays have burst out from the center of the sun and toward the end of the burst run out of energy and disappear.

18. On the Window menu, choose Toolbars, Controller and click the play button to watch the animation. To see the animation loop (that is, to play it over and over again), choose Control, Loop Play Back and then click the play button again.

This is frame-by-frame animation. Typically, frame-by-frame animation is used in character animation. By drawing on each frame, you can achieve more fluid, life-like animation. This is especially true when used in conjunction with a Wacom or pressure-sensitive palette.

> **NOTE**
>
> When doing keyframe animation, it is important to know that not every frame needs to be a keyframe. You can have every other frame be a keyframe for general animation, and for parts of the animation that need more detail, switch to every frame being a keyframe for that section.

## Shape Tweening

After creating the sun animation, you can really appreciate the hard work that goes into creating a feature-based animation film. However, feature animation films are truly an art form; you probably don't have a few years to complete your projects. Let's take the Walt Disney Company for example. Disney will typically have an artist painting key cells within an animated sequence. If a character is at bat in a baseball game, for instance, this artist would paint the character waiting for the pitch and then probably another cell after the character takes a swing. To complete the animation, a team of "in-betweeners" would paint all the cells in between the first and last key cells.

Flash has this functionality built in. You can set two keyframes, much like the artist painting those key cells, and let Flash build the animation in between, just like the team of in-betweeners. This process is known as **tweening**. To add to the confusion, there are two different types of tweening in Flash: shape tweening and motion tweening. The differences aren't exactly black and white, at least at this point in the book. When you've finished Chapter 5, "Symbols and the Library," the differences will be very apparent. Each type of tweening has very strict rules. For example, the biggest rule for shape tweening is that the item must be a primitive object; it cannot be a grouped object or a symbol.

### Creating an Animation with Shape Tween

The point of this exercise is to get you more familiar with creating a shape-tween animation. We're going to start by doing something simple—moving a square across the stage. Here are the steps to follow:

1. Draw a square on the stage using the Rectangle tool. Select a fill color but no stroke color. Position the square in the top-left corner of the stage.

2. Click inside frame 20, not on the play head, but rather physically in the open frame space, as shown in Figure 4.5. Choose Insert, Timeline, Frame or press F5 on your keyboard.

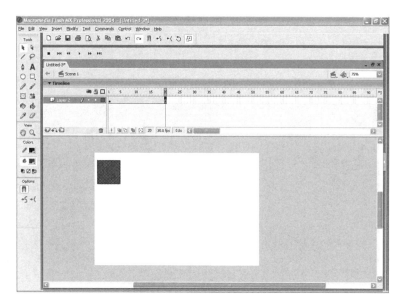

**FIGURE 4.5**   Frame 20 is selected by clicking the empty cell.

Notice that frame 20 and all the frames from 1 through 20 become populated. This means that the square is visible for 20 seconds. It is, however, in the same location, and we want an animation.

3. With the play head set to 20, using the Arrow tool, double-click and drag the square to the opposite side of the stage. Notice that you may have left a stroke behind if you didn't

double-click the square when you selected it to move it. That's okay; just delete the stroke left behind.

4. Select frame 1 by clicking it. Notice that the frame becomes highlighted in black. In the Properties Inspector, use the Tween drop-down menu and choose Shape. Notice that the frames have turned green with an arrow pointing from frame 1 to frame 20.

5. Click the play button on Window, Toolbars, Controller or press the Return (Mac) or Enter (Windows) key to play the animation. See the square move its position over time.

    One of the great things about shape tweening is the ability to morph objects. We could actually make this square morph into a circle while it's moving to its new position! All we have to do is modify our previous animation slightly.

6. Move the play head to frame 20. Highlight the square on the stage with the Arrow tool. When the square is highlighted, press the Delete or Backspace key on your keyboard. Notice that the square has disappeared on that frame but is still present on all the other preceding frames. The arrow has also turned into a dashed line, indicating a broken tween, as noted in Figure 4.6.

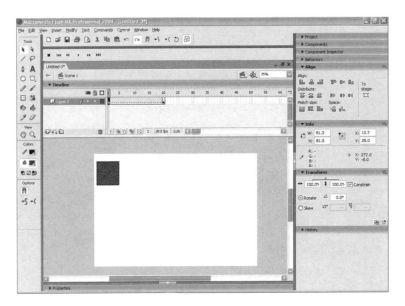

**FIGURE 4.6**    Notice the dashed line indicating a broken tween.

7. With the play head still on frame 20, choose the Oval tool in the Tools panel. This time pick a different fill color while still leaving the stroke color empty. Draw a circle anywhere on the stage that's a good distance from the square.

    When the circle has been drawn on frame 20, notice that the dashed lines have turned back into an arrow.

8. Click the play button in Window, Toolbars, Controller or press the Return (Mac) or Enter (Windows) key on your keyboard. Your animation has already been updated, and the square slowly morphs into a circle and changes color!

You may want to save this file in a handy location because we'll refer to it later. It will be used as a starting point for other animations we're going to create in this chapter.

## Controlling Your Tweens

Now that you understand the basics of shape tweening, we can move on to how to manipulate tweens. The first thing we can do is control the speed of the animation from the beginning and at the end. This can really help in the visual mood you are trying to set. For example, suppose you have a small drawing of a car, and you want to animate that car taking off from a stoplight. Unless you are one of the few people who own a Ferrari F-50, the car will take off from the stop light at a slower speed than what it will cruise at. To achieve this effect in Flash, you would use **easing**. You can either ease into an animation or ease out of it. In the case of your car animation, you'd choose to ease in, which means Flash will slowly start the animation before bringing it up to full speed. Of course, I don't have a Ferrari, so I will use a square as an example. With the slider in the Properties Inspector, you can make the adjustments. The lower the number's value, the more dramatic (or slow) the ease-in will be. Just the opposite applies for easing out: The greater the value, the slower the animation will get towards the end of the animation.

Another important option is to have either angular or distributive tweening. Angular is best used with objects that contain a lot of corners, whereas distributive provides a smoother tween among items. Distributive is the default because it generally yields better results for most tweens.

### Making a Shape-Tween Animation Fade Away

A common question I get is: How do I make my object fade away in the shape tween? The answer may not be that obvious, but keep in mind we are working with primitive shapes, so there is only one logical way. Open the animation you created earlier with the square morphing into the circle and then follow these steps:

1. Move your play head to the last frame in the animation, which should be frame 20.
2. With the Arrow tool selected, click the circle to select it.
3. If your Color Mixer panel is not open, select Window, Design Panels, Color Mixer. Notice that the fill swatch is the same color as the selected circle.
4. If the fill swatch is not selected in the Color Mixer panel, click the Paint Bucket icon just to the right of the swatch in the Color Mixer panel.
5. In the Alpha text box, type in **0** or choose 0 with the slider box (see Figure 4.7). At first it may look as if nothing has happened, but as soon as you click away from the circle, the circle will become invisible.

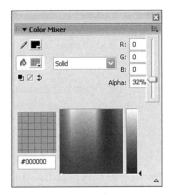

**Figure 4.7**    The Alpha slider bar in the color swatches.

6. In the controller, click the play button to see the animation. Notice that toward the end of the animation, the square not only turns into a circle and a different color, but it also fades away!

## Shape Hinting

So you can change the shape, color, and transparency of your items during tweening, but what if you want more control? Well, more control is on the way. In fact, you can even dictate how an item's corners and points will morph into the other item's corner and points.

This wonderful feature is called **shape hinting**. When you shape-hint, you have more control of the object's morphing appearance by placing anchors. This anchors a point in item A to a point in item B. To further illustrate this, let's do one more exercise.

**Shape-Hinting Your Shape Tween**

In this exercise, we are going to turn a star shape into the letter A using shape hints.

1. First, draw a basic five-point star on the stage using the polystar tool (don't worry, it doesn't have to be perfect) as shown in Figure 4.8.

2. Then, select frame 15 by clicking in the empty slot. Choose Insert, Timeline, Blank Keyframe or press F7 on your keyboard. Notice that the frame becomes white and that frames 2 through 19 become populated.

3. On this frame, type the letter **A** with the Type tool in the same general location where the star was. If you forget where the star is located, turn on Onion Skin. Use a sans-serif type-face and a larger size (for example, Trebuchet at a size of 200).

4. With the letter A selected, choose Modify, Break Apart (PC–Ctrl+B, Mac–Open Apple+B) to convert the A to a primitive item. This letter is no longer editable with the Type tool. Flash now considers this letter a shape and not a typed letter.

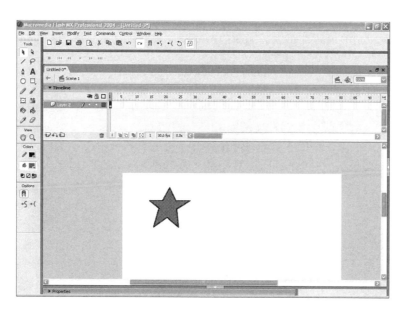

**FIGURE 4.8**    The star symbol after it has been broken apart.

5.  Select frame 1 and in the Properties Inspector choose Shape Tween. Play the animation.

    Notice how the star almost disappears before morphing into the letter A, as in Figure 4.9. We're going to fix the appearance of this tween using shape hinting.

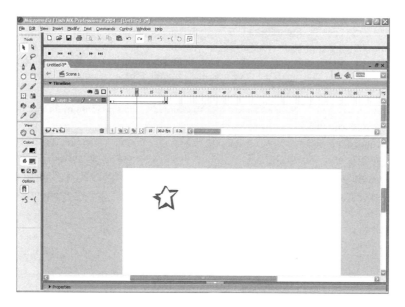

**FIGURE 4.9**    Unpredictable morphing effects without shape hinting.

6. With the play head set back to frame 1, choose Modify, Shape, Add Shape Hint (PC–Ctrl+H, Mac–Shift+Open Apple+H). Notice the little red circle that appears with the letter A. This is the shape-hint anchor.

7. Place the anchor on the top point of the star, as shown in Figure 4.10.

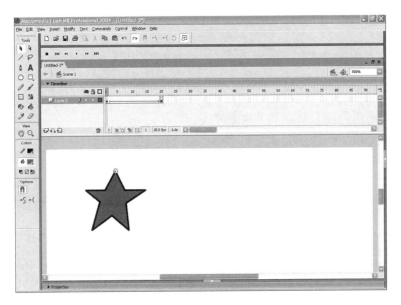

**FIGURE 4.10**   Placing the shape-hint anchor on top of the star.

8. Move the play head to frame 15. Notice the same little anchor. Drag the anchor to the top of the letter A. Notice that the color changes to green. If the color does not change to green, check to make sure you have Snap to Objects turned on in the arrow's options on the toolbar. At this point, we have essentially mapped these two points together. The top of the star will join to the top of the A.

9. Play the animation. Notice that the morph is already solid and looks more natural, as shown in Figure 4.11.

10. We'll add one more hint. Move the play head back to frame 1. On the Modify menu, choose Shape, Add Shape Hint. Notice the new anchor point that appears on the stage.

11. Drag the new anchor point to the bottom part of the middle line of the star.

12. Move the play head to frame 15 and place the anchor point at the bottom part of the middle line of the A. Notice that the anchor changes color.

15. Play the animation to see how smooth it is.

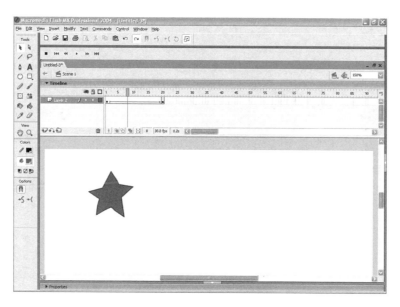

**FIGURE 4.11**   Animation after a shape hint has been applied.

Finally, suppose you like the shape hints, but you think they're a lot of work to use. For many animations, there is no other way to change the blending appearance of the morph. However, in this situation, where the star is turning invisible before turning into the letter A, there is a quick fix. One of the biggest issues with this type of tween is that one object has a hole and the other doesn't. The center portion of the A is hollow, and there is nothing in the star to compensate for it—unless, of course, we do something to fix that.

If you want to remove a shape hint, you can right-click (Windows) or Control-click (Mac) on the hint. In the contextual menu, choose Remove Hint. In our case, we are going to choose Remove All Hints to bring us back to square one in our tweened animation. You can also choose Modify, Shape, Remove All Hints.

To fix the problem at this point, all we have to do is insert a keyframe on frame 2. Here are the steps to follow:

1. Move the play head to frame 2 and press F6 on your keyboard or choose Insert, Frame.

2. Select the Eraser tool in the Tools panel and choose the smallest brush.

3. With the play head still on frame 2, erase a small circle in the center of the star, as shown in Figure 4.12. The animation now looks normal (see Figure 4.13).

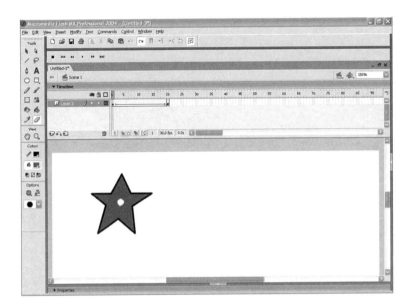

**FIGURE 4.12**    Erase a small hole in the star.

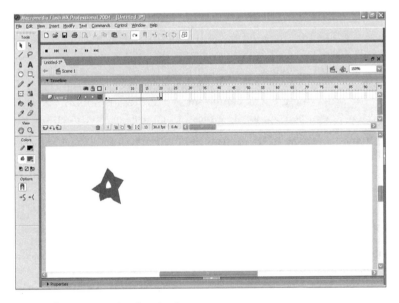

**FIGURE 4.13**    Perfect tweened animation!

That's shape tweening in a nutshell. In the next chapter, we'll look at motion tweening. You'll see that in many ways motion tweening is a bit more conducive to Web animation.

## Changing Timeline Views

For most people, the standard timeline view is the best for most projects. However, Flash offers flexibility in terms of how you can view the timeline. In some cases, you may want a preview of what your animation is going to look like over time, and in others you may want the frames to appear very small so you can fit more on your screen. Whatever the case may be, the ability to change frame styles is a nice option to have, so let's review what each style looks like and the advantages and disadvantages of those styles.

As shown in Figure 4.14, you have options for changing the size, color, and style of the frames. Generally these different views are used for cartoon animators, to get a preview of what their animation will actually look like. You can also scale down the size of the frames to allow more viewable timeline space.

The top choices are for modifying the size options, as detailed in the following list:

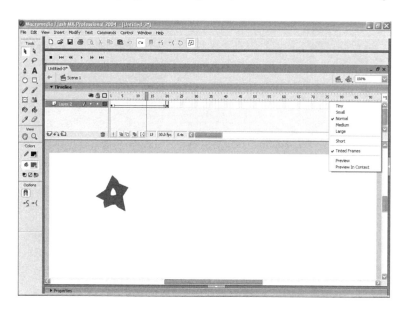

**FIGURE 4.14**   The frame view options menu.

- **Tiny**, **Small**, **Normal**, **Medium**, and **Large**. These options are for adjusting the width of the frames.

- **Short**. This option changes the height of the frames to afford more room to view more layers within the same Timeline panel size.

- **Tinted Frames**. This option turns the tint of the frames on or off. If this option is turned on, populated frames are indicated by a gray fill, blank or unpopulated frames are indicated by a white fill, and motion and shape tweens display blue and green, respectively. The Tinted Frames option is on by default. Otherwise, when it's turned off, frames will display white, unless they're tweened, in which case they'll show a gray checkered background.

- **Preview**. This view displays a thumbnail preview of the animated subject for each frame, as shown in Figure 4.15.

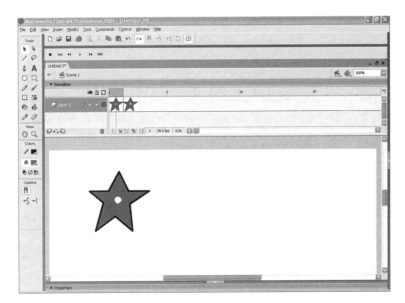

**FIGURE 4.15**    Timeline displaying an animation in Preview view.

- **Preview in Context**. This view still offers a thumbnail preview of each frame; however, it does not just focus on the animated subject. Instead, this view displays the subject in context to the placement on the stage, as shown in Figure 4.16.

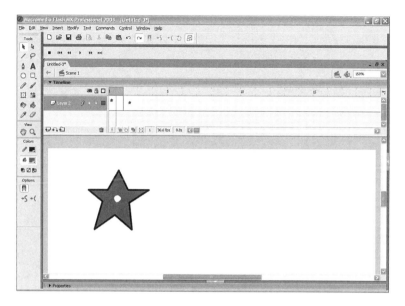

**FIGURE 4.16**   Timeline displaying an animation in Preview in Context view.

## Summary

In this chapter we covered some of the basics of animating in Flash and using tweens. In the next chapter, we talk about using nonprimitive objects on the stage, and get into another type of tween in Flash called motion tweening.

CHAPTER **5**

# Symbols and the Library

So far we have been dealing with primitive objects on the stage, such as shapes or groups (which are just groups of shapes).

In this chapter we are going further with objects on the stage including the three basic symbol types: graphics, buttons, and movie clips. We are also going to discuss instances of these symbols as well as the library where all symbols are kept.

## What Is a Symbol?

A **symbol** is an item stored in the library to be used once or multiple times throughout your Flash file. This is a benefit of symbols not only because of smaller file size, but also because changes are more easily made. If you edit a symbol, all copies of that symbol will reflect the changes made to the original. All symbols are kept in the library (which we discuss later in this chapter) and can be accessed through the library at any time during authoring. When you drag a symbol from the library onto the stage, you create an instance of that symbol.

## What Is an Instance?

An **instance** is nothing more than a copy of a library symbol that has been placed on the stage. When a symbol is changed, the instances of that symbol will change accordingly. Also, because you are using an instance of the symbol, you can adjust certain settings of that instance such as size, coloring, and alpha without affecting other instances of the same symbol. Just remember that changing symbols affects all instances of that symbol, but manipulating an instance only affects that one instance.

Also, each instance will have a unique name, which enables you to control it via ActionScript. Later in this chapter, you will begin using ActionScript to control the appearance and movement of instances.

So remember, symbols are items held in the library and instances are copies of symbols that have been placed on the stage.

# An Overview of the Graphic Symbol

The graphic symbol is the first symbol we will discuss because it is the most basic. Graphic symbols have a **synced timeline**. This means that when a graphic is rendered on the main timeline, if the graphic has several frames of animation, it will only play ahead if the timeline it is residing in moves ahead also. Also, ActionScript (which is discussed in Chapter 8, "Welcome to ActionScript 2.0") will not work within graphic symbols.

## When Should You Use a Graphic?

When you draw on the stage, you are creating primitive objects that will have to be rendered at runtime by Flash. Even groups are just several shapes, instances of symbols, or other groups all grouped together that will also have to be rendered at runtime.

This is where graphic symbols come in. They behave differently from primitive items in that animated primitive items are calculated for each keyframe for Flash to render the contents. Graphic symbols simply call the library item and ask the library to draw the contents of the symbol in any given region on the stage based on the animation. This helps reduce processor usage and in some cases can help with complex animation speeds.

Therefore, graphic symbols are better than primitive graphics for static and animated content. However, in the world of Flash, graphic symbols are best suited for static use because, as mentioned earlier, when a graphic symbol is animated, Flash must continually point the instance to the library item on every single frame. Needless to say, this statement becomes rather long and complex. The best choice for behaviors when it comes to animated symbols is a movie clip, which we'll review later in this chapter in the section "The Movie Clip."

### Creating Graphic Symbols

Let's take a look at some of the many ways to create symbols in Flash—and more specifically, how to create graphic symbols. Follow these steps to create a graphic symbol:

1. Choose Insert, New Symbol (PC–Ctrl+F8, Mac–Open Apple+F8). This will launch the Create New Symbol dialog box, as shown in Figure 5.1.

2. In this dialog box is a whole series of choices. If your Create New Symbol dialog box is slightly different from Figure 5.1, click the Basic button to switch the dialog box to the basic view. Notice that the additional options are now hidden.

3. Select the Graphic radio button to give the new symbol the graphic symbol behavior.

4. Name the graphic by typing **circle** in the Name text field.

**FIGURE 5.1**   The Create New Symbol dialog box.

**5**

---

**NOTE**

It is good practice to name a symbol something that is easy to remember and relates to the content of the symbol. For instance, we named this symbol `circle` because we are drawing a circle, not a square.

---

5. Click OK. Notice that the screen changes to a new view. You can tell by looking at the icons at the top of the timeline, indicating that you are now inside the graphic symbol, as shown in Figure 5.2.

6. The crosshair in the center of the stage, as shown in Figure 5.2, represents the center point of the symbol.

7. Draw a circle over the crosshair, thus placing the circle in the center of the symbol.

   Note that the center of the symbol is important to locate for many reasons. This point defines the center for the axis of any rotation animation. It's also considered when scaling numerically and is used to return feedback about the symbol's placement on the stage.

8. When you're happy with the appearance of the artwork, you're done editing this symbol. Let's go back to scene 1, also known as the **main timeline**, by clicking the scene 1 link (refer to Figure 5.2 if you forget where the tabs are).

9. Now that we're back in scene 1, you'll notice that the circle has disappeared...or so it seems. Remember, we've created a symbol, so all our artwork is stored in the library under a symbol named circle. If your library isn't already open, as it is in Figure 5.3, choose Window, Library (PC–F11, Mac–F11). The Library panel is now visible.

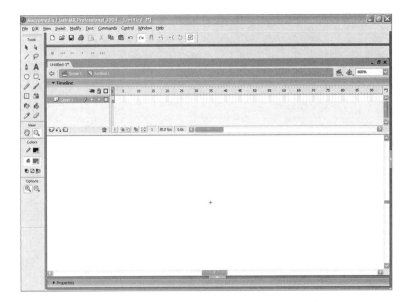

**FIGURE 5.2**    The crosshair in the stage represents the center of the symbol.

**FIGURE 5.3**    The Library panel with the circle graphic symbol.

**10.** Click the symbol in the Library panel and drag it anywhere on the stage. This is an instance of our circle symbol.

This exercise demonstrates how you go about creating a new symbol from scratch. However, there is a good chance you may want some existing artwork on the stage to also become a symbol. To deal with that, all you have to do is select the artwork on the stage and choose Insert, Convert to Symbol (PC–F8, Mac–F8). This will launch a dialog box, called Convert to Symbol, that's similar to the Create New Symbol dialog box. The one exception is displayed in Figure 5.4—you have a choice as to where you want the center point to be on the new symbol. Just click one of the small squares in the Registration icon to select the center point. Often you'll want to choose the center box as the center point, unless you have certain requirements that dictate otherwise. An example of choosing a registration point other than the center point would be if you intend to create a rotating animation and you want the axis point to be something other than the center of the object.

**FIGURE 5.4**    Use the Registration icon to choose the center point of the symbol.

## An Overview of the Button Symbol

The button symbol is the least complex symbol in terms of understanding its purpose. It is designed for creating buttons! This symbol's timeline has predefined states for making it easier to design and develop a button. Buttons are important symbols when it comes to creating interactivity between a Web site and a user. You can place ActionScript on a button, but you cannot place it in the button.

### Building a Button Symbol

Here are the steps to follow to build a button symbol:

1. Draw a shape anywhere on the stage.
2. Choose the Arrow tool and double-click the shape to select it.
3. With the shape now selected, choose Insert, New Symbol. The Create New Symbol dialog box pops up.
4. Select the Button radio button to give the symbol the button behavior. Also choose a center point for the symbol in the Registration icon. And give it a symbol name of myShape.
5. Click OK. Notice that the shape no longer has a speckled selection but rather a blue box with a crosshair for the center point.
6. Double-click the new symbol. Notice that you are brought into button symbol editing mode. Also notice that the first four frames are predefined button states, as shown in Figure 5.5.

   The four states are Up, Over, Down, and Hit. Up is the state the button will have when the movie loads. Over is what the button will change to when the end user moves the mouse over the button. Down is the state the button will have when the end user presses the mouse button (but does not release it). When the user releases the mouse button, the state returns to Up. Finally, Hit defines the active area of the button. It's typically best to have a Hit state at least the size of the button. If the button is text, be sure to draw a solid box over the text in the Hit state. The Hit state is invisible, but if text is the subject for the end user to click, this could cause some buggy problems for the user. Remember that many characters have "holes" in them, such as the letter *O*, for example. In theory, the mouse could be clicked in that empty area of the *O* without ever clicking the Hit state of the button. If you draw a solid box over your text, the Hit state problem is solved.

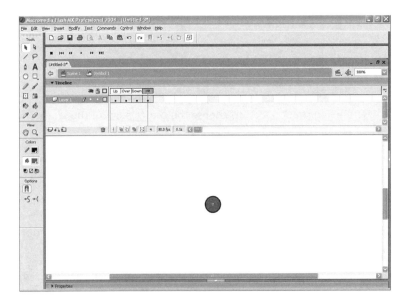

**FIGURE 5.5**    Button symbol timeline.

7. Because we've converted an existing shape to a symbol, we automatically have content in frame 1, also known as the Up state. If you want, you can modify any part of the shape to better suit your liking.

8. Choose Insert, Keyframe or press F6 to insert a keyframe to move to the Over state. Notice that a keyframe has been inserted into the Over state, carrying over the attributes of the previous frame.

9. Now that we're in the Over state, all we're going to do is change the fill color of the shape. Select the shape using the Arrow tool and choose a different color in the Fill Color swatch of the Tools panel.

10. Press F6 to insert another keyframe. Make some similar modifications to the artwork in the Over state.

11. Press F6 one last time to insert a keyframe on the Hit state. Remember, the Hit state is invisible; it just defines the active area of the button. Simple shapes you can pretty much just leave alone; however, if the shape has a hole in it, like the letter *O*, draw a solid shape over it.

12. Come back to scene 1 by clicking the Scene 1 link, or you can use the Scene Select drop-down menu, as shown in Figure 5.6.

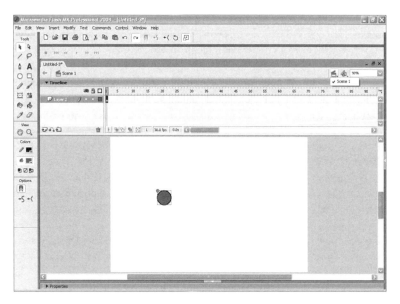

**FIGURE 5.6**    Select a scene by using the Scene Select drop-down menu.

You can preview the button you just built within the Flash authoring environment. Choose Control, Enable Simple Buttons. Move your mouse over the button on the stage and click it to see the previews. To turn it off, choose Control, Enable Simple Buttons again.

The real power of buttons is the ability to communicate with the timeline and other objects. For example, if we had an animation, we could create play and stop buttons to control the animation. Furthermore, we haven't discussed motion tweening.

Now that you know how to create a graphic symbol, we can animate it on our main timeline and have it follow a motion guide. The use of motion guides is one of the advantages of motion tweening. In the next few exercises, you'll learn how to create a motion tween, and we'll look at the advantages of motion tweening as well as controlling the timeline with buttons.

## Motion Tweening

### Creating a Motion Tween

In this exercise, we are going to create an animation of a circle moving from one side of the stage to the other. During this animation, the circle will fade out toward the end of the sequence and follow a motion guide during the tween. For the first time, we are going to be using motion tweening instead of a shape. Remember, the key difference is that when you motion-tween, you are tweening a symbol as opposed to a primitive shape. Here are the steps to follow for this exercise:

1. Double-click layer 1 to rename it. Name it **animation**. Draw a circle on the stage with a fill and stroke color of your choice. With the Arrow tool, double-click the circle to select its fill and stroke.

2. Choose Insert, New Symbol. Be sure to give this symbol a graphic behavior and name it **circle**. Notice the new symbol, called circle, in the library.

3. Select frame 20 and press F6 to insert a keyframe. With the play head on frame 20, select the circle and drag it down to the bottom-right corner of the stage. At this point, in frames 1 through 19, the circle is in the top corner, but on frame 20, it jumps down to the bottom-right corner.

4. To have this movement happen over time, select the first frame; then, in the Properties Inspector, choose Motion from the Tween drop-down menu. Notice that the frames turn blue with an arrow pointing from the first frame to the last. You've just created a motion tween!

   Now that you have a motion tween, you can add a motion guide. This way, the animation will now follow a path that you draw, as opposed to the circle just moving from one side to the other.

5. To add a motion guide, click the Add Motion Guide button, as shown in Figure 5.7. Notice the new guide layer added above the animation layer. Also notice that the animation layer is indented, illustrating that this layer is now a slave to the motion guide layer.

6. With a new guide layer selected and the play head moved to frame 1, choose the Pencil tool. With the Pencil tool, draw a curvy line across the stage, being sure not to intersect the line at any point because this could confuse the animated item. With frame 1 in the animation layer selected, in the Properties Inspector, make sure the Snap check box is selected (see Figure 5.8). When Snap is checked, notice how the circle "snaps" to the beginning of the guide.

   If you play your animation and it does not follow the guide, it's because the item is falling off the guide before it gets to the last frame. To fix this problem, move the play head to the last frame. Click the center of the circle and drag it to the end of the guide. When you have the circle in snapping range, the symbol center of the circle increases in size. This size increase is an indication that the circle will snap to the guide in that location.

   To make the circle disappear over time, you need to apply a color effect. We have already done something similar with shape tweening, but the process is a bit different for motion tweening. In shape tweening, we took down the alpha of the fill color. We can't do that to a symbol, and if we edited the symbol to apply a lower alpha fill, we would be applying it to the entire symbol, thus causing the circle to appear invisible the whole time. Therefore, we'll apply a color effect to the symbol instead.

7. With the play head on the last frame of the animation, select the instance of the circle on the stage. In the Properties Inspector, use the Color drop-down menu and choose Alpha. Drag the Alpha slider down to 0, as shown in Figure 5.9.

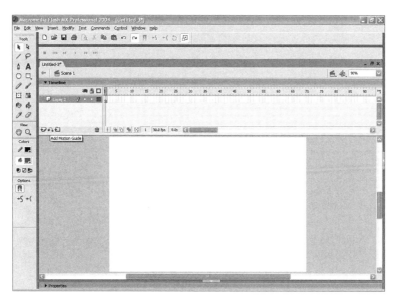

**FIGURE 5.7**    The Add Motion Guide button.

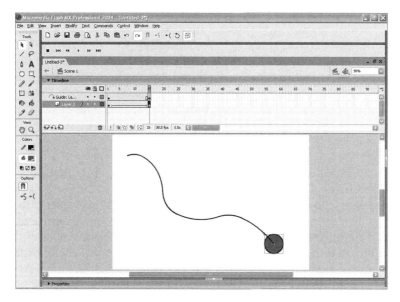

**FIGURE 5.8**    The guide layer and the Snap option are checked in the Properties Inspector.

8. Play your animation. Notice the circle moving across the stage, following the guide and fading out over time.

9. Save this file as mtween.fla. We will refer to it later.

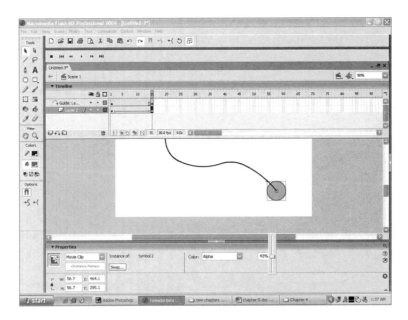

**FIGURE 5.9**    The color effect—alpha.

Some additional options are available in the Properties Inspector for motion tweening, as shown in Figure 5.10. Orient to Path, for example, not only makes the object follow the path, but it causes the baseline of the symbol to orient itself to the path. For instance, if the moving object was a car, the car would continually face the direction it is moving.

You can also set how many times you'd like the instance to rotate during your animation—either clockwise or counterclockwise.

Also, a shortcut is available for creating a motion tween. Draw a primitive item on the stage and insert a frame (F5) in a later frame. Right-click (PC) or Control-click (Mac) and, in the pop-up menu, choose Create Motion Tween. Notice that the frames turn blue. The series of dotted lines indicate a broken tween. To fix the tween, simply move the play head to the last frame, select the item on the stage, and drag it somewhere else on the stage. The frame will turn into a keyframe, and the dotted lines will change into a solid arrow. Scrub the play head (that is, drag it back and forth through the frames) to see the animation. Flash will also put the item into your library, naming it tween1.

**FIGURE 5.10**    Motion tween options in the Properties Inspector.

### Combining Motion and Shape Tweens

In development, you may find it necessary to have a morphing animation, but at the same time you may need the animation to follow a guide. In this exercise, we are going to take a look at how we can use both of these techniques to complete the desired effect. This will also reinforce the concept of keyframes.

We are going to create an animation of five squares, animating them across the stage. As they animate, they will follow a path. After following the path, they will proceed to morph into the letters *F, L, A, S, H* respectively. Here are the steps to follow:

1. Draw a square at the top-left corner of the stage without a stroke color but with a fill color of your choice. Convert it to a symbol by selecting it and pressing F8 on your keyboard. Give it a graphic behavior and name it **square**.

2. Insert a keyframe in frame 15. With the play head on frame 15, move the square to the bottom-right corner. Highlight keyframe 1 and, in the Properties Inspector, choose Motion Tween. This will create an arrow from frame 1 to 15, and the frames will turn blue. Scrub the play head to see the animation. Be sure to check Snap, because we are going to create a motion guide in the next step.

3. Name layer 1 **F**. Click the Add Motion Guide button to create a new guide layer. Notice the new guide layer above the F layer. With the Pencil tool, draw a guide in the shape of a half square, as shown in Figure 5.11.

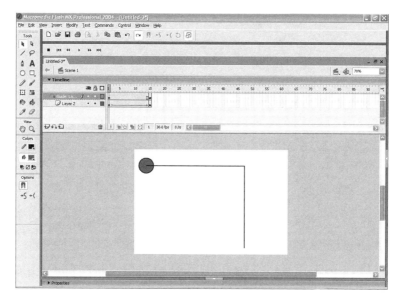

**FIGURE 5.11**    A half-square motion guide.

4. Scrub the play head to make sure the square is snapped to the motion guide. If not, be sure to fix the last frame, just as you did in the preceding exercise.

   Now that you have the motion tween working, you have the first part of your animation. In the next part, we want the square to morph into the letter *F*. To do this, you need to break apart the symbol. However, if you break apart the symbol in frame 15, you will break the motion tween. Remember, a tween is from keyframe to keyframe. In order to have a motion tween, you need the same symbol in two different keyframes. Therefore, you cannot break apart the symbol in frame 15. You can, however, insert a new keyframe in frame 16. A keyframe represents a major change within an animation. In this case, on frame 16 the major change is that the item is no longer a symbol but rather a primitive item.

5. In frame 16 of the F layer, insert a keyframe by pressing F6 on your keyboard. In this new keyframe, highlight the square by clicking it. Choose Modify, Break Apart. Notice that the symbol changes into a primitive item. Primitive items can be morphed.

6. In frame 20 of the F layer, insert a blank keyframe (F7). This will clear the layer of all its contents.

7. With the Type tool selected, type **F** on the left side of the stage using a sans-serif typeface. Editable text behaves much like a grouped item. You cannot morph grouped items, so the letter *F* also needs to be broken apart.

8. If you are happy with the style and size of the type, choose Modify, Break Apart. The letter is no longer editable text and is a primitive shape (see Figure 5.12).

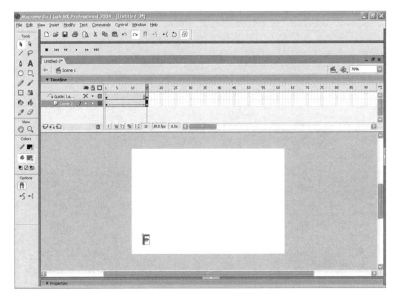

**FIGURE 5.12**   An animation with a guide layer and text that has been broken apart.

9. Highlight keyframe 16 and in the Properties Inspector, choose Shape Tween. This completes the first letter of the animation. With the controller, click the play button or press Return (Mac) or Enter (Windows) to see the animation. The next step is to copy this layer and animation.

   Instead of going through all these steps again, you can just copy your work onto a new layer and modify the last frame to change the letter that the square morphs into.

10. Click the Add New Layer button to create a new layer. Click the name of the F layer to highlight all the frames. You'll notice that they're all highlighted in black, indicating that all frames in that layer are selected. Hold down the Option (Mac) or Alt (Windows) key and then click and drag the highlighted frames from the F layer to layer 2 and stagger the layer over four frames. Notice the little plus sign next to your cursor as you drag, as shown in Figure 5.13. This indicates that you are in fact copying the layers and not just moving them.

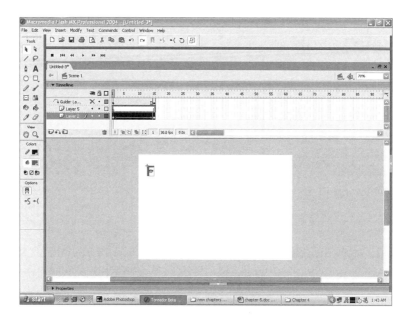

**FIGURE 5.13**    Duplicating a layer.

11. Rename layer 2 **L**. In frame 20 of the L layer, delete the *F* and, with the Type tool, type **L**. This shape tween will not work because the letter *L* is still editable and is not a primitive shape. With the letter *L* selected, choose Modify, Break Apart. Now the shape tween will work.

12. In the F layer, insert a frame (F5) in frame 20 so that the letter *F* lasts throughout the animation, as displayed in Figure 5.14.

13. Repeat steps 10 through 12 until the word *FLASH* is spelled out.

    When the animation is complete with all the squares flying across the stage and then morphing into their respective letters to spell FLASH, there is still one problem. The *A* turns hollow in the animation because there is a hole in the *A* (note that I could have said this backwards—that there is an A... well, you get the point). Therefore, you need to fix this by putting a hole in the square.

14. On frame 25 of the A layer, you need to insert a keyframe by pressing F6. On this new keyframe, choose the Eraser tool with the smallest eraser size. Erase a small hole in the center of the square. Problem solved!

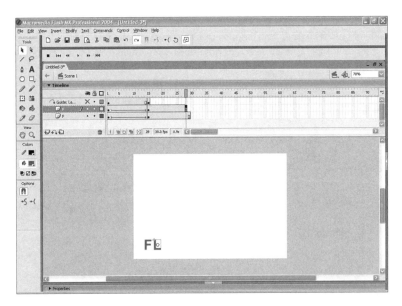

**FIGURE 5.14**    Extending the timeline for the bottom layer.

Again, this exercise further illustrates the importance of proper keyframing. It also shows what will be a very common technique in development—combining the shape and motion tweens.

## Creating Interactivity with Buttons

For true interactivity, the end user must have some input as to how the Flash movie or animation will unfold. The easiest way to do this is with buttons. Buttons can control certain elements in a Flash movie. For example, a button can play or stop an animation. Buttons can also trigger other events, such as opening up a browser window, setting volume for a sound, or even controlling a spaceship in a video game. Understanding how buttons work and how buttons interact with different Flash objects is fundamental to interactive Web design.

**Controlling the Animation with Buttons**

When you're adding interactivity, it is important to allow the end user to control how an animation is played. Here are the steps to follow to control an animation with buttons:

1. Open `mtween.fla`, the file you created earlier in this chapter. Create a new layer and name it **Button**. Lock the animation layer so that you don't edit it by accident. Create a new button symbol by choosing Insert, New Symbol. Make sure to choose Button for the behavior and name the symbol **button**. Then add keyframes to all the button's states.

2. Return to the main timeline. If the library isn't already open, choose Window, Library or press Cmd+L (Mac) or Ctrl+L (PC) to open it. Drag out two instances of button and place them anywhere on the stage on the Button layer.

3. With the Type tool, type **Play** over the first button and **Stop** over the second.

4. With the Play button selected (be sure to have the button selected and not the text *Play*), select Window, Development Panels, Behaviors. This will bring up the Behaviors panel, as similar to Figure 5.15.

**FIGURE 5.15**   The Behaviors panel.

5. In the Behaviors panel, click on the plus sign to add some actions to the play button. Select Movieclip, Goto and Play at Frame or Label. When that is selected, a window will appear with options similar to Figure 5.16. The options include the frame number we want to start on, and the path to the movie clip we want to play. For this example, the defaults are fine, so click OK. The action will now be in the Behaviors panel.

**FIGURE 5.16**   Options for the Goto and Play at Frame or Label behavior.

This will have placed actions in the button. To see the actions, make sure the play button is still selected, and open up the Actions panel by going to Window, Development Panels, Actions (PC–F9, Mac–F9). Then you will see the actions in the play button like these:

```
on (release) {
    //Movieclip GotoAndPlay Behavior

    this.gotoAndPlay("1");
    //End Behavior
}
```

The event handler on (release) can be changed. At this point, the release of the mouse will trigger the event (in this case, play). If you want to change this to press or some other event, simply go back to the Behaviors panel, and you will see the action that has been placed in the play button. In the Behaviors panel, there are two columns, Event and Action. Under the Event column, you will see On Release. To change this, click in that column, and a drop-down menu will appear with several choices as shown in Figure 5.17.

**FIGURE 5.17**    Additional events in the Behaviors panel.

Before we test the script, the animation will automatically start playing. All movies in Flash will play and loop by default. Therefore, you need to fix this so that the Play button will actually serve a purpose.

6. Highlight frame 1 in either layer and choose Window, Development Panels, Actions. Notice that the Actions panel reads "Actions – Frame." In the Actions panel, type these actions to stop the movie from automatically playing:

   stop();

7. Now you can test the movie. Choose Control, Test Movie. Notice that the animation does not start playing by default. Click the Play button. Your animation should now be playing!

8. Watch the entire animation.

   This animation looks okay; however, the movie will stop playing, even though we didn't ask it to. The reason why it has stopped is that the play head is looping. Looping simply means that when the play head reaches the end of the animation, it will come back to the beginning. In our case, the first frame has a stop action causing the animation to stop.

   Therefore, we need to come up with a workaround for this problem. We can't remove the stop action from the first frame because it is stopping the animation from playing automatically.

9. Highlight the last frame in your animation. With it highlighted, open the Actions panel. In the Actions panel, type these actions:

```
gotoAndPlay(2);
```

This will fix the problem because when the play head hits the last frame, the play head will read the script and send it back to frame 2, thus avoiding frame 1 altogether.

It's important to point out that when you're dealing with ActionScript, you should test your movies often. From this one example, you can see the benefit of testing frequently. It is easier to build on good scripts and make minor adjustments where needed, as opposed to debugging longer ActionScript code.

10. All you need to do now is add functionality to the Stop button. This task is a bit easier. Highlight the button with the Arrow tool. With the Stop button selected, go to the Behaviors panel, and click the plus sign again. This time choose Movieclip, Goto and Stop at Frame or Label, and click OK.

11. Test your movie! See how easy that was?

12. Save this movie as `control1.fla`.

---

This exercise illustrates the first step in creating interactivity between your site and an end user. Much of what we'll cover in the rest of this book builds on these basic principles.

## The Movie Clip

The movie clip symbol is by far the most important symbol in Flash. When we get into advanced ActionScript, we'll refer to the movie clip as an object. For now, we'll review the differences between a movie clip and a graphic symbol. For starters, ActionScript can be placed on a movie clip, as well as in a movie clip.

You create a movie clip symbol the same way you create a graphic or button symbol. To create one from scratch, you simply choose Insert, New Symbol. In the Create New Symbol dialog box, select Movie Clip for the behavior. Of course, if you have some artwork already drawn on the stage, you can convert it to a movie clip symbol. When you've created a new movie clip symbol, you'll be placed in movie clip symbol editing mode. The crosshair in the center of the stage indicates the center of the symbol.

However, the most compelling thing about the movie clip is that it has its own timeline, just like the button symbol and the graphic symbol, but the key difference is that this timeline will play independently of the main timeline. This offers huge advantages in Flash development. For instance, the main timeline doesn't get clogged with all sorts of animations. Instead, animations can reside inside movie clips. Also, your buttons can communicate with the movie clips, with some additional syntax.

**Nesting Symbols and Controlling a Movie Clip with Buttons**

Here, as in the last exercise, we are going to control the play head, telling it when to stop and when to play. The biggest difference in this exercise, however, is that we need to communicate with the movie clip's play head and not the main timeline's. Therefore, our syntax will change slightly.

Also, in this exercise you are going to take your first step in nesting symbols. Nesting a symbol simply means placing one symbol inside another symbol. Nesting has many advantages, but for our purposes, the advantage is that inside the movie clip will be a graphic symbol that's animated, as opposed to a primitive shape. Remember, during an animation with a primitive shape, each keyframe must be redrawn. With a graphic symbol, the keyframe simply points to the library when it needs graphical information. Here are the steps to follow for this exercise:

1. Choose Insert, New Symbol. Be sure to give the new symbol a graphic behavior. Name this symbol `square_graphic` and click OK. You'll then be placed inside the graphic symbol.

2. Draw a square in the center of the symbol. Choose a fill and stroke color.

3. Click back to scene 1 to get to the main timeline. Notice that the square is not on the stage. Open the Library panel by choosing Window, Library. Drag out an instance of square_graphic and place it anywhere on the stage.

4. Highlight square_graphic and press F8 to convert it to a symbol. Yes, it already is a symbol; however, by converting to a symbol, you are placing the existing square_graphic symbol inside this new symbol you're defining. Name this symbol `squareMC` and give it the movie clip behavior. Click OK.

5. Double-click the squareMC to go into the editing mode for the square. Create a small motion tween of the square moving from one side of the stage to the other. Remember, you are in the movie clip, which means that this is an animated symbol.

6. After creating the motion tween, come back to scene 1. You'll notice that the main time-line has only one frame. If you press Enter (Windows) or Return (Mac), the animation will not play, even though your movie clip has an animation. In order to see animated movie clips, you must test the movie. Choose Control, Test Movie, and the animation should start playing.

7. Close the test window. Then highlight the instance of the movie clip. In the Properties Inspector, name the movie clip `anim_mc` in the Instance Name field as in Figure 5.18. As with symbol names, it is good practice to give instance names that mean something to you. Also, it is good practice to use suffixes for movie clips and buttons to better interact with ActionScript. For movie clips, use _mc and for buttons use _btn.

8. We now want to create some buttons to stop and play this animation. But first, remember that the animation will play and loop by default. To fix this problem, you need to go into the editing mode for the anim_mc movie clip and then place a `stop` action on the first frame and a `gotoAndPlay frame 2` action on the last frame. This will keep the animation from playing automatically and from stopping when it tries to loop. Refer to the exercise in this chapter titled "Controlling the Animation with Buttons."

9. Next, create a new layer and name it `buttons`.

10. Choose Library, Common Library, Buttons to open the Buttons common library. Drag out two instances of your favorite button.

11. With one of the buttons selected, open the Behaviors panel, click the Add Behavior button and choose Movieclip, Goto and Play at Frame or Label. This time when the Behavior Options window pops up, instead of using the default settings, choose anim_mc from the list as in Figure 5.19, and leave the frame number at 1.

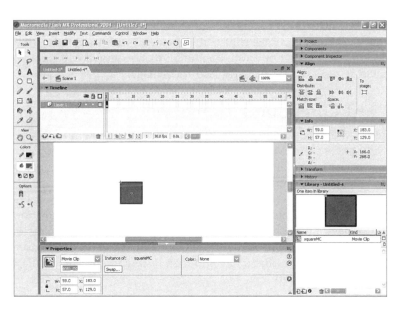

**FIGURE 5.18**    You can name the instance `anim_mc` in the Properties Inspector.

**FIGURE 5.19**    Choose `anim_mc` from the list.

12. Test the move by pressing Cmd+Return (Mac) or Ctrl+Enter (Windows) or choosing Control, Test Movie.

13. To apply a `stop` action to the next button, follow step 10 again, except use a Goto and Stop at Frame or Label behavior instead of a Goto and Play at Frame or Label behavior.

The ability to control and communicate with movie clips is the basis for ActionScript. The more you practice and understand the concepts in this section, the easier writing ActionScript will be. Although the code in the preceding exercise is proper, it might not be the most efficient. In Chapter 11, "The MovieClip Object," we'll discuss how movie clips work and what they are. The movie clip is an object, and with that comes an easier syntax structure. Right now, though, don't worry about all this because it will soon make more sense as we start to deconstruct the ActionScript language.

# Nested and Compound Animation

We've covered how to take a symbol and place it inside another symbol, thus creating a nested symbol. One of the real powers of nesting symbols is the ability to create compound animation, which means, in not so many words, animating an animated symbol. In the preceding exercise, we nested a graphic symbol inside a movie clip. When you tested the movie, the movie clip actually animated, even though the main timeline was only one frame long, because the movie clip was made up of an animation. In the next exercise, we have a movie clip on the main timeline that doesn't animate unless we test the movie. The main timeline contains only one frame, but we'll add more. By inserting a keyframe and tween into that frame and then testing the movie, you'll notice you have animated your animation!

### Creating an Animated Button

You can nest movie clips within buttons, and vice versa. By nesting a movie clip within a button, you can create an animated button. In this exercise, we are going to take a look at how to animate a button as the end user moves a mouse over it. Here are the steps to follow:

1. Open a new document by choosing File, New. In the new document, create a new button symbol by choosing Insert, New Symbol. Give the symbol a button behavior and name it **button**. Click OK to be placed in button symbol editing mode.

2. Draw a circle filled with any color of your choice. Add keyframes in the Over, Down, and Hit states. Change the color slightly on each keyframe.

3. Name the layer **button** and click the Add Layer button. Name this new layer **glow**.

4. Insert a keyframe in the Over state of the glow layer. If, at this point, you add content to this frame, you would then populate the Down and Hit states as well, and we don't want that. To avoid this, insert a blank keyframe (F7) in the Down state, thus clearing anything on the frames before it.

5. Drag the glow layer underneath the button layer so that the glow layer is on the bottom, as shown in Figure 5.20.

6. On the glow layer, draw a small yellow circle without a stroke underneath the button. When you let go of the mouse to finish drawing the circle, it will look as if nothing has happened because the circle you just drew is hidden under the button. To see the circle, turn on the visibility of the button layer by clicking the bullet under the eye column.

7. Highlight the circle and convert it to a movie clip symbol by pressing F8. Name this symbol **glowMC**.

8. Click OK. Double-click the small yellow circle to go into movie clip symbol editing mode.

9. Highlight the circle by clicking it and open the Color Mixer if it isn't already open. To open the Color Mixer, choose Window, Design Panels, Color Mixer. In the Color Mixer (see

Figure 5.21), choose the fill swatch and bring the Alpha setting down to 0%. This will make the circle invisible when you deselect it by clicking away from it.

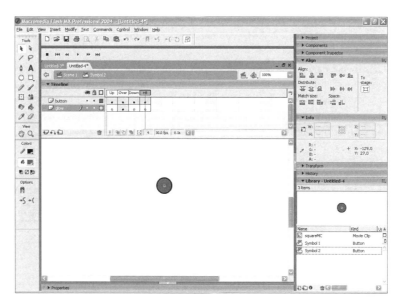

**FIGURE 5.20**     The glow layer underneath the button layer.

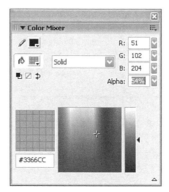

**FIGURE 5.21**     In the Color Mixer, you can fill a symbol with a color that has an Alpha setting of 0%, thus filling it with an invisible color.

10. Insert a keyframe on frames 7 and 14 by pressing F6. Notice that the black circle representing the keyframe appears in both frames. Then create a shape tween from frame 1 to 7 and from frame 7 to 14.

11. Move the play head back to frame 7. In frame 7, select the circle and then choose Modify, Transform. In the dialog box that appears, you can scale the item numerically. Scale the circle up 400%.

12. With the circle still selected in frame 7, open the Color Mixer. Bring the fill's Alpha setting back up to 100%.

    It is important to remember that movie clips play and loop by default. Therefore, the glow movie clip will always be playing. However, glow will only be visible in the Over state of the button. Therefore, only when an end user moves the mouse over the button will he see the animated glow.

13. Click the Scene 1 link to come back to the main timeline. Open up the Library panel and drag out an instance of the button symbol. By dragging out an instance of button, you are also dragging out an instance of glow, because glow is nested inside the button.

14. Choose Control, Test Movie. This will launch a Flash player. In the Flash player, move your mouse over the button to see the animation play (see Figure 5.22).

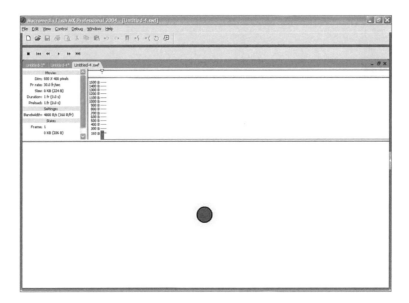

**FIGURE 5.22**    An animated button symbol.

# The Library

So far, we've been adding items to the library. Now we'll dive deeper into organizing and managing the library. We're going to be looking at some of the more advanced techniques in handling symbols. The Library panel, as displayed in Figure 5.23, is an area for organizing, storing, and accessing your symbols.

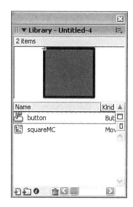

**FIGURE 5.23**   The Library panel.

Each movie contains a library. Every symbol, movie, sound, and bitmap image in that file becomes a part of that movie's library. You can even open up other files' libraries to get their items by going to File, Import, Open External Library. A library is made up of these basic components:

- **Item Preview**. This area of the library gives you a thumbnail of the artwork in the library. If it is a sound, you will see a waveform. Movie clips and sounds have play and stop buttons so that you can preview the animation or sound within the library!

- **Sort Order**. Sorts the llibrary items in either ascending or descending order, depending on which column you have selected (Name, Kind, Use Count, or Linkage).

- **Wide State**. Use this option to set the visibility of the library in its wide state, maximizing the Library to view all its contents horizontally.

- **Narrow State**. This is the more common state, taking less screen real estate. It's a slimmed-down version of the wide state that just shows the essentials.

- **Delete Item**. This button deletes an item or folder from the library. Use it only if you are sure you want to remove the contents for the library (this action is not undoable).

- **Item Properties**. This button launches a dialog box that gives you specific feedback about a particular item. If you get item properties for a bitmap, for example, the dialog box returns information such as the path, dimensions, the date the file was created, and compression options. The properties change depending on the type of item you've selected.

- **New Folder**. This button creates a new folder in the library for organizational purposes.

- **New Symbol**. This button creates a new symbol and launches the Create New Symbol dialog box. This is the equivalent to choosing Insert, New Symbol.

You may also manage and organize your library by using folders. This can maximize your efficiency and workflow when using Flash assets.

For example, you could create a Graphic Symbols folder, a Buttons folder, and a Movie Clips folder. This would allow you quicker access to the symbols you're looking for. To create a new folder, just click the New Folder button at the bottom of the library and then type in a name for the folder in the highlighted area. If the Name area is not highlighted, just double-click it as you would to rename a layer. You can also sort the stacking order, just like layers. Click and drag up the folder that you want to have on top. To move a library item into the folder, just drag the icon of the library item on top of the folder icon and drop it. You'll notice the difference between an empty folder and folder that has items in it by their appearance—an empty folder appears "empty" where a filled folder appears to have a document in it.

When a folder has content in it, you can collapse or open the folder by double-clicking the folder's icon. Alternatively, you can choose Expand Folder or Collapse Folder from the Library Options menu.

You can also create a folder by right-clicking (Control-clicking on Macs) an item in the library and selecting Move to New Folder. This will pop up a window asking the name of the new folder. When you click OK, the library will create the folder, and move the item into it.

You can also easily find content within the library that is not used in the movie. For organizational purposes, you should delete this data. However, Flash will not export any data not used in the movie. Therefore, removing unused items from the library does nothing to conserve file size. To select or find unused items, use one of the following methods:

- Under the Library Options menu, choose Select Unused Items, as shown in Figure 5.24. This will highlight all the unused Library items. With the items highlighted, click the trash can button to remove them all.

- Sort the items by use counts. If the Use Counts column is not active, choose Options, Update Use Counts Now. If you would like the use counts to update continually, choose Keep Use Counts Updated.

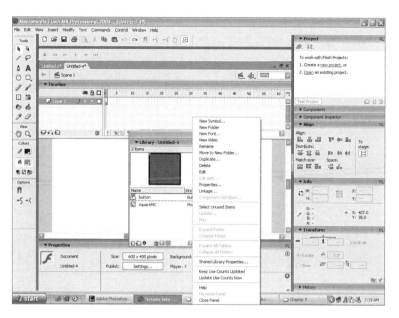

**FIGURE 5.24**  Choose the Select Unused Items option in the Library Options menu.

## Summary

This chapter covered all the basics with regard to symbols and instances. Concepts to take away from this chapter are that instances are copies of the original symbol and making changes to symbols affects all instances, but changes made directly to instances only affect that one instance. We also went over how to motion-tween certain symbols to create animation as well as how to use the motion guide.

And at the end of this chapter the library was covered. The library is where all symbols from the Flash file are held and organized.

It's important to understand the fundamentals from this chapter because they will be used throughout the rest of this book.

CHAPTER **6**

# Publishing

When all your work is finished, you still aren't quite done. The Flash authoring environment is created within a file with an extension of .fla. When you save your work, your entire Flash project is included in that FLA file. The problem is that if you don't publish your work, no one can view it unless they also own Flash. This is also impractical because then anyone with Flash will be able to open your project and use your graphics, library items, or any other authored asset. What's more, anyone without Flash would never be able to see your work. Luckily, the developers at Macromedia have stepped in to save the day with **publishing**. In Flash, publishing is easier and more versatile than most other authoring environments. Publishing in Flash also allows you to show your project to millions of online users while giving you the security of knowing your work is protected.

Publishing protects your work, while simultaneously letting the masses view your project. Let's take a look at how to access the publishing settings and give your end users the ability to see your work.

## Where to Find Publishing

On your menu bar, choose File and then one of the following three items (see Figure 6.1):

• **Publish Settings (Ctrl+Shift+F12).** Choosing this option allows you to customize publish settings for the FLA file currently open. You can choose the file format and file-specific options desired for your final output. Be aware that some settings will not work with one another.

- **Publish Preview**. This option allows you to preview the published FLA file in the format of your choice. Only those items selected in Publish Settings can be chosen here for preview.

- **Publish (Shift+F12)**. This option publishes the results of your FLA file without letting you preview your output. You can also do this by going into Publish Settings and clicking the Publish button at the bottom of the Publish Settings dialog box.

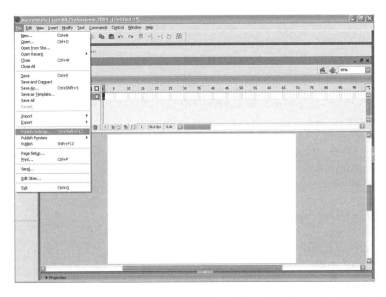

**FIGURE 6.1**   Under the File drop-down menu, you'll find the Publish Settings, Publish Preview, and Publish items.

## Versatile Formats

When you're publishing in Flash, you have the option to create multiple formats. The default publishing settings include SWF and HTML documents. The SWF document, which is short for *Shockwave Flash* (or Small Web Format if you are a Web history buff), is viewable in the Macromedia Flash Player. The HTML document that accompanies the SWF document is set up with OBJECT and EMBED tags that embed the SWF document into the HTML document. We'll talk more about this later in the chapter.

Flash is highly versatile. It not only publishes to its own format (SWF) but will also publish to the following "alternative" formats: GIF, JPEG, PNG, and QuickTime. The first three formats are graphic formats. If you have created artwork in Flash on a frame or group of frames, you can export it to be viewable as an image online or for use in other applications.

The QuickTime format is viewable with Apple's QuickTime Player and is a video format. With this format you can import a QuickTime movie into Flash. You simply overlay your own Flash graphics and animations and then publish the whole thing to be viewable in the QuickTime Player.

Flash also has the ability to publish to either a Mac or PC standalone projector. This gives you the ability to place your project in a single, self-contained executable file. The project does not rely on the Flash Player to be viewed, nor do you need any application at all to view it. Simply opening a standalone projector allows end users to view your work on their computers.

One of the truly wonderful points in Flash's favor over many other authoring tools is its ability to publish to a multitude of formats. You can use Flash as an authoring tool for an entire project or Web site, or simply to create portions of projects for use in other authoring environments or for the Web. As you get further into the publishing aspects of Flash, you will begin to realize the impact Flash has as a tool for your overall creativity. Flash is not simply a Web development tool, a graphics tool, or an animation tool. Instead, it is all three of these tools wrapped up into one.

## Publishing Profiles

The first new thing you will notice in the Publish Settings dialog box (see Figure 6.2) is the available profiles. You can create, duplicate, edit, and remove profiles for publishing. This can come in handy if you like to create custom file options, and you do not feel like making the changes manually—you can use profiles to store your publishing information.

To create a new publishing profile, follow these steps:

1. Click the Create New Profile button, which is the button with the plus sign.

2. Give your profile a name.

3. Make all the necessary changes to the options you would like, and you're done.

Now, you can return to the settings whenever you like, select the profile you created, and all of your settings will be made.

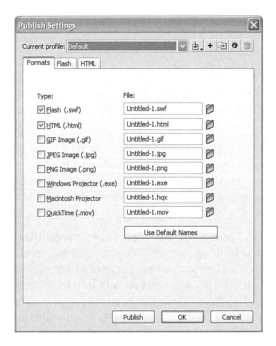

**FIGURE 6.2**    The Publish Settings dialog box.

## Macromedia Flash Player 7 and the SWF File Format

As mentioned earlier, the SWF file is used for deploying Flash content. It can be read in each of the following ways:

- In Internet browsers that are equipped with the Flash Player. The SWF document must be embedded into an HTM, HTML, or HTML-compatible format (such as ASP or PHP) file in order for the browser to read it.

- Inside Macromedia Director or Authorware, as long as the Flash Xtra is included with the final Director or Authorware project.

- With the Flash ActiveX control in Microsoft Office and other ActiveX hosts.

- Inside the QuickTime Player. Note that depending on which version of QuickTime is being used, some Flash functionality may be lost.

- As a standalone movie called a **projector**.

Let's take a look at the first bulleted point for a moment. Internet browsers require the end users to install a plug-in that allows them to view SWF content online. Not all users will have the most current version of the plug-in for the browser. This means that content created in the current player version may not be viewable to all users. Also, any content created in a player version greater than the one on the user's system will not be displayed. You can get the latest Flash Player penetration statistics here:

```
http://www.macromedia.com/software/player_census/flashplayer/
version_penetration.html
```

And you can of course get the most recent player at

```
http://www.macromedia.com/shockwave/download/
download.cgi?P1_Prod_Version=ShockwaveFlash
```

Not only do you need to be concerned with player version, but you also need to consider the player's subversion. In the Flash 6 Player, there were several releases fixing security holes, adding features, and increasing performance.

Fortunately, many of the new features in Flash MX 2004 are compatible with Flash Player 6 (if not, an error message will appear in the Output panel to let you know, like the one in Figure 6.3).

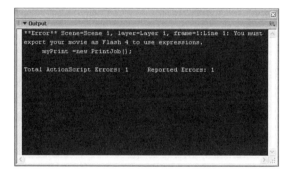

**FIGURE 6.3**    When you attempt to use a script that is not supported by your selected player version, you will receive an error.

As an easy way to tell whether an ActionScript action is supported by a given player, you can use the ActionScript dictionary in the Help panel to check the player availability as in Figure 6.4.

Not to worry—Flash MX 2004 and the new Flash Player 7 have ways of helping you out. The first is an automatic player version detection that can be included when you publish (which is discussed later in the section covering the HTML tab of the Publish Settings dialog box). Also, to keep users up to date with the latest player, the new Flash 7 Player now has an autoupdate built in, as you can see in Figure 6.5.

**FIGURE 6.4**     Checking the player availability for an ActionScript action in the Help panel.

**FIGURE 6.5**     The autoupdate alert for the Flash 7 Player.

Before you worry about making sure your code works with the selected version, you first have to select the version in the Publish Settings dialog box.

## Version Field

Flash has provided a way to go back in time, enabling you to choose the version of your Flash document. The resulting SWF document will be tailored to use only the functions of that version and previous versions of the Flash authoring environment. Therefore, choosing Flash Player 7 will be inclusive of all version 7 Player options and ActionScript.

However, publishing in the targeted version is important because it allows you to use code targeted to work with that particular version of Flash and those that precede it. You can select the version you would like to use at the top of the Flash tab in the Publish Settings dialog box; the Version drop-down menu should look similar to Figure 6.6. You can choose any version, from 1 to 7 as well as Flash Lite 1.0.

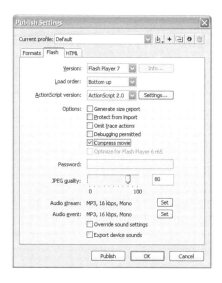

**FIGURE 6.6**    The Flash Version field enables you to publish your final SWF file for previous versions of the Flash Player.

## Sound Settings

Several compression options are available for the sounds you import into Flash. Also, it is best to compress your sound on a case-by-case basis. This will ensure the best quality for your sounds, and you will not have only a single setting throughout your movie. However, if you still choose to have a single setting, Flash does provide this option for you. Here are the steps to follow:

1. Choose File, Publish Settings and click the Flash tab.

2. At the bottom of the Flash tab you will see settings for streaming and settings for event sounds. The difference between event sounds and streaming sounds is that event sounds must be fully downloaded before played, and that they can only be stopped manually, whereas streaming sounds can start playing immediately. Click the Set button next to either of these options. Figure 6.7 shows the Sound Settings dialog box.

**FIGURE 6.7**    The default values for the sound settings.

3. Your first option will be the type of compression (refer to Chapter 7, "Working with Sound and Video," for a listing of types of compressions to use). Select Disable if you want to set the sound settings on individual sounds in your project. Select another option if you want to change the compression of your sounds globally.

4. Also, based on the type of sound you are using, you may choose a particular sampling rate, level of quality, or bit rate for sound. Then click OK in the Sound Settings dialog box, which will return you to the Publish Settings dialog box.

5. Finally, under the Audio Stream and Audio Event options, you have the choice to override the sound settings. Clicking the Override Sound Settings box will throw out the settings you have created in the library and will use the compression you chose earlier in this dialog box. And in Flash MX 2004 Professional edition, you also have the last check box, Export Device Sounds, for exporting sounds specifically for devices, such as mobile devices and handhelds.

## Other Flash Tab Settings

So far you have learned about the Version menu, and we've gone over the sound settings, but what other controls are present in our Flash SWF creation? Refer to Figure 6.6 to see the entire Flash tab and the options found there. Here's a list that describes each of them:

- **Load Order**. Use this option to decide how your timeline will load onto the end user's computer. Your choices are limited to top-down and bottom-up (which is the default). However, the main thing to keep in mind is your initialization of variables in ActionScript. If you have items loading before your initialization that rely on some of those variables, your frame might not load correctly. Your use of variables is where you will run into the most problems with the load order. Therefore, it is important to keep your initialization of variables as close to the first thing loaded as possible.

- **ActionScript Version**. This option is for setting the ActionScript version to run in the SWF file. The default is version 2.0, and you can also select version 1.0 (the previous version of ActionScript). If you do select ActionScript version 2.0, you can also create the classpath for external ActionScript files (.as), which hold classes you have built.

- **Options and Password**. These options allow you to maintain your project. For example, you may want to restrict some users from being able to debug your project or find out some statistics about the file after publishing. Here are the options:

  - **Generate Size Report**. This is useful in trying to determine which frames are causing problems in your SWF document, which frames are largest, and which frames load fastest. It's also useful for determining the overall size of your project. If your client requests a specific size for a project, you can use this report to target frames and reduce the overall size of a project. It is useful in identifying areas of your project that may be too large to load for your users.

  - **Protect File from Import**. This is highly useful to keep envious designers from stealing your creativity. You can also choose to have a password to allow certain users to view your work (the Password field will become active when you select this option).

  - **Omit Trace Actions**. Trace actions are ActionScript code useful in testing parts of your movie. The results of trace actions will appear in the Output window. Omitting them is only a good idea on your final publication to your end users. It is not a good idea before this because you may want to use trace actions in the debugging and development of your project.

  - **Debugging Permitted**. This option provides end users with the ability to debug your project from a remote server. This option can be useful if you need outside assistance with your project in the debugging stage. This is also password-enabled (so the Password field will become enabled).

  - **Compress Movie**. This option is only available with Flash Players 6 and 7. It attempts to compress your movie to the smallest size possible. It is set to On by default.

  - **Optimize for Flash Player 6 r65**. This option is only available when choosing the Flash Player 6. It is used to improve performance for the Flash Player 6 subversion 65 and later versions of the Flash Player only.

- **JPEG Quality**. This option refers specifically to the JPEG quality within your Flash movie. You have an option range of 0 to 100 for the quality of bitmapped images in your Flash SWF document. Remember, you will have the tradeoff of a larger file size the higher the setting you select. Generally, I like to keep my images up around 90%.

## Alternative File Settings (JPEG, GIF, and PNG)

Alternative file options are intended to allow you the choice of using a frame (or frames) in your Flash piece outside the project in another a graphical format. Often you may create artwork in your Flash piece that you want to use in other print pieces or in HTML online. You can publish selected frames from your Flash piece and convert them into workable artwork in JPEG, GIF, or PNG format. This can also be useful if you want to blur objects in Flash. Simply export a frame from Flash, bring it into Photoshop to apply a blur appearance to it, and import it as a PNG file back into Flash. You can then use the blurred image on in-between frames of your animation to create a blurred look for animation styles. In this section we'll take a look at how to publish a frame or group of frames to alternative formats.

## JPEG Settings

JPEG files will export only the frame your playback head is currently in. Therefore, if your playback head resides on frame 20, frames 1–19 will not be exported. Figure 6.8 shows a Flash document that is currently resting on frame 10. No other frames will be able to export to JPEG; only frame 10 will export because that is the playback head's location.

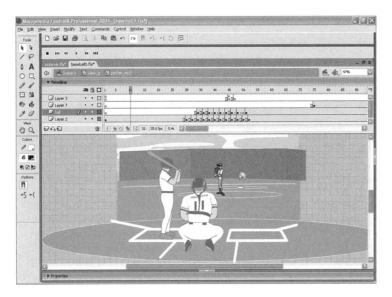

**FIGURE 6.8**    Frame 10 is the frame where the playback head of this FLA rests. When this file is published to the JPEG format, only frame 10 will export. All other frames will be ignored.

To get to the JPEG settings choose File, Publish Settings, and in the Formats tab, check the box next to the JPEG Image (.jpg) option. If you want the JPEG to possess the same name as the FLA file, use the default filenames, as displayed in Figure 6.9. You can change the filename manually or, using the browsing folders to the right of the text fields, you can browse to the folder you would like to create it in, and even select a file to overwrite. And you can, of course, click the Use Default Names button to restore all the filenames back to their defaults.

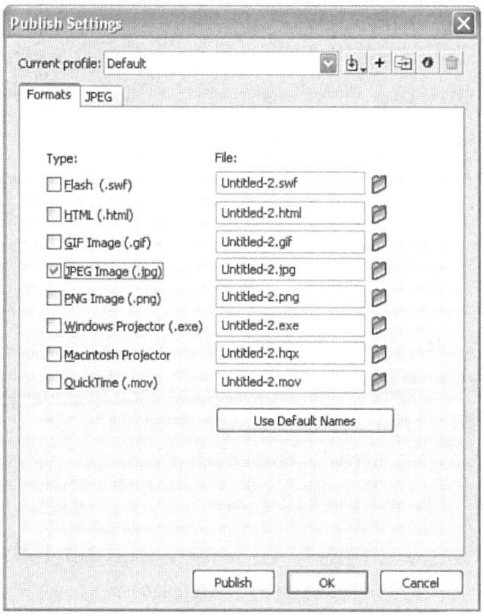

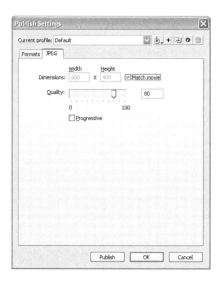

**FIGURE 6.9**   Notice that we are using the default filename.

Immediately after selecting JPEG Image in the Formats tab, you will notice that a tab for JPEG appears alongside Formats at the top of the Publish Settings dialog box. Clicking this tab will allow you to choose the settings you want for your JPEG image. Figure 6.10 displays the options available under this tab. These settings are also described in the following list:

**FIGURE 6.10**   The options of the JPEG tab in the Publish Settings dialog box include the choice of dimensions and the quality of the image to be output.

- **Dimensions**. You can choose to have your dimensions match the Flash movie settings (accessible under Modify, Document in your menu bar), or you can pick your own settings for this file. As always with JPEGs (or any image for that matter), the larger the dimensions the bigger the file size will be. Checking the Match Movie box will gray out the dimensions. Because you already chose the dimensions in the movie settings, there's no need to specify dimensions. If you leave this box unchecked, the Width and Height categories are now editable.

- **Quality**. Based on a value of 0 to 100, this option determines the quality of your image. You need to decide what your objective with the JPEG is. If you are using this image on the Web, you will most likely want to choose a setting in the 50%–90% range. This way, the image will not look as clean but will load faster over the Internet. If you are creating a JPEG that will eventually be used in a print format, nothing short of 100% will be acceptable.

- **Progressive**. This allows your JPEG to load incrementally in a Web browser with a slow connection, which makes your JPEG image appear to load faster over a slow connection. Again, depending on your audience this option may be useful. However, if you select progressive for the JPEG image, it cannot be loaded back into Flash dynamically by means of the `loadMovie` or `loadMovieNum` methods in ActionScript.

## GIF and PNG Settings

The GIF file format is ideal for images that are simple and contain few colors. Examples of these images are cartoons, logos, and signs. The use of fewer colors creates better GIFs in terms of download time and visibility. A GIF generally gives less photorealistic quality than that of JPEG images. GIFs, when properly optimized, create very small files that load quickly over slower connections.

When you're publishing images in Flash to the GIF format, Flash will automatically publish the first frame in the file. If you want a different frame marked for export, you must put a frame label in the frame you want exported. That label must be named `#Static`. If you are exporting a series of frames for a GIF animation, Flash will export all the frames of your movie. To select a range of frames to be exported to GIF format, create two frame labels. `#First` specifies the first frame you want published, and `#Last` represents the name of the last frame you want published to the GIF. All frames between these two frames will be published, ignoring all other frames in your movie.

Flash can also export an image map for use in specifying URL links in your HTML documents. `#map` specifies in which frame the map information is located for your GIF file.

Keeping this in mind, let's take a look at the GIF options by clicking the check box next to the GIF Image (`.gif`) option in the Formats tab again. Then click the GIF tab at the top of the Publish Settings dialog box to open the GIF options. These options are described in the following list and displayed in Figure 6.11:

**FIGURE 6.11**    The options under the GIF tab in the Publish Settings dialog box offer a choice between an animated or static GIF and a choice of palettes for the resulting GIF.

- **Dimensions**. Similar to the JPEG settings, you can also choose the size of your GIF image. Again, you have the choice of Match Movie or your own dimensions. Leaving this check box blank will allow you to enter a width and height for your GIF file.

- **Playback**. Unlike other image formats, GIFs allow you to choose an animation (series of images) or a single image to be included in your file. Choosing Static will gray out the options on the right because the image will only contain one frame. Choosing Animated will allow you to determine whether you want your animation to loop continuously or to repeat a specified number of loops. Animated GIFs are generally used for ad banners. Just be judicial in your use of animation on a static HTML page because your users can be easily annoyed by multiple items moving at the same time on your page.

- **Optimize Colors**. This option removes any unused colors from the GIF file's color table, which means it will only use those colors essential for the image. This is similar to locking in the colors that are needed for your image to look a certain way (locking is used in programs such as Photoshop and Fireworks).

- **Interlace**. Allows the image to display incrementally as it downloads in a browser. This may appear to download the GIF faster on slower browsers. Do not interlace animated GIFs. This is similar to the Progressive option under the JPEG settings.

- **Smooth**. This option applies antialiasing to an exported bitmap to increase the quality of a bitmap image. It also improves text quality. Beware though, because images placed on a colored background may gain a gray halo around them. If this occurs, republish the image with Smooth unchecked.

- **Dither Solids**. Applies dithering to solid colors as well as to gradients. Dithering is the way in which colors not in the GIF color palette are read.

- **Remove Gradients**. Turns all gradients to a solid color, using the first color in the gradient as the default. Gradients are often the cause of large file sizes in GIFs because they require many colors to make a smooth transition between two colors.

- **Transparent**. Gives you the ability to make your GIF image transparent or opaque, or possess an alpha value.

    - **Opaque**. Leaves the image's background intact.

    - **Alpha**. Allows you to choose to have a background semitransparent by choosing a value between 0 and 255. A lower value, such as 10, will result in a more transparent background as opposed to a higher value, such as 200.

    - **Transparent**. Removes the background completely from the image.

- **Dither**. Dithering tries to simulate how colors that are not present in a palette will be displayed in your image. This increases your file size but can improve color quality.

    - **None**. This option will approximate the analyzed color to the closest color in the palette.

    - **Ordered**. Dithers your file with good balance between quality and file size.

    - **Diffusion**. Dithers your file with the best quality but gives up some ability to limit the file size.

- **Palette Type**. The kind of palette is determined by how many colors you want or how you will display your image over the Web. Your choices of palettes include the following:

    - **Web 216**. Uses the standard 216 colors that are safe to use across the most popular browsers.

    - **Adaptive**. Analyzes colors and comes up with a unique set of colors used to produce the best possible image.

    - **Web Snap Adaptive**. A mix between Web 216 and Adaptive. This option tries to maximize the image quality while using Web 216 colors whenever it deems necessary.

    - **Custom.** Palettes can be imported into Flash and used from programs such as Fireworks. They must be imported using the ACT format. The advantage here is that you get to determine the exact colors you want. Although time-consuming, this can be the best alternative, especially for small colored pictures.

PNG files follow almost the same format as GIF, with a few minor differences. You can find a graphical display of the options for PNG files in Figure 6.12.

**FIGURE 6.12**   The options under the PNG tab in the Publish Settings dialog box offer the ability to choose a bit depth and a palette for the resulting PNG file.

PNG files work primarily on a bit-depth system that allows you to have transparency within a bitmap format for the image. To enable the transparency, you must select 24-bit with Alpha for your Bit Depth setting. If your image does not call for a transparent effect, choose either 16- or 24-bit to reduce the size of your PNG file.

The other option that PNG provides that GIF does not is the ability to choose a filter. This option attempts to make the bitmap more compressible. It's a system that looks at neighboring pixels to get a sense of what the overall pixel value should be through a line-by-line filtering system. Here are the options available to you for filtering:

- **None**. Turns the filtering option off.

- **Sub**. Evaluates the difference between the pixel prior to the current pixel and the current pixel to gain a value.

- **Up**. Examines the current pixel and the adjacent pixel above it to evaluate the current pixel value.

- **Average**. Takes the adjacent pixels above and to the left of the current pixel to predict a value for the current pixel.

- **Path**. Creates a function out of the top, left-top, and left pixels to arrive at a value for the current pixel.

- **Adaptive**. Analyzes the colors needed to produce the best-quality picture. The file size of an adaptive filtering system can be reduced by reducing the number of colors in your image. However, this option is usually intended for use on machines with millions of colors.

> **NOTE**
>
> When trying to decide which filter to use, test each of them to figure out which one best suits your needs.

## HTML

Early in the lifespan of Macromedia Flash, back when it was known as Future Splash, the product had little use because ActionScript was not yet a language. However, it was a great graphics tool, and many early developers talked of how Flash worked well as a tool for creating animated GIFs and images for the Web. When Macromedia introduced Flash 3, the game started to change a little bit. Not only were graphic designers finding a use for the tool, but programmers had some leeway by being able to design some interactivity into their projects. That interactivity exploded with Flash 4, when ActionScript was brought into the mix. Flash was now a tool developers could use to create entire Web sites.

Well, not exactly an *entire* Web site, because the Web site still has to get from an SWF file format to your Web page in order for end users to view it. This is where the HTML tab in the Publish Settings dialog box comes into the picture. Flash, upon publishing HTML, will create a document that embeds the Flash SWF into the HTML code to allow the SWF document to be seen by the browser. The code it creates is made up of OBJECT and EMBED tags, which allow you to specify a Flash SWF to be viewed. Here's an example:

```
<object classid="clsid:d27cdb6e-ae6d-11cf-96b8-444553540000"
codebase="http://download.macromedia.com/pub/shockwave/cabs/
flash/swflash.cab#version=4,0,0,0" width="600" height="400"
id="Untitled-1" align="middle">
<param name="allowScriptAccess" value="sameDomain" />
<param name="movie" value="Untitled-1.swf" />
<param name="quality" value="high" />
<param name="bgcolor" value="#ffffff" />
<embed src="Untitled-1.swf" quality="high" bgcolor="#ffffff"
width="600" height="400" name="Untitled-1" align="middle"
allowScriptAccess="sameDomain" type="application/x-shockwave-flash"
pluginspage="http://www.macromedia.com/go/getflashplayer" />
</object>
```

> **NOTE**
>
> The OBJECT tag appears between the body tags in an HTML document. When you publish this HTML file, an HTML file with the basic preceding code will be created.

Let's try publishing this HTML file. First, make sure the HTML box is checked under the Formats tab of the Publish Settings dialog box. If it is checked, you will notice that immediately the Flash box becomes checked as well (if it wasn't already checked before). This is because Flash needs to know what Flash SWF will be used in the code of the HTML. Therefore, it will use the FLA file you have opened as the template for the creation of its code. Your window should look similar to Figure 6.13. Now click the HTML tab at the top of the Publish Settings dialog box. Here are the options you'll find there:

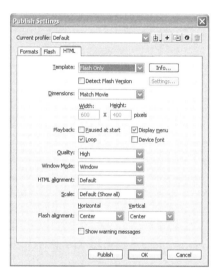

**FIGURE 6.13**    The options in the HTML tab in the Publish Settings dialog box will custom-tailor an HTML or HTM file to your specifications. The resulting file must be published in addition to a SWF file.

- **Template**. This is the format Flash will use to create the HTML code for you. This is also helpful for creating code on higher-end Flash/HTML scripting. However, if you are just starting out in Flash, use the default Flash-only template. The default template is set up simply to enter OBJECT and EMBED tags into your HTML to embed the document into the code. Other templates include the following:

  - **Flash for Pocket PC 2003**. Displays Flash content in HTML with Pocket PC–specific alignment.

  - **Flash HTTPS**. Displays Flash content in HTML. If the player is not detected, the user is directed to an HTTPS (secure HTTP) server to obtain it.

- **Flash Only**. Only places a Flash SWF document in an HTML file.

- **Flash w/AICC Tracking**. Embeds a Flash file with support for AICC tracking when using Macromedia's Learning component.

- **Flash w/SCORM Tracking**. Embeds a Flash file with support for SCORM tracking when using Macromedia's Learning component.

- **Flash w/FS Command**. Embeds Flash in HTML but also lends support for JavaScript in coordination with FS commands. FS commands allow interaction between the Flash movie and the player or HTML holding the player.

- **Flash w/Named Anchors**. Embeds Flash in HTML but allows you to set up labels as anchor points to be used with the Back button of the end user's browser and for bookmarking capabilities.

- **Image Map**. Sets up image maps (to be used with the PNG or GIF files you create).

- **QuickTime**. Displays the SWF in a QuickTime movie from the browser (you must use this template in coordination with the QuickTime tab).

For the purposes of this example, we will work with the default template, but feel free to use a different template to see what code is created with that particular template.

- **Detect Flash Version**. This is a new option for publishing in Flash MX 2004. It is used to create a detection system for the Flash Player, as well as a routing system for when a user either does or does not have the required player version or greater. After you select the check box, you can select the Settings button, which will launch the Version Detection Settings dialog box, which has these options:

  - **Requirements**. This sets the version of the Flash Player you are requiring the user to have.

  - **Detection File**. This file will be the first HTML page a user hits. It will contain the detector.

  - **Content File**. This is the HTML file that the user goes to if they have the correct player version or greater. By default, this is where the Flash content will be loaded.

  - **Alternate File**. This is the HTML page the user goes to if they do not meet the player requirements. By default, it has a link to get the latest Flash Player.

  - **Generate Default/Use Existing**. This section will allow you to either use your own alternative HTML page or have Flash create one.

  - **Dimensions**. This dialog box will ask you to input the size of your project. A very interesting effect of Flash is that you can choose to have your Flash movie match the movie size, fix it to a different size, or let the browser size determine the size of your piece for you. If you choose Percentage, the size of your browser will be the size of your final project. This is a useful feature when you want every user to see all of your project because it tailors your project to the size of the browser. The drawback to this feature is that your presentation can get stretched. Therefore, if your movie is 640×480 and your user has a browser height greater than the browser width, your presentation will get squeezed to fit the browser size. To prevent this from happening, read about the Scale property, further along in this section.

- **Paused at Start**. Do you want your movie to be paused at the start or run automatically? I'm not sure what reason you would have to pause at the start, but you may let your users choose when they want to start the movie by either clicking a button in the presentation or right-clicking and then clicking Play within the Flash Player. This feature is not used in professional presentations, where navigation will stop and start the presentation and control is in the end user's hand.

- **Loop**. Turning this feature off will stop the SWF at the end of the movie. This is also an irrelevant feature if your navigation is well thought out. Usually Flash programmers like to choose when the movie stops and starts using Flash ActionScript, but if you have a continuously looping cartoon, you may want to activate this feature. If it is activated, Flash will replay from frame 1 when it reaches the end of the movie.

- **Display Menu**. This option allows your end users to have the full menu of items available to them by right-clicking your SWF in the Flash Player. This is a key feature because many developers like the idea of keeping the control in their hands, not in the hands of the Flash Player. Deselecting this option will result in just the choice About Flash Player appearing by right-clicking in the Flash Player environment. (But don't forget, the context menu can be controlled with ActionScript.)

- **Device Font**. For Windows machines, you may also want to use Device Font to substitute antialiased system fonts for fonts not installed on the user's computer. This ensures the best quality of legibility for your end users for those text pieces that are set to display with device fonts.

- **Quality**. Lets you determine how well Flash will play back the items in the SWF. If you choose Low Quality, you are favoring the playback speed and performance on slower machines (but giving up appearance quality for items on the screen). Choosing High quality favors better-looking graphics, but your movie could take a performance hit on some slower machines. Check your target audience to see what kind of machines will be used. If their machines tend to have fast processors, you may select the High quality setting here. If you are not sure, you can choose either Auto High or Auto Low. This will favor either quality of images (High) or speed (Low) and will attempt to improve the opposite feature whenever it deems necessary for better playback. Medium will attempt to give good quality and good speed, but it will not choose on a case-by-case basis. The Best option will give you the best quality available, which sacrifices the speed of the project.

- **Window Mode**. Allows you to change the transparency, positioning, and layering of the Flash movie in question. It does this through changing the WMODE tag in the OBJECT tag and the EMBED tag of your HTML document. I would highly recommend leaving this option set to Window. This mode attempts to place the Flash piece in its own rectangular window on the Web page and attempts to play back the movie faster than the other options. However, if you plan to deliver your presentation in Internet Explorer 4.0 with ActiveX control, you may want to use the other options. The Opaque Windowless option allows you to place items behind the Flash piece without letting them show through. The Transparent Windowless option allows you to display objects on your HTML page behind the Flash SWF.

- **HTML Alignment**. Positions the Flash piece within the HTML window. The Flash alignment looks at how the Flash movie is placed within the movie window. These tags are highly important when you are attempting to bump your Flash piece up against the edge of your HTML window (for example, if you are opening a pop-up window for your SWF to appear in). If you are attempting to do this, you must choose the Left or Top options so that your movie will move as close to the edge of the browser window as possible.

- **Scale**. Determines how your Flash piece will scale if you did not choose Match Movie in the Dimensions property earlier.

  - **Default**. Tries to display the entire movie without distorting the original image while maintaining the original aspect ratio of your movie.

  - **No Border**. Scales your movie to fill the specified area but may crop your movie in order to keep the aspect ratio of your movie.

  - **Exact Fit**. Displays the entire movie in the area specified, without taking into consideration the aspect ratio. This option may cause distortion of your project on some machines.

  - **No Scale**. Prevents the movie from scaling when the Flash Player is resized.

- **Flash Alignment**. This will attempt to position or crop (if necessary) the Flash piece within the window specified by other alignments.

- **Show Warning Messages**. Checking this option causes Flash to warn you if your options conflict in any way. Flash will let you know whether your settings will generate errors in code.

## Standalone Projectors

Keep in mind that Flash is versatile—a point that has resonated throughout this chapter. This means you don't have to use the Web at all to display your creation. You can choose to deliver your project on CD-ROM or over a kiosk. This is where the use of standalone projectors is highly useful. You will find the option to publish them by choosing either Macintosh Projector or Windows Projector (.exe) from the check boxes on the Formats tab, shown in Figure 6.14. Publishing with one of these options checked will create either a file with the extension .exe for the PC or .hqx for the Mac.

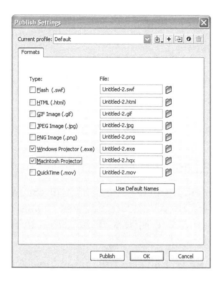

**FIGURE 6.14**   Under the Formats tab of the Publish Settings dialog box, you can choose to publish either Mac or PC standalone projector files. You can also give each file its own unique name.

The Mac file cannot be opened on your PC but can be transferred to the Mac to be opened on that platform. The great thing about these projector files is that they will execute or play the Flash file you created in its own self-contained format, meaning there's no need for the Flash Player (any version) on the end user's computer in order to play back the project.

## FS Commands

If you just double-clicked your executable file, you may have noticed that the project still appears within a window, looking similar to the Flash Player. This is because the project has not been set to Full Screen. In order to give your newly created, self-contained project special features such as Full Screen, you must issue FS commands to Flash to tell it to perform such actions.

FS commands are a series of commands that can, in some cases, pass arguments to the host program of the Flash Player. In this instance, we will be looking at the self-contained executable host. However, you could be using an FS command to send messages to JavaScript within a browser. You may want to use FS commands to talk to Director through strings or events. You can even use FS commands to pass information through to Visual Basic or C++ applications.

To access the FS commands, click the first frame of your movie and then go to the Actions panel. Now type in the following command:

```
fscommands("fullscreen","true");
```

And now the projector will launch in full screen mode.

Here is a list of supported FS commands:

- Quit. Closes the program and accepts no arguments.

- Fullscreen. Setting this to true will show your projector full screen on the end user's computer. This means it will fill the screen at any cost.

- Allowscale. This command, when set to true, will scale your project to reach the corners of your user's screen. A false setting will always reset the project to the size of your movie, leaving the outer spaces of the screen the same color as your document's background color.

- Showmenu. This command is similar to the option Display Menu in the HTML dialog box. Setting this to true will provide the whole set of menu items when right-clicking the Flash presentation. Setting it to false will only display the About Flash Player option.

- Exec. Requires the path to the application to open as the argument. This command will open a document from the projector, or can run batch files on Windows.

- Trapallkeys. Sends *all* key events to the onClipEvent handler.

## QuickTime Settings

Often, you can use QuickTime to create a solution to problems with sound synchronization. As an example, my company was working on an interactive kiosk in Director. Each module contained information about wetlands and an activity to teach this information was presented at the front of the module. One activity included cartoons, and we chose to create them in Flash because of its superior animation capabilities. When I imported the Flash SWF cartoons into Director, I ran into a problem. Both Flash and Director are frame-based applications, and I found keeping the synchronization difficult. The more computers we tested on, the more the problem intensified because one computer's processor could interpret the frame rates of Flash in Director totally differently than another computer did. Our solution was to publish our Flash document as a QuickTime file and import the time-based product into Director. This way, a time-based movie could drop frames to keep up with the frame rate on slower computers. Presto! Problem solved.

This story demonstrates the flexibility of Flash projects. It also demonstrates one way you can use QuickTime in your projects. Another important use for QuickTime is to add more animation to your movies. Suppose you have a movie to which you would like to add a Flash animation you already have completed in your MOV (the file extension for QuickTime movies). You can import the MOV into Flash and then perform your animation in Flash. When it is published, Flash will place the MOV onto the movie track and the Flash animation on a separate, new track. Now your animation is incorporated into your MOV.

Figure 6.15 shows the default options for the QuickTime tab. Here are the options you need to publish your MOV:

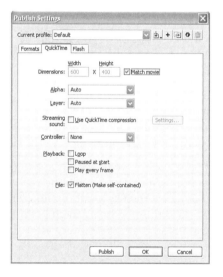

**FIGURE 6.15**    The options on the QuickTime tab in the Publish Settings dialog box offer various layering and playback options for your resulting MOV file.

- **Dimensions**. As with the Dimensions options on the other tabs, here you have the option to match the movie or choose your own dimensions.

- **Alpha**. Choosing Auto (the default) will make sure that when you have no other tracks in your movie (outside of the Flash track), the movie will be opaque. If other tracks are behind the Flash track, the Flash track will be made transparent to show the other tracks. Choosing Alpha-Transparent, obviously, makes the Flash track transparent throughout the MOV. The Copy option will make the Flash track opaque.

- **Layer**. This option determines where your Flash track is located. Top places it in front of all other objects, whereas Bottom places it behind all other tracks in your movie. The Auto option determines whether any movie items are in front of your movie in the movie's timeline. If so, your Flash track will play in front. Otherwise, it will play behind the movie track.

- **Streaming Sound**. Do you have sound in your Flash movie? If you do, that sound can be compressed in the QuickTime Player and placed on its own track. Just check this box and fill in the options you need for your sound.

- **Controller**. Specifies the type of controller that will be associated with this MOV file. Here are the options:

  - **None**. Creates a MOV that is a simple file with no control bar attached. This is a useful choice when you're incorporating the QuickTime movie into a Director presentation, where you can use Lingo to control the interface of the MOV.

  - **Standard**. Includes the standard toolbar that allows the user to interact with the MOV file.

  - **QuickTimeVR**. If your Flash file is going to be used in a QuickTimeVR format, choose this option to export your MOV with the QuickTime interaction tools available to the end user.

- **Playback**. As with the GIF settings, you can choose to have your MOV paused at start, loop at the end of the movie, or play every frame. The last of these three settings could put a strain on your computer's processor because it forces the MOV to play every frame of your SWF, not marrying it to the timeline.

- **File**. Choosing Flatten (Make Self-Contained) will make sure you have one single document at the end of the publishing process. The resulting file will be a single MOV document that "contains" the Flash information within it. Deselecting this option forces you to keep all imported items (such as your original QuickTime movie) in the same locations so that the resulting MOV can reference these items.

## Summary

Flash is a highly versatile program. It can create files ready for the Web (SWF and HTML files), self-contained projector files (EXE and Mac projector), images (GIF, JPEG, and PNG), and QuickTime movies with interactivity (MOV). The power of publishing is recognizing the correct medium for your target audience. Picking the proper mix of elements is the key to a successful project. Although publishing is one of the last steps in the process of creating a Flash project, you should have an overall sense of which formats you will be using before ever opening the Publish window for your final test. Now that you know the power that Flash possesses, you can utilize its power to the advantage of your clients.

CHAPTER **7**

# Working with Sound and Video

This chapter covers two topics that are important for enhancing a user's experience when viewing your Flash content: sound and video. Both offer a little more than the basic Web viewing experience you still find in conventional Web sites. We start off with sound.

## Working with Sound in Flash

Adding sounds to your Flash movie can often make or break it. For example, I tend to caution people about using hip-hop and techno music unless their Web sites cater to an audience for which this type of music is appropriate. As another immediate bit of advice when it comes to sound, in a professional development situation, *never* use the stock sounds. Yes, some are nice, but people recognize these sounds and know they're built into the program, which ultimately makes you a lame-o for using them. Be creative. Create your own sounds and music; if that's not reasonable, use a Flash resource on the Web, such as Flashkit.com, which offers tons of free sounds and music for you to use in your projects—all royalty-free.

You can import three different sound file types: WAV format (most commonly found on Windows), AIFF (a Macintosh format), and last but not least, MP3. The sounds can be either 8-bit or 16-bit and have sample rates of 11KHz to 44KHz.

This chapter is based on the fundamental concepts of sound in Flash. In addition, ActionScript is an object-oriented programming language, and within the ActionScript model, there's actually a Sound object you can use to do a lot of cool stuff, such as changing the volume, and so on. If you want to know how to do that stuff but you've never worked with sound before, you're in the right place. But first you need to understand how the basics of sound in Flash work before you can move into these more advanced topics.

# Adding Sound to Your Movie

The first thing you need to know is that sounds must be attached to a keyframe. Whether you're dealing with a keyframe in a timeline or a keyframe in a button state, the sounds must be placed a keyframe. With that established, let's get in and get our hands dirty.

---

**Adding Sound to a Button**

The point of this exercise is to get you more familiar with how sounds work and where you put them in your movie. In this exercise we will add a sound to a button so that when the end user clicks the button, a small camera sound will play. This does two things: First, it's an aural indicator to end users that they successfully clicked the button. Second, if used properly, it will create an experience for the end users that make them believe the button has physical qualities and actually makes that noise when clicked! This is the ultimate goal in Flash development—making the end users forget for a moment that they are actually sitting at their desks, believing that they're in the space you created. Sound can play a huge role in creating this illusion.

To add sound to a button, follow these steps:

1. Create a new document. Save this file as `loudButton.fla`.

2. You can either create your own button or use a stock one from the common libraries. Choose Window, Other Panels, Common Libraries, Buttons. Choose any button you like and drag an instance of it out onto the stage.

3. Even though I just gave you a speech about not using stock Flash sounds, that's exactly what we're going to do here! However, I am not recommending that you publish this project. It's simply a learning tool.

4. Choose Window, Other Panels, Common Libraries, Sounds to open the Sounds common library. Notice that you can preview the sound by clicking the Play button in the Preview window of the library, as shown in Figure 7.1. Preview the various sounds until you find the one you like.

**FIGURE 7.1**    Preview sounds by clicking the Play button. Stop them by clicking the Stop button.

5. Double-click the button to go into the button symbol's editing mode. Inside the button, create a new layer and name it **sound**.

6. Insert a keyframe in the Down state on the sound layer. Notice the hollow circle in the frame, which indicates that there is no content in this frame and on this layer. This is the frame we're going to use to add the sound.

7. With the sound layer still active and the play head on the Down state, drag the sound from the library and drop it on the stage. Notice the small waveform inside the Down state, as shown in Figure 7.2, indicating that there is a sound on that frame. If you have the frame selected, notice that the Properties Inspector offers some sound options.

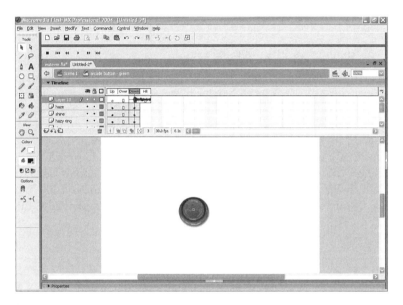

**FIGURE 7.2**    The waveform indicates that there is indeed a sound on the frame.

8. Come back to scene 1 and test the movie by choosing Control, Test Movie.

9. Click the button to hear the sound. Not bad, huh?

## The Sound Sync Menu

You may have noticed in the Properties Inspector some options for synching sound. If you do not see these options, be sure to select the frame holding that sound. In the drop-down menu are four different settings, and each of these settings will make the sound behave in a different way. Let's go ahead and take a look at what these settings are and when would be the right time to choose one over the other:

- **Event**. The most important concept to learn here is that once the sound has been triggered, it will play independently of the timeline. On our button, we have a short sound, probably about half a second in length. Now suppose the sound was three seconds long. You can probably click the button about 10 times within a span of three seconds. Because this is set to an event, the sound will play each time the event happens (in this case, clicking the mouse button). Therefore, the three-second sound will overlap and play on top of itself. The moral of this story is: Don't use a sound of any real length for an event sound.

- **Start**. The great thing about Start is that the second instance of the sound cannot begin playing until the first instance has finished. Therefore, if you do need to use a longer sound for an event situation, such as for a button, this is the solution.

- **Stop**. This simply stops the indicated sound.

- **Stream**. This is the sync setting to use if you are doing character animation or any type of animation that has to be synchronized with sound. Stream literally forces the movie to keep pace with the sound. If, for some reason, it can't (for example, the end user has a slow machine or low bandwidth), Flash will drop frames or skip them. If Flash skips an animation frame, it will also drop or not play the corresponding sound for that frame. This way, everything stays synced. The sound is dependent on the timeline, so if you stop the animation, the sound will stop as well. Stream also has its advantages during the development process. You can scrub the play head and hear the sound as you scrub. Stream is the only sync option that adds this functionality.

## Sound Effects

Also in the Properties Inspector are some options for effects you can apply to your sound, as shown in Figure 7.3. Here's a list of these options:

- **Left Channel**. This effect will only play the sound in the left speaker if the end user's computer has stereo sound.

- **Right Channel**. This effect will only play the sound in the right speaker if the end user's computer has stereo sound.

- **Fade Left to Right**. With this effect selected, the sound will gradually fade out in the left speaker and gradually fade in on the right speaker. Of course, the end user must have stereo speakers in order to benefit from this option.

- **Fade Right to Left**. With this effect selected, the sound will gradually fade out in the right speaker and gradually fade in on the left speaker. This effect will only be heard on stereo systems.

- **Fade In**. With this effect the sound gradually fades in at the beginning.

- **Fade Out**. This effect will gradually fade the sound out toward the end of the sound.

- **Custom**. This option allows you to edit the sound envelope manually. After you modify the sound, the Effect drop-down menu will still display Custom because it's a custom configuration that you set up.

- **None**. This option disables any sound. No sound will be selected when the None option is chosen.

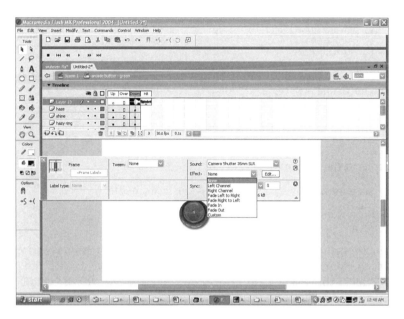

**FIGURE 7.3**    Effect options for sound in the Properties Inspector.

To open the Edit Envelope dialog box, you can choose Custom in the Effect drop-down menu or you can click the Edit button to the right of the drop-down menu. Go ahead and click Edit to open the Edit Envelope dialog box, as shown in Figure 7.4.

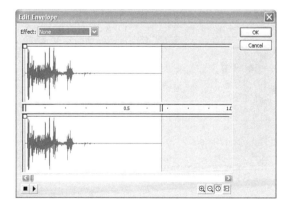

**FIGURE 7.4**    The Edit Envelope dialog box.

Let's go ahead and deconstruct the interface of the Edit Envelope dialog box so that you know what all the buttons stand for.

The four small buttons at the bottom-right corner of the window, from left to right, are as follows:

- **Set Scale to Frames**. This will scale the waveform's length size to the number of frames used in the animation.

- **Set Scale to Time**. This will scale the waveform's length size to the amount of time used in the animation.

- **Zoom Out**. Choose this button to increase the amount of time that spans the waveform in the visible area of the dialog box.

- **Zoom In**. Choose this button to decrease the amount of time that spans the waveform in the visible area of the dialog box.

The two buttons at the bottom-left corner of the window are

- **Play**. This button allows you to preview the custom effect.

- **Stop**. This button stops the preview.

The small bars shown in Figure 7.5 are for setting the in and out points. An **in point** is the start point for the sound. If you didn't like the first couple of chords, you can cut them off! The small hollow boxes are handles, as shown in Figure 7.6, for the volume control bars. You add a new handle by clicking a space in the volume bar that isn't already occupied by a handle. A new handle will just appear.

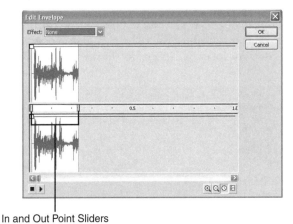

In and Out Point Sliders

**FIGURE 7.5**    To adjust the in and out points, move the slider bars back and forth.

Volume Handlers

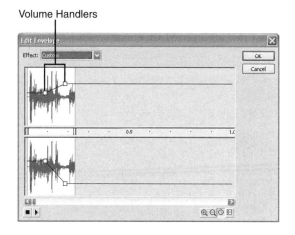

**FIGURE 7.6**   You can use these handles to adjust the volume for the area of the waveform.

## Looping Music

Looping music simply means to play it over and over again. In fact, most music you hear on Web sites consists of loops. The sound is probably under three seconds, just played over and over again. This is why techno and hip-hop music are so popular, because they consist of small, simple loops. The longer the sound you try to loop, the larger the file size. Not to imply that looping adds file size, because it doesn't. The longer the sound itself is, however, the more the file size will ultimately be bumped up.

How do you loop music? In Flash MX 2004, sound looping has been upgraded and now has two different options:

- **Repeat**. Allows the sound to loop through a set number of loops and then stop

- **Loop**. Makes the sound loop continuously

As shown in Figure 7.7, you type a value in the Repeat text field.

**FIGURE 7.7**   The Repeat text field for sound in the Properties Inspector.

You can type any value in this text field, as long as it is a whole number. For background music, something like 9999 should be fine. After you type a value, click the Edit button to show the envelope. You'll notice, as displayed in Figure 7.8, that you can tell how many times it loops. The more you loop it using Repeat, the more necessary it may be to zoom out a bit.

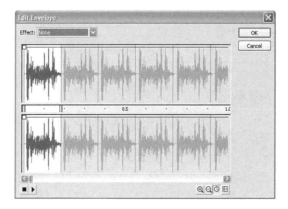

**FIGURE 7.8**    Notice how the appearance of the edit envelope changes when you loop the sound.

## Compression

When Flash exports your movie, it compresses the sound. Four different compression methods are available: Raw, ADPCM, MP3, and Speech. You can compress each sound individually, or you can apply a global compression to any sound you do not compress manually. I highly recommend compressing each sound, especially if it's a looping song, manually. This will ensure optimum file size and fidelity.

Let's first look at how you can optimize each sound manually. First, you must download a looping sound file. You can download a file at Flashkit.com. The best file format to download is MP3; however, WAV and AIFF files will work as well. After you download the file, import it into Flash by choosing File, Import, Import to Stage. When the file is imported, it should be visible in the Library. Highlight the sound in the Library and click the info icon in the bottom-left corner of the panel (or in the Library Options menu, choose Properties). This will launch the Sound Properties dialog box, as shown in Figure 7.9.

In the Compression drop-down list, you have five choices:

- **Default**. This option uses whatever compression settings have been set in the Publish Settings dialog box.

- **Raw**. This option resamples at the specified rate. However, no compression will be applied, thus yielding a larger file size than what's appropriate for the Web. However, the sound quality is very high and can be used for CD-ROM development.

- **ADPCM (Advanced Differential Pulse Code Modulation)**. This compression is used for 8-bit and 16-bit sound data. ADPCM is not as optimal as MP3; however, if for some reason you need to cater to the Flash 3 player, this would be your choice. The Flash 3 player cannot read MP3 files. Otherwise, MP3 would be a better choice than ADPCM.

- **MP3**. This compression method can be heard by the Flash 4 player and above. MP3 yields the best compression at the highest sound fidelity. In most cases, you will be using MP3.

- **Speech**. Speech may offer a smaller size than MP3 for voiceovers and straight speech without any music.

**FIGURE 7.9** The Sound Properties dialog box.

A nice feature in the Sound Properties dialog box is the ability to test the compression, to make sure the audio quality is still acceptable after the compression. When you choose a compression method, Flash gives a small readout about the end file size and how the file size compares to the original, as shown in Figure 7.10.

### Setting Compression in the Publish Settings Dialog Box

Although I don't recommend using this feature, you can set a global compression for sound files that you don't individually compress. Choose File, Publish Settings, which will open the Publish Settings dialog box, as shown in Figure 7.11.

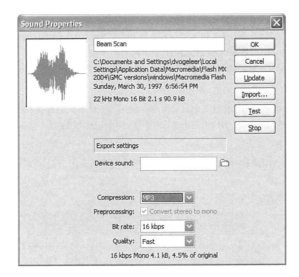

**FIGURE 7.10**  Compression feedback within the Sound Properties dialog box.

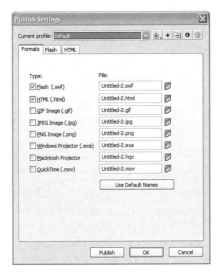

**FIGURE 7.11**  The Publish Settings dialog box.

Click the Flash tab to set the sound compression. When you select the Flash tab, the dialog box will change to give you options for the SWF file, as shown in Figure 7.12.

Notice the options toward the bottom portion of the dialog box for setting the stream and event sounds. Click the Set button to launch the Sound Settings dialog box, as displayed in Figure 7.13.

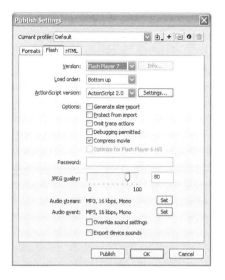

**FIGURE 7.12**    The Flash tab in the Publish Settings dialog box.

**FIGURE 7.13**    The Sound Settings dialog box.

When returned to the Publish Settings dialog box, notice the Override Sound Settings check box. This option ignores all the settings we defined in the dialog box we accessed from the Library.

## Updating a Music File in the Sound Properties Dialog Box

You can easily update or replace a sound file in the Library. If you've used instances of that sound file, they'll automatically be updated. If you're not still in the Sound Properties dialog box, select the sound in the Library and click the little blue properties button to launch the dialog box again. Click the Import button. This will launch the Import Sound dialog box, as shown in Figure 7.14.

Search for a file to replace the current one with and then choose Import (Mac) or Open (Windows). You can also automatically bring in a newer version of the sound by choosing the Update button. This is good, for example, if you decide to tweak the sound in a third-party sound-editing program. Instead of having to import it again and delete the original file, you can just update it.

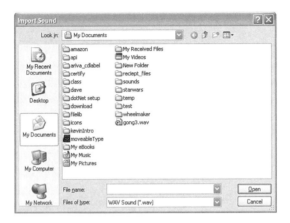

**FIGURE 7.14**    The Import Sound dialog box, for replacing an existing sound in a Flash movie's timeline.

### Importable File Formats

You can import a few different file formats into Flash for sound. Regardless of what format your sound files come in as, they must be exported using one of these compression types:

- **MP3 (MPEG-1 Audio Layer 3)**. MP3 can improve workflow between different developers on different platforms. The other advantage is, of course, all the available MP3 files. Over the past couple of years, MP3 has become the standard for storing digital music because its file size is generally smaller than other music formats.

- **WAV**. WAV files are most commonly used in the Windows world. What's great about being able to import WAV files is that you can bring in audio created in third-party sound-editing/creation programs such as SoundForge, Rebirth, and Acid. WAV files are not normally compatible with Macs; however, with the help of QuickTime 4 or 5, Flash on the Mac can import WAV files.

- **AIFF (Audio Interchange File Format)**. This is the WAV equivalent for the Mac. Therefore, sounds created or edited with applications such as Rebirth, Peak, or Deck can be completely imported into Flash. Normally, Windows machines cannot read AIFF files, but again with the help of QuickTime 4 or 5, it's not a problem.

## Sound with ActionScript

Although we have not covered ActionScript much thus far, it is important to understand some of the basic ideas and uses of the Sound object, a native object in ActionScript.

Before you can use the Sound object, it must be initialized like this:

```
var mySound:Sound = new Sound();
```

The preceding code creates a new instance of the Sound object.

Once you have a sound object initialized, you can do several things. But the first thing you want to do with a new Sound object is to get the sound into it. There are two methods for doing this, the attachSound() method and the loadSound() method. ActionScript is still new to you at this point in the book, so we will focus on the simpler method, attachSound(), which will grab the sound file from the library after it has been imported and you have set the linkage property. By contrast, the loadSound() method grabs an external sound source in the form of an MP3.

In the following example, we are going to import an MP3 song, set its linkage property, and use ActionScript to start and stop it.

1. Start by creating a new Flash document.

2. Select File, Import, Import to Library, and then choose your favorite MP3 song, or use the one from the accompanying Web site.

3. When your file has been imported, go to the library, select the song you just imported, choose the Panel Properties button, and select Linkage from the drop-down.

4. Select the Export for ActionScript check box, and give it a linkage name of **sample**.

5. Now we want to add play and stop buttons to the stage. You can get them from the Common Libraries, or create your own—just make sure they have the instance property names of play_btn and stop_btn respectively.

6. Create a new layer, name it **actions**, and then open the Actions panel in the first frame of this new layer (F9) and place these actions in it:

```
//create the new sound object
var mySound:Sound = new Sound();
//attach the song we want to this sound object
mySound.attachSound("sample");
//when release, the song will play
play_btn.onRelease=function(){
    mySound.start(0,0);
}
//when released, the sound will stop
stop_btn.onRelease=function(){
    mySound.stop();
}
```

The two zeros passed as arguments in the start() method represent that the sounds should start at the beginning (point 0) and have zero loops.

Now you can test the movie, and when you click the play button, the song will begin to play. When you click the stop button, the song will stop.

That was just a simple way to make play and stop buttons with sound. Another great thing you can do with the sound object is to control the volume and pan of the sound itself. Pan is the left and right speaker control. Basically, you can make a sound appear to be coming more from the left or right speaker using the pan controls.

Building on the last example, we are going to make the sound play automatically, but this time, as it starts playing, it will fade out and to the left (if you have stereo speakers).

Simply replace the code in the Actions layer with this code:

```
//create the new sound object
var mySound:Sound = new Sound();
//attach the song we want to this sound object
mySound.attachSound("sample");
//start the sound
mySound.start(0,0);
//set the initial pan
mySound.setPan(100);
//this function will fade it from the left to the right, and the volume to zero
this.onEnterFrame=function(){
    if(mySound.getVolume()>0){
        mySound.setVolume(mySound.getVolume()-.5);
        mySound.setPan(mySound.getPan()-3);
    }
}
```

Now when you test the movie, the sound will automatically play, and as it does, it will fade out gradually from right to left.

There are a lot more things you can do with the Sound object, such as get the current position in a song and ID3 information about a song such as title, artist and album. This information is included in most MP3s. For more information on the Sound object, check the ActionScript reference in the Help panel.

## Video in Flash

Video on the Web is one of the most exciting (and high-bandwidth) types of content out there. And Flash has not forgotten this in Flash MX 2004 Professional. With a new import wizard and the ability to cut segments from imported videos and string them back together as one, Flash has never looked better when it comes to video integration.

## Importing Video into Flash

Flash MX has new, powerful support for video. Video can play natively inside the Flash 7 Player. Flash supports DV, MPEG, WMV, MOV, AVI, and Flash Video FLV. Once the video is in the authoring environment, you can scale, skew, distort, mask, and rotate it, and make it interactive using scripting. Both the Flash 6 and 7 players can support video. It is important to note that the support for video in Flash is ideal only for short video pieces, no longer than a few minutes or a few megabytes in file size. By no means is the Flash Player going to act as a substitute for any of the media players, such as QuickTime or Windows Media Player in the way they handle large video files.

To import a video, follow these steps:

1. Select File, Import, Import to Stage.

2. Choose any video you want (or use one from the companion site).

3. When the Video Import Wizard pops up, similar to Figure 7.15, it asks you to either link or embed the video as before and if you were to link, you'd have to export the Flash movie as a QuickTime movie in order to see the video. By embedding it, the video will play inside the Flash 7 player. Choose Embed and click Next.

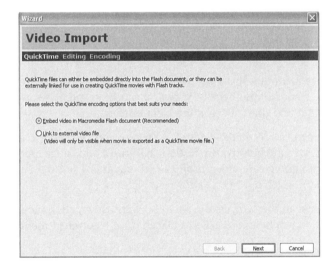

**FIGURE 7.15**   The Video Import Wizard.

4. At this point, you can choose to embed the entire video, if it is exactly how you want it, or you can edit it by slicing it into the pieces you want, and then embedding it, so choose Edit the Video First to continue through the wizard.

5. Now the screen should look similar to Figure 7.16. In the video's progression bar, the top arrow represents the position in the video you are viewing, and the bottom two

represent the starting and ending points of the segment of the video you would like to create. You can use the controls to go through and preview your selection, and then use the Create Clip button to make the video slice, which will then appear in the video list box.

**FIGURE 7.16**    The video-editing interface.

6. After you have made the slices you want, you can string them together by selecting the Combine List of Clips check box, or you can keep them as separate library items by deselecting it and then clicking the Next button.

7. Now your screen will look like Figure 7.17 where you can select the compression and quality (the lower the quality, the faster it will run), and in the bottom section, you can select, edit, and create video profiles with advanced settings such as color, dimensions, and track options as shown in Figure 7.18.

8. When you have all the settings the way you want them, click the Finish button, and the entire video will be imported and placed on the current timeline you are in.

Play around with different video settings until you find the right settings for you.

Now that you see how the Video Import Wizard works, the next example will take it a step further by showing how easy it is to control your video.

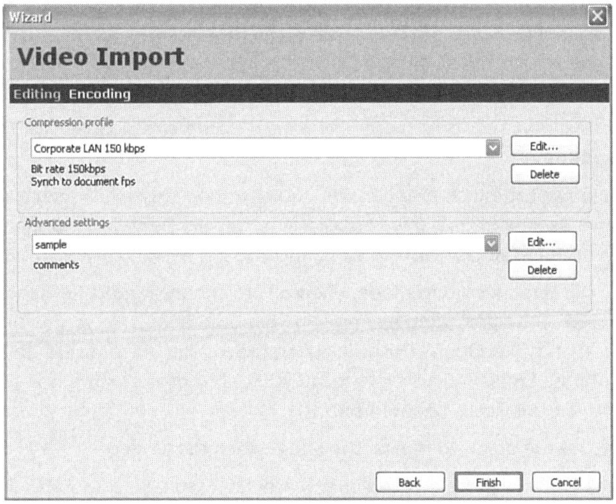

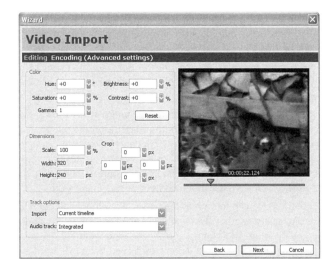

**FIGURE 7.17**   Final options for the Video Import Wizard.

**FIGURE 7.18**   Editing Encoding (Advanced Settings) dialog box.

**Creating Controls to Play and Stop Video**

In this exercise, we will be working with the same video you imported in the preceding example. This time, we will be controlling the video with some basic functionality:

1.  Start by creating a new document. In the new document, double-click the first layer and name it **video**.

2.  Create a movie clip by choosing Insert, New Symbol. This will launch the New Symbol dialog box. Be sure to give this symbol the movie clip behavior and then name it **video_source**. Click OK, which will bring you inside the movie clip symbol.

3.  In movie clip symbol editing mode, choose File, Import, Import to Stage. Search for the file you used in the preceding example, or any other video file you would like to use. Highlight it and click Open. This will launch the Import Video dialog box that we saw before. Choose Embed and click Next. (If you're prompted with a box asking whether to import or edit the video, choose Import.)

4.  This time, we are going to import the entire video to the stage.

5.  And in the final dialog box, we will use the default settings, so go ahead and click Finish.

6.  After you choose OK, a dialog box may warn you that there are more frames in the video than in your Flash movie. It asks you whether you want it to automatically extend the timeline. This is a huge timesaver—back in Flash 5, you would have to calculate how many frames a video file has by multiplying the frame rate by the duration of the clip. But since Flash MX, Flash does this automatically. Choose Yes. Notice the movie clip's timeline is now full of video.

7.  Click Scene 1 to get back to the main timeline. Open up this movie's Library by choosing Window, Library. Drag out an instance of the video source symbol to the stage and give it an instance name of **video_mc**.

8.  Now you're going to set up the controls to stop and play the movie. Create a new layer and name it **buttons**. Make sure the buttons layer is on the button. Open the Buttons Common Library by choosing Window, Other Panels, Common Libraries and choose Buttons. Choose the play and stop buttons you want (or you can create your own), and drag out an instance of each onto the stage in the buttons layer. Give them instance names of play_btn and stop_btn respectively, as shown in Figure 7.19.

9.  Double-click the video clip to go into the movie clip symbol-editing mode. Once inside the movie clip, create another layer and call it **actions**. Then highlight the first frame in that layer and open up the Actions panel by choosing Window, Development Panels, Actions, and put this action within it, which will keep the movie from playing automatically:

    ```
    stop();
    ```

10. Now go back to the main timeline, create another layer, and name it **actions**. Then highlight the first frame of this layer, open the Actions panel (if it is not still open) and place these actions in it:

    ```
    //this is for the play button
    play_btn.onRelease=function(){
        video_mc.play();
    ```

```
    }
    //this is for the stop button
    stop_btn.onRelease=function(){
        video_mc.stop();
    }
```

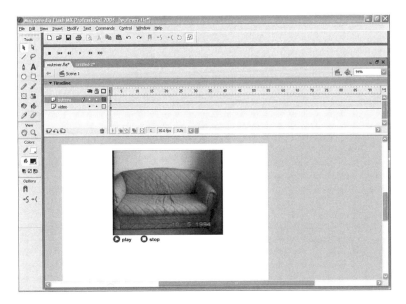

**FIGURE 7.19**   The Play and Stop buttons under the video clip.

11. Test your movie! Notice that it takes a second to export. In a real-world situation, you would create a preloader for this. A **preloader** is a visual object that will let the user know content is being loaded in the background.

Of course, you can also add fast-forward and rewind buttons using the goto action. This should give you a good understanding of how video is handled in Flash. Remember, you always have the options of animating, scaling, and rotating the video, just to name a few. As long as the video is in a movie clip, everything you can do to a movie clip, you can now do to the video. In fact, if you're not satisfied with the quality of the video, you might consider taking down the alpha of the video, which seems to take away some of the compression artifacts.

## Summary

This chapter covered two areas of Flash that help enrich your files. One thing to keep in mind with both video and sound is that the lower the quality, the lower the file size and generally the better the performance.

Remember that you can edit both video and sound in Flash MX 2004 Professional to some extent without the need for third-party applications. And you can set the properties of sound both with individual sound properties, or with global sound properties in the Publish Settings dialog box.

For more on video in Flash, see Chapter 25, "Streaming Media."

# PART II

# ActionScript

## IN THIS PART

CHAPTER **8**

# Welcome to ActionScript 2.0

So far in this book, you've learned how to create different things in Flash manually, how to publish Flash documents, and how to do basic animation and interactivity. This chapter begins a new world of understanding for Flash. In this chapter we cover ActionScript, the native language of Flash. We go over the basic principles of programming in Flash as well as the differences between ActionScript 1.0 and ActionScript 2.0.

Before we start talking about the fundamentals of programming, it is important to understand what the language itself is.

## What Is ActionScript?

ActionScript is the programming language of Flash. It is based on the European Computer Manufacturers' Association (ECMA) scripting language model. Other languages such as Java and JavaScript are based on the same model. ActionScript has been around since early versions of Flash, but really began to take form in Flash 5. Then in Flash MX, ActionScript really stepped into the object-oriented programming (OOP) arena (don't worry, we go over what OOP means in the next section). Now Flash MX 2004 comes along with ActionScript 2.0—more objects, stricter syntax, and stronger OOP.

The next section will help you become familiar with the object-oriented programming model.

## Object-Oriented Programming

Object-oriented programming is more than a type of programming language; it is how you approach a problem in the context of programming.

Back in the early days of programming, everything ran in a straight line with hundreds of conditionals to check to see if something should happen or not. For instance, let's say driving is the program; the program would start by going to the car, opening the door, putting the key in the ignition, and turning the key (which would start the car). It then would go through a series of conditional statements checking to see if the user wants their headlights on or not, if they want the radio on or not, and if the emergency brake is on or not (see Figure 8.1). Already this program is long and painstakingly slow, and we haven't even begun to drive yet.

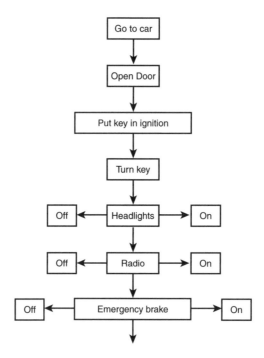

**FIGURE 8.1**   The old way of programming.

This is where object-oriented programming can come in handy. Instead of having all of these steps and conditional checks, you could have a single object on which all the code could be based.

## What Is an Object?

An **object**, as it relates to programming, is a self-contained chunk of code containing the three very important elements that all objects contain: properties, methods, and events.

These three elements of objects are what makes them so powerful and gives them the ability to be self-contained.

## Properties of an Object

A **property** of an object is raw data. Basically, each property of an object holds information about that specific instance of an object. Some properties can be read and changed, but others are read-only.

Here are some examples of built-in object properties in Flash:

- `movieClip._x`—The horizontal position of a movie clip object, read and write editable.

- `array.length`—A read-only property of the `Array` object that holds the number of elements in a given array.

- `textField.text`—A read-write property for getting and setting the text of a text field object.

- `Math.PI`—A constant property of the `Math` object, which is read-only; it translates to 3.14159265358979 roughly.

- `textformat.bold`—A read-write property of the `TextFormat` object, and can be set to either `true` or `false`.

These are just a few of the many properties already built into Flash and its objects.

Going back to the driving program, if we were to build an object for it, the object would be a `Car` object.

Some of its properties might be the following:

- `Car.type`—The type of car being driven; Mustang, Liberty, or 911 Carerra Twin Turbo.

- `Car.color`—The exterior color of the car; red, blue, or green.

- `Car.speed`—This property would constantly change depending on how fast the car is being driven.

- `Car.passengers`—This property could be either the number of passengers in a car or the names of each passenger in the car.

Of course, the `Car` object could have literally hundreds more properties.

But that's just the information about the car. What about what the car does?

## Methods of an Object

If properties are the "adjectives" of objects, then methods are the "verbs." Methods make things happen. A method, when it comes down to it, is nothing more than a function that is associated with a specific object.

Here are a few built-in methods for objects in Flash:

- `movieClip.stop()`—This method stops the play head for a specific movie clip's timeline.

- `array.reverse()`—This method reverses the order of elements in a given array.

- `textField.getDepth()`—This method returns the depth number of a specific text field.

- `Math.random()`—This method returns a random number between 0 and 1.

- `color.getRGB()`—This method returns information on a `Color` object's color.

Again, methods are what make objects do things.

With the `Car` object, you could have many methods to make the car do things:

- `Car.start()`—This method would start the car.

- `Car.brake()`—This method would apply the brakes.

- `Car.honkHorn()`—This method would let the person in front of you know you don't appreciate them cutting you off.

- `Car.accelerate()`—This method would accelerate the car.

Of course, these methods do a specific thing, no variance whatsoever. When the `Car.start()` method is called, the car starts; when the `Car.honkHorn()` method is called, the car honks. But that is not the limit of methods: They can have parameters in which you pass information to them that can dictate what will happen and to what degree.

For instance, the movie clip object has a method called the `gotoAndStop()` method. By itself, it can do nothing, but if you pass it information, it can run that specific task.

Here are some examples of this method with parameters:

- `movieClip.gotoAndStop(2)`—This method will take the play head to frame 2 and stop.

- `movieClip.gotoAndStop("end")`—This method will take the play head to the frame labeled "end" and stop.

With this in mind, we could make our methods for the `Car` object more reuseable. For instance, we could make the `accelerate()` method accelerate to a certain speed like this:

```
Car.accelerate(55);
```

Now the car will accelerate to 55 miles per hour and hold that speed.

So now you see the power of methods, the code that makes things work. The last element that objects are made of is events.

## Events of an Object

Properties are information about objects. Methods do things with objects. **Events** tell Flash when certain things have occurred with objects. This is the most difficult aspect of objects to understand, which is why a whole chapter is devoted to events (Chapter 14, "Events"). Events usually have code associated with them that will function when triggered through either a callback or a listener. This makes it easy to call code at only certain points.

For example, here are some built-in events of Flash objects:

- `movieClip.onEnterFrame`—This event fires as close to the frame rate of a given movie clip as possible, for instance, if the frame rate is 12 frames per second (the default setting), the event will fire approximately 12 times per second.

- `textField.onChanged`—This event fires when a user or ActionScript changes the content in a specific text field.

- `button.onRelease`—This event fires when a user releases a button after it has been clicked.

- `XML.onLoad`—This event is triggered when an XML document has completely loaded into Flash.

- `click`—This is an event for the `Button` component.

You can see why these events are very important to objects. If events did not exist, you would have to use looping conditional statements to check to see if something has occurred, but with events, you can have code ready whenever the event fires.

Here is an example of loading content into Flash and checking to see if it has loaded without events:

```
//there is a property coming in called "done"
var sample:LoadVars = new LoadVars();
//load the file in
sample.load("test.txt");
//use a loop to see if "done" has been received
this.onEnterFrame = function(){
    if(sample.done == "true"){
        //do something
        //get rid of the loop
        delete this.onEnterFrame;
    }else{
        //continue to wait
    }
}
```

∞

The preceding block of code uses a movie clip event to continuously check to see if the variable done has been loaded into the LoadVars object we created. If it has been loaded, the code executes on the information, placing it either in a component or a text field, and then it destroys the looping statement.

Now here is the code with the onLoad event:

```
//create the LoadVars object
var sample:LoadVars = new LoadVars();
//the event for the LoadVars object
sample.onLoad = function(){
    //do something
}
//load the file in
sample.load("test.txt");
```

This block of code, besides being much shorter, is more efficient. Instead of having a looping statement look to see if the content has loaded, an event triggers and lets Flash know when the content is loaded.

Now that you see the benefit of events, let's take that approach back to the Car object. Although it's hard to imagine because we take them for granted, a car has a great many events. Here are a few of them:

- Car.onStart—Lets Flash know when the car starts.

- Car.onDoorOpen—This event triggers when any of the doors open.

- Car.onBrake—Lets Flash know the brake has been applied so that it knows to turn on the brake lights.

- Car.onCrash—This event could trigger the air bag to be released and notify other "emergency objects" to come see if everyone is okay.

Events have a high priority when writing object-oriented code.

Now that we've discussed the three major features of objects, we're going to learn how objects are created.

## Where Do Objects Come From?

When two objects have known each other for a long time, and are very much in love, they.... Wait a minute, that's something else. Objects come from classes.

A **class** acts as a blueprint from which object instances of that class can be created. It states what properties that object has and what things that object can do (methods).

There are two ways of building objects: One is the old way that can still be done in the Flash authoring environment. The other is new to Flash, and must be done in an external ActionScript file, which is beyond the scope of this chapter, but is covered in detail in Chapter 19, "External ActionScript."

To create an object class in Flash, you give the object class a name (in our examples, "Car"). Although it is not a necessity, it is good coding practice to capitalize object class names. Once you have stated the object class name, set it equal to a function and enclose all properties, methods, and events within the function like this:

```
//create the class
Car = function(){
//stuff
}
```

Now, this example doesn't have any properties, methods, or events. Nor are there any instantiated properties. The instantiated properties are passed to the object by means of parameters in the constructor function. So now we will add some parameters to the function, and instantiate them within the function.

```
//create the object class constructor
Car = function(color:String, speedLimit:Number, startSpeed:Number){
    //instantiate a few properties
    this.color = color;
    this.speedLimit = speedLimit;
    this.speed = startSpeed;
}
```

This block of code is a little more advanced than the previous. We pass three parameters into the constructor function and then instantiate them to the object within the function. Of course, there could be several more properties, but for now we are just sticking with three; the color of the car, its maximum allowable speed, and its start speed.

We now have an object class. From this we can create several Car objects, which are called **instances**, and set their individual properties.

This next block of code would be written after the class is constructed:

```
//create a mustang
mustang = new Car("silver", 140, 35);
//create a jeep
liberty = new Car("silver", 90, 45);
//create a 86 pinto
lemon = new Car("green", 25, 10);
//now get the current speed of the jeep
trace(liberty.speed);
//Output: 45
```

As you can see, we created three individual instances of the `Car` object. We gave them each individual properties and even retrieved the current speed of the Jeep instance we made.

So far, our object constructor just has properties. Of course, we want any car we make to be able to do things, so now let's add a method to the constructor:

```
//create the object class constructor
Car = function(color:String, speedLimit:Number, startSpeed:Number){
    //instantiate a few properties
    this.color = color;
    this.speedLimit = speedLimit;
    this.speed = startSpeed;
    //create a method for the Car class
    this.accelerate = function(amount:Number):Number{
        //increase the speed
        this.speed += amount;
        //return the current speed
        return this.speed;
    }
}
```

In this block of code, we take our object class a bit further by creating a method that has one parameter, the amount to increase the speed by. Notice that after we increase the speed, we also return the current speed to the object calling the method.

Now we can create a car, call the method, and see what happens. Again, the next block of code is after the `Car` constructor:

```
//create a mustang
mustang = new Car("silver", 140, 35);
//get the current speed
trace(mustang.speed);
//call the accelerate method
mustang.accelerate(10);
//now get the current speed
trace(mustang.speed);
//call the accelerate method, and get the new speed
trace(mustang.accelerate(15));
//Output: 35
//       45
//       60
```

This time, we create an instance of the `Car` object. We then send the current speed to the Output panel. After that, we call the `accelerate` method, and then send the current speed again to the Output panel. Finally, we call the `accelerate` method and send the new speed to the Output panel at the same time; this is where the `return` action comes in handy.

Now we can create cars and increase their speed, but what if they go over their designated speed limit? This is where the events come in.

This time, in the `accelerate` method, we will put a conditional to check if the car has gone over its designated speed limit.

```
//create the object class constructor
Car = function(color:String, speedLimit:Number, startSpeed:Number){
    //instantiate a few properties
    this.color = color;
    this.speedLimit = speedLimit;
    this.speed = startSpeed;
    //here is the event
    this.onSpeedLimitBreak = function(){};
    //create a method for the Car class
    this.accelerate = function(amount){
        //increase the speed
        this.speed += amount;
        //check to see if the car is going to fast
        if(this.speed > this.speedLimit){
            //trigger the event
            this.onSpeedLimitBreak();
        }
        //return the current speed
        return this.speed;
    }
}
```

This time, we create the constructor in the same way as before. We create the properties and set them to the parameters. We then create what looks like a method, but it is in fact our event to be called. You can tell it is meant to be an event because it starts with "on". Then in the `accelerate` method, we still increase the car's speed, but then we check to see if the `speed` is above the `speedLimit`. If so, we call the empty event. Then the current speed is returned.

So now let's create an instance of the `Car` object. Create a callback event method (events are covered in greater detail in Chapter 14). Then use the `accelerate` method to push the car's speed past its speed limit.

```
//create a mustang
mustang = new Car("silver", 55, 35);
//create the event callback for this Car
```

```
mustang.onSpeedLimitBreak=function(){
    //send a message to the output panel
    trace("slow down lead foot");
}
//call the accelerate method
trace(mustang.accelerate(40));
//Output: slow down lead foot
//          75
```

As just mentioned, we create the instance of the Car object. Then we create a callback method that will send a message to the Output panel in the event that the car goes beyond its speedLimit property. Finally, we call the accelerate method to increase the car's speed.

Now you have created your own object class with properties, methods, and events. You have created an instance of that object and used its methods and events. There is one more way to add information to an object class without having to place it in the constructor function.

## Prototyping an Object

Most of the time when you hear the word "prototype," it means a first working draft of a project. And in Flash, that can be true as well, but it can also mean the prototype chain.

The prototype chain in Flash starts with the Object object. All other objects are based on this supreme parent object. This means that if you add a property or method to the Object object, all other objects in Flash will then have the ability to use this property or method. But the Object object is already instantiated, so how do you add things to its constructor class after the fact? By using the prototype property.

The prototype property is designed to be able to add methods and properties to any and all object classes after the object class has already been instantiated. It's easy to use; you just call the object class's name, add the prototype property, and then add the new property or method name.

Here is an example of adding a method to the Array class that will, when called, send back a message saying hello:

```
//add the method to the Array class
Array.prototype.hello = function(){
    return "Hello there, how are you?";
}
//now create a new Array
var myArray:Array = new Array();
//send the message to the output panel
trace(myArray.hello());
//Output: Hello there, how are you?
```

The preceding code adds a new method to the Array class that will send a message back using the return action. We then create a new array and use the trace action to send the message to the Output panel.

But now let's say we want all object classes to able to instantly know what kind of object they are. We could add a new method to the Object object like this:

```
//add a method to the Object object
Object.prototype.whatAmI = function(){
    return typeof this;
}
//now create a new Array
var myArray:Array = new Array()
//now using the new Object method
//trace what kind of object the array and the _root timeline are
trace(this.whatAmI());
trace(myArray.whatAmI());
//Output: movieclip
//        object
```

The preceding code adds a method to the Object object. Then we create an array. After that, we call the new method on the array we created as well as the root timeline and send the results to the Output panel.

So far, we have added methods to objects already created in Flash. Now we will go back to our Car object and add a new method using the prototype property.

```
//create the object class constructor
Car = function(color:String, speedLimit:Number, startSpeed:Number){
    //instantiate a few properties
    this.color = color;
    this.speedLimit = speedLimit;
    this.speed = startSpeed;
    //here is the event
    this.onSpeedLimitBreak = function(){};
    //create a method for the Car class
    this.accelerate = function(amount){
        //increase the speed
        this.speed += amount;
        //check to see if the car is going to fast
        if(this.speed > this.speedLimit){
            //trigger the event
            this.onSpeedLimitBreak();
        }
        //return the current speed
```

∞

```
            return this.speed;
    }
}
//add the new method to the Car class
Car.prototype.decelerate = function(amount){
    //put a conditional to make sure we can't decelerate passed 0
    if(this.speed-amount >= 0){
        this.speed -= amount;
    }
    return this.speed;
}
```

We created the constructor class the same way as before. After the constructor has been created, we create another method for the Car class using the prototype property. The new method will decelerate the Car by the amount parameter. And there is a conditional inside the method to make sure the speed does not drop below zero.

Now that we have the method, let's use it. The following code is meant to be placed after the Car constructor and the prototype method decelerate().

```
//create a new Car
mustang = new Car("silver",140,55);
//get the current speed
trace(mustang.speed);
//decelerate the mustang
trace(mustang.decelerate(25));
//Output: 55
//        30
```

The preceding code creates a new instance of the Car object. Then we send the current speed to the Output window. Finally, we decelerate the Mustang and send the new speed to the Output window.

Now that you have an understanding of how the object-oriented programming model works and the benefits it has, we can go over some of the new features and differences in ActionScript 2.0 from ActionScript 1.0.

## Introduction to ActionScript 2.0

Those of you who have been coding in Flash will find this section very useful; it covers some of the differences and advantages in the new version of Flash's programming language.

Several changes have been made to ActionScript to hold closer to ECMA standards. Some of these changes include strict data typing, function return data typing, and parameter data typing. Also, there is a new way to build class constructors, but that is covered in more detail in Chapter 19.

But not to worry—those of you still wanting to code in ActionScript 1.0 (Flash MX style coding) still have this option as you can see in Figure 8.2. Go to the publish settings; choose File, Publish Settings(Ctrl+Shift+F12), choose the Flash tab, and choose ActionScript 1.0. Be warned, it's not only possible, but likely that you will run into conflicts using ActionScript 1.0 with ActionScript 2.0 anywhere in the file. You can also see which version of ActionScript you are running in your file by selecting the stage and viewing the Properties Inspector as in Figure 8.3.

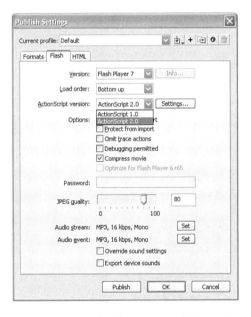

**FIGURE 8.2**   Use the Publish Settings dialog box to set which version of ActionScript you would like your file to support.

**FIGURE 8.3**   Use the Properties Inspector to quickly see which version of ActionScript you are using.

But the first new feature we will discuss in ActionScript 2.0 is the case-sensitive structure.

Back in Flash MX, you could easily declare a variable `myVariable` and then call it by using `MYVARIABLE`; they both would have been considered the same variable. But now, all internal and external ActionScript is case sensitive.

For example, in Flash MX/ActionScript 1.0, you would write this:

```
var myVariable = "test";
trace(MYVARIABLE);
//Output: test
```

Now in Flash MX 2004/ActionScript 2.0, you would write this:

```
var myVariable = "test";
trace(MYVARIABLE);
//Output: undefined
```

It is the same when passing parameters into functions:

```
//create the function
function myFunction(sample){
    trace(SAMPLE);
}
//call the function
myFunction("testing");
//Output: undefined
```

As you can see, in ActionScript 2.0, the preceding code would return `undefined`. So remember to always check your case.

### Declaring Variables and Instance Names

Other new features of ActionScript 2.0 that bring it more in line with ECMA standards are shown in Table 8.1.

**TABLE 8.1**    New Features of ActionScript 2.0

|  | ActionScript 2.0 | ActionScript 1.0 |
|---|---|---|
| Undefined numbers | Resolve to `NaN`. | Resolve to 0. |
| Undefined strings | Resolve to `undefined`. | Resolve to empty strings, "". |
| When converting strings to Boolean values | Resolve to `true` if the string has a length greater than 0, `false` if the string is empty. | The string is first converted to a number, and the Boolean value is `true` if the number is a non-zero number, `false` if it is zero. |

# Strict Data Typing Variables

Another new feature in ActionScript 2.0 is strict data typing. **Strict data typing** is the ability to declare the data type of a variable when that variable is initialized. This helps a great deal in debugging large applications. For instance, if you have a login variable that will hold the user's login name as a string, you do not want it accidentally changing to a number or hexadecimal color by accident later in the code.

In ActionScript 1.0, it was possible to have a variable change data types constantly through an application. This is not good coding practice.

This was allowed in Flash MX/ActionScript 1.0:

```
var myName = "David";          //declares the variable myName with a String
myName = 12;                //places a number in myName
myName = 0xff0000;           //changes myName to a hexadecimal color of red
myName=function(){}           //changes myName to a function
```

And, truth be told, this is still allowed in Flash MX 2004, but that is because we have not used the strict data typing features yet.

To use the new strict data typing features when declaring variables, first use the keyword var and then the name of the variable followed by a colon. At this point a pop-up list of all the available data types including component data types appears, as you can see in Figure 8.4.

**FIGURE 8.4**    The pop-up list of all available data types in the Actions panel.

You can also see the list of allowable data types by choosing the Add a New Item to the Script button in the Actions panel, and going down to Types.

Here is a correct declaration of a variable in ActionScript 2.0:

```
var myName:String = "David";
//declares the myName variable as type String
var myAge:Number = 23;
//declares the myAge variable as type number
var myObject:Object = new Object();      //declares a new object type Object
```

Now that these variables are declared, if at any time within the code, we attempt to change the variable's data type, when we either test the movie or check the syntax, we will receive an error.

To see this error, try this code:

```
var myName:String = "David";
myName = 23;
```

Now test this code, and you should see an error in the Output panel as shown in Figure 8.5.

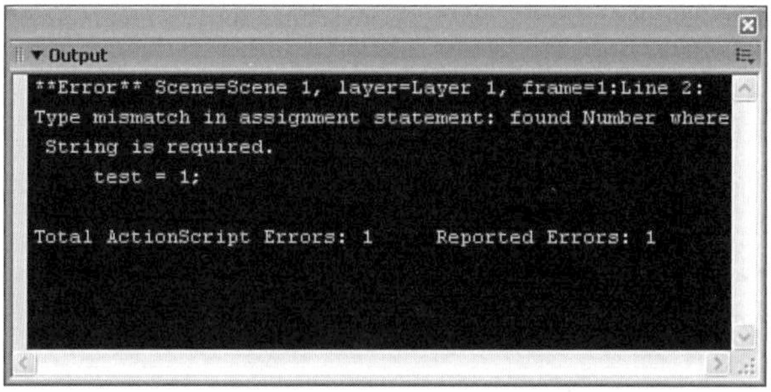

**FIGURE 8.5**    The error seen when a strict data type of a variable is changed.

Strict data typing is not limited to variables, however; they can be very useful in functions.

## Strict Data Typing with Functions

A common problem in ActionScript 1.0 is building a function that is supposed to return a certain data type, a number for example, but, somehow it sends out a Boolean value instead. Or worse yet, you have parameters set to receive a certain data type, but another developer passes it a different data type, and then that developer cannot figure out where the error is.

Strict data typing in functions comes to the rescue. You can not only data type the result of a function, but also all parameters in that function.

To data type the parameters of a function, you simply place a colon after each parameter name, and the data type pop-up list appears where you can choose which data type this parameter is meant to be.

To data type the return value of a function, you place a colon after the closing parenthesis of the parameters, and then choose which data type the return value is to be in.

Here is an example of data typing a function:

```
//create the function
function square(num:Number):Number{
    return num*num;
}
//call the function
trace(square(3));
//Output: 9
```

The preceding code creates the function with a single parameter, num. Both num and the result are set to the Number data type.

If the result does not match the strict data type, as in this case, a similar error message will appear in the Output panel as in the preceding example.

```
//create the function
function square(num:Number):Number{
    return "num*num";
}
//call the function
trace(square(3));
```

And what if the parameters placed in a calling function do not match the strict data types they were assigned, like this?

```
//create the function
function square(num:Number):Number{
    return num*num;
}
//call the function
trace(square("3"));
```

This time the function is declared correctly, but when invoked, we use a string instead of a number.

Another error will appear, as shown in Figure 8.6.

**FIGURE 8.6**    Strict data typing can even make sure parameters match the correct data type declared.

And because you can have strict data typing in both functions and variables, there is increased debugging when combining them, as in the following example:

```
//create the function
function square(num:Number):Number{
    return num*num;
}
//call the function
var myName:String = square(3);
```

This code creates the function we have been using, and this time sets the result to a variable that has a different data type from the one declared on the result.

Run this code, and again you will receive another error message as in Figure 8.6.

That concludes the discussion on the differences and new features of ActionScript 2.0 for this chapter. Again, there is more on class construction in Chapter 19.

You have seen a lot of ActionScript already in this chapter, but what about all the features of the Actions panel?

## The Actions Panel

The Actions panel is where you can manually type in ActionScript. To access the Actions panel, choose Window, Development Panels, Actions.

The Actions panel, as seen in Figure 8.7, has three main sections:

- **The Actions window**. This is where you will type in your ActionScript code.

- **The quick reference**. This holds all the snippets of code in a categorized hierarchical format. To choose a code, find the one you want and double-click it, or click and drag it into the Actions window.

- **Go to Action window**. This window acts like a small Windows Explorer panel for finding actions anywhere in the Flash movie. To go to one, simply map to it and click on it, and the Actions window will go to that frame of object.

Those are the three main sections of the Actions panel. You can close and resize them with the small arrows on their sides.

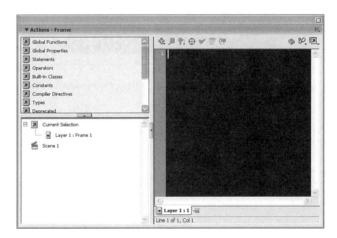

**FIGURE 8.7**    The Actions panel.

The main Actions window of the Actions panel is where all of your actions will be. It has several buttons across the top, and their functions are as follows:

- **Add Script**. This button, when clicked, will show a drop-down menu with the same categories as the quick reference. You can map to a specific action, and select it for it to appear in the Actions window.

- **Find**. This button, when clicked, will open the Find dialog box, as shown in Figure 8.8, for finding specific sections or words in your ActionScript.

- **Find and Replace**. This button will launch the Replace dialog box, shown in Figure 8.9, where you can find and replace specific scripts or words in your ActionScript. This is very useful for changing a variable name in every instance of ActionScript at once.

- **Insert Target Path**. This opens the Insert Target Path dialog box, shown in Figure 8.10, which is used to map to individual objects on the stage from within ActionScript.

- **Check Syntax**. This will quickly check your code for basic errors.

- **Auto Format**. This button will turn on and off the Auto Format features of the Actions panel.

- **Show Code Hints**. This button will turn on and off the code-hinting features of the Actions panel.

- **Reference**. This button will launch the Help Panel and map to highlighted code for easy search.

- **Debug Options**. Used in debugging ActionScript (for more on debugging, see Chapter 18, "Debugging").

- **View Options**. This button will allow you to select or deselect the following options.

  - **View Escape-Shortcut Keys**. Shortcut keys are used to shorten the number of keystrokes necessary to place an action in the Actions panel.

  - **View Line Numbers**. This will display line numbers on the left side of the Actions window, which makes it easier to track down malfunctioning code.

  - **Word Wrap**. A newfeature to Flash MX 2004; you can now wrap your code to the next line without errors occurring. This is a very useful feature if you do not have a lot of screen room.

A new feature in the Flash MX 2004 Actions panel is the ability to pin multiple scripts. This is very useful in that you can select multiple frames and objects containing ActionScript at once and simply choose the corresponding tab at the bottom of the Actions panel to move between them. To pin a script, follow these steps:

1. Choose a frame or object containing ActionScript so that the code will display in the Actions panel.

2. Select the icon of a pushpin in the bottom left corner of the Actions window or go to the Actions panel Options menu and chose Pin Script.

3. Now you will see a corresponding tab at the bottom of the Actions panel that you can select at any time to return to the actions of that specific frame or object.

**FIGURE 8.8**    The Find dialog box for finding words in ActionScript.

**FIGURE 8.9**    The Replace dialog box used to find and replace items in ActionScript.

**FIGURE 8.10**    The Insert Target Path dialog box for helping to map to specific objects on the stage in ActionScript.

There are several options that you can change with the Actions panel to help developers program better. The first is the Auto Format Options dialog box, as seen in Figure 8.11. This will help in setting rules for things such as line spacing with brackets, spacing with operators, and other visual aspects of coding. You can select each of the options to see what it would look like in the Preview window. And you can always select the Reset to Defaults button to return to default settings.

Another place where you can make changes to the layout of the Actions panel is the preferences for the Actions panel.

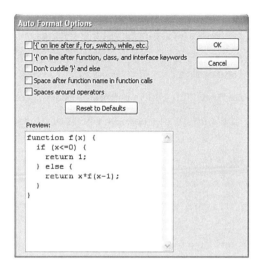

**FIGURE 8.11**    Use the Auto Format Options dialog box to make changes in the layout of auto formatted code.

## Actions Panel Preferences

If you don't like the default settings of the Actions panel, you can change them. You can get to them by choosing the Options drop-down for the Actions panel and selecting Preferences. A window will pop up as shown in Figure 8.12.

**FIGURE 8.12**    The preferences for the Actions panel.

The preferences for the Actions panel have three main sections for settings; Editing, ActionScript appearance options, and ActionScript 2.0 settings.

The Editing section allows you to select options and settings to control the flow of writing ActionScript, and it has these options:

- **Automatic Indentation**. This allows automatic spacing for lines following brackets.
- **Tab Size**. This sets the amount of space each press of the tab key (used in spacing) will take.
- **Code Hints**. This turns on or off the code-hinting features of the Actions panel.
- **Delay**. The number of seconds before a code hint appears.
- **Open/Import**. This sets the encoding of ActionScript files being opened or imported.
- **Save/Export**. This sets the encoding of ActionScript files being saved or exported.

The ActionScript appearance options section of the Actions panel preferences is used to control the color, size, and font of every piece of ActionScript code in the Actions panel. It has these options:

- **Font**. This controls the font of the ActionScript in the Actions panel.
- **Size**. This controls the font size of the ActionScript in the Actions panel.
- **Syntax Coloring**. This turns on or off the ability to distinguish certain keywords in ActionScript from the rest; you should leave this option on.
- **Syntax Color Settings**. This section allows you to choose the color of every aspect of ActionScript as well as the background of the Actions panel.

---

**NOTE**

By personal preference, many developers choose the background to be a dark color or black, and all of the code itself to be a lighter color. This makes the code easier to see from farther away from the screen.

---

The last section of the preferences for the Actions panel is the ActionScript 2.0 settings. This button will open the Class Path dialog box, which is used to map to external ActionScript files. This option is covered in more detail in Chapter 19.

There are over a thousand different commands and actions that can be placed in ActionScript. It is nearly impossible to remember all of them and their parameters. This is where the Reference button comes in.

## Reference/Help Panel

With this new version of Flash, Macromedia has decided to get rid of the reference panel. Don't panic—it has simply been replaced by the Help panel.

You can open the Help panel by either selecting the reference button in the Actions panel, or choosing Help, Help (see Figure 8.13).

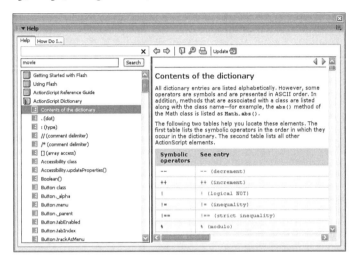

**FIGURE 8.13**   The Help panel now includes the reference panel.

The Help panel has two tabs, the Help tab and the How Do I tab. We will be focusing on the Help tab, but the How Do I tab is for tutorials and long explanations of new Flash features.

The Help panel allows you to go through the most frequently asked questions, or you can search for what you are looking for. The search option will return results based in different categories including the ActionScript reference. You can also print right from the Help panel and run the update from there as well.

> **NOTE**
>
> It is important to update at least once a month to get the latest in definitions and help material available.

## Behaviors and the Behaviors Panel

Those who have worked in previous versions of Flash will notice something missing from the Actions panel—normal mode. Normal mode was a GUI interface for putting ActionScript in the Actions panel. It has since been replaced somewhat by the Behaviors panel.

Behaviors are small pieces of code that can be placed in frames or within objects them-selves. When a behavior is selected, an interface will pop up for certain parameters of the behavior to be chosen or filled in. When placing actions within objects, behaviors have events associated with them that can be adjusted directly from the Behaviors panel. Flash comes with a certain number of built-in behaviors, and you can download more from select vendors or from Macromedia. You can also create your own behaviors, which is covered in Chapter 26, "Extending the Flash Authoring Environment."

You can open the Behaviors panel by selecting Window, Development Panels, Behaviors. You can see the Behaviors panel in Figure 8.14.

**FIGURE 8.14**   The Behaviors panel.

Follow these steps to place a behavior in a button:

1. Create a new Flash document.

2. Choose Window, Other Panels, Common Libraries, Buttons, and choose your favorite button to drag out onto the stage.

3. Give this button the instance name of `button_btn`.

4. Open the Behaviors panel by selecting Window, Development Panels, Behaviors.

5. With the button selected, click the Add Behavior button in the Behaviors panel and choose Web, Go to Web Page. The Go to URL dialog box will pop up as shown in Figure 8.15.

6. Type `http://www.sams.com` in the URL field, choose "_blank" as the Open In choice, and click OK.

7. Now the Behaviors panel will show the behavior you just placed in the button, and under the Event column, it will say On Release, which is fine.

8. Now open up the Actions panel and select the button on the stage. You should see the following code:

```
on (release) {
    //Goto Webpage Behavior
    getURL("http://www.sams.com","_blank");
    //End Behavior
}
```

Now test the movie by going to Control, Test Movie and then clicking the button. It should take you to something like Figure 8.16 if you are connected to the Internet.

FIGURE 8.15    The interface for the Go to Web Page behavior.

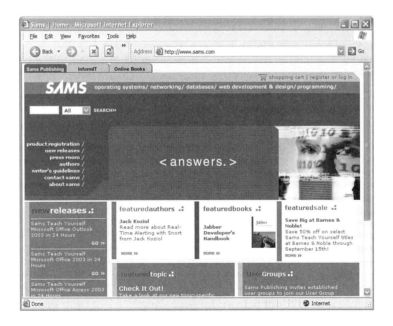

FIGURE 8.16    Use behaviors to quickly add ActionScript to your files.

That was an easy and fast way to add some interactivity to the Flash file. Now we will begin to delve into the fundamental aspects of ActionScript itself including some of the built-in objects and good practices.

# ActionScript Fundamentals

ActionScript, as mentioned throughout this chapter, is the programming language of Flash, but do not let that intimidate you. Unlike many other languages, ActionScript allows its programmers to write minimal amounts of code and still see results.

You can type in this simple line of code, test the movie, and something will happen:

```
trace("something happened");
```

Now granted, it is not doing much—just simply sending a message to the Output panel—but it is still doing something. You can see the results of your hard work in writing that line instantly, and that's what ActionScript is about. Of course, the more ActionScript you put in, the more results you will get out of it. And that is what this section is for.

In this section, we will briefly go over many pieces of ActionScript that are covered in more detail as you continue through this book. But this section will show the simple uses of these pieces to get simple results.

Looking back at that one line of code we just used, if I hadn't mentioned what it was going to do, the only way you might have known is by testing the movie. When you see the results, you know what the trace action does; it sends messages to the Output panel. Of course, there was only one line of code, so it was easy to see which line sent the message, but what if you had 500 lines of code instead? It would be that much more difficult to figure out which line of code sent the message to the Output panel. This is why developers use comments.

# Comments

**Comments** are lines of code the ActionScript reader skips over, but they are visible to people who open the file in the authoring environment. Comments are used to tell the story of ActionScript to the next person who looks at your code, (or to tell yourself later if you have to go back into the file). They are placed with variables to tell what those variables are used for. Comments are placed with functions to tell what the parameters are and what should go in them. And they are used to help narrow down bugs in code by commenting out specific lines.

To make a comment, you simply put two forward slashes (//) in front of your comment like this:

```
//this is a comment
```

You can put comments on their own line like the preceding one, or you can put them at the end of a line after some code, like these:

```
this.stop(); //this stops the movie clip
var name:String = "David" //declares a variable
function myFunction (){ //start of a function
     this.stop();     //the guts of a function
}                     //the end of a function
```

You can even comment out several lines at once using /* in the beginning and */ at the end of the comment like this:

```
    /*
this entire section is commented
I know, because I commented it
ok, that's enough...
*/
```

And as mentioned, they are used to tell someone looking at your ActionScript (including yourself) what the code is doing and why.

You can also comment out lines of code for debugging as previously mentioned, like this:

```
this.stop();
function myFunction(){
     this.gotoAndStop(2);
     myVariable = 15;
//     myNumber = myVariable/Math.PI;
}
```

Notice that when you put the comment in front of the line of code, it changes the entire line's color, meaning that the ActionScript reader will skip it because it is now a comment.

Another very important point is naming conventions.

## Code Hints and Naming Conventions

Even though commenting is very helpful, and is good coding practice, sometimes you take a variable for granted and think that anyone will be able to tell what that variable is with or without a comment. And that may be true if you practice good naming conventions.

When naming variables, instances, functions, methods, and events, it is important to use names that can be easily understood. For instance, if you have a variable that represents the beginning horizontal position of an object on the stage, which of the following would you be more apt to recognize as what it is?

```
var startX = myMovie._x;

    or
var s1 = myMovie._x;
```

Obviously the first variable is named something appropriate to what it is holding, whereas the second variable, even though it is holding the same information, does not give you a clue about what it holds. As its creator, you will remember (at least for a short time) what the variable is, but the next person to look at your code will have no idea what the variable is for.

Some rules to follow when naming instances and variables:

- They must start with either a letter or an underscore (_).

- They may not have any spaces within them.

- They cannot be one of the reserved keywords such as var or this.

- Although this is not a rule, but more of a warning, you should also not give variables the same name as object classes such as Color or Date, which can cause errors in your coding in certain situations.

Also, when creating instances of objects, there are special suffixes that can be added to the ends of the names to make the code hints pop up. Code hints are used to assist developers when working with objects. When the Actions panel knows what object type you are working with, it can give you a list of all the available methods, properties, and events of that object so that you don't have to remember them all.

To see an example of code hints, follow these steps:

1. Create a new Flash document.

2. Open the Actions panel in the first frame of the main timeline and create a string like this:

```
var myString_str = "test";
```

3. Now, after that line of code, begin typing the string's name (myString_str) and then type a period after the last character of the name. The code hints will pop up.

If the code hints do not appear, make sure they are turned on by going to the Show Code Hint button in the Actions panel.

What controls these code hints?

## AsCodeHints.xml

The code hints for objects are controlled in an XML file at `C:\Program Files\Macromedia\Flash MX 2004\en\First Run\ActionsPanel\AsCodeHints.xml` for Windows users and `Applications\Macromedia\Flash MX 2004\en\First Run\ActionsPanel\AsCodeHints.xml` for Mac users. You can view all of the suffixes as well as other hinting tools in those files. Or you can use this list to see the available suffixes:

- MovieClip—_mc
- Array—_array
- String—_str
- Button—_btn
- Text Field—_txt
- Text Format—_fmt
- Date—_date
- Sound—_sound
- XML—_xml
- XML Node—_xmlnode
- XML Socket—_xmlsocket
- Color—_color
- Context Menu—_cm
- Context Menu Item—_cmi
- Print Job—_pj
- Movie Clip Loader—_mcl
- Error—_err
- Camera—_cam
- LoadVars—_lv
- LocalConnection—_lc
- Microphone—_mic
- NetConnection—_nc
- NetStream—_ns
- Shared Object—_so
- Video—_video

8

Of course, using suffixes is not the only way to trigger code hints. You can also declare the data type in comments.

### Triggering Code Hints with Comments

You do not have to use the suffixes with object names to get code hints to work; you can also declare the object's data type in a commented line. After that, the object's name will pop open the code hints for that object.

To declare a data type of an object on a commented line, you first put the two forward slash marks (//), followed by the object class name (Array, String, Color), then a space followed by the object's instance name, and finally a semicolon to end the line.

For example, place this code in the first frame of the main timeline in the Actions panel:

```
//Color myColor;
```

Now whenever myColor is used, it will pop open the code hints for the Color object.

There is one final way to trigger the code hints, and we have already used it: strict data typing.

### Strict Data Typing to Trigger Code Hints

You can trigger code hints by declaring the object's data type in a commented line because you are declaring the object's data type. Strict data typing does the same thing without the commented line.

Place this line of code in the first frame of the main timeline in the Actions panel:

```
var myString:String = "test";
```

Now when you use the myString string, when you place a period after its name in the Actions panel, the code hints for the String object will appear.

# Dot Syntax

With every programming language, there are rules and guidelines to using it correctly also known as its syntax. ActionScript is no exception to this; its has its own syntax called dot syntax.

The idea behind dot syntax is simple. When using properties, methods, or events with objects, the name of the property, method, or event must be separated from the object by a dot (period), like the following:

```
myMovie.stop();     //Stops the play head for the movie clip
myString.length;    //this is the read only length property of a string
myText.text="test";    //sets the text of a text field
myStuff.onLoad=function(){};//declares the onLoad event for a LoadVars object
```

As you can see, each time a property, method or event is associated with an object, a dot is used to separate them. Also, if you are going to use a target path to a child movie clip, you must use dot syntax to separate the movie clip's instance names, like this:

```
parentMovie.childMovie.gotoAndPlay(10);

//tell the child movie clip to go to frame 10 and play
```

Another thing to notice about the preceding line of code is the use of the semicolon (;). In ActionScript, semicolons tell the ActionScript reader that the line is done. They are not necessary, but it is good practice to include them.

Another piece of the ActionScript language to mention is the use of parentheses () and curly brackets {}.

Parentheses are used for the following reasons:

- To group segments of math together so that they are calculated first:

```
trace(5+4*3);      //returns 17
trace((5+4)*3);    //returns 27
```

- To enclose parameters when creating or calling functions:

```
function addNumbers(num1,num2){
      return num1+num2;
}
trace(addNumbers(1,3));      //returns 4
```

- To enclose a conditional:

```
if(5 < 10){
      trace("5 is less than 10");
}
```

Curly brackets are used for the following reason:

- To enclose ActionScript to run as a block of code:

```
// with a conditional
if(5 < 10){
      trace("5 is less than 10");
}
//with a loop
while(i<10){
      trace(i);
      i++;
}
```

```
//with an event
button.onPress=function(){
    trace("the button was pressed");
}
```

Those are some of the basic pieces that are used in ActionScript. Now we will begin to cover some of the basic objects and actions of ActionScript starting with the movie clip.

## The Movie Clip Object

The movie clip object is unique among all other objects because it can be created manually or with ActionScript. It also has a timeline that is independent from the main timeline. This means that you can have content on a movie clip's timeline that runs on its own, unconnected from its parent timeline.

The movie clip object also has an extensive list of properties, methods, and events. It can also handle button events, so you can see why it is the most popular object to use in Flash.

In this example, we will create a movie clip manually, and then control it with ActionScript.

1. Create a new Flash document.

2. Draw a circle on the stage about 100 pixels in width and height.

3. Highlight the circle both stroke and fill, and choose Modify, Convert to Symbol.

4. Give it a symbol name of `circleMC` and make sure the behavior is set for Movie Clip.

5. Back in the main timeline, give the instance of the circle an instance name of `circle_mc`.

6. Create a new layer called **actions**.

7. In the first frame of the actions layer, open up the Actions panel, and place this code in it:

```
//create the speed variable
var speed:Number = 10;
//the event to move the circle
circle_mc.onEnterFrame=function(){
    //get the distance between the mouse and the circle
    xDist = _xmouse-this._x;
    yDist = _ymouse-this._y;
    //set the circles position
    this._x+=xDist/speed;
    this._y+=yDist/speed;
}
```

The preceding code first creates a variable to control the speed of the circle. Then it simply creates a callback function that continually fires. In this callback, we get the distance between the circle and the mouse on both the horizontal and vertical plane. We then set the circle's position based on that distance.

Now test the movie and move the mouse around on the screen. You will see that the circle_mc movie clip follows the mouse wherever it goes while still on the screen.

You can find more information on the movie clip object in Chapter 11, "The MovieClip Object."

# Functions

Functions are an important part of programming. The basic idea behind a function is to create one when you have repetitive blocks of code. For instance, if you are constantly getting the area of a rectangle, that is a perfect opportunity for a function.

You create a function with the keyword function and then the name of the function followed by an opening parenthesis, which will hold any parameters you may want to put in the function, followed by a closing parenthesis. Then an opening curly bracket ({), after that, any code that you want to run, and then a return statement to send information back out of the function, followed, finally, by a closing curly bracket (}) on its own line.

> **NOTE**
>
> Not all functions need return statements, as you will see in Chapter 12, "Functions."

Here is an example of creating and using a function to get the area of a rectangle:

```
//create the function
function getArea(width:Number, height:Number):Number{
    //return the area in pixels
    return width * height;
}
//now call the function, and send the results to the output panel
trace(getArea(20,31));
//Output: 620
```

The preceding code creates the function getArea, which has two parameters, width and height. In the function, it returns the width by the height. Then we call the function and send the result to the Output panel.

You can clearly see the benefit of using functions. Now we can get the height of any rectangle on which we use the function. We could even send it information about a movie clip's width and height, and it will send back its area.

For more on functions, see Chapter 12.

## Conditionals

Conditionals are what make programming smart. Conditionals ask questions, and based on the answer, they either do or do not execute code associated with them. The type of question they ask is a simple yes or no, or rather a true or false question such as whether one number is greater than another.

When building a conditional, such as the `if` statement, you put a condition within parenthesis that the conditional looks at. If the condition is met, in other words, if it is true, then the code associated with the `if` statement is run. If it is not met, or is false, the entire code within is skipped over.

Programmers use conditionals to set boundaries, verify information, and make logical decisions. For instance, if we had a simple login for a page, we would want to verify if the user's name and password were correct. The code for that might look something like this:

```
if(userName == corectUserName){
    if(userPass == password){
        trace("welcome");
    }else{
        trace("password incorrect");
    }
}else{
    trace("no user found");
)
```

The preceding code checks to see if the username given is the correct user. If so, it then checks to see if the password is correct as well. If both are correct, a welcome message is sent to the Output panel. If the `userName` is correct, but the password is not, another message is sent to the Output panel. And if the user has not entered the correct user name, a different message is sent to the Output panel for that as well.

You can see how conditionals follow a path of logic and can be used in many circumstances, as you will see as you work through the other chapters.

You can find more information on conditionals in Chapter 10, "Statements and Expressions."

## Loop Statements

Conditionals are used to check something once, and then move on. **Loop statements** are used until the condition is no longer true.

Conditionals are often used with numerical values to see if a certain number of objects are present, or if a certain object has reached a designated spot on the stage. For instance, if we have an array of information, and we want to know each element in that array, we could use a loop statement to cycle through each element in an array until there are no more, like this:

```
//create an array
var myArray:Array = new Array("David","Ben","Lesley","Missy","Micki");
//now loop through the entire array and display each element in the output panel
for(var i:Number = 0; i<myArray.length; i++){
     trace(myArray[i]);
}
//Output: David
//          Ben
//          Lesley
//          Missy
//          Micki
```

The preceding code creates an array full of names. Then a loop statement is created that will loop through the entire array and display each element in the Output panel.

Loop statements can be very powerful, but also very processor-intensive, so make sure the loop does not continue forever.

For more on loop statements, see Chapter 10.

## Summary

This chapter covered a lot of information on ActionScript. Do not feel alarmed if some concepts were difficult—they are covered in more detail as you continue through the following chapters.

A few key points to remember are

- Objects have three features:

    - **Properties**. Information about the object

    - **Methods**. What the object does

    - **Events**. Let Flash know when something happens with the object

- Use strict data typing to help debug applications early in development.

- Comment your code. If you're in doubt whether or not it's important enough to comment, comment it.

- Set the preferences of the Actions panel to your liking. You are going to be using it a lot from here on out, and it should be just the way you want it.

- Use code hints to help keep track of individual objects' code.

# CHAPTER 9

# Strings, Numbers, and Variables—In Depth

In this chapter we discuss different types of data and variables that store data.

Data, simply put, is anything and everything you want it to be, including text, numbers, and logical representations (known as Boolean data). In its most raw form (binary code), data is represented as a bunch of zeros and ones, which comprise the basic data computers use as their primitive language. For instance, this next excerpt is the binary translation of "Flash MX 2004 Professional":

```
0100011001101100011000010111001101101000001000000010011010
1011000001000000011001
0001100000011000000110100000100000010100000111001001101111
0110011001100101011100
11011010010110111101101110011000010110110

```

## Types of Data Types

Before we get into any major details about any of the data types, let's briefly look at the different data types in Flash:

- `String`. Any piece of data to be listed as basic text (for example, "This is a string data type"). Notice the quotation marks, which signify that this is a string.

- `Number`. Any piece of data to be listed as an integer, or floating-point with a numeric value (for example, 1, 44, -10, 21.7, and -0.8 are all legal number data types).

- `Boolean`. This is a logical representation used for conditions and results of certain functions (`true` and `false` are the only two Boolean data types).

- Null. This data type is used to show the absence of data having a value of null.

- Undefined. This data type is used to show the absence of value in a variable; its value is undefined.

- Array. This is used for lists of data (it is its own data type); the data itself can be a certain type such as String, or Number, or it can also be mixed within the array.

The two most commonly used data types are strings and numbers. We will go into greater detail on these two and discuss the different parts of both data types.

First, let's take a look at these data types and see how easily they can be misinterpreted:

```
"My name is David."      // this is a string datatype
1234                     // this is a number datatype
"1234"                   // this is a string datatype
1+2+3                    // this is a number datatype
"My name "+"is David"    // this is a string datatype
'Single quote marks'     // this is a string datatype with single quote marks
```

These are the basic forms of the string and number data types. The text to the right with the double forward slashes (//) just represents comments in the code (the interpreter skips this text completely).

## The String Data Type

The string data type can be categorized as any amount of text between quotes. This includes characters, numbers, and certain properties of movie clip instances such as the _name property.

### Creating a String

To create a string, place some text between quotation marks, as shown here:

```
"this is a string literal"
"this is also a string"
//that was simple enough
```

Another way of creating a string using the string data type is to declare a new string with the new constructor, which will make an instance of an object, in this case the String object:

```
new String("this is a string literal")
```

Also, you can set a variable equal to a string (which we will discuss later in this chapter):

```
var myString:String = new String("this is a string literal");
```

And you don't even need to use the new constructor; you can set a string to a variable like this:

```
var myString:String = "another string";
```

## Empty Strings

You do not have to put anything between the quotes for it to be a string literal. You can just place an opening and closing set of quotes to create an empty string, as shown here:

```
""       // an empty string with double quotes
''       // an empty string with single quotes
```

Although this is an empty string, it is not equal to the null or undefined data types. In the following example, we first start a new file by going to File in the menu bar, choosing New (PC–Ctrl+N, Mac–Open Apple+N), and then choosing Flash Document. Here we use an if statement in the actions of the first frame in the main timeline and test it by going to Control in the menu bar and selecting Test Movie (if statements are discussed in Chapter 10, "Statements and Expressions"):

```
if ("" != null) {
      trace ("An empty string is not equal to null");
}
// output: An empty string is not equal to null
```

Notice that we use a trace action that, when the movie is tested, displays our output in the Output panel. You'll see how to use this empty string, like the one found in the if statement, at the end of this chapter.

## Quotes

As you have seen, all string literals must be surrounded by quotes. These quotes can be single quotation marks (') or double quotation marks ("), but you must close with the same type of quotation mark you started with. Here are some examples:

```
"double quotes"       //legal string
'single quotes'       //legal string
"double to single'    //illegal string
'single to double"    //illegal string
```

If you do not close with the same quotation mark you opened with, you will receive this error:

```
String literal was not properly terminated
```

However, you can put quotation marks inside quotation marks, as shown here:

```
'Then David said: "These are quotes inside a string"'
//this is a legal string containing a quote within it
```

You do need to be careful, though, because a single quotation mark can also be used as an apostrophe. This can cause errors if you are not paying attention. Here's an example:

```
'He wasn't going to go'
//the interpreter reads this as 'He wasn' and throws an error message
```

If we had used opening and closing double quotation marks instead of single quotation marks here, the interpreter would not have thrown the error. However, let's say we want to use single quotation marks anyway. In this case, there is a workaround: the escape sequence.

### Escape Sequences

Escape sequences are string literals used with a backslash (\). This tells the interpreter to consider the following character or character representation as a character and not part of an action.

Here are some basic escape sequences:

```
\"       double quote escape sequence
\'       single quote escape sequence
\\       backslash escape sequence using the backslash not as an escape sequence
```

Let's take a look at our example again, but this time using the escape sequence:

```
'He wasn't going to go'
//as before, this will cause errors and not display the proper text
'He wasn\'t going to go'
//now using an escape sequence, the problem is solved, and the
//interpreter reads it correctly
```

Now the interpreter reads the string correctly. Remember, you only have to use the quote escape sequences when you have quotation marks (double or single) that you want to display in between the opening and closing quotation marks of a string.

## Manipulating Strings

String manipulation includes creating new strings, joining strings, and much more. In this section, we'll start with the easy tasks and work our way up.

## Joining Strings

Joining strings is as simple as putting a plus operator (+) between two string literals. Here's an example:

```
"This is " + "a string literal"
// the interpreter translates this as "This is a string literal"
```

Notice the space after "is" in the preceding example. This space is necessary in strings; otherwise, the string would appear like this: `"This isa string literal"`. Alternatively, we could use a space string to make the code look clearer, as shown here:

```
"This is" + " " + "a string literal"
// the interpreter translates this as "This is a string literal"
```

Note that the space string is not equal to the empty string we discussed earlier:

```
if (" " != '') {
        trace ("A space string is not equal to an empty string")
}
// output: A space string is not equal to an empty string
```

Also, even though it has been deprecated back in Flash MX, you can use the operator add to join strings together:

```
"This is " add "a string literal"
// the add operator works just like the + operator
```

You can also add strings by setting them to variables:

```
var fName:String = "David";
var lName:String = "Vogeleer";
var space:String = " ";
trace (fName + space + lName);
// output: David Vogeleer
```

Here, all we did was set each string to a variable and then add the variables.

Another way to add strings with variables is to set the same variable to an additional string with an assignment operator. Here's an example:

```
var name:String = "David ";
name += "Vogeleer";
trace (name);
// output: David Vogeleer
```

6

Notice that we added the string to the variable, but you cannot add the variable from within a string. The following example shows this:

```
var fName:String = "David ";
var lName:String = "Vogeleer";
var fullName:String = "fName + lName";
trace (fullName);
// output: fName + lName
```

So keep in mind that you cannot use variables from within a string.

You can, however, create a new string by adding a string to a variable that contains a string, as shown here:

```
var fName:String = "David ";
var fullName:String = fName + "Vogeleer";
trace (fullName);
// output: David Vogeleer
```

### The concat Function

Using dot syntax, the concat function acts similarly to the assignment variable (+=) we looked at earlier. Simply attach it to a string with another string in the brackets:

```
var name:String = "David ".concat("Vogeleer");
trace (name);
// output: David Vogeleer
```

And, of course, you can attach the concat function to a variable:

```
var fName:String = "David ";
var fullName:String = fName.concat("Vogeleer");
trace (fullName);
// output: David Vogeleer
```

Now let's put a variable in the parentheses instead of a string literal:

```
var fName:String = "David ";
var lName:String = "Vogeleer";
var fullName:String = fName.concat(lName);
trace (fullName);
// output: David Vogeleer
```

This technique can even handle multiple expressions:

```
var myString:String = "This is ".concat("a"+" ".concat("string " + "literal"));
trace (myString) ;
// output: This is a string literal
```

Not only can you use multiple joining expressions, but you can also embed `concat` functions within `concat` functions.

You can use the `concat()` method in place of the plus sign (+) in order to add strings together, but it is not necessary. As you can see in the previous examples, even though the end result is the same, using the plus sign to add strings reads better when you are looking over your code.

## Indexing Characters in Strings

Characters inside of strings can be indexed, stored, and displayed. Each character in a string has a specific index, starting with the first character at the index zero (0). The indexing of strings always starts with 0 instead of 1 in Flash; therefore, the second character has an index of 1 and the third character has an index of 2, and so on (see Figure 9.1).

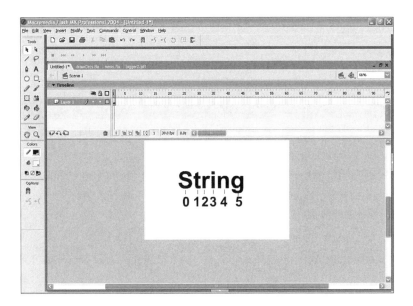

**FIGURE 9.1**    Indexing strings start with index 0 for the first character.

### The `charAt` Method

You can use the `charAt` method with strings to see characters at a defined index. Just attach the method to a string and place a number in the parentheses that represents the index you want to grab. Here's an example:

```
trace("David".charAt(2));
// output: v
```

This function can also be attached to a variable holding a string:

```
var name:String = "David";
trace (name.charAt(2));
// output: v
```

What's more, you can use a variable in place of the number in the parentheses:

```
var place:Number = 2;
var name:String = "David";
trace (name.charAt(place));
// output: v
```

### The `length` Property

The `length` property provides a way to determine the number of characters in a given string. Simply attach it to a string, and it will return a numeric value. Here's an example:

```
trace ("Unleashed".length);
// output: 9
```

> **TIP**
>
> The index of the last character in a string will always be *string*.`length` minus one.

Of course, this property can also be attached to a variable holding a string, as shown here:

```
var myTitle:String= "Unleashed";
trace (myTitle.length);
// output: 9
```

Even though you might not consider a space to be a character, ActionScript does:

```
var myTitle:String = "Flash Unleashed";
trace (myTitle.length);
// output: 15
```

In this example, the output is 15 instead of 14 because the space is counted as a character.

Using the `length` property combined with the `charAt` method, we can identify every character in a word based on a defined function (more on functions in later chapters). Here's an example:

```
//first create the function
list = function (myString:String) {
   //use a loop statement to cycle through
   //all the characters in the string
```

```
    for(var i:Number = 0; i < myString.length; i++){
         trace (myString.charAt(i));
    }
}
//create our string
var myTitle:String = "Unleashed";
//run the function on our string
list(myTitle);
// output: U
//         n
//         l
//         e
//         a
//         s
//         h
//         e
//         d
```

### The indexOf Method

The indexOf method takes a given character, looks for it in a string, and returns the character's index. As before, you can attach it directly to a string or a variable holding a string. Place the character you are looking for in the parentheses as a string literal, like so:

```
//attach the function directly to a string
trace ("Flash".indexOf("a"));
// now create a variable and attach the function to the variable
var myTitle:String = "Unleashed";
trace (myTitle.indexOf("e"));
// output: 2
//         3
```

In the second part of the preceding example, the indexOf method found the first index of *e*, but let's say we now want to find the next one. To do this, we just place a starting index in the function after the character we are looking for and separate them with a comma:

```
var myTitle:String = "Unleashed";
trace (myTitle.indexOf("e",4));
// output: 7
```

In this case, we put in the index of the character following the first *e* and the indexOf method found the next one with no problem.

You can also look for certain strings of characters with the indexOf method. Just place the string in quotes, as you would a single character. The indexOf method will return the first index of the first character in the string you are looking for:

```
var myTitle:String = "Unleashed";
trace (myTitle.indexOf("she"));
// output: 5
```

The Output panel displays the index of the first character in the string you're looking for (in this case, *s*).

Here's another nice feature of the indexOf method: If it does not find the character or characters in the string, it will display -1 in the Output window when you trace it:

```
var myTitle:String = "Unleashed";
trace (myTitle.indexOf("o"));
// output: -1
```

Let's take a look at what happens when we look for the letter *u* in the same string:

```
var myTitle:String = "Unleashed";
trace (myTitle.indexOf("u"));
// output: -1
```

The indexOf method could not find *u* in this case because Flash reads upper- and lower-case letters as completely different characters.

This can be useful when you're using forms in Flash. For example, let's say your company is willing to pay for in-state shipping to its customers, but if the recipient is outside the state, he or she must pay the shipping. Therefore, when users enter another state in the shipping form, they are greeted with a message reminding them to include shipping costs (otherwise, a thank-you message appears):

```
//first create our variables
var homeState:String = "VA";
var thankYou:String = "Thank you for your order";
var reminder:String = "Please remember to include shipping";
//now create the if statement
if (enteredState.indexOf(homeState) == -1) {
    message = reminder;
} else {
    message = thankYou;
}
```

This code determines whether the variable homeState is in enteredState and sends the appropriate message.

### The lastIndexOf Method

Like the indexOf method, the lastIndexOf method searches a string for a character or group of characters. However, unlike the indexOf method, which starts at the beginning of the string and moves toward the end, the lastIndexOf method starts at the end and works toward the beginning.

Also, this method works the same as the indexOf method in that you simply attach it to a string or variable holding a string and place the desired character or characters in parentheses, followed by a comma with a starting index. If no starting index is defined, the starting index automatically becomes the last character in the string. Here's an example:

```
var myTitle:String = "Unleashed";
trace (myTitle.lastIndexOf("e"));
// output: 7
```

Although this method may not seem like much, consider that the following code is what it would take to do the same thing without the built-in lastIndexOf method:

```
theLastIndexOf=function(myString:String,searchFor:String){
     for (var i:Number = 0; i < myString.length; i++){
          if (myString.charAt(i) == searchFor) {
               found = i;
          }
     }
     trace (found);
}
var myTitle = "Unleashed";
theLastIndexOf(myTitle,"e");
// output: 7
```

### The substring **Method**

Many times, it is necessary to pull more than one character from a string. Flash has a few built-in methods for this task. One of them is the substring method.

The substring method attaches to strings and variables like other methods. However, in the parentheses, you put the starting and ending index, separated by a comma. Here's an example:

```
trace("Unleashed".substring(2,7))
// output: leash
```

Now let's attach it to a variable and leave out the ending index:

```
var myTitle:String = "Unleashed";
trace (myTitle.substring(2));
// output: leashed
```

As you can see, without an ending index, the substring method grabs all the characters from the starting index onward.

So far we have put in numbers representing the starting and ending indexes. Now let's use a variable instead of a number. This will make the function more dynamic. For example, let's say you would like to pull the ZIP Code out of the last line of an address:

```
var line3:String = "Richmond, VA 23866";
var finalSpace:Number = line3.lastIndexOf(" ");
var zip:String = line3.substring(finalSpace+1);
trace (zip);
// output: 23866
```

This takes the last space in the third line and makes it the starting point. It then grabs everything after that, which in this case is the ZIP Code.

If, by mistake, you place the ending index first and the starting index second, the interpreter will switch them for you:

```
var myTitle:String = "Unleashed";
trace (myTitle.substring(7,2));
// output: leash
```

Even though the numbers were reversed, the interpreter still retrieves the correct information.

### The substr Method

The substr method acts similarly to the substring method. However, in place of an ending index, you put the desired number of characters to be returned. The substr method still uses a starting index like the substring method. Here's an example:

```
var myTitle:String = "Unleashed";
trace (myTitle.substr(2,5));
// output: leash
```

If you have a starting index but not a designated number of characters to pull, the substr method will begin at the starting point and pull all the following characters:

```
var myTitle:String = "Unleashed";
trace (myTitle.substr(2));
// output: leashed
```

You can also place a negative number in the starting index, and the substr method will start counting from the end toward the beginning using the specified number of spaces:

```
var myTitle:String = "Unleashed";
trace (myTitle.substr(-4,2));
// output: sh
```

### The `slice` Method

The `slice` method acts similarly to the `substring` method, except you can use negative numbers in the starting and ending indexes, as shown here:

```
var myTitle:String = "Unleashed";
trace (myTitle.slice(-7,-2));
// output: leash
```

### The `split` Method

The `split` method is a unique method when it comes to manipulating strings. It divides a string into separate strings that can be stored in an array (more on arrays in Chapter 13, "Arrays").

Attach the `split` method to a string or variable and in the parentheses place the delimiting character. Here's an example:

```
var myTitle:String = "Unleashed";
trace (myTitle.split("e"));
// output: Unl,ash,d
```

The preceding example separates the original string based on the letter *e*. This is very powerful because you can take apart a sentence and store each individual word as its own variable or within an array as elements. Let's take a look:

```
//first, create a variable holding the string
var myTitle:String = "Flash MX Unleashed";
// then set an array equal to the string with the function attached
var myArray:Array = myTitle.split(" ");
//display the entire array
trace (myArray);
//display just the first element in the array
trace (myArray[0]);
// output: Flash,MX,Unleashed
//         Flash
```

Now you can see some of the capabilities this method has. You can sort, store, and send all this data in a nice, clean format thanks to the `split` method.

### The `toLowerCase` Method

Earlier, we ran into a problem when trying to find a lowercase *u* in the word *Unleashed* because Flash does not treat lowercase characters the same as uppercase characters. This problem can be overcome with either the `toLowerCase` method or the `toUpperCase` method. Both work the same, except one converts characters to lowercase and the other to uppercase.

Let's go over toLowerCase first. When you want to find a letter in lowercase format in a string with uppercase letters, you must first convert all the uppercase letters to lowercase so that Flash will be able to find the lowercase version of the letter you are looking for. This can be done on an individual basis with a lot of tedious coding, or you can simply attach the toLowerCase method directly to the string. Here's an example:

```
var myTitle:String = "Unleashed";
myTitle = myTitle.toLowerCase();
trace (myTitle);
// output: unleashed
```

In this case, we converted the uppercase *U* to a lowercase *u*. Now we can run the indexOf method as before and view the results:

```
var myTitle:String = "Unleashed";
myTitle = myTitle.toLowerCase();
trace (myTitle.indexOf("u"));
// output: 0
```

### The toUpperCase Method

The toUpperCase method is identical to the toLowerCase method, except instead of lower-casing a value in a string, it uppercases it. Attach this method as you would any other method with nothing in the parentheses:

```
var myTitle:String = "Unleashed";
myTitle = myTitle.toUpperCase();
trace (myTitle);
// output: UNLEASHED
```

Like the toLowerCase method, the toUpperCase method affects the entire string.

### The charCodeAt Method

We've talked about how Flash reads upper- and lowercase letters as different letters. This is because Flash doesn't see them as letters at all but rather as code points. The String object has two built-in methods for dealing with code points: the charCodeAt method and the fromCharCode method.

The first method, charCodeAt, takes characters at defined indexes of strings and returns the code point value in a numeric form. Attach this method as you would any other, and in the parentheses put the index of the character you're interested in. Here's an example:

```
var myTitle:String = "Unleashed";
trace (myTitle.charCodeAt(2));
// output: 108 (the code point for the letter "l")
```

The following code goes through any string and displays each character's code point in the Output window:

```
//create the function
listCodePoints = function (myString:String){
//set the loop statement to run through each character
     for(var i:Number=0; i < myString.length; i++){
     //trace each character's code point
          trace (myString.charCodeAt(i));
     }
}
//create the variable to hold the string
var myTitle:String = "Unleashed";
//run the function
listCodePoints(myTitle);
// output: 85
//         110
//         108
//         101
//         97
//         115
//         104
//         101
//         100
```

Putting a negative value in the index place will always return the value NaN (Not a Number, covered later in this chapter in the "NaN" section):

```
var myTitle:String = "Unleashed";
trace (myTitle.charCodeAt(-2));
// output: NaN
```

### The fromCharCode Method

Unlike the charCodeAt method, the fromCharCode method allows you to put code points in parentheses, and it translates them back to their string characters. Attach this method to a string data type and put the code points you would like to see in parentheses, separated by commas:

```
//create the variable to hold our string
var myTitle:String ;
myTitle = String.fromCharCode(85,110,108,101,97,115,104,101,100);
trace (myTitle);
// output: Unleashed
```

> **TIP**
>
> The `fromCharCode` method must be attached to a `String` data type when it is run; otherwise, it will return Undefined.

## Unicode-Style Strings

Another way to create a string is by using Unicode-style escape sequences. Because Flash does not exactly support the Unicode style, it emulates this style instead. The basic form of a Unicode escape sequence starts with a backslash character, then a lowercase u, followed by a four-digit number:

```
var myTitle:String = "\u0055\u006e\u006c\u0065\u0061\u0073\u0068\u0065\u0064"
trace (myTitle);
// output: Unleashed
```

Now you can type data in Unicode format into strings. The only real reason you would want to do this is to get those characters you can't simply type from the keyboard, such as the copyright symbol (©), which in Unicode is \u00A9.

You can also type Unicode in shorthand format by replacing the \u00 with \x, as shown here:

```
trace ("\u0068");
trace ("\x68");
// output: h
//         h
```

## The `Number` Data Type

The next data type we'll discuss is the `Number` data type. Numbers come in all sorts of forms and are used for lots of different reasons, ranging from counting, to mathematical properties of movie clips, to expressions. Let's look at a few examples:

```
1                //legal number
4.998            //legal number
3+4              //legal number
_x               //legal number representing a horizontal position
string.length    //legal number representing the length of a string
0123             //legal number representing an octal number
10e2             //legal number using exponents
0x000000         //legal hexadecimal number
"1234"           //not a legal number, but a string literal
```

The two basic types of numbers supported by Flash are integers and floating-point numbers. Integers are whole numbers (positive or negative). Floating-point numbers are also positive or negative, but they include decimal points as well as fractional values (which are converted to decimal values).

Integers have two basic rules:

- They cannot contain decimals or fractional values.

- They cannot go below `Number.MIN_VALUE` or above `Number.MAX_VALUE`.

Some of the basic integers are raw numbers, such as 428 and 1200. These numbers are plain and simple. However, another example of an integer is a hexadecimal number, which is often used in color-coding (0x6F9AB1, for instance). Yet another form of integer is an octal number, such as 0123, which translates to the following:

```
(1*64) + (2*8) + (3*1)
```

Floating-point numbers include decimal values, fractional values, and exponents. Exponents are defined by using the letter *e* followed by a number. This number represents the number of zeros to be added to the preceding number. Here's an example:

```
trace (10e2);
// output: 1000
```

## Creating a Number

One way to create a number is to simply type it:

```
4
```

You can also use the `Number` data type in conjunction with the `new` constructor to create a number:

```
new Number(4);
```

Now you can set it equal to a variable:

```
var myNumber:Number = new Number(4);
trace (myNumber);
// output: 4
```

You can also create numbers without the `new` constructor like this:

```
var myNumber:Number = 4;
trace(myNumber);
//output:    4
```

## Solving the Problem of Repeating Decimal Points

Because computers have difficulties with defining repeating decimal places and can some-times misrepresent a number with multiple decimal places, it's a good idea to round or drop the decimal places with the built-in methods `Math.round` and `Math.floor`.

When using the `Math.round` method, simply place the number or variable holding the number in parentheses, and the method will round it to its nearest whole value, thus creating an integer:

```
trace (Math.round(1.23333));
trace (Math.round(1.566666));
// output: 1
//         2
```

The `Math.floor` method, on the other hand, completely drops the decimal places from the number and returns an integer. Its use is the same as the `Math.round` method:

```
trace (Math.floor(1.23333));
trace (Math.floor(1.566666));
// output: 1
//         1
```

## Predefined Values for Numbers

Even though you can create almost any number manually, Flash has a few values for numbers built into it. Ironically, the first predefined value for a number is Not a Number (NaN).

### NaN

Rarely would you set a number equal to NaN, but occasionally you might see this value in the Output panel when the number you are trying to use is not a number. A NaN value can be the result of placing text inside a `Number` data type or trying to divide zero by zero. Here's an example:

```
var seatsAvailable:Number = new Number("lots");
trace (seatsAvailable);
// output: NaN
```

Because NaN is not a number, variables with this value cannot be equal to each other:

```
//create our variables
var seatsAvailable:Number = new Number("lots");
var seatsTaken:Number = new Number ("a few");
//create the if statement to see if it is not equal
if (seatsAvailable != seatsTaken) {
      trace("These two are not equal");
}
```

You can also test to see if a number is NaN by using the `isNaN` function as in the following example:

```
var myNum:Number = new Number("not a number");
if(isNaN(myNum)){
    trace("the number is NaN");
}
//output: the number is NaN
```

But this does not mean that NaN is a string. For instance, you cannot do this:

```
var myNum:Number = new Number("not a number");
if(myNum == "NaN"){
    trace("the number is NaN");
}
//output: (nothin)
```

### MAX_VALUE and MIN_VALUE

Flash has limitations as to what a number can be. Two of these limitations are MAX_VALUE and MIN_VALUE. Currently, the maximum allowable value for a number is 1.79769313486231e+308, and the minimum allowable value is 4.94065645841247e-324.

This doesn't mean a number has to be between these two values. For example, a number can be lower than MIN_VALUE, as shown here:

```
//create our variable
var myNumber:Number = -1;
//create an if statement to see if myNumber
//is lower than the MIN_VALUE
if (myNumber < Number.MIN_VALUE) {
    trace ("myNumber is lower than MIN_VALUE");
}
// output: myNumber is lower than MIN_VALUE
```

This is because MIN_VALUE is the minimum value a number can be in Flash, not the largest negative number. To see the largest negative number, set MAX_VALUE, the largest number Flash can handle, to negative and run the same code:

```
//create our variable
var myNumber:Number = -1;
//create an if statement to see if myNumber
//is lower than the -MAX_VALUE
if (myNumber < -Number.MAX_VALUE) {
    trace ("myNumber is lower than -MAX_VALUE");
}
// output: (nothing because -1 is not smaller than -MAX_VALUE)
```

POSITIVE_INFINITY **and** NEGATIVE_INFINITY

If, by some chance, you create a number greater than Number.MAX_VALUE, the value will be Infinity. Likewise, if you create a negative number larger than -Number.MAX_VALUE, the value will be -Infinity.

Predefined values are built into Flash that represent Infinity and -Infinity. They are Number.POSITIVE_INFINITY and Number.NEGATIVE_INFINITY.

Using these predefined values, we can test whether a number is infinite in the code:

```
//create our variable
var myNumber:Number = Number.MAX_VALUE * Number.MAX_VALUE;
//create the if statement
if (myNumber == Number.POSITIVE_INFINITY){
        trace ("Both numbers are infinite");
}
// output: Both numbers are infinite
```

## Bonus Numbers

Here's a list of more predefined Math constants:

- Math.E. The natural base for a logarithm. The approximate value is 2.71828.

- Math.LN2. The natural logarithm of 2. The approximate value is 0.69314718055994528623.

- Math.LN10. The natural logarithm of 10. The approximate value is 2.3025850929940459011.

- Math.LOG2E. The base-2 logarithm of MATH.E. The approximate value is 1.442695040888963387.

- Math.LOG10E. The base-10 logarithm of MATH.E. The approximate value is 0.43429448190325181667.

- Math.PI. The ratio of the circumference of a circle to its diameter, expressed as pi. The approximate value is 3.14159265358979.

- Math.SQRT1_2. The reciprocal of the square root of one half. The approximate value is 0.707106781186.

- Math.SQRT2. The square root of 2. The approximate value is 1.414213562373.

Numbers are the basis of almost all object-oriented programming. In Chapter 10, you'll see a lot of ActionScript that involves using numbers.

## Boolean **Data Type**

The next data type we'll discuss is Boolean. Boolean data types are logical answers in the form of true or false. Also notice that these words cannot be used as variable names or identifiers in ActionScript because they are strictly Boolean data types. Let's take a look at a use of Boolean:

```
var alarm:Boolean = true;
if (alarm == true) {
     trace ("Wake me up!");
}else{
     trace ("Let me sleep in.");
}
// output: Wake me up!
```

Because alarm is set to true, the if statement is true and traces the appropriate message. If the alarm had been set to false, the else statement would have taken effect.

The Boolean data type can be used in many ways, and we'll examine it in more detail in Chapter 10.

## Null **Data Type**

The null data type is a representation that a variable has no data or definable data (string, number, boolean, and so on). Null will not show up in the Output window unless assigned in the code.

> **TIP**
>
> Null must be assigned manually; the interpreter will not assign it.

Because null is a representation of no data, it is only equal to itself and the undefined data type. Here's an example:

```
if (null == undefined) {
     trace ("no data equals no data");
}
// output: no data equals no data
```

## Undefined Data Type

Much like null, undefined represents the absence of data. However, unlike null, undefined can be assigned in several ways:

- It can be manually assigned in the Actions panel.

- The interpreter will assign it if a variable does not exist.

- The interpreter will assign it if a variable has no value.

Let's take a look at the `undefined` data type in action.

```
var myTitle;
trace (typeof(myTitle));
// output: undefined
```

Like `null`, because `undefined` represents the absence of data, it is only equal to itself and `null`.

## Array Data Type

Arrays are used to hold lists of data and sometimes even lists of lists. Here's an example of an array:

```
var myArray:Array = new Array("David","Mike","Bart");
```

For more on arrays, see Chapter 13.

## Variables

Now that we have covered data, let's take a look at what holds this data—variables.

Data without variables only lives for a second; once the interpreter has passed it, its lifespan is over. Variables are like Tupperware: They can hold data for long periods of time, and whenever you want that data, you just go to the variable and it's still there. A variable can hold any type of data, including strings, numbers, Boolean values, and even other variables.

A downside to variables is that they can only hold one piece of data. Arrays, on the other hand, can hold multiple pieces of data (see Chapter 13 for more information).

### Making a Variable

A variable can be created in several different ways. Let's start with the easiest method, which is the one we will be using most often. You simply use the keyword var to start the process, name the variable, and finally assign it a type. You close the line with a semicolon so that the interpreter knows the line has finished. Here's an example:

```
var myVariable:String;
```

That's easy enough. Now let's do the same thing, but this time assign it some data:

```
var myVariable:String = "Unleashed";
//we set myVariable to the string literal "Unleashed"
```

Although it is possible to create variables without setting the data type, it is good practice to assign the data type when the variable is created. Also, after you declare the data type, you cannot change the type of data being held within the variable without receiving an error.

You do not actually need the keyword var to declare a variable (although the code is easier to follow when you're looking through it, and you cannot declare a data type without the keyword var); the interpreter will recognize that a variable has been declared when data is assigned. Here's an example:

```
myVariable = "Unleashed";
//we still declared a variable, but without the keyword var
```

Another way to declare a variable is by using the set identifier. In the parentheses, you declare the variable's name with a string literal and then set its value after a comma:

```
set ( "myVariable", 6 );
trace (myVariable);
// output: 6
```

We have looked at assigning variables with single pieces of data; now let's look at one assigned with an expression:

```
var myVariable:Number = 2+4;
trace (myVariable);
// output: 6
```

This time, we are going to assign a variable to another variable:

```
var myVariable:String = "Unleashed";
var variable2:String = myVariable;
trace (variable2);
// output: Unleashed
```

You can create multiple variables with the same data using equality marks to separate them, as shown here:

```
var myVariable = variable2 = variable3 = "Unleashed";
trace (myVariable);
trace (variable2);
trace (variable3);
// output: Unleashed
```

6

```
//        Unleashed
//        Unleashed
```

Even though each variable has the same value, the last two variables are not bound by the data type, and can be changed without an error popping up, but it is good practice to not change the data type of variables during runtime.

You can even assign a variable to an expression using other variables:

```
var myVariable:Number = 4;
var myVariable2:Number = 2;
var addedVariables:Number = myVariable + myVariable2;
trace (addedVariables);
// output: 6
```

## Changing Data in Variables

Now that you have seen how to create variables and add data to them, let's see how to change the data in them.

The process is as simple as reassigning data to the variables:

```
var myVariable:String = "Unleashed";
trace (myVariable);
myVariable = "Flash";
trace (myVariable);
// output: Unleashed
//         Flash
```

Another way to change a variable is to add to it. Here's an example:

```
var myVariable:String = "Flash";
trace (myVariable);
myVariable = myVariable + " Unleashed";
trace (myVariable);
// output: Flash
//         Flash Unleashed
```

Here, all we did was set the variable equal to itself plus another string. There is an easier way of doing this—by using an assignment operator, called the **addition assignment operator** (+=).

We'll use the same code as before but replace the long, written method of adding additional text with this new way:

```
var myVariable:String = "Flash";
trace (myVariable);
```

```
myVariable +=  " Unleashed";
trace (myVariable);
// output: Flash
//         Flash Unleashed
```

Now let's look at another variable that uses an incremental operator to increase its value.

## Incrementing and Decrementing Variables

As you have just seen, you can add to already created arrays. Now let's look at how to do it with numbers.

First, create a new Flash document, and then open the Actions panel on the first frame of the main timeline and place the following code in it:

```
//let's create our variable
var i:Number = 0;
//this event will continue to run
 this.onEnterFrame=function(){
//let's increase our variable one at a time
   i = i + 1;
   trace (i);
}
// output: (it will start with 1, and increase by 1 constantly)
```

That was the old way of adding to variables; now let's do it the new way:

```
//let's create our variable
var i:Number = 0;
//this event will continue to run
this.onEnterFrame=function(){
//let's increase our variable one at a time
   i += 1;
   trace (i);
}
// output: (it will start with 1, and increase by 1 constantly)
```

That looks better, but there's still an easier way to increase a variable by one each time, and that's by using the increment operator (++):

```
//let's create our variable
var i:Number = 0;
//this event will continue to run
this.onEnterFrame=function(){
//let's increase our variable one at a time
    i++;
```

6

```
    trace (i);
}
// output: (it will start with 1, and increase by 1 constantly)
```

That was great! However, if we want to increase our variable by more than one at a time, we'll have to go back to the addition assignment operator because the increment operator only increases at a rate of one at a time.

Now that we have these numbers, let's make them move a movie clip to the right. So now create a small circle on the left of the stage and convert it to a movie clip symbol, and then give it an instance name of `circle_mc`, and finally, make this change to the actions:

```
//let's create our variable
var i:Number = 0;
//this event will continue to run
this.onEnterFrame=function(){
//let's increase our variable one at a time
    i = i + 1;
    circle_mc._x = i;
}
// output: (it will start with 1, and increase by 1 constantly)
```

Now when you test the movie, the little circle will move to the right one pixel at a time.

Technically, you could have written the preceding code like this:

```
this.onEnterFrame=function(){
        circle_mc._x++;
}
```

We've covered increment variables, so now let's review decrement variables. These variables are the exact opposite of increment variables because they take away one at a time.

Let's look at our previous code with the circle move clip. Using the same code, replace instances of ++ with --, which will cause the variable to decrease:

```
//let's create our variable
var i:Number = 0;
//this event will continue to run
this.onEnterFrame=function(){
//let's increase our variable one at a time
    i--;
    circle_mc._x = i;
}
```

Now the circle moves to the left one pixel at a time.

## Empty Variables

As you know from previous sections, an empty variable has a value of `undefined`. We can use this to test whether a variable is being used. We use an `if` statement to test whether a variable is equal to `undefined`; if it is, the variable needs to be filled. Let's take a look at an example:

```
var title:String;
if (title == undefined) {
      trace ("This variable is empty");
}else{
      trace ("This variable has information in it");
}
// output: This variable is empty
```

Because the variable we created has yet to be assigned any data, it is automatically valued as `undefined` and the `if` statement value is `true`.

## Comparing Variables

Often, when using variables, you'll want to compare one against another (for password verification, memory games, and high score validation, for example).

When you're comparing variables, it's important that they are the same data type. Keep that in mind until we get to the next section.

Let's start with a password-verification example. We'll use a predefined password and a user input password and compare them. If they are equal, we'll run some specific code; if they are not equal, we'll run different code. Here are the steps to follow:

1. Start a new file by going to File, New and then choosing Flash Document.

2. Create two more layers on the main timeline and label the layers Actions, Input, and Validate, respectively top to bottom.

3. Now create a movie clip symbol called "validate" that has a rectangle in it with the text "Validate" over top of it. Place this movie on the Validate layer of the main timeline and label its instance name `validate_mc`.

4. In the Input layer, choose the Text tool and draw a text box. Change the type to Input Text and choose Show Border Around Text so you can easily see the text box when we test the movie. Then choose Password for the line type instead of Single Line (this will place asterisks instead of characters in the text box). Then give the text field an instance name of `password_txt`. The settings should look like Figure 9.2.

5. Now for the actions. In the first keyframe of the Actions layer, place this code:

```
//We first create the password
var password:String ="flash";
```

```
//Now we set the button actions for the validate movie
validate_mc.onRelease = function (){
//this will check to see if the password and the input match
    if(password_txt.text == password){
        trace("You may enter");
    }else{
        trace("You do not have clearance");
//This clears the input field
        input="";
    }
}
```

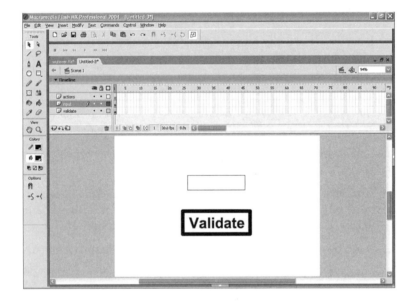

**FIGURE 9.2**    The stage for the validate example.

When you test the movie, note that if you enter the correct password, it issues a welcome message in the Output window; otherwise, the Output window displays a different message and clears the user input field.

As another example of using variables, let's try to determine whether a new score is the high score.

Create a new file as before in previous examples (PC–Ctrl+N, Mac–Open Apple+N) and put the following code in the first frame of the main timeline:

```
//first create the current high score
var highScore:Number = 1200;
```

```
//then create a new score to rival the high score
var newScore:Number = 1300;
//now create the if statement that will determine and adjust the high score
if (newScore > highScore){
    highScore = newScore;
    trace ("congratulations, the new high score is " + highScore);
}else if (newScore == highScore) {
    trace ("You are now tied for 1st at " + highScore);
}else{
    trace ("Your score of " + newScore + " was not good enough");
}
// output: congratulations, the new high score is 1300
```

Test the movie. Then go back and change the variables to see different results.

## Combining Types of Values in Variables

You may have noticed in the preceding high-score example that we were adding two different types of values into one statement. So, what does that make the value of the statement? That depends on what was combined and how. Because in the preceding example we added a string with text in it to a number, the interpreter automatically converted the entire thing to a string.

Now let's take a look at using the typeof function to check the value of a given variable:

```
var name:String = "Kevin ";
var age:Number = 35;
var combined:String = name + age;
trace (typeof(combined));
// output: string
```

Let's suppose we have two variables (one a number and the other a string containing numbers):

```
var year:String = "1967"
var age:Number = 35;
var combined:String = year + age;
trace (typeof(combined));
// output: string
```

This still comes back as string. However, if we subtract them, the result changes, as shown here:

```
var year:String = "1967"
var age:Number = 35;
```

```
var combined:Number = year - age;
trace (typeof(combined));
// output: number
```

When the variables are subtracted, the interpreter converts the combination to a number.

Although the conversion has taken place in the combined variable, it has not affected the original values. Automatic conversion only works when evaluating an expression.

When using a Boolean in an expression involving a number, the conversion will always be to a number, as shown here:

```
var answer:Boolean = true;
var age:Number = 35;
var combined:Number = answer + age;
trace (typeof(combined));
// output: number
```

The same goes for a Boolean and a string. Both data types will always convert to a string:

```
var answer:Boolean = true;
var age:String = "35";
var combined:String = answer + age;
trace (typeof(combined));
// output: string
```

As far as conversion goes, what does the interpreter convert each element to? To find out, let's take a look at the next few lists.

These rules apply to string conversions:

- A number converts to a string literal equal to that number (for example, 123 to "123").
- A boolean converts to true if true and false if false.
- Undefined converts to undefined.
- Null converts to null.
- NaN converts to NaN.
- An array converts to a list of elements separated by commas.

These guidelines apply to number conversions:

- A string containing numbers converts to a numeric value represented in those numbers.
- A string not containing numbers converts to NaN.

- Undefined converts to NaN.

- Null converts to NaN.

- A Boolean converts to 1 if true and 0 if false.

- NaN converts to NaN.

- An array converts to NaN.

These are the rules for Boolean conversions:

- A string with a length greater than 0 converts to true.

- An empty string converts to false.

- A number converts to true if it's a nonzero number and false if it's zero.

- Undefined converts to false.

- Null converts to false.

- NaN converts to false.

- An array converts to true.

## Converting Variables Using Functions and Methods

Now that you know what values convert to, let's see how to convert them. We will start the conversions by using the toString method. Remember, you are only converting the data type within the variable to another data type, not the variable itself.

### The toString Method

This method acts like any of the previous methods we've discussed. Simply attach it directly to a data type you would like to convert to a string or attach it to a variable you would like to convert. There are no arguments in the parentheses. Here's an example:

```
var age:Number = 35
var myString:String = age.toString();
//Converts the variable age to a string
var myString:String = false.toString();
 //Converts the boolean datatype false to a string
var myString:String = (50).toString();
//Converts the number 50 to a string
// the parentheses are there so as not to
// confuse the interpreter into
//thinking it was a decimal point
```

### The `String` Function

To use the `String` function, simply place the variable or data type you would like to convert in the parentheses, and the function will convert it to a string:

```
var myString:String = String(myVariable);
var myString:String = String(123);
var myString:String = String(null);
// the String function converts all of these datatypes to a string datatype
```

### Using Operators

You have already seen that using a plus sign (+) will convert numbers and variables to a string, as shown here:

```
var myString:String = 500 + "string";
//Converted to a string
var myString:String = myVariable + "";
//Using an empty string to convert variables to a string
```

### The `Number` Function

This function acts nearly identically to the `String` function. Place the variable or data you want to convert in between the parentheses, and the function will convert it to a number:

```
var myNum:Number = Number(myVariable);
//Converts value of myVariable to a number
var myNum:Number = Number("Unleashed");      //Becomes NaN
var myNum:Number = Number("1234");           //Becomes the number 1234
```

This function is great for converting input fields that are string literals.

### The `parseInt` and `parseFloat` Methods

These methods convert strings to numbers much like the `Number` function. However, unlike the `Number` function, these two methods can pull numbers out of text, as long as the first non-space character is a number.

Let's take a look at the `parseInt` function, which is for pulling whole integers (remember from earlier, integers have no decimals or fractional values). Just attach this function as you would any other function and place the variable or string you want to convert in the parentheses:

```
var idNumber:String = "123abc";
trace (parseInt(idNumber));
// output: 123
```

The `parseFloat` function works in much the same manner, but it pulls floating numbers instead of integers:

```
var idNumber:String = "123.487abc";
trace (parseFloat(idNumber));
// output: 123.487
```

If the first non-space character is anything but a numeric value, the function returns NaN:

```
var idNumber:String = "abd123.487";
trace (parseInt(idNumber));
// output: NaN
```

In case you're wondering what happens when you use `parseInt` on a floating number, the following example shows that the function will return everything up to the decimal point:

```
var idNumber = "123.487abc";
trace (parseInt(idNumber));
// output: 123
```

However, if you use the `parseFloat` function on an integer, it will return the same value as the `parseInt` function:

```
var idNumber:String = "123abc";
trace (parseFloat(idNumber));
// output: 123
```

### The `Boolean` Function

Converting to a Boolean is as easy as using the `String` or `Number` function. Place the variable or data type in the parentheses, and the `Boolean` function converts it to a Boolean:

```
var mySample:Boolean = Boolean(myVariable);
//Converts the value of myVariable to Boolean
var mySample:Boolean = Boolean(123);            //Converts to true
var mySample:Boolean = Boolean(0)               //Converts to false
```

## The Scope of a Variable

So far, we have placed variables on the main timeline and in a movie on the main timeline. It's now time for you to learn about the scope of variables and how to overcome the shortcomings of the local scope of variables.

### Timeline Variables

Whenever a variable is created or defined on a timeline, it is available to every frame on that timeline as well as any buttons that have been placed on the stage associated with that timeline.

Any code placed in the object actions of a movie clip instance can access variables on the timeline of that movie, but not the timeline the movie is in. Here's an exercise to make this clear:

1. Start a new file as you did before.

2. On the main timeline, place the following code:

```
var myVariable:String = "Success";
```

In the second frame of the main timeline, place this code:

```
//this will stop the movie from looping
stop();
trace (myVariable);
```

3. Now create a new layer called rectangle and place a rectangle on that layer. Highlight the rectangle and press F8 on your keyboard to convert it to symbol (or select Insert, Convert to Symbol). Then choose Button. And give this button an instance name of myButton_btn.

4. Go back into the actions of the first frame, and place these actions in:

```
myButton_btn.onRelease=function(){
      trace(myVariable);
}
```

You're done, so test it.

You should see the word *Success* pop up in the Output window, and when you click the rectangle button, the variable should appear again (see Figure 9.3).

### Dot Syntax

Dot syntax enables code to see from one timeline to the next, either by direct route with the use of instance names or with special predefined identifiers such as _root and _parent. Just remember that each level must be separated by a dot, hence *dot syntax*.

The _root and _parent identifiers are constants: _root is always the main timeline and will never change (however, you can define the _root of a movie clip using the _lockroot property of a movie clip), but _parent is relative to where you are using it, and it always goes up one level.

Another part of dot syntax involves using the instance names of symbols. For example, if you want to know the horizontal position of myMovie_mc on the main timeline, you would type the following:

```
_root.myMovie_mc._x;
```

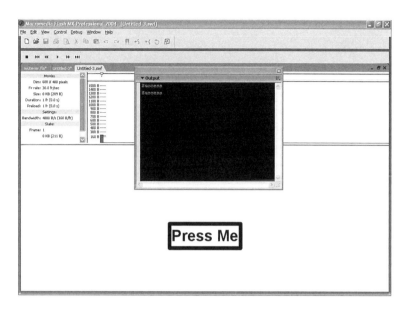

**FIGURE 9.3** A successful implementation of a timeline variable.

If you need to know the value of myVariable in the movie myMovie_mc, which is embedded in theMovie_mc, which in turn is on the main timeline, you would use this:

```
_root.theMovie_mc.myMovie_mc.myVariable
```

### The _root Identifier
The _root identifier represents the main timeline; everything on it can be accessed like so:

```
_root.whatever
```

Let's look at an example of this:

1. In the movie you created earlier, create a movie clip on the main timeline with these actions on its timeline:

```
trace (theVariable);
trace (_root.theVariable);
```

2. On the main timeline in the first frame, place this code:

```
var theVariable:String = "theRoot";
```

Now test the movie again. Here's the output:

```
// output: undefined
//          theRoot
//          Success
```

The movie came back with undefined because the variable could not be found in its local scope, but in the root it found the variable with ease.

### The _parent Identifier
The _parent tag is used in dot syntax to refer to one step up. Parents can be overlapped like this:

```
_parent._parent
```

Now go back into the actions of the movie you created earlier and replace its code with the following:

```
        trace (_parent.theVariable);
```

Now test again:

```
// output: theRoot
//          Success
```

This time, the _parent part of the dot syntax looks up one level and finds the variable.

Although this may seem tedious and difficult to understand, thanks to the _global identifier, many of these problems can be solved.

### The _global Identifier
Introduced back in Flash MX, the _global identifier creates data types that can be seen from all parts of the Flash movie without the use of dot syntax and target pathing.

Just attach the _global identifier to what you would like to make global; then you can access it from anywhere in the Flash movie.

1. Start a new Flash movie. Then on the main timeline, in the first frame, place this code:

```
_global.myVariable = "Omnipotent";
```

2. On the stage, draw a rectangle and convert it to a movie clip symbol (F8) with the symbol name draw1.

3. Convert it again, this time with the symbol name draw2.

4. Convert it for a third time, with the symbol name draw3.

5. Open up your library (PC–Ctrl+L, Mac–Open Apple+L) and go into draw1. In the first frame of the timeline, place the following code:

```
trace (myVariable);
```

Now test the movie:

```
// output: Omnipotent
```

Is that powerful or what? You have just traced a variable on the main timeline from another timeline that is embedded into three separate movies.

If you happen to create a local variable with the same name, only ActionScript attempting to access it locally will be affected; it will not affect the global variable.

### The this Identifier

The this identifier is used to refer to the current timeline, or object it is being placed in. It acts in the same way the understood "you" does in English. To better understand the this identifier, here is an example:

1. Create a new Flash document.

2. Draw a circle about 50×50 on the left side of the stage

3. Convert it to a movie clip with the symbol name circleMC.

4. Back on the stage, give the circle an instance name of circle_mc.

5. Add a new layer called actions and place this code in the first frame of that layer:

```
//this variable is placed on the main timeline
this.myTime = getTimer();
//this event is for a movie clip on the main timeline
circle_mc.onEnterFrame=function(){
    //this variable refers to the timeline of circle_mc
    this._x += 1;
}
```

The this identifier is not necessary in most cases, but it is good practice to use it to make it easy when going back over code to see which timeline or object it is referring to.

## An Applied Example

You have learned a lot of fun stuff in this chapter (and some not-so-fun stuff). Let's end with an easily applied example of how to use variables. Follow these steps:

1. Start a new Flash movie and make its dimensions 400×400 in the stage properties.

2. Now draw a circle on the main stage, but not too big—about 50×50 should do. Convert this circle to a movie clip symbol. Then give it an instance name of circle_mc.

3. Create a new layer called `actions`, open the Actions panel in the first frame of that layer, and then put these actions in:

```
//create all our variables
var friction:Number = .5;
var pointX:Number = Math.round(Math.random()*400)
var pointY:Number = Math.round(Math.random()*400);
//create the event
this.onEnterFrame=function(){
//set our if statements to move at different speeds
//based on distance, and to pick a new spot once the
//designated spot has been reached
    if (Math.round(circle_mc._x) != pointX){
        circle_mc._x+=(pointX-circle_mc._x)*friction;
    }else if (Math.round(circle_mc._x) == pointX){
        pointX = Math.round(Math.random()*400);
    }
    if (Math.round(circle_mc._y) != pointY) {
        circle_mc._y+=(pointY-circle_mc._y)*friction;
    }else if (Math.round(circle_mc._y) == pointY){
        pointY = Math.round(Math.random()*400);
    }
}
```

Now test the movie.

In this example, the `if` statements are saying that if the object is not at its designated spot yet, adjust its position based on the distance it is from the designated spot. Then, once it has reached the spot, pick a new spot and keep moving the circle.

Note that you can adjust the friction to achieve some interesting effects.

## Summary

This chapter covered all the basics of the major data types and variables. Remember that variables are used as containers for data, and when creating them, even if they are left empty, it is good practice to give them a data type.

Also, use caution when changing the data type of variables. It is better to create a separate variable to hold the value as a different data type than to keep swapping the data type throughout your code.

In the next chapter, you will begin to use conditionals and loop statements to better understand the flow of ActionScript in Flash.

CHAPTER **10**

# Statements and Expressions

This chapter covers statements and expressions. Even though we have not formally gone over statements, you have already used them. A **statement** is simply a small piece of code made up of keywords, operators, and identifiers. Statements can belong to one of six different categories:

• **Declaration statements**. These statements involve declaring variables, creating functions, setting properties, declaring arrays, and so on. Here's an example:

```
var myVariable:String;                 // declares a
➡variable
myObject._x = 235;        //sets the horizontal position
var myArray:Array = new Array ();  //creating an array
function myFunction (){          //creates a function
```

• **Expressions**. These include any type of legal expression. Here's an example:

```
i++;                         //increase a variable
lName + space + fName;    //combining variables
```

• **Flow modifiers**. These include any statement that disrupts the natural flow of the interpreter reading the ActionScript. There are two subtypes of flow modifiers: conditional statements and loop statements.

Conditional statements use Boolean answers to determine what to do next or what *not* to do next. Here's an example:

```
if (inputName == userName){
     if (inputPassword == password){
```

```
        gotoAndPlay("startPage");
   }else {
            displayMessage = "Double check your password";
      }
  }else if (inputName != userName){
     if (inputPassword == password){
            displayMessage = "Double check your user name";
     }
  }else{
      displayMessage = "Double check your all your information";
  }
```

Loop statements run until a defined condition has been met. Here's an example:

```
for (var i:Number=0; i<30; i++) {
    trace (i);
}
```

- **Predefined functions**. ActionScript provides some functions that are predefined for you. Here's an example:

```
trace ("function");          //a simple trace function
gotoAndStop (2);             //a playback function
getProperty ( myMovie, _x );  //gets the horizontal position
```

- **Object statements**. These are statements that deal with and manipulate objects. Here's an example:

```
var myGrades:Object = { tests: 85, quizzes: 88, homework: 72 };
for (name in myGrades) {
    trace ("myGrades." + name + " = " + myGrades[name]);
}
//output: myGrades.tests = 85
//         myGrades.quizzes = 88
//         myGrades.homework = 72
```

- **Comments**. This last category is one of a kind. It includes comments used in code merely as information for the user while in the Actions panel; the interpreter will skip over these comments. Here's an example:

```
//this is a comment used in ActionScript;
```

Breaking up statements into these simple categories is only to help you understand the different types and uses of statements. We will go over a few of these categories in more detail later in this chapter.

Now, let's look at some of the basics of building these statements.

# Statement Syntax

As you've seen, statements are keywords, operators, and identifiers joined together to accomplish certain tasks. For instance, in the following code, `var` and `new` are the keywords, `Array ()` is the identifier, `Array` is the data type, which follows a colon (:) separating it from the variable name, and the equal sign is the operator:

```
var myArray:Array = new Array();
```

As you'll notice, a semicolon has been placed at the end of this statement. This semicolon tells the interpreter that the statement is complete and to move to the next one. The semicolon is not required, and the interpreter will move on without it. However, it is good coding etiquette to place one there.

Also, it is good etiquette to place each new statement on its own line. Again, this is not necessary, but it is a good practice to follow. However, if you do not use semicolons, each statement must appear on its own line or the interpreter will not be able to read it. You can see for yourself the benefits of having each statement on its own line by examining the following two segments of code. Which code section is easier to read?

```
var myVariable:String = "Flash";
myVariable += " Unleashed";
trace (myVariable);
//output: Flash Unleashed


myVariable = "Flash"; myVariable += " Unleashed"; trace (myVariable);
//output: Flash Unleashed
```

Although the output is the same, the first section of code is much easier to read than the second. Note the spacing between each part of the statement. Often this is a necessity for the interpreter to correctly identify each part. However, even if this spacing is not always required, it is *always* a good rule to follow.

## Statement Block

Some statements have multiple statements associated with them, particularly **flow modifiers**. These statements have statements within them that appear between brackets. Let's take a look at an example:

```
if (book == "Flash Unleashed") {
    trace ("You're on the right track");
}
```

The first statement is an `if` statement (if statements are discussed in greater detail later in this chapter) that contains a function statement. Notice that not only is the `trace` function held between brackets, but it is indented as well. This indentation is not a

10

requirement but is used for improved readability. You can, however, turn on the option to have statements indent automatically: Choose Auto Format under the ActionScript preferences or press Ctrl+Shift+F. You can even adjust the settings of the automatic formatting under Auto Format preferences.

Also, note that the lines with curly brackets do not have semicolons. You can put semicolons after closing curly brackets, but it is not necessary. What's more, the closing bracket is aligned with the beginning of the line that the opening bracket is on. Again, this is not a requirement; the brackets are just placed this way for ease of readability.

The closing bracket is required if an opening bracket is used; otherwise, the interpreter will send an error message like this one:

```
Statement block must be terminated by '}'
```

Even though the earlier code is in brackets, because only one statement is held within the `if` statement, the use of brackets is not required. Instead, the code can be written like this:

```
if (book == "Flash Unleashed") trace ("You're on the right track");
```

As a personal preference, I use brackets in conditional statements, even if they are not required, just for consistency.

Another type of statement that uses brackets is a user-defined function. Here's an example:

```
function myFunction (myVariable:String){
      trace (myVariable);
}
var name:String = "David";
myFunction (name);
//output: David
```

Again, the statement held within the function appears between brackets and is also indented for easy reading and consistency.

Now that we have gone over some of the basic syntax of statements, let's cover some of the statement categories in more detail.

## Object Statements

This section covers a couple of the statements associated directly with objects (which were discussed in Chapter 8, "Welcome to ActionScript 2.0"). These include the `with` statement and the `for in` statement.

### The `with` Statement

The `with` statement is for controlling multiple properties or methods of an object without the hassle of typing the object over and over again. Just place the object's name in the parentheses, and the properties and methods listed between the brackets are those affected for that object. Here's an example:

```
//first create an object
var myObject:Object = new Object();
with (myObject){
    //set 2 properties
      height = 50;
      width = 100;
    //call a method
      setName("Ben");
}
```

Another use of the with statement involves associating it with a movie clip and using some of the drawing API features available in Flash.

In this example, we will create an empty movie clip on the main stage. Then, using the onEnterFrame event, we will make it possible for a line to be drawn wherever the mouse goes. We will also use a simple Math.random() method to make the line change color constantly to add a little style.

```
//create the empty movie clip
this.createEmptyMovieClip("line_mc",1);
//now the event that will allow a line to follow the mouse
line_mc.onEnterFrame=function(){
    with(line_mc){
        lineStyle(5,Math.random()*0x10000000,100);
        lineTo(_xmouse,_ymouse);
    }
}
```

As you can see, using with allows you to associate the drawing actions with a single movie at once, instead of having to associate each action individually, like this:

```
//create the empty movie clip
this.createEmptyMovieClip("line_mc",1);
//now the event that will allow a line to follow the mouse
line_mc.onEnterFrame=function(){
    line_mc.lineStyle(5,Math.random()*0x10000000,100);
    line_mc.lineTo(_xmouse,_ymouse);
}
```

As you have seen, the with statement can be very powerful, especially if it's used in conjunction with a function, as in this example:

```
function myFunction (myMovie:MovieClip){
     with (myMovie){
          _x=50;
          _y=20;
          trace (myMovie._name);
     }
}
```

Now, all you have to do is call the function with any movie clip and all the properties and functions associated with the with statement will be applied to that clip.

## The for in Statement

The for in statement is an advanced loop statement that's associated directly with objects. Unlike other loop statements, which run based on a defined condition, the for in statement runs until all properties of the assigned object are evaluated.

The syntax for this statement can be difficult, so it's important that you read this section carefully. Start with the for keyword; then add an opening parenthesis and the keyword var. Following that, name the variable that will hold each property for the object; then add the keyword in. Next, place the name of the object you are using followed by a closing parenthesis and an opening bracket. Between the brackets is where you'll place the code that will use the properties of the object. Let's take a look at a generic template:

```
for (var myProp in myObject){
     //the code to use the properties;
}
```

This seems simple enough, so now let's go over how to use the properties. There are two types of property calls: One calls the property's name, and the other calls the property's value.

The first type of property call simply uses the variable you created to hold the properties. An example will help make this clearer.

First, let's create an object we can use for the rest of the exercise; then we'll use the for in statement to call each property's name in this object:

```
var contact:Object = new Object();
contact.name = "David";
contact.age = 23;
contact.state = "VA";
for (var myProp in contact){
     trace (myProp);
}
//output: state
```

```
//       age
//       name
```

In the preceding example, we traced the variable we created to hold each property in our object. As you'll notice, it does not start at the beginning but rather at the end, and it moves toward the beginning.

Now that you know how to pull the names of the properties, let's go over how to pull the values of each property. To get the value of each property, use the object's name (in this case, contact) and connect it to the variable we created inside of the brackets. Here is the example:

```
var contact:Object = new Object();
contact.name = "David";
contact.age = 23;
contact.state = "VA";
for (var myProp in contact){
    trace (contact[myProp]);
}
//output: VA
//       23
//       David
```

You know how to get the names of the properties, and you just saw how to get the values. Now let's combine the two:

```
var space:String = " "
var contact:Object = new Object();
contact.name = "David";
contact.age = 23;
contact.state = "VA";
for (var myProp in contact){
    trace (myProp + ":" + space + contact[myProp]);
}
//output: state: VA
//       age: 23
//       name: David
```

Let's not stop there; let's take a big step forward and set the for in statement to a function. Then we'll place all the properties of the object in an array with named elements (see Chapter 13, "Arrays," for more on arrays):

```
var contact:Object = new Object();
contact.name = "David";
contact.age = 23;
```

10

```
contact.state = "VA";
var myArray:Array = new Array();
function makeArray (myObject:Object){
     for (var myProp in myObject){
          myArray[myProp] = myObject[myProp];
     }
}
makeArray(contact);
trace (myArray.name);
//output: David
```

While we are on the subject of arrays, note that you can also pull each element out of an array using the for in statement, as if it were a property of an object. Here's an example:

```
var myArray:Array = new Array ("David",23,"VA");
var space:String = " ";
for (var element in myArray){
     trace (element + ":" + space + myArray[element]);
}
//output: 2: VA
//        1: 23
//        0: David
```

The for in statement also works on named array elements, as you can see here:

```
var myArray:Array = new Array ("David",23,"VA");
myArray.city = "Richmond";
var space:String = " ";
for (var element in myArray){
     trace (element + ":" + space + myArray[element]);
}
//output: city: Richmond
//          2: VA
//          1: 23
//          0: David
```

Now that we have discussed object statements, let's move on to flow modifiers.

## Flow Modifiers

So far, we have gone over ActionScript as a language that executes code, one line after another, without stopping. Now we are going to go over some statements that redefine how ActionScript functions.

Flow modifiers are statements that adjust the natural order the interpreter takes when reading ActionScript. When the interpreter hits a flow modifier, it doesn't just run the statement and move on. Instead, it runs the statement to see whether a condition has been met. If the condition hasn't been met, sometimes the interpreter will move on, but other times it will stay at that spot until the condition has been met. In most cases, this condition is user-defined.

The first category of the flow modifiers we'll cover is the conditional statement.

## Conditional Statements

Conditional statements are statements that are executed only when their conditions have been met. These conditions are based on Boolean values (either `true` or `false`). Here's an example of how a conditional statement acts:

```
if (true){
    //do something;
}
```

You'll often use conditional statements in situations where you want to test whether to run certain code. Without these conditional statements, every piece of ActionScript you place in the Actions panel would run without being checked for whether it is necessary or even correct.

An example would be in a game; after the user has finished, the ActionScript checks whether this user's score is higher than the present high score. If it is, the user's score becomes the new high score. However, if the user's score is not higher than the present high score, the new score will not replace the present one.

The code for this might look something like the following:

```
if (userScore > highScore) {
    highScore = userScore;
}
```

Everything between the parentheses is the **condition**, and the symbol between the two variables is the **comparison operator**. Before going on with more examples of conditional statements, we should go over each of the comparison operators and their uses.

## Comparison Operators

Everything between the parentheses in a conditional statement is the condition, and the comparison operator is the type of condition. This operator tells the conditional statement how to evaluate the data in the condition. Here's a list of the comparison operators:

- Equality (==)
- Inequality (!=)

- Less than (<)

- Less than or equal to (<=)

- Greater than (>)

- Greater than or equal to (>=)

- Strict equality (===)

- Strict inequality (!==)

### Equality Operator (==)
This operator determines whether two pieces of data are equal to one another. Here are some examples:

```
var title:String = "Unleashed";        //creates our variable

if (title == "Unleashed"){         //evaluates to true

if (title == "Not Unleashed"){     //evaluates to false
```

### Inequality Operator (!=)
This operator determines whether two pieces of data are *not* equal (note the exclamation point before the equal sign). Here are three examples:

```
var title:String = "Unleashed";        //creates our variable

if (title != "Unleashed"){         //evaluates to false

if (title != "Not Unleashed"){     //evaluates to true
```

### Less Than Operator (<)
This operator determines whether the variable on the left has a lower value than the variable on the right. Here are three examples:

```
var myAge:Number = 23;
var yourAge:Number = 24;
var myName:String = "David";
var yourName:String = "Jen";    //creates all the variables we need
if (yourAge < myAge){          //evaluates to false

if (myName < yourName){        //evaluates to true
```

> **NOTE**
>
> Keep in mind that strings are evaluated based on their ASCII code point, not the letter itself. Therefore the upper- and lowercase versions of the same letter will not be equal to each other.

### Less Than or Equal To Operator (<=)

This operator evaluates whether the data on the left is less than the data on the right. If this is true, or if they are equal, the condition will evaluate to true. Here are a few more examples:

```
var myAge:Number = 23;
var yourAge:Number = 23;
var myName:String = "David";        //creates all the variables we need


if (myAge <= yourAge){        //evaluates to true


if ("David" <= myName){        //evaluates to true
```

### Greater than Operator (>)

This operator determines whether the data on the left is greater than the data on the right. Here are three examples:

```
var myAge:Number = 23;
var yourAge = 22;
var myName = "David";
var yourName = "Ann";      //creates all the variables we need


if (myAge > yourAge){        //evaluates to true


if (yourName > myName){        //evaluates to false
```

### Greater than or Equal to Operator (>=)

If the data on the left side of this operator is greater than or equal to the data on the right side, the condition will evaluate to true. Here are three examples:

```
var myAge:Number = 22;
var yourAge:Number = 24;
var myName:String = "David";          //creates all the variables we need


if (myAge >= yourAge){        //evaluates to false


if ("David" >= myName){        //evaluates to true
```

### Strict Equality (===)

This operator not only determines whether the values are equal but also whether they are the same type of value. Notice the triple equal sign, as opposed to the double equal sign for the regular equality operator. Here are four examples:

```
if (5 == 5){       //evaluates to true

if (5 == "5"){     //evaluates to true

if (5 === 5){      //evaluates to true

if (5 === "5"){    //evaluates to false
```

Notice that with an equality sign, the string value `"5"` is evaluated as being equal to the number 5, but with strict equality, they are not equal.

### Strict Inequality (!==)

This operator not only determines whether the values are not equal but also determines whether the values are not the same type (note the exclamation point in front of the double equal signs). Here are four examples:

```
if (5 != 5){       //evaluates to false

if (5 != "5"){     //evaluates to false

if (5 !== 5){      //evaluates to false

if (5 !== "5"){    //evaluates to true
```

Strict equality and strict inequality are very useful, not only for determining whether two values are the same but also whether they are being used the same way.

Now that we have gone over the comparison operators, let's get back into the conditional statements, starting with the `if` statement.

## The `if` Statement

You have been using the `if` statement for some time without a formal introduction, so let's start with the basics of how this statement works.

The `if` statement works like a simple "yes or no" questionnaire: If the condition specified in the `if` statement evaluates to `true`, run the code in the curly brackets; if it evaluates to `false`, skip the code in the curly brackets and move on.

The `if` statement starts out with the keyword `if` and is followed by a condition, which is any comparison expression held within parentheses. This is followed by an opening curly bracket, which is followed by all the actions that ActionScript is to run if the condition evaluates to true. Finally, a closing curly bracket finishes the statement.

The simplest of if statements involves actually placing a Boolean value right into the condition, as shown here:

```
if (true){
      trace ("True");
}
if(false){
      trace ("False");
}
//output: True
```

In this case, only "True" will be traced, because that is the only condition that comes back true. The statements within the condition that was set to false are skipped after the condition is evaluated.

You can also use the numeric equivalent to the Boolean representation to accomplish the same effect:

```
if (1){
      trace ("True");
}
if(0){
      trace ("False");
}
//output: True
```

Again, only "True" is traced because 0 is equal to the Boolean value false. This is a good tool for evaluating numbers because any non-zero number will be considered true. Here's an example:

```
var myScore:Number = 80;
var previousScore:Number = 86;
if (myScore-previousScore){
      trace ("Something's changed");
}
//output: Something's changed
```

You can also use variables in if statements that hold values that translate to Boolean values or are Boolean values themselves:

```
var myVariable:Number = 1;
if (myVariable){
      trace ("True");
```

10

```
}
//output: True
```

Another great feature of the `if` statement is that it can check whether a movie clip instance exists. Simply place the name of the instance in the condition, and if this instance exists, the `if` statement will evaluate to `true`; otherwise, it will evaluate to `false`.

Let's look at an example of this. First, create a shape on the main stage and then convert it to a symbol by selecting Insert, Convert to Symbol (F8). Then, name the instance `myMovie_mc`.

Next, create a new layer and call the layer **actions**.

Then place the following code in the first frame on the main timeline in the actions layer:

```
if (myMovie_mc){
     trace ("myMovie_mc exists");
}
//output: myMovie_mc exists
```

This is great, but if we want to check for a certain movie on the go, we set it to a function, as shown here:

```
function findMovie (movie:MovieClip){
     if (movie){
          trace (movie +" exists");
     }
}
findMovie(myMovie_mc);
```

Now whenever the movie exists on the same timeline as the function, when the function is invoked with the proper name, the phrase will be displayed in the Output window.

You can also test a single variable to see whether it is "not true" in a conditional statement using the logical NOT operator.

### The Logical NOT Operator (!)

The logical NOT operator is used to show inequality or to test whether something is false. Place an exclamation point in front of the variable or expression you want to evaluate as "not true," as shown here:

```
var myVariable:Boolean = false;
if (!myVariable) {
     trace ("myVariable is false");
}
//output: myVariable is false
```

This, when used in conjunction with the function we just created, can determine whether there is no instance of a specific movie on the stage:

```
function findMovie (movie:MovieClip){
    if (!movie){
        trace ("the movie does not exist");
    }
    }
findMovie(myMovie_mc);
```

The function we created determines whether the movie does not exist, and if it doesn't, the trace function is run.

Now that you've seen the basic workings of the if statement, we'll cover nested if statements.

### Nested if Statements

Nested if statements are if statements held by other if statements to check more than one condition. You simply put the nested statement in as if it were a regular statement held within the original if statement. Here's an example:

```
var bookTitle:String = "Unleashed";
var name:String = "David";
if (bookTitle == "Unleashed"){
    if (name == "David"){
        trace ("They both match");
    }
}
//output: They both match
```

If the nested if statement evaluates to false, even with the original if statement evaluating to true, the trace function will not be run. Here's an example:

```
var bookTitle:String = "Unleashed";
var name:String = "David";
if (bookTitle == "Unleashed"){
    if (name == "Kevin"){
        trace ("They both match");
    }
}
//output: (nothing)
```

If the original if statement evaluates to false, the nested if statement will not even be evaluated. Again, the trace function will not be run. Here's an example:

10

```
var bookTitle:String = "Unleashed";
var name:String = "David";
if (bookTitle == "Flash"){
    if (name == "David"){
        trace ("They both match");
    }
}
//output: (nothing)
```

Now that you have seen how to evaluate multiple conditional statements using nested `if` statements, let's do the same thing the easy way, using a logical operator.

### The AND Operator (&&)

In the condition part of an `if` statement, you can place multiple conditions using the short-circuit AND operator. After the first condition, place a space, followed by two ampersands (&&) and then the second condition. Let's look at our previous example using this operator:

```
var bookTitle:String = "Unleashed";
var name:String = "David";
if (bookTitle == "Unleashed" && name == "David"){
    trace ("They both match");
}
//output: They both match
```

As with nested `if` statements, both conditions must evaluate to `true` in order for the entire condition to evaluate to `true`. Here's an example:

```
var bookTitle:String = "Unleashed";
var name:String = "David";
if (bookTitle == "Flash" && name == "David"){
    trace ("They both match");
}
//output: (nothing)
```

Notice how the previous example does not send the message to the Output panel. Even though the second condition would evaluate to `true`, it was never evaluated because the first condition evaluates to `false`.

You can place many of these operators in a single conditional statement for checking multiple conditions, as shown here:

```
var bookTitle:String = "Unleashed";
var name:String = "David";
var age:Number = 23;
```

```
if (bookTitle == "Unleashed" && name == "David" &&  age >= 10){
     trace ("Everything is working");
}
//output: Everything is working
```

> **NOTE**
>
> Although you can see the benefits of using the AND operator (&&) as far as readability versus using nested if statements, there is a benefit to using nested if statements sometimes. When using a nested if statement to check multiple conditionals at once, you can actually have code run from the first condition independent of the results of the second condition; however, with the AND operator, both conditions must be met.

Now that you know how to check multiple conditions to see whether each is true, let's see whether any of the conditions are true using another logical operator.

### The OR Operator (||)

Often you'll want to see whether any one of a set of conditions is correct. To do this without the logical OR operator requires multiple if statements with the same response over and over again, if any of the conditional statements are met. Let's take a look at what this would look like:

```
var name:String = "David";
var age:Number = 23;
if (name == "David"){
     trace ("One of them is correct");
}
if (age == 33) {
     trace ("One of them is correct");
}
//output: One of them is correct
```

Because the first conditional statement evaluates to true, the trace function is run. But what if both the if statements evaluate to true?

```
var name:String = "David";
var age:Number = 23;
if (name == "David"){
     trace ("One of them is correct");
}
if (age == 23) {
     trace ("One of them is correct");
}
//output: One of them is correct
//        One of them is correct
```

The problem we encounter using multiple `if` statements to determine whether one of them evaluates to `true` is that if they are both correct, both sections of code are executed, thus creating duplication. We could overcome this by using a test variable to hold a value if the first conditional statement is met. Instead, however, we are going to use the logical OR operator. The syntax of this operator is || (Shift+\). Place this operator between conditions in the condition statement, separating them with a space on both sides. Let's take a look at this using our previous example:

```
var name:String = "David";
var age:Number = 23;
if (name == "David" || age == 23){
      trace ("One of them is correct");
}
//output: One of them is correct
```

Now the interpreter reads the statement and checks to see whether the first condition is met. If so, it skips the second condition because of the OR operator and runs the `trace` function. If the first condition is not met, the interpreter evaluates the second condition, and if this condition is met, the `trace` function is run. If neither condition is met, the interpreter simply moves on.

With the OR operator, you can check to see whether any one of multiple conditions will be met. Here's an example:

```
var name:String = "David";
var age:Number = 23;
if (name == "Kevin" || age == 33 || true){
      trace ("One of them is correct");
}
//output: One of them is correct
```

Because neither of the first two conditions evaluates to `true`, the third condition is evaluated to `true` and the `trace` function is run.

Another type of conditional statement is known as the **conditional**. We'll cover this type of conditional statement before moving on because it acts very similar to an `if` statement.

### The Conditional (?:)
The conditional is more of an expression than a conditional statement, although it does have a conditional statement in it.

The syntax is a condition followed by a question mark, a value (which we'll call *value 1*), a colon, and then another value (which we'll call *value 2*). It looks like this:

```
(condition) ? value 1 : value 2;
```

If the condition evaluates to true, the expression's value is equal to *value 1*. If the condition does not evaluate to true, the expression's value is equal to *value 2*.

This is nice if you want to run a simple conditional statement without typing a lot. Here's an example:

```
var myVariable:Number = 1;
var myVariable2:Number = 2;
var myVariable3 = (myVariable < myVariable2) ? myVariable : myvariable2;
trace (myVariable3);
//output: 1
```

Let's look at another applied example:

```
var myPassword:String = "flash";
var userPassword:String = "flash";
trace ((myPassword == userPassword) ? "Correct": "Incorrect");
//output: Correct
```

As you'll notice, the previous conditional statement not only does something if the condition evaluates to true but also if it does not evaluate to true. We can also create a statement that will run if the conditional is not met. These statements are called else statements.

## The else **Statement**

An else statement is used with an if statement. If the if statement does not evaluate to true, the else statement runs its code.

The syntax for else statements is like the syntax for other conditional statements, except it has no conditions. It runs when the evaluator reaches it. Here's an example:

```
var name:String = "David";
if (name == "Kevin"){
      trace ("The name is Kevin");
}else{
      trace ("The name is not Kevin");
}
//output: The name is not Kevin
```

Because the if statement does not evaluate to true, the else statement is run. If the if statement does evaluate to true, the else statement is not read by the interpreter. Here's another example:

```
var name:String = "David";
if (name == "David"){
```

```
    trace ("The name is David");
}else{
    trace ("The name is not David");
}
//output: The name is David
```

Now let's take a look at a more practical example of using the `else` statement, this time as an age-verification check:

```
//create a date object
var date:Date = new Date();
//get the year
var year:Number = date.getFullYear();
var inputYear:Number = 1982;
//see the difference in inputYear and year
var age:Number = year-inputYear;
//evaluate if they are old enough
if (age>=21) {
    gotoAndPlay("welcome");
} else {
    gotoAndPlay("tooYoung");
}
```

Now that you have seen what the `else` statement can do when joined with an `if` statement, let's look at the `else if` statement to see how it works in conjunction with the other two.

## The `else if` Statement

The `else if` statement allows you to run through several conditional statements in your code, and each is only read if the preceding conditional statement does not evaluate to true.

The syntax for the `else if` statement is nearly identical to the `if` statement, except that it has a preceding keyword of `else`, as demonstrated here:

```
var bookTitle:String = "Unleashed";
if (bookTitle == "Flash") {
    trace ("The title is Flash");
}else if (bookTitle == "Unleashed") {
    trace ("The title is Unleashed");
}else {
    trace ("We don't know what the title is");
}
//output: The title is Unleashed
```

Now that you understand the significance of the `else if` statement, let's take a look at the same code but *without* the `else if` statement:

```
var bookTitle:String = "Unleashed";
if (bookTitle == "Flash"){
     trace ("The bookTitle is Flash");
}else{
     if (bookTitle == "Unleashed") {
           trace ("The title is Unleashed");
     }else{
           trace ("We don't know what the title is");
     }
}
//output: The title is Unleashed
```

In addition to fewer lines being required, the code is much easier to read in the first example than it is in the second one.

So far we have covered the `if` statement, the `else` statement, and the `else if` statement. Now let's go over another type of conditional statement: `switch`. We'll also discuss some of its methods.

### switch, case, default, and break

A `switch` statement is used much like an `if` statement: It evaluates a condition and runs the code associated with that condition if the condition evaluates to `true`.

The syntax is difficult to understand, so don't feel bad if you don't get it the first time around.

The statement starts with the keyword `switch`, followed by a value in a set of parentheses and then an opening curly bracket. The value in the parentheses is usually a variable that you are looking for in strict equality (`===`) in your set of cases.

After the opening curly bracket, you begin to use the keyword `case`, followed by a space and another value and a colon. After the colon, you can put in any code you want to execute if the case evaluates to `true`. The value before the colon is what the switch is searching on, and it can be any data type. After the code you want to execute, place the keyword `break` to stop the code from going on to the next case without evaluating it.

Then, after all your cases, place the keyword `default` and a colon and then the code to be executed if none of the cases evaluate to `true` (in much the same way the `else` statement works).

That's a lot to do, so before we look at an applied example, let's see what this looks like:

```
switch (mainValue) {
     case value1:
```

```
        //code to be executed;
        break;
    case value2:
        //code to be executed
        break;
    case value3:
        //code to be executed
        break;
    default:
        //default code to be executed
}
```

The preceding example is fairly generic. Now let's see it using real information:

```
var name:String = "Damon";
switch (name) {
case "Damon":
    trace ("Damon is the name");
    break;
case "Steve":
    trace ("Steve is the name");
    break;
case "Margaret":
    trace ("Margaret is the name");
    break;
case "Shelley":
    trace ("Shelley is the name");
    break;
case "Elizabeth":
    trace ("Elizabeth is the name");
    break;
default:
    trace ("There isn't a name");
}
//output: Damon is the name
```

As previously stated, the break keyword plays a big part in executing this code smoothly. To prove this point, let's see what happens without it:

```
var name:String = "Damon";
switch (name) {
case "Damon":
    trace ("Damon is the name");
```

```
case "Steve":
     trace ("Steve is the name");
case "Margaret":
     trace ("Margaret is the name");
case "Shelley":
     trace ("Shelley is the name");
case "Elizabeth":
     trace ("Elizabeth is the name");
default:
     trace ("There isn't a name");
}
//output: Damon is the name
//        Steve is the name
//        Margaret is the name
//        Shelley is the name
//        Elizabeth is the name
//        There isn't a name
```

And of course, if the variable is not found, the `default` keyword will execute its code:

```
var name:String = "Doug";
switch (name) {
case "Damon":
     trace ("Damon is the name");
     break;
case "Steve":
     trace ("Steve is the name");
     break;
case "Margaret":
     trace ("Margaret is the name");
     break;
case "Shelley":
     trace ("Shelley is the name");
     break;
case "Elizabeth":
     trace ("Elizabeth is the name");
     break;
```

```
default:
     trace ("There isn't a name");
}
```

```
//output: There isn't a name
```

We have covered the basics of conditional statements. Now it's time to move to the next group of flow modifiers: loop statements.

## Loop Statements

Much like conditional statements, loop statements use conditions to modify the flow of ActionScript. Unlike conditional statements, loop statements run continuously until the condition has been met.

We have already seen one loop statement—the for in loop statement used with objects. This statement is specific to objects; the other loop statements we'll cover have a different syntax than the for in loop statement.

Let's jump right in with our first loop statement: the while loop.

### The while Loop

The while loop runs similarly to an if statement: If the condition is true, the statement runs its code. Unlike an if statement, however, a while loop starts over and runs again until the condition is no longer true.

The while loop's syntax is very similar to that of the if statement as well, except it uses the keyword while, followed by the condition and an opening curly bracket that encloses the ActionScript to be run while the condition is true, along with a closing curly bracket that ends the statement.

Because the statement will run until the condition is not true, you must make sure the loop will eventually end. Otherwise, processor power can be affected and errors can occur. Let's take a look at an example:

```
var i:Number = 0;
while (i < 4) {
     trace (i);
     i++;
}
//output: 0
//        1
//        2
//        3
```

Notice that we put an incremental variable in the code to be run while the condition is true. This incremental variable is what shuts down the loop. Let's see what would happen if we didn't have that incremental variable:

```
var i:Number = 0;
while (i < 4) {
      trace (i);
}
//output: (an error message that says that a script in the movie is causing
//the flash player to run slowly, and then it asks do you want to abort)
//as well as a bunch of zeros one on each line indicating the script never finished
running
```

This is why ending a loop statement at some point is very important. Another way to cause the loop statement to end is to use a break script. We covered the keyword break in the previous section on switch statements. Now we're going to use it to end loops.

### The break Keyword

The break keyword is often used to end long-running loop statements. The syntax is simple: Place the keyword break at the end of the code you would like run while the condition is true and follow it with a semicolon to end the line.

Let's take another look at our previous unstopping loop statement, but this time with the break keyword added:

```
var i:Number = 0;
while (i < 4) {
      trace (i);
      break;
}
//output: 0
```

Because the condition is true, the loop statement is run until the point where the interpreter hits the break keyword. After reaching break, the interpreter moves as if the condition is no longer true.

The while loop can also be used to duplicate movie clips much easier than manually duplicating them, as you will see in the next example.

1. Create a new Flash document.

2. Draw a small rectangle (about 100×100) in the top left corner of the stage as shown in Figure 10.1.

3. Convert the rectangle to a movie clip symbol (F8) and then give it an instance name of rec_mc.

**4.** Now create a new layer, name it **actions**, and in the first frame, place this code:

```
var i:Number = 0;
var amount:Number = 7;
while (i<=amount) {
        duplicateMovieClip("rec_mc", "rec_mc"+i, i)
        rec_mc._y =i * rec_mc._width;
        rec_mc._x =i * rec_mc._width;
        i++;
}
//this simply cleans the first duplicated movie
rec_mc0._visible = false;
```

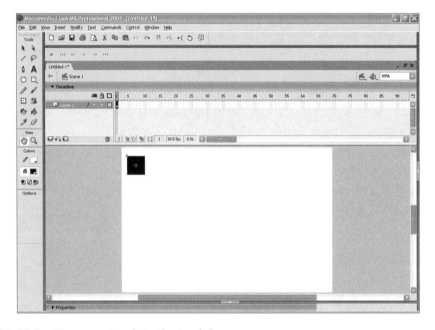

**FIGURE 10.1**    Draw a rectangle in the top left corner.

Now test the movie by selecting Control, Test Movie (Ctrl+Enter).

Now you have steps (see Figure 10.2). Even if you wanted to duplicate each instance of the movie clip manually, you would have a line for each single time you created a new instance.

You can also set the condition to something a little more dynamic, such as the `length` property of a string or array. Let's take a look:

```
var date:Date = new Date();
var fullDate:Array = new Array();
```

```
fullDate.push(date.getDate());
fullDate.push(date.getMonth()+1);
fullDate.push(date.getFullYear());
var i:Number = 0;
var myDate:String = "";
while (i < fullDate.length){
     myDate +=fullDate[i];
     if (i < fullDate.length-1){
          myDate += "-";
     }
     i++;
}
trace (myDate);
//output: 16-10-2003 (this just represents a possible date)
```

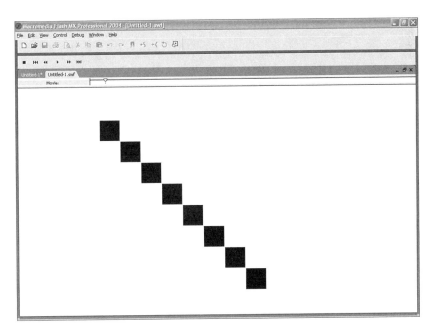

**FIGURE 10.2**   After the movie is tested, it should look similar to a staircase effect.

Now you have a nice-looking full date that's dynamic! These are just a few of the hundreds of ways the while loop can be used. Other examples might include running a game "while" the character has enough energy or having a date- and time-sensitive security lock on a site so that "while" the date is before a set date, no one can enter the site.

Next, we'll take a look at another type of loop statement: the do while loop.

10

**The** do while **Loop**

The do while loop works identically to the while loop in that it runs its code while the set condition evaluates to true. The syntax, however, is completely different.

The syntax for the do while loop starts with the keyword do, followed by an opening curly bracket. Then comes the code to be executed while the condition evaluates to true. On the next line, following the last line of code to be executed, is a closing curly bracket followed by the keyword while, which is then followed by the condition inside a set of parentheses. Finally, a semicolon is used to end the line. Let's take a look at a generic template:

```
do {
      //code to be executed while the condition is true
}while (condition);
```

That's the basic format of the do while loop. Now let's revisit a couple of previous examples to see how they can be used with do while. Here's the first example:

```
var i:Number = 0;
do{
      trace (i);
      i++;
}while (i<4);
//output: 0
//        1
//        2
//        3
```

This is just a basic loop with an incremental variable. Now let's revisit the duplicate movie example and see how it would work with a do while loop:

```
var i:Number = 0;
var amount:Number = 7;
do{
      duplicateMovieClip("rec_mc", "rec_mc"+i, i)
      rec_mc._y =i * rec_mc._width;
      rec_mc._x =i * rec_mc._width;
      i++;
} while (i<=amount);
//this simply cleans the first duplicated movie
rec_mc0._visible = false;
```

Just like before, the staircase appears (see Figure 10.3).

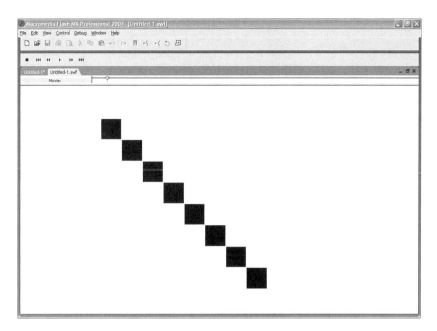

**FIGURE 10.3**    Here again is the staircase effect after you test the movie.

As you can see, the do while loop works similarly to the while loop, except that the do while loop will always run once no matter what, and the while loop may not run if the condition never evaluates to true.

Let's move on to our next loop statement: the for loop.

### The for Loop

The for loop works like the other loop statements. It has a condition as well as code to be executed while the condition evaluates to true. The difference is that the condition as well as the incremental variable are held in the same area.

The syntax of the for loop begins with the keyword for, followed by an opening parenthesis. However, instead of placing the condition first, you create an incremental variable and set a value to it. This variable is followed by a semicolon. After the first semicolon, you create your condition, which again is followed by a semicolon. After the second semicolon, you adjust your incremental variable according to how you want it to work so that the loop will have an end. Then use a closing parenthesis and an opening curly bracket to end the line. The code to be executed begins on the following line, and the statement ends with a closing curly bracket. Here's the generic template of the for loop:

```
for (incremental variable; condition; adjustment of our variable){
    //code to be executed
}
```

You may find this difficult to understand without real information, so let's put some in:

```
for (var i:Number = 0; i<4; i++){
      trace (i);
}
//output: 0
//        1
//        2
//        3
```

In this case, we created our incremental variable, i, and put a condition in i<4. Then we increased our variable so that the loop will end eventually.

This is all pretty basic, but we can put it to a function and make it more dynamic by attaching the function to whatever we want.

Next, we'll create a basic function using our for loop, and we'll separate each character in a string, place each character in an array that we create (more on arrays in Chapter 13), and then reverse the array and place it back into a variable as a string. Here's the code:

```
//create a function with just one variable
function reverseString(string:String){
//create a blank array
    var myArray:Array = new Array();
//get each character and put it in the array
      for (var i:Number=0;i<string.length;i++){
            myArray[i] = string.charAt(i);
      }
//reverse the array
      myArray.reverse();
//use an empty string to join each character
//then set it equal to the original string
      string = myArray.join("");
      trace (string);
}
//create a variable holding a string literal
var name:String = "David";
//call function
reverseString(name)
//output:divaD
```

In this function, we use the for loop to make sure we retrieve each character in our string.

You can also use nested for loops to pull even more information out of data types. This next example takes strings in an array and counts each one. Then it returns the string that appears most often (notice the use of nested for loops). Here's the code:

```
//create the function
function stringCount(theArray:Array){
//sort the array
     theArray.sort (1);
//create the variables we need
     var preCount:Number = 1;
     var count:Number = 0;
     for(var i:Number=0; i<=theArray.length-1; i++){
          for(var j:Number=(i+1); j<=theArray.length-1; j++){
//change the element with the .toUpperCase () method when counting
//because flash distinguishes between upper case and lower case letters
               if(theArray[i].toUpperCase()==theArray[j].toUpperCase()){
                    preCount+=1;
//check to see if the new element has a higher frequency than the previous
                    if (preCount > count) {
                         count = precount;
                         preCount = 1;
                         name = theArray[i];
                    }
               }

          }

     }
//then the answer is changed  to upper case and displayed in the output window
     trace (name.toUpperCase());
}
//example array
var myArray:Array = new Array
("David","fred","George","John","Mike","fred","mike","Fred");
//run the function
stringCount (myArray);
//output: FRED
```

You can also place multiple variables and conditions in loop statements, but this tends to produces surprising results.

### Multiple Conditions in Loop Statements

Using multiple conditions in loop statements can serve a variety of purposes when you are dealing with multiple objects. For instance, we'll create two variables, i and j, and set them to 0 and 3, respectively. Then we'll increase each by 1 and test them both with a "less than 5" condition. First, we'll use the logical OR operator and test it; then we will use the short-circuit AND operator and test it. Finally, we'll discuss the results.

When placing multiple variables in `for` loops, separate them with commas, as shown here:

```
for (var i = 0, j = 3; i<5 || j<5;i++,j++){
      trace ("j="+j);
      trace ("i="+i);
}
```

```
//output j=3
//i=0
//j=4
//       i=1
//       j=5
//       i=2
//       j=6
//       i=3
//       j=7
//       i=4
```

Now we will use the short-circuit AND operator:

```
for (var i = 0, j = 3; i<5 && j<5;i++,j++){
      trace ("j="+j);
      trace ("i="+i);
}
//output j=3
//       i=0
//       j=4
//       i=1
```

This time, j counts up to 4 and i counts to 1.

This seems almost backward to what you learned about these two operators as they relate to conditional statements, because in loop statements, as long as a condition is true, the code will run. Therefore, in the case of the OR operator, as long as either of the conditions evaluates to true, the statement will run. When we used the AND operator, on the other hand, they both had to evaluate to true for the statement to continue to run.

That just about covers loop statements. However, you should know that using loop statements is not the only way to create loops in Flash. There are also event handler loops as well as timeline loops. Let's discuss them next.

### Event Handler Loops

In Chapter 14, "Events," we will cover event handlers in more detail. For now, though, we're just going to cover one: the onEnterFrame event. This clip event is placed on the timeline of a movie clip instance (or the main timeline) and runs constantly. You can use conditional statements to create a mock loop, if you want.

For example, let's say you want to wait a little bit before moving on to the next frame of a movie. You could use this code by placing it in the frame actions on the main timeline:

```
var i:Number = 0;
this.onEnterFrame=function(){
      if (i>=50){
            trace ("go to next frame");
            delete this.onEnterFrame;
      }else{
            trace ("not yet");
      }
      i++;
}
```

Now, because of the onEnterFrame event, the movie will not move on until i is equal to 50.

Another type of loop is the timeline loop, which is covered next.

### The Timeline Loop

A timeline loop uses a timeline and a set number of frames in that timeline to continuously play through a movie. Let's see one in action.

First, go to the second frame of the main timeline and insert a blank frame by choosing Insert, Timeline, Blank Key Frame (F7).

Now, in the first frame of the main timeline (on the same layer, because there should only be one layer), place the following code:

```
      trace ("This is a loop");
```

Now when you test this code, you will see "This is a loop" a bunch of times, until you stop the movie from running.

You can also use goto functions to create a conditioned timeline loop. As an example, place three keyframes on the main timeline and use the following lines of code on the indicated frames. Here's the code for frame 1:

```
var i:Number = 0;
```

Here's the code for frame 2:

```
i++;
```

Finally, here's the code for frame 3:

```
if (i<5){
      trace (i);
```

10

```
      gotoAndPlay (2);
}else {
      stop();
}
```

The output are the numbers 1–4.

## Summary

In this chapter, we have covered expressions including conditionals and enough loops to make anyone dizzy. One of the major points to remember about loops and conditionals is that they run on Boolean values or expresions that evaluate to Boolean values. Also, remember that any statement block you open with a curly bracket must be closed by one as well. And lastly, remember when comparing strings, Flash will interpret a lowercase letter differently than the same letter in uppercase because Flash evaluates the ASCII code points of the character, not the character itself.

Continue to play with the structure and conditions of loops to really get a good feel for them and what can be accomplished using them.

CHAPTER **11**

# The Movie Clip Object

The movie clip object is the most powerful object in Flash. Not only is it the only symbol that has its own timeline similar to but independent of the main timeline, but also it is the only symbol that can have actions on its timeline.

But there is more to the movie clip object than just its independent timeline. Movie clips have properties, methods, and events that set them apart from all other objects.

Throughout this chapter, we will be exploring the many different ways to use and manipulate movie clips including using the Drawing API, Flash's way of drawing shapes and lines with ActionScript.

To start with, we are going to cover the different ways to create movie clips.

## Creating Movie Clips

We covered how to create a movie clip manually back in Chapter 5, "Symbols and the Library," but just for review we will go over it quickly.

### Creating Movie Clips Manually

To create a movie clip symbol manually, follow these steps:

1. Choose Insert, New Symbol.

2. In the Create New Symbol dialog box, give the symbol a symbol name, choose Movie Clip as the behavior, and then click OK.

3. Now you are inside the newly created movie clip.

That was pretty simple; you just created a movie clip manually. Now if you want to use it, all you have to do is drag an instance of it out from the library onto the stage and give it an instance name.

> **NOTE**
>
> Although technically you do not need to give every instance of movie clip objects an instance name unless you plan to refer to it with ActionScript, it is good practice to do so.

Creating movie clips manually is not the only way to create them. You can also create them on the fly with ActionScript.

## Creating Movie Clips with ActionScript

Since the MX version of Flash, users have been able to create movie clips with ActionScript. Before then, when you wanted an empty movie clip on the stage, you would have to create one manually and drag it onto the stage, and then give it an instance name.

To create empty movie clips in ActionScript, use the `createEmptyMovieClip()` method, which looks like this:

```
movieClip.createEmptyMovieClip(instanceName, depth);
```

The parameters of this method are as follows:

- `movieClip`—The instance name of the movie clip where the empty clip will be created.

- `instanceName`—This is a string literal that represents the instance name of the movie clip being created.

- `depth`—This is a numerical value that represents the stacking order of the movie clip being created (more on `depth` later in this chapter).

That is the basic layout of the `createEmptyMovieClip()` method. The next example shows how to implement it.

1. Create a new Flash document.

2. In the first frame of the main timeline, place these actions:

   ```
   //this refers the main timeline
   this.createEmptyMovieClip("sample_mc", 1);
   ```

3. Now test the movie by choosing Control, Test Movie.

4. Notice that when the movie runs, there isn't anything on the stage. This is because we created an empty movie clip; there is nothing inside it, but you can tell it's there.

When you're in the test movie screen, choose Debug, List Objects, and you should see in the Output panel something similar to Figure 11.1.

The movie is listed in the Output panel.

**FIGURE 11.1** Using the List Objects option under Debug, you can see the movie clip you created with ActionScript.

Now that you have seen the different ways to create movie clips, continue on to see how to manipulate them.

## Manipulating Movie Clips

There are several different aspects of movie clips that can be manipulated to change the appearance of the movie clips. Some of them can be used to move the movie clip across the stage, and others can be used to change the color of the movie clip. There are even several different properties of movie clips that control the visual aspects of the object.

Here is a short list of those properties with descriptions:

- _x—The horizontal position of a movie clip on the stage
- _y—The vertical position of a movie clip on the stage
- _xscale—The horizontal scale of a movie clip represented as a percentage; above 100% enlarges the clip, below 100% shrinks the clip
- _yscale—The vertical scale of a movie clip represented as a percentage; above 100% enlarges the clip, below 100% shrinks the clip
- _height—The height of a movie clip in pixels
- _width—The width of a movie clip in pixels
- _alpha—The transparent level of a movie clip from 0 to 100
- _rotation—The rotation of a movie clip in degrees
- _visible—A Boolean value representing whether a movie clip is visible (true) or not (false)

Now that you have a list of some of the basic visual properties of movie clips, we can begin using them to animate movie clips.

## Animating Movie Clips with ActionScript

Animating movie clips with ActionScript has many benefits that manually animating them does not, file size reduction being one of the major benefits.

When you create tweens, you are requiring Flash to not only create the necessary animation between the two points, but to also remember it when the .swf file is compiled. This will cause the file size to increase. Even if you use keyframe animation without any tweening, the file size will increase with each key frame. Using ActionScript to control movement of movie clips is an easy way to trim file size because Flash only has to remember the original position of the movie clip, and then ActionScript will execute the movement at runtime.

Here is a basic example of scripted movement:

1. Create a new Flash document.

2. Draw a small circle on the left side of the stage about 50 pixels in width.

3. Select the drawn circle (including the circle's stroke) and convert it to a symbol by choosing Modify, Convert to Symbol.

4. Give it a symbol name of `circleMC` and choose Movie Clip as the behavior.

5. Give the circle on the stage an instance name of `circle_mc`.

6. Create a new layer and name it `actions`.

7. In the first frame of the actions layer, open the Actions panel and place these actions within it:

```
//this event will make the circle move
this.onEnterFrame = function(){
     //move the circle 5 pixels at a time
     circle_mc._x += 5;
}
```

   What we did was to use the `onEnterFrame` event, which will continually trigger throughout the entire run of the movie at the same pace as the frames per second (fps). Within the `onEnterFrame` event, we are moving the `circle_mc` movie clip by 5 pixels each time the event fires.

8. Now test the movie and see the circle moving across the screen as shown in Figure 11.2.

That was a simple example of moving a movie clip from one side of the screen to the other, but the problem is that the `circle_mc` continues to move well past the end of the stage. So we will continue the example by adding a conditional statement to see if the `circle_mc` has moved far enough, and then it will stop moving. We are also adding a trace action, which we will discuss later.

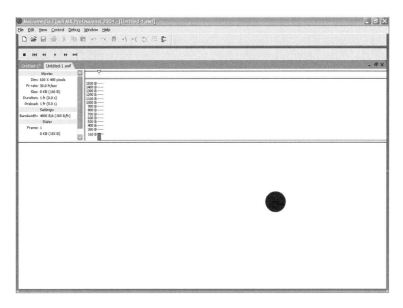

**FIGURE 11.2** Using ActionScript, you can animate movie clips just as smoothly as using tweens, and the file size stays tiny.

Follow these steps to continue the example:

1. Close the test movie screen and return to the authoring environment.

2. In the first frame of the actions layer, replace the actions in the Actions panel with these:

```
//this event will make the circle move
this.onEnterFrame = function(){
    //this trace function lets us know it is working
    trace("working");
    //if it hasn't gone too far, move the circle 5 pixels
    if(circle_mc._x < 550){
        circle_mc._x += 5;
    }
}
```

What this code is doing is taking the original code and placing a conditional statement to check whether `circle_mc` has passed 550 in its horizontal position (550 being the default width of the Flash stage). If it has not yet reached that point, the movie clip will continue moving to the right. Also, we put a `trace` action in the code, which will be discussed in the next section.

3. Now test the movie.

Notice that as before, the `circle_mc` movie clip moves across the screen, but this time, when it reaches a certain point it stops moving. Also, the `trace` action continues to run even after the circle has stopped moving, as you can see in Figure 11.3. This is because even though the circle has stopped moving, the `onEnterFrame` event is still being triggered.

Even though it's hard to tell, the `onEnterFrame` event is still taking up valuable processor power that can be taken back. In the next extension of this example, we will remove the `onEnterFrame` event and regain the processor power.

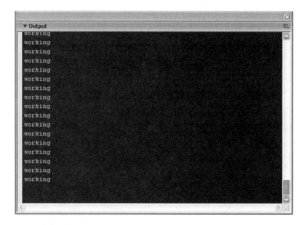

**FIGURE 11.3**    Even though the `circle_mc` movie clip has stopped moving, the trace action continues to work while the `onEnterFrame` event fires.

The final step in this example is to remove the `onEnterFrame` event when we no longer need it, and regain the processor power. To do this, we will use the `delete` statement in conjunction with our conditional statement.

Follow these steps:

1. Close the test movie screen and return to the authoring environment.

2. In the first frame of the actions layer, replace the actions in the Actions panel with these:

```
//this event will make the circle move
this.onEnterFrame = function(){
    //this trace function lets us know it is working
    trace("working");
    //if it hasn't gone too far, move the circle 5 pixels
    if(circle_mc._x < 550){
        circle_mc._x += 5;
    }else{
```

```
        //destroy the onEnterFrame
        delete this.onEnterFrame;
    }
}
```

The changes were small; all we did was add an else statement to coincide with the if statement. When the circle_mc movie clip reaches the correct position, the else statement is triggered, the onEnterFrame event is destroyed, and the processor power is returned to the user.

3. Test the movie.

This time when the movie is tested, the circle_mc acts exactly the same way it has been acting, moving from the left side of the stage to the right side. This time, however, when the circle_mc reaches the horizontal position of 550 or greater, the circle_mc movie clip stops moving and the onEnterFrame event is deleted there by stopping the trace action from occurring.

Even though this example was a little boring, it is very powerful. What we have done is move a movie clip from one side of the screen to the other, stop, and destroy the action that was moving it in the first place.

We are going to take the basic fundamentals from the preceding example, and do a more advanced example of a movie clip moving from spot to spot on the stage. We will use some basic math to make it slow down and speed up.

## Using Math to Help Animate Movie Clips

So far we have just moved a movie clip using a static number. Using math, you can improve the appearance of animating movie clips. You can make them appear to have a bouncy momentum. You can make them appear to be bound by gravity. You can even make them appear to be easing in and out each time they move, and that is what we are going to cover in this next example, which extends the preceding example.

1. Close the test screen and return to the main timeline.

2. In the first frame of the actions layer, open the Actions panel, and replace the code with this:

```
//the easing control
var friction:Number = 0.5;
//the starting positions
var currentX:Number = circle_mc._x;
var currentY:Number = circle_mc._y;
//set the boundaries
var xBoundary:Number = 550;
var yBoundary:Number = 400;
```

```
//set some initial go to points
var newX:Number = Math.floor(Math.random()*xBoundary);
var newY:Number = Math.floor(Math.random()*yBoundary);
```

These actions declare some variables we will be using in the event. The friction variable is what will control the speed of how the movie clip eases in and out of position. The currentX and currentY variables hold the current position of our movie clip. The boundary variables are used in setting the next position. The newX and the newY variables use the Math object to choose new positions at random based on the boundaries, for the movie clip to move to. Now let's add the code to do the actual moving.

3. After the code already in the Actions panel, place this code:

```
//this is the event for the motion
this.onEnterFrame=function(){
    //continually get the current position
    currentX = Math.floor(circle_mc._x);
    currentY = Math.floor(circle_mc._y);
    //check the horizontal position
    if(currentX != newX){
        circle_mc._x += (newX-currentX)*friction;
    }else{
        newX = Math.floor(Math.random()*xBoundary);
    }
    //do the same with the horizontal position
    if(currentY != newY){
        circle_mc._y += (newY-currentY)*friction;
    }else{
        newY = Math.floor(Math.random()*yBoundary);
    }
}
```

This code constantly checks the current position of the movie clip and stores it in two of the variables we created earlier. It then checks to see if the movie clip's current position is at the new position. If it is not, it moves it closer to the new position based on the friction that we declared earlier. If it is at the new position, it then creates another new position for the object to move to.

4. Test the movie.

Now when the test movie screen appears, you will see the circle_mc movie clip moving all over the stage from spot to spot, slowing down as it gets closer. Play with the friction variable to get some surprising results.

That example was not only powerful but cool. You can try not only playing with the friction variable, but using other movie clip properties in conjunction with or without the _x and _y properties to see what else you can do. We will come back to this concept in later examples, but first we are going to cover another way you can manipulate movie clips. This time we are going to change their color.

## Using the `Color` Object with Movie Clips

The `Color` object is an object used to change the color or tint of a movie clip. It is unique among all other objects. Most objects, when created, have no association by default with other objects. The `Color` object, on the other hand, must be associated with a movie clip when the `Color` object is created.

Here is an example of creating a `Color` object:

```
var myColor:Color = new Color(myMovie);
```

The `myMovie` parameter refers to a movie clip that is either already on the stage or has been created with ActionScript.

The `Color` object has four basic methods, but we are going to focus on two of them, the `setRGB()` method and the `setTransform()` method. Both have unique differences that make them suitable for different situations.

We will start with the `setRGB()` method because it is slightly easier to implement.

### The `setRGB()` Method

The `setRGB()` method is used to set the RGB color of a movie clip. When called, it will change the color of the movie clip specified when the `Color` object was created to any legal hexadecimal color.

Here is the generic layout of the method:

```
colorObj.setRGB(hexColor);
```

The parameter it accepts, `hexColor`, can be any legal hexadecimal color such as `0x000000` (black), `0xffffff` (white), or `0xff0000` (red). It can also be a variable that is holding a legal hexadecimal color.

Here is an example of using the `setRGB()` method:

1. Create a new Flash document.

2. Draw a square somewhere on the stage with the fill color some shade of red.

3. Highlight the square, including the stroke, and convert it to a movie clip symbol by choosing Modify, Convert to Symbol.

4. Give it a symbol name of `squareMC` and make sure the behavior is set to Movie Clip.

5. Give the instance of the square on the stage an instance name of square_mc.

6. Create a new layer and call it **actions**.

7. In the actions layer, open the Actions panel in the first frame, and place these actions within it:

```
//create the color object, and pass it the square_mc
var myColor:Color = new Color(square_mc);
//set the color to a light shade of blue
myColor.setRGB(0x397dce);
```

The preceding code creates a color object and associates itself with the movie clip we already created. Then it calls the setRGB() method and passes it a hexadecimal color that translates to a light shade of blue.

When you test the movie, you will see that the square_mc movie clip has changed from the red color it was originally in, to a light shade of blue (see Figure 11.4). Notice that it did not just change the fill color, but also the stroke color has now become the same shade of blue. The setTransform() method will do something a little bit different.

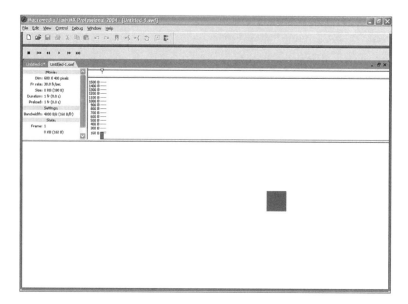

**FIGURE 11.4**   You can use the setRGB() method to change the color of an entire movie clip.

## The setTransform() Method

The setTransform() method is slightly different in the way it changes the color of a movie clip from the setRGB() method. Instead of changing the entire movie clip to a flat color, the setTransform() method tints the movie clip.

Here is the generic layout of the setTransform() method:

```
myColor.setTransform(transformObject);
```

This method has only one parameter when called, the transformObject. The transformObject is an object you create prior to calling the method that has special properties set. Here is a list of the available properties you can set for the transformObject:

- ra—The percentage for the red coloring ranging from –100 to 100

- rb—The offset for the red coloring ranging from –255 to 255

- ga—The percentage for the green coloring ranging from –100 to 100

- gb—The offset for the green coloring ranging from –255 to 255

- ba—The percentage for the blue coloring ranging from –100 to 100

- bb—The offset for the blue coloring ranging from –255 to 255

- aa—The percentage for alpha ranging from –100 to 100

- ab—The offset for alpha ranging from –255 to 255

That might be a little confusing until you see how to create one of these transformObjects. As with most things in Flash, there is more than one way to accomplish this.

Here is the long way:

```
//first create the object
var transformObject:Object = new Object();
//now set some of the properties of that object
transformObject.rb = 200;
transformObject.gb = 100;
transformObject.bb = 50;
transformObject.ab = 50;
```

And here is the short way:

```
//first create the object
var transformObject:Object = {rb: '200', gb: '150', bb: '50', ab: '50'};
```

As a personal preference, I tend to use the long way merely because it is easier to read and make corrections.

Now that you have seen the basic layout of not only the setTransform() method, but also the transformObject we pass to the method, an example will bring it all together.

1. Create a new Flash document.

2. Draw a square somewhere on the stage with the fill color some shade of gray, and the stroke color being black.

3. Highlight the square, including the stroke, and convert it to a movie clip symbol by choosing Modify, Convert to Symbol.

4. Give it a symbol name of squareMC and make sure the behavior is set to Movie Clip.

5. Give the instance of the square on the stage an instance name of square_mc.

6. Create a new layer and call it **actions**.

7. In the actions layer, open the Actions panel in the first frame, and place these actions within it:

```
//create the color object, and pass it the square_mc
var myColor:Color = new Color(square_mc);
//create the transformObject
var transformObject:Object = new Object();
//now set some of the properties of that object
transformObject.rb = 200;
transformObject.gb = 100;
transformObject.bb = 50;
//finally call the setTransform() method
myColor.setTransform(transformObject);
```

The preceding code creates a Color object and associates it with our movie clip. Then it creates an object that we will use as the transformObject in our method. After that, it sets a few basic properties of the transformObject. And finally, the code calls the setTransform() method using the transformObject.

Now when you test the movie, the square_mc movie clip will appear with a pinkish tint. Notice that this time, the stroke is not the exact same color as the fill, but it is the same tint.

> **NOTE**
>
> If the setRGB() method is called, it will override the settings of the setTransform() method.

That was just another way movie clips can be manipulated. So far we have covered how to move and adjust them using the built-in properties of the movie clips. We have also discussed how to change their color using the Color object. The next section covers how to change their stacking order with regard to other movie clips.

## Depth and the Stacking Order

We briefly mentioned depth earlier in this chapter when we were creating movie clips with ActionScript. To recap, depth is a numerical value representing the stacking order of objects on the stage during runtime. And because each object, whether created manually or dynamically, has its own depth, no two objects can exist at the same depth.

Flash has some old methods for working with depth, as well as some new ones. The first method is the `getDepth()` method.

### The `getDepth()` Method

The `getDepth()` method will return a numerical value representing the depth of the object on which you call the method.

The generic layout is as follows:

```
myMovie.getDepth();
```

This method has no parameters; it just needs to be associated with an object on the stage.

In the following example, we will create a movie clip manually and then use the `getDepth()` method to see what depth it is residing on.

1. Start a new Flash document.

2. Draw a circle on the stage.

3. Convert the circle to a movie clip symbol by choosing Modify, Convert to Symbol.

4. Give it a symbol name of `circleMC` and make sure the behavior is set to Movie Clip.

5. Give the instance of the circle on the stage an instance name of `circle_mc`.

6. Create a new layer and name it **actions**.

7. In the first frame of the actions layer, open the Actions panel and place this code in it:

   ```
   //send the depth of the movie clip to the output panel
   trace(circle_mc.getDepth());
   ```

The preceding code merely retrieves the depth of the `circle_mc` movie clip, and sends it to the Output panel.

Test the movie and you should see the number –16383 in the Output panel. This is the first depth where objects created manually reside.

The `getDepth()` method just retrieves information about an object's depth, but if you want to change an object's depth, you have to use the `swapDepths()` method.

**The** swapDepths() **Method**

The swapDepths() method, as mentioned, is used to change the depth of movie clips whether created manually or with ActionScript. This method has two ways of working. Here are both of them in generic layouts:

```
myMovie.swapDepths(depth);
myMovie.swapDepths(target);
```

Both uses have the myMovie in front of the method. This is the movie clip that you want to change its depth.

Using the depth parameter, you will swap depths with the object in the depth parameter. If that depth is empty, myMovie will simply be placed there.

Using the target parameter, myMovie will change depths with the target movie clip. Both myMovie and target must reside within the same parent movie clip in order for the method to work correctly.

In this example, we will create two movie clips manually, align them slightly over one another, and then swap their depths so that at runtime, they will appear to have switched stacking orders.

1. Start a new Flash document.

2. Draw a circle on the stage.

3. Convert the circle to a movie clip symbol by choosing Modify, Convert to Symbol.

4. Give it a symbol name of circleMC and make sure the behavior is set to Movie Clip.

5. Give the instance of the circle on the stage an instance name of circle_mc.

6. While still in the same layer, draw a square shape (preferably with a different fill color, but that is not necessary).

7. Convert the square to a movie clip symbol by choosing Modify, Convert to Symbol.

8. Give it a symbol name of squareMC and make sure the behavior is set to Movie Clip.

9. Give the instance of the square on the stage an instance name of square_mc and align it so that it is partially covering up the circle_mc movie clip as in Figure 11.5.

10. Create a new layer and name it **actions**.

11. In the actions layer, open the Actions panel in the first frame, and place these actions in it:

```
//swap the two movie clips depths
square_mc.swapDepths(circle_mc);
```

This code is simply swapping the two movie clips' depths with one another.

Test the movie, and you will see that now the circle movie clip appears above the square as in Figure 11.6.

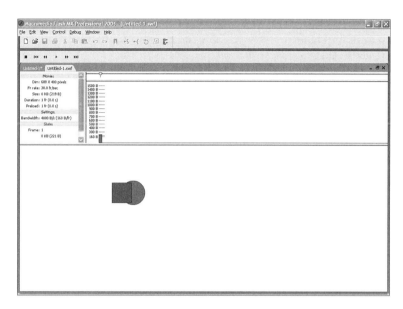

**FIGURE 11.5**   Place the square over the circle on the stage.

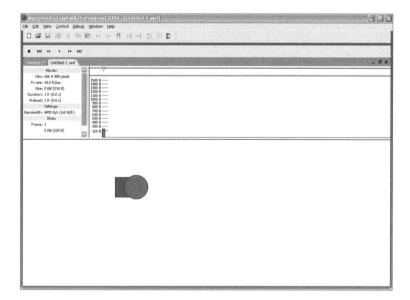

**FIGURE 11.6**   Now the circle appears above the square.

As you can see, it is important to know what depth movie clips are residing on, especially if you want to create them in ActionScript. Remember, two objects cannot reside on the same depth. In previous versions of Flash, it was difficult to know whether a depth you were creating a movie clip on was available or not. You would have to build complex loop statements to look through every movie clip's depth. Now, thankfully, Flash has introduced the `getNextHighestDepth()` method.

### The `getNextHighestDepth()` Method

The `getNextHighestDepth()` method is used when creating movie clips in ActionScript. It will return the next available depth for a movie to be placed on as a numerical value starting with zero.

The generic layout is this:

```
myMovie.getNextHighestDepth();
```

The `myMovie` in the code represents the movie clip you are checking for the next available depth.

Here is a short example:

1. Create a new Flash document.

2. In the first frame of the main timeline, open the Actions panel and place these actions in it:

   ```
   //send the first available depth to the output panel
   trace(this.getNextHighestDepth());
   //create a movie clip on the first available depth
   this.createEmptyMovieClip("test",this.getNextHighestDepth());
   //send the next available depth to the output panel
   trace(this.getNextHighestDepth() );
   ```

The preceding code gets the first available depth and sends it to the Output panel. Then it creates a movie clip on the very same depth. And finally it sends the next available depth to the Output panel.

Test the movie, and you should see an Output panel similar to Figure 11.7. Also, if you check the objects by clicking Debug, List Objects, you will see the movie clip we created in the Output panel as well.

Sometimes you know a movie clip is on a certain depth, but you just cannot remember which one. Flash has a new method for that as well, the `getInstanceAtDepth()` method.

### The `getInstanceAtDepth()` Method

The `getInstanceAtDepth()` method is used to find out what object is residing on a certain depth. It will return the instance name of the object residing in the depth specified.

**FIGURE 11.7**    Using the `getNextHighestDepth()` method, you will never have to worry if you are overwriting another movie clip's depth.

Here is a generic layout of the `getInstanceAtDepth()` method:

```
myMovie.getInstanceAtDepth(depth);
```

The only parameter the `getInstanceAtDepth()` method has is the `depth` parameter. This is the numerical value representing the depth you would like to check. If there is no instance on that depth, `undefined` will be returned.

Here is an example of using the `getInstanceAtDepth()` method:

1.  Create a new Flash document.

2.  In the first frame of the main timeline, open the Actions panel and place these actions in it:

    ```
    //create three movie clips on their own depth
    this.createEmptyMovieClip("sample1_mc",this.getNextHighestDepth());
    this.createEmptyMovieClip("sample2_mc",this.getNextHighestDepth());
    this.createEmptyMovieClip("sample3_mc",this.getNextHighestDepth());
    //now check to see what is on depth 1
    trace(this.getInstanceAtDepth(1));
    ```

The foregoing code creates three instances of movie clips, and then returns the instance of the movie clip on depth 1.

Test the movie, and you will see in the Output window the instance name of the second movie clip we created. Remember the `getNextHighestDepth()` method starts at zero, not one.

We have covered many different ways to manipulate movie clips including their visual properties, color and now their depth. The next section continues the controlling of movie clips, but goes in a different direction by talking about how to make copies of them during runtime.

## Duplicating Movie Clips

Duplicating movie clips can be useful, and more file-size efficient than manually creating each new movie clip. When you manually duplicate movie clips, the `.swf` file increases in size because not only does it include each new movie clip, but also all the code each of the extra movie clips contain. Using ActionScript to duplicate movie clips is more efficient because it will duplicate the movie clips on runtime when the actions are run.

The method used in ActionScript for duplicating movie clips is the `duplicateMovieClip()` method.

### The `duplicateMovieClip()` Method

The `duplicateMovieClip()` method was introduced back in Flash 5, and has the ability to take movie clips created manually or with ActionScript, and make duplicate copies on the stage during runtime.

Its generic layout is this:

```
myMovie.duplicateMovieClip(instanceName, depth, initObject);
```

The `myMovie` is the movie clip to be duplicated. As you can see, the `duplicateMovieClip()` method has three parameters:

- `instanceName`—A string literal representing the instance name given to the duplicated movie clip being created
- `depth`—The depth of the duplicated movie clip as a numerical value
- `initObject`—An optional parameter referring to a movie clip that the duplicated movie clip will retain all actions from

The `duplicateMovieClip()` is usually used in conjunction with a loop statement so that several copies can be made with one instance of the method.

Here is an example using the `duplicateMovieClip()` method:

1. Create a new Flash document.
2. Draw a square in the upper left corner of the stage about 50 pixels in width.
3. Highlight the entire square including the stroke, and convert to symbol by choosing Modify, Convert to Symbol.
4. Give it a symbol name of `squareMC` and make the behavior movie clip.
5. On the main stage, give the square an instance name of `square_mc`.
6. Create a new layer and give it the name **actions**.
7. In the first frame of the actions layer, open the Actions panel, and place these actions within it:

```
//create a loop statement to control the duplication
for(var i:Number = 0; i<10; i++){
```

```
        //duplicate the movie clip
        square_mc.duplicateMovieClip("square"+i+"_mc",i);
    }
```

The preceding code uses a for loop statement to control the duplication of the movie clip. Then, in the duplicateMovieClip() method, we use the variable i that was created in the loop statement to give each instance of the duplicated movie clip a unique instance name as well as putting them on individual depths because remember, they must be on unique depths.

Test the movie and notice that it appears that the duplication did not take place. But in fact it did work; select Debug, List Objects and the Output panel will show all of the duplicated movie clips as you can see in Figure 11.8.

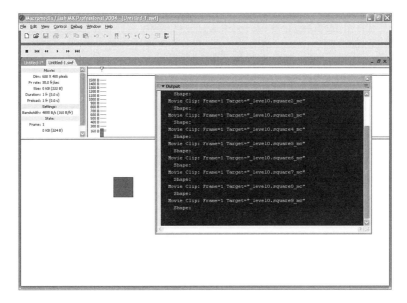

**FIGURE 11.8**   The Output panel shows that the duplicateMovieClip() method was successful even if the results on the stage appear to be otherwise.

Let's go back into the code to create a visual indicator that the duplicateMovieClip() method is working.

1. Close the test movie screen, and go back to the main timeline.

2. Open the Actions panel in the first frame of the actions layer, and change the code to this:

```
//create a loop statement to control the duplication
for(var i:Number = 0; i<10; i++){
```

```
        //duplicate the movie clip
        square_mc.duplicateMovieClip("square"+i+"_mc",i);
        //the following code will show visual appearance of the other movies
        this["square"+i+"_mc"]._x += square_mc._width*i;
    }
```

The preceding code is very similar to the code that was there before. The only difference is the code that will move each new square over and the line of code commenting it.

Test the movie again, and you should see that the `duplicateMovieClip()` method did in fact work with each square being spaced out across the stage as shown in Figure 11.9.

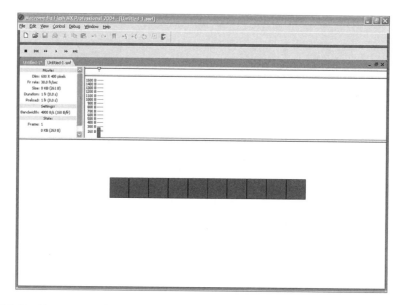

**FIGURE 11.9**    You can see the `duplicateMovieClip()` method worked as the squares are spaced along the stage.

The next example is going to take into consideration all that we have covered thus far. We will use the code that will make movie clips move around on the screen as well as the `Color` object and the `duplicateMovieClip()` object.

1. Create a new Flash document.

2. Draw a circle on the stage.

3. Convert the circle to a movie clip symbol by choosing Modify, Convert to Symbol.

4. Give it a symbol name of `circleMC` and make sure the behavior is set to Movie Clip.

5. Give the instance of the circle on the stage an instance name of `circle_mc`.

6. Create a new layer and name it **actions**.

7. In the first frame of the actions layer, open the Actions panel, and place this code in it:

```
//place some variables associated with circle_mc
circle_mc.friction = 0.3;
circle_mc.xBoundary = 550;
circle_mc.yBoundary = 400;
circle_mc.newX = Math.floor(Math.random()*circle_mc.xBoundary);
circle_mc.newY = Math.floor(Math.random()*circle_mc.yBoundary);
```

The preceding code creates variables associated with the circle_mc movie clip. Next we will add the coloring code.

8. After that section of code, we will create a Color object, and use the Math object to select a random color. Place this code after the preceding code:

```
//this will color the circle_mc
circle_mc.newColor = new Color(this);
//set the RGB using the Math.random() method
circle_mc.newColor.setRGB(Math.random()*0x1000000);
```

This section of code creates a Color object within the circle_mc movie clip. You will see later why we are putting the variables and Color object in the circle_mc. After the Color object is created, we call the setRGB() method and pass it a random hexadecimal value by using the Math.random() method.

You can test the movie at this point if you like. Every time the movie is run, the color of the circle will change to a random color.

The next block of code will be used to move the circle around.

9. After the preceding block of code in the Actions panel, add these actions:

```
//this is the event for the motion
circle_mc.onEnterFrame=function(){
    //continually get the current position
    currentX = Math.floor(this._x);
    currentY = Math.floor(this._y);
    //check the horizontal position
    if(currentX != this.newX){
        this._x += (this.newX-currentX)*this.friction;
    }else{
        this.newX = Math.floor(Math.random()*this.xBoundary);
    }
    //do the same with the horizontal position
    if(currentY != this.newY){
```

```
            this._y += (this.newY-currentY)*this.friction;
        }else{
            this.newY = Math.floor(Math.random()*this.yBoundary);
        }
    }
}
```

This code creates the function that will control the movement of the circles. You can test again here if you like to see that the `circle_mc` is moving around. Now all we have to do is make copies.

10. Now we'll create the final part of the code, the duplicating part. Add these actions to the bottom of the code we already have:

```
//this will duplicate the movie
for(var i=0; i<10; i++){
    circle_mc.duplicateMovieClip("circle"+i+"_mc",i, circle_mc);
}
```

This code merely duplicated the movie clip we have already built, and uses the `circle_mc` as its initializing object, which means each duplicate movie clip will take on the same characteristics as the object we place in there.

Now test the movie again, and you should see a bunch of circles flying around the screen as shown in Figure 11.10. And each time you run this movie, their color will change.

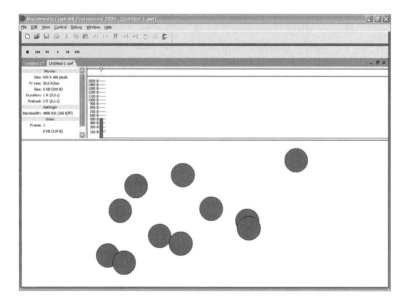

**FIGURE 11.10**    Using the `duplicateMovieClip()` method, you can create some cool effects.

We have seen how to create movie clips two different ways as well as duplicate them. But what if we want to remove them?

# Removing Movie Clips

Sometimes movie clips need to be removed from the stage because they are no longer necessary, and you would prefer that the users have their virtual memory and resources back for other objects on the stage to function more efficiently.

The method to use is the removeMovieClip() method.

### The removeMovieClip() Method

The removeMovieClip() method is used to remove movie clips that have been created manually or with ActionScript.

It has two basic layouts:

```
myMovie.removeMovieClip();
removeMovieClip(myMovie);
```

Both generic uses have myMovie either as a parameter, or as the object the method is being called on. Both uses when called will accomplish the same thing, removing myMovie from the stage.

Here is an example of removing movie clips from the stage:

1. Create a new Flash document.

2. Draw a square somewhere on the stage.

3. Highlight the entire square including the stroke, and convert it to a symbol by choosing Modify, Convert to Symbol.

4. Give it a symbol name of **squareMC** and make the behavior Movie Clip.

5. On the main stage, give the square an instance name of **square_mc**.

6. Create a new layer and give it the name of **actions**.

7. In the first frame of the actions layer, open the Actions panel, and place these actions within it:

   ```
   //create an empty movie clip
   this.createEmptyMovieClip("test_mc",1);
   //remove the square_mc movie clip
   square_mc.removeMovieClip();
   //remove the test_mc movie clip
   removeMovieClip(test_mc);
   //see if the test_mc movie clip is still available
   trace(test);
   ```

The preceding code creates an empty movie clip, and then removes the square_mc movie clip we created manually. After that, it removes the test_mc movie clip we created with code, and finally it uses a trace action to check to see if the test_mc movie clip is still available.

Test the movie and you should see nothing on the stage, and the Output window should say undefined, showing there isn't a test_mc movie clip available any more.

So far in this chapter, we have covered how to create movie clips, manipulate movie clips, and remove movie clips. The final section will cover the Drawing API for movie clips.

# The Drawing API

The Drawing API is Flash's way of being able to draw shapes and lines with ActionScript. The Drawing API can be used in conjunction with any movie clip including the _root timeline.

We are going to cover some of the methods used in the Drawing API starting with the lineStyle() method.

## The lineStyle() Method

The lineStyle() method is used to define the stroke size, color, and transparency of a line before you start drawing with the other methods.

Its generic layout is this:

```
movie.lineStyle(thickness, color, alpha);
```

This method has three parameters:

- thickness—A numerical value used to declare the weight of the line
- color—A hexadecimal value used to declare the color of the line
- alpha—A numerical value representing the transparency level of the line

The method alone will not show anything, so the example will have to wait until we draw a line.

The next method you would use with the Drawing API is the moveTo() method.

## The moveTo() Method

The moveTo() method is used to create a starting point for the drawing API. It can also be used to move the drawing point without drawing a line. If the moveTo() method is skipped, the Drawing API begins drawing at points (0,0) of the movie clip it is being drawn in.

Here is the generic layout of the `moveTo` method:

```
movie.moveTo(X,Y);
```

This method has two parameters:

- X—A numerical value representing the horizontal position the drawing point is moved to without a line being drawn

- Y—A numerical value representing the vertical position the drawing point is moved to without a line being drawn

Like the `lineStyle()` method, the `moveTo()` method does not do anything that can be seen, so the example of its use can be seen in the next section covering the next method: the `lineTo()` method.

## The `lineTo()` Method

The `lineTo()` method is used to draw a line from the preceding point created by either the `moveTo()` method or another `lineTo()` method to the next point. The line drawn will have the characteristics created by the `lineStyle()` method.

The generic layout for this method is

```
movie.lineTo(X,Y);
```

The two parameters for this method are

- X—A numerical value representing the horizontal position to draw the line to

- Y—A numerical value representing the vertical position to draw the line to

Now that we have covered three of the basic methods for the drawing API, here is an example that will bring them together.

1. Create a new Flash document.

2. In the first frame of the main timeline, open the Actions panel, and place these actions in it:

```
//create the line style
this.lineStyle(2,0x000000,100);
//move the starting point
this.moveTo(100,100);
//draw a line
this.lineTo(200,200);
```

The preceding code does three things. First, it creates the line style with a weight of 2 pixels, black as its color, and a 100 alpha setting. After that, it moves the starting point to (100,100). Then it draws a diagonal line to point (200,200).

Test the movie and your screen should look similar to Figure 11.11 with a diagonal line. You can go back in and add more lineTo() methods to make the line go from point to point.

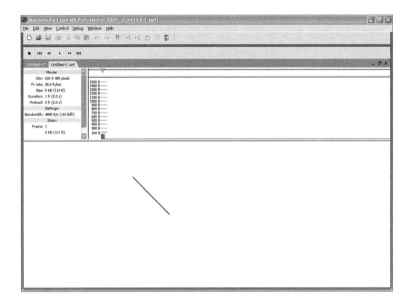

**FIGURE 11.11**    Use the Drawing API to draw lines right from ActionScript at runtime.

That was a simple enough example. Next is a more advanced example, which will allow the user to draw lines during runtime all over the stage. To accomplish this, follow these steps:

1. Create a new Flash document.

2. In the first frame of the main timeline, open the Actions panel, and place these actions in it:

```
//this event will trigger when the user presses the mouse button
this.onMouseDown = function(){
    //declare the line style
    this.lineStyle(4,Math.random()*0x1000000,100);
    //set the starting point
    this.moveTo(this._xmouse,this._ymouse);
    //this event will fire as the user moves the mouse
    this.onMouseMove=function(){
        //draw a line
        this.lineTo(this._xmouse,this._ymouse);
        //re-style the line
```

```
        this.lineStyle(4,Math.random()*0x1000000,100);
    }
}
//this event triggers when the user releases the mouse
this.onMouseUp = function(){
    //destroy the onMouseMove event
    delete this.onMouseMove;
}
```

The preceding code does many things. First, it creates an event for when the user clicks the mouse button, which in turn creates another event that triggers continuously while the user moves the mouse. While the user is moving the mouse, a line is drawn to where the mouse is, and the line continuously changes color. Finally, we create an event for when the user releases the mouse. When that event is triggered, the onMouseMove event is destroyed and the line will not follow the mouse any more.

Test the movie and you will see when you click the mouse, and move the mouse around, a constantly color-changing line will follow the mouse around.

Now that you know how to draw a line, the next step is how to draw a shape and fill it with the beginFill() method.

## The beginFill() Method

The beginFill() method is used to fill shapes drawn with drawing API. Whenever you use the beginFill() method, when you are done filling the shape, you should always have the endFill() method to tell the Drawing API you are done filling.

Here is the generic layout of the beginFill() method:

```
movie.beginFill(color,alpha);
```

This method has two parameters:

- color—A hexadecimal value used in declaring the color of the fill
- alpha—A numerical value representing the transparency of the fill

In the next example, we will draw a square and fill it with a light green color.

1. Create a new Flash document.

2. In the first frame of the main timeline, open the Actions panel, and place these actions in it:

```
//create the line style
this.lineStyle(2,0x000000,100);
//move the starting point
```

```
this.moveTo(100,100);
//begin the fill
this.beginFill(0x00ff00,50);
//draw a line
this.lineTo(100,200);
this.lineTo(200,200);
this.lineTo(200,100);
this.lineTo(100,100);
//end the fill
this.endFill();
```

The preceding code started out similar to previous examples, but this time after we went to the starting point, we began to fill the shape. After that we drew the square. And finally, we ended the fill with the endFill() method.

Test the movie, and you should see a square with a light green color for the fill as shown in Figure 11.12.

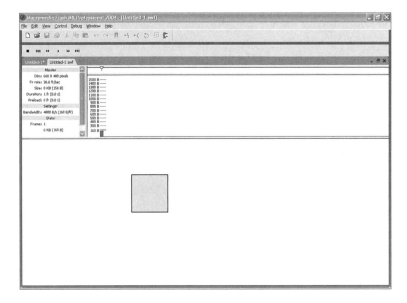

**FIGURE 11.12**    You can use the drawing API to draw shapes, and color them in.

So far, we have drawn straight lines, but the next section will go over how to draw curved lines with the curveTo() method.

## The `curveTo()` Method

The `curveTo()` method is used to draw curved lines with the drawing API. It works similarly to the `lineTo()` method in that it starts from the previous point created by either a `moveTo()` method or a `lineTo()` method.

Its generic layout is as follows:

```
movie.curveTo(controlX,controlY,X,Y);
```

This method has four parameters:

- `controlX`—This represents the horizontal position toward which the line will curve.

- `controlY`—This represents the vertical position toward which the line will curve.

- `X`—This is the horizontal position where the curved line will end.

- `Y`—This is the vertical position where the curved line will end.

The generic layout is a little difficult to grasp without an example, so here is one:

1. Create a new Flash document.

2. In the first frame of the main timeline, open the Actions panel, and place these actions in:

```
//declare the line style
this.lineStyle(2,0x000000,100);
//create the start point
this.moveTo(100,100);
//draw the curved line
this.curveTo(200,100,200,200);
```

The preceding code creates the line style, then declares a starting point, and finally draws the curved line.

Test the movie and your screen should have a curved line on it similar to Figure 11.13.

That example was pretty simple. The following example shows off the `curveTo()` method a little further.

1. Create a new Flash document.

2. In the first frame of the main timeline, open the Actions panel, and place these actions in it:

```
//declare the line style
this.lineStyle(3,0x000000,100);
//go to the start point
```

```
this.moveTo(300,260);
//start the fill
this.beginFill(0xff0000,100);
//start drawing the shape
this.curveTo(300,200,250,200);
this.curveTo(200,200,200,260);
this.curveTo(220,350,300,400);
this.curveTo(398,350,400,260);
this.curveTo(400,200,350,200);
this.curveTo(300,200,300,260);
//end the fill
this.endFill();
```

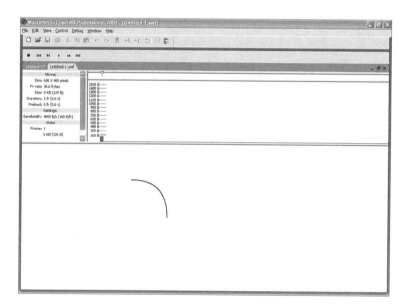

**FIGURE 11.13**    Use the `curveTo()` method to draw curved lines with the drawing API.

The preceding code doesn't really do anything special. It declares the line style we want to use. Then it sets a start point using the `moveTo()` method. After that, it begins the fill with a shade of red as its color. Then it begins to draw the shape using a few `curveTo()` methods. It finishes by ending the fill with the `endFill()` method (which is good practice).

Now test the movie, and you will see a shape on your screen similar to the one in Figure 11.14. Now that you see what can be accomplished with the Drawing API, you can start creating your own custom shapes all with ActionScript.

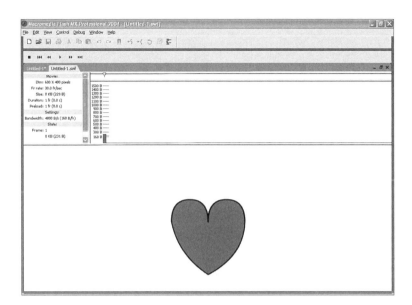

**FIGURE 11.14**  A heart is just one of the many shapes that can be drawn with a little math and the Drawing API.

## Summary

This chapter covered a lot of information regarding the movie clip object. It started with how to create it manually (which was more review than new material) and also how to create them with ActionScript. Then it went on to show some of the many different ways movie clips can be manipulated. After that you learned how to remove movie clips from the stage during runtime using the removeMovieClip() method. And finally, we went over some of the ways to use the Drawing API.

The next chapter covers functions. Try combining that chapter with the Drawing API and you can start creating functions to draw shapes for you.

CHAPTER **12**

# Functions

So far we have covered some of the basics of ActionScript, including variables, statements, and movie clip objects. Now we'll get into functions.

A **function** is basically a reuseable piece of code. After a function is created, it can be used over and over again, without rewriting the code. This is very powerful, not only because it can save on file size but also because it will make your code much more scalable and portable.

This chapter covers the topics of creating functions, using functions, and creating methods and objects with functions. Let's jump right in and create a function.

## Creating a Function

Creating a function is as easy as using the keyword function, providing a name for the function followed by a pair of parentheses for parameters (we discuss the topic of parameters in more depth later), and placing whatever code you want between two curly brackets. It looks something like this:

```
function myFunction(){
    //script to run in function
}
```

Now that you know what a function looks like, you can create one of your own. To begin, open a new Flash movie, click the first frame in the timeline, open the Actions panel (F9), and place the following code:

```
function myFunction (){
    trace ("My first function");
}
```

Now you have your own function, with a simple `trace` statement placed within the curly brackets. However, if you tested your movie at this point, nothing would happen. This is because all you have done so far is create the function; now you need to run it.

## Running the Function

Now that you have your function, let's make it work for you. To run this function (also called **invoking** or calling the function), you start with your function name, followed by a set of parentheses to hold your parameters, and you finish with a semicolon to end the line, as shown here:

```
function myFunction (){
    trace ("My first function");
}
myFunction();
//output: My first function
```

That was easy. You simply created a function and then invoked it to see the statements run and the message displayed in the Output panel.

Let's now look at another way of creating functions. This way starts with the function name that we set to the Function type. Then you set it equal to the keyword `function`, followed by a set of parentheses and the curly brackets for holding your code. Here's an example using a generic template:

```
var myFunction:Function = function(){
    //script to run in function
}
```

Now let's put this into practice with the previous example:

```
var myFunction:Function = function(){
    trace("My second function");
}
myFunction();
//output: My second function
```

Now you have seen two basic ways of creating functions and running them. So far, all you have done is run a simple `trace` statement. Now let's put some script in it that you can really use. We'll start with a function that fades out a movie:

```
var fadeOut:Function = function(){
    myMovie_mc._alpha -= 5;
}
//now invoke the function
fadeOut();
```

Every time this function is invoked, the movie clip `myMovie_mc` will decrease its `_alpha` value by 5. You would normally place this function within a looping event such as an `onEnterFrame` event. (For more on events, see Chapter 14.)

That was simple, but what if you only wanted to fade to a certain point? You can place conditional as well as loop statements within functions to perform a condition test.

Here's the same example, but this time we're using an `if` statement to only allow `myMovie_mc` to fade to a certain point:

```
var fadeOut:Function = function(){
    if(myMovie_mc._alpha >50){
        myMovie_mc._alpha-=5;
    }
}
//now invoke the function
fadeOut();
```

Now the function will check whether the movie clip has faded to the designated point yet. If it has reached the designated point, the function still runs, but the code in the `if` statement will not.

Now, suppose you want to set the point where the alpha will fade differently for two different functions that are invoked. This is where parameters come in.

## Using Parameters in Functions

So far you have seen how to create functions and place scripts inside them. This is not very dynamic, though, in that once the information is in the function, it cannot be adjusted for different situations. Now we'll use parameters to change this limitation.

Parameters in a function act similarly to variables in ActionScript. They can be changed on the fly whenever the need arises. You place the parameters in parentheses following the name of the function, which looks something like this:

```
function myFunction(parameter){
    //script involving parameter;
}
```

You can also set the type for the parameters, which is very helpful in debugging, as you will see in the next example.

The preceding code is simply a generic template, so let's look at some examples next. The first example runs a simple `trace` statement:

```
//create a function with a string parameter
function myTrace(name:String){
    trace(name);
}
```

```
//now we will run the function twice with two different parameters
myTrace("Doug");
myTrace("Paul");
//output: Doug
//        Paul
```

You can see that we used the `String` data type to make sure that is the type of data being passed into the parameters. If you change one of the parameters to the number 15, you will receive this error in the Output panel when you test the movie, or check your code:

```
    **Error** Scene=Scene 1, layer=Layer 1, frame=1:Line 7: Type mismatch.
     myTrace(15);
    **Error** Scene=Scene 1, layer=Layer 1, frame=1:Line 7: Type mismatch.
myTrace(15);
```

The preceding code will not create an error if you put quotes around the number because then it would still be a string.

Now let's return to the previous fading example and see how to use parameters with conditional statements.

As before, you want to set a point that your movie clip will fade to, but this time you'll use three parameters—the instance name of the movie clip, the point to fade the movie to, and the amount to fade the movie by. In this example, you'll use a loop statement instead of a conditional statement:

```
function fade(movie:MovieClip, fadePoint:Number, amount:Number){
    while(movie._alpha > fadePoint){
        movie._alpha -= amount;
    }
}
//now that the function is made, let's run it on a couple of movies
fade(myMovie_mc,50,5);
fade(myMovie2_mc,20,2);
```

The preceding code would be placed in the timeline where both movies reside.

> **NOTE**
>
> It's important to understand that declaring the parameter types is not necessary, but it is good practice and can help prevent future errors.

So far we have used functions to perform basic repetitive tasks using code that we want to consolidate and use whenever we want without having to rewrite the entire script. Now let's make the functions give us back information.

# Functions That Return Values

Currently we are using functions to run repetitive code using parameters, but all the functions are doing is running code. Now let's make them give back some information. To do this, we'll use the `return` statement.

The `return` statement does two things. First, when the interpreter reaches the `return` statement, it causes the function to end. Second, it returns the value of an expression assigned to it, but the expression is optional. Here is a generic template:

```
function functionName (parameters){
    //script to run when function is invoked
    return expression;
}
```

And thanks to ActionScript version 2.0, we can set the strict type of the return value to any data type as you can see in the next example.

Now let's look at an example of using the `return` statement to end a function. This example contains a conditional statement, and if the condition is met, the function will end and will not run the remaining code:

```
function myFunction (num:Number){
    if(num>5){
        return;
    }
    trace(num + " is smaller than 5");
}
//Now we invoke the function twice
myFunction(6);
myFunction(3);
//output: 3 is smaller than 5
```

Even though the function is run twice, because the conditional statement in the first function call is met, the `return` statement is run and the function is ended before the `trace` statement is called. In the second function call, the conditional statement is not met, and the `trace` statement is run.

This time, let's use the `return` statement to return a value to us based on an expression we apply to the `return` statement:

```
function fullName (fName:String,lName:String):String{
    return fName+" "+lName;
}
//now we set the variable to the function
var myName:String = fullName("David", "Vogeleer");
trace(myName);
//output: David Vogeleer
```

12

All we did was set the function to a variable, and the `return` statement returned the value of the expression we assigned to it to the variable. Notice, after the parameters, we use a colon (:) and then the data type `String`. This is where we tell the function what type of data will be returned, and if the return value is not that data type, we will get a type mismatch error.

Using `return` statements, you can nest functions within functions and even use them as parameters.

## Nested Functions

Nested functions can be a great tool if you want to run a repetitive set of scripts within a function but use the result differently in each function. Let's take a look at a couple of functions—the first will square a user-defined number, and the second will combine two squared numbers by using the return value from the first function:

```
function square(num:Number):Number{
    return num*num;
}
//Now create the second function
function combineSquares():Number{
    square1 = square(2);
    square2 = square(3);
    return square1 + square2;
}
//Set the variable to the second function
myNum = combineSquares();
trace(myNum);
//output: 13
```

The preceding code uses the first function (square) and nests it within a second function (combineSquares) to return a value that uses the returned value of the square function.

Now let's create a function that uses another function as a parameter. We'll use the same example as before, but this time we'll set the square function as a parameter:

```
function square(num:Number):Number{
    return num*num;
}
//Now create the second function
function combineSquares(square1:Number, square2:Number):Number{
    return square1 + square2;
}
//Set the variable to the second function
myNum = combineSquares(square(2),square(3));
trace(myNum);
//output: 13
```

As stated, you can nest functions within themselves for repetitive use if you want to use the result differently in each function.

We have talked about creating and using functions in many different ways; now let's see the scope of a function.

## Function Scope

The scope of a function is like the scope of a variable; the function is only directly available (called by name, instead of dot syntax mapping to the function) in the following situations:

- If the function is called on the same timeline it was created in.

- If the function is called from a button where the function resides on the same timeline as the button that called it.

In previous versions of Flash, if none of these criteria were met, you had to use dot syntax to map to the function you created. Since Flash MX, you can use the `global` identifier to create a function that is available throughout the entire Flash movie and all its timelines. (We will discuss the `global` identifier later in this chapter.)

First, let's discuss how to map to functions using dot syntax.

## Mapping to a Function

There are two basic ways of mapping to a function:

- **Using relative or absolute identifiers**. In this case, *root* refers to the root timeline of the current level the script is run on, and *parent* refers to the movie clip or object that contains the movie clip or object with the script. If a script using the _parent object is placed within a movie, the script looks to the movie containing itself. Also, _level*N* refers to the *n*th level in the standalone Flash player or the Flash movie.

- **Using direct movie names**. An example is `myMovie.myFunction();`. Notice that every movie object or movie name used in dot syntax is separated by a period.

---

**NOTE**

Although it is possible to call functions created on other timelines, it is good practice to keep all functions on the main timeline, or in an external `.as` file so that you will always know where to find them.

---

Now that you have seen some generic tags for using dot syntax to map to functions, let's look at a few examples of using them:

```
_root.myFunction()            //invokes the function in the root timeline
_parent.myFunction()          //invokes the function in the parent timeline
_parent._parent.myFunction()  //invokes the function in the parent of the
                              //parent timeline
_root.myMovie.myFunction()    //invokes the function in myMovie which is
                              //located on the root timeline
```

As mentioned before, using dot syntax is no longer a necessity when trying to reach a function from a timeline that's different from the one it was created on due to the _global identifier.

# The _global **Identifier**

The _global identifier, which was introduced back in Flash MX, has the power to allow functions and other data types to be reached from the entire movie. It can transform any variable, array, function, or object into a globally available data type. This way, you can create all the variables, functions, and whatever else you need to call upon in the main timeline and reuse them over and over again being called from anywhere in the Flash file.

The generic template looks like this:

```
_global.datatype
```

We could go on for several pages talking about this object, but for this chapter, we'll use it in the context of functions. Therefore, let's look at the generic template:

```
_global.functionName = function(parameters){
    //script to be run
}
```

Now that you have seen the general form of a global function, let's jump right in and create one.

We'll start with a simple trace function, with no parameters this time, and place this script in the main timeline:

```
_global.myFunction = function(){
    trace("My first global function");
}
```

You can now call this function from anywhere in the entire Flash movie and on any timeline, provided there is not a local function with the same name, which will cause the interpreter to use the local function instead.

The preceding example was straightforward, and so is the next one. This time, we are going to use parameters with the function but still use a `trace` statement as the script:

```
_global.myFunction = function(name:String){
    trace(name);
}
```

Now whenever this function is invoked from anywhere, whatever string is placed as its parameter will be displayed in the Output window when the movie is tested.

These two examples are great, but they do not show the true power of what the `global` object can do. The next example requires a little more effort and understanding to see how the object works.

First, create a new Flash document. On the main stage, draw a circle and then convert it to a movie clip symbol (F8), give it an instance name of `circle_mc`, and place it on the far left side of the stage.

Now in the timeline that your circle resides in, create another layer, name it **actions**, and place the following actions in the first frame of the new layer:

> **NOTE**
>
> This layer should be blank. Technically, you can place code in layers where symbols reside, but this is not a good habit.

```
_global.frictionSlide = function(friction,movie,distance,startX){
    newX = startX + distance;
    if(movie._x <= newX){
        movie._x+=(newX-movie._x)*friction;
    }
}
```

Now that this code is on the main timeline, you can put the function and a variable in your symbol. So, double-click `circle_mc` to edit it. Create a new layer called actions, and place these actions in the first frame of that layer:

```
var currentX = this._x;
//now invoke our function
this.onEnterFrame=function(){
    frictionSlide(.2,this,300,currentX);
//notice how the function can be invoked without a direct path to the function
}
```

When you test the movie, the circle will slide slightly to the right and then slow down.

You can adjust the parameters for when you call the function to have it do different things. Here's what we did in the actions of the `circle_mc` movie clip: First, we get the current X position, and store it in the variable. Then, we call our global function inside the `onEnterFrame` event so that it will continually be called to make the circle look like it is sliding, but it is really just changing its X position over and over again.

Of course, because this function is global, it can be called from anywhere, and the parameters can be changed for each movie clip.

Also note that, as shown in the preceding code, the global function calls a local variable. The next section covers some rules involved with calling variables regarding functions.

## Variables and Functions

When using variables in conjunction with functions, you need to follow several rules to avoid errors and increase consistency.

First, you should be cautious when using a variable name that's the same as the name of a parameter in the function when they both reside in the same script. This should be common sense (if for no other reason than for the sake of organized code), but let's say it happens anyway.

Create a variable and call it `myVariable`; then create a function and have it trace `myVariable`:

```
var myVariable:String = "Flash";
//now create the function with no parameters
function myFunction (){
    trace(myVariable);
}
//now run the function
myFunction();
//output: Flash
```

In this instance, the interpreter does not find `myVariable` anywhere in the function, so it begins to look outside the function, and it runs into the variable you created, which is named `myVariable`, and grabs the value of that variable.

Now let's see what happens when you use a parameter with the same name. Using the same code as before, simply add a parameter with the same name as the variable you created:

```
var myVariable:String = "Flash";
//now create the function
function myFunction (myVariable:String){
    trace(myVariable);
}
```

```
//now run the function
myFunction("2004");
//output: 2004
```

This time, the interpreter found myVariable within the function itself, as a parameter name, and ignored the variable that was created before the function was created.

Finally, let's add a variable inside the function with the same name as the parameter and the variable you created before the function (again, using the same code as before):

```
var myVariable:String = "Flash";
//Now create the function
function myFunction (myVariable:String){
    var myVariable:String = "Unleashed";
    trace(myVariable);
}
//Now run the function
myFunction("2004");
//output: Unleashed
```

This time the interpreter found the variable myVariable inside the function and didn't bother with the parameter or the variable you created before you created the function.

So now you know how the interpreter looks for variables: First, it looks in the function itself; then it looks at the parameters, and finally it looks outside the function.

The variables available within the function are not available outside the function. Let's take a look at an example:

```
//First create the function
function myFunction (myVariable:String){
    var myVariable:String = "Unleashed";
    trace(myVariable);
}
//call the function
myFunction();
//trace the variable
trace(myVariable);
//output: Unleashed
//        undefined
```

Notice that you cannot pull the variable name out of the function, even after the function has been invoked. This is important because it means that the scope of variables created inside a function is local to that function. Thus, after the function is run, the variable is no longer in existence, and you regain some (a small amount of) virtual memory.

The next section will take functions a step further. As far as parameters are concerned, all we have covered involves using them to pass information to a function. Now you'll see how to use them as objects.

## The Arguments Class

Each time a function is invoked, an Arguments object is created automatically, and can be referenced using the local variable arguments, which is automatically included within the scope of the function. Basically, arguments are the parameters you define when you invoke any function. The arguments variable of any function is more like an array (refer to Chapter 13, "Arrays," for more on arrays). And as with an array, you can call specific parameters as well as the number of total parameters. The arguments variable can be used to get information about any and all of the parameters being passed to that function. You might want to double-check to make sure the user has passed the correct number of parameters or the correct type of parameters.

Let's start with the number of arguments in a given function. Gathering this information is as easy as using the length property of the arguments object.

### The length Property

The length property of the arguments object found in all functions returns a value that represents the number of parameters a user has defined when a function is invoked. The generic template looks like this:

```
function functionName(parameters){
    //code to be run in the function
    arguments.length;
}
```

As you'll notice, you must use the length property as well as the arguments object inside the function. (The length property is also a property of arrays as well as a property of strings and can be used outside a function only in that context.)

Now let's see this property in a real example. Create a function with two basic parameters and trace the length of the arguments, like so:

```
function myFunction (x:Number,y:Number){
    trace (arguments.length);
}
//now run the function
myFunction(5,6);
//output: 2
```

The function runs, and the number of parameters are displayed in the Output window.

However, as mentioned before, the `length` property returns the number of arguments when the function is invoked, not created. To see what that means, here is an example:

```
//create a function with two parameters
function myFunction(x:Number,y:Number){
    trace(arguments.length);
}
//now invoke the function, but add a parameter
myFunction (5,6,7);
//output: 3
```

Now that you have seen how to find the number of arguments, the next step is to pull individual arguments out of the entire set.

To call individual arguments, you use the `arguments` object and a numerical value held in brackets. The generic template looks like this:

```
function functionName(parameters){
    //code to be run in the function
    arguments[N]
}
```

With this generic template, place a number (*N*) in the brackets that represents the argument in that position. However, note that arguments begin counting at 0 instead of at 1, like arrays, so the first element looks like this:

```
arguments[0]
```

Here is an example using this method of pulling individual arguments:

```
//create a function with three parameters
function myFunction(x:Number,y:Number,z:Number){
    trace(arguments[1]);
}
//now invoke the function
myFunction(2,4,6);
//output: 4
```

Because arguments begin counting at 0 instead of at 1, the second argument is labeled [1] instead of [0].

Now, using this method combined with the `length` property, you can create some amazing code. Let's take a look at an example that creates a function that adds all numbers placed as parameters:

```
//first create a function with no parameters
```

```
function addArgs(){
//now use a loop statement to total the argument values
    var numTotal:Number = 0;
    for(var i:Number = 0; i<arguments.length; i++){
        numTotal += Number(arguments[i]);
    }
//display the total in the output window
    trace (numTotal);
}
//now invoke the function with as many numbers as you like
addArgs(1,2,3);
//This can also work with combining strings.
//first create a function with no parameters
function combineStrings(){
//create a variable that will hold a string literal space
    var space:String = " ";
    var total:String = "";
//now use a loop statement to combine the strings
    for(var i:Number = 0; i<arguments.length; i++){
//now convert each argument to a string for consistency
        total +=arguments[i].toString()+space;
    }
    trace (total);
}
//now invoke the function with as many strings as you like
combineStrings("Flash","MX 2004 Pro","Unleashed");
//output: 6
//      Flash MX 2004 Pro Unleashed
```

Another great use of this technique involves creating an array that can hold the arguments outside of the function, because, as previously stated, the Arguments object cannot be used outside the function. Here's an example:

```
//first create a function with no parameters
function createArray():Array{
//create an array to hold the arguments
    var myArray:Array = new Array();
    for(var i = 0; i < arguments.length; i++){
        myArray.push(arguments[i]);
    }
    return myArray;
}
//set a variable equal to the returned array
```

```
var argsArray:Array = createArray(1,2,3,"One","Two");
//display new array in output window
trace(argsArray);
//output: 1,2,3,One,Two
```

These are just a few examples of using the `length` property combined with pulling individual arguments. There are two more properties of the `Arguments` object, and they are the `callee` property, which refers to the function being called, and the `caller` property, which refers to the `Arguments` object of the calling function.

Here is a small example using the `callee` property of the `Arguments` object. It will take a number, add it to itself, and then subtract one, and continue until the number reaches one.

```
//create the function
addNums = function (num) {
  if (num <= 1) {
    return 1;
  } else {
    return num + arguments.callee(num-1);
  }
}
//send the value returned to the output panel
trace(addNums(4));
//output: 10
```

So far, you have seen functions used as easily repeatable code that can be changed, as needed, by using parameters. However, you can also use them for more than just actions because they can also be considered objects.

## Functions As Objects

Using a function as an object may seem a bit unorthodox, but this actually greatly increases the useability of a function. This process was covered in Chapter 8, so the following is mostly for review purposes.

To create a function object, you assign it without the parentheses and use it like an expression. Also, because the function is becoming an object, you can move it around like any other type of data.

Here is an example using the built-in function `trace()` (built-in functions are discussed in the "Functions Built Into Flash" section):

```
//First, we set a variable to the trace function, but without parentheses
var myFunction:Function = trace;
myFunction("This function is also an object");
```

```
//output: This function is also an object
```

As you can see, the `trace` function is sent to the variable `myFunction` as an object, and because the variable is equal to the function, we invoked the function using the variables name.

Now let's look at another way of using the `trace` function as an object—this time we'll create our own function and set what we want displayed as a property of it:

```
//First, create the function
function myInfo (){
    trace(myInfo.name);
}
//Assign a property called name to the function
myInfo.name = "David";
//Run the function
myInfo();
//output: David
```

Assigning properties to functions is easy because of the built-in `function` object. You can even assign multiple properties to your functions. Now, suppose you would like to see a list of all the properties in a function. You can use the `for in` loop statement to pull properties of objects. (For more on loop statements, see Chapter 10, "Statements and Expressions.")

To use the `for in` loop statement, place the keyword `for` ahead of an opening parenthesis. Then place the keyword var followed by your variable's name (in this case, `functionProp`). Then place the keyword in followed by the name of the object (the function's name, in this case). Finally, place a closing parenthesis, then opening and closing curly brackets enclosing the script you want to run while the loop looks through the properties. Here's what it looks like:

```
//First, create the function
function myInfo (){
}
//Now assign properties to it
myInfo.fName = "David";
myInfo.lName = "Vogeleer";
myInfo.age = "23";
myInfo.location = "Virginia";
//now use the for in statement to look through our properties
for(var functionProp in myInfo){
    trace("The property "+functionProp+" equals "+myInfo[functionProp]);
}
//output: The property location equals Virginia
//         The property age equals 23
```

```
//          The property lName equals Vogeleer
//          The property fName equals David
```

Notice that, in this example, we not only called the name of the property but also the value by using the function's name and the property we wanted to call in brackets. Because we used a dynamic variable, we did not have to put it in quotes. However, to get or set a single property of a function using brackets, you must place the name of the property in quotes, as shown in the following code:

```
//First, create the function
function myInfo (){
}
//Now assign the property to it
myInfo.age = "23";
trace(myInfo["age"]);
//output: 23
```

Let's take it another step forward by creating multiple functions with multiple properties. Then we'll store each function in an array. (As mentioned earlier, arrays are covered in greater detail in Chapter 13.) After that, we'll call all the properties of all the functions to be displayed in the Output window, and because we stored the functions in the array as objects, we can invoke the functions by using the array.

First, we'll create the functions we need and, in the first one, store the trace statement we'll use at the end of the code. After that, we'll assign the properties to the functions. Then we'll create the array and store the functions in the array as objects. Finally, we'll run a script that looks through each element of the array as well as displays each property in each element.

After that, we'll invoke our first function using the array as a shortcut. Here's the code:

```
//First, create the functions
function myInfo (){
//This script is for later use
    trace("Traced from myInfo");
}
function flashInfo (){
}
//Create the properties for each function
myInfo.fName = "David";
myInfo.age = "23";
flashInfo.version = "2004 Pro";
flashInfo.player = 7;
//Now create the array to hold the functions as objects
var functionArray:Array = new Array();
```

```
//Place the functions in the array
functionArray[0] = myInfo;
functionArray[1] = flashInfo;
/*
Finally we create the script to search through the array
and trace all of our properties with their values
*/
for (var myElement in functionArray){
    for (var functionProp in functionArray[myElement]){
        trace("Property "+functionProp);
    }
}
//and because the function is stored as an object in the array
//we can call it using the array
functionArray[0]();
//output: Property player
//          Property version
//          Property age
//          Property fName
//            Traced from myInfo
```

In the preceding code, we used only two functions and two properties for each function. You can, however, increase both, and the script will still function properly.

Now that you have seen functions used as repeatable sets of code and as objects, let's move on to using them as methods to be used in conjunction with other objects.

## Functions As Methods

Before we get into using functions as methods, we need to review what a method is. A method is a function used in conjunction with an object. A method can perform a desired task on that object or can be used to gather information from that object.

We call methods in the same way we call functions, using parentheses; however, methods are attached to objects using dot syntax. Here is a generic template for calling a method:

```
object.method();
```

The preceding template is just for calling a method; to assign a method, you drop the parentheses, like this:

```
object.method;
```

Now that you have the generic templates to go by, let's start creating a few methods. First, we'll place a simple trace function within a function we create. Then we'll create a generic object, called gObject, and assign a property of gObject to our function. Then we'll invoke it by using the entire name, including the property. Here's the code:

```
//First, the function
function myFunction(){
    trace("Flash MX 2004 Unleashed");
}
//Then the generic object
var gObject:Object = new Object();
//Now the property of the object
gObject.title = myFunction;
//Now invoke the method
gObject.title();
//output: Flash MX 2004 Unleashed
```

Using a method is stronger than using a function when dealing with an object in that the method can manipulate the object itself. Take a look at the following code to see the function created and then reworked to change the object's method:

```
//First, the function
function myFunction(){
    trace("Flash MX 2004 Unleashed");
}
//Then the generic object
var gObject:Object = new Object();
//Now the property of the object
gObject.title = myFunction;
//Now create a new property
gObject.name = "David";
//Rewrite the function
function myFunction(){
    trace(this.name);
}
//Invoke the method
gObject.title();
//output: David
```

In this code, you can see how changing the function completely changes the method title of the gObject object.

Functions can also get information from objects when used as methods. Let's start by looking for a single property in an object and then have the function return its value instead of tracing it directly. Then we'll trace the method. Here's the code:

```
//First, create the object
```

```
var gObject:Object = new Object();
//Now add two properties to our object
gObject.age = 23;
gObject.ageVerify = getAge;
//Here, create the function, and have it look for the property
function getAge (){
    return(this.age);
}
trace(gObject.ageVerify());
//output:23
```

That was a lot of work for not a big payoff. We could have simply traced the property itself. Therefore, let's build on the preceding example and combine multiple properties in an expression that we may want to use again and again.

In this example, we'll create an object called `myCircle`. Then we'll create a function that gets the circumference and the area of the object. The idea is that no matter how often the properties we use change, the function will perform the same calculation on our object. Here's the code:

```
//First, create the object
var myCircle:Object = new Object();
//Now add a property and two methods to our object
myCircle.radius = 5;
myCircle.circumference = getCircumference;
myCircle.area = getArea;
//Here, create the functions
function getArea():Number{
    return Math.round(Math.PI*Math.pow(this.radius,2));
}
function getCircumference():Number{
    return Math.round(Math.PI * 2 * this.radius);
}
//Finally, invoke the methods
trace(myCircle.area());
trace(myCircle.circumference());
//output: 79
//         31
```

Note that we use `Math.round()` in these functions to keep the answers smaller. The preceding code shows that methods can be quite powerful when used in an expression. You can change the value of `radius` to verify that the formula will still calculate correctly, or you can even apply the functions as methods to other objects for the same results.

Flash does have built-in methods as well as custom methods that you create. As a matter of fact, it is difficult to write ActionScript without using methods. They are too numerous to list here, because nearly each object has its own set of methods. You can review Chapter 8, or look into the reference for more on methods.

Here is a list of a few of the methods that are built into Flash:

```
myArray.push();        //adds an element to an array

myMovie.stop();        //stops a movie clip's playhead

myXML.load();          //loads an XML document into an XML object

Math.sqrt();           //returns the square root of a number
```

## Functions Built into Flash

We have covered ways of creating and manipulating user-defined functions thus far. Now we'll focus on some of the built-in functions Flash has to offer. We'll briefly go over some basic built-in functions. Finally, we'll discuss some of the deprecated functions, which are functions that still work in Flash, but may not be supported in the next version.

Because you know what functions look like, I'll only briefly label the parts:

```
stop()             //stops a movie clip from playing, and has no parameters
play()             //plays a movie clip, and has no parameters
gotoAndStop(5)     //goes to a specified frame (the parameter) and stops
trace("Flash")     //displays parameter in output window
```

This list just goes on and on.

However, there are a couple of functions that deserve mention. One of them is the `call` function.

### The `call` Function

The `call` function is an interesting function that's brought all the way from Flash 4. This function can run code from any given frame without moving to that frame. It is a deprecated function, and Macromedia recommends using the keyword `function` to make code available throughout the timeline, as we discussed earlier. However, it's still good to know how to use the `call` function in case you ever need to.

The generic template is straightforward. Use the keyword `call`, followed by a string representing the frame label or a number representing a frame number, enclosed in parentheses. Here is the generic template:

```
call(frame);
```

Now that you know what it looks like, let's use the `call` function in an example.

1. Start a new Flash document

2. Then create a new layer. Name the top layer **labels** and the bottom layer **actions**. Then place two more keyframes in each layer (F6).

3. Open the Actions panel for the first frame on the actions layer and place this code there:

```
stop();
```

This will stop the play head from moving past this frame.

4. Next, in frame 2 of the same layer, place this `trace` statement:

```
trace("This is code from frame two");
```

5. Then in the final frame of the actions layer (frame 3), place this `trace` statement:

```
trace("This is code from the third labeled frame");
```

6. Now we turn our attention to the labels layer. Give the first frame the label of "one"; in the second frame, give it the label "two"; and in the third frame of this layer, place the label "three." When you're done, your screen should look similar to Figure 12.1.

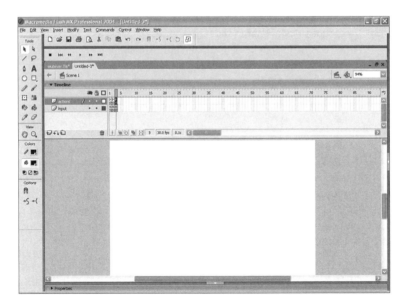

**FIGURE 12.1**    The project thus far.

7. If you were to test this movie right now, nothing would happen. This is because of the stop function in frame 1. If stop were removed, both trace statements would run repeatedly, over and over again, while the movie loops through. However, when you place these next actions after stop, both statements will be run, but only once, and the frames still will never be reached by the play head. Therefore, place the following code in the first frame of the actions layer, and at the end, it will look like this:

```
stop();
call(2);
call("three");
//output: This is code from frame two
//        This is code from the third labeled frame
```

Test the movie. There you have it—the code that was placed in frame 2 as well as the third frame, which was labeled "labeled," runs without the play head ever reaching these frames.

Now that we have covered this unique function, let's move on to some more built-in functions. Flash has predefined a couple of categories for functions in the Actions panel. The first category is conversion functions.

## Conversion Functions

Conversion functions perform a specific task on objects: they convert objects. Each of the five main data types has its own conversion script that will change it to another data type.

The generic template utilizes the keyword of the object you are trying to convert to, and the expression you are trying to convert follows, enclosed in parentheses, as shown here:

```
converter(expression);
```

We will use the following example to change some data from one type to another. After each step, we will use the trace statement and the typeof operator to display the data type of each object following the conversion. Here's the code:

```
//Start off with a simple string
myString = "string";
trace (typeof myString);
//Now we begin converting the same object
//again and again while checking after each time
myString = Number(myString);
trace (typeof myString);
myString = Array(myString);
trace(typeof myString);
myString = Boolean(myString);
```

```
trace(typeof myString);
myString = Object(myString);
trace(typeof myString);
//Finally back to a string
myString = String(myString);
trace(typeof myString);
//output: string
//          number
//          object
//          boolean
//          object
//          string
```

> **NOTE**
>
> When converting to an array with the `Array` conversion function, whatever is being converted will be placed in the first element of the array, and not separated into individual elements.

Converting data types is an important part of using ActionScript, however, the preceding code will not work with strict data typing, so keep that in mind if you want to change the data type of a variable over and over (which is bad practice). You can convert numbers from input text fields (all types of information from input text fields are strings; see Chapter 17, "Working with Text," for more information) into true number data types. You can convert Boolean data types into strings to use in sentences.

Let's now move on to the next category of functions: mathematical functions.

## Mathematical Functions

Mathematical functions execute mathematical operations on expressions you assign to them. You may be thinking addition, subtraction, and so on, but these operations are much more advanced. Only four mathematical functions are listed in ActionScript:

- `isFinite`

- `isNaN`

- `parseFloat`

- `parseInt`

The first two of the mathematical functions, `isFinite` and `isNaN`, act more like conditionals because they return a Boolean value. Let's see how they work individually.

The first, isFinite, checks to see whether the expression entered is a finite number. If the number is finite, the function returns True. If the expression is not finite (or infinite), the function returns False. Here is an example in which we test two numbers and trace the results:

```
trace(isFinite(15));
//evaluates to true
trace(isFinite(Number.NEGATIVE_INFINITY));
//evaluates to false
```

The second of these two functions, isNaN, works in the same manner. It checks to see whether the expression entered is not a real number. If the expression is not a real number, the function returns True. If the expression is a real number, the function returns False. Let's take a look:

```
trace(isNaN(15));
//evaluates to false
trace(isNaN("fifteen"));
//evaluates to true
trace(isNaN("15"));
//evaluates to false
```

Even though the last example is in fact a string, the interpreter converted it to a number when it was evaluated. Keep this in mind when evaluating numbers as strings.

The next mathematical function is parseFloat. This function takes numbers out of a string literal until it reaches a string character. Then it converts what it has removed into a true number data type. Here are a few examples:

```
trace(parseFloat("15"));
//output: 15
trace(parseFloat("fifteen"));
//output: NaN
trace(parseFloat("20dollars"));
//output: 20
trace(parseFloat("12.14"));
//output: 12.14
trace(parseFloat("5+10"));
//output: 5
```

As you can see in the last example, the function only takes the number and drops the rest of the string.

The last mathematical function is parseInt. This function can perform the same task as the parseFloat function, but it can also use a radix, which is useful when working with octal numbers. Here is an example:

```
trace(parseInt("15", 8));
//output: 13 (a representation of the octal number 15
//that has been parsed)
```

Although there are only four mathematical functions, there are many methods associated with the Math object—remember, methods are functions that are associated with objects.

A few more functions are defined directly in ActionScript, which can be called without any object, including getProperty(), getTimer(), targetPath, and getVersion(), all of which return information. There is also eval, escape, and unescape, which perform their desired tasks on expressions.

We have covered a great deal of information about functions; now let's look at some deprecated functions and alternatives to their use.

## Deprecated Functions

If you have worked in Flash 4 or even Flash 5, you may notice that some of the functions are not where they used to be. No, they are not completely gone, but they are deprecated, which means that ActionScript provides new ways of performing the same tasks, and although these functions are still available for use, they might not be in the next release. Therefore, it is a good idea to get out of the habit of using them.

We'll go over each deprecated function briefly and discuss alternatives to their use.

chr

The chr function converts a numeric value to a character based on ASCII standards. It has been replaced by String.fromCharCode. Here are examples of both:

```
//The old way
trace(chr(64));

//The new way
trace(String.fromCharCode(64));

//output @
//       @
```

int

The int function takes a number with a decimal point and drops the decimal point. It has been replaced by Math.floor. Here are examples of both:

```
//the old way
trace(int(5.5));
```

```
//the new way
trace(Math.floor(5.5));

//output: 5
//         5
```

length

The length function returns the number of characters in a string or variable holding a string. It has been replaced by String.length. Here are examples of both:

```
//First create a variable holding a string
myString = "Flash";

//the old way
trace(length(myString));

//the new way
trace(myString.length);

//output: 5
//         5
```

mbchr

The mbchr function, like the chr function, converts a numeric value to a character based on ASCII standards. It has been replaced by String.fromCharCode. Here are examples of both:

```
//the old way
trace(mbchr(64));

//The new way
trace(String.fromCharCode(64));

//output @
//        @
```

mblength

The mblength function, like the length function, returns the number of characters in a string or variable holding a string. It has been replaced by String.length. Here are examples of both:

```
//First create a variable holding a string
myString = "Flash";
```

```
//the old way
trace(mblength(myString));

//the new way
trace(myString.length);

//output: 5
//       5
```

### mbord

The `mbord` function converts a character to a number by using the ASCII standard. There is no replacement, but this function is still deprecated. Here is an example:

```
trace(mbord("@"));
//output: 64
```

### mbsubstring

The `mbsubstring` function removes a set number of characters from a string. It has been replaced by `String.substr`. Here are examples of both:

```
//First, create a variable to hold a string
myVar = "Unleashed";

//the old way
trace(mbsubstring(myVar, 0, 2));

//the new way
trace(myVar.substr(0, 2));

//output: Un
//        Un
```

### ord

The `ord` function, like the `mbord` function, converts a character to a number by using the ASCII standard. There is no replacement, but this function is still deprecated. Here is an example:

```
trace(ord("@"));
//output: 64
```

### random

The `random` function returns a random number from a expression given. It has been replaced by `Math.random`. Here are examples of both:

```
//the old way
trace (random(5));

//the new way
trace (Math.floor(Math.random()*5));
//output: (2 random numbers between 0-4)
```

substring
The substring function, like the mbsubstring function, removes a set number of characters from a string. It has been replaced by String.substr. Here are examples of both:

```
//First, create a variable to hold a string
myVar = "Unleashed";

//the old way
trace(substring(myVar, 0, 2));

//the new way
trace(myVar.substr(0, 2));

//output: Un
//        Un
```

This is the last of the deprecated functions.

# Summary

That's it for all the functions. We have gone over everything, from creating functions to
using deprecated functions. We have even covered using functions as objects and
methods.

Just remember that functions are mainly used as blocks of repetitive code, parameters are
used to slightly modify functions for different uses, you can use the return statement to
return a value from a function, and methods are functions attached directly to objects.

As you go through the rest of the book, you will really begin to see where functions can
come in handy.

CHAPTER **13**

# Arrays

## What Is an Array and How Does It Work?

Back in Chapter 9, "Strings, Numbers, and Variables—In Depth," we discussed different data types, including variables. Variables can hold one piece of data or another data type, including another variable. Like variables, arrays can hold any type of data, including strings, integers, and Booleans. They can also hold other data types, including variables and other arrays (called nested arrays), which we will discuss later in this chapter.

In this chapter, we go over what an array is, how to create one, and how to retrieve, manipulate, and delete data from arrays with an applied example at the end.

So let's jump right in and see how an array is made.

## Deconstructing an Array

As stated earlier, an array is a data type that can hold multiple pieces of information. Here's an easy way to imagine this: A variable is like a chair, and it can hold one person (one piece of data). On the other hand, an array is more like a bench, and it can hold multiple people (multiple pieces of data).

Each piece of data in an array is called an **element**. Each element is automatically assigned the name of the array and a unique number called its **index**, which is enclosed in brackets. However, the first element in an array is not assigned the number 1; it is instead assigned the number 0 because arrays start counting at zero instead of one.

Therefore, the first element in the array myArray is labeled myArray[0]. Likewise, for the seventh element in the same array, you would use myArray[6].

This indexing is great for holding and retrieving sequential information.

The number of elements in an array is known as its **length**, and we will cover this topic in greater detail later in the chapter when the properties of an array are discussed.

## Creating an Array

Now that you know what an array is and what it does, let's discuss how to create one. There are several different ways to create an array; however, we will be dealing mainly with the new operator and the Array constructor to build our sample array.

Open a new movie, click the first frame of the main timeline, and open the Actions panel. When creating arrays using the new operator and the Array constructor, start by setting a variable. Then make the variable equal to the new operator combined with the Array constructor, followed by a set of parentheses and then a semicolon (to end the line of code). Here's an example:

```
var myArray:Array = new Array();
```

You're done! You just created your first array, so let's take a look at it. Start by adding the following to your code:

```
var myArray:Array = new Array();
trace(myArray);
```

Now test your movie by choosing Control, Test Movie. When you test your movie, an output window will open because of the trace function in the code. However, nothing appears in the window, as shown in Figure 13.1. That's because there is nothing in our array. Let's go back and add some data to the array.

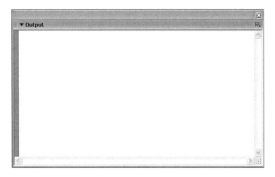

**FIGURE 13.1**    An empty output window for your movie.

Each element in an array is labeled with the array's name and an integer that represents its position inside of the array. The first element in an array will always have an index of 0, followed by the second element indexed as 1, and so on. Because you have already created the array, you will label the new elements manually. On the next line after the line in which you created the array, type the array name and then **0** in brackets, like this:

```
var myArray:Array = new Array();
myArray[0] = "fName";
myArray[1] = "lName";
trace(myArray);
//output: fName, lName
```

Now that you have data in the array, you can continue to add elements. However, it's much easier to create the elements right in the beginning. So let's do that next. Also, notice that this time the output of the code is preceded by comment marks (//). Such comments do not affect the code at all and are merely for explaining some of the actions in it. The output will appear in the code like this from now on.

You will still be using the original code, but when you create the array this time, you will create it with data inside. Elements in an array can be of any data type, as discussed earlier. Let's use a couple of strings to start with. When putting elements in an array when you create them, place them in the parentheses and separate them with commas, like this:

```
var myArray:Array = new Array("fName","lName");
trace(myArray);
//output: fName, lName
```

Another way of creating an array with information doesn't involve the new operator or the array constructor. You can simply set a variable equal to the elements you want in the array, but instead of putting them inside parentheses, place them between brackets, as shown here:

```
var myArray:Array = ["fName","lName"];
trace(myArray);
//output: fName, lName
```

This traces the same as the other examples. However, just remember that when you do not use the new operator and the array constructor, you must place the elements in brackets.

You can even put just one piece of data in the array when you create it, but make sure it is not an integer. Otherwise, some surprising results will happen. Let's take a look.

Use the same code as before but replace what is in the parentheses with the number 5 (note that the output of the code is shown within the code using comment marks):

```
var myArray:Array = new Array(5);
trace(myArray);
//output: undefined,undefined,undefined,undefined,undefined
```

When you test the movie, notice that it doesn't display the number 5 but instead displays five elements as undefined. This is because when you place only an integer in an array, it creates that many blank elements.

You can also store variables in arrays just like any other type of data, and the data stored in the variables will display in the array:

```
var myName:String = "David";
var myAge:Number = 22;
var myArray:Array = new Array(myName, myAge);
trace(myArray);
//output: David, 22
```

Besides variables, arrays can also hold other arrays (called **nested arrays**). Nested arrays are useful for holding multiple lists in one place. Just place the name of the array as an element, as you would a variable:

```
var myNames:Array = new Array("fName","lName");
var myArray:Array = new Array("age",myNames);
trace(myArray);
//output: age, fName, lName
```

The second array simply encompasses the first array. However, if you trace the last element in myArray, you will see that it doesn't separate the elements from myNames. Let's take a look at this:

```
var myNames:Array = new Array("fName","lName");
var myArray:Array = new Array("age",myNames);
trace(myArray[1]);
//output: fName, lName
```

As you can see, even though it appears that when we added myNames to myArray, the elements came over as individual elements, in fact the entire array came over as one element. Just keep this in mind when you add arrays to arrays.

## Retrieving Information from an Array

When retrieving information from an array, use the index of the array element to pull that specific piece of data, as shown here:

```
var myArray:Array = new Array("fName","lName","age");
trace(myArray[1]);
//output: lName
```

In this example, we simply call the second element in myArray, which has the index of 1 because arrays start counting at 0.

There is a way to count the number of elements within an array—using the `length` property. It is the only property that an array has. Just attach the `length` property to any array with a period, and it will return the length. Here's an example:

```
var myArray:Array = new Array("fName","lName","age","location");
trace(myArray.length);
//output: 4
```

> **TIP**
>
> Remember, the index of the last element in any array will always be the value of `array.length` minus 1.

When combined with loop statements, the `length` property can be used to retrieve sequential information.

This example lists each element vertically in the Output window, as opposed to all in one line. Place this code in the first frame of the main timeline actions of the movie:

```
var myArray:Array = new Array("fName","lName","age","location");
//the loop statement to cycle through the Array
for(var i:Number = 0; i < myArray.length; i++){
    trace(myArray[i]);
}
//output: fName
//        lName
//        age
//        location
```

This is just a simple example of how to use a loop statement and the `length` property.

## Adding Elements to Arrays

So far we have created an array and placed elements in the array; now let's add elements to an array. There are a couple of ways of accomplishing this. Let's start with the simple method and move into the more dynamic method.

You can start by setting the `length` property of an array. Setting the `length` property of an array will add as many blank elements to that array as you specify—but again, the last blank element will have the index of the length minus 1. Here's an example:

```
var myArray:Array = new Array();
myArray.length = 5;
trace(myArray);
//output: undefined,undefined,undefined,undefined,undefined
```

Using the length property to add elements will only add undefined elements to the beginning.

Now we will add elements that actually have data in them. Start by creating an array and adding elements using the index of the elements, as shown here:

```
var myArray:Array = new Array("fName","lName");
trace(myArray);
myArray[2] = "age";
myArray[3] = "location";
trace(myArray);
//output: fName, lName
//        fName, lName, age, location
```

That was pretty easy. All we did was add elements manually by looking at the next index of the array and assigning an element to it.

Now we will make it more dynamic. Create a button and place it on the main stage. Give it an instance name of myButton_btn. Then add these actions to the first frame of the main movie:

```
var myArray:Array = new Array();
var i:Number = 0;
myButton_btn.onPress = function(){
        var thisLength:Number = myArray.length;
        myArray[thisLength] = i;
        i++;
        trace(myArray);
}
//output: (depending on how many times you click the button, increasing
//output continued:          numbers starting at 0)
```

Let's take a look at what we did. First, we created an array and a variable that equals zero. Then, we added actions to a button on the main timeline so that, when the button is clicked, the action will set the element with the index of the array's length to the variable i. The variable i will be increased by 1 each time the button is clicked. Finally, we traced the array.

Well, that was pretty dynamic, but we had to write some code that lets us know what the next index of the array should be. Now we're going to talk about an array method that will do the checking for us: the push method.

## The push Method

The push method is great when you want to add elements to the end of an array without checking the length. Just assign the method to the array using a period and put what you want to add in parentheses following the push. Take a look at the following example.

Start a new Flash document and add these actions to the first frame of the main timeline:

```
var myArray:Array = new Array();
//create the object to listen for the event
var keyListen:Object = new Object();
//create the event
keyListen.onKeyDown=function(){
    var theKey:String = String.fromCharCode(Key.getAscii());
    myArray.push(theKey);
    trace(myArray);
}
//Add the listener
Key.addListener(keyListen);
//output: (every key you press depending on how many
// and which key(s) you press)
```

This example is a simple keystroke recorder to show how easily the push method works. It simply "pushes" the keystroke to the end of the array.

When you're pressing keys in the test screen, if you do not see anything at first, click the mouse on the stage. Even though a keyDown event is taking place, sometimes the mouse must be clicked inside at least once for the event to take place.

You can also push more than one element at a time into an array. In this example, we will add two pieces of data at the end of the array using the push method:

```
var myArray:Array = new Array("fName","lName");
trace(myArray);
myArray.push("age","location")
trace(myArray);
//output: fName, lName
//        fName, lName, age, location
```

Here, we just added two elements to myArray simultaneously using the push method.

You can add any kind of data type using the push method, as shown in the following example:

```
var myArray:Array = new Array("fName","lName");
trace(myArray);
var x:Number = 10;
var anotherArray:Array = new Array("age","location");
var y:Number = 5 + x;
myArray.push(x,y,anotherArray);
trace(myArray);
//output: fName, lName
//        fName, lName, 10, 15, age, location
```

Here, we've added a variable, an expression, and even another array to our original array using the push method.

As an interesting aside to what the push method for arrays can do, you can check the new length of an array while using the push method to add elements, as shown here:

```
var myArray:Array = new Array("fName","lName");
trace(myArray.push("age","location"));
trace(myArray);
//output: 4
//        fName, lName, age, location
```

You can even substitute this method of returning the length for the length property in some cases. Here's an example:

```
var myArray:Array = new Array("fName","lName");
trace(myArray.push(myArray.push()));
trace(myArray);
//output: 3
//        fName, lName, 2
```

Because this method adds the number before it checks the length using the push method, it adds the number 2, representing the length of the array, instead of 3.

The push method is great for gathering repetitive information for retrieval. Some examples might be providing back and forward control inside the Flash movie and recording users' information for the next time they visit.

Another example is a search function that searches inside an array and returns the frequency and positions of the element you are looking for:

```
//First, create the function and label your variables
searchArray = function(theArray:Array,lookFor:String) {
//Then create an array to hold the positions
        var position:Array = new Array();
    //Use a for loop statement to check through each element
        for (var i:Number = 0; i <=theArray.length-1; i++) {
//Use an if statement to compare each element to what you're looking for
            if (theArray[i] == lookFor) {
//If the element matches, add to the position array
                position.push([i]);
            }
        }
    //Lastly, trace the results
        trace("The frequency is " + position.length);
        trace("In position(s) " + position);
```

```
}
var myArray:Array = new Array("fName","lName","age","location","age");
searchArray(myArray,"age");
    //output: The frequency is 2
    //        In position(s) 2, 4
```

This is just another example of how to use the push method and the length property to retrieve elements from an array.

Another method you can use to add elements to an array is the unshift method.

## The unshift Method

The unshift method works identically to the push method, except that, instead of adding elements to the end, it adds them to the beginning. Here's an example:

```
var myArray:Array = new Array("fName","lName");
trace(myArray);
myArray.unshift("age");
trace(myArray);
//output: fname, lName
//        age, fName, lName
```

Again, the unshift method adds elements to the beginning of an array. Therefore, each of the original elements' indexes is increased. For instance, fName will go from myArray[0] to myArray[1], and age will become myArray[0].

Also, like the push method, the unshift method can be used to show the length of an array:

```
var myArray:Array = new Array("fName","lName");
trace(myArray.unshift("age","location"));
trace(myArray);
//output: 4
//        age, location, fName, lName
```

Like the push method, unshift traces the new length and adds elements to the array, but unlike push, it adds them to the front of the array.

## The splice Method

The splice method is one of the more powerful methods of arrays. Not only can it add elements to an array, but it can also delete elements and place elements in the middle of arrays. Its syntax is very similar to the other methods we have talked about, except it has multiple parts:

```
myArray.splice(startingIndex,deleteNumber,itemsToAdd);
```

Let's take a look at the first part, the part that will delete items from the starting point forward. Attach the method as you would any other, and in the parentheses, place the index of where you want to start deleting items from the array:

```
var myArray:Array = new Array("fName","lName","age","location","phone");
myArray.splice(2);
trace(myArray);
//output: fName, lName
```

The method started with the second index, which was age, and deleted all remaining elements. The elements were permanently removed. As a matter of fact, if you check the length of myArray after the splice, the value will be 2.

Now that you know how to delete from one index to the end, let's see how to remove a certain number of elements from a starting point. Use the same code, only this time, in the parentheses place a comma after the starting point and put in however many elements to remove. Here's an example:

```
var myArray:Array = new Array("fName","lName","age","location","phone");
myArray.splice(2,2);
trace(myArray);
//output: fName, lName, phone
```

This time the method removed elements from the starting index we assigned and permanently removed the number of elements we assigned. If you check the length, it will return the value 3.

The last step of the splice method is to add elements in the middle of the array, beginning with the starting point. Again, we will be using the same code as before. This time after the number representing the number of elements to remove, we'll place another comma and then add the elements while separating them with commas:

```
var myArray:Array = new Array("fName","lName","age","location","phone");
myArray.splice(2,2,"fax","email");
trace(myArray);
//output: fName, lName, fax, email, phone
```

This time, the splice method removed the number of assigned elements at the assigned starting point and added elements at the starting point. Again, when adding elements, you can add any type of data, including variables and other arrays.

Now let's add elements to the middle of an array without deleting any elements. This time, we'll use the same syntax but set the number of items we want to delete to zero:

```
var myArray:Array = new Array("fName","lName","age","location","phone");
myArray.splice(2,0,"fax","email");
```

```
trace(myArray);
//output: fName,lName,fax,email,age,location,phone
```

Because we set the number of items to delete to zero, the method simply adds the elements in at the index we listed and slides the other elements over.

The splice method has yet another great use. It can return the values of the items removed. Here's an example:

```
var myArray:Array = new Array("fName","lName","age","location","phone");
trace(myArray.splice(2,2));
//output: age,location
```

In this case, instead of showing what the array looks like after the splice, the method shows which elements were removed. At this point, if you trace the array, it will show the new array with these elements removed. This is really useful if you want to remove certain information from one array and place that information in another array. Here's an example:

```
var myArray:Array = new Array("fName","lName","age","location","phone");
var anotherArray:Array = myArray.splice(2,2);
trace(anotherArray);
trace(myArray);
//output: age, location
//        fName, lName, phone
```

This time, we removed items from an array and placed them in a new array called anotherArray.

You can even add elements to the original array while removing elements from it and placing them into a new array. Using the same code as before, this time we'll add an element to the original array:

```
var myArray:Array = new Array("fName","lName","age","location","phone");
var anotherArray:Array = myArray.splice(2,2,"fax");
trace(anotherArray);
trace(myArray);
//output: age, location
//        fName,lName,fax,phone
```

That was simple enough. We removed two elements and placed them in a new array while adding an element to the original array.

To summarize, the splice method can almost do it all. You can use it to add, remove, and change the elements inside an array. It can even be used to create new arrays.

Another method used for adding elements to arrays is the concat method.

## The `concat` **Method**

The concat method works similarly to the push method in that it adds elements to the end of an array. However, it does not affect the original array. Instead, it creates a new array with the new elements.

To demonstrate the concat method, let's use our sample array. Now we can create another array by adding elements to the original with the concat method:

```
var myArray:Array = new Array("fName","lName","age");
var anotherArray:Array = myArray.concat("phone","fax");
trace(anotherArray);
//output: fName, lName, age, phone, fax
```

The new array, anotherArray, has both the elements from the original array, myArray, and the new elements we add to the end. If you trace myArray, nothing changes because the concat method only affects the new array it creates.

One nice thing about the concat method is that when adding an array to another array, it separates the elements and adds them as singular elements. Let's take a look at two examples: one using the push method and the other using the concat method.

Here's the example that uses the push() method:

```
var myArray:Array = new Array("fName","lName");
var anotherArray:Array = new Array("age","location");
myArray.push(anotherArray);
trace(myArray[2]);
//output: age, location
```

And here's the example that uses the concat() method:

```
var myArray:Array = new Array("fName","lName");
var anotherArray:Array = new Array("age","location");
myArray = myArray.concat(anotherArray);
trace(myArray[2]);
//output: age
```

In the first example, we used the push method to add the second array to myArray. Notice that it doesn't separate the elements into their own individual elements. Instead, it places the entire array in myArray[2]. In the second example, we used the concat method to add the second array to myArray. When the concat method is used, array elements are separated into individual elements.

---

> **NOTE**
>
> Unless you set the array equal to itself, the concat method will not permanently affect the original array.

---

Even though concat will separate the elements in an array into individual elements, it will not separate nested arrays. Here's an example:

```
var myArray:Array = new Array(["fName","lName"],["age","location"]);
var anotherArray:Array = myArray.concat(myArray);
trace(anotherArray[0]);
//output: fName, lName
```

# Naming Array Elements

Most array elements are numbered, but they can also be named. Naming array elements is an easy way to keep information organized within an array. None of these named elements can be manipulated by array methods, nor can they be seen when the array is traced.

There are two ways to create named array elements. The first uses dot syntax, and the second uses brackets and string literals. Here's an example of both methods:

```
var myArray:Array = new Array();
myArray.fName = "David";
myArray["age"] = 22;
trace(myArray);
//output: (nothing)
```

> **NOTE**
>
> When you use dot syntax with any other object in Flash, the word that follows the dot is referred to as a property. However, because the Array is a unique class of object, when you use dot syntax, the elements are called named array elements.

We first created an array to hold the named elements and then we attached the first element using dot syntax and set it equal to a string. Then we attached the next named element using brackets and a string to name it, and we set its value to a number. Finally, we traced the array, but there were no results. This is because, as previously stated, when you trace an array, named elements will not appear. You have to call the named elements individually. Therefore, using the same code as before, we will trace both named elements individually when tracing the array:

```
var myArray:Array = new Array();
myArray.fName = "David";
myArray["age"] = 22;
trace(myArray["fName"]);
trace(myArray.age);
//output: David
//        22
```

This time, when we traced the elements individually, the trace was successful.

Named array elements will also not show up in the array's length. Here's an example:

```
var myArray:Array = new Array();
myArray.fName = "David";
trace(myArray.length);
//output: 0
```

Now that you know how to add elements to an array, let's cover how to remove them.

# Removing Array Elements

Just like adding elements, removing them has several different options. We will start with the simple options and then move into using the array methods.

The first option for removing elements from an array is using the `delete` operator.

### The `delete` Operator

The `delete` operator is misleading. It does not actually delete the element in the array; it merely sets the element to `undefined`. To use this operator, type **delete** and then use a space to separate the array element you want to "delete" by using its index. Here's an example:

```
var myArray:Array = new Array("fName","lName");
trace(myArray[0]);
delete myArray[0];
trace(myArray[0]);
//output: fName
//        undefined
```

As you can see, when we traced the first element in `myArray` before we used the `delete` operator, it displayed `fName`. Then after we used the `delete` operator, the output of the first element became `undefined`. Also note that the length of an array after the use of the `delete` operator will stay the same—even though the operator removes the data in the element, it does not remove the element itself.

The `delete` operator can also be used on named array elements, as shown here:

```
var myArray:Array = new Array();
myArray.fName = "David";
trace(myArray.fName);
delete myArray.fName;
trace(myArray.fName);
//output: David
//        undefined
```

Just like indexing array elements, the delete operator simply removes the value of the element, but the element is still in the array.

To remove the element itself, we have a few choices. The first involves using the length property. Then there are the pop, shift, and splice methods.

## Removing Elements Using the length Property

Using the length property to remove elements in an array is very similar to using it to add elements. Just create an array and set its length, like so:

```
var myArray:Array = new Array("fName","lName","age","location");
trace(myArray);
myArray.length = 2;
trace(myArray);
//output: fName, lName, age, location
//        fName, lName
```

Using the length property to remove elements is a very simple way to get rid of everything that comes after the desired length of the array.

## The splice Method Revisited

The splice method was already covered earlier in this chapter. This time, however, we'll use it for the removal of elements in an array.

You can use the splice method in two different ways when removing elements. The first way removes all elements beginning with the starting index you define. The second way sets the number of elements to remove at the starting index. Here's an example:

```
var myArray:Array = new Array
("fName","lName","age","location","phone","fax","email");
trace(myArray);
myArray.splice(5);
trace(myArray);
myArray.splice(2,2);
trace(myArray);
//output: fName, lName, age, location, phone, fax, email
//        fName,lName, age, location, phone
//        fName, lName, phone
```

The first splice sets the starting index and removes all elements at and beyond that point. The second splice sets the starting index and the number of elements to remove and then actually removes those elements. Another method used for removing array elements is the pop method.

## The pop **Method**

The pop method can be thought of as being the "archenemy" of the push method. Whereas the push method adds elements to the array, the pop method removes singular elements from the end of the array. Its syntax is the same as the other methods—just attach the method to the array you want to remove elements from, as shown here:

```
var myArray:Array = new Array("fName","lName","age","location");
myArray.pop();
trace(myArray);
//output: fName, lName, age
```

In this example, the pop method simply dropped the last element in the array completely and changed the length of the array.

The pop method can also return the value of the element it removes. Here's an example:

```
var myArray:Array = new Array("fName","lName","age","location");
trace(myArray.pop());
//output: location
```

The next method for removing array elements is the shift method.

## The shift **Method**

If the pop method is the archenemy of the push method, the shift method is the archenemy of the unshift method. The shift method removes one element from the beginning of an array and decreases its length by one:

```
var myArray:Array = new Array("fName","lName","age","location");
myArray.shift();
trace(myArray);
//output: lName, age, location
```

Also like the pop method, the shift method returns the value of the element it removes:

```
var myArray:Array = new Array("fName","lName","age","location");
trace(myArray.shift());
//output: fName
```

But what if we don't want to get rid of the elements in an array and instead just want to change them?

# Changing Elements in Arrays

Now that you know how to add and remove elements, let's discuss how to change them. We will create an array, trace it to see the original, change the first element to something

else by using the index, and then trace it again to see the difference as shown in the
following code:

```
var myArray:Array = new Array("fName","lName");
trace(myArray);
myArray [0] = "age";
trace(myArray);
//output: fName, lName
//         age, lName
```

That was pretty simple. We just renamed the first element, like renaming a variable.
What's more, changing named array elements is just as easy, as shown here:

```
var myArray:Array = new Array();
myArray.age = 23;
trace(myArray.age);
myArray.age = 24;
trace(myArray.age);
//output: 23
//         24
```

The next section covers nested arrays in greater detail and how they can be used and
manipulated.

## Advanced Nested Arrays

Earlier in this chapter, we briefly discussed nested arrays (arrays held within other arrays).
Now we are going to discuss some advantages to using these nested arrays. First, let's go
over again how to create one. The example we'll use here involves the starting five of a
basketball team by position. This example shows the following information:

- Points scored

- Shots taken

- Total rebounds

We will start with just the first two positions and combine them, as shown here:

```
var pG:Array = new Array(12,15,4);
var sG:Array = new Array(20,22,5);
var team:Array = new Array(pG,sG);
trace(team);
//output: 12,15,4,20,22,5
```

Now that we have the data entered, we could get the point guard's rebounds from the `team` array, without showing the other elements. To do this, we assign an index to the indexed element. This may sound complicated, but it's not. We want to know how many rebounds the point guard has (the third element in the first element of the `team` array). Here's the code we'll use:

```
var pG:Array = new Array(12,15,4);
var sG:Array = new Array(20,22,5);
var team:Array = new Array(pG,sG);
trace(team[0][2]);
//output: 4
```

Success! We retrieved an individual element from a nested array. This is a very powerful tool when you have massive arrays with many nested arrays. Now let's take this a step further. We'll add the rest of the team and this time get the total for each category and place this information in an array called `totals`. We'll also divide the totals, as they are being calculated, by the main array's `length` property to get the averages for the players and then place that information into another array called averages. Here's the code:

```
//First, get all the players ready with their stats in their own array
var pG:Array = new Array(12,15,4);
var sG:Array = new Array(20,22,5);
var sF:Array = new Array(11,13,8);
var pF:Array = new Array(18,14,16);
var c:Array = new Array(20,17,21);
//Now combine all the players arrays into one array called "team"
var team:Array = new Array(pG,sG,sF,pF,c);
var totals:Array = new Array();
var averages:Array = new Array();
//Now let's create the loop statement that will perform all the necessary
//tasks we want
for(var i:Number = 0; i<team[0].length; i++){
    //reset the holders
    var tempTotal:Number = 0;
    var tempAvg:Number = 0;
  for(var j:Number = 0; j<team.length; j++){
    tempTotal += team[j][i];
//Place the total of each tempElement into the totals array
    totals[i]=tempTotal;
//Divide the total of each sub-element by
//the main array's length to get the average
    tempAvg +=(team[j][i])/team.length;
    averages[i] = tempAvg;
  }
}
trace(totals);
```

```
trace(averages);
//output: 81, 81, 54
//       16.2,16.2,10.8
```

In this example, we drew information in sequence from the nested arrays, totaled each column, and placed the totals in another array. We also successfully got the averages for all the players and placed them in another array. This is just one of the many possibilities for using this method.

# Additional Array Methods

So far we have gone over methods for adding and removing elements. Now we will go over some other array methods for manipulating elements within an array.

### The toString Method

Often, you might want to set an array equal to a variable, but when you set a variable equal directly to an array, the script simply copies the array over to that variable and stores each element as its own element. We'll use the toString method, which you saw before in Chapter 9, to convert an entire array to one string, with each element separated by commas:

```
var myArray:Array = new Array("fName","lName");
var anotherArray:Array = myArray;
var myVariable:String = myArray.toString();
trace(anotherArray[0]);
trace(myVariable[0]);
//output: fName
//        undefined
```

This example shows that when we copied myArray into anotherArray, an exact copy of the original array was created. Then we copied the same array to myVariable, but attached the toString method to it. When we tried to trace a singular element out of myVariable, undefined was returned. So now let's drop the index of myVariable and see what happens:

```
var myArray:Array = new Array("fName","lName");
var anotherArray:Array = myArray;
var myVariable = myArray.toString();
trace(anotherArray[0]);
trace(myVariable);
//output: fName
//        fName, lName
```

Notice that the elements are separated with commas and spaces when the array becomes a string. But what if you want to separate each element with some other character? The join method can accomplish this.

## The `join` Method

Similar to the `toString` method, the `join` method converts all elements in an array to one string to place in a variable. Unlike the `toString` method, however, the `join` method separates each element the way you want it to. Again, just set this method to an array as you would any other method and then place whatever data type you want to separate the elements with between the parentheses. It can be a string, a number, a variable, or any other type of data. Here's an example:

```
var myArray:Array = new Array("fName","lName","age","location");
var myVariable:String = myArray.join("--");
trace(myVariable);
//output: fName--lName--age--location
```

Alternatively, you can leave the parentheses blank, which causes `join` to act just like the `toString` method:

```
var myArray:Array = new Array("fName","lName","age","location");
var myVariable:String = myArray.join();
trace(myVariable);
//output: fName,lName,age,location
```

You can even put in an expression, as shown here:

```
var myArray:Array = new Array("fName","lName","age","location");
var myVariable:String = myArray.join(2+2);
trace(myVariable);
//output: fName4lName4age4location
```

Now let's look at another method for arrays—the `slice` method.

## The `slice` Method

Like the `splice` method, the `slice` method can grab elements from an array and place them into a new array. Unlike the `splice` method, however, the `slice` method does not affect the original array. Here's an easy way to think of these methods: The `splice` method is like cutting, and the `slice` method is like copying.

The syntax for the `slice` method is the same as the `splice` method—you can set the starting point and how many elements you want to copy. Here's an example:

```
var myArray:Array = new Array("fName","lName","age","location");
var anotherArray:Array = myArray.slice(2);
trace(anotherArray);
trace(myArray);
//output: age, location
//        fName, lName, age, location
```

The `slice` method copies the elements, starting with the declared index, to the last element of the original array and places them in a new array without affecting the original array.

You can also set the ending index of the elements you want to copy:

```
var myArray:Array = new Array("fName","lName","age","location");
var anotherArray:Array = myArray.slice(2,3);
trace(anotherArray);
//output: age
```

So far, these methods have removed, added, and shifted elements. Now let's change the order of them with the reverse method.

### The `reverse` Method

The `reverse` method is exactly what it sounds like—it's a method for reversing the order of all the elements in an array. After you've created an array, you can attach the `reverse` method to it, like so:

```
var myArray:Array = new Array("fName","lName","age","location");
myArray.reverse();
trace(myArray);
//output: location, age, lName, fName
```

The `reverse` method is used mainly for reversing already sorted arrays. The next section shows you how this method is used.

## Sorting Arrays

Sorting plays an important role in using arrays. With sorting, you can put names in alphabetical order, put prices from greatest to least, and even see who has the highest score so far in a video game.

There are two types of sorting: One involves a general sort of the elements in an array, and the other involves the sorting of nested arrays.

Let's go over the general `sort` method. Just attach this method as you would any other method, and it sorts somewhat alphabetically. Here's an example:

```
var fName:Array = new Array("David","Mike","George","Matt","Kim");
fName.sort();
trace(fName);
//output: David,George,Kim,Matt,Mike
```

The sort worked fine. So why did I mention it will sort "somewhat" alphabetically? As you'll notice, all the strings in the `fName` array start with a capital letter. However, change the first letter in "David" to a lowercase *d* and see the results:

```
var fName:Array = new Array("david","Mike","George","Matt","Kim");
fName.sort();
trace(fName);
//output: George,Kim,Matt,Mike,david
```

This time, "david" is moved to the back, even though it's the same name. The sort method does not recognize "david" as being the same as "David" because it doesn't look at the letters themselves; instead, it looks at their ASCII code points (discussed in Chapter 9), in which capital letters come before lowercase letters. There are solutions to this, however, and that is where the arguments to the sort method come in. You can pass arguments to control how the sort method will sort. There are three arguments you can pass:

- 1—When A appears after B in the sorted sequence

- -1—When A appears before B in the sorted sequence

- 0—If A is equal to B

If you pass the sort method 0 as an argument, it is the same as leaving it blank.

Let's see what each does to our example:

```
var fName:Array = new Array("david","Mike","George","Matt","Kim");
fName.sort(1);
trace(fName);
fName.sort(-11);
trace(fName);
fName.sort(0);
trace(fName);
//output: George,Kim,Matt,Mike,david
//        david,George,Kim,Matt,Mike
//        George,Kim,Matt,Mike,david
```

In this example, we created an array filled with people's first names, except that one of them was not capitalized, which confused the sort method. We passed it three different arguments to see which way we wanted it sorted.

## The sortOn Method

The sortOn method is an extremely tricky method to use. This method sorts nested arrays by the value of a specific named element in each array. The syntax is similar to other methods covered so far, but in the parentheses, you put the named field you want to sort all the nested arrays by. Each of the nested arrays you want to sort must have that named field in it. Let's take a look at an example:

```
var one:Array = new Array();
one.a = "a";
one.b = "b";
```

```
one.c = "c";
var two:Array = new Array();
two.a = "b";
two.b = "c";
two.c = "a";
var three:Array = new Array();
three.a = "c";
three.b = "a";
three.c = "b";
var myArray:Array = new Array(one,two,three)
trace(myArray[0].a);
myArray.sortOn("b");
trace(myArray[0].a);
//output: a
//        c
```

In this example, we first created the three arrays we are going to put in our main array. In each of the nested arrays, we created three named array elements: one, two, and three. Then we set each of the three named elements to three different string literal letters: a, b, and c. Next we shuffled each of the values so that the arrays will not be equal to each other. Then, we placed each of these three arrays in myArray. After that, we traced the named element a in the first nested array of myArray. Then we ran the sort based on the named element b in all the nested arrays. After the sort, we traced myArray again based on the named element a in the first array element, and this time it was c. Therefore, the sort was successful.

## Applied Example

We have gone over lots of code and different examples of how to use some of the methods of arrays. Now let's look at an applied example of arrays at work. We are going to create a mouse recorder that, after a certain length of recording, will replay the recorded positions of the mouse.

First, we must create the necessary symbols for the movie:

1. Create a movie symbol with an arrow graphic that's centered at the point of the arrow. Name this symbol **arrow** (see Figure 13.2).

2. Create a button symbol to move from frame to frame (I used one from the common libraries under Window, Other Panels, Common Libraries, Buttons). Name this symbol **button** (see Figure 13.3).

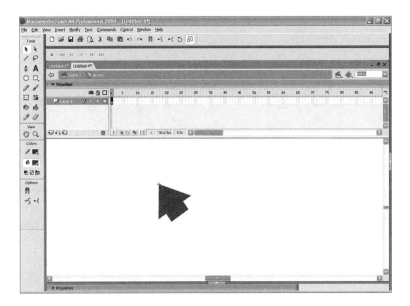

**FIGURE 13.2**    The "arrow" symbol.

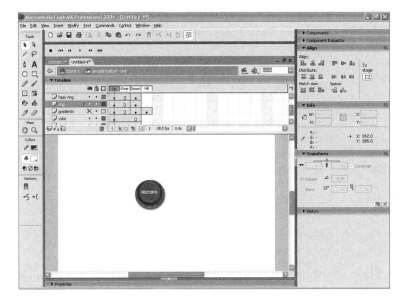

**FIGURE 13.3**    The "button" symbol.

Next, on the main stage, create four layers with the following labels:

- Actions
- Labels
- Arrow
- Button

The movie will consist of three keyframes. In the Labels layer, label the frames like this:

- `frame 1—start`
- `frame 10—record`
- `frame 20—playRecord`

In the Button layer, place a copy of the button we created and give it an instance name of `record_btn`.

Now we will move to the Actions layer. In the first frame, place this code:

```
stop();
//Create our arrays to hold our data
var mouseX:Array = new Array();
var mouseY:Array = new Array();

//this is the event for the button
record_btn.onRelease = function(){
        gotoAndStop("record");
}
```

Next, create a second keyframe in frame 10 of the Actions layer. Place the following code within that frame:

```
//Create a variable to adjust the length of the recording
//in seconds
var time:Number = 10;
var startTime:Number = getTimer();

this.onEnterFrame=function(){
//Then use a loop statement to check if time is up
    if(time >= Math.floor((getTimer()-startTime)/1000)){
//Record the positions of the mouse and place them
//in the arrays on the main stage
        mouseX.push(_xmouse);
```

```
        mouseY.push(_ymouse);
    }else {
//When time is up
        gotoAndStop("playRecord");
        delete this.onEnterFrame

    }
}
```

Then, on the Arrow layer, place an arrow instance on the main stage with an instance name of arrow_mc in the third keyframe (frame 20). Then create another keyframe in the Actions layer and place these actions in it:

```
//create the incramental variable
var i:Number=0;
this.onEnterFrame=function(){
//as long as the you are not at the end of the array
//keep playing
    if(i<mouseX.length){
//Set the positions of this arrow equal to positions
//held in arrays on the main timeline
        arrow_mc._x = mouseX[i];
        arrow_mc._y = mouseY[i];
        i++;
    }else {
//When it's over, go to the beginning
        _root.gotoAndStop("start");
    }
}
```

That's it! Now test the movie and have some fun coming up with your own experiments using arrays. Also note that the higher the frame rate, the smoother the animation will play.

## Summary

We have gone over all the basics of arrays including how to create them. We have also covered the methods used in Flash to control arrays including adding and removing data as well as re-sorting data on command. Also covered in this chapter is the only property of an array, the length property. Remember that the number of elements in an array is the array's length minus 1.

After going over the fundamentals and theories behind the structure of arrays and when to use them, we then applied them in a real-world example.

CHAPTER **14**

# Events

Back in Chapter 8, "Welcome to ActionScript 2.0," we went over the three basic elements that all objects in Flash have:

- **Properties**. Information about an object, held within the object

- **Methods**. These are the "verbs" of objects; they are what the object does.

- **Events**. Events tell Flash when something has occurred with that object.

For instance, with a movie clip, here are the three elements:

- **Property**. _x

- **Method**. gotoAndPlay(2)

- **Event**. onEnterFrame

This chapter goes into more detail about the third thing that objects have, events.

An event, simply put, is when something happens. Every day you go through several hundred events. Every time you get email, that is an event. When you eat lunch, that's another event. And when you go home on Friday, you know that's an event.

So you see, events happen all the time in almost everything we do. So what's the big deal with events? Well, events in Flash are used to tell us when something occurs so that we can run a certain block of actions or go to a certain frame in the movie. To put it in real-world terms, sometimes people want to be notified when a certain event happens. For instance:

- "Let me know when she calls."

- "Let me know when lunch is here."

- "Let me know when the next meeting is."

These are just a few events that people want to be notified about in everyday life. When these events occur, the individual who is notified will do something about it. For instance, if someone is notified when lunch arrives, that person will probably want to eat it. This is what that event would look like in ActionScript:

```
onLunchArrival = function(){
    eatLunch();
}
```

That looks simple enough, and it is. In Flash, you have events, which we will cover in detail throughout this chapter, that you might want your movie or application to listen for so that it will know when to execute a block of code. But before we cover some of the events of different objects, it's important to know how to handle these events in Flash when they occur.

# Handling Events

Knowing how to handle an event is very important. Just the fact that an event occurs doesn't mean anything in itself. In order to do something with that event, you must capture it first. Flash has two basic means of capturing events: the callback and the listener.

The first one we will discuss is the callback.

## The Callback

For those who have been programming in Flash for some time, callbacks will seem more familiar and therefore easier to use and implement in your code. **Callbacks**, simply put, are functions tied directly to a particular event.

Because you can create and destroy as well as overwrite any and every variable, function, and method in Flash on the fly, callbacks are basically functions written directly to the event.

For instance, the movie clip object has an event called onMouseDown that is triggered every time the user presses the mouse button on the stage. But if you were to run a blank movie (remember, the main timeline is nothing more than the _root movie clip) and click the mouse on the stage, nothing would happen. This is because no function has been created with the onMouseDown event.

So to handle the event, you need to build a function around the event itself like this:

```
//this refers to the main timeline
this.onMouseDown = function(){
    trace("the mouse is down");
}
```

Usually you would want to do more than simply send a message to the Output panel. Sometimes, you may want the event to interact with other objects, and that's where the downside of callbacks comes in.

Because callbacks are associated directly with events of a specific object, in this case the _root timeline, you cannot always refer directly to other objects on the stage if they are not enclosed in the object of the event being called.

For instance, if you have two movie clips on the stage (movie1_mc and movie2_mc), and you have a onMouseDown event for the movie1_mc movie, you cannot directly access movie2_mc from within that event:

```
movie1_mc.onMouseDown = function(){
    movie2_mc.gotoAndPlay("start");      //this will not work
}
```

The preceding code will not run properly because the onMouseDown event is in the scope of the movie1_mc and not in the scope of movie2_mc. The following code will fix this problem.

```
movie1_mc.onMouseDown = function(){
    _parent.movie2_mc.gotoAndPlay("start");      //this will work
}
```

Just keep in mind the scope of the object you are referring to inside the event.

Another point to note is that some events pass information to the callback. For instance, the onLoad event for the LoadVars object sends the callback a Boolean value based on its success or failure in loading content.

Here's an example of how to get information from events with callbacks:

```
//create the LoadVars object
var myStuff:LoadVars = new LoadVars();
//create the call back
myStuff.onLoad = function(success){
    if(success){
        //it worked
    }else{
        //it didn't work
    }
}
//load the content
myStuff.load("theStuff.txt");
```

Notice that we passed the information coming from the event as a parameter in the function. That's how we get information from events using callbacks. And in this case, the

14

event is a Boolean value that is used in conjunction with conditional statements inside the event.

Now that you see how to create a callback, it is important to know how to destroy them as well.

### Removing Callbacks

Sometimes you will want callbacks to stop firing. For instance, if you are using a callback in conjunction with the onEnterFrame event of movie clips, you may only want that event to fire so many times. You can use conditionals to stop the event from affecting anything on the stage, but to regain processor power and virtual memory you need to destroy the callback itself. To do this, you use the delete action.

Here is an example using a loop statement and a delete action:

```
//create a variable we will use in the callback
var i:Number = 0;
//create the callback
this.onEnterFrame = function(){
    //this will trace independant of the conditional
    trace("working");
    if(i < 10){
        trace(i);
    }else{
        delete this.onEnterFrame;
    }
    //increase the variable
    i++;
}
```

The preceding code first creates a variable that is used in the callback. Then it creates the callback and uses a conditional to decide when to destroy itself with the delete action.

Run this code, and you should see an Output panel similar to Figure 14.1. The code runs ten times and then stops completely. To see what would happen if the delete action had not been used, just the conditional, go back and comment out the line containing the delete action. You will see that even though the numbers stop being sent to the Output panel (because of the conditional), the other trace action is still working because the event is still triggering the callback.

Using a callback is just one way of capturing events; the other is using listeners.

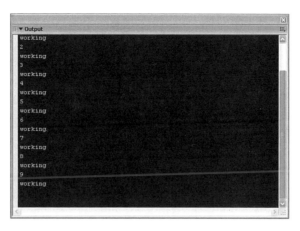

**FIGURE 14.1**   Use the `delete` action to destroy callbacks.

14

## Listeners

If you are new to programming, listeners may appear difficult to use at first, but they are quite powerful when you get used to building them. Listeners take a completely different approach to handling events than callbacks do.

**Listeners** differ from callbacks in two very important ways. First, listeners do not care where the event is coming from (that is, a movie clip, button, or component)—they only care about who is receiving the event. In the case of the `onMouseDown` event, the event is coming from the _root timeline, but the `Mouse` object is actually receiving the event. The other way listeners differ from callbacks is that using a callback with an event will only work with that object, but with listeners, which are objects themselves, you can have several objects "listening" at the same time for the event to fire.

Using listeners is also different from using callbacks. Unlike callbacks, where you just apply a function to that object's event, listeners require you to "subscribe" to the event or object containing the event, or "unsubscribe" from the event or object containing the event. This means that you ask the object to let you know when the event occurs, or you tell it to stop letting you know.

Not all objects support listeners for their events. Those that do have two methods, `addListener()` and `removeListener()`. These two methods are how other objects "subscribe" and "unsubscribe" to the events.

Here is an example using the `Mouse` object's event `onMouseDown`:

```
//create the object to listen
var listenClick:Object = new Object();
//create the event that looks similar to callback
listenClick.onMouseDown = function(){
```

```
     trace("the mouse is down");
}
//now subscribe the listener
Mouse.addListener(listenClick);
```

All the preceding code does is create a generic object to "listen" for the event. It adds the event to the object (it looks like a callback, but without the listener, it won't work). Then it subscribes the object to the Mouse object as a listener.

Now if you test this code, every time the mouse is pressed, the message will be sent to the Output panel.

Also, remember that multiple objects can listen to a single event source. In this next example of code, we will extend the preceding example by creating another object to listen for when the mouse is released:

```
//create the object to listen
var listenClick:Object = new Object();
//create the event that looks similar to callback
listenClick.onMouseDown = function(){
     trace("the mouse is down");
}
//now subscribe the listener
Mouse.addListener(listenClick);
//create another object
var listenUp:Object = new Object();
//create the event similar to before
listenUp.onMouseUp = function(){
     trace("and the mouse is back up again");
}
//now add the new object to the event source as a listener
Mouse.addListener(listenUp);
```

This code merely extends the preceding block of code. It creates another object that will listen to the onMouseUp Mouse event. And then we subscribe it to the Mouse object.

Every time you press and release the mouse button, you will receive two messages in the Output window as shown in Figure 14.2.

Now that you know how to subscribe listeners to objects, the next ysection shows how to unsubscribe them.

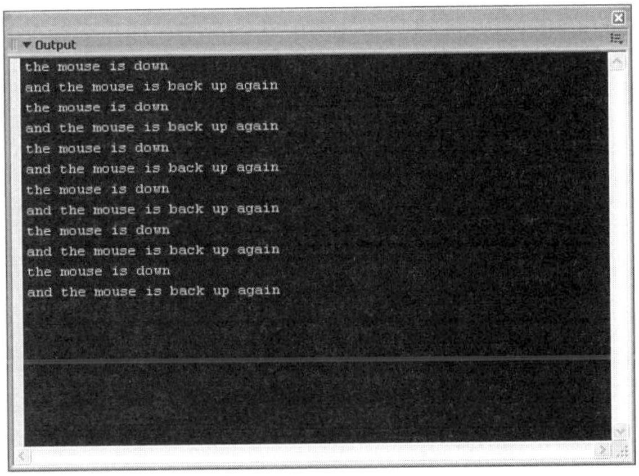

**FIGURE 14.2**   Using listeners can increase efficiency for capturing events.

### Unsubscribing Listeners

Unsubscribing an object uses the method `removeListener()` in conjunction with the object it is currently listening to. This example shows how to use this method:

```
//create the object to listen
var listenClick:Object = new Object();
//create the event that looks similar to callback
listenClick.onMouseDown = function(){
    //send a message to the output panel
    trace("the mouse is down");
    //remove the listener
    Mouse.removeListener(this);
}
//now subscribe the listener
Mouse.addListener(listenClick);
```

This code starts the same way the preceding code does, but the first time the event fires, the listening object removes itself from the `Mouse` object. After the first click, no messages will be sent to the Output panel.

Components also use listeners to trigger events associated with them, although the coding is slightly different from what we have used so far.

### Components' Special Listeners

Back in Flash MX, components used a form of callbacks to refer to functions on the timeline of which the component itself resided. However, in Flash MX 2004, components' events are now centered on using listeners.

To add listeners to components, you use the component's instance name and the `addEventListener()` method.

The generic layout of the addEventListener() method is as follows:

```
component.addEventListener(event, listenerObject);
```

This method has two parameters:

- event—A string literal representing the event you want to listen for
- listenerObject—The object being added as a listener

Here is an example of how to add an event listener to the button component:

1. Create a new Flash document.
2. Drag an instance of the Button component onto the stage.
3. Give the button an instance name of **myButton**.
4. Create a new layer and name it **actions**.
5. In the actions layer, open the Actions panel, and place the following code within it:

```
//create the object
var clickListen:Object = new Object();
//create the event
clickListen.click = function(){
    trace("the button was clicked");
}
//now add the listener
myButton.addEventListener("click", clickListen);
```

The preceding code creates a listener object. Then it creates the event-handling method for that object, which has a trace action in it so it will send a message to the Output panel. Then you add the event listener to the instance of the button.

Now test the movie, and you will see that every time you click the button, the event is triggered, and the listener fires, sending a message to the Output panel.

You can create your own events with components, but that is discussed in more detail in Chapter 16, "Components."

## Duplicating Effort

Some objects will support both callbacks as well as listeners. For instance, you can create a callback with the onMouseDown event and then add a listener to the Mouse object at the same time. Doing this will produce some surprising results, as you will see in the next example of code.

```
//create the callback
this.onMouseDown = function(){
     trace(" the mouse is down");
}
//Now add the listener to the Mouse object
Mouse.addListener(this);
```

The code creates the callback that we have been using in this chapter. After that, it adds the _root timeline as a listener to the Mouse object.

Now test the movie, and you will see that every time you press the mouse button on the stage, the message appears twice in the Output panel. Keep this in mind when dealing with both callbacks and listeners.

Now you have seen the two ways Flash handles events, and I bet you are wondering which one you should use.

### Callbacks Versus Listeners—Showdown

We have covered both sides of capturing events, the callbacks and the listeners. Now comes the moment of truth—which one should you use in which situation? Well, if the truth be told, most of the time the choice is already made for you. Most of Flash's built-in object classes support either callbacks or listeners. A few, however, do support both.

The point to keep in mind is that objects that might have other objects wanting to listen for events will support listeners. The Key object and the Mouse object (which you have already seen) both support listeners because other objects may want to be notified when events occur with these two objects.

Although callbacks are faster to build, it is important to understand listeners, both for better object-oriented programming and because Flash MX 2004 is more listener-based than previous editions of Flash.

Throughout the rest of the chapter, we will be going over many of the events for Flash's built-in object classes, starting with the Button class.

## Button Events

Table 14.1 shows events associated with buttons, but it is important to note that both the Button and the MovieClip classes of objects support ActionScript in frames, as well as in the object itself.

**TABLE 14.1**    Button Events

| Event Handler Object Action | Event Handler Frame Method | Action Description |
|---|---|---|
| on (press) | onPress | The event triggered when a user presses a button |
| on (release) | onRelease | The event triggered when a user releases a button after pressing it |
| on (releaseOutside) | onReleaseOutside | The event triggered when a user releases the mouse button outside the hit area of a button that has received an onPress event |
| on (rollOver) | onRollOver | The event triggered when a user's mouse cursor moves over a button without the mouse button being pressed |
| on (rollOut) | onRollOut | The event triggered when a user moves the mouse cursor outside a button's hit area |
| on (dragOver) | onDragOver | The event triggered when a user moves the mouse cursor over a button's hit area while the mouse button is depressed |
| on (dragOut) | onDragOut | The event triggered when the mouse cursor is moved outside the button's hit area while the mouse button is depressed |
| on (keyPress"...") | onKeyDown, OnKeyUp | The event triggered when a user presses or releases a key on the keyboard that has been specified in the event |
| N/A | onSetFocus | The event triggered when a button receives focus from a keyboard interaction (for example, if a user uses the Tab key to gain focus on the button) |
| N/A | onKillFocus | The event triggered when a button loses keyboard focus |

Now that you've seen all the available events for buttons, let's use some of them in the following example:

1. Create a new Flash document.

2. You learned how to create a button in earlier chapters, so we will use one from the common libraries. Choose Window, Other Panels, Common Libraries, Buttons. Choose your favorite button and drag it out to the stage.

3. Give the button on the stage an instance name of **myButton**.

4. Create another layer and name this layer **actions**.

5. In the actions layer, place these actions:

```
//the event for rollover
myButton.onRollOver = function(){
    trace("rollOver occurred");
}
//the event for press
myButton.onPress = function(){
    trace("press occurred");
}
//the event for release
myButton.onRelease = function(){
    trace("release occurred");
}
//the event for release outside
myButton.onReleaseOutside = function(){
    trace("release outside occurred");
}
//the event for rollout
myButton.onRollOut = function(){
    trace("rollOut occurred");
}
//the event for dragOver
myButton.onDragOver = function(){
    trace("dragOver occurred");
}
//the event for dragOut
myButton.onDragOut = function(){
    trace("dragOut occurred");
}
```

The preceding code creates several event callbacks to use with the button we created on the stage.

Test the movie, and do everything you can to the button. You will notice a series of messages in the Output panel depending on what events you trigger with the button. Figure 14.3 shows some of the messages sent to the Output panel.

A button is just one of the objects that can handle events on an independent timeline frame or within the object itself. The other object that can do the same is the movie clip object.

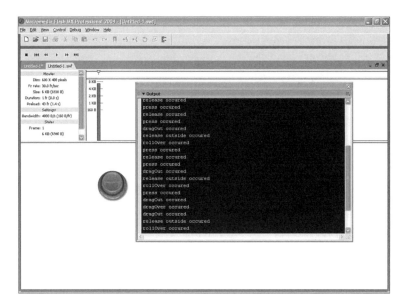

**FIGURE 14.3**    Use callbacks for button events.

## Movie Clip Events

Movie clips are another object that uses events regularly. They have several events that may look like duplicates of the button events, but they are independent of them.

Table 14.2 shows the events supported by movie clips.

**TABLE 14.2**    Movie Clip Events

| Event Handler Actions | Event Handler Methods | Action Description |
|---|---|---|
| onClipEvent (load) | onLoad | The event that is triggered when a movie clip loads |
| onClipEvent (unload) | onUnload | The event that is triggered when a movie clip is unloaded |
| onClipEvent (enterFrame) | onEnterFrame | The event that is triggered as close to the frame rate of a movie clip as possible (the frame rate can be found in the Properties Inspector when the stage has focus) |
| onClipEvent (mouseDown) | onMouseDown | The event that is triggered whenever the mouse button is pressed anywhere on the stage |
| onClipEvent (mouseUp) | onMouseUp | The event that is triggered whenever the mouse button is released anywhere on the stage |
| onClipEvent (mouseMove) | onMouseMove | The event that is triggered whenever the mouse moves anywhere on the stage |

**TABLE 14.2**  Continued

| Event Handler Actions | Event Handler Methods | Action Description |
|---|---|---|
| onClipEvent (KeyDown) | onKeyDown | The event that is triggered whenever the user presses a key (after the stage has received focus) |
| onClipEvent (keyUp) | onKeyUp | The event that is triggered when a user releases a key (after the stage has received focus) |
| onClipEvent (data) | onData | The event that is triggered when the movie clip receives data |

Now that you've seen the events associated with movie clips, here is an example of how to use them:

1. Create a new Flash document.

2. Open the Actions panel in the first frame of the main timeline, and place these actions in it:

```
//create the event for when a user presses the mouse button
this.onMouseDown = function(){
     //create the event for when the user moves the mouse
     this.onMouseMove = function(){
     //send the mouse coordintates to the output panel
     trace("x="+this._xmouse+",y="+this._ymouse);
     }
}
//create the event for when the user releases the mouse
this.onMouseUp = function(){
     //destroy the onMouseMove event
     delete this.onMouseMove;
}
```

The preceding code creates a callback for the onMouseDown event which, when triggered, will create another callback with the onMouseMove event that will continually trace the mouse position while the mouse moves. Then we created a callback for the onMouseUp event, which will destroy the onMouseMove callback so that when the user releases the mouse, the trace action will no longer send the mouse position to the Output panel while the mouse moves.

Test the movie, and you will see that if you drag the mouse cursor around the stage, the position will continually be sent to the Output panel. When you release the mouse, the position will no longer be traced.

Even though we listed all the events associated with the movie clip object, those are the events that are associated solely with the movie clip object. The movie clip object itself actually shares other events with the button object.

## Movie Clips Handling Button Events

The movie clip object can use all events associated with the button, as well as the movie clip events. Something to note about using button events with movie clips is that if you create a callback for a movie clip object with a button event, the movie clip will display the "button hand" when the mouse cursor is over the top of it.

Here is an example using a movie clip with button events:

1. Create a new Flash document.

2. Draw a square with both width and height of about 100 pixels.

3. Highlight the square you just created, including the stroke, and choose Modify, Convert to Symbol.

4. Give the square a symbol name of **squareMC** and choose Movie Clip for behavior.

5. Back on the stage, give the instance of the square an instance name of square_mc.

6. Create another layer and name the layer **actions**.

7. In the actions layer, open the Actions panel, and place these actions in it:

```
//stop the square_mc's playahead
square_mc.stop();
//create the release function
square_mc.onRelease = function(){
      trace("movie clipped released");
}
```

The first thing the preceding code does is to stop the play head of the square_mc movie clip. Normally, this is not necessary because the movie clip only has one frame, but it will become necessary in the next example. The next thing the code does is create a callback event for the square_mc with the button event onRelease.

Now test the movie, and you will see that every time you click the square_mc movie clip, the message will be sent to the Output panel, as you can see in Figure 14.4.

But it's not just the events of buttons that are supported by movie clips;—you can also use the special button frames within movie clips. All you have to do is create four keyframes and label each keyframe with these labels:

• _up—This is the frame representing the up state of the button/movie clip.

• _over—This is the frame representing the over state of the button/movie clip.

• _down—This is the frame representing the down state of the button/movie clip.

• _hit—This is the frame representing the hit area of the button/movie clip.

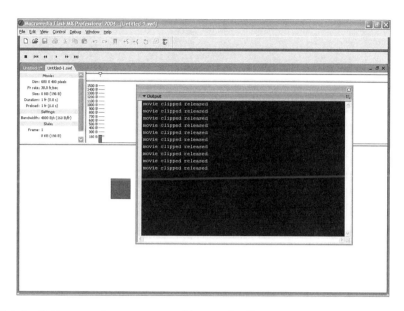

**FIGURE 14.4**  Button events are supported by movie clips.

Now we are going to continue the preceding example by creating the button states in the movie clip:

1. Close the test movie screen and return to the main timeline.

2. Double-click the instance of the square to go into it, and edit it.

3. Create three more keyframes, preferably spaced apart a bit so that you can easily read the states.

4. Create a new layer and name it **labels**.

5. Make sure the labels layer has the same keyframes as the other layer in the movie clip.

6. Label each key frame in the labels layer; "_up", "_over", "_down", and "_hit".

7. Then in each keyframe, change the fill color of the square (your screen should look similar to Figure 14.5).

8. Now test the movie.

Test the movie, and you will see that when you roll your mouse over or press the mouse over the square_mc movie clip, the button changes color to the colors we used in the keyframes.

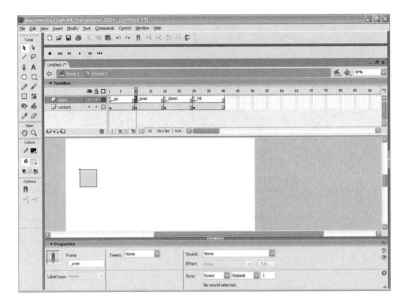

**FIGURE 14.5**   Using special frame labels, you can create button states within movie clips.

Now you have seen the events for both buttons and movie clips, but they are not the only objects that have events. Many other objects have events, and here are a few of them starting with the Mouse object.

# Events of the Mouse Object

The mouse is one of the most frequently used objects for interactive interfaces because the only ways a user can interact with Flash are with either the mouse or the keyboard.

Table 14.3 shows the events for the Mouse object.

**TABLE 14.3**   Mouse Events

| Event Handler Methods | Action Description |
|---|---|
| onMouseDown | This event occurs if the user presses the mouse button on the stage. |
| onMouseUp | This event occurs when the user releases the mouse button over the stage. |
| onMouseMove | This event occurs when the user moves the mouse over the stage. |
| onMouseWheel | This new event occurs when the user uses the mouse wheel. |

> **NOTE**
>
> Even though the onMouseWheel event is new to Flash, it is supported, along with the other Mouse object events, in the Flash 7 player. It is, however, Windows only.

Now that you've seen all the events for the `Mouse` object, here is an example using the `addListener()` method and the `onMouseWheel` event.

Here is the code block used to detect the mouse wheel:

```
//create the listener object
var wheelListen:Object = new Object();
//create the event
wheelListen.onMouseWheel = function(amount){
    trace(amount);
}
//add the listener to the Mouse object
Mouse.addListener(wheelListen);
```

In this code block, we create a listener object. Then we create the event-handling method for listening to the mouse wheel. Notice that you pass the event-handling method a parameter. The `amount` parameter is a numerical value representing which direction the mouse wheel is spinning, and at what speed. We send this numerical value to the Output panel with the `trace` action. After that, we add the listener to the `Mouse` object.

Now when you test the movie, if the event doesn't fire when you spin the wheel, click the stage once to make sure it has focus. When the mouse wheel spins, you will see negative and positive numbers in the Output panel.

The other object that is most often used for user interaction is the `Key` object.

## Events of the `Key` Object

The keyboard is the most important way users interact with applications. It is the only way to enter pertinent information into forms. The `Key` object is the object that captures events associated with keyboard interaction.

Table 14.4 shows the events for the `Key` object.

**TABLE 14.4**    Key Events

| Event Handler Methods | Action Description |
| --- | --- |
| onKeyDown | This event occurs when the user presses a key on the keyboard. |
| onKeyUp | This event occurs when the user releases the key that has been pressed. |

Now that you've seen the two events associated with the `Key` object, here is a code example using the `onKeyDown` event:

```
//create the object to listen to the Key
var keyListen:Object = new Object();
```

```
//create the event
keyListen.onKeyDown = function(){
    //trace the character you pressed
    trace(String.fromCharCode(Key.getAscii()));
}
//add the listener
Key.addListener(keyListen);
```

The preceding code creates the listener object. Then it creates the event-handling method that includes the `trace` action that will send the character the user presses to the Output panel using the `String` object with the `Key` object.

Run the code, and if nothing happens at first, give the focus to the stage by clicking on it once. Then, when you use the keyboard, you should begin to see letters appearing in the Output panel.

Another object that uses events is the `TextField` object.

## Events of the `TextField` Object

Flash uses text fields as a means of gathering and displaying information. And because they are objects, they also have events associated with them.

Table 14.5 lists those events.

**TABLE 14.5**   TextField Events

| Event Handler Methods | Action Description |
| --- | --- |
| onChanged | The event invoked when the text in a text field changes |
| onScroller | The event triggered when the scroll property of a text field changes |
| onSetFocus | The event called when a text field receives keyboard focus (for example, if a user uses the Tab key to gain focus on the text field) |
| onKillFocus | The event called when a text field loses keyboard focus |

`TextField` objects support listeners and callbacks.

Here are two examples doing the same thing using both means of capturing an event.

First, the callback way:

1. Create a new Flash document.

2. Draw an input text field on the stage.

3. Give the text field an instance name of **input_txt** and make sure the border option is selected (so that you can see it on the stage).

4. Create a new layer and name it **actions**.

**5.** In the actions layer, open the Actions panel and place these actions in it:

```
//create the callback
input_txt.onChanged = function(){
   trace("changes have been made");
}
```

The preceding code creates a callback such that when a user makes changes to the content in the input_txt text field, a message will be sent to the Output panel.

That example used a callback to capture the onChanged event. This example uses a listener:

**1.** Create a new Flash document.

**2.** Draw an input text field on the stage.

**3.** Give the text field an instance name of **input_txt** and make sure the border option is selected (so that you can see it on the stage).

**4.** Create a new layer and name it **actions**.

**5.** In the actions layer, open the Actions panel and place these actions in it:

```
//create the object to listen for the event
var changeListen:Object = new Object();
//create the event method
changeListen.onChanged = function(){
   trace("changes have been made");
}
//add the listener to the TextField
input_txt.addListener(changeListen);
```

The preceding code creates the listener object. Then it creates the event-handling method, which, when triggered, will send a message to the Output panel. Finally, we add the listener object to the text field instance.

Both of these examples accomplish the same tasks, but in different ways. You choose to use the one you feel most comfortable with.

You do not have to just use certain events with certain objects. In some circumstances, you can use events with objects that they were not meant for.

## Cross-Object Events

In HTML forms, when a user has finished entering data, he or she can click the submit button or press the Enter key while in the last text field. Well, Flash, by default, does not have the capability for users to simply press the Enter key and move on through an application or form. So how does a Flash developer overcome this dilemma? Use a Key object listener with the TextField object.

This example will create a text field that will listen for the Enter key to be pressed:

1. Create a new Flash document.

2. Draw an input text field on the stage.

3. Give the text field an instance name of **input_txt** and make sure the border option is selected (so that you can see it on the stage).

4. Create a new layer and name it **actions**.

5. In the actions layer, open the actions panel and place these actions in it:

```
//create the listener with the text field
input_txt.onKeyDown = function(){
//check to make sure its the ENTER key being pressed
    if(Key.isDown(Key.ENTER)){
        //send a message to the output panel
        trace("I detect an ENTER");
    }
}
//add the text field as a listener
Key.addListener(input_txt);
```

The preceding code uses anI~objects;cross-object;events> event-handling method on a text field with a Key object event. Inside the event, it uses a conditional to check to see which key has been pressed and whether it is in fact the Enter key, and then a message is sent to the Output panel. And finally, it adds the text field as a listener to the Key object.

Test this code and you will see that not only will the event be triggered with the text field as the listener, but the focus must be in the text field itself in order for it to trigger.

That is just one of the many cross-object events that can be accomplished with listeners. Play around with some of the other objects and see ifI~objects;cross-object;events> you can build your own custom events.

## Summary

This chapter has covered all the basics and even some advanced uses of events. It has covered the major objects that use events, and the different ways to capture these events.

Just remember what events are. They are tattle-tales. They tell Flash exactly when things occur so that as developers, you know when and how to execute certain blocks of code.

The next chapter will cover how to handle another event: loading external files into Flash.

CHAPTER **15**

# Loading Movies

Thus far in the book, we have only dealt with things right on the stage. This chapter goes outside the realm of the stage and shows you how to load external files in at runtime. Not to be confused with importing, which takes place during authoring, loading external files at runtime has many advantages, which will be covered.

Also covered in this chapter is the delicate art of creating preloaders for content, a "must-have" for any heavy Flash content. Preloaders are what developers use to keep the user occupied while large amounts of content load in the background. They can also be used to show the progress of content being loaded, as you will see later in this chapter.

## Why Load External Content?

Why use external files? Everything we have done so far seems to be working fine with no problems, so what are the benefits of externalizing content?

For starters, file size is a major factor to anyone serious about developing for the Web. With broadband connections crawling to a few new areas every month, dial-up is still the prevalent bandwidth for Internet users. Keeping content external from the Flash movie will speed the process of loading the Flash file itself because the file will be smaller.

Another benefit of externalizing content is user experience. Imagine going to a car dealership for a specific car, and the salesperson starts telling you about every single model they have. You would lose patience with him for wasting your time and go to a different salesperson, or maybe a different dealership. Well, that's what happens when you give users more than they want. With externalizing content, you can load specific content based on the user's choices instead of loading all the content and overloading the user with information.

When you create a Flash file, and you have all your content in that one file, it will take much longer to load than if you only load content that the user wants. This way, the users can come to your site, get the information important to them, and leave knowing that if they need more content, they can always come back.

So think of loading external files as a content-on-demand service.

Another thing to keep in mind is fresh content. Keeping everything inside Flash means that any time you want to update an image or a section of the Flash file, you have to open the entire file. But if you load pieces from external sources, you only have to update those pieces. For instance, if you like to keep an image of yourself somewhere on your site (I know I do), you may want to update it often. Keeping the image in Flash means that you have to upload the new version of your site every time you want to change the image. But if you load the image into Flash with ActionScript, you only have to upload the new image every time you want to make a change.

## What Content Can Be Loaded and Where?

Since Flash MX, Flash has the ability to load in external `.swf` files (Flash Movies) and JPEG images. You can also load in `.flv` (Flash Video) files and MP3s, but that is beyond the scope of this chapter. (More on `.flv` and MP3 loading in Chapter 25, "Streaming Media.")

You can load `.swf` files and `.jpg` files into three places:

- **Level Number**. You can load content directly into a level of the Flash player.

- **Movie Clip**. You can load content into any movie clip created manually, or with ActionScript including the _root.

- **Text Fields**. New to Flash MX 2004, the ability to load not only images, but also SWF files directly into dynamic text fields.

We will go over each method of loading in external files, but first, let's look at the difference in file size whether we load a file externally or we have it on the stage all the time.

Look at Figures 15.1 and 15.2. There is no difference in image quality, but notice the file size difference. Figure 15.1 was brought into Flash manually, and then the Flash file was compiled at a file size of 154 kilobytes. Now look at Figure 15.2, which shows exactly the same image, but it is being loaded in from an external source. The file size there is 104 bytes, not even one kilobyte in file size.

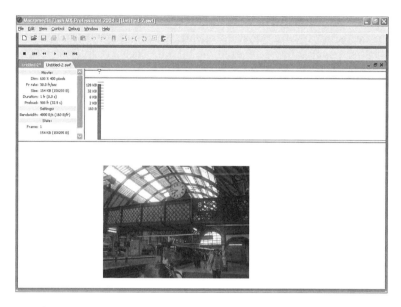

**FIGURE 15.1** The image is within the Flash document.

**FIGURE 15.2** The image has been loaded in dynamically.

Now, these figures have to be taken with a grain of salt. It is true that the file size of the Flash movie is decreased, but that does not mean that the image is smaller. In fact, the image size may be greater with an external file because Flash compresses JPEGs further.

So what does this mean if the file could have actually been smaller inside the Flash file rather than keeping it on the outside? Simple—the Flash file loaded the image when I told it to, and not before: content-on-demand.

And as far as large files from external sources taking a while to load, later in this chapter we cover preloaders for such an event.

Now you have seen it, but how do you do it?

> **NOTE**
>
> For all examples, you can use your own external files, but for everything to be exactly as it is in the book, you should download the files for this chapter from the Web site.

## Loading JPEGs Dynamically

We will start with JPEG images first because they are simpler to work with; they have no "moving parts" so to speak, as Flash files do.

There is one rule that must be followed or errors will occur when loading JPEGs. They *cannot* be progressive. If they are, they will not load correctly.

Flash uses certain methods to load content in dynamically, and the first one to cover is the loadMovie() method.

### The loadMovie() Method

The loadMovie() method is used to load external files directly into a MovieClip object. It can be called either by the ActionScript reader hitting it, or on an event such as a button being clicked.

This method has two layouts; the first is the independent action:

```
loadMovie(URL, movieClip, method);
```

The second is the movie clip method:

```
movieClip.loadMovie(URL, method);
```

Both usages do the exact same thing, and both have the same parameters basically:

- URL—A string literal representing either a relative or absolute path to an external .swf or .jpg file.

- movieClip—This is a reference to the movie clip object that will receive the content.

- method—An optional parameter used for sending or receiving variables; it can take either GET or POST as its argument; GET will append variables to the end of the URL, and POST will send the variables in a separate header.

Now that you see the basic usage and parameters, let's do an example:

1. Create a new Flash document.

2. Save this document as loadImage1.fla in the same directory as the external images.

3. Name the layer in the main timeline **actions**.

4. Go to the first frame of the actions layer, open the Actions panel, and place this code within it:

```
//load the image
this.loadMovie("bigBen.jpg");
```

All this code does is call the loadMovie() method.

Run this code, and your screen should look like Figure 15.3. That's it—that's all the code necessary for loading a JPEG file into Flash at runtime. You could even take out the comment if you wanted to, but that wouldn't be good coding practice.

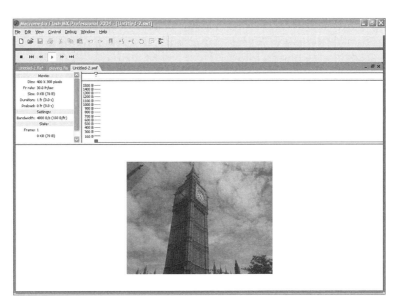

**FIGURE 15.3**    Loading external files is as easy as adding one line of code.

That was pretty simple. Now let's go back and add a button, and change the way we load the image in.

1. Continuing from the preceding example, close the test movie screen and go back to the main timeline.

2. Create a new layer and name it **button**.

3. Choose Window, Other Panels, Common Libraries, Buttons.

4. Choose your favorite button and drag it from the library to the bottom right of the stage in the button layer.

5. Give the button an instance name of **myButton_btn**.

6. Go back into the actions layer, and replace the code with this:

```
//create the event for the button
myButton_btn.onRelease = function(){
     //load the image
     loadMovie("bigBen.jpg",_root);
}
```

This code creates an event for the myButton_btn button on the stage. When triggered, it will accomplish the same thing that the preceding code did—load an image into the _root timeline. Also notice that we used _root this time instead of this because we were calling code from inside a button event. If we had used this, it would have meant we were trying to load the image into the button instead of the _root timeline.

Test the movie; click the button and see what happens. The image still loads, but the button disappears. Welcome to the first limitation of loading external content into movie clips; it replaces everything in that movie clip, which is why the button was removed.

Let's fix that by creating an empty movie clip with ActionScript as you learned in Chapter 11, "The Movie Clip Object."

1. Go back into the actions layer, and change the code to this:

```
     //create the event for the button
   myButton_btn.onRelease = function(){
        //create a movie on the main timeline
        _root.createEmptyMovieClip("target_mc",1);
        //load the image
        loadMovie("bigBen.jpg",_root.target_mc);
   }
```

This time, we created an empty movie clip on the _root timeline and loaded the image into that. We could have made the empty movie clip outside the button event, but in keeping with the content-on-demand mindset, it was better to create the movie clip when we needed it, and not before.

Test the movie, and as you can see in Figure 15.4, the image loads in when the button is clicked, and the button remains on the stage. As a matter of fact, you can continue to click the button, and it will refresh the image every time.

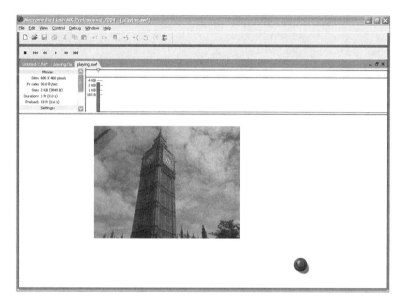

**FIGURE 15.4**    External files should be loaded into empty movie clips, or content within the movie clip being loaded into will be overwritten.

Now that we are loading content into movie clips other than the _root timeline, it is important to understand inheritance.

## Inheritance

The idea of **inheritance** may be difficult to grasp at first, until you see an example. The idea is that any content loaded into a movie clip will inherit its parent's properties.

For instance, if you load an image into a movie clip that has an alpha of 50, the image in turn will also have an alpha of 50.

Let's take a look at an example of inheritance:

1. Create a new Flash document.

2. Save this document as inheritance1.fla in the same directory as the external images.

3. Go to the first frame of the main timeline, open the Actions panel, and place this code within it:

```
//create the empty movie clip
this.createEmptyMovieClip("holder_mc",1);
//set the position of the holder_mc movie clip
holder_mc._x=250;
holder_mc._y=200;
//rotate the holder_mc movie clip
holder_mc._rotation=180;
//load the image
holder_mc.loadMovie("bigBen.jpg");
```

This code creates an empty movie clip on the _root timeline to load the image into. We set a few of its properties including the _rotation set to 180, which will flip the empty movie clip. Then we load the image into the empty movie clip just as before.

Now test the movie, and you will see that the image is completely upside down just like the one in Figure 15.5. This is very useful for aligning images or sizing them before they are even loaded.

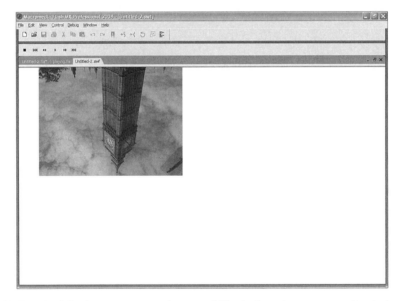

**FIGURE 15.5**    Use inheritance to control external files before they are even loaded.

You are not limited to movie clip properties, however, as you will see in this next example. We will create a color object, change the tint of the empty movie clip, and then load the image into it.

1. Continuing from the preceding example, close the test movie screen and return to the actions on the main timeline.

2. Replace the code in the first frame with the following:

```
//create the empty movie clip
this.createEmptyMovieClip("holder_mc",1);
//create a color object
var myColor:Color = new Color(holder_mc);
//create a transform object
var blueObj:Object = new Object();
//set its blue property to the maximum
blueObj.bb=255;
//change the tint
myColor.setTransform(blueObj);
//load the image
holder_mc.loadMovie("bigBen.jpg");
```

The preceding code creates an empty movie clip as it did before. Then it creates a `Color` object associated with the `holder_mc` movie clip. After that, another object is created that will be used in conjunction with the `Color` object. We set a special property, and then pass the `blueObj` to the `setTransform()` method of the `Color` object, changing the tint of the empty movie clip to a shade of blue. Finally, we load the image into the empty movie clip.

Test the movie again and you will see that the image is right side up again (because we removed the rotation code), but this time the image is a shade of blue.

So far we have loaded images directly into movie clips. Now we will see how to load them into levels of the Flash player directly using the `loadMovieNum()` method.

## The `loadMovieNum()` Method

The `loadMovieNum()` method, like the `loadMovie()` method, loads external files into Flash, but unlike the `loadMovie()` method, the `loadMovieNum()` method loads the files into a specific level of the Flash player directly.

This is the generic layout of the `loadMovieNum()` method:

```
loadMovieNum(URL, level, method);
```

This action has three parameters:

- URL—A string literal representing either a relative or absolute path to an external `.swf` or `.jpg` file.

15

- level—A numerical value representing the level of the Flash player the content is to be loaded into.

- method—An optional parameter used for sending or receiving variables; it can take either GET or POST as its argument.

Although the loadMovieNum() method will not remove everything in a movie clip as the loadMovie() method does, it will remove anything on the level number it is being loaded into, so keep that in mind.

Now that you've seen see the parameters and layout of this method, let's start using it.

1. Create a new Flash document.

2. Save this document as loadMovieNum1.fla in the same directory as the external images.

3. Go to the first frame of the actions layer, open the Actions panel, and place this code within it:

```
//load the movie into the Flash player
loadMovieNum("bigBen.jpg",1);
```

The preceding code loads content into the first level of the Flash player.

Test this code and you will see that the image has loaded in once again.

> **CAUTION**
>
> It is possible to load external content into the level zero (0) of the Flash player; however, that is the _root level of the timeline so all content in the Flash movie will be replaced.

Now you know how to load images into Flash, but how do we get rid of them?

## The unloadMovie() Method

The unloadMovie() method is designed to clean out movie clips containing any content (but in this case, content that has been loaded into it).

Like the loadMovie() method, the unloadMovie() method has two basic layouts, the first being the independent action:

```
unloadMovie(movieClip);
```

The other use is as a MovieClip method:

```
movieClip.unloadMovie();
```

Both of these actions perform the same thing and have the same basic parameter, movieClip. The movieClip parameter is the movie to be cleaned.

Here is an example of removing a loaded image from the Flash movie:

1. Create a new Flash document.

2. Save this document as unloadMovie1.fla in the same directory as the external images.

3. Name the layer in the main timeline **actions**.

4. Create a new layer and name it **button**.

5. Choose Window, Other Panels, Common Libraries, Buttons.

6. Choose your favorite button and drag it from the library to the bottom right of the stage in the button layer.

7. Give the button an instance name of **myButton_btn**.

8. Go into the first frame of the actions layer, and place this code within it:

```
//create an empty movie clip to house the image
this.createEmptyMovieClip("holder_mc", 1);
//load the image
holder_mc.loadMovie("bigBen.jpg");
//use the button to remove the movie clip
myButton_btn.onRelease = function(){
    //clean the movie clip
    holder_mc.unloadMovie();
    //check to make sure the movie is still there
    trace(holder_mc);
}
```

The preceding code creates an empty movie clip to house the image being loaded into it. Then an event is created to remove the loaded content from that movie, and also to check to see if the movie is still there.

Run this code, and you will see that the image does load in, and when you click the button, the image disappears, and the Output panel shows a reference to the holder_mc movie clip that is still present.

There is another way to remove loaded content from movie clips: to remove both the clip and the content. Although it is a little more definite: the removeMovieClip() method will accomplish this.

## The `removeMovieClip()` Method

The `removeMovieClip()` method can be used to remove loaded content from movie clips, but the difference between it and the `unloadMovie()` method is that the `removeMovieClip()` method will completely remove the movie clip it is referencing, not just the loaded content.

Like the `unloadMovie()` method, the `removeMovieClip()` method has two ways of being written. The first is the independent action:

```
removeMovieClip(movieClip);
```

And the second way is the `movieClip` method:

```
movieClip.removeMovieClip();
```

Both ways of writing this action accomplish the same task: They both remove the `movieClip` completely from the Flash player.

We will continue the preceding example by merely changing the code to use the `removeMovieClip()` method.

1. Return to the first frame of the actions layer, and change the code to this:

```
//create an empty movie clip to house the image
this.createEmptyMovieClip("holder_mc", 1);
//load the image
holder_mc.loadMovie("bigBen.jpg");
//use the button to remove the movie clip
myButton_btn.onRelease = function(){
    //remove the movie clip
    removeMovieClip(holder_mc);
    //check to make sure the movie is still there
    trace(holder_mc);
}
```

The only thing changed in the code was that the method `unloadMovie()` was replaced with `removeMovieClip()`.

Test this movie, and again when the button is clicked, the image is removed. However, this time in the Output panel, there is no reference to the `holder_mc` movie clip because it was also removed.

Those two methods are used to remove loaded content from movie clips, but to remove content from level numbers you must use the `unloadMovieNum()` method.

## The `unloadMovieNum()` Method

The `unloadMovieNum()` method works the same way as the `unloadMovie()` method except that it cleans levels, not movie clips.

Here is the layout of this method:

```
unloadMovieNum(level);
```

The only parameter this method has is the `level` parameter representing which level is to be cleaned.

Returning to the same example, we will replace the code to show how the `unloadMovieNum()` method works.

1. Return to the first frame of the actions layer, and change the code to this:

   ```
   //load the image into level 1
   loadMovieNum("bigBen.jpg",1);
   //use the button to remove the movie clip
   myButton_btn.onRelease = function(){
       //clean level 1
       unloadMovieNum(1);
   }
   ```

The preceding code loads the image into level 1 of the Flash player. Then it creates the event for the button so that when the button is clicked, it will clean out the level.

Test this movie, and just like before, the image loads in fine, and when the button is clicked, the image is removed.

After all that work and coding to load images into Flash, now is the perfect time to tell you that there is an easier way.

## The `Loader` Component

This is one of the simplest components shipping with Flash MX 2004. The `Loader` component is designed to make it easy for designers and developers to load JPEGs and SWF files into Flash dynamically.

It has three parameters:

- `autoLoad`—This is a Boolean value representing whether the component should automatically load the content or wait to be told.

- `contentPath`—The relative or absolute path to the image or SWF file you are loading in. You can also use URLs to load content.

- `scaleContent`—This parameter, if set to `true`, will scale the content being loaded into it to its physical parameters (which are set during authoring). If this parameter is set to `false`, the component simply acts as a point to load files to.

That's the basics of how these components work. Now let's see them in practice in this next example.

1. Create a new Flash document.

2. Save this document as `unloadMovie1.fla` in the same directory as the external images.

3. Drag an instance of the `Loader` component onto the stage.

4. Give it an instance name of **loader**.

5. Set the parameters as follows:

   - `autoLoad—true`

   - `contentPath—bigBen.jpg`

   - `scaleContent—true`

Now test the movie, and your screen should look like Figure 15.6. You can go back into the main timeline and change the size of the `Loader` component with the Free Transform tool (Q), retest the movie, and the image will reflect the changes made to the `Loader` component.

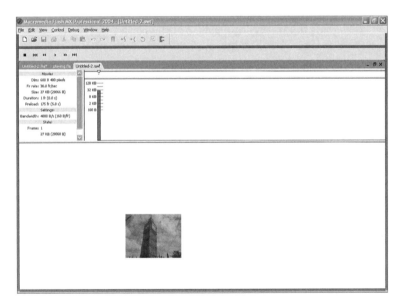

**FIGURE 15.6**    The `Loader` component makes it almost too easy to load dynamic images into Flash.

All we have done so far is load JPEG images into Flash. Next we begin to load other .swf files into Flash.

## Loading SWF Files into Flash

The methods used to load JPEG images into Flash can also be used to load other Flash-created SWF files. In fact, this is more powerful than loading simple images into Flash because loading other Flash content can help teams of designers and developers to work together better. It can allow custom interfaces to be used based on individual tastes. It can even allow objects in the parent timeline to interact with objects in the loaded timeline.

There are a couple of things to consider when loading external Flash content into another Flash movie. First is the frame rate. When Flash content is completely loaded into a new Flash movie, it takes on the parent timeline's frame rate whether it's faster or slower than its own, so timing of animations may be off if the two movies are on different frame rates in their individual form.

Another thing to consider is the _root. There can only be one _root to rule them all, so to speak. If code inside the loaded Flash file refers to its _root with absolute identifiers, errors will occur within the code that make it difficult to debug.

Because the methods used in loading images are the very same for loading Flash content, we can go right into examples.

The first one will load a digital clock that you can download from the Web site.

1. Create a new Flash document.

2. Save this document as loadingSWF1.fla in the same directory as the external files.

3. Go to the first frame of the main timeline, open the Actions panel, and place this code within it:

```
//load the clock in
this.loadMovie("clock.swf");
```

This code is similar to the code we originally used to load an image in except that it uses a different URL.

Test the movie, and on your screen you should see a small digital clock face similar to the one in Figure 15.7.

That was just a simple example of loading Flash content back into Flash. The next section will go over how to manipulate Flash content that has been loaded in.

15

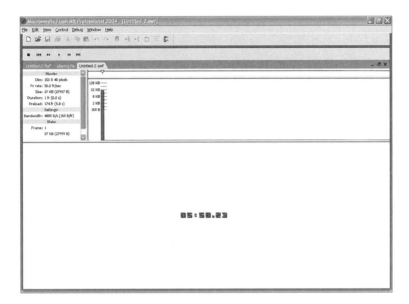

**FIGURE 15.7**    Use the `loadMovie()` method to load external Flash content back into Flash.

## Manipulating Loaded SWF Files

If you load in Flash content from external sources, you are going to want to know how to control the Flash elements and objects that have been brought in.

Working with loaded content is just as easy as working with content that is created on the stage manually. You simply reference the movie clip the content is residing in, and there you can control variables, manipulate objects, and work with anything in that file.

Here is an example that will load in an external SWF file with a text field in it. When we click a button, it will notify the text field.

1. Create a new Flash document.

2. Save this document as `controlSWF1.fla` in the same directory as the external files.

3. Name the layer in the main timeline **actions**.

4. Create a new layer and name it **button**.

5. Choose Window, Other Panels, Common Libraries, Buttons.

6. Choose your favorite button and drag it from the library to the bottom right of the stage in the button layer.

7. Give the button an instance name of **myButton_btn**.

8. Go into the first frame of the actions layer, and place this code within it:

```
//create an empty movie clip to house the SWF file
this.createEmptyMovieClip("holder_mc",1);
//load the SWF file in
holder_mc.loadMovie("textBox.swf");
//create the event for the button
myButton_btn.onRelease = function(){
    //send text to the text field
    holder_mc.myText_txt.text = "Clicked";
}
```

The preceding code first creates a movie clip for the SWF file to reside in. It then loads the content in. After that, it creates a callback function for the onRelease event of the myButton_btn button so that when the button is released, text will be placed into the text field.

Test the movie and you will see immediately that the SWF file has indeed been brought in because the text field is clearly visible. When you click on the button, the word "Clicked" appears in the text field as in Figure 15.8.

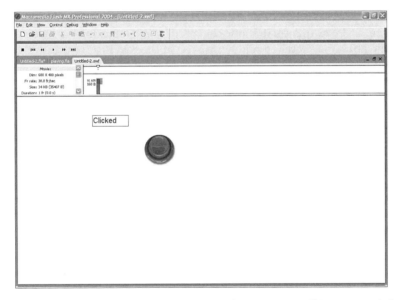

**FIGURE 15.8**    Accessing content on a loaded SWF file is as easy as if it were made in the host movie clip.

That example loaded a SWF file into an empty movie clip. We will continue the same example by changing the code to put the SWF file in a player level number. We will also change the text sent to the text field.

You access information on a player's level by using the _level*n* identifier where *n* represents the level you are referring to.

1. Continuing from the preceding example, return the first frame of the actions layer, and replace its code with the following:

```
//load the SWF file in
loadMovieNum("textBox.swf",1);
//create the event for the button
myButton_btn.onRelease = function(){
     //send time elapsed to the text field
     _level1.myText_txt.text = getTimer();
}
```

The preceding code loads the SWF file into level 1 of the Flash player. It then creates the callback function, which we have already seen, but this time instead of sending a generic message to the text field, it sends the milliseconds that have elapsed since the movie started playing, using the getTimer() method.

Test the movie, and you will see that once again, the SWF file is loaded successfully, and every time the button is clicked, a number is seen in the text field representing the amount of milliseconds elapsed.

So far we have placed external content in movie clips and levels of the Flash player. Next we will begin to put them in text fields.

## Loading External Content into Text Fields

New to Flash MX 2004 is the ability to embed images as well as SWF files, right into dynamic text fields. This is accomplished with the use of the <img> tag. And as you can see, because the files are brought in by means of an HTML tag, the text fields must be HTML-enabled.

The <img> tag has several attributes that can be changed and manipulated:

- src—This attribute is the path to the file to be brought in.
- id—The instance name of the movie clip being created by the Flash player to hold the embedded file; it is useful if you want to manipulate the movie clip with ActionScript.
- width—The width of the file being embedded, in pixels.
- height—The height of the file being embedded, in pixels.

- `align`—Controls the horizontal alignment of the embedded file; `left` or `right` are the allowable parameters, and the default is `left`.

- `hspace`—Specifies the horizontal space around the embedded file between the file and the text. The default value is 8.

- `vspace`—Specifies the vertical space around the embedded file between the file and the text. The default value is 8.

Those are all the attributes for the `<img>` tag, so let's go over an example of loading in an image:

1. Create a new Flash document.

2. Save this document as `imageInText1.fla` in the same directory as the external files.

3. Name the layer in the main timeline **actions**.

4. Create a new layer and name it **text**.

5. In the text layer, draw a dynamic text field about 400×400 in the middle of the stage.

6. Give the text field the instance name of **imageText_txt**.

7. Make sure that the Render Text as HTML property is turned on in the Properties Inspector, as well as the border, and that it is set for Multiline.

8. Go into the first frame of the actions layer, and place this code within it:

```
//set the html text to the text field
imageText_txt.htmlText =
➡"<img src='bigBen.jpg' width='200' height='200'>Big Ben!!!";
```

The preceding code simply sets the `htmlText` property of the text field to the text we want to display, plus the image tag that will embed the image.

Test the movie, and you will see a text field with an image and some text in it as shown in Figure 15.9.

To continue with this example, we are going to embed the clock SWF file under the image.

1. Return to the actions layer, and add this line of code to what is already there:

```
//add the clock SWF file
imageText_txt.htmlText += "<img src='clock.swf'
➡width='150' height='50' align='right'>What time is it?";
```

This line of code adds the `clock.swf` file to the text field, as well as some more text.

Test the movie again, and now you will see the clock in the text field as well as the image, as in Figure 15.10.

15

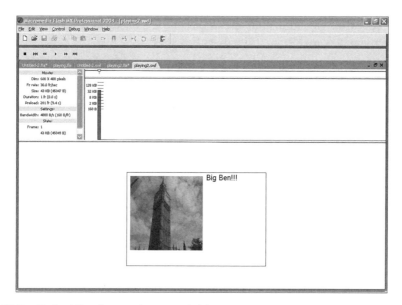

**FIGURE 15.9**    Embedding images into text fields is a great way to liven up boring text.

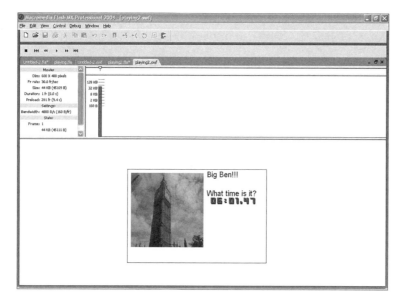

**FIGURE 15.10**    You can also embed external SWF files right into text fields.

Now we have embedded files into text fields. What if we want to manipulate them?

### Manipulating Embedded Content in Text Fields

You can control embedded content in text fields using the *id* attribute within the <img> tag. You simply give the movie clip that is containing the embedded content an instance name, and then you can refer to it in ActionScript.

Follow these steps continuing from the preceding example:

1. Close the test screen and return to the main timeline.

2. Go into the first frame of the actions layer, and replace the code with this code:

```
//set the html text to the text field
imageText_txt.htmlText =
➥"<img src='textBox.swf' id='myContent'> _ text field";
//now create the function that will continually run
this.onEnterFrame = function(){
    //constantly send information to the text field
    imageText_txt.myContent.myText_txt.text = getTimer();
}
```

The preceding code uses the <img> tag to place a SWF file in the text field along with some text. Then we create a callback function that will fire continually, thereby sending the result of the getTimer() method to the text field constantly.

Test the movie and you will see the text field within the text field constantly being updated by the getTimer() method.

We have covered a lot of different ways you can bring content into Flash, but so far, all the examples we have used have brought content into Flash while Flash was running locally on our computer. This means that the transfer has been almost instant. In the real world, this would not be the case because SWFs and JPEGs take time to load, and that's where preloaders come in.

## Preloaders

Preloaders are movie clips or blocks of code meant to show the user how much content has loaded, and how much there is left to load. It is important to keep the user engaged in something while the content loads in the background. This section will cover several methods of gathering the necessary information to build preloaders, starting with the basic getBytesLoaded() and getBytesTotal() methods.

### The getBytesTotal() and getBytesLoaded() Methods

The getBytesTotal() method returns the total file size of the associated movie clip in bytes. The getBytesLoaded() method returns the size of the associated movie clip's file that has been loaded into the Flash player.

Here they both are in their respective forms:

```
movieClip.getBytesTotal();
movieClip.getBytesLoaded();
```

Both of these methods return numerical values.

They both seem simple enough, so let's jump right into an example.

In this example, we will place a large image in the timeline, and use the `getBytesLoaded()` and `getBytesTotal()` methods to determine the percentage of content loaded while we wait.

1. Create a new Flash document.

2. In the main timeline, create a second keyframe.

3. In the second key frame, place an image that is of considerable file size, 50 kilobytes or more.

4. Return to the first frame of the main timeline, open the Actions panel, and place these actions in it:

```
//this gets the total file size
var bT = this.getBytesTotal();
//this event will continually check to see how much has loaded
this.onEnterFrame = function(){
    //create the variable we need to see how much has loaded
    var bL = this.getBytesLoaded();
    if(bT != bL){
        //send the percentage loaded to the output panel
        trace("Percentage Loaded = "+Math.floor((bL/bT)*100)+"%");
    }else{
        //go to the second frame
        this.gotoAndStop(2);
        //destroy the event we no longer need
        delete this.onEnterFrame;
    }
}
```

The preceding code first gets the total file size of the main movie. Then it creates a callback that will constantly check to see how much has loaded. It uses a conditional that determines whether the loaded amount is equal to the total amount. If not, it displays a message in the Output panel with the percentage loaded. If they are equal, the play head is moved to frame 2, and the `onEnterFrame` callback is destroyed because it is no longer necessary.

Test the movie, and you will see that it jumps right to the second frame, so go to View and choose Simulated Download to see the preloader working. We will have to do that each time we test our preloaders because that is the only way to simulate an Internet download.

That example worked well, but it only sent information to the Output panel. And the user will never see the Output panel. You can, however, use ActionScript to create a preloader that a user will see.

### Creating a Preloader with ActionScript

The idea of a preloader is to give the user something to look at, or interact with, while the main chunk of content is being loaded in the background.

We will continue the preceding example by changing the code in the first frame to this:

```
//stop the play head
stop();
//create the movie clip to hold the preloader
this.createEmptyMovieClip("preLoader_mc",1);
//put the preloader in the right spot
preLoader_mc._x = 200;
preLoader_mc._y = 200;
//create some variables for the preloader
preLoader_mc.tBytes = this.getBytesTotal();
preLoader_mc.startX = 0;
preLoader_mc.startY = 0;
//create the text field to display the information
preLoader_mc.createTextField("loader_txt",10,0,-40,200,40);
//create a text format and set some properties
var loadFormat:TextFormat = new TextFormat();
loadFormat.font="_sans";
loadFormat.bold=true;
loadFormat.size=14;
preLoader_mc.loader_txt.setNewTextFormat(loadFormat);
//this callback will run the preloader
preLoader_mc.onEnterFrame = function(){
    this.clear();
    //create the lineStyle
    preLoader_mc.lineStyle(2,0x000000,100);
    //get the amount of loaded bytes
    lBytes = _root.getBytesLoaded();
    //create the percentage variable
    var percentLoaded = Math.floor((lBytes/this.tBytes)*100);
    if(lBytes != this.tBytes){
```

```
            //insert the text into the text field
            this.loader_txt.text="Loaded "+lBytes+" of "
➥           +this.tBytes+"\nat "+percentLoaded+"%";
            //start the fill
            this.beginFill(0x397dce,60);
            //draw the loader
            this.moveTo(this.startX,this.startY);
            this.lineTo(this.startX,this.startY+25);
            this.lineTo(this.startX+(percentLoaded*2),this.startY+25);
            this.lineTo(this.startX+(percentLoaded*2),this.startY);
            this.lineTo(this.startX,this.startY);
            this.endFill();
    }else{
            //go to the second frame
            _root.gotoAndStop(2);
            //remove this preloader
            this.removeMovieClip();
    }
}
```

This code does a lot of things. First, it creates an empty movie clip for the preloader to reside in. Then it sets some of the positioning properties of the empty movie clip. Next, it sets some variables for the preloader, and then creates a text field within the empty movie clip. After that, a TextFormat is created to control the format of our text field. Then the event that will run the preloader for us is created. In the callback, we constantly check the amount loaded, convert it to a percentage, and use a conditional to detect whether the loaded bytes are equal to the total bytes. If not, we put text in the text field and create a rectangle to show the percentage loaded. If the loaded bytes do equal the total bytes, the movie goes to the second frame, and the preLoader_mc movie clip is removed.

Test the movie, and then choose View, Simulate Download. Then you should see a preloader similar to the one shown in Figure 15.11.

That was one way to show a preloader, but we had to build it in ActionScript. There is an easier way to have a preloader using the ProgressBar component.

### The ProgressBar **Component**

The ProgressBar component can be used in conjunction with the Loader component to create a preloader with a dynamic content loader without having to type a single line of ActionScript.

Follow these steps to load in a JPEG image and have it preload:

1. Create a new Flash document.

2. Save this document as progressBar1.fla in the same directory as the external files.

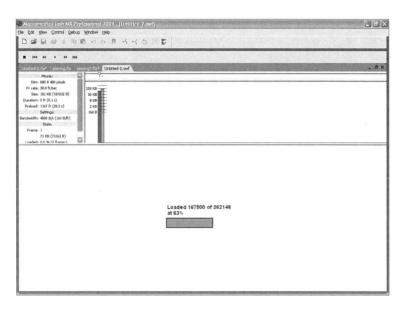

**FIGURE 15.11**  Use ActionScript to create visual preloaders.

3. Drag an instance of the Loader component onto the stage and give it an instance name of **loader**.

4. Set its parameters to the following:

   - autoLoad—true

   - contentPath—bigBen.jpg

   - scaleContent—true

5. Now drag an instance of the ProgressBar above the Loader component and set the parameters to the following:

   - conversion—1

   - direction—right

   - label—LOADING %3%%

   - labelPlacement—top

   - mode—event

   - source—loader

The source is the most important parameter; it refers to the Loader component we placed on the stage.

Test the movie, and you will see the image and loader on the stage. Choose View, Simulate Download to see the progress bar work as shown in Figure 15.12.

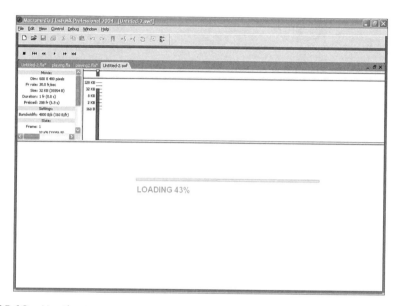

**FIGURE 15.12**    Use the `ProgressBar` component with the Loader component for a quick and easy dynamic content and preloader combo.

## Summary

This chapter went over some of the benefits of using dynamic content including better user experience and smaller file size. We went over the different approaches to loading content, as well as the different file formats, which can be loaded into Flash dynamically.

Then we covered the need for preloaders and the different ways to make them.

We even covered the two components that make it easy to load in content as well as create a preloader without any ActionScript whatsoever.

In later chapters, we cover more on dynamic content including loading in data from external text files and from servers, as well as how to stream video.

CHAPTER **16**

# Components

Components are nothing new to Flash. They were introduced in Flash MX, but version 2.0 is yet another major step forward in their design and function.

This chapter goes over what components are and how to use them, including many of the built-in components in Flash MX 2004 Professional. It covers the new ways to connect components to one another as well as how to skin them. And this chapter will even show you how to create your own component.

## What Is a Component?

Even though components were introduced in Flash MX, the idea behind them started back in Flash 5 with smart clips.

Smart clips were the original components—a reuseable movie clip that needed only a few parameters set for anyone to customize and use, or such was the plan. In reality, smart clips were not only difficult to use, but were hardly scalable at all. Each time a component needed to be used in a different situation, the designer or developer using them would have to actually go into the code to tweak it slightly so that the smart clip would work. Not only that, but they were tremendous in file size compared to what they were capable of doing.

The next step was Flash MX components; they were scalable, reuseable, customizable, and smarter than any smart clip ever created. The components that came with Flash MX were very well-designed and developed to be used in any situation. And building custom components was not a difficult task either.

Now, with Flash MX 2004, we have components, version 2.0.

# The Next Step in Components

Components version 2.0 is not just a simple upgrade with ActionScript 2.0, but a step forward in performance, scalability, and continuity.

Components now support listeners instead of callbacks, which are more object-oriented. Also, components now support data binding, the ability to easily connect properties of components to one another. And all new UI components now have a slick new look.

Let's start working with some components.

# Getting Started with Components

Before you start creating applications using components, you need to know where to find them, and how to control them. All components can be found in the Components panel (Window, Development Panels, Components).

## The Components Panel

As you can see in Figure 16.1, Flash MX 2004 Professional comes with three distinct sets of components:

- Data components
- Media components
- UI components

This chapter focuses mainly on the UI components, but the other components are covered in other chapters where applicable.

## Adding Components to the Stage

Adding components to the stage is as simple as dragging them from the Components panel onto the stage. You can also double-click any one of them, and it will appear in the stage.

> **NOTE**
>
> If you need multiple copies of a single component, drag one instance onto the stage and either copy and paste it, or drag other instances from the library. Do not drag multiple instances of the same component onto the stage from the Components panel because it may increase file size unnecessarily.

After you have brought a component onto the stage, you can also attach more instances to the stage using the `attachMovie()` method.

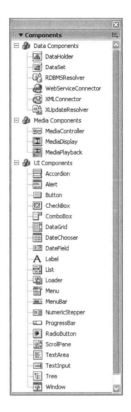

**FIGURE 16.1** The Components panel where all components that come with Flash as well as any you create can be found.

## The `attachMovie()` Method

The `attachMovie` method will use the component's linkage identifier to create a new instance of the component on the stage at runtime.

The generic template for this method is as follows:

```
movieClip.attachMovie(linkageID, newName, depth, initObj);
```

The `movieClip` in the preceding code represents which movie clip the component will reside in. This method has four parameters:

- `linkageID`—The linkage identifier of the movie clip or component being attached.

- `newName`—A string literal indicating the instance name of the new movie clip or component.

- `depth`—A numerical value representing the depth of the new movie clip or component.

- `initObj`—This optional parameter is an object containing properties, events, and methods with which to initialize the new movie clip or component.

All components, by default, have a linkage identifier that is the same as the component's name. To view it, drag an instance of any component (in this case a `Button` component) onto the stage, open the library and right-click (Mac–Ctrl-Click) the component, and choose Linkage from the menu. You will see the Linkage Properties dialog box as shown in Figure 16.2. You cannot change the linkage identifier of any components.

**FIGURE 16.2**   The Linkage Properties dialog box.

Follow these steps to attach a new `Button` component to the stage:

1. Create a new Flash document.

2. Drag an instance of the `Button` component to the center of the stage.

   This step will also add the `Button` component to the library.

3. Create a new layer called **actions**.

4. In the first frame of the actions layer, open up the Actions panel and place this code in it:

```
//attach the Button
this.attachMovie("Button", "myButton", 1);
//give it a label
myButton.label = "Click me";
```

The preceding code first attaches the new `Button` component and then gives it a label.

If you test the movie, you will see that a second `Button` component has indeed been brought to the stage. If a label was not assigned to it at runtime, it would be blank, so keep that in mind.

Now that you know how to add components to the stage, you should know how to control certain aspects of them.

## Setting Parameters

Each component has a set of parameters that can be set to adjust the visual aspects of the component, how they operate, or what data they contain. You can set these parameters two different ways: by selecting the Parameters tab in the Properties Inspector, or by using the Component Inspector.

## The Properties Inspector Panel

The Properties Inspector panel will change when you select the Parameters tab for a component, as shown in Figure 16.3 for the `Button` component.

**FIGURE 16.3**    The Properties Inspector panel showing the parameters for the `Button` component.

The following sections list all the parameters with descriptions for all the UI components: `Accordion`, `Alert`, `Button`, `CheckBox`, `ComboBox`, `DataGrid`, `DateChooser`, `DateField`, `Label`, `List`, `Loader`, `Menu`, `MenuBar`, `NumericStepper`, `ProgressBar`, `RadioButton`, `ScrollPane`, `TextArea`, `TextInput`, `Tree`, and `Window`.

### Accordion **Component**

- `childIcons`—An array of linkage identifiers representing symbols to be used as icons in the headers of the `Accordion`'s panels.

- `childLabels`—An array of text strings to use as headers for the `Accordion`'s panels.

- `childNames`—An array of text strings used as the instance names of the child symbols for the `Accordion` component.

- `childSymbols`—An array of linkage identifiers representing the symbols to be used for the `Accordion`'s children.

### Alert **Component**

The `Alert` component has no parameters and must be adjusted with ActionScript.

### Button **Component**

- `icon`—A linkage identifier to the symbol to be used as an icon with the `Button` component.

- `label`—A text string representing the text to appear in the `Button` component.

- `labelPlacement`—A drop-down menu of choices representing where the text will be placed relative to the icon.

- selected—A Boolean value representing the state of the Button; selected if true, unselected if false.

- toggled—A Boolean value representing whether a toggle button is toggled; if true, it is toggled on; if false, it is toggled off.

### CheckBox **Component**

- label—A text string representing the text of the check box.

- labelPlacement—A drop-down menu of choices representing the position of the label to the check box itself.

- selected—A Boolean value representing the initial state of the check box; if this parameter is true, the box is selected; if it is false, the box is unselected.

### ComboBox **Component**

- data—An array of data to coincide with each item in the ComboBox.

- editable—A Boolean value indicating whether the items in the ComboBox are editable or not; editable if true, not editable if false.

- labels—An array of text strings representing the label of each item in the ComboBox.

- rowCount—A numerical value representing the maximum number of rows to be shown when the ComboBox is selected.

### DataGrid **Component**

- editable—A Boolean value indicating whether the information in the DataGrid can be edited by a user.

- multipleSelection—A Boolean value indicating whether a user can select more than one row of information at a time. If this parameter is true, selecting multiple rows is allowed; if false, it is not allowed.

- rowHeight—The height in pixels of the rows in a DataGrid.

### DateChooser **Component** (Calendar **Component**)

- dayNames—An array of letters representing the name of each day of the week; by default, the names of days are already there.

- disabledDays—An array of numerical values (0–6) representing which days to disable, meaning they cannot be selected.

- firstDayOfWeek—A numerical value (0–6) representing which day of the week should be considered the first; by default, the value is 0, Sunday.

- monthNames—An array of text strings representing the names of each month to display (by default, the month names are already there).

- showToday—A Boolean value indicating whether or not to automatically highlight the current date; highlight date if `true`, do not highlight date if `false`.

### DateField **Component**

- dayNames—An array of letters representing the name of each day of the week; by default, the names of days are already there.

- disabledDays—An array of numerical values (0–6) representing which days to disable, meaning they cannot be selected.

- firstDayOfWeek—A numerical value (0–6) representing which day of the week should be considered the first; by default, the value is 0, Sunday.

- monthNames—An array of text strings representing the names of each month to display (by default, the month names are already there).

- showToday—A Boolean value indicating whether or not to automatically highlight the current date; highlight date if `true`, do not highlight date if `false`.

### Label **Component**

- autoSize—A drop-down menu indicating how the text in the `Label` component will resize. It has these parameters:

  - none—The label will not resize at all.

  - left—The right and bottom sides of the label resize to fit.

  - right—The left and bottom sides of the label resize to fit.

  - center—The bottom side of the label resizes to fit.

- html—A Boolean value indicating whether the label supports HTML or not.

- text—A text string that will appear in the label.

### List **Component**

- data—An array of data to coincide with each item in the `List` component.

- labels—An array of text strings representing the label of each item in the `List` component.

- multipleSelection—A Boolean value indicating whether a user can select more than one row of information at a time. If this parameter is `true`, selecting multiple rows is allowed; if `false`, it is not allowed.

- rowHeight—The height in pixels of the rows in a `List` component.

### Loader **Component**

- autoLoad—A Boolean value indicating whether to automatically load the content or not. If this value is true, the content will load automatically. If it is false, the Loader component will wait until told through ActionScript to load the content.

- contentPath—A text string representing the absolute or relative path to the content being loaded, either a SWF or JPG file.

- scaleContent—A Boolean value indicating whether to scale the content to the size of the Loader component (true), or to scale the Loader component to the size of the content (false).

### Menu **Component**

- rowHeight—The height in pixels of the rows in a Menu component.

### MenuBar **Component**

- labels—An array of text strings representing the label of each button in the MenuBar component.

### NumericStepper **Component**

- maximum—A numerical value representing the maximum allowable value.

- minimum—A numerical value representing the minimum allowable value.

- stepSize—A numerical value representing the amount the value moves up or down.

- value—A numerical value representing the initial value.

### ProgressBar **Component**

- conversion—A number to divide the %1 and %2 values of the label being displayed. It is used to display different types of measurements of file sizes such as bytes or kilobytes.

- direction—A drop-down menu indicating which direction the loader should move toward, either right or left.

- label—This is a text string of particular characters used to give feedback to the user as to how much of the content has loaded; here are the special characters to use with the ProgressBar component:

  - %1—The number of bytes loaded

  - %2—The total number of bytes loading

  - %3—The percentage that has been loaded

  - %%—The percentage sign (%)

The default value of %3%% will show the percentage loaded with a percentage sign (%).

- labelPlacement—A drop-down menu indicating where the label will appear in the ProgressBar component.

- mode—A drop-down menu indicating which mode the ProgressBar will operate in.

- source—A text string representing the source of the download where the loader can get the total file size of the content being loaded, and the current amount loaded (the Loader component for example).

### RadioButton **Component**

- data—A text string representing the value associated with the RadioButton.

- groupName—A text string indicating which RadioButton group the individual RadioButton belongs to.

- label—A text string indicating the label of the individual RadioButton.

- labelPlacement—A drop-down menu representing the position of the label in the RadioButton component.

- selected—A Boolean value representing the initial state of the radio button; selected (true), unselected (false).

---

**NOTE**

Only one RadioButton in a given group can be selected at a time.

---

16

### ScrollPane **Component**

- contentPath—A text string representing the relative or absolute path to the content being loaded, either a SWF file or a JPG file.

- hLineScrollSize—A numerical value representing the number of units the horizontal scrollbar moves each time a scroll button is clicked.

- hPageScrollSize—A numerical value representing the number of units the horizontal scrollbar moves each time a scroll track is clicked.

- hScrollPolicy—This is a drop-down menu representing whether the horizontal scrollbars will be visible; it will show the bar (on), it will not show the bar (off), or it will decide if it is necessary (auto).

- scrollDrag—A Boolean value indicating whether users can drag the content around (true) or not (false).

- vLineScrollSize—A numerical value representing the number of units the vertical scrollbar moves each time a scroll button is clicked.

- vPageScrollSize—A numerical value representing the number of units the vertical scrollbar moves each time a scroll track is clicked.

- vScrollPolicy—This is a drop-down menu representing whether the vertical scroll-bars will be visible; it will show the bar (on), it will not show the bar (off), or it will decide if it is necessary (auto).

### TextArea **Component**

- editable—A Boolean value representing whether the user can edit the TextArea component at runtime (true) or not (false).

- html—A Boolean value indicating whether the TextArea component will display HTML text as HTML (true) or not (false).

- text—A text string that will initially appear in the TextArea component.

- wordWrap—A Boolean value indicating whether to wrap text to the next line when it reaches the border (true) or not (false).

### TextInput **Component**

- editable—A Boolean value representing whether the user can edit the TextInput component at runtime (true) or not (false).

- password—A Boolean value indicating whether the text will be legible (false) or just a bunch of asterisks (true).

- text—A text string that will initially appear in the TextInput component.

### Tree **Component**

- multipleSelection—A Boolean value indicating whether a user can select more than one node of information at a time; selecting multiple nodes is allowed if true and is not allowed if false.

- rowHeight—The height in pixels of the nodes in a Tree component.

### Window **Component**

- closeButton—A Boolean value indicating whether the close button at the top right of the Window component will be visible (true) or not (false).

- contentPath—A text string representing either a linkage identifier to a symbol in the library, or a relative or absolute path to either an external SWF or JPG.

- title—A text string that will appear in the drag bar of the Window component.

## Changing the Parameters of a Component

Changing the parameters of a component is easy with the Properties Inspector. Follow these steps to set up the Button component:

1. Create a new Flash document.

2. Drag an instance of the Button component onto the stage.

3. Select the Button component, and change the parameters to the following:

   - icon—leave blank

   - label—"My First Button"

   - labelPlacement—right

   - selected—false

   - toggle—true

Now test the movie, and you will see that you now have a toggle button.

Buttons are pretty easy, but notice that some of the parameters for certain components were arrays, such as the labels parameter for the List component.

Arrays in component parameters have their own special dialog box, as you will see in this next example where we will add some labels to the List box.

1. Create a new Flash document.

2. Drag an instance of the List component onto the stage.

3. Select the List component, and go to the Properties Inspector. Select the labels parameter. Then you will see a small magnifying glass at the end of the field; select it.

4. The Values dialog box appears as in Figure 16.4. Click the Add Value button (the plus sign) three times, and you will see three items appear in the dialog box, all labeled "defaultValue".

5. Select each of these three items, and change the text to the following:

   Flash

   Dreamweaver

   Fireworks

6. Click OK, and you will see that the component on the stage shows the new values you just added.

Test the movie, and you will see that the three items are still there.

Of course, the Properties Inspector is not the only place to control the parameters of a component; you can also change parameters in the Component Inspector panel.

**FIGURE 16.4**    The Values dialog box for array parameters in components.

## The Component Inspector Panel

You can find the Component Inspector panel by going to Window, Development Panels, Component Inspector. As you can see in Figure 16.5, the Component Inspector has three tabs; Parameters, Bindings, and Schema. The Bindings tab is used to control data binding between components, and will be covered later in this chapter. The Schema tab controls all the properties of the component and is based on an XML document. In the Parameters tab, you can adjust component parameters as in the following example.

In this example, we are going to use a simple TextInput component and change a couple of its parameters using the Component Inspector panel.

1. Create a new Flash document.

2. Drag an instance of the TextInput component onto the stage.

3. Select the TextInput component and open the Component Inspector. Then choose the Parameters tab.

    Notice in Figure 16.6 that when you use the Component Inspector, you will see many more parameters than you do when using the Properties Inspector. This is because the Component Inspector allows access to more of the component's properties.

4. Set the parameters of the TextInput component to the following:

    - editable—true

    - password—true

    - text—topSecret

The rest of the parameters we will leave to default values.

**FIGURE 16.5**    The Component Inspector panel, which is used to control components.

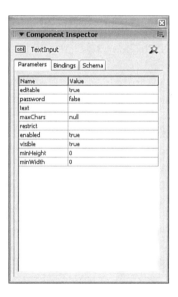

**FIGURE 16.6**    The Component Inspector provides direct access to more parameters than does the Properties Inspector.

As you change the `password` parameter, and then place text in, notice that the component on the stage again changes before the movie is even tested. Also, the parameters in the Properties Inspector change to match the Component Inspector panel.

Test the movie, and you now have half of a login; all you need is a user name field.

There is a third and final way you can change the parameters of a component, but these changes will not take effect until runtime.

## ActionScript

Because component parameters are nothing more than direct links to component properties, we can control them from within ActionScript at runtime.

Follow these steps to create a combo box and fill it with labels all from within ActionScript:

1. Create a new Flash document.

2. Drag an instance of the `ComboBox` component onto the stage.

3. Give it an instance name of `myCombo_cb` so that we will be able to access it from ActionScript.

4. Create a new layer called **actions**.

5. In the first frame of the actions layer, open the Actions panel, and place this code in it:

```
//add some data to the ComboBox
myCombo_cb.addItem("ASP");
myCombo_cb.addItem("PHP");
myCombo_cb.addItem("ASP.NET");
myCombo_cb.addItem("ColdFusion");
myCombo_cb.addItem("CGI");
myCombo_cb.addItem("Perl");
//change the width of the drop down
myCombo_cb.dropdownWidth = 200;
```

The preceding code first adds some labels to the `ComboBox`, and finally changes the width of the `ComboBox`'s drop-down menu to twice its size.

Test the movie, and when you select the `ComboBox`, you will see that the drop-down is twice its default size.

> **NOTE**
>
> Even if you change a component's parameters manually, because ActionScript runs at runtime, ActionScript will override any manual settings.

Another great way ActionScript interacts with components is when you need to capture a component's event, such as if a user clicks a button. You need to know when that happens to run whatever code is associated with that button.

## Capturing Component Events

In Flash MX, component events were easy to control. There was a callback function associated with each instance of a component that would look on the timeline for any function with that name, and then run all the code associated with that function.

Version 2.0 of components is slightly more complicated. In order to capture an event of a component, you must create a listener object. A listener object is a generic object whose sole purpose is to sit around and "listen" for a given event to occur. When this event does occur, it calls its associated callback method.

But first, you have to add the event listener to the component using the `addEventListener()` method.

### The `addEventListener()` Method

The `addEventListener()` method is used to add event listener objects to components. Each time it is used, it is basically subscribing the listener object to listen for a component's event.

Here is the generic layout for the `addEventListener()` method:

```
myComponent.addEventListener(event, listener);
```

One parameter of this method is the *event* parameter, which is a string literal name of the event being listened to. The other parameter is the *listener*, a reference to the event object. As you start to build applications with components, you will learn how important it is to be able to capture these events.

For instance, if you wanted to get the label of an item in a List component whenever the user chooses one, you would use code that looks similar to this:

The following code is in a frame on the same timeline where a List component with an instance name of `myList` resides.

```
//create the listener object
var listListen:Object = new Object()
//create the event callback for the event you're listening for
 listListen.change = function(){
    trace(myList.selectedItem.label);
}
//then add the event listener to the instance of the List component
myList.addEventListener("change", listListen);
```

16

All the preceding code does is create the generic object. Then it creates the callback function for the event it was listening to. Finally, it adds the event listener to the List component.

It is possible to replace the preceding code by putting this code directly into the actions of the component itself:

```
//the event
on(change){
    trace(this.selectedItem.label);
}
```

Even though the preceding code would yield the exact same results, it is bad practice to put code directly in the object actions of components, or any other object for that matter, because it makes it difficult to find code hidden in objects when you need to find it. So throughout the rest of this chapter, we will be using event listeners on the timeline.

You can also use the handleEvent() method, which will allow an event listener to handle multiple events, but you have to pass it the event, and then use conditionals to tell which event was called.

The following is an example of using the handleEvent() to handle multiple events:

```
//create the listener object
var listListen:Object = new Object()
//create the event callback for the event your listening for
listListen.handleEvent = function(eventName){
    if(eventName.type == "change"){
        trace(myList.selectedItem.label);
    }else if(eventName.type == "scroll"){
        trace("scrolling");
    }
}
//then add the event listener to the instance of the List component
myList.addEventListener("change", listListen);
myList.addEventListener("scroll", listListen);
```

As you can see from the preceding code, it is possible to have a single event listener listen to multiple events, but the code is quite messy, and not flexible.

Now that you understand the concepts of capturing events in components, work through the following example to see how to capture the "click" event for a button:

1. Create a new Flash document.

2. Drag an instance of the Button component onto the stage.

3. Give the button an instance name of **myButton_pb** and change the label to "Now".

**4.** Create a new layer called **actions** and place this code in the first frame of it:

```
//create the event listener object
var clickListen:Object = new Object();
//create the event callback for the click event
clickListen.click = function(){
    trace(getTimer());
}
//now add the event listener to the Button instance
myButton_pb.addEventListener("click", clickListen);
```

The preceding code creates the event listener object, and then creates its event callback method. Every time this event callback is called, it will send the number of milliseconds that have occurred since the beginning of runtime. Finally, we add the event listener to the Button component.

Test this movie out, and every time you click the button, a number will be sent to the Output panel representing the number of milliseconds that have occurred since you tested the file.

Now you know how to put data into a component, and how to capture events from components. The next step is getting data from components.

## Getting Data from Components

Even though we have done some useful examples so far, we haven't really gathered information from components yet, which is a major point to using components to quickly build applications.

You can access most data by means of either a method, or more likely a property of a component. And in list type components, you can access properties of the selected item.

In the next example, we will use a NumericStepper component to control the _alpha property of a movie clip.

**1.** Create a new Flash document.

**2.** Drag an instance of the NumericStepper component onto the top left of the stage; give it an instance name of myStepper and set its parameters to the following:

- maximum—100
- minimum—0
- stepSize—1
- value—100

**3.** Now draw a rectangle in the center of the stage.

4. Highlight the entire rectangle including the stroke and choose Modify, Convert to Symbol.

5. Give it a symbol name of **recMC** and make sure the behavior is set to Movie Clip.

6. Give the instance of the rectangle still on the stage an instance name of **rec_mc**.

7. Create a new layer called **actions**.

8. In the first frame of the actions layer, open the Actions panel and place this code in:

```
//create the listener object
var stepListen:Object = new Object();
//add the event callback to the listener
stepListen.change = function(){
    //set the rectangles alpha
    rec_mc._alpha = myStepper.value;
}
//add the listener to the component
myStepper.addEventListener("change", stepListen);
```

The preceding code is nothing new. It creates the event listener. Then it creates the event callback method for the *change* event of the NumericStepper. In that event, every time the user adjusts the NumericStepper component, the _alpha property of the rectangle changes to the value of the NumericStepper. Finally, we add the event listener.

When you test this movie, you will see the transparency of the rectangle change as you change the value in the NumericStepper component.

Now that you have seen how to use components, you need to know how to make them look good.

## Skinning Components

Back in Flash MX, skinning components was pretty simple—a lot of work, but simple. When you drag a component onto the stage, the component's skins were added to the library, and you could go in and adjust them any way you wanted. Now in version 2.0 of components, it's not as easy. When you drag a component onto the stage, just the component itself is sent to the library, and you cannot go into it and change it manually. There are, however, a couple of options starting with manually changing the skins.

### Manually Skinning a Component

Manually skinning components is not as difficult as it may sound, but it is time-consuming unless you want to keep the default gray colors.

To manually skin components, you have to drag a new "theme" into your current project's library. You get the other theme in the components folder of the first run directory. Follow these steps to begin manually skinning components:

1. Create a new Flash document.

2. Drag instances of the following components onto the stage:

   - `Button`

   - `TextArea`

   - `RadioButton`

   - `CheckBox`

   - `Window`

3. From `C:\Program Files\Macromedia\Flash MX 2004\en\First Run\ComponentFLA`, open `SampleTheme.fla`.

4. In the library of the SampleTheme file, drag the Movie Clip symbol "Sample Theme" into the library of the other file.

5. You will then see a couple of new folders in the library. The `themes` folder is where all the assets reside, and you can manipulate any visual aspect of the components now.

Notice that when you brought the new theme in, the components on the stage did not change. Only at runtime will the visual aspects of the components change.

Test the movie, and you will see that the components on the stage have changed to an older-looking style.

But that is not the only way to change the visuals of a component; you can also adjust its theme.

## Using the `style` Property

All components support the `style` property, which allows users to control certain aspects of components ranging from coloring all the way to the speed of the drop-down list in the `ComboBox` component.

To set a style to a component, you use the `setStyle()` method like this:

```
component.setStyle(style, value);
```

This method uses two parameters, the `style` parameter, which is a string literal representing the style property being changed, and the `value` parameter, which is the value that the style is being changed to.

You can also set global style properties by using the `_global` identifier, and the keyword `style`, like this:

```
_global.style.setStyle(style, value);
```

Setting global style properties will affect all components throughout the Flash file. Table 16.1 lists some of the styles that most components will support.

**TABLE 16.1**    Style Properties That Can Be Used with Components

| Style | Description |
| --- | --- |
| BackgroundColor | Controls the background color of the component. |
| BorderColor | Represents the dark corner aspect of three-dimensional objects such as the Button. |
| borderStyle | Controls the border of components and has four possible values: inset, outset, solid, none. |
| buttonColor | The color of the Button face, and any component that uses the Button component will inherit this property. |
| Color | The text color of the Label component. Any component using the Label component (such as the Button or CheckBox) will inherit this value. |
| disabledColor | The color of text when the component is disabled. |
| fontFamily | Controls the font used by components. |
| fontSize | Controls the font size of components. |
| fontStyle | Controls the style of fonts used by components; it has two values: normal, italic. |
| fontWeight | Controls the weight of fonts used by components; it has two values: normal, bold. |
| highlightColor | Controls the highlight portion of the three-dimensional aspects of components. |
| marginLeft | Controls the left margin of text in components. |
| marginRight | Controls the right margin of text in components. |
| scrollTrackColor | Controls the track color of the scrollbar used by components. |
| shadowColor | Controls the shadow portion of the three-dimensional aspects of components. |
| symbolBackgroundColor | Controls the background color of both the CheckBox and RadioButton components. |
| symbolBackgroundDisabledColor | Controls the background color of both the CheckBox and RadioButton components when disabled. |
| symbolBackgroundPressedColor | Controls the background color of both the CheckBox and RadioButton components when clicked. |
| symbolColor | Controls the check color of the CheckBox and the dot color of the RadioButton. |
| symbolDisabledColor | Controls the check color of the CheckBox and the dot color of the RadioButton when disabled. |
| textAlign | Controls the text alignment of components. Its values can be left, center, or right. |
| textDecoration | Controls the underlining of text in components. Its values are either none or underline. |
| TextIndent | Controls the indentation of text in components. |

And there is one more property to use when using the `style` property: the `themeColor` property.

The `themeColor` property controls the three-dimensional aspects of components such as the `Button` component, all at once. You can pass it any hexadecimal color such as `0xff0000` for red or `0x000000` for black. You can also pass it three different prebuilt coloring themes:

- `haloBlue`
- `haloGreen`
- `haloOrange`

To see an example of the `themeColor` at work, follow the steps in this example:

1. Create a new Flash document.

2. Drag an instance of the `Button` component onto the stage.

3. Create a new layer called **actions** and place this code in the first frame of that layer:

```
//set the global themeColor to orange
_global.style.setStyle("themeColor","haloOrange");
```

Now test the movie, and you will notice that when you hover your mouse over or click the `Button` component, the button's color changes to a light orange.

This completes the discussion of the basics of components. The next few sections build on what we have covered so far and take it beyond just fundamentals.

## The `dataProvider` Property

So far, we have filled out components that can handle data either manually through their parameters, or by using the `addItem` method to add individual items. You can also use the `dataProvider` property.

The `dataProvider` property is used with some data-ready components such as the `List` and the `ComboBox` components. This property can be set to any array, and the component will fill with the array's data.

Here is an example of filling a `ComboBox` with an array using the `dataProvider` property:

1. Create a new Flash document.

2. Drag an instance of the `ComboBox` component onto the stage and give it an instance name of `myCombo_cb`.

3. Create a new layer called **actions**, and place the following code in the first frame:

```
//create an array full of names
var names:Array = new Array("David","Ben","Eddie","Todd","Doug","Paul");
//now set the dataProvider property to this array
myCombo_cb.dataProvider = names;
```

The preceding code creates an array and fills it with names. Then we set the dataProvider property to the array.

Test the movie and you will see the ComboBox has filled with data. You can also add elements to either the array, or the ComboBox at runtime and it will show up in the ComboBox.

The array we just used is a simple array that just filled the label array property of the ComboBox. To really see what the dataProvider can do, you have to send it an array with named elements. The two names to use for named elements are

- label—Elements with this name will go to the labels array.

- data—Elements in this array will be the value of the item.

Let's extend the previous example by adding not only names, but also ages into an array, and then setting that array to the dataProvider. We will also add an event listener to get the age from the ComboBox.

Go back into the actions layer and replace the code with this:

```
//create the necessary arrays
var names:Array = new Array("David","Ben","Eddie","Todd","Doug","Paul");
var ages:Array = new Array(23,23,25,28,30,20);
//create an array to hold all the data
var people:Array = new Array();
//now create a loop statement to combine these two arrays into one
for(var i=0; i < names.length; i++){
    //push the object with the label and data names into the main array
    people.push({label: names[i], data: ages[i]});
}
//now create the event listener for the
var listListen:Object = new Object();
//create the callback event for the listener
listListen.change = function(){
    trace("age - "+myCombo_cb.value);
}
//add the event listener to the ComboBox
myCombo_cb.addEventListener("change", listListen);
//now set the dataProvider property to this array
myCombo_cb.dataProvider = people;
```

Here's what this code does: First, it creates two different arrays to hold the names and ages of people. Then it creates an array to hold all the data at once. After that, it creates a loop statement that will take one element at a time from both the names and the ages arrays and place them in as a single element in the main array people. Then we create the listener for our ComboBox. After that, we create the callback function that, when triggered, will pull the selected element's value, in this case the age. Then we add the event listener to the ComboBox and set the dataProvider property to the people array.

Test the movie and you will see that not only was the data again successfully placed in the ComboBox, but also when you select an item from the ComboBox, it sends the age of the selected person to the Output panel, not the label.

There is another component that uses the dataProvider property, but in a slightly different way. The DataGrid component will take a dataProvider and create the necessary columns based on the elements provided.

Follow these steps to see how easy it is to fill the DataGrid with data:

1. Create a new Flash document.

2. Drag an instance of the DataGrid component onto the stage.

3. Set its dimensions to about 350×150 and give it an instance name of myDataGrid.

4. Create a new layer called **actions**, and place the following code in the first frame:

```
//create the necessary arrays
var names:Array = new Array("David","Ben","Eddie","Todd","Doug","Paul");
var ages:Array = new Array(23,23,25,28,30,20);
var locations:Array = new Array
➥("Prince George","Sussex","Richmond","Philadelphia","Hopewell",
➥"Hopewell");
//create an array to hold all the data
var people:Array = new Array();
//now create a loop statement to combine these two arrays into one
for(var i=0; i < names.length; i++){
    //push the object with the label and data names into the main array
    people.push({Name: names[i], Age: ages[i], Location: locations[i]});
}
//now set the dataProvider property to this array
myDataGrid.dataProvider = people;
```

Just like before, we created a few arrays and filled them with data. Then we used a loop statement to fill a main array with one element from each array at a time. Then we set the dataProvider property of the DataGrid to the main array people.

When you test the movie, you should see something like Figure 16.7. This time, the DataGrid used the names of the named elements in the main array as column headers.

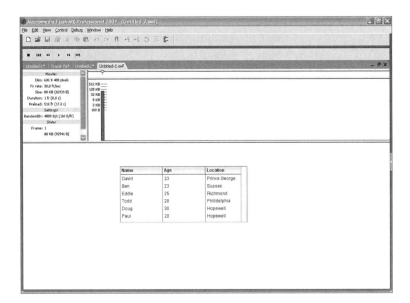

**FIGURE 16.7**    Use the `DataGrid` component to easily display large amounts of data at a time.

While on the subject of controlling data and values of components, the next section covers data binding.

## Data Binding

Data binding is one of the nicest new features of components. It allows you to link components together without having to use ActionScript.

To data bind one component to another, you use the Bindings tab in the Component Inspector panel, as shown in Figure 16.8. You select the Add Binding button, and the Add Binding dialog box will appear with a list of all the available data binding values (see Figure 16.9). Next, return to the Component Inspector panel, open the Bindings tab, select your new binding, and click the Bound To field where a magnifying glass will appear. Select the magnifying glass, and the Bound To dialog box will appear (see Figure 16.10), which will allow you to choose which component to bind to as well as which of its binding values.

**FIGURE 16.8**   The Binding tab in the Component Inspector.

**FIGURE 16.9**   The Add Binding dialog box for choosing which data binding element you want to bind.

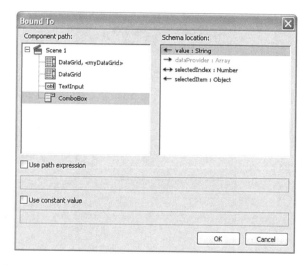

**FIGURE 16.10** The Bound To dialog box to choose which data binding element to bind to.

It is difficult to grasp until you do it yourself, so follow these steps to data bind a List component to a TextInput component:

1. Create a new Flash document.

2. Drag an instance of the List component onto the left part of the stage, and give it an instance name of myList.

3. Drag an instance of the TextInput to the right of the List component, and give it an instance name of myText.

4. Select the List component, open up the Component Inspector, and then select the Bindings tab.

5. Choose the Add Binding button.

6. From the list in the Binding dialog box, choose selectedItem : Object and click OK.

7. Now select the Bound To field in the Component Inspector and click the magnifying glass that appears.

8. Select the TextInput component in the left window, and then choose text : String in the right window and click OK.

9. Now create a new layer called **actions**, and place this code in the first frame:

```
//create the necessary arrays
var names:Array = new Array("David","Ben","Eddie","Todd","Doug","Paul");
//now set the dataProvider property to this array
myList.dataProvider = names;
```

The code creates an array of names, and fills the `List` component by means of the `dataProvider` property.

Test the movie, and you will see that when you select a name from the `List` component, that name appears in the `TextInput` component automatically.

Data binding is a great way to quickly and easily link different components together to share data.

Now that you have seen a great deal about the components that come with Flash, it's time to create one.

## Creating a Version 2.0 Component

Creating components with Flash MX 2004 Professional can be difficult, but very rewarding.

Back in Flash MX, to build a component, you placed information in a movie clip, and then converted it to a component. Version 2.0 of components goes a lot further.

In this example, we will create a small component that will have a property specifically designed for data binding. What it will do is allow developers to test information by sending it to this component, which will then automatically send it to the Output panel. Keep in mind that this component will only work in the test mode of the authoring environment and is not meant to be used outside of that.

The first part will be done in Flash, so follow these steps:

1. Create a new Flash document called `Tracer.fla` and save it to the desktop.

2. Using the Text tool, create a letter "T" on the stage and set its size to 16×16.

3. Select the "T" and choose Modify, Convert to Symbol.

4. Give it a symbol name of `tracerG` and make sure the behavior is set for Movie Clip, and set its registration point to centered.

5. Right-click (Mac–Ctrl-click) the tracerG movie clip in the library and choose Linkage.

6. Select the Export for ActionScript check box, and uncheck the Export in First Frame check box to save file size. Leave the AS 2.0 Class blank and click OK.

7. Back on the main stage, highlight the movie clip "T" and choose Modify, Convert to Symbol again.

8. Give it a Symbol name of "Tracer", make sure the behavior is set to Movie Clip, and set its registration point to centered.

9. Right click (Mac–Ctrl-click) the Tracer in the library and choose linkage.

10. Select the Export for ActionScript check box, and uncheck the Export in First Frame check box to save file size. Set the AS 2.0 Class to "Tracer" and click OK.

11. Now double-click the new movie clip symbol to enter edit mode.

12. Name the layer the "T" is residing on **Bound**.

13. Align the left edge and the top edge to the stage using the Align Panel (Windows, Development Panels, Align).

14. Create a second layer under the Bound layer called `assets_mc` and give it an extra keyframe, so there should be two blank key frames on the assets_mc layer.

15. Make a copy of the first frame in the Bound layer, and paste it exactly the same in the second frame on the assets_mc layer.

    This is so that when the component gets dragged onto the stage, the user will be able to see it.

16. In the first frame of the Bound layer, open the Actions panel and place in a `stop` action like this:

    ```
    stop();
    ```

    This will stop the movie clip from looping back and forth, and should always be done in every component you make.

    Your stage should now look like Figure 16.11.

17. Return to the main timeline. We are done with Flash for the time being.

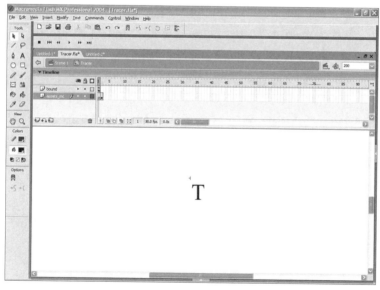

**FIGURE 16.11**    The stage after step 16 after we have created all the content on the stage needed.

The next section requires us to make a class file. Class files are new to Flash in how they work and how they are built. All functionality of components are kept in external class files. For more on external class files, see Chapter 19, "External ActionScript."

The next step requires the use of a text editor such as Notepad or SciTe. You can also use the AS file builder built into Flash by choosing File, New and choosing ActionScript File.

18. When your new file is open, save it to the same directory as our Flash file as Tracer.as.

19. Drop in this code and save the file again:

```
[TagName("Tracer")]
[IconFile("Tracer.png")]

class Tracer extends MovieClip{
    private var tracerInfo:String;

    function Tracer(){
        this._visible = false;
    }

    [Inspectable(name="Trace What" defaultValue="")]
    [Bindable("writeonly")]
    function get tracerI():String{
        return this.tracerInfo;
    }
    function set tracerI(t:String):Void{
        this.tracerInfo = t;
        if(tracerInfo.length > 0){
            trace(tracerInfo);
        }
    }
}
```

Let's break this code into sections so you can see what is happening.

The first section uses what are called MetaData tags. These tags are used in processing the component and set certain options. In this case, they are setting the TagName and the IconFile.

```
[TagName("Tracer")]
[IconFile("Tracer.png")]
```

The next section begins our class, which will extend the `MovieClip` class. Then it creates a private method, `tracerInfo`, that is the data we are going to trace.

```
class Tracer extends MovieClip{
    private var tracerInfo:String;
```

The section after that creates the constructor function that will be called when the component initializes at runtime.

```
function Tracer(){
        this._visible = false;
    }
```

After that, we use two more MetaData tags. The first declares the parameter of our component. The second declares that the following functions are used with data binding.

```
[Inspectable(name="Trace What" defaultValue="")]
    [Bindable("writeonly")]
```

Finally, we create two getter/setter methods to control the variable. And we also send the variable to the Output panel here. And finally, we close off the class with a closing curly bracket.

```
    function set tracerI(t:String):Void{
        this.tracerInfo = t;
        if(tracerInfo.length > 0){
            trace(tracerInfo);
        }
    }
}
```

Once that is saved, you can return to Flash.

> **NOTE**
>
> The PNG file mentioned in the class file is a 16×16 picture of the letter "T," which can be downloaded from the accompanying site, or you can create your own. Just make sure it is residing in the same directory as the FLA and the class file.

1. Back in the Flash file, open the Library (Window, Library).

2. Select the Tracer movie clip, right-click, (Mac–Ctrl-click) and choose Component Definition.

   If you have built components before in Flash MX, the dialog screen will be familiar to you (see Figure 16.12).

3. Set the AS 2.0 Class to "Tracer" and check the Display in Components Panel check box.

4. Type **The Tracer Component** in the Tool Tip Text Field and click OK.

5. Now select the component you just made, and right-click again (Mac–Ctrl-click). This time choose Convert to Compiled Clip.

   Converting to a compiled clip is a new way of creating components. It will actually return a compiled SWF file to the library, which will be the actual component and will be included in your SWC file. This saves a great deal on file size.

6. Select the component you created again, and right-click again (Mac–Ctrl-click). This time choose Export SWC File, and save it to the desktop as Tracer.swc.

That was it! Now go to the components directory and create a new folder called Unleashed Components, copy the SWC file into it, and restart Flash.

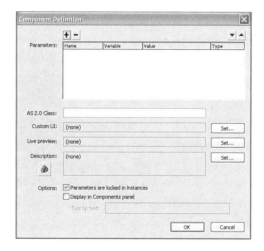

**FIGURE 16.12**   The Component Definition dialog box where certain parameters of the component are set.

To test the component, follow these steps after you have restarted Flash:

1. Create a new Flash document.

2. Drag an instance of the Tracer component onto the stage and give it an instance name of myTracer.

3. Set the Trace What parameter to test and press Enter, which should pop open the Output panel, showing that it is working.

4. Now drag an instance of the Button component, give it an instance name of myButton, and set the toggle parameter to true.

5. Select the `Tracer` component, open the Component Inspector, and select the Bindings tab.

6. Click the Add Binding button, choose `tracerI:String`, and click OK.

7. Select the Bound To field and click the magnifying glass that appears.

8. Choose the `Button` component in the left window, choose `selected : Boolean` in the right window, and click OK.

9. Test the movie and you will see "test" appear in the Output panel from the parameter we set when creating the file. And every time you toggle the button, it will display a Boolean value in the Output panel as well.

That was awesome! You have created a component that has data bindings, which will help you test other applications in the future.

## Summary

This chapter covered a lot of information about components. We talked about what a component is and when you should use one. We covered the basic fundamentals of components including

- How to set parameters
- How to capture their events
- How to extract data from them

We also went into some more advanced features of components and how to use them including

- The `dataProvider` property
- Data binding

And we finished up by creating a debugger component that can data bind to other components to test data.

To further your study on components, use online resources and always check the Macromedia Exchange for components people have built.

CHAPTER **17**

# Working with Text

Text is one of the earliest forms of media communication, and Flash has not forgotten this. Back in Flash MX, text fields became full-fledged objects with properties, methods, events, and even instance names. This chapter explores the many ways to create and manipulate text fields, as well as some new things added to the object with this version of Flash.

Some of the topics to be covered are

- The text field interface
- Creating the three basic types of text fields
- Formatting text fields
- Working with HTML text

Let's start with the interface.

## The Text Field Interface

To get to the Text Field interface, you first have to select the Text tool either by going to the large letter *A* on the toolbar, or by pressing the letter *T* on the keyboard. When you have selected the Text tool, the Properties Inspector will look like Figure 17.1.

Most of the options are the general variety of font options such as size, font type, font size, alignment, and color. Some of the other options that you may not be familiar with are on the Text Field type drop-down menu, which includes three options:

- **Static Text**. This text is exactly the way it sounds; all the text to be seen in this text field must be placed in it during authoring, and cannot be manipulated by ActionScript during runtime.

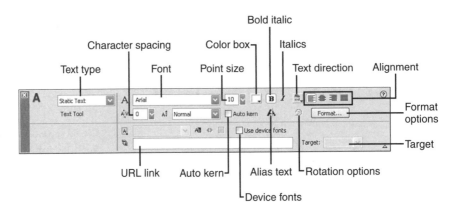

**FIGURE 17.1**   The text field interface.

- **Dynamic Text**. This text field type is as it says, dynamic, meaning that it can be manipulated and adjusted not only during authoring, but also at runtime.

- **Input Text**. This text field is nearly identical to the dynamic text field, except that not only can it be changed at runtime by ActionScript, but the user can enter text into this type of text field to be used with ActionScript.

All three of these types of text fields will be reviewed in greater detail in the next section.

Another option on the text field interface you may not be familiar with is the text direction option that will allow text to be both horizontal and vertical. Under that option is the text rotation option, which will rotate the text field when it has been set to a vertical direction. Text direction and text rotation options are only available to static text fields. Continuing with the options, there is also the auto kern feature, which will adjust spacing between the letters automatically. There are also three buttons in the middle of the interface that control certain features of text fields:

- **Selectable**. This option controls whether or not a user can select and highlight text in a text field. It is available to static and dynamic text fields only. Input text fields have this set to true automatically.

- **Render Text as HTML**. This option can turn a normal text field into an HTML text field (more on HTML text in text fields later in this chapter). This option is available to dynamic and input text fields.

- **Show Border Around Text**. This option will create a black rectangle around the text field. It is available to dynamic and input text fields only.

There are also URL options, which allow you to place a link inside the text field as well as choose the URL target type. You can also select the Use Device Fonts option. That will allow the text field to look for a font on the user's system that is similar to what you are using in the text field, while still keeping the overall file size small. The three built-in device fonts that Flash has are

- **_sans**. Similar to Helvetica or Arial

- **_serif**. Like Times Roman

- **_typewriter**. Like Courier

Using device fonts will only work with static, horizontal text fields.

To make sure your text field is using the correct font on other users' systems with input or dynamic text fields, you must embed the font outline. To do this, you select the character button from the Properties Inspector (remember, it will only show up when the text field type is set to Dynamic Text or Input Text). Then the Character Options menu will appear as in Figure 17.2. You can specify a range of characters such as Uppercase or Numerals. You can also include only a few select characters you type in, or have the menu select the characters you are already using by clicking the Auto Fill button.

**FIGURE 17.2**   The Character Options menu for dynamic and input text fields.

But remember, embedding fonts will increase the file size roughly 100 bytes or more per glyph, so only embed the characters you are sure you will use.

And in the properties of dynamic and input text fields, there is also the Var field, which allows you to place a variable name to associate the content of the text field to a variable on the timeline. However, because text fields are now objects, there is a more up-to-date way of doing that, which we will discuss later in this chapter.

## Alias Text

A new option in Flash MX 2004 is the Alias Text option. This option allows text inside text fields to be more readable, especially at smaller sizes. See Figure 17.3 for an example.

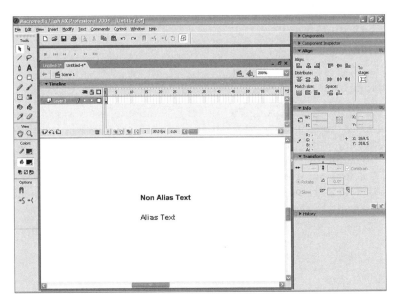

**FIGURE 17.3**    You can easily see the difference between alias text and nonalias text.

This option is available for all three text field types. However, it will display static, dynamic, and input text fields with alias text with the Flash 7 Player and higher, but it will only display alias text in static text fields with Player versions 6 and below.

> **NOTE**
>
> Even though alias text will make smaller text appear easier to read, it will slow down page rendering minimally because of the sharpness of the text especially with large amounts of text being aliased, even if antialiased is enabled for the entire document.

Also notice that many of the options available in the Properties Inspector are also available on the menu bar under Text as well as a much-needed addition to the Flash authoring environment, spell checking.

## Spell Text Fields

One of the hardest things to do from a designer/developer standpoint while building Web sites and Web applications is to spell check. This has plagued Flash users for some time now, and Macromedia has answered with a built-in spellchecker for text fields.

Before you start using it, you need to make sure it is set up the way you want. To get to the setup, go to Text, Spelling Setup. The Spelling Setup window will pop open as in Figure 17.4. Some of the options include what you want to spell check (it is good practice to have text fields and strings checked), which of the built-in dictionaries you would like to use, and which words to suggest, as well as which words to completely ignore. You can also set up your own dictionary and edit it from within Flash.

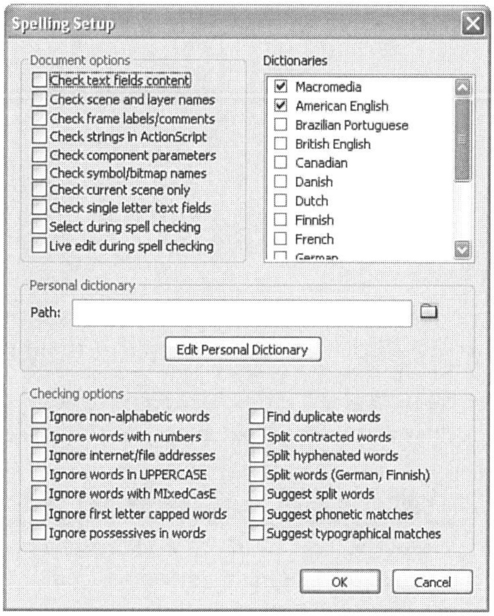

**FIGURE 17.4**    The Spelling Setup menu.

When you have your setup the way you want it (and it may take some time to get it just right), go ahead and create a static text field on the stage by choosing the Text tool and clicking somewhere on the stage. When the text field has been created, type in the word *thier,* which was meant to be *their*, but is a common spelling mistake (at least by me). Now go to Text and choose Check Spelling, and the Check Spelling dialog box appears as in Figure 17.5. One of the first options should be the correct spelling of the word *their*. Make sure that is selected and click Change. A pop-up will tell you that you're done, and now the word is spelled correctly.

So we've covered the text field interface as well as the new Spell Checker. Now let's talk a little more about each type of text field starting with static text fields.

**FIGURE 17.5**    The Check Spelling dialog box.

# Creating Text Fields

In this section, we'll go over the basic ways to create and use all three types of text fields manually, and then we'll go over how to create a couple of them with ActionScript.

The basic way to manually create a text field is to select the Text tool from the toolbar (T on the keyboard) and click and draw the text fields on the stage.

---
**CAUTION**

After a text field has been created, you can still go back and resize it manually using the Text tool. You should not, however, use the Free Transform tool to adjust the size of a text field because it will actually stretch and resize the text inside the text field as well.

---

## Static Text

Static text, again, can only be manipulated in the authoring environment. You can, however, do some interesting things with it such as distribute each individual character to its own layer. This can be useful if you want to do some interesting animation with words because each object would have to be on its own layer.

To push letters from a single text field into individual layers, you will first want to create a text field by selecting the Text tool, setting the text type to Static Text, and clicking on the stage. After you have created the text field, you can simply type something in, like your name. When the text field is on the stage, and has some text in it, you can select it with the Selection tool, and either right-click (Mac–control-click) and then select Break Apart, or you can choose Modify, Break Apart. After it has been broken apart, make sure all the text fields are still selected, and choose Modify, Timeline, Distribute to Layers (PC–Ctrl+Shift+D, Mac–Shift+Open Apple+D). Now each letter has its own timeline named for that letter, as you can see in Figure 17.6.

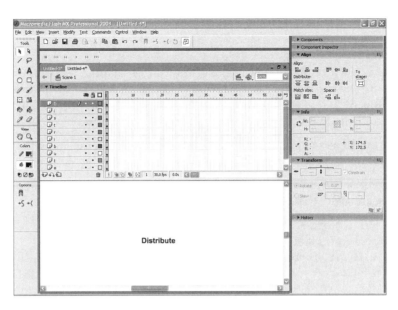

**FIGURE 17.6**    After you select Distribute to Layers, each letter receives its own layer.

This technique can actually be done with all three types. When dynamic or input text fields are broken apart, they are turned into static text fields, but there isn't really anything special you can do with static text.

## Dynamic Text

This type of text field is much more advanced than the static text field because it can be changed and manipulated at any point during authoring or runtime via ActionScript. As a matter of fact, you do not even need to type a single character in the text field itself to have text appear, as you will see in the first example.

For this first example, we are going to put text in a dynamic text field.

1. Start a new Flash document.

2. Create a second layer, and name the top layer **actions** and the bottom layer **text** (remember from Chapter 8, "Welcome to ActionScript 2.0," that it's good practice to have a layer dedicated to ActionScript).

3. In the text layer, create a dynamic text field, make sure the Show Border option is selected, set the Var property to myText, and give it an instance name of textField_txt.

4. Now we are going to go to the first frame of the actions layer, open the Actions panel (F9), and put these actions in:

```
//this will set the first text field's Var property
var myText = "Testing";
```

Now test the movie (Control, Test Movie) and you will see that the text is now in the text field. It does this by sharing a variable name in ActionScript and the Var property in the text field's properties. This was the way it was done way back in Flash 5. It still works, but now we are going to do it the new way because text fields are now objects in ActionScript.

1. Using the same example, go to the text field's properties in the Properties Inspector and clear out the Var property box so that it is completely blank.

2. Now go back to the actions in the first frame of the actions layer, delete all of the actions, and place these in instead:

```
//this will create a string to hold our text
var myString:String = "Test 2";
//this will set the text field's text property to the string
textField_txt.text = myString;
```

Now test the movie again, and you will see that the text field is displaying our text. This way of doing it is much easier to read because instead of having a blind variable, you actually are setting text to a specific text field. This makes it much easier to go back and read. Because it is good practice to set text to the text field's text property, that is the way we will continue to do it.

So far, the two examples we have done using dynamic text were not very dynamic. We could have just written that text in right on the stage. In this next example, you will see why dynamic text fields are so important.

In this example, we are going to build a mouse tracker to show where the mouse is whenever the mouse moves.

1. Start out by creating a new Flash document.

2. As you did before, create two layers, the top one named **actions** and the bottom one **text**.

3. In the text layer, create two dynamic text fields about 100 pixels wide and 20 pixels high. Make sure they both have Show Border turned on, and give them instance names of x_txt and y_txt.

4. Now in the first frame of the actions layer, place these actions:

```
//this event will update everytime the mouse moves
this.onMouseMove=function(){
    x_txt.text="x="+Math.floor(_xmouse);
    y_txt.text="y="+Math.floor(_ymouse);
}
```

Test the movie and you will see that whenever the mouse moves, the text fields will show its position on the main stage.

Now that you see how powerful and easy it is to update dynamic text fields, we are going to move on to our last text field type, input text fields.

## Input Text

As mentioned earlier, input text fields are exactly like dynamic text fields in how we can set text to them. But unlike dynamic text fields, the user can actually put text into input text fields to interact with our Flash document. Input text fields also have a few extra options that the other two text types do not. The Linetype option can be set to Multiline just like dynamic text fields, but it can also be set to Password, which would make any character in it appear to be an asterisk. That comes in handy when building login systems. Another option is the Maximum Characters field, which you can set to keep the length of what the user can input at a certain length or less.

You will begin to feel comfortable with input text fields as we go through the next example.

In this example, we are going to allow users to input information into one text field, and when they submit it, we will place that exact same string in another field capitalized.

1. Start by creating a new Flash document.

2. Create two more layers so that you have three in total.

3. Name the layers from top to bottom—**actions**, **button**, and **text**.

4. In the text layer, create a dynamic text field, make sure the Show Border option is selected, and give it an instance name of `output_txt`.

5. On the same layer, create an input text field, make sure it has Show Border selected, and give it an instance name of `input_txt`.

6. On the button layer, create a button, and give it the instance name `submit_btn`.

7. Finally, in the actions layer, place these actions:

```
//this event will occur when the submit button is released
submit_btn.onRelease=function(){
    output_txt.text=input_txt.text.toUpperCase();
}
```

Test the movie, type something in the input text field, and then click the submit button to see the same text displayed in our dynamic text field, but in uppercase format. Also, notice in our code that we get text out of text fields using the exact same property we use to set text to text fields, the `text` property.

So far, all we have done when we create a text field is to select the Text tool and draw the field on the stage. Now we are going to go through how to create one dynamically with ActionScript.

## Creating Text Fields in ActionScript

One of the nice things about text fields is that now because they are actual objects in ActionScript, you can create and destroy them dynamically. And to create them in AS, we use the `createTextField()` method, which works like this:

```
Movie.createTextField(instanceName, depth, x, y, width, height);
```

Because text fields must be placed within movie clips, `Movie` represents the movie clip that the text field will reside in. The first parameter we set is the instance name; remember to use the suffix "_txt" to activate code hints. The next parameter is the depth, or stacking order, of the text field. The next two parameters are its coordinates, and they represent the top left corner of the text field. The final two parameters are the width and height of the text field.

Let's jump right in and create one in ActionScript.

1. Start off by creating a new Flash document.

2. In the first layer, in the first frame, open the Actions panel and put these actions in:

   ```
   //this will create a text field on the root layer
   this.createTextField("myText_txt",1,0,0,120,20);
   ```

3. Now test the movie and notice that you don't really see anything. This is because even though we have created a text field, we haven't put any text in it. But it is there, and you can see it in the object's list by going to Debug, List Objects while still in the test movie screen. You will see it listed there.

   We already know how to put text in text fields, so let's go back and do that.

4. After we create the text field in the actions, put these actions in:

   ```
   //this will put text in the text field
   myText_txt.text = "I created this with code";
   ```

Now test the movie once more, and you will see the text in the text field at the top left corner of the screen.

Notice that the letters are black and appear to be in Times New Roman. That is because when you create text fields in ActionScript they have a few default values:

- type—"dynamic"
- border—false

- `borderColor`—`0x000000` (black)

- `background`—`false`

- `backgroundColor`—`0xffffff` (white)

- `textColor`—`0x000000` (black)

- `password`—`false`

- `multiline`—`false`

- `html`—`false`

- `embedFonts`—`false`

- `variable`—`false`

- `maxChars`—`false`

Now you know how to change some of the features, so let's go back into our example and give it a border and a background, as well as change the text color.

1. Building on the preceding example, go back into the actions of the first frame and add these lines at the bottom:

```
//this will add a border around the text field
myText_txt.border = true;
myText_txt.borderColor = 0xff0000;
myText_txt.background = true;
myText_txt.backgroundColor = 0x397dce;
myText_txt.textColor = 0xffffff;
```

When you test the movie again, you will see a border around the text field. And the text field formatting could have been applied before setting the `text` property. But in order to be able to change the color of the border and the background, both properties must be set to `true` or the border will not show.

Now that you've seen how to create text fields manually as well as with ActionScript, and you know how to change properties of the text field itself, let's look at how to change the formatting of the text in the text field.

## Formatting the Text in Text Fields

We've already gone over the interface, so you know how to make changes to text manually, but now we will go over how to change the formatting of the text with ActionScript.

We will start out with the built-in object that Flash has for formatting text fields, called the `TextFormat` object.

## The `TextFormat` **Object**

Before you can start creating these `TextFormat` objects, you should know that when you create a text field with ActionScript, a default `TextFormat` object is applied to it with these values:

- font—"Times New Roman"
- size—12
- color—0x000000 (black)
- bold—false
- italic—false
- underline—false
- url—"" (empty string)
- target—"" (empty string)
- align—"left"
- leftMargin—0
- rightMargin—0
- indent—0
- leading—0
- bullet—false
- tabStops—[] (an empty array)

Notice that the `textColor` property in the `TextField` object does the same thing as the `color` property of the `TextFormat` object, so if all you want to do is change the color of the text, the `TextFormat` object is overkill; just use the `textColor` property of the `TextField` object.

To create a new `TextFormat` object, you basically create a variable and set it to a new `TextFormat` object like this:

```
var myFormat_fmt:TextFormat = new TextFormat();
```

Now we can start setting properties of this new `TextFormat` object like this:

```
myFormat_fmt.align = "center";
myFormat_fmt.bold = true;
myFormat_fmt.color = 0x00ff00;
```

We still have to apply the format we want to a text field before it can be rendered. There are two options for applying TextFormats to text fields. The first one is setTextFormat(), which has several different ways of being used:

- textField.setTextFormat(textFormat)—This way sets the textField to the textFormat.

- textField.setTextFormat(index,textFormat)—This way sets the textFormat to the character at index.

- textField.setTextFormat(startIndex, endIndex, textFormat)—This way sets the textFormat to all characters from startIndex to endIndex.

It is also important to know that this method can only be applied after the text field has text in it. Also note that indexing strings start at 0, not 1. So the first character in any string has an index of 0.

Let's go over a few examples of how to use this method.

In the first example, we are going to put a small phrase in a text field, and then format that text field to look nice.

1. Star by creating a new Flash document.

2. In the first frame, open the Actions panel, and put these actions in:

```
//this will create the text field
this.createTextField("phrase_txt",1,0,0,100,50);
//this will set the text field to multiline, and wrap words
phrase_txt.wordWrap = true;
//here we put text in the text field
phrase_txt.text = "Every cloud has a silver lining";
//now create the text format object and set some of its properties
var myFormat_fmt:TextFormat = new TextFormat();
myFormat_fmt.color = 0x0000ff;
myFormat_fmt.bold = true;
myFormat_fmt.align = "center";
//now apply the format
phrase_txt.setTextFormat(myFormat_fmt);
```

Now test the movie, and you should see your text formatted similar to Figure 17.7.

17

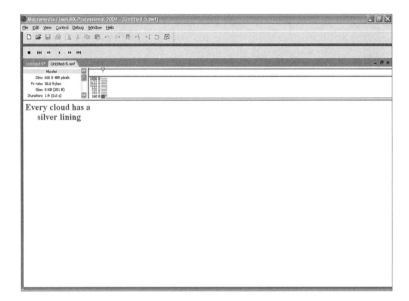

**FIGURE 17.7**    Using the `TextFormat` object can produce great results.

In the next example, we are going to use the same method, but change it a bit, and use a loop to gradually change the characters to the format.

1. Using the preceding example, go back into the actions on the first frame and remove the last two lines.

2. Now put these actions in at the bottom.

```
//this variable is for our loop
var i:Number = 0;
//this is the looping function that we will use
this.onEnterFrame=function(){
    if(i < phrase_txt.text.length){
        phrase_txt.setTextFormat(i, myFormat_fmt);
        i++;
    }else{
    //this will get rid of the looping function
        delete this.onEnterFrame;
    }
}
```

Now when you test the movie this time, it will gradually change over to the format instead of all at once as it did before.

The final example of using the `setTextFormat()` method will set the text format to just one word.

1. Still building on the preceding example, remove all of the code up to `myFormat_fmt.bold = true`.

2. Now add these actions at the bottom:

```
//this will set the text format to the word "silver"
phrase_txt.setTextFormat(18,24,myFormat_fmt);
```

This time when you test the movie, it will look like Figure 17.8.

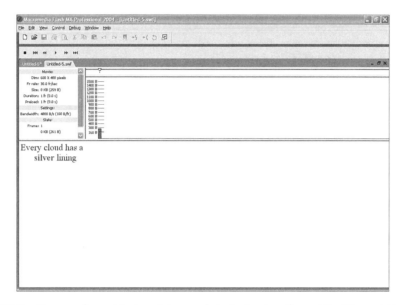

**FIGURE 17.8**    You can format just certain words in text using the `setTextFormat()` method.

As I mentioned earlier, there are two ways to set a `TextFormat` object to a text field, and the second way is using the `setNewTextFormat()` method, which is applied only one way, like this:

```
textField.setNewTextFormat(textFormat);
```

The difference between this method and the preceding one is that this method will work now and forever on text fields. Basically that means that unlike the `setTextFormat()` method where it has to be used only after text has been placed inside a text field, any text put in after that will not only not have the text format, but will also clear the text format back to default values. But if you use the `setNewTextFormat()` method, all text from then on will use that format.

17

Here is an example to help:

1. Start a new Flash document.

2. In the first frame, open the Actions panel and place these actions in:

```
//create the text field, and put some text in it
this.createTextField("phrase_txt",1,0,0,150,20);
phrase_txt.text = "Every dog has";
//create the text format object and set some properties
var myFormat_fmt:TextFormat = new TextFormat();
myFormat_fmt.color = 0xff0000;
myFormat_fmt.underline = true;
//now set the format to the text field
phrase_txt.setNewTextFormat(myFormat_fmt);
//now add more text to it
phrase_txt.text += " his day";
```

Now when you test it, you won't see anything terrific—it will have just done what you had done before, but this time, you added text to the text field after you applied the format. That would have caused the loss of the format if you had used `setTextFormat` instead of `setNewTextFormat`. To see what it is meant by that, go back to the line that we set the format on, and change it:

```
phrase_txt.setTextFormat(myFormat_fmt);
```

Now when you test, it looks as if the format was never applied, but in actuality it was applied and then it was cleared when you added text.

Now you've seen how to format text inside text fields using the `TextFormat` object, but there are two more ways to format text. One is to use HTML (which we discuss later in this chapter) and the other way is brand new to Flash MX 2004: Cascading Style Sheets.

## Cascading Style Sheets

Cascading Style Sheets (CSS) are not new in and of themselves, but now that Flash can use them, it makes setting formats to text fields completely dynamic because you can actually create the style sheets in a text editor, save them as `.css` files, and load them in at runtime. Another great thing about their being dynamic is that you can have an HTML site and a Flash site all formatted with the same CSS.

For those of you who are new to CSS, it was designed to help keep content and design separate in HTML. What that means is that you can create content, label the type of content it is (title, body, footnote, and so on), and then create a CSS to format those particular types of content and set the CSS to the content. That way whenever you want to update content, you don't have to worry about it not being in the right format, and if you want to update the format, the content does not have to be touched.

An example of this would be a newspaper. There is tons of content in a newspaper ranging from headlines, text body, writers' names, and even comments. But if there were no way of telling which was which, it would make the newspaper almost impossible to read with the title of the story, the writer's name, and the story itself all the exact same size and format. But the writers do not have time to set up format while they are writing the articles; they simply say this section is a headline, and that section is the body.

Taking that concept over to cascading style sheets, the CSS is the formatter, and all it needs is definitions. So let's take a look at setting up some CSS inside ActionScript.

The first thing you have to do is create a new `StyleSheet` object like this:

```
myStyle = new TextField.StyleSheet();
```

Now that you have your `StyleSheet`, it's time to make some definitions for it using the `setStyle()` method like this:

```
styleSheet.setStyle(styleName, theStyle);
```

In this method, the first parameter is the name of the specific style (which we will go into when we start implementing the style sheets) and the second is an object that has style properties set. There are two ways of implementing this.

The first way is to create the style name and add attributes of that style all in the same method like this:

```
myStyle.setStyle("title", {color: "#ff0000", fontSize: "20px"});
```

And the second way to implement the same method is to create a generic object, set the properties of the object the same way you would set style properties, and then pass the entire object to the style, like this:

```
var tempStyle:Object = new Object();
tempStyle.color = "#ff0000";
tempStyle.fontSize = "20px";
//now pass the object to our already created StyleSheet
myStyle.setStyle("title",tempStyle);
//get rid of the temporary style object
delete tempStyle;
```

Both of these implementations will work with our style sheet, so whichever you feel more comfortable using is what you should go with. Just remember, if you create temporary objects to hold your style properties, get rid of them when you are done to regain memory.

Now that you've seen how to create the style sheet objects and how to set some styles to them, let's look at how to set them to our text, and how our text should be formatted to accept the styles.

There are several different ways of setting text to the StyleSheet. The first one we will cover will use already supported tags such as <p> and <span>. You can use their built-in class attribute to set each class to an already specified style class like this.

```
<p class="title">This is<span class="smaller"> small </span></p>
```

And here is an example pulling the StyleSheet and the text together:

```
//create the text field
this.createTextField("phrase_txt",1,0,0,150,20);
//set the html property to true
phrase_txt.html = true;
//create the StyleSheet object
myStyle = new TextField.StyleSheet();
//create 2 style classes and set them to myStyle
myStyle.setStyle(".title",{color: "#397dce", fontSize: "16px"});
myStyle.setStyle(".body",{color: "#000000", fontSize: "10px"});
//set the text field to the StyleSheet
phrase_txt.styleSheet = myStyle;
//set the text
phrase_txt.htmlText="<p class='title'>This is<span class='body'> small </span>
➥</p>";
```

A couple of things to notice in the preceding example; first, "styleSheet" beginning with a lowercase "s" is a property of the text field, and "StyleSheet" beginning with an upper-case "s" is an object class, so don't get those confused. And when we create style classes, we put a "." in front of the name and when we use them in our string, we don't need the period. Also, span tags are used inside the paragraph tag, and therefore must be closed before the paragraph tag.

Here we used classes of styles, but we can also style an entire HTML tag so that anything residing in that tag will inherit the style we apply.

Table 17.1 lists HTML tags in Flash that support having styles applied to them.

**TABLE 17.1**   Supported HTML Tags in Flash

| Style Name | Supported Tag |
|---|---|
| p | All <p> tags. |
| body | All <body> tags, but the <p> tag will override this setting. |
| li | All <li> list item (bullet) tags. |
| a | All <a> anchor tags. |
| a:link | All <a> anchor tags, after the a style. |
| a:hover | All <a> anchor tags when the mouse is hovering over it, after the a and a:link styles have been applied. It will go back when the mouse goes off hover. |
| a:active | All <a> anchor tags when they are clicked on, after the a and a:link styles have been applied. When the mouse is released, the style will be removed. |

Here is an example using the a style name.

```
//create the text field
this.createTextField("link_txt",1,0,0,100,20);
//set the html property to true
link_txt.html = true;
//create the StyleSheet object
linkStyle = new TextField.StyleSheet();
//set the styles of the style sheet
linkStyle.setStyle("a:link",{color: "#ff0000"});
linkStyle.setStyle("a:hover",{color: "#0000ff"});
linkStyle.setStyle("a:active",{color: "#00ff00"});
//set the StyleSheet to the text field
link_txt.styleSheet = linkStyle;
//set the text to the text field
link_txt.htmlText = "<a href='http://www.sams.com' target='_blank'>
➥Sams Publishing</a>";
```

Now you have seen how to format classes of tags as well as how to format the entire class. You can of course mix them together. For instance, you can define the entire <p> tag, and then define classes so that the main <p> tag acts more like a default setting.

You can even create your own tags, and have them formatted to your own style names, as you will see in this next example.

```
//create the text field
this.createTextField("news_txt",1,0,0,200,80);
//set some of the properties
news_txt.html = true;
news_txt.wordWrap = true
//create the StyleSheet object
myStyle = new TextField.StyleSheet();
//define the styles
myStyle.setStyle("title", {color: "#ff0000", fontSize: "20px"});
myStyle.setStyle("body",{color: "#000000", fontSize: "12px"});
//set the StyleSheet to the text field
news_txt.styleSheet = myStyle;
//now set the text
news_txt.htmlText="<title>This just in</title><br><body>
➥Flash supports CSS in text fields</body>";
```

So far in CSS we have talked about creating the styles inside ActionScript, but that really isn't the point. The whole idea is to create the CSS files and store them outside of the Flash file to be loaded in. The method StyleSheets use to load external files is the load()

method, and when the CSS has been loaded, it triggers the onLoad event, which we will also be using in the following example.

1. The first thing you want to do is create a new Flash document, and save it somewhere called CSSTest.fla.

2. After that, open up your favorite text editor, Notepad, or SciTe and put this text in it:

```
title {
    color: #000000
    font-size: 20px;
    display: block;
    textDecoration: italic;
}
body {
    color: #333333;
    font-size: 12px;
}
emphasized {
    color: #000000;
    font-weight: underline;
    display: inline;
}
```

3. When the text is in, save the file to the same directory as the Flash file you just saved as myCSS.css.

4. Go back into Flash, and in the first frame open up the Actions panel and place these actions within it:

```
//create the text field
this.createTextField("news_txt",1,0,0,200,80);
//set some of the properties
news_txt.html = true;
news_txt.wordWrap = true
//create the StyleSheet object
myStyle = new TextField.StyleSheet();
//create the event for when the CSS is loaded
myStyle.onLoad = function(done){
    if(done){
        news_txt.styleSheet = myStyle;
        news_txt.htmlText = "<title>Read all about it
➥</title><br><body>Can you <emphasized>believe
➥</emphasized>this<body>";
    }else{
```

```
            trace("there was an error");
        }
    }
    //now load the CSS
    myStyle.load("myCSS.css");
```

We have covered a lot of different ways to format a text field (and we will cover one more in the HTML section later in this chapter). We have even covered how to keep content and design separate from one another using Cascading Style Sheets and loading them in from outside our Flash file.

In this next section, we are going to cover how to manipulate the position using scroll properties, and we are going to cover the new `Mouse` event that will make scrolling a lot easier.

## Scrolling Text Fields

Many times when you fill text fields with information, the text field just is not large enough to handle it all. You can, of course, make the text field larger, but you can also scroll the text. Scrolling the text will allow you to keep the text field the original size, but still be able to display all of the information.

You can scroll a text field two different sets of directions with two different properties. The first is the `scroll` property, which controls up and down motion and starts at position 0. The second property is the `hscroll` property, which controls left and right scrolling and also starts at position 0. And both of these properties have limits, which are `maxscroll` and `maxhscroll` oddly enough. With these properties, you can control the positioning of text in text fields.

Let's jump right in with an example of using the `scroll` property.

1. Start a new Flash document.

2. Create two more layers, and name the top layer **actions**, the middle layer **buttons**, and the bottom layer **text**.

3. In the text layer, create a dynamic text field about 200 by 100 with the Show Border option turned on, change the line style to Multiline, and give it an instance name of `info_txt`.

4. Then go into the actions of the first frame of the actions layer and set `info_txt.text` equal to the preceding paragraph (or any large amount of text).

5. Now when you test the movie, you should not be able to see all of the text in the text field because the text field is too small. We are going to fix this by making it scroll.

17

6. Go into the buttons layer, create two buttons with instance names of up_btn and down_btn, and place them beside the text field as in Figure 17.9.

7. Now go back into the actions layer, and put these actions in under where you set the text to the text field:

```
//this will control the upward motion
up_btn.onPress=function(){
    if(info_txt.scroll != 0){
        info_txt.scroll--;
    }
}
//this will control the downward motion
down_btn.onPress=function(){
    if(info_txt.scroll < info_txt.maxscroll){
        info_txt.scroll++;
    }
}
```

Now test the movie to see that the scroll buttons are working.

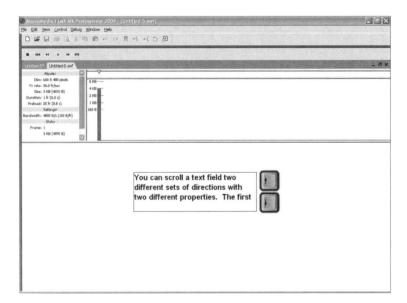

**FIGURE 17.9**    Position the scroll buttons beside the text field.

Now that you can scroll text, let's take a step further and use the new Mouse Event.

### The Mouse Wheel Event

Back in Flash MX, if you wanted to make text fields scrollable by using the wheel mouse, you had to do some fancy JavaScripting. Now it's as easy as hovering over the text field and spinning the mouse wheel.

Going back to our preceding example, save the file somewhere, publish it, and then open up either the .html or the .swf file, hover over the text field, and scroll the text field with your mouse wheel.

But you don't need a text field to get the event. Here is an example that will actually listen for the event, and tell you how fast and which direction the mouse wheel is going.

1. Create a new Flash file.

2. Open up the actions in the first frame and place these actions inside:

```
//create an object to listen for the event
var wheelListen:Object = new Object();
//add the event to the object
wheelListen.onMouseWheel = function(amount) {
//send the speed and direction to the ouptut window
    trace(amount)
}
//add the lisenter to the Mouse Object
Mouse.addListener(wheelListen);
```

Now test the movie (and remember to click on the stage in test mode). When you move the mouse wheel up and down, it will send the speed to the Output window. All positive numbers are scrolling up on the wheel, and all negative numbers are scrolling down on the mouse wheel.

In the next section, we are going to cover HTML text in text fields, which isn't really new because we used some HTML text when we were applying StyleSheet objects.

## HTML Text in Text Fields

So far, we have focused on putting raw text directly into text fields and then formatting that text with either a TextFormat object or a StyleSheet object. With HTML text, you can put content and formatting in one package using supported HTML tags.

Here is a list of the supported HTML tags in Flash:

• Anchor tag—<a>—Creates a hyperlink with these attributes:

href—The URL to be loaded

target—The window type to be used when opening a link

This example creates a link to Macromedia in its own window:

```
<a href="http://www.macromedia.com" target="_blank">click here</a>
```

- Bold tag—<b>—Creates bold text between the tags:

```
<b>This is what I call bold</b>
```

- Line Break tag—<br>—This tag creates a new line in HTML text fields.

    This example creates two lines of text:

```
This is one like<br>this is another line.
```

- Font tag—<font>—This tag can control some properties of text using these attributes:

    color—This attribute controls the hexadecimal color of text as in this example:

```
<font color="#0000ff">I am blue</font>
```

    face—This attribute controls the actual font type of text, and can also handle multiple font names separated by commas. It will choose the first font available on the user's machine.

    This example uses Arial text as our first choice and Courier as our second:

```
<font face="Arial, Courier">I am Arial</font>
```

    size—This attribute controls the size of the text in pixel points.

    This example sets text to a point size of 20:

```
<font size="20">This is big text</font>
```

- Image tag—<img>—This tag is new to Flash and allows outside JPGs and SWFs to be brought into HTML text fields as well as internal movie clips with their linkage set. It supports a number of tags:

    src—This attribute is the only required attribute and is the URL to the SWF or JPG; it can also be the linkage to an internal movie clip. Both JPGs and SWFs will not display until completely loaded and Flash does not support the loading of progressive JPGs.

    id—This attribute gives the movie clip that holds the external JPG or SWF (which is automatically created by Flash). It is good if you want to be able to manipulate the embedded image with ActionScript.

    width—Used to set the width of the JPG, SWF, or internal movie clip you load in.

`height`—Used to set the height of the JPG, SWF, or internal movie clip you load in.

`align`—This attribute controls which side the content you load in to the text field will be on. `left` and `right` are the only allowable settings, and the default is `left`.

`hspace`—This attribute controls the horizontal space in pixels around the loaded content between the content and the text. The default is 8.

`vspace`—This attribute controls the vertical space in pixels around the loaded content between the content and the text. The default is 8.

This example places a JPG on the left, with default spacing as well as an id.

```
<img src="local.jpg" width="320" height="240" id="image_mc">
```

For more on embedding images into text fields, look at the section titled "The Image Tag" later in this chapter.

- Italics tag—`<i>`—This tag italicizes text:

```
<i>Here is some italicized text</i>
```

- List Item tag—`<li>`—This tag is used to create bulleted lists:

```
Software<li>Flash MX 2004 Pro<li>Dreamweaver<li>Freehand
```

This example would appear like this:

  - Software
  - Flash MX 2004 Pro
  - Dreamweaver
  - Freehand

- Paragraph tag—`<p>`—This tag begins a new paragraph and usually holds a large amount of text. It has two attributes:

`align`—Controls the horizontal positioning of text between the `<p>` tags. You can use `left`, `right`, and `center`.

`class`—This attribute is used with the `StyleSheet` object to control format.

This example creates a new paragraph and sets its alignment to center:

```
<p align="center">New paragraph</p>
```

- Span tag—`<span>`—This tag is only useful when setting text to `StyleSheets`. It used to have a different class of style within a `<p>` tag. It has one attribute:

`class`—Used to name the certain style within the `StyleSheet` to use for formatting.

17

In this example we use a span tag to change some text in a <p> tag:

```
<p class="Body">This is <span class="Emphasize">really </span>cool</p>
```

- Text format tag—`<textformat>`—Is used to allow a certain set of the `TextFormat` object's properties to be used with HTML text. It has many attributes:

  `blockindent`—This attribute is used to control the block indentation in points.

  `indent`—This attribute controls the indentation from the left side of the text field in points for the first character in the paragraph.

  `leading`—This attribute controls line spacing.

  `leftmargin`—This attribute controls the margin on the left in points.

  `rightmargin`—This attribute controls the margin on the right in points.

  `tabstops`—This attribute creates custom tabbing points (creates a mock table). An example using this attribute is provided later in this chapter.

  This example creates some text with 2-point line spacing and a 3-point indentation for paragraphs:

  ```
  <textformat leading="2" indent="3">
  ```

- Underline tag—`<u>`—This tag underlines text and it has no attributes:

  ```
  <u>I am underlined</u>
  ```

Now that you have seen all the tags HTML text fields will support, let's start using some.

First, if you are creating the text field manually, you must make sure the HTML option in the Properties Inspector is turned on. If you are creating your text fields with ActionScript, make sure you change the `html` property to `true` like this:

```
myTextField_txt.html = true;
```

Also, we have been using the `text` property to set text to text fields. If we did that with HTML text fields, it would display the actual HTML tags and the text, so instead we set HTML text to text fields using the `htmlText` property like this:

```
myTextField_txt.htmlText = "<b>This is a bold statement</b>";
```

Okay, now you know some basic rules of HTML text fields. Let's jump right into an example.

In this example, we will create a text field and put some HTML into it.

1. Create a new Flash document.

**2.** Open the Actions panel in the first frame and place these actions in it:

```
//create the text field
this.createTextField("myText_txt",1,0,0,200,200);
//set of its properties
myText_txt.html = true;
myText_txt.wordWrap = true;
//create the html string we want to use
var myString:String = "<p align='center'><b>Extra Extra</b>
➥<br>Read <u>all</u> about it</p>";
//now set the text to the text field
myText_txt.htmlText = myString;
```

Test the movie, and it should appear like Figure 17.10. Nothing too spectacular, but you can of course add as much HTML as you want, and play around to see what else you can do.

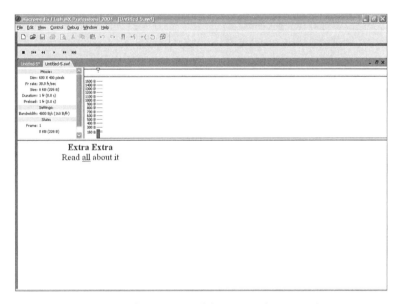

**FIGURE 17.10**    Use HTML to hold content and format at the same time.

This next example will be a little more advanced. We are going to create a "mock table" with the <textformat> tag to display sets of information. We are going to create three basic field names: name, age, and location. Then we'll add four different people to the table. After that, we will set all of the text to the text field.

**1.** Create a new Flash document.

**2.** Open the Actions panel in the first frame and put these actions in:

```
//create the text field
this.createTextField("myText_txt",1,0,0,250,200);
//set its properties
myText_txt.html = true;
myText_txt.multiline=true;
myText_txt.wordWrap = true;
```

This created our text field and set some of the necessary properties.

3. Now we create the string and add all the information we need, so add these actions in:

```
//now create the string to hold the headers
var headers:String = "<u>Name\tAge\tLocation</u>";
//now the string to hold all the rows
var rows:String = "Ben\t23\tVirginia<br>";
rows += "Lesley\t24\tBarcelona<br>";
rows += "Missy\t24\tLondon<br>";
rows += "Micki\t31\tNew Hampshire";
```

4. Finally, create the text format tag and add all the strings to the text field by adding these actions:

```
//add the textformat tag
myText_txt.htmlText = "<textformat tabstops='[70, 120]'>";
//add the headers
myText_txt.htmlText += headers;
//add the rows
myText_txt.htmlText += rows;
//close the text format tag
myText_txt.htmlText += "</textformat>";
```

Now test the movie, and it should appear like Figure 17.11.

That was a pretty powerful example showing how you could display data inside HTML text fields and make it appear to be organized into tables using the <textformat> tag.

Another tag that is very useful is the <img> tag.

## The Image Tag

The image tag, <img>, is a new tag for Flash HTML text fields, and is extremely useful, as you will see in the next example.

In this example, we are simply going to load in a JPG from the outside and put some text around it. You can use any image because we are going to size it in the tag.

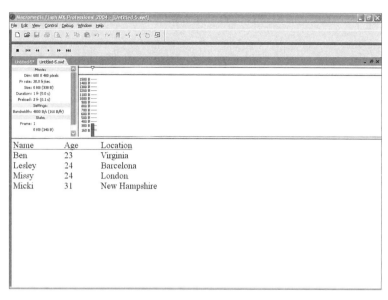

**FIGURE 17.11**    Use the `<textformat>` tag to create HTML text that appears to have tables.

1. Start a new Flash file.

2. Save as `imageLoader.fla`.

3. We are going to load a JPG image into the text field, so make sure there is one in the same directory where you just saved this file.

4. Open the Actions panel in the first frame and put these actions in:

```
//create the text field
this.createTextField("imageAndText_txt",1,0,0,300,300);
//set its properties
imageAndText_txt.html = true;
imageAndText_txt.wordWrap = true;
imageAndText_txt.border = true;
```

This created our text field and set some necessary properties.

5. Now let's create the string to hold the HTML and insert it into the text field with these actions:

```
//create the string to hold the html
var myString:String = "Picture 1<br><img src='image.jpg'
➥width='200' height='200'>This is a picture of platform 9 3/4 in london."
//set the text in the text field
imageAndText_txt.htmlText = myString;
```

17

Now test the movie, and you should see something similar to Figure 17.12.

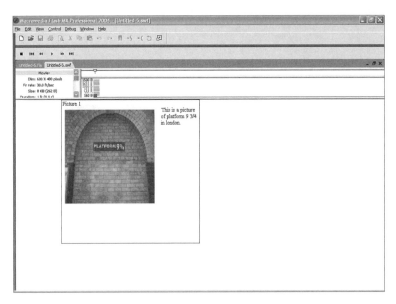

**FIGURE 17.12**    You can now load images directly into a text field.

That example showed how to load a JPEG from outside the Flash file, and loading SWFs works the exact same way, but now we are going to show how to load a movie clip symbol from the Flash file into the text field.

In this example, we are going to create a rectangle and then load it into the text field we create.

1. Start a new Flash file.

2. Go to Insert, New Symbol.

3. Make sure it is a movie clip you are creating. Give it a Symbol name of `rectangleMC` and check the Export for ActionScript check box (also make sure the Linkage Identifier is the same as the Symbol name).

4. When you're in this new movie clip, draw a rectangle with any stroke and fill color, but make sure it is aligned to the left, and to the top of the Movie Clip (its top left corner is on the cross hair) or it will not sit correctly in the text field. Make it about 150×150, but again, because we will size it with the `<img>` tag, it is not that important here (although the closer it is to the actual size, the clearer it will appear).

5. Go back to the main timeline, open the Actions panel in the first frame, and put these actions in:

```
//create the text field
this.createTextField("imageAndText_txt",1,0,0,300,300);
//set its properties
imageAndText_txt.html = true;
imageAndText_txt.wordWrap = true;
imageAndText_txt.border = true;
```

This will create the text field and set some of its necessary properties.

6. Now that we have our text field, we will create the string and set it to the text field with these actions:

```
//create the string to hold the html
var myString:String = "<img src='rectangleMC' width='150'
➥height='150' align='right'>Now we loaded something from inside of Flash";
//put the text in the text field
imageAndText_txt.htmlText = myString;
```

Now test the movie to see the rectangle load into the text field.

In this example, we embedded the movie clip we created earlier, and set it to the right side of the text box. But let's say we wanted to do something with the rectangle after it has been loaded into the text field. That's where the id attribute of the <img> tag comes in, as you will see as we continue.

Building on our preceding example, we are going to make it so that if a user clicks on the image tag, they will open a link.

1. Go back into the actions, and in the line of code where we create the HTML string, change the image tag to this:

```
<img src='rectangleMC' id='rectangle_btn' width='150' height='150'
➥align='right'>
```

Now we are using the id attribute, so we can interact with the rectangle in ActionScript.

2. Now that we have an id we can use in AS, let's create a function that will open a link when the user clicks on the rectangle, by adding these actions to the bottom:

```
//this will add the event to the rectangle
imageAndText_txt.rectangle_btn.onRelease=function(){
    getURL("http://www.macromedia.com","_blank");
}
```

Now, when you test the movie, you can click on the rectangle, and it will open up a browser window with the link. This example showed how to interact with loaded content in HTML text fields using the id attribute, but if the truth be told, you can also hyperlink these files by using an anchor tag <a> around the image tag <img> like this:

```
<a href="http://www.macromedia.com"> <img src='image.jpg' ></a>
```

We have covered the image tag, and all that can be done with it. Of course, because you can embed outside SWFs as well as movie clips you create inside, you can do a lot of interesting things, such as having a constantly running clock inside a text field. The possibilities are endless.

In the next section, we are going to cover how to interface these HTML text fields with JavaScript, another Web language.

## HTML Text Fields and JavaScript

JavaScript, like ActionScript, is an object-oriented programming language, so if you are not familiar with it, it is easy to pick up if you are comfortable with ActionScript. And JavaScript can do many things that ActionScript cannot because it is a browser language. We are going to show two examples of what can be done with JavaScript and Flash. The first is a simple alert that will pop up when a link is selected. The second is a bit more powerful, and therefore more complicated; we will use JavaScript to open a custom window to load content in.

This first example is fairly simple because we will use the JavaScript inside the ActionScript.

1. Start a new Flash file.

2. Open the Actions panel in the first frame and place these actions within it:

   ```
   //create the text field
   this.createTextField("alert_txt",1,0,0,100,20);
   //set its properties
   alert_txt.html = true;
   alert_txt.border = true;
   //now put the text inside the text field
   alert_txt.htmlText = "<a href='javascript:
   ➥alert(&quot;You made an alert!&quot;);'>Alert Me</a>"
   ```

Now test the movie and click the link. A browser will open so that the JavaScript can be run (remember, JavaScript must run within a browser). Note that the browser Safari on the Mac platform sometimes does not allow this code to work properly.

In this next example, we are actually going to publish the HTML, and add some JavaScript to it so we can create custom pop-up windows. But we will build the Flash part first.

1. Start a new Flash document.

2. Save the document as **popup.fla**.

3. Open the Actions panel in the first frame, and place these actions in it:

```
//create the text field
this.createTextField("popUp_txt",1,0,0,100,20);
//set some properties
popUp_txt.html = true;
//place the html in the text field
popUp_txt.htmlText = "<a href=\"javascript:
➥popUp(&quot;http://www.sams.com&quot;,500,500)\">Open POP-UP</a>";
```

Now that we have all the script we need for Flash, we are calling a JavaScript function (that we have yet to build) and passing a few parameters to the function.

4. Go to File, Publish (Shift+F12), which will create the .swf file as well as the .html file.

5. Open the .html file we just created in a text editor (like Notepad or SciTe).

6. The first thing you will want to do is remove the line of HTML code that says

```
<param name="allowScriptAccess" value="sameDomain" />
```

That single line of code will prevent us from using JavaScript in our Flash movie, so make sure it is gone.

7. Now, between the <head> tags, place this JavaScript:

```
<script language="JAVASCRIPT" type="TEXT/JAVASCRIPT">
<!--
if(screen){
topPos=0
leftPos=0
}
function popUp(thePage,wt,ht){
leftPos= (screen.width-wt)/2
topPos = (screen.height-ht)/2
newWin1 = window.open(thePage,'aWin','toolbars=no, resizeable=no,
➥scrollbars=no,left='+leftPos+',top='+topPos+',width='+wt+',height='+ht)
}
// -->
</script>
```

When that text is in the HTML file, you can save the file and close it. Then launch it in a browser and you will see the text we put in the text field. When you click on it, it will open a custom window 500×500 in the center of the screen.

17

## Summary

This chapter covered a lot of things you can do with text in Flash from drawing text fields on the stage all the way to creating them in ActionScript with images, tables, and even some JavaScript. We also went over the best ways to format the text. Cascading Style Sheets are the best way to go because they make it easy to update multiple text fields without ever having to open Flash.

CHAPTER **18**

# Debugging

## Writing Proactive ActionScript

The first and best way to debug is to write code that does not create errors. This means planning your project from start to finish. The first day you sit down to create your project, start thinking about mapping out the way in which interaction will be created. That means thinking about the placement of variables, thinking about a hierarchical structure for your movie clip objects, and also thinking about how your graphics will work in coordination with the code you write. The trick is to have as much as possible of this planning process mapped out before you even open Flash. Flash is a tool that assists in creating interactive programs. It is not a tool that dictates creativity; that comes from the human brain—your human brain. Therefore, your project should have a starting map that will be referred to constantly throughout the project's lifespan. This is not to say that the map is unchangeable; however, following a road map will help you steer clear of pitfalls and the dreaded "bug."

Another common programming technique is to comment your code. This not only helps in writing ActionScript but also assists any other designers or programmers viewing the project to contribute their work. Comments are delineated in Flash with the // sign. For multiline comments, place /* at the beginning of the text and */ at the end of the text to be commented. You place comments to divulge the purpose of a variable, to show how a block of code works, and to show why a function is called in a particular place, among other things. There is almost no limit to the number of comments you can place in a project. Don't write paragraphs of comments, but little single-line notes that will greatly explain your code. Even the most experienced coders will run into mental blocks as to what they were trying to accomplish on projects they worked on in previous years. Comments can clear up these mental speed bumps.

Comments can also come in a variety of colors. Flash allows you to change the color codes on the various types of code you write. Go to Edit, Preferences and click the ActionScript tab. Under the option for syntax coloring you can change the color of your ActionScript text, background, comments, keywords, strings, and identifiers. I highly recommend sticking with the default colors, which would make your comments gray, but if you do decide to change the color of your ActionScript, make sure you remain consistent from one Flash document to another, and make sure the text colors make sense. For example, if you are going to change the comment color, don't make it a color that closely resembles the color of keywords. Furthermore, I recommend making the color of your commented text red so that any person viewing your code would know that red text is a warning that a comment is being used. Using green or purple text for comments might not get the point across as well as red would. Regardless of the color of your comments, your ActionScript should be littered with commented, colored text throughout.

Another great tool for basic debugging is the `trace` action. In many cases, using `trace` actions is even better than using the debugger for following the values of variables and checking code with notes in your project—especially if you already know that an area of code has proved problematic. A `trace` action can be called in the following manner:

```
trace ("any text here to display a message");

trace (myVariableName);
```

The first line of the preceding code uses a `trace` action that will place the exact message in the Output panel. The second `trace` action will place the variable's value in the Output panel. The second example is more useful when you're trying to track what a value is at a particular point in your code. The first example can be used when you're just trying to figure out how an action in Flash works. Then you can just replace the `trace` action for the code you want placed in a particular code block. If you don't want end users to view `trace` actions in your project, choose File, Publish Settings, click the Flash tab, and check the box labeled Omit Trace Actions. You can see the Omit Trace Actions check box in Figure 18.1.

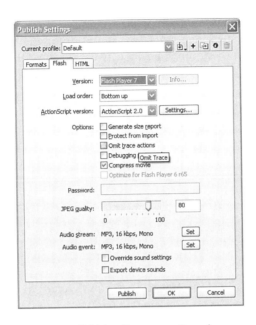

**FIGURE 18.1**    Omit Trace Actions will hide all trace actions from your end users.

## Naming Conventions

If you run into problems in Flash concerning your addressing of movie clips, make sure you have named every clip in the target path correctly. This means ensuring there are no extra spaces at the end of the instance names. Also, make sure your movie clips are in the correct order. Be meticulous about the hierarchy and make sure to follow it exactly when writing code in the target path. Any mistyping of letters, different capitalization, or additional spaces will throw the path off and will prevent the code from running properly.

While writing your code, make sure your ActionScript does not conflict with itself. By this I mean that you should place actions on the top layer of every timeline, and name this layer "actions" for good practice. Also, it's usually helpful to not include any graphics, buttons, or movie clips on the top layer. Otherwise, you could mistakenly put two conflicting actions on the same frame. Make sure your variables are set up in a particular way to ensure the success of your project. A variable is set to make sure your project navigates in a certain way. If you have two variables that cancel each other out, parts of your project may become defunct.

Make sure your items in Flash are all unique. You will run into fewer errors if every object has its own identifier. And make sure to give every object on the stage an instance name. More often than not, after you have coded several hundred lines of code, and nothing happens the way it is supposed to, it is due to either a naming conflict or a complete lack of instance naming.

18

Don't provide a movie clip with a name and then provide a variable with the same name. It will be harder to track down items when you are scanning the Movie Explorer for an object or piece of code. Furthermore, follow a convention in writing your code. Commonly, ActionScript programmers like to name variables and objects with lowercase letters for the first word in a name and use a capital letter to start the second word in the object's name, with no space in between the words. For example, a variable would be written as

```
myVarName
```

but not

```
myvarname
```

or

```
My Var Name
```

Remember, this is just a style of preference. Using underscore characters (_) for your spaces is a matter of choice. Just stay consistent in coding ActionScript. Do not mix and match styles; this causes harder searches of code and makes the process more difficult for other programmers who may be looking at your work.

Also, save your work constantly. It is good to have several versions of your project. Constantly save your work that you know to be functioning properly to a "current" or "final" file. That way, old versions of your project can be used as a guide or a fallback. If you only work in one file, you are highly likely to save some code you didn't necessarily want. Going back one or two versions can save many headaches.

Finally, remember that bugs happen! They are as inevitable as death and taxes. Bugs are often due to an oversight in coding. At other times bugs are caused by a game plan gone wrong. The key to catching bugs is paying attention to the flow of your project. Understand how your project is expected to work and how your project currently flows in relation to the code. This will often accentuate what bugs may be present in the project.

The next section identifies ways of finding and fixing the bugs in your projects. These techniques will help you to be more efficient in solving problems related to bugs and allow your project to be error-free when you go to publish it.

# Identifying Bugs

As mentioned earlier, there are several ways to restrict the number of bugs that occur in your project. However, we all know that bugs are going to happen anyway. For example, you may have a button that isn't responding to an action, or a handler might be missing some syntax, or your variables might not be changed based on a mislabeled target path. Whatever the problem, tools are available to rescue you—tools such as the Output panel with `trace` actions and the `Error` object class. You can also use the Watch, strict type settings in ActionScript, the Bandwidth Profiler, and the Debugger to assist you in identifying bugs in your project.

One problem with discovering bugs is that code blocks are read by Flash in a very short period of time. Within milliseconds, Flash tries to accomplish the tasks set out in a code block. Just watching a movie in the Flash Player will not always allow the human eye to pick up what problems are currently in the project. Furthermore, variables are used in basically all the projects in which you write ActionScript, and you cannot see these variable values simply by watching the movie in the Flash Player.

Let's open the `ECdebug.fla` file and work through some of the debugging techniques to find values for the variables and decipher what bugs may be present in the project. This file is an example built to show regions and states within those regions to users in an easy-to-follow, interactive format. The `ECdebug.fla` file is a tampered file, in which the programmer has taken a lackadaisical approach to writing code. The use of debugging techniques and the Flash interface will help clean up the code and place objects to perfect the project. Currently none of the buttons work. However, when we finish cleaning up the FLA file, there should be a working preloader, buttons labeled "Choose Region" and "Choose State" that reveal more buttons underneath them, and buttons corresponding to each state and region within the U.S., which animate their particular part of the East Coast. Currently, none of that functionality is working, but code has been written in an attempt to make it work. In the next few sections, we will pinpoint the problems with this file.

## Output Panel

The Output panel allows Flash to talk to the programmer. When ActionScript errors are created in code, the Flash Output panel alerts you to the facts associated with the error in the test movie screen. The test movie screen is the only place the Output panel will be active. When you need to know the variables or objects in your code, the Flash Output panel will list those items for you when those options are selected from the Debug menu option in the test screen. Finally, when you want to know whether a particular piece of code is working, `trace` actions as well as error object messages can appear in the Output panel to let you know that the code is being executed. For the next exercise, we'll open up the `ECdebug.fla` file and use the Output panel to find problems with this code.

### Using the Output Panel in Debugging

In this exercise, we will go through some of the steps that can be taken to debug a basic Flash file. We will continue to work through the different steps throughout the rest of this chapter.

1. Immediately upon opening `ECdebug.fla`, save the movie and call it `ECdebugCorrectSample.fla` so that you do not confuse it with the original file.

2. Test the movie by choosing Control, Test Movie.

3. The Output window should immediately appear, alerting you to an error in the code. The window should produce the error shown in Figure 18.2.

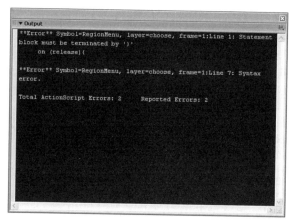

**FIGURE 18.2**    The Output panel assists you in finding the line and object where incorrect ActionScript syntax occurs.

4. Close the Flash Player and leave the Output panel open so that you can refer to it while changing your code in the Actions panel during authoring mode.

5. The Output panel has instructed you to go to the symbol named RegionMenu in the library. Therefore, double-click the symbol in the movie with that name. This symbol happens to correspond to the movie clip symbol that houses the buttons for the region names and is located on the upper-right area of the stage.

6. Upon entering this movie clip symbol, check the layer names for the layer "choose." In this layer you will find one button. It has an instance name of myChoiceReg. Click once on this button and open the Actions panel to investigate the code attached to the button. *Be careful not to click on the text field above the button on the same layer!*

7. The Output panel shows you that line 1 needs to have a symbol to terminate the code block.

8. In your Actions panel, turn on the line-numbering feature. You can do this by pressing Ctrl+Shift+L (or Cmd+Shift+L on the Mac) or by clicking the Actions panel menu options and choosing View Line Numbers. This step really isn't necessary for this code, but it shows you how you can now easily locate line number 1 in the code block to identify where the problem is occurring.

9. Look at this statement. Notice that there is a curly bracket ({) to open the on release statement, a curly bracket to start the conditional statement, and a curly bracket to start the else statement. However, if you look at the closing brackets (}), you'll see that indeed we are missing one to complement the on release statement. Therefore, in the final line of code, add a closing curly bracket to end the statement.

10. Test the movie. This should remove the error from the Output panel. In fact, because this was the lone syntax error in this project, the Output panel will appear empty if it is still open. Leave the Flash Player open for our next exercise.

## Bandwidth Profiler

The Bandwidth Profiler allows you to view streaming as if you were looking at a file using a particular modem speed. It also gives you vital statistics about the size of frames and the overall size of a project. The value of the Bandwidth Profiler is that you can target parts of your project to optimize and rework certain sections of it.

Now, simply looking at this movie, it might appear to be perfectly normal. However, our programmer has missed some key components, which you'll fix in the next exercise.

### Using the Bandwidth Profiler in Debugging

This exercise will go through how to use the Bandwidth Profiler in debugging Flash applications as well as how to preload content. Here are the steps to follow for this exercise:

1. Test the Flash movie again, and without clicking any of the buttons, click View, Bandwidth Profiler (if the Profiler is not already open). This will bring up a bar graph view of what the project looks like. Now you can view how many bytes are located in the movie on any given frame. Your Bandwidth Profiler should look similar to the one shown in Figure 18.3.

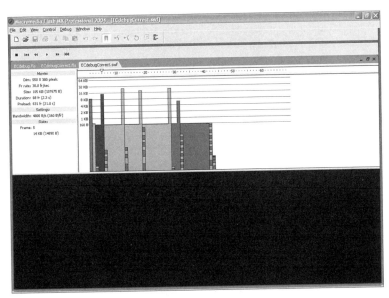

**FIGURE 18.3**  The Bandwidth Profiler allows you to see the graphical representation of a project in bytes per frame.

This lets you know what frames have a lot of information and may need further optimization. It also tells you which frames will trip up the pace of the presentation if the project is not preloaded.

2. Now choose View, Download Settings, 56K (4.7 KB/s). This will allow you to test the project as though you were an end user looking at the project streaming over a 56K modem. If you want to target other stream rates, you can choose View, Download Settings, Customize to specify another rate. For now, we will test using 56K.

3. Choose View, Simulate Download. Now your project will run as if it were streaming over a 56K modem. Notice how the project stutters on all the frames that have a lot of content. This means Flash cannot load the project faster than the animation of the objects on the screen. This is a perfect opportunity for a preloader to be built into the project. Therefore, let's leave the Flash Player for a moment.

4. Save your FLA as `ECdebugCorrect.fla`.

5. Go to the second frame of the root-level movie timeline and let's look at the code under the layer named "actions."

6. Notice a function initialization and some initialization of variables. After that, you'll find a block of code that is surrounded by comment marks. Apparently the programmer of this piece of code neglected to take out the comment marks, which must be done before running the preloader. Therefore, delete the instances of `/*` and `*/` from the code block. Now we have a preloader. This is important for halting the movie while it loads the necessary pieces to run smoothly over a 56K modem. Also, you will notice that the percentage of the bytes loaded is calculated in the variable named `percentLoaded`, which is also associated with the dynamic text box object named `percentPre_txt`.

7. Test the movie using Ctrl+Enter (Cmd+Return on the Mac).

8. Go to your Flash Player menu bar and click View, Simulate Download again. Notice how the percentage of the movie will show after the first frame is loaded and your user has a graphical representation of how long until the program is started. Also notice how the play head remains on frame 1 while the rest of the movie loads; this is also represented graphically in Figure 18.4. When it gets to 100%, the movie plays the rest of the animation on the main timeline.

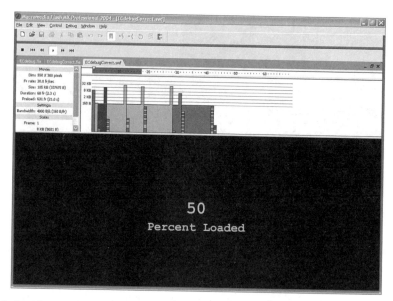

**FIGURE 18.4**   The newly created `ECdebugCorrect.swf` file with a preloader added to the code. Notice the location of the play head.

You can see how valuable a tool the Bandwidth Profiler can be for viewing a project's flow. It allows you to test your movies under ideal end-user modem specifications without having to physically hook up any connections or alternate machines.

Now, the next step is to optimize the graphics in frames where the kilobytes seem to be high.

9. Open up the Bandwidth Profiler in the Flash Player environment for `ECdebugCorrect.swf`. Notice that frame 31 is right around 4KB.

10. Go to frame 31 of the outlines layer in the root-level timeline of the FLA. Click the frame that holds the content for the outlines of the states.

11. With the Arrow tool selected, click on the lines of the states, and then click the Straighten button until you feel all the lines are straightened out sufficiently. Disregard the look of this piece for the moment. You should have several straight lines surrounding the states, causing the states to look incorrect. However, for the purpose of this demonstration, you'll want to see the states with optimized lines.

12. Test the movie and look at the Bandwidth Profiler for frame 31. Notice how the kilobytes for this frame now hover around 2KB. Other frames may also be affected by the line straightening, but for now we're just looking at frame 31.

13. Go back to your FLA and press Ctrl+Z (Cmd+Z on the Mac) a number of times to undo the straightening you did in step 11.

14. Save your work.

If you get this graphical representation below the red line in the Bandwidth Profiler, no preloader will be necessary for the frame. This is less important for this movie because our programmer decided to leave preloading code for us. However, if a file needs to be a specific size for a client (say, under 100KB), the Bandwidth Profiler could decipher which frames are too high in size and target those frames for optimization, as it did for frame 31.

The project is not finished yet. We still haven't checked to see whether all the parts of the project work yet. Go to the end of the project's timeline in the Flash Player and click around on the various buttons. Notice that none of them work. Clicking the Animate All button, for instance, animates nothing. Also, we want to get the Choose State button to react much the same way the Choose Region button reacts (you already fixed the Choose Region button when you completed the first exercise in this chapter).

## Identifying Values Attached to Variables

Often the bugs in a project remain because variables are not being tracked correctly. You may have wanted to change a variable at a point in your project but forgot to change it. Sometimes you may be changing variables in places where it is unnecessary. Luckily, Flash allows you to track the values of variables during the runtime of your projects.

18

For the purposes of the next exercise, we are going to target the Choose State button to determine why it does not toggle between showing and hiding other buttons' options.

### Identifying Variables When Debugging

In this exercise, we will go through how to get information about variables at runtime. Here are the steps to follow for this exercise:

1. Open the `EcdebugCorrectSample` file, if it isn't already opened.

2. Double-click the `StateMenu` movie clip. Look around at how the piece is set up. Click the actions. Notice the variable named open. It is set to 0 in two places. This should be a red light already, but we are going to investigate this variable using the Flash Player. Also notice that there are two labels: one named open, and one named `close`. Click the various buttons in this movie clip to familiarize yourself with the clip's structure. Do not change any code attached to the buttons; just observe them and how the project is set up.

3. Go back to the root-level timeline and test the movie. When your movie has loaded all the objects, select Debug, List Variables. Notice that all the timeline variables present in the project are listed and show the value associated with each variable. All the global variables would also be listed here, if the project had global variables associated with it. The local variables in functions would not be listed here. However, toward the end of the list, you'll notice that open is listed twice and has the value of 0 in both cases. We now know that the variables are being read correctly in both movie clips.

4. Press Ctrl+Enter (Cmd+Return on the Mac) to test the movie in the Flash Player. Click the Choose Region and Choose State buttons in your SWF.

5. Choose Debug, List Variables again. Your Flash Player should look similar to Figure 18.5.

**FIGURE 18.5**    The Output panel containing the values of variables and movie clips located currently on the timeline. Notice the value of open.

Notice that the value for the Choose Region button has changed to 1, whereas the value for Choose State has remained at 0. This is the second time we have been clued in to a mislabeled variable causing the code to be faulty.

Before we fix the variable value, let's look at one more maneuver for finding values of variables during testing in the Flash Player. Go back to authoring mode.

6. Open the `StateMenu` movie clip you investigated earlier. On the button for Choose State, place the following code in the on (release) event handler:

   `trace(open);`

7. This will show you what the value is whenever the Choose State button is clicked.

8. Test the movie. Notice that the Output window appears with the value `0` for the `open` variable every time the Choose State button is clicked.

9. Go back to authoring mode and into the movie clip `StateMenu`. You have now seen three times that the `open` variable is not changing values properly. Therefore, go to the frame labeled "open" and look at the code in the Actions panel. Change the value of `open` to `1`. If you are confused as to why we are changing it here, check the way in which the variables are set up in the `RegionMenu` movie clip. That clip toggles back and forth properly.

10. Test the movie. What happened? The variable still didn't work. Something else must be wrong. We will fix this second problem in the next exercise.

11. Save your work to `ECdebugCorrectSample.fla`.

---

**NOTE**

When you selected Debug, List Variables, you may have noticed an option called List Objects. As you might expect, this option allows you to view all the objects included in the SWF file in the Output window.

---

## The Debugger

The Debugger is a tool that allows you to track values of variables, follow hierarchies of objects, and "watch" values throughout your project. It provides yet another way in which you can follow values to analyze bugs in your projects. In the next exercise, you will use the Debugger to track problems remaining in the project.

**Using the Debugger**

This exercise will walk through some of the basics in using the debugger. Here are the steps to follow for this exercise:

1. Open the movie `ECdebugCorrectSample.fla`.

2. In the Flash authoring environment, choose Control, Debug Movie. Notice that the SWF opens with the Debugger available for viewing. It also pauses the movie at the start of the project.

3. Using the Script pull-down menu on the right side of the panel, choose the script for the button named `chooseStateBU`, which should look similar to this:

```
on (release){
  if (open1){
          gotoAndStop("close");
        }else{
```

18

```
                        gotoAndStop("open");
                    }
            }
```

4. Next, place a breakpoint on the second line of this code by clicking to the left of the line number or by right-clicking a line of code and choose Set Breakpoint. This will pause the project when this point in the code is reached. Your debugger should look like the one shown in Figure 18.6. However, the gold arrow in the figure will not show up until this piece of code has been "broken," meaning that you executed the statement in the project and Flash is now executing this line of code.

**FIGURE 18.6**    The Debugger stopping at a breakpoint on the second line of the problematic button script.

5. Now click the play button on the debugger to run the movie.

6. Test the problematic Choose State button and watch the Debugger pause the movie at the breakpoint you set.

7. In the Debugger, an indicator is located over the top of your breakpoint. This shows the location where Flash is reading the code. Flash is slowing down the processing of the script and allowing you to see its thought process.

8. If you click the State button in the display window, you can also see the open1 variable under the Variables tab to follow the progress again of how it is being set.

9. Note that the conditional is evaluating open1 to be not equal to 1. Therefore, Flash will skip the first conditional of the statement. Instead, when you click the Step In Script button, the Flash script will go to the else option of the conditional. This is expected for the first time running through the script.

> **NOTE**
>
> The Step Over button is only useful for stepping over the script of a user-defined function. In all other instances, it reacts the same exact way the Step In Script button does.

10. Click the Choose State button again to determine the thought process of Flash for the second run through the script. The second time, notice that open1 is still being interpreted by Flash as not equal to 1. This means Flash will skip over moving the playback head at this point in the code.

11. With this new information, you can return to authoring mode, now that you know open1 is not the correct variable. In fact, the programmer shouldn't have named the variable open1. Perhaps his hand slipped while typing and he accidentally typed 1 at the end of line 2 of the button's code. Therefore, go to the StateMenu button and change the conditional to search for the value open, not open1.

12. Test the movie. You will find that both buttons now toggle. Save the ECdebugCorrectSample.fla file.

The bug in this code may have been easy to pick out. However, sometimes it takes a couple of passes for your eyes to locate a bug in your project. Sometimes you will see the variable values in the Output window but not pick up on why the code doesn't work until you look in the Debugger. Sometimes it will take "watching" a variable in the Watch to pick up on a problematic piece of code. The important thing to remember is not to give up. The errors you make in coding can be solved with a combination of logic and patience.

## The Watch

Now that you know both the buttons work, let's watch the two open variables using the Watch. This will ensure that the variables are working correctly. The next exercise shows you another way to track the variables in a movie. Much like the trace action, the method used in this exercise will target a single variable of your choice; however, unlike the trace action, the Watch will follow the progress of the variable as its value changes for the duration of the movie playback.

### Using the Watch in Debugging

In this exercise, we will use the Watch feature in the debugger. Here are the steps to follow for this exercise:

1. Open the ECdebugCorrectSample.fla file and choose Control, Debug Movie to open ECdebugCorrectSample in the Flash Player 7 environment. You will notice a series of tabs on the Debugger as well as a window that displays a list of all the objects in a scene. Figure 18.7 shows the display list and the Variables tab.

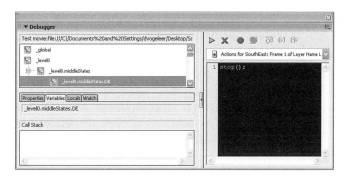

**FIGURE 18.7**    The display list and Variables tab in the Debugger.

Click the `_level0.regChoice` movie clip object in the display list.

2. Click the Variables tab.

3. Right-click the variable `open` and choose Watch to set this variable to be watched by the Debugger.

4. Click the `_level0.stateChoice` movie clip object and in the Variables tab, right-click the variable `open` and choose Watch to watch this variable as well.

5. Click the Watch tab in the debugger. Notice how both the variables just selected appear in the Watch. Your Watch tab should look similar to Figure 18.8. Now click both buttons in the SWF and notice how the values change.

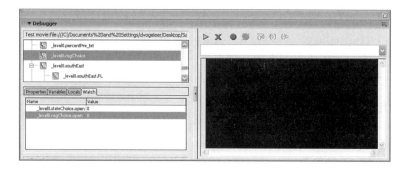

**FIGURE 18.8**    The Watch tab, looking for the value of each `open` variable.

The Watch can be a valuable tool when you know a variable is not acting right. It allows you to click around your SWF and test to see changing values of variables, without needing to place several `trace` actions throughout your code.

## Mislabeled Target Paths

One common mistake programmers make involves not being able to keep names straight. You have the name of the movie clip symbol, the name of any instances of that symbol, and the names of any variables on the timeline inside the movie clip—and that's just movie clips. Add button instances, nested clips, and other objects in the scene, such as sound, and things can get cluttered quickly. That's why the naming convention for your items is of paramount importance in your programming.

Naming conventions help you keep track of items and enable you to avoid problems in the future. However, you'll most likely encounter a slip in your foolproof plan for naming movie clips (especially because every clip needs an instance name for addressing, and you are probably going to have several dozen movie clips in your projects). The next exercise will assist you in finding problems with misnamed target paths. In testing the sample movie, you may have noticed that some of the region names and all the states did not target the correct paths.

## Target Paths

In this example, we will focus on target paths and the errors they can cause. Here are the steps to follow for this exercise:

1. Open the movie `ECdebugCorrectSample.fla`.

2. Open up the movie and click the movie clips in the scene. Look at the instance names assigned to each clip.

3. Double-click each of the region movie clips and look at the names of the states.

4. Write all the instance names down on a piece of paper so you can remember exactly how they are spelled.

5. Double-click the `RegionMenu` movie clip to see what code is written for the buttons of the three different regions.

6. Notice the path for the Northeast region:

   `_root.northEast.Maine.play();`

   This is in conflict with attempting to play the northEast timeline. In fact, it won't play any timeline because there is no movie clip named Maine in the FLA.

7. Delete `Maine` from the target path.

8. In testing the SWF, we noticed that the `middleStates` movie clip plays as expected when the button is clicked. Therefore, check the target path of the final button, southEastBU, in the `RegionMenu` movie clip. Figure 18.9 displays the Actions panel and shows how going back to the panel and checking codes can often reveal misspellings of paths or misrepresented paths in your addressing of movie clips. Make sure that your target path matches the target path of your instance names for movie clips and objects.

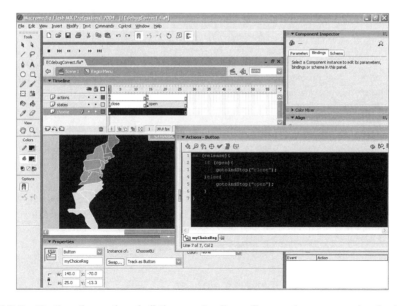

**FIGURE 18.9**  Testing the paths of all the movie clips will smooth out many beginning programming problems.

9. You will find that this target path is also suspect:

   ```
   _root.southEast.play;
   ```

10. Instead of the movie clip being referenced incorrectly (the clip being targeted is southEast), this time the method needs to be finished. Therefore, insert two parentheses after the word play, like so:

    ```
    _root.southEast.play();
    ```

    This will complete the method for this button.

11. Now that we have fixed some errors in the RegionMenu movie clip, let's investigate the target paths for the StateMenu movie clip. Double-click the movie clip and investigate the path on the button for Maine.

12. Earlier we noticed that the path has an error in the way in which the instance of Maine is referenced. If you open the Library, you'll notice that our programmer forgot to reference the movie clip instance and instead referenced the movie clip symbol name. Therefore, make sure to change this to the instance name, which happens to match the initials for the state. In other words, change the path

    ```
    _root.northEast.maine.play();
    ```

    to now read as follows:

    ```
    _root.northEast.ME.play();
    ```

13. Now do the same for the rest of the state buttons (our programmer has absentmindedly made the same mistake on all the state buttons):

    Massachusetts—MA

    New York—NY

    Pennsylvania—PA

    Virginia—VA

    North Carolina—NC

    Florida—FL

14. The one other problematic target path in this movie is on the Animate All button. Therefore, check the code included on that button:

    ```
    animateAll();
    ```

    Even though this is a function being called, it still needs to follow a target path.

15. Add the target path we need to make the function work correctly by changing the above code to this:

    ```
    _root.animateAll();
    ```

16. Test the movie. Now all the buttons are working in this project. I have left one final problem in the project for a later example. Save your ECdebugCorrectSample.fla file and ponder that tidbit while we discuss changing values.

## Changing Variable and Property Values

Most of the techniques discussed in this chapter have focused on discovering bugs in your project. Keep in mind, though, that debugging shouldn't always be about the eradication of "bugs." It should be about making your project perfect—finding the best appearance for your project, with the interactivity that keeps users coming back to use it. This can also be achieved through the use of the Debugger. The Debugger allows you to change values of properties (size, position, height, width, and so on) and values of variables to see how your project would look with those changed values. To learn more about this, proceed to the next exercise.

**Changing Values at Runtime**

Here are the steps to follow for this exercise:

1. Open and test your `ECdebugCorrectSample.fla` file to view the `ECdebugCorrectSample.swf` file in the Flash Player. Choose Window, Debugger.

2. Within the Debugger window, you have already been to the Variables tab. Note that a tab labeled Properties is available to you as well. Select the Continue button. Click a movie clip object in the display list. In this case, choose `_level0.northeast`.

3. Click the Properties tab. All the properties of the `_level0.northeast` movie clip object are available for you to edit, except for the ones shown in gray. These cannot be changed.

4. Select the `alpha` property and change its value to `40`.

5. Select the `_x` value and change it to `150`. Your Debugger should look something like Figure 18.10.

**FIGURE 18.10** The properties of the northEast movie clip in your SWF. These values can change the appearance of your SWF for testing purposes but will not change the values within your FLA.

Notice how the properties of your clip have changed for the purposes of the SWF.

6. Close the SWF in the Flash Player and look at your FLA.

All the properties are still the same as they were previously. Changing property values in the Debugger will not change values in the FLA. This gives you the ability to look at how a project could look using different colors, placements, and sizes, without damaging the original content.

To access the variables, you can click the Variables tab of any timeline that possesses a variable, or you can click the _global button in the display list to get a list of all the global variables in the project. All the variables you see in the Variables tab can be edited. Just as with the properties, this will not change the value of the variables in the FLA. It will only temporarily change the values for testing purposes. In the previous example, where the toggle's variable open needed to be changed to 1, we could have changed the variable's value during runtime to see how the toggle would react to the value being 1 at a particular moment. This would have given us another clue as to why the value was not working properly. This is important because you can save valuable time by being able to change variables during runtime and not have to go back, change them, and retest over and over until they are right.

# Debugging from Remote Locations

Troubleshooting should come from many different sources. Your learning should never end. One day you might solve a problem by reading a newsgroup online. Reading Macromedia tech notes can help you solve many of the general troubleshooting problems you'll encounter. Sometimes you may have an effect you want to get exactly right, which may be found in an online reference. Other times you may find the answer you're looking for in the reference materials in this and other books. The point is that you have an endless source of knowledge to tap into while debugging your projects. One such source can come in the form of help from other programmers. Are you out of luck with transmitting your file to them to test and debug? Of course not. Macromedia allows you to share your project with users who want to look at your project from a remote server location.

## Enabling Flash with the Ability to Debug Remotely

The next exercise shows you how to debug movies that are located on a server away from your computer. However, before you can place files on a server for the world to see, you must follow some steps to enable the file to be debugged remotely. This exercise goes over the items that need to be included in your project to allow for debugging remotely.

### Enabling Remote Debugging

Here are the steps to follow for this exercise:

1. Select File, Publish Settings in your ECdebugCorrectSample.fla file.

2. On the Flash tab of the Publish Settings dialog box, in the Options group, select Debugging Permitted. If you want your project to be protected from theft, provide a password in the Password box. This box is displayed in Figure 18.11.

3. Open the Debugger using any of the following menu commands:
   - Control, Debug Movie
   - File, Export Movie
   - File, Publish Settings, Publish

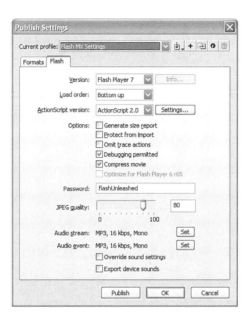

**FIGURE 18.11**   The publish settings needed to enable debugging in your SWF file.

4. Flash creates two files: a SWF file, which is the file needed for viewing the project, and an SWD file, which is needed for viewing breakpoints in the Debugger of the SWF.

5. Both the SWF and SWD files must remain alongside each other on the server location you choose. Place both files on the server.

## Activating the Debugger from the Server

The preceding exercise looked at enabling Flash to use a server. The next exercise shows you how to use a server to debug a file that is not located on your computer. You will need access to a server to debug the movie in this exercise, so if you do not have access to a server, you can skip this exercise.

### Using Remote Debugging

Here are the steps to follow for this exercise:

1. In Flash, choose Window, Development Panels, Debugger.

2. From the Options pull-down menu in the upper-right corner of the panel, choose the Enable Remote Debugging option.

3. Open either a browser window or the Flash Player standalone application.

4. Open the remote file using its location path.

5. This should open the Remote Debug dialog box. Choose either the Localhost or Other Machine option. Here are explanations of these options:

   - **Localhost**. If the Debug Player and the Flash authoring environment are on the same computer as the one on which you are viewing the file, choose Localhost.

   - **Other Machine**. Allows you to debug from a computer that lacks the proper authoring and debugging tools or lacks Flash. Refer to Figure 18.12 to view the dialog box that appears with these options.

**FIGURE 18.12**    The Remote Debug dialog box prompts you to enter the location of the Flash authoring environment.

6. Enter the password for the Debugger, as shown in Figure 18.13.

**FIGURE 18.13**    Enter the same password initialized in the Publish Settings dialog box for the file.

Remember the problem we had at the end of the exercise titled "Target Paths"? Let's try to find that bug. Start by looking at the function script we wrote in the second frame of the movie.

7. Place a breakpoint in the first line of the function.

8. Play the Debugger and click the Animate All button.

9. The Debugger will show each of the actions in the statement block as you click the Step In script button. You'll notice that the `middleStates` movie clip did not play. Check the target path of the middleStates line in the custom function. Here's how it currently reads:

```
_middle.play();
```

10. Change the value so that the path includes the entire `middleStates` instance name. It should now read as follows:

```
_middleStates.play();
```

11. Publish the movie and place it back on the server for any further testing you would like to perform.

You've now finished debugging a file using many of the debugging techniques included in the Flash Player and the Flash authoring environment. Of course, in the real world your debugging wouldn't finish until you and many of your coworkers approve the project. Testing is important, and it must be done often and thoroughly. Make sure you let as many people use the project as possible before calling your project complete.

# Strict Data Typing

As mentioned in Chapter 8, "Welcome to ActionScript 2.0," ActionScript now has the ability to have strict data typing. This means that you can declare a data type on variables, objects, parameters and results. If the data type changes after you have labeled a strict data type, Flash will produce an error in the Output panel.

Here is the basic way to declare a data type on a variable:

```
var myString:String = "David";
```

Now if we were to change the data type to say a number by adding this code to what we already have:

```
myString = 4;
```

you would then receive an error when you either check the syntax of the code, or attempt to test the movie. The error can be seen in Figure 18.14.

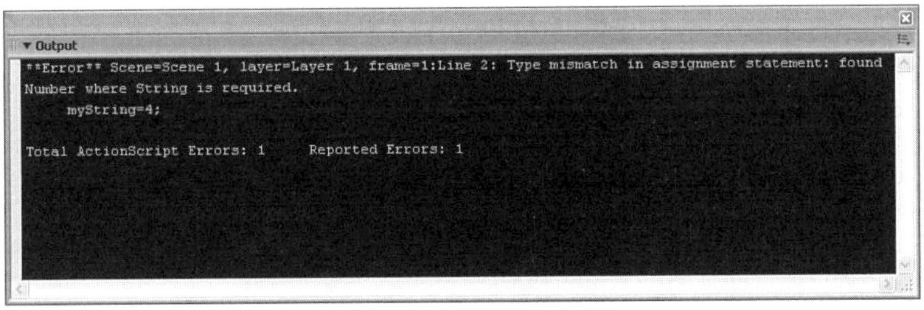

**FIGURE 18.14** The error message received if a data type is changed from its original type.

## The Error **Object**

The Error object is new to Flash and is used to hold error messages that can either be thrown directly to the Output panel, or be caught by a catch or finally action while inside a try statement. Error messages are most commonly used with testing functions.

In this example of code, we will create a try statement, and then use conditionals to trigger the error.

```
//create a password
var myPass:String = "testing";
//test the password using a try statement and a conditional
try{
   if(myPass != "password"){
      throw new Error("Incorrect password");
   }
}
//last resort
finally{
   //everything is fine
}
//simple trace action to see if the reader gets this far
trace("test");
```

When you test this code, the error will be thrown to the Output panel. Notice that the trace action at the end of our code was not sent to the Output panel. This happens because when an error is thrown, it stops the ActionScript interpreter from moving forward. If you change the myPass variable to "password", the error will not be thrown, and the trace function will be run.

In the next example of using the Error object, we will use it inside a function we build, and then capture the error message using try and catch statements.

```
//create the function
function greaterThan(num1:Number, num2:Number){
//compare the numbers
  if(num1 < num2) {
    throw new Error("The first number is not greater than the second");
  }
}
//try the function
try {
  greaterThan(12,15);
} catch (e) {
```

```
   //trace the error if there is one
   trace(e.toString());
}
```

Notice that this time, because we are using the throw statement inside a function, in order for the error to be shown, it must be captured with the catch statement.

Those are just two ways the Error object can be used to improve debugging. You can also use them inside functions to return specific values in the finally statement.

## Summary

Proper debugging involves many steps. Furthermore, these steps begin when your project begins, not simply at the end of your project. Using tools in Flash, you can decipher which problems are occurring. What's more, you can stop Flash from executing each line of code to determine which objects are holding variable and property values at runtime. This will allow you to determine whether your interactivity map at the beginning of your project is matching the logic that Flash interprets in your ActionScript.

18

# PART III

# Outside of Flash

## IN THIS PART

# CHAPTER **19**

# External ActionScript

In earlier chapters, we covered the fundamentals of ActionScript including the new features of AS 2.0 and debugging. Now we can begin to start taking ActionScript out of Flash and put it in external .as files. Some of the benefits include scalability and reuseability; because the ActionScript is outside of Flash, it can be used by several different Flash files without your having to rewrite the code.

External .as files can be created with any text editor such as Notepad or SciTe. And now, with Flash MX 2004 Professional, they can also be created within Flash.

To create an external ActionScript file in Flash, choose File, New and choose ActionScript File. The stage will change to a large version of the Actions panel, which functions in much the same way as the standard Actions panel does in Flash, as you can see in Figure 19.1.

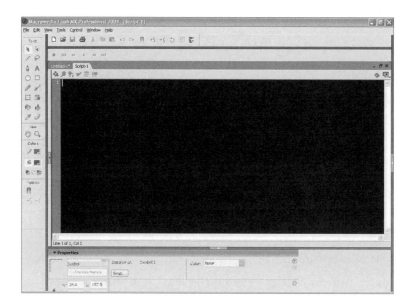

**FIGURE 19.1**    Create external ActionScript files from within Flash.

# Why Use External ActionScript?

Thus far in this book, you have seen that external ActionScript files are not necessary. In fact, creating external AS files would be yet another step in the process of building an application in Flash, so what would be the reason behind it?

ActionScript, as mentioned in previous chapters, is an object-oriented language, meaning that every piece of code is based on an object class. But this doesn't directly address the reason behind creating external ActionScript files; it is just the basis behind the reason.

It's no secret that Flash MX 2004 is designed to be used by design and development teams in harmony, and that is where externalizing core ActionScript requirements for a given application comes in handy. A developer can create object classes to be used by designers or other developers easily and quickly at the same time that the designer is creating the visual aspects of the application, thus keeping design, content, and function all separate.

Using external AS files also allows multiple applications to use the same file at the same time. Think of it this way: Imagine having to define the `MovieClip` object in each file you wanted to use it. It would be very difficult to create the exact same class each time you needed a movie clip, not to mention the repetitiveness of it. But because the `MovieClip` object is defined already, we can simply use it in Flash and not have to worry about how the movie clip was actually created.

As we go through this chapter, all of this will begin to make more sense and you will begin to see the advantages in creating external ActionScript files.

# #include **Versus Classpath**

External ActionScript files are not new to this version of Flash, but what's new about them is the way they are brought into Flash at compile time.

In previous versions of Flash, if you wanted to include an external AS file, you would use a pound sign (#) followed by the keyword include, and the path to the AS file as a string literal like this:

```
#include "myFile.as"
```

Notice that this line of code is not followed by a semicolon like most lines in ActionScript. An include statement cannot be followed by a semicolon or errors may occur. Also, do not put code directly below an include statement or errors might occur. Put at least one line of space between include statements and other code.

That was the old way of including external ActionScript in Flash files. The new way is much simpler and it is called classpath.

The **classpath** is a path or group of paths to where external ActionScript files can be found. And to include information from within one of the files, you simply call the constructor of the object class and Flash will look for a reference to that object in the classpath.

Here is an example of an external AS file:

```
class myClass{
    //class definition
}
```

And provided that this external AS file is within the classpath, the ActionScript to use it in Flash would be as follows:

```
    sampleClass = new myClass();
```

When this action is called, it will look through the classpath to see if there is a class named myClass in it. You can also keep external AS files in the same directory as the Flash file that is trying to use them, and if the class being referred to in Flash cannot be found in the defined paths of the classpath, it will then look in its own directory, which is also controlled by the classpath.

> **NOTE**
>
> External ActionScript files are compiled directly into the SWF file when the SWF file is created, so if an external AS file is updated, the Flash file using it must be recompiled before the changes will take effect.

19

You can set the classpath in your preferences by going to Edit, Preferences and choosing the ActionScript tab (see Figure 19.2). Then choose the ActionScript 2.0 Settings button and the ActionScript Settings dialog box pops up as shown in Figure 19.3. Here you can add classpaths, remove them, or edit them. You can also sort the order in which they are checked. Notice that it has two directories by default. The first is where Flash's built-in classes are kept—in the `Classes` directory of the user's configuration directory. And the second, ".", represents the current directory that the Flash file you are working with is in.

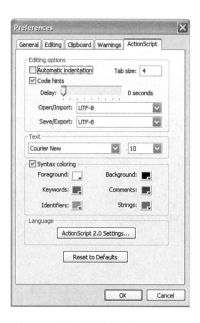

**FIGURE 19.2**    ActionScript preferences for all Flash documents.

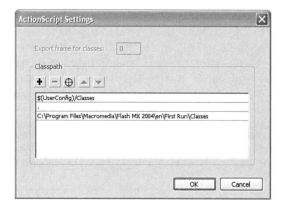

**FIGURE 19.3**    ActionScript Settings dialog box where you can control your classpaths.

At the top of the ActionScript settings box, there is a field labeled Export Frame for Classes, and it has the number 0 as its value, which means that before the first frame of ActionScript is reached, it will compile the external code that is necessary. But the field is grayed out and cannot be adjusted. This is because there is another spot where you can adjust your classpath settings, in the Publish Settings dialog box, in the Flash tab, as shown in Figure 19.4. If you have the ActionScript version set to ActionScript 2.0 (the default), you can click the Settings button, and an ActionScript settings dialog box appears as in Figure 19.5. The difference is that there are no default classpaths, and you can adjust the export frame. This ActionScript setting is for the current file only and will not be kept from file to file (unless you save it as part of your publishing profile). And even though you can adjust the export frame, it will not let you go lower than the number zero.

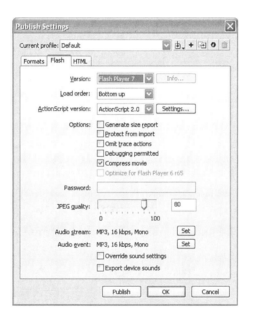

**FIGURE 19.4**    Publish settings for the Flash tab.

19

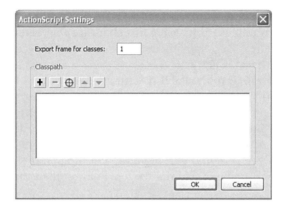

**FIGURE 19.5**    ActionScript settings for the publish settings.

Now that you have seen where to create external ActionScript, and how to use it, let's start creating these files.

# Getting Started with External Class Files

As mentioned earlier, custom class construction is nothing new, but the manner in which it is done is completely different. In previous versions of Flash, you could create classes of objects either externally or internally in the Flash file. But with the introduction to ActionScript 2.0, the only way to correctly build object classes is externally in .as files. And there is a different method of creating classes than before.

Here are two examples of building the same class, one in ActionScript 1.0 and the other in ActionScript 2.0.

Here's how you would do it in ActionScript 1.0:

```
function Bird (){
    //create an event
    this.onLand=function(){};
    //create a fly method
    this.fly=function(speed, distance){
        //fly
    }
    //create a method to check altitude
    this.checkAltitude=function(){
        if(this.altitude <= 0){
            //call the event for when the bird lands
            onLand();
        }
        return this.altitude
    }
}
```

And this is what you would do in ActionScript 2.0:

```
//get the ability to use listeners
import mx.events.EventDispatcher;

class Bird{
//declare the methods and properties
    public var altitude:Number;
    public var addEventListener:Function;
    public var removeEventListener:Function;
    private var dispatchEvent:Function;
//initialize the ability to have listeners
    function Bird(){
        EventDispatcher.initialize(this);
    }
    //create a fly method
    function fly(speed:Number, distance:Number){
        //fly
    }
    //create a method to check altitude
    function checkAltitude():Number{
        if(this.altitude <= 0){
            //trigger the listener
            dispatchEvent({type:"onLand"});
        }
        return this.altitude;
    }
}
```

You can definitely see the difference in complexity in the ActionScript 2.0 version compared to the ActionScript 1.0 version, but with that complexity comes much more power, flexibility, and scalability than ever before. Don't worry if you do not understand everything in the preceding code; as we move through the chapter, each part will be covered.

## Defining a Class

The concept of object-oriented programming was covered back in Chapter 8, "Welcome to ActionScript 2.0," so there is no need to repeat that information here. When creating a class, you are defining what the class has in it, what it can do, and what events are taking place.

Defining a class in ActionScript 2.0 is as simple as using the keyword `class`, the name of the class, and opening and closing curly brackets like this:

19

```
class MyClass{
    //class instructions
}
```

Of course this class does not do anything, nor does it have any properties, but we will get to that soon enough.

And when defining a class, you do not always have to start from scratch. If there is a class already made, you can extend that class with a subclass (child class), like this:

```
class Shape extends MovieClip{
    //extends the MovieClip class
}
```

Now the new class Shape extends the MovieClip class, and therefore has all of the MovieClip properties and methods plus whatever is created within the Shape class itself.

> **NOTE**
>
> Notice that all of the classes we have built thus far are capitalized. This is not necessary, but it is good coding practice to capitalize class names for easy readability. And remember, ActionScript 2.0 is case sensitive, so when you create instances of the new object, use the same case.

> **NOTE**
>
> Another thing of note when building external classes is that the filename must match the class name. For instance, if you have a class called Bird, it must reside in a file named Bird.as.

That covered how to build a class, but so far our classes do not have anything in them. Let's start placing methods and properties in them.

## Public, Private, and Static

Before we start creating properties and methods, it's important to know a few keywords that describe how these properties and methods interact in Flash.

When you declare properties and methods, you can use the keywords public or private to set boundaries for their use.

Public means that they can be used within the class itself, or in conjunction with an instance of the object in Flash.

Private means that the property or method can only be used internally in the object class itself.

Here are a few small examples of public and private:

```
class Bird{
    public var birdType:String;
    public var weight:Number;
    public var feathers:Number;

    public function fly (speed:Number, distance:Number){
        //fly
    }
    private function featherCount(){
        return this.feathers;
    }
    public function molt(){
        this.feathers = this.featherCount()-25;
    }
}
```

You can see that we create three public properties for the Bird class of object. We then create a public method to allow the bird to fly. After that, we create a private method that can only be used in this class file. Then we use the private method from within a public method to remove some of the bird's feathers.

The benefit of using public and private is that sometimes in object classes, you don't want certain properties or methods to be callable directly from ActionScript: Instead, they are called from within other methods, properties, or events. If you do not declare whether a method or property is either public or private, it will be public by default.

There is another keyword that can be used when creating properties or methods with object classes: the static keyword. Making a property static means that it can only be accessed by using the object's class name, not an instance of that object. Static methods and properties are not new to Flash; in fact, here are a few examples using them with the Math object:

- Math.PI—Approximately 3.1415926

- Math.E—Approximately 2.71828

- Math.tan(0)—Returns tangent of number 0

Notice that when we call either a property or method of the Math object, we use the class name, not an instance of the object.

Most static methods and properties are used with object classes that have just static methods or properties, and they rarely have events. Classes with static elements are used to perform certain tasks where instances of that object class would not be necessary, such as the Math class.

19

And when creating static properties or methods of objects, they can be either private or public like the following code, which would appear within a class:

```
private static var age:Number = 23;
public static function square(num:Number){
    return num*num;
}
```

Those are the keywords that will help define properties and methods in external ActionScript files.

## Declaring Properties with a Constructor Function

Sometimes when you create an instance of an object, you want to set some of the properties of that object right when it is being created. To do so, you need a constructor function inside the class definition.

A constructor function uses the class's name as the function name within itself, so when an instance of that object is created, everything within the constructor function will be done.

Here is an example of using a constructor function to build a House object:

```
class House{
    //declare some properties
    public var houseWidth:Number;
    public var houseHeight:Number;
    public var stories:Number;
    public var houseType:String;
//create the constructor function
    function House(width,height,stories,houseType){
        this.houseWidth = width;
        this.houseHeight = height;
        this.stories = stories;
        this.houseType = houseType;
    }
}
```

And you can then create an instance of the House object in Flash like this:

```
    var homeSweetHome = new House(50,50,2,"rancher");
```

Now you see not only how to create properties, but also how to create them when an instance of the object is created. Next is how to declare methods.

## Creating Methods

If properties are information about an object, methods are what objects do. A method is nothing more than a function directly associated with an object.

When creating a function, it is important to remember to declare whether it is private or public. Otherwise, it will automatically become public, which may not be what you want. It is good practice to always declare which type of method it is.

Also note that you cannot declare a blank function and then redefine it. Here is an example that will cause an error trying to accomplish this:

```
class Bird{
    public var fly:Function;

    function fly(){
        //fly
    }
}
```

If you attempt to use this code, an error will occur saying that the function cannot be created twice; just something to keep in mind.

Also, when you declare a function, you can set the type of data to be returned. Here is an example of that:

```
class Bird{
    private var altitude:Number;
    public function getAltitude():Number{
        return this.altitude;
    }
}
```

As you can see, in the preceding example, the method getAltitude() will return the current altitude of any instance of the Bird object, and it will always be a number.

But if you are creating a method that will not return a value, you can declare that as well, as you can see in this next example:

```
    class Bird{
    private var altitude:Number;
    private function increaseAltitude(amount:Number):Void{
        this.altitude += amount;
    }
}
```

19

Notice that we used the keyword Void instead of a data type to declare that this method will not return any data. If a method with the Void return type attempts to return data, an error message will appear.

There are also two types of methods that are unique and can be created within external AS files.

## Creating Getter/Setter Methods

Getter and setter methods are unique among other methods created in object classes because when they are accessed, they are not accessed in the same way most other methods are. When methods are called, they have a set of parentheses following the name of the method; this is how you can distinguish methods. Getter/setter methods are created in much the same way other methods are created, but they are accessed like properties.

The reason behind this is that it is bad practice for a user to directly access a property of an object, so developers often create methods to both get the information from a property and set information to that property. But setter/setter methods alleviate this problem by creating methods that can be accessed like properties.

Here is an example of creating a getter method using the keyword get:

```
class Bird{
    //declare a property
    public var birdWeight:Number;
    //create the constructor function
    function Bird(weight){
        this.birdWeight = weight;
    }
    //create the getter method
    public function get weight():Number{
        return birdWeight;
    }
}
```

And here is the code that will create a new instance of the Bird object and then get the weight. The code is in a Flash file that resides in the same directory as the Bird.as file:

```
//create a new Bird
myBird=new Bird(40);
//get the birds weight
trace(myBird.weight);
```

As you can see if you test this code, the weight of the bird is returned because we called the getter method, but it looks like a property, not a method.

Here is an example, extending the preceding example to now include a setter method:

```
class Bird{
    //declare a property
    public var birdWeight:Number;
    //create the constructor function
    function Bird(weight){
        this.birdWeight = weight;
    }
    //create the getter method
    public function get weight():Number{
        return birdWeight;
    }
    //create the setter method
    public function set weight(amount:Number):Void{
        this.birdWeight = amount;
    }
}
```

And here is the update to the Flash code that will create an instance of the `Bird` object, get its current weight, then reset it, and finally get the current weight again:

```
//create a new Bird
myBird=new Bird(40);
//get the birds weight
trace(myBird.weight);
//now reset the weight
myBird.weight = 25;
//now get the weight again
trace(myBird.weight);
```

Again, we access the getter and setter methods to control the properties of the `myBird` instance, but they appear to be properties we are calling, not methods.

> **NOTE**
>
> With getter methods, there are never any parameters, just the result being returned. And with setter methods, there is one parameter, and nothing is being returned.

Now we have covered both properties and methods, and the final step is events.

## Creating Events

Properties are pieces of information about an object. Methods are what objects do. Events are notifications about objects.

There are two ways to create events so that they can be used in Flash. You can create a callback event or a listener event. In this section, we will go over both.

## Creating Callback Events

Callback events are blank methods that can be reassigned to individual instances of objects, but are called from within the object class.

Here is an example of creating a callback event:

```
class Bird{
    //create the callback event method
    public var onLand:Function;
    //create a method that will land the bird
    public function landBird():Void{
        //call the event
        this.onLand();
    }
}
```

As you can see, we create a blank function in the beginning of our class. We then create a method that will trigger the event automatically (normally, an event would be triggered within a condition, but in this example, we want it to be triggered no matter what).

Here is the code that will reside in the Flash file that is in the same directory as the preceding .as file:

```
//create a new Bird
myBird=new Bird();
//set the callback event for this instance
myBird.onLand=function(){
    trace("the bird has landed");
}
//call the method that will trigger the event automatically
myBird.landBird();
```

In this example, we create an instance of the Bird object. We then set up the callback method for this particular instance for when the onLand event fires. Finally we call the method that will automatically trigger the event. If you test this movie, you will see that the message has been sent to the Output panel.

That was one way to create an event. The other way is a bit more complicated than callbacks, but is much more scalable and flexible to use when you get used to it.

## Creating Listener Events

Listeners are another way your objects can have events captured. The difference between listeners and callbacks is that for callbacks, you are creating an event method on the instance of the object. For listeners, you create an object whose sole purpose is to listen to a certain event, and then you add that object to the instance as a listener.

It's a little complicated at first, but after we go through the example, it will be easier to understand.

To create listeners in external object classes, you need to import the `EventDispatcher` class using the `import` keyword, like this:

```
import mx.events.EventDispatcher;
```

Importing classes is an important part of creating external AS files. It allows you to use methods from other classes within your own class without having to extend the class you import. You import classes directly from the `Classes` directory in the `First Run` directory of Flash MX 2004. You separate subdirectories with dot syntax.

> **TIP**
>
> You can import all external AS class files of a directory by using a wildcard on that directory like this:
>
> ```
> import mx.controls.*
> ```
>
> Now all class files in the directory `mx/controls` will be imported.

Now that you know how to import the class we need, let's see how to use it.

This is the code for creating an event that has listener support. We will use the `dispatchEvent()` method of the `EventDispatcher` object after we initialize it in our constructor function.

```
//import the object class we need
import mx.events.EventDispatcher;

class Bird {
//create two methods that will be used in Flash
public var addEventListener:Function;
        public var removeEventListener:Function;
    //declare the event we will use from the EventDispatcher object
private var dispatchEvent:Function;
    //declare the constructor function
function Bird() {
        //initialize the EventDispatcher to work with this object
                EventDispatcher.initialize(this);
        }
    //create the method that will automatically trigger the event
```

```
function landBird():Void {
dispatchEvent({type:"onLand"});
}
}
```

The preceding code first imports the object class we need to have listeners. It then declares the object class as `Bird`. After that, it declares two methods that will be used in the Flash file. Then it declares another method from the `EventDispatcher` object to be used in this object. Then the constructor function is created, initializing the `EventDispatcher` object to work with the `Bird` object. Finally, the method that will automatically trigger the event is created and it uses the `dispatchEvent()` method to send the event name to Flash.

That was the external AS file; here is the code for the Flash file:

```
//create a new Bird
myBird=new Bird();
//create an object to listen for the onLand event
var birdListen:Object = new Object();
//create the event for this object
birdListen.onLand = function(){
    trace("the bird has landed");
}
//add the object to the instance of the bird as a listener
myBird.addEventListener("onLand", birdListen);
//now call the method to automically trigger the event
myBird.landBird();
```

This code creates an instance of the `Bird` object. Then it creates a generic object that we will use as the listener. We then create the event with the generic object that will send a message to the Output panel when called. We then add the generic object to our instance of the `Bird` object class as an event listener. Finally we call the method that will automatically trigger the event.

Test the movie, and you will indeed see the message sent to the Output panel.

That ends the basic fundamentals of creating external AS files. Let's move on to an applied example.

## Bringing It All Together

In this section, we are going to build an applied example of using external AS files by building a creature that will follow the mouse around wherever it goes.

We will begin with the `Creature` object class.

1.  Create a new `.as` file called `Creature.as` and save it to the desktop.

2. Place this code within it:

```
//import the EventDispatcher object class
import mx.events.EventDispatcher;

class Creature extends MovieClip {
    //create a couple of properties
    private var xDist:Number;
    private var yDist:Number;
    private var creatureSpeed:Number;
    //create a couple of methods to use in Flash
    public var addEventListener:Function;
    public var removeEventListener:Function;
    //create the method to trigger the event
    private var dispatchEvent:Function;

    function Creature() {
        this.changeColor();
        //initialize the EventDispatcher
        EventDispatcher.initialize(this);
        //place it at a random spot
        this._x = Math.random()*550;
        this._y = Math.random()*400;
        //set the initial speed
        this.speed = 10;
        //where all the magic happens
        this.onEnterFrame=function(){
            xDist = _root._xmouse-this._x;
            yDist = _root._ymouse-this._y;
            this._x+=xDist/creatureSpeed;
            this._y+=yDist/creatureSpeed;
            if(this.hitTest(_root._xmouse,_root._ymouse)){
                dispatchEvent({type:"onGotcha"});
            }
        }
    }
    //create the getter setter methods
    public function get speed():Number{
        return this.creatureSpeed;
    }
    public function set speed(amount):Void{
        this.creatureSpeed = amount;
    }
```

19

```
//create the method to change its color
public function changeColor():Void{
    //give it a random color
    var myColor:Color = new Color(this);
    myColor.setRGB(Math.random()*0x10000000);
    delete myColor;
}
}
```

The preceding code may look like a lot, but it really is just all of the things we have covered in this chapter combined. It first imports the EventDispatcher class so that we can have listeners. Then we declare the class, which is an extension of the MovieClip class. After that, we create a few properties that we use within the class. Then we start to create some of the methods we will use in Flash. Then, of course, is the constructor function where we call a method to change the object's color to a random color. Then we initialize the EventDispatcher object so that it will work with our Creature object. We then set the object at a random spot in the stage and using the onEnterFrame event, we move the creature around following the mouse. After that, we declare a couple of getter/setter methods to control the speed, and finally create the method to randomly change the color of the creature.

3. Next comes the Flash part. Create a new Flash document and save it also on the desktop as creatureExample.fla.

4. Draw a circle about 75×75 on the stage.

5. Select the entire circle including the stroke and choose Modify, Convert to Symbol.

6. Give it the same options as in Figure 19.6, which are as follows:

   - Name—creatureMC

   - Behavior—Movie Clip

   - Identifier—creatureMC

   - AS 2.0 Class—Creature

   - Linkage—Export for ActionScript

   Notice that we are setting the class of this movie clip right in its symbol properties. This means that this symbol will now have all of the characteristics of the Creature object.

7. Give the circle an instance name of myCreature.

8. Create a new layer called action.

9. In the action layer, place this code:

```
//create the object to listen for the event
var creatureListen:Object = new Object();
//create the event
creatureListen.onGotcha=function(){
    //we will change the color rapidly
    myCreature.changeColor();
}
//add the listener
myCreature.addEventListener("onGotcha", creatureListen);
```

What the preceding code does is create a new object we will use as a listener for our instance of the Creature object. We then set the event to the listener that, when triggered, will change the color of the creature. Finally, we add the listener to our Creature object.

**FIGURE 19.6**    Set ActionScript 2.0 classes directly to movie clips in the Symbol Properties dialog box so they automatically have all of the specified class's methods and properties.

Now, when you test the movie, the circle will follow your mouse around the stage changing color constantly as long as it is touching the mouse.

## Summary

This chapter introduced you to the idea of keeping ActionScript outside of Flash for faster, more scalable, and more reuseable code. We went over how the new version of Flash looks for these files as well as the old way of incorporating external ActionScript. We covered all

19

the fundamentals of creating your own external classes including the differences between `public` and `private` as well as `static`. This chapter also covered the three basic elements each object has:

- Properties
- Methods
- Events

And we finished off with a large example that brought the fundamentals together.

It's important to experiment with external ActionScript and see where you and your team can benefit from using it to achieve greater scalability and reuseability.

CHAPTER **20**

# Introduction to Data Integration

We have discussed dynamic content in Chapter 15, "Loading Movies," and Chapter 19, "External ActionScript," but this chapter is different. All we have brought into Flash externally has been ActionScript classes we have built, which can only be brought in during compiling of the .swf file. And we have also brought in other .swf files as well as .jpg files, which can be brought in during runtime. But that does not do the concept of dynamic content justice.

In this chapter, we talk about the basics of bringing data into Flash and sending data out from Flash, as well as the format the data needs to be in to be successfully interpreted.

Before we go through some of the fundamental ways Flash handles data transfer, it is important to fully understand the benefits of dynamic content.

## Why Dynamic Content?

A quick definition of dynamic content could be: to always have current information, or to update regularly. For a better explanation of the importance of dynamic content, here are some of my own experiences with static and dynamic content.

When I first started building applications in Flash, way back in Flash 4, I used to create the interface, all the buttons, text fields, and movie clips right on the stage. And all the content would also either be on the stage with the other elements, or held in ActionScript waiting to be called. As clients began to request changes (and they always do), I would have to then go into the Flash document (because none of them would have Flash to be able to open the source file), find where the content was, and change it, hoping that I would not have to make another change, which of course I would.

After doing this several times, I decided to start keeping major content in outside .txt files or in databases (which is discussed in later chapters). That way, whenever I needed to change content, all I would have to do is change a text file or a database entry. The client could make changes to text files because they would only need a text editor, and then the application or Web site would reflect those changes. This way, if I had to make changes, I could do them quickly, and would not have to reupload the entire application. Even better, the client had much more control over their own site (which may or may not be a good thing).

So, as you can see, dynamic content is invaluable in building quality, content-driven sites or applications.

To get started with dynamic content, we will cover the getURL() method, the simplest way to send data out of the Flash environment.

## The getURL() Method

Sending data out of Flash is one of the most exciting ways to show interaction. When any user can fill in a form, click a submit button, and see a Web page open with their results, the possibilities are endless. The getURL() method was the earliest means of accomplishing this goal.

Its general usage looks something like this:

```
getURL(URL,window,variables);
```

Let's go over what each part is for:

- URL—This is the path to the Web page you would like to go to.
- window—This is an optional parameter specifying the window or frame from which to load the content, and it has four specific keywords:
  - _self—The current frame in the current window the Flash file is residing in
  - _blank—Creates a new window
  - _parent—The parent frame of the current frame that the Flash file is residing in
  - _top—The top-level frame in the window that the Flash file is residing in
- variables—Optional parameter for sending variables to the URL with either the GET or POST method

The getURL() method is most often used for links to other pages, but you can use it to send data to other Web pages as well. Here is an example of using the getURL() method to accomplish this goal. Place this code in the actions of the first frame on the main time-line:

```
getURL("http://slashdot.org/search.pl?query=apple","_blank");
```

This example, when run, will open up a browser window, and the results from searching slashdot.org will display. You can replace the last part, "apple", with something else, and when you rerun the file, it will open up a browser window with the new results.

In the preceding example, we can change what we are looking for in the code itself and then see the results each time the code is run. This is not interactive at all, in fact, the user cannot control what is being searched for. Therefore, the next example will take the preceding one a step further.

In this example, we are going to create an input text field for the user to type in search terms. We will also put a submit button in the file so that the user can perform several different searches.

1. Start a new Flash document.

2. Create a second layer, and name the top layer **actions** and the bottom layer **content**.

3. In the content layer, create an input text field with the border turned on, and give it an instance name of **search_txt**.

4. In the same layer, create a button (or use one from the common libraries, by choosing Window, Other Panels, Common Libraries, Buttons). Give it an instance name of **search_btn**, and align it to the right of the text field (as in Figure 20.1).

5. Now, in the first frame of the actions layer, open up the Actions panel and place these actions within it:

```
//the event for the button
search_btn.onRelease=function(){
     //call the search URL with the search term
     getURL("http://slashdot.org/search.pl?query="+search_txt.text,
➡      "_blank");
}
```

What the actions are doing is calling the getURL() method and in the URL part, we put the path to the search section of slashdot.org, and then combined it with the search term that the user will place in the text field.

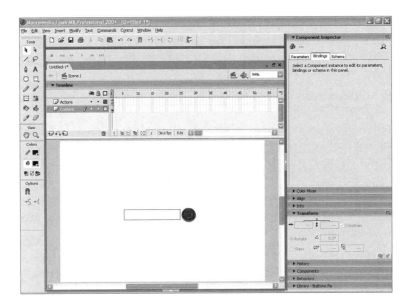

**FIGURE 20.1**   Place the search button beside the search field.

Test the example, and you will see that when you put a search term in the text field, and click the search button, a browser window will open with the results of the search, as shown in Figure 20.2.

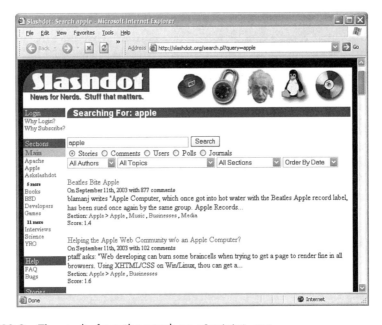

**FIGURE 20.2**   The results from the search on `slashdot.org`.

That was a good example of how to move data out of Flash with user interaction. The downside is that when we use the getURL() method, we are actually going outside of Flash with the results. In the following sections, we are going to go over how to get data into Flash using several built-in methods as well as the LoadVars object class.

Before we start loading data in, however, we need to go over what form the data needs to be in.

# The MIME Format

The standard MIME format is the format that data being loaded into Flash by means of loadVariables(), loadVariablesNum() or the LoadVars class must be in. It is in application/x-www-form-urlencoded format and is basically a bunch of name/value pairs.

Here is a basic example of a name/value pair in MIME format:

```
name=David
```

Unlike ActionScript, here we do not put the value of the variable name in quotes. Also, there is no space after the equal sign; this is because if there were a space the value would include the space, making "David" become " David".

The preceding example had only one name/value pair. To separate multiple name/value pairs, the ampersand (&) is used like this:

```
name=David&age=23
```

And you can of course put ampersands on either side of the name/value pair just to make sure there are no errors, like this:

```
&name=David&age=23&
```

This way, you can clearly tell where each name/value pair begins and ends.

You can also create URL-encoded strings in Flash for special characters such as the ampersand using the escape() function.

### The escape() and unescape() Functions

Because an ampersand is used to separate individual name/value pairs in URL-encoded content, they cannot be within the content itself or Flash will read it as a separator, which can cause errors. Using the escape() function, you can encode the ampersand in a URL-encoded format as in the following code:

```
//create the string
var myString:String = escape("title = War & Peace");
//send the encoded string to the output panel
trace(myString);
//output: title%20%3D%20War%20%26%20Peace
```

As you can see, the string being created is URL-encoded and stored in a variable. Then the string is sent to the Output panel where you can see that the ampersand, as well as the spaces in the string, have been replaced with special characters. To get the string back to normal, use the unescape() function, which will convert URL-encoded strings back to their original format like this:

```
//create the string
var myString:String = escape("title = War & Peace");
//send the encoded string to the output panel
trace(myString);
trace(unescape(myString));
//output: title%20%3D%20War%20%26%20Peace
//            title = War & Peace
```

Now that you have seen the basic format that the data we are going to load needs to be in, let's make a file to hold the information that we will be using in several examples throughout this chapter.

1.  Open a text editor such as Notepad or SciTe and put this code in it (you can replace my information with yours if you like):

    ```
    &name=David&
    &age=23&
    &location=Richmond&
    ```

    Notice that they are on separate lines. This is not necessary; it simply makes it easier to read. And each line begins and ends with an ampersand to make sure that none of the name/value pairs accidentally join another.

2.  Save this file as **sample.txt**.

Now that we have a file we can work with, let's start going over some of the methods used to bring in data from external sources starting with the loadVariables() method.

## The loadVariables Method

The loadVariables() method was introduced back in Flash 4, and it has the ability to load data from external files (like the sample.txt file we are going to be using) as well as from middleware such as PHP and Cold Fusion, which are discussed in later chapters. It loads the data directly into a movie clip object that must be specified when called. Its general layout looks like this:

```
loadVariables(URL,target,method);
```

And here is what each part means:

- URL—This is the string path to either the file holding the data, or to the middleware that will send back the data. It can either be an absolute path or a relative path to the file. (The URL must reside on the same domain as the Flash file when on the Web.)

- target—This is the name of the movie clip object that will receive the data.

- method—This is an optional parameter for use with middleware that tells how the data will be sent and received from the Web server with either GET or POST.

Now that you see what it looks like, let's start using it.

In the next example, we are going to call the text file we have previously created from within Flash using the loadVariables() method. We will store the data in the _root timeline by using the keyword this.

1. Create a new Flash document.

2. Save this document as **sample-20-1.fla** in the same directory as the text file we have already created.

3. Open the Actions panel in the first frame of the main timeline and place these actions within it:

```
//get the data from the text file
loadVariables("sample.txt",this);
```

We call the text file we have already created that resides in the same directory as the Flash movie, and we place the variables on the main timeline using this. We are not interfacing with middleware, so the method parameter is left out.

Now test the movie. You'll see that it appears that nothing has happened, but on the contrary—while still in the test movie screen, select Debug, List Variables, and you will now see the variables that have been brought in displayed in the Output window, as shown in Figure 20.3.

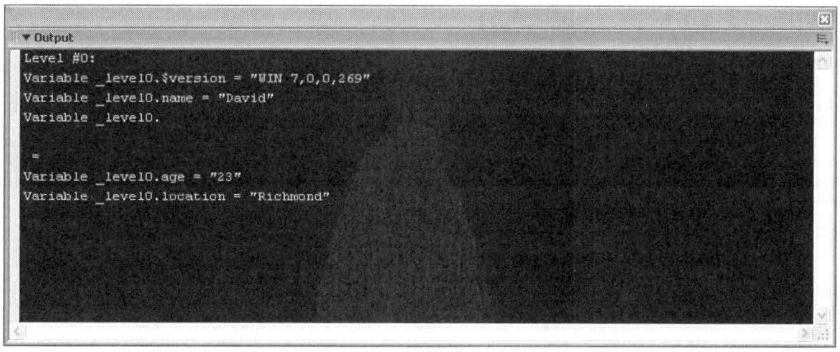

**FIGURE 20.3**  The Output window lists the variables that are available in the movie.

20

Now that you can see that the variables are being brought in and parsed correctly, we are going to use them. But before we can use them, we have to know when they have loaded in completely. Even though they appear to have loaded in instantly, they did not, and on the Web, it is even more important to know when the variables have completed loading because over some dial-up connections, it may take a while.

Fortunately, there is already an event built into Flash to let us know when data has been fully received in a movie clip: the onData event.

## The onData Event

The onData event is an event that is triggered whenever the associated movie clip receives data using the loadVariables() or the loadVariablesNum() method. And when used in conjunction with the _root timeline, it will receive this event automatically.

We can set a function to this event the same way we have been setting functions to events:

```
movieClip.onData = function(){
    //do something
}
```

The MovieClip can be any movie clip created either manually or with ActionScript including the _root timeline.

Now that you see what the event is supposed to do, let's put it into practice with this next example.

1. Start a new Flash document.

2. Save this document as **sample-20-2.fla** in the same directory where the sample.txt file is saved.

3. Name the layer **actions**, and in the first frame of that layer, place these actions:

```
//create the movie clip to hold the data
this.createEmptyMovieClip("holder_mc",0);
//get the data from the text file
loadVariables("sample.txt",holder_mc);
//when the movie receives the data
holder_mc.onData = function(){
    trace("my name is - "+this.name);
    trace("my age is - "+this.age);
    trace("my location is - "+this.location);
}
```

Notice that this time, we create a movie clip object in our code to be the data holder for the data coming in.

Now test the movie, and when the data is received, the Output panel should appear similar to Figure 20.4, with all of the information from the text file.

**FIGURE 20.4**    The onData event is triggered when the movie clip receives data.

That was awesome! We loaded some basic information into Flash, and then had an event let us know when the data had been fully loaded.

But what if we want to have multiple pieces of data in a single name/value pair? You cannot use arrays in the text file; they are not supported to be loaded in that way. There is a workaround for this bottleneck.

Even though you cannot store data in arrays in a text file to be loaded in, you can separate data in a single name/value pair with unused characters such as "~" or "$", and then separate them and store them in an array after they have been received by Flash.

In this example, we will need another text file named `sample2.txt` stored in the same directory as the other text file with this data in it:

```
&names=David~Ben~Doug~Paul~Lesley~Todd~Missy&
```

Notice that we used the "~" character to separate each name in the single name/value pair.

Now that we have the text file we need, we can do another example. This example will have several stop points so that we can see the progression all the way until we fill a ComboBox component with the names.

1.  Start a new Flash document.

2.  Save this document as **sample-20-3.fla** in the same directory as the text file you just created.

3.  Create another layer and name the top layer **actions** and the bottom layer **content**.

4.  In the first frame of the actions layer, open the Actions panel, and place these actions in it:

    ```
    //create the movie clip to hold the data
    this.createEmptyMovieClip("holder_mc",0);
    ```

20

```
//get the data from the text file
loadVariables("sample2.txt",holder_mc);
//when the movie receives the data
holder_mc.onData = function(){
     trace(this.names);
}
```

This code should look familiar; we created the movie clip to handle the data coming in. Then we called the text file with the data within it, and placed the data in the holder_mc movie clip. If you test the movie, when data is received, the variable that is brought in, names, is traced, showing all the names in the text file separated by "~" characters.

1. Now that we know the data is coming in, we can go to the next step, which will separate the names variable, and store the information in an array. Then we will trace the array. To do this, we will use the split() method. Replace the function for the onData event with this one:

```
//when the movie receives the data
holder_mc.onData = function(){
     //create an array to hold the data
     var myNames:Array = new Array();
     //put the data in the array
     myNames = this.names.split("~");
     trace(myNames);
}
```

Now if you test the movie, instead of the names being separated by "~" characters, they are separated by commas showing that they have indeed been placed into the array.

2. The next step is to select the content layer, and drag a ComboBox component onto the stage. Give it an instance name of myCombo_cb.

3. Finally, replace the trace statement in the onData event with this line of code:

```
myCombo_cb.dataProvider = myNames;
```

The preceding line of code takes the array that was filled with the data we brought in and sets it as the dataProvider for the ComboBox component.

Now test the movie, and the end result should look like Figure 20.5, with all the names inside the ComboBox. Now you can really begin to see the benefits of dynamic data. All you have to do is add, change, or remove names from the text file sample2.txt, and the movie when run will display the new information without any more work needing to be done in Flash.

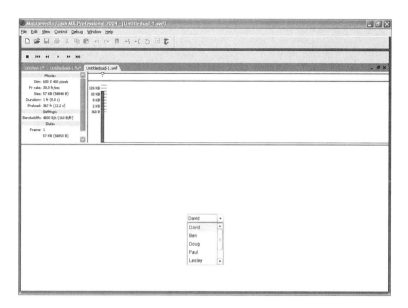

**FIGURE 20.5**    You can use dynamic content in conjunction with interface pieces quickly and easily.

There is another way to load content into a movie clip from an external source: the `loadVariablesNum()` method.

# The `loadVariablesNum()` Method

The `loadVariablesNum()` method is similar to the `loadVariables()` method in that it loads external variables into Flash, but unlike the `loadVariables()` method, the `loadVariablesNum()` method loads the variables into a level instead of directly into a movie clip.

The basic layout of this method looks like this:

```
loadVariablesNum(URL, level, method);
```

And here are the parameters that `loadVariablesNum` will accept:

- `URL`—The path to either the text file being loaded, or the middleware page being called.

- `level`—The level in the Flash player to receive the variables when they are loaded.

- `method`—This is an optional parameter used to define the method used when transferring data to and from middleware.

It also supports the `onData` event as a means of announcing when data has been fully loaded.

Here is an example using the `loadVariablesNum()` method:

1. Create a new Flash document.

2. Save this document as **sample-20-4.fla** in the same directory as the text files we have been working with.

3. In the first frame on the main timeline, open the Actions panel and place these actions in it:

```
//get the data from the text file
loadVariablesNum("sample.txt",0);
//when the movie receives the data
this.onData = function(){
    if(init){
        trace("my name is - "+this.name);
        trace("my age is - "+this.age);
        trace("my location is - "+this.location);
    }else{
        init=true;
    }
}
```

Notice that this time, we use a conditional statement to make sure that the event is not accidentally being triggered by the main timeline's initialization. Also notice that we are calling the original text file we created, not the one we used to put in an array.

Now test the movie, and you will see in the Output window the variables from that text file, as shown in Figure 20.6.

**FIGURE 20.6**    Using the `loadVariablesNum` method is as simple as the `loadVariables` method.

But the two methods we have covered in regards to loading external data are not the end. There is even a built-in object specifically designed for interfacing with external data.

# The LoadVars **Object**

The LoadVars object, introduced back in Flash MX, is an object whose sole purpose is to send and load data in and out of Flash. And, because it is its own object with its own events, properties, and methods, you do not have to create a movie clip object to hold the data (which would take up more memory).

Creating a LoadVars object is the same as creating any other object. Create a variable, give it a name, and set it, using the constructor, to the LoadVars() object like this:

```
var myLoader:LoadVars = new LoadVars();
```

There you have it—you have just created your first LoadVars object. Now let's see how to use them.

The LoadVars object has three basic methods for sending and loading data:

- load—This method will load content from either a text file, or middleware.
- sendAndLoad—This method will send data out of Flash to middleware, and return the results created by the middleware back to Flash.
- send—This method posts variables to a specified URL and does not return anything.

The last two methods are beyond the scope of this chapter as they deal strictly with middleware, which are scripts that run on Web servers designed to create dynamic content when requested. You will be exposed to them in later chapters.

The method that will be covered in this chapter in regard to the LoadVars object is the load() method.

## The load() **Method**

The load() method for the LoadVars object is used to load content into Flash. The format for the content is the same as we have been using, the MIME format.

Here is the load() method's basic usage:

```
loadVars.load(URL);
```

There is only one parameter for this method:

- URL—A path to the text file or middleware to load variables from

Now that you see what it looks like, let's use it.

1. Create a new Flash document.

2. Save this document as **sample-20-5.fla** in the same directory we have been working in.

20

**3.** Open up the Actions panel in the first frame of the main timeline, and place these
actions within it:

```
//create the LoadVars object
var myLoader:LoadVars = new LoadVars();
//load the content
myLoader.load("sample.txt");
```

Now test the movie, and notice that, as before, nothing appears to have happened, but if
you select Debug, List Variables, you will see that the variables have been loaded from the
original text file you created (see Figure 20.7).

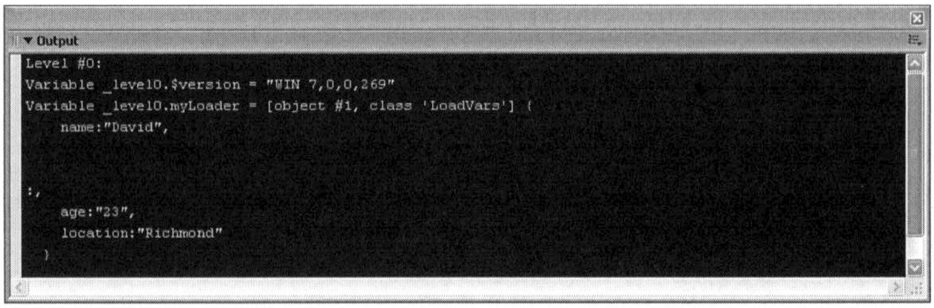

**FIGURE 20.7**    The variables have loaded into the LoadVars object via the load() method.

Because LoadVars is its own object, it has its own event for when the variables have
completely loaded, the onLoad event.

## The onLoad **Event**

The onLoad event is the only supported event for the LoadVars object. It is triggered when
data has been loaded into the LoadVars object the event is associated with, and the data
has been parsed. It is only called when either the load() or the sendAndLoad() methods
have finished running.

Its generic layout is

```
LoadVars.onLoad = function(success){
}
```

Notice, that unlike the onData event we used earlier, the onLoad event has a parameter that
can be passed through the function. This parameter, success, is a Boolean variable, and if
the data loaded correctly, it will be true. If there was an error, success will be false.

The success parameter can be useful, especially when dealing with middleware, which is a
bit more complex than the examples we have done in this chapter. You can see its use in
the next example, which builds on the preceding one.

1. After the code that has already been placed in the Actions panel, place this:

```
//the event for when the variables have loaded
myLoader.onLoad = function(success:Boolean){
    if(success){
        trace("my name is - "+this.name);
        trace("my age is - "+this.age);
        trace("my location is - "+this.location);
    }else{
        //there has been an error
        trace("an error has occurred");
    }
}
```

Notice that we used the success parameter to detect whether everything loaded and was parsed correctly.

To see an example of what would happen if success had been false, change the line of code that says

```
myLoader.load("sample.txt");
```

to

```
myLoader.load("doesntExist.txt");
```

Now when you test the example, instead of all of the variables being displayed in the Output panel, the error message is displayed along with an error message from Flash, as you can see in Figure 20.8.

**FIGURE 20.8**  Because Flash could not find the file we were looking for, the error message we created is displayed.

The onLoad event is the only supported event for the LoadVars object. However, it is not the only event in general for the LoadVars object.

20

## The Undocumented onData Event

There is an undocumented event for the LoadVars object that is actually triggered long before the onLoad event is ever triggered: the onData event. This event is called when data is first received by the LoadVars object. It then parses the data into individual properties of the LoadVars object and triggers the onLoad event. You can, however, use this event for your own use, and it can come in quite handy when debugging, especially when working with middleware.

Here is the basic layout of the onData event:

```
loadVars.onData = function(src){
    //do something
}
```

Notice in this event, we use a parameter called src. This parameter, when used inside the callback function, is all the variables being returned in their raw format, before they are parsed. That means that you will be able to see everything coming back from the text file (or middleware) including all the variable names, the values, equal signs, and ampersands.

Let's do an example using this event.

1. Start a new Flash document.

2. Save this document as **sample-20-6.fla**.

3. In the first frame of the main timeline, open the Actions panel, and place these actions in it:

```
//create the LoadVars object
var myLoader:LoadVars = new LoadVars();
//load the content
myLoader.load("sample.txt");
//the event for when the LoadVars object first receives data
myLoader.onData = function(src:String){
    trace(src);
}
```

Now test the movie. This time, instead of getting the usual trace message that we have seen before, we get the entire string of information coming from the text file, as you can see in Figure 20.9.

But what if we want to use the onLoad event in conjunction with the onData event?

Take a look at this next example to see what happens:

1. Start a new Flash document.

2. Save this document as **sample-20-7.fla**.

**FIGURE 20.9**    Using the onData event, you can see the entire string coming back to the LoadVars object.

3. In the first frame of the main timeline, open the Actions panel, and place these actions in it:

```
    //create the LoadVars object
var myLoader:LoadVars = new LoadVars();
//load the content
myLoader.load("sample.txt");
//the event for when the LoadVars object first receives data
myLoader.onData = function(src:String){
    trace("onData");
}
//the event for when the variables have loaded
myLoader.onLoad = function(success:Boolean){
    trace("onLoad");
}
```

Now test the movie and notice that only the onData is sent to the Output panel when the onData event is triggered, but the onLoad was not sent to the Output panel because the onLoad event was never triggered. This is because the onData event by default will trigger the onLoad event; however, because we have overwritten the onData event, the onLoad event is never triggered. Like everything else, you can work around this, too.

To trigger the onLoad event from the onData event, two things have to occur. First, the string of information coming to the LoadVars object must be decoded using another undocumented feature of the LoadVars object, the decode() method. The decode() method will take the raw name/value pairs passed to it and change them into properties and values for the LoadVars object receiving the data. It looks like this:

```
loadVars.decode(src);
```

The second thing that needs to be done is the actual triggering of the onLoad event by passing a true Boolean value to it like this:

```
loadVars.onLoad(true); and
```

20

Now that you've seen the two actions that need to be called within the `onData` event before the `onLoad` event can be called, let's take a look at that example again.

1. Start a new Flash document.

2. Save this document as `sample-20-8.fla`.

3. In the first frame of the main timeline, open the Actions panel, and place these actions in it:

```
    //create the LoadVars object
var myLoader:LoadVars = new LoadVars();
//load the content
myLoader.load("sample.txt");
//the event for when the LoadVars object first receives data
myLoader.onData = function(src:String){
    trace("onData");
    //the two actions that need to be called
    this.decode(src);
    this.onLoad(true);
}
//the event for when the variables have loaded
myLoader.onLoad = function(success:Boolean){
    trace("onLoad");
}
```

Now test the movie again, and notice that both `trace` actions are executed and both messages are sent to the Output panel.

Now that you know how the undocumented `onData` event works, you should have no problems debugging your applications when you run into data integration issues.

## Summary

This chapter was dedicated to showing not only the ways in which you can begin to interact with data, but also the reasons why a developer or designer might want to interact with data, and the benefits.

We started out with the `getURL()` method, the quickest and easiest way to have user interaction with Flash and data. Then we moved on to some of the fundamental ways to bring in data, and what form that data needs to be in. And we finished up with the object that is designed to handle data integration and all of its documented and undocumented events.

The next chapter will cover the basics of another form of data integration using Flash and XML. The chapters following that are devoted to more advanced means of data integration with middleware, databases, and Web services.

CHAPTER **21**

# XML and Flash

The preceding chapter introduced you to data integration. It used name/value pairs to keep data in text files that would be brought into Flash with most likely the LoadVars object.

This chapter introduces another way to keep data separate from Flash in an external file: XML.

XML is a buzzword on the Internet, a W3C standard, and more importantly, another language that Flash can work with and understand natively. But what is XML really?

## What Is XML?

XML stands for Extensible Markup Language. I know what you're thinking; extensible starts with an "e," not an "x." Well, the reason behind using the "x" instead of "e" is that XML sounds more important and techie than EML.

Now that we have established that the name does not really use the correct letters, we can begin to go over what exactly **extensible** means.

The extensible part of XML is the fact that XML is much more of a format than a language. By that I mean it is a metalanguage. XML is meant to be written in such a way that there are no boundaries for what it can be—it just has simple rules. This is because XML is actually a simple form of SGML that allows you to create your own set of tags for different situations, as you will see while you move through the chapter.

Many languages used today are based on XML, such as Extensible HyperText Markup Language (XHTML), Scalable Vector Graphics (SVG), RDF Site Summary (RSS), and Wireless Markup Language (WML).

XML, in its most raw form, does not have conditionals and loop statements like some other languages; it is merely a very strict data holder.

So now you know what its definition is, but how does it work?

# Formatting XML

Before we go over the basic rules and formatting of XML, you should know that you will want to use a text editor such as Notepad for building the XML files. Also, XML files can be opened in a browser such as Internet Explorer 5 (or better) and will show errors in the form, so it is good to test your XML in browsers first to make sure it is well formed.

Here is a basic snippet of XML:

```
<root>
    <sample>
        the stuff
    </sample>
</root>
```

The first thing you will notice in this XML is that XML uses tags. If you are familiar with HTML, you know what tags are. If you are not familiar with HTML, **tags** describe the data held between them. If the data in between the tags is supposed to be a title, you would use the tags `<title>` and `</title>` on either end of the data. And in XML lingo, these tags with their data are called **elements** and that is how we will be referring to them. So you see, elements are data holders and the data they hold.

In the preceding snippet of code, you see that the first element, `<root>` has a subelement, `<sample>`, which then contains some data. And that's XML really, just a bunch of tags and data. Of course, it can get more complicated, and we will be going over how to extend the elements and data later in the chapter.

Notice that the structure of the XML is very tree-like with its hierarchy. As we continue to move forward in building out the XML documents, you will begin to see the structure more easily.

That small example showed you the basic layout. Now we will create a larger XML document, and then discuss some of the rules for XML.

Here is the code that you should type into a text editor such as Notepad or SciTe. Save this code as `team1.xml`.

```
<team>
  <player>
      <name>Paul</name>
      <number>15</number>
      <position>Point Guard</position>
  </player>
  <player>
      <name>Matt</name>
      <number>21</number>
      <position>Small Forward</position>
  </player>
```

```
    <player>
        <name>Doug</name>
        <number>33</number>
        <position>Center</position>
    </player>
    <player>
        <name>Todd</name>
        <number>51</number>
        <position>Power Forward</position>
    </player>
    <player>
        <name>Eddie</name>
        <number>11</number>
        <position>Shooting Guard</position>
    </player>
</team>
```

And to make sure everything is fine with your XML file, open it in Internet Explorer, and you should see a layout similar to Figure 21.1.

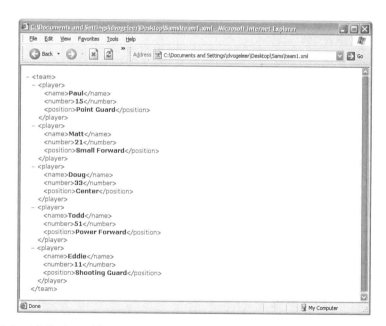

**FIGURE 21.1**  XML viewed in Internet Explorer will help weed out possible bugs or typos in making sure your document is well formed.

You can use the handles on the left side of the elements to collapse or expand their substructure.

Now that you have a better idea of the structure of XML, it's time to go over some basic rules.

## Rules of XML

There are several rules to creating well-structured XML. And it is very important that your XML be as perfect as possible when bringing it into Flash. The first rule concerns the first line in the document.

### XML Declaration

Although we have not yet done so in our XML, it is good practice to put a line of code in the beginning that declares what the document is, and what version the document is in.

The declaration line looks like this:

```
<?xml version="1.0"?>
```

Notice that the line may look like an XML element, but in fact, it is not; it is a processing instruction because of the <?  ?> surrounding it. It is used to tell the browser or parser that the content is XML, and should be viewed that way.

From here on out, all of our XML documents will have this line in it.

### Open-and-Shut Case

Another rule that you may have noticed we are already implementing is that all elements that open must also close. Notice in our last example each new element started with a <team> tag and ended with a </team> tag.

Here is an example of an element:

```
<name>David</name>
```

There are elements that open and close in one single tag, and they are called empty elements, meaning they do not have any data, or subelements.

Here is an example of an empty element:

```
<empty/>
```

The difference is that instead of the closing slash being at the front, it is at the end of the element name.

### No Overlapping

HTML is pretty soft when it comes to elements being within other elements, and the order in which they close. XML, however, is not. If you open a child element within a parent element, the child element must be closed before the parent element is closed.

21

Here are two examples of what I mean:

```
<parent><child>this is legal</child></parent>
<parent><child>this is not legal</parent></child>
```

The latter of the two code lines will produce an error because it is not permitted.

Those are a couple of rules about how the elements work; there are also naming convention rules associated with elements.

### Element-Naming Conventions

The elements themselves do have some rules and guidelines to follow when creating them.

- Element names, much like variables in Flash, are case sensitive, meaning that element, ELEMENT, and Element are completely different elements.

- Element names must begin with a letter or an underscore.

- Element names cannot begin with a number or a special character (@,#).

- Element names cannot begin with "xml" in upper- or lowercase.

- Element names cannot have spaces in them (you will see why when we discuss attributes).

### Commenting XML

Not all information in an XML document has to be elements or data within elements: XML does support the use of comments. Comments in XML have the same syntax as comments in HTML.

Here is an example of a comment found in an XML document

```
<!--here lies a comment-->
```

They are not allowed to be within tags, however, so the following code is illegal:

```
<team <!--this won't work--> >data</team>
```

The preceding code will cause errors.

There is another part of XML we have yet to cover: attributes.

## Attributes

Those familiar with HTML know what attributes are. They are snippets of data stored within tags (or in this case, within elements). They are used to distinguish between elements of the same name. After the element name, use a space, then the attribute name followed by equal signs "=" and the attribute value in quotes.

Here is an example of using attributes:

```
<root>
    <element number="1">stuff</element>
    <element number="2">more stuff</element>
</root>
```

Notice that you still close the element with the element name only.

You can also put multiple attributes in a single element separated by spaces like this:

```
<element number="1" name="David" type="author">stuff</element>
```

And empty elements can also have attributes.

```
<element style="none" color="blue"/>
```

### No Duplicating Attributes

There is one strict rule for attributes; they cannot be duplicated in the same element.

Here is an example of an illegal use of attributes:

```
<element number="1" number="2">stuff</element>
```

The preceding code cannot be used in well-formed XML documents.

Now that you understand attributes, we can revisit the XML document we created earlier.

Here is the first of two new versions of the team XML document. Save this one as team2.xml.

```
<?xml version="1.0"?>
<team>
    <player name="Paul">
        <number>15</number>
        <position>Point Guard</position>
    </player>
    <player name="Matt">
        <number>21</number>
        <position>Small Forward</position>
    </player>
    <player name="Doug">
        <number>33</number>
        <position>Center</position>
    </player>
    <player name="Todd">
        <number>51</number>
        <position>Power Forward</position>
    </player>
```

```
    <player name="Eddie">
        <number>11</number>
        <position>Shooting Guard</position>
    </player>
</team>
```

The preceding code removes the child element <name> and creates a name attribute in the player element. You can immediately see the benefits of using attributes: Now when you look through the player elements, you can see which one is which immediately without having to look to its child node. Also notice that we now include the XML declaration line in the beginning. You can see the output of this XML document in the browser in Figure 21.2.

Here is another version of the team XML document. Save it as team3.xml.

```
<?xml version="1.0"?>
<team>
    <player name="Paul" number="15" position="Point Guard"/>
    <player name="Matt" number="21" position="Small Forward"/>
    <player name="Doug" number="33" position="Center"/>
    <player name="Todd" number="51" position="Power Forward"/>
    <player name="Eddie" number="11" position="Shooting Guard"/>
</team>
```

In this version, we removed all the child elements and replaced them with attributes in the player elements. Also notice that all of the player elements are empty elements. You can see the output of this document in the browser in Figure 21.3.

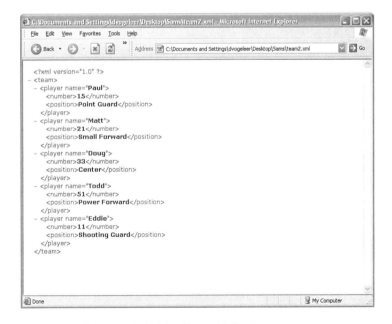

**FIGURE 21.2**   Use attributes to help identify multiple elements.

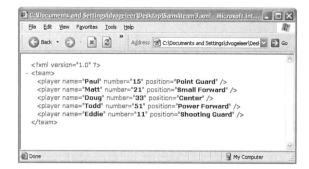

**FIGURE 21.3**    You can have all attributes and no child elements, and the document is still well-formed.

Now you have seen elements and attributes, but you might be confused as to which to use when.

## Elements Versus Attributes

Because attributes can handle data and so can elements, the question often arises: Which one should be used for which situation? Back in Flash 5, the built-in XML parser would cycle through attributes faster than data held in elements. But with the Flash 7 Player, they parse at virtually the same speed, so now it is a matter of preference.

Personally, I tend to use attributes only to keep track of which element is which. I keep most data as element data. And, in the Web services chapter, you will see that Web services format their XML in a similar fashion.

## XML and Flash

Now that you have seen the structure of the XML document, and how to create elements and attributes, it's time to go over what Flash can do with it.

Before we start loading XML into Flash, it is important to understand the XML class of object in Flash as well as some of its methods, properties, and events.

### The XML Object

Introduced back in Flash 5, the XML object is Flash's means of loading, parsing, and handling XML data. You create XML objects the same way you create any other object.

Here is the generic code for creating XML objects:

```
var myXML:XML = new XML();
```

Now that you have a new XML object, you will need to know the methods, events, and properties that make it work. And the first thing you will want to know is how to get XML into Flash with the load() method.

21

### The load() Method

Similar to the LoadVars load() method, the XML load() method goes to an assigned URL and brings the entire XML document back into Flash using HTTP. When the method is called, it sets the property loaded in the XML object to false until the document is completely loaded. Any XML data held within the XML object prior to the load() method being called will be disregarded completely.

The generic layout of the code for the load() method is as follows:

```
myXML.load(URL);
```

The URL parameter is a string literal path that is either relative or absolute to the XML document you want to load either locally, or from a remote server.

When the data has completely loaded, the onLoad event method will be called.

### The onLoad Event

The onLoad event method is called when the entire XML document has been loaded. It is best used as a callback for the XML object.

Here is the generic layout of the onLoad event:

```
    myXML.onLoad = function(success){
        //do something
    }
```

This event has a single parameter that it passes into the function, the success parameter. The success parameter is a Boolean value that represents whether the XML document loaded without errors (true) or with errors (false).

When the onLoad event fires, several properties of the XML object data is being loaded into change.

### The loaded Property

Although it is obvious that when the onLoad event triggers, the loaded property will change, it is still important to know that this property can be monitored. The value of this property will always be a Boolean value. When the load() method is called, the property is set to false; when the content has loaded, it is changed to true.

```
myXML.loaded;
```

### The hasChildNodes() Method

When called, the hasChildNodes() method will return a Boolean value stating whether or not the loaded XML content has child nodes.

A **node** is another name for element.

```
myXML.hasChildNodes();
```

This method is good for determining whether you have loaded a blank XML document.

### The status Property

The status property is very important when debugging XML-driven applications in Flash. This property returns a numerical value indicating whether the XML document loaded successfully. If it does not load successfully, it will return a number representing the error that occurred.

This is the generic layout of the property:

```
myXML.status;
```

And here is the list of the possible values it will return:

- 0—No error has occurred; the information was parsed successfully.
- -2—Termination error with CDATA.
- -3—Termination error with the XML declaration.
- -4—Termination error with the DOCTYPE declaration.
- -5—Termination error with a comment in the XML document.
- -6—An ill-formed XML element was detected.
- -7—Not enough memory is available.
- -8—Termination error with an attribute in the XML document.
- -9—There is an opening element without a matching closing element.
- -10—There is a closing element without a matching opening element.

Now you have seen a few of the properties, methods, and events associated with the XML class (we will go over more as we continue through the chapter). Here is an example that will load an XML document that has been previously created into Flash, and then send messages about its loading success (or failure, but we hope not) to the Output panel.

1. Create a new Flash document.

2. Save the document in the same directory as the team1.xml file you created earlier, as **sample1.fla**.

3. In the first frame of the main timeline, open the Actions panel, and place this code in it:

   ```
   //create the XML object
   var myXML:XML = new XML();
   ```

```
//create the event for when it loads content
myXML.onLoad=function(success){
    if(success){
        trace("loaded - "+this.loaded);
        trace("has child nodes - "+this.hasChildNodes());
        trace("status - "+this.status);
    }else{
        trace("there was a major error");
    }
}
//now load the content
myXML.load("team1.xml");
```

The preceding code does a great deal. First, it creates the XML object that will be doing all the work and holding all the data. Then it creates a callback event for when the data is loaded in. In that callback function, it checks to make sure the load went successfully, and if so, it sends the properties of `loaded` and `status` as well as the result from the `hasChildNodes()` method to the Output panel. If there was a major error, it will send an error message to the Output panel. After the callback is finished, it calls the `load()` method to bring in the content.

Test the movie, and as long as you have the XML file and the Flash file in the same directory, you should have an Output panel similar to Figure 21.4.

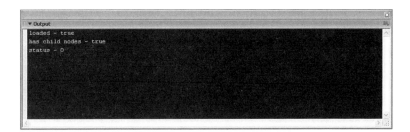

**FIGURE 21.4**   Use the `onLoad` event to alert your code when the XML has loaded.

When you have successfully brought XML data into Flash, you will want to do something with the data. And the first thing you will want to get out of the XML document you are loading is the `firstChild`.

### The `firstChild` **Property**

The `firstChild` property in the XML object represents the root node (element) in the XML document. This property not only contains the root node, but also all other nodes and their data as well. Basically, the `firstChild` property is the entire XML document.

Let's look back at our preceding example, and this time, we will send the `firstChildNode` to the Output panel.

1. Create a new Flash document.

2. Save the document in the same directory as the `team1.xml` file you created earlier, as **`sample2.fla`**.

3. In the first frame of the main timeline, open the Actions panel, and place this code in it:

```
//create the XML object
var myXML:XML = new XML();
//create the event for when it loads content
myXML.onLoad=function(success){
     if(success){
          trace(this.firstChild);
     }else{
          trace("there was a major error");
     }
}
//now load the content
myXML.load("team1.xml");
```

This code is nearly identical to the preceding, except that this time, we send the XML object's `firstChild` property to the Output panel.

When this code is run, you will see all the XML data displayed in the Output panel.

The next step is to go through the other nodes and get the data you need out of them. This is referred to as "walking the tree."

Walking the tree means that we will go through each node and pull out the data or child nodes of that node, and then continue until we have walked the entire XML document. To do this, we use the `childNodes` property.

### The `childNodes` **Property**

We use the `childNodes` property in the XML object to walk the tree of our XML data. It returns an array of the current node's children nodes. That's a little confusing; what this means is that the property will return an array of every node (element) held within a specific node. Each element in the array is in fact an XML element and can be manipulated as such.

Before we start using this property, it is important to look at the XML we are working with again.

```
<team>
<player>
     <name>Paul</name>
     <number>15</number>
```

21

```
            <position>Point Guard</position>
        </player>
        <player>
            <name>Matt</name>
            <number>21</number>
            <position>Small Forward</position>
        </player>
        <player>
            <name>Doug</name>
            <number>33</number>
            <position>Center</position>
        </player>
        <player>
            <name>Todd</name>
            <number>51</number>
            <position>Power Forward</position>
        </player>
        <player>
            <name>Eddie</name>
            <number>11</number>
            <position>Shooting Guard</position>
        </player>
</team>
```

This is the XML file we created and used in previous examples. And as mentioned, using the childNodes property, it converts this information into arrays of information, so let's take a look at what that might look like if we kept our data in arrays instead of XML.

Here is the exact same information (minus the data itself) in array format:

```
team[0]
team[0].player[0]
team[0].player[0].name[0]
team[0].player[0].number[0]
team[0].player[0].position[0]
team[0].player[1]
team[0].player[1].name[0]
team[0].player[1].number[0]
team[0].player[1].position[0]
team[0].player[2]
team[0].player[2].name[0]
team[0].player[2].number[0]
team[0].player[2].position[0]
team[0].player[3]
```

```
team[0].player[3].name[0]
team[0].player[3].number[0]
team[0].player[3].position[0]
team[0].player[4]
team[0].player[4].name[0]
team[0].player[4].number[0]
team[0].player[4].position[0]
```

I'm just glad we can use XML instead of having to create the array structure like that. Although this setup is difficult to read, you can easily see the tree-like structure our XML documents have.

So now that you've seen the structure, there is one more thing to cover before we start walking the tree: white space.

### White Space

Even though we can tell just by looking at the XML structure where one node ends and the other begins, the computer has more difficulty. It uses white space, the empty space between each node, as its own node value. If we were to attempt to walk the tree without taking white space into consideration, we would receive many hard-to-find bugs.

Thankfully, Flash's XML object does have a solution, the `ignoreWhite` property. By default, this property is set to `false`, meaning the parser takes the white space into consideration. We will want to ignore that white space by setting this property to `true` like this:

```
myXML.ignoreWhite = true;
```

Put this with the code that creates the XML object, and you do not have to worry about white space any longer.

> **NOTE**
>
> If you are compiling to the Flash 5 Player, be careful; the `ignoreWhite` property sometimes does not work properly. Just make sure to test carefully when using it in that version of the player. It works fine in the Flash 6 Player and up, however.

That's everything we need to know to begin walking the tree. Let's begin using the `childNodes` property in the following example.

1. Create a new Flash document.

2. Save this document as **sample3.fla** in the same directory as the XML files we created.

3. Open the Actions panel in the first frame of the main timeline and place these actions in it:

```
//create the XML object
var myXML:XML = new XML();
//ignore the white space
myXML.ignoreWhite = true;
//create the event for when it loads content
myXML.onLoad=function(success){
     if(success){
          //trace the first player's stuff
          trace(this.firstChild.childNodes[0]);
          //trace the first player's name element
          trace(this.firstChild.childNodes[0].childNodes[0]);
     }else{
          trace("there was a major error");
     }
}
//now load the content
myXML.load("team1.xml");
```

This code works the same as previous examples, but this time when the XML has finished loading, if there are no errors, the first player node is sent to the Output panel along with the first player's name node.

Now when you test the movie, the entire first player's node was traced along with the entire first player's name node. We will extend this example by pulling the data itself out with the nodeValue property of the node. The nodeValue property is a text node containing the actual data of the element.

Each individual node has its own set of properties:

- nodeName—This is the element name, for example, the nodeName of <team> is "team", but if the node is a text type node, the value is null.

- nodeType—This is a numerical value representing the type of node:

  - 1—An XML node containing an XML element

  - 3—A text node containing data

- nodeValue—This property returns the data held between nodes, for example, the nodeValue of <name>Paul</name> is "Paul".

So now we will go back into the code in the main timeline and replace what is there with this:

```
//create the XML object
var myXML:XML = new XML();
//ignore the white space
```

```
myXML.ignoreWhite = true;
//create the event for when it loads content
myXML.onLoad=function(success){
     if(success){
     //trace the first player's, first elements value, name and type
trace(this.firstChild.childNodes[0].childNodes[0].childNodes[0].nodeValue);
          trace(this.firstChild.childNodes[0].childNodes[0].nodeName);
          trace(this.firstChild.childNodes[0].childNodes[0].nodeType);
     }else{
          trace("there was a major error");
     }
}
//now load the content
myXML.load("team1.xml");
```

The preceding code should look familiar by now except that we have changed what is being sent to the Output panel. This time we are sending the name of the node we are looking at, its value, and the type.

Run this code, and you should see in the Output panel the name "Paul", the node name "name", and the node type "1" meaning that it is an XML node.

Now we will go a step further and incorporate a loop statement to walk the entire tree and return all of its values.

Still in the same example, replace the code in the main timeline with the following:

```
//create the XML object
var myXML:XML = new XML();
//ignore the white space
myXML.ignoreWhite = true;
//create the event for when it loads content
myXML.onLoad=function(success){
   if(success){
   //this will search through the players
     for(var i:Number = 0; i<this.firstChild.childNodes.length; i++){
     //this will search through the players' nodes
        for(var j:Number = 0;
➥    j<this.firstChild.childNodes[i].childNodes.length; j++){
           var nodeName:String =
➥    this.firstChild.childNodes[i].childNodes[j].nodeName;
           var nodeValue:String = this.firstChild.childNodes[i].
➥    childNodes[j].childNodes[0].nodeValue;
           trace(nodeName+"="+nodeValue);
        }
```

```
        }
    }else{
        trace("there was a major error");
    }
}
//now load the content
myXML.load("team1.xml");
```

This code takes a giant step forward from what we have done so far. Now instead of hard-coding the function to walk through each node, we use two looping statements to go through each node and return not only the node's value, but also the node's name. This has tremendous implications because now we can extend our XML document not only by adding players, but also by adding information about each of those players. For instance, if you were to return to the XML document we are using in this example, give each player a new child node that represents the height of the player, and place a value for the nodes, you could still go back to Flash and run the identical code to get all the information.

Run this code and you will see all the players and their information in the Output panel.

So far, all we have done is use information in the nodes. Now let's go over how to get attributes out of the nodes.

### The attributes Property

The attributes property of the XML object is used to get all known attributes of a single node, and return them in the form of an array with named elements.

For example, the following node has three different attributes:

```
<player name="Paul" number="15" position="Point Guard"/>
```

The attributes property of this node would return an array with three elements: name, number, and position.

Before we continue with the example, we should look at the XML we will be working with. You have already created it and called it team3.xml:

```
<?xml version="1.0"?>
<team>
    <player name="Paul" number="15" position="Point Guard"/>
    <player name="Matt" number="21" position="Small Forward"/>
    <player name="Doug" number="33" position="Center"/>
    <player name="Todd" number="51" position="Power Forward"/>
    <player name="Eddie" number="11" position="Shooting Guard"/>
</team>
```

Notice that this XML has no data in the nodes, only attributes. We will be working with this file in a similar fashion as the previous one.

In this example, we will grab the information from a single attribute:

1. Create a new Flash document.

2. Save this document as **sample4.fla** in the same directory as the XML files we created.

3. Open the Actions panel in the first frame of the main timeline and place these actions in it:

```
//create the XML object
var myXML:XML = new XML();
//ignore the white space
myXML.ignoreWhite = true;
//create the event for when it loads content
myXML.onLoad=function(success){
    if(success){
        //trace each attribute individually
        trace("name="+this.firstChild.childNodes[0].attributes.name);
        trace("number="+this.firstChild.childNodes[0].attributes.number);
        trace("position="+
            this.firstChild.childNodes[0].attributes.position);
    }else{
        trace("there was a major error");
    }
}
//now load the content
myXML.load("team3.xml");
```

This code creates the XML object as before. And as before, it creates the callback for the onLoad event, but this time, we send the attributes in the nodes to the Output panel.

Run this code and you will see the same information we have covered before, but this time it was derived from attributes, not node values.

You can also get all the attributes with a specific node using the following example.

Go back into the main timeline and replace the code with this:

```
//create the XML object
var myXML:XML = new XML();
//ignore the white space
myXML.ignoreWhite = true;
//create the event for when it loads content
myXML.onLoad=function(success){
    if(success){
        //create the loop statement to look through the players' attributes
```

```
            for(attribute in this.firstChild.childNodes[0].attributes){
                trace(attribute);
            }
        }else{
            trace("there was a major error");
        }
}
//now load the content
myXML.load("team3.xml");
```

What this code does is to use a `for` loop to look through the array of attributes, and it sends each attribute name to the Output panel.

Run this code and you will see all three attributes in the Output panel.

Now that we have seen how to create the XML, load the XML and walk the tree, the next example will use some visual elements on the stage and bring it all together.

In this example, we will be using the `team2.xml` file we created before:

1.  Create a new Flash document.

2.  Save the document as **teamStats.fla** in the same directory where the `team2.xml` file resides.

3.  Drag a `List` component onto the stage and place it in the top left corner. Give it an instance name of **myList_lb**, and leave the parameters with their default settings.

4.  Drag an instance of the `TextArea` component and place it to the right of the `List` component, give it an instance name of **number_ta**, and change its properties to the following:

    *   editable—false

    *   html—false

    *   text—Number

    *   wordWrap—false

5.  Copy the `TextArea` component, paste a copy under the `number_ta` TextArea component, give it an instance name of **position_ta**, and leave the parameters the same.

6.  Your screen should look similar to Figure 21.5.

7.  Create another layer and call it **actions**.

8.  In the actions layer, open the Actions panel and place this code in it:

    ```
    //create the XML object
    var myXML:XML = new XML();
    ```

```
        //ignore the white space
        myXML.ignoreWhite = true;
        //create the event for when it loads content
        myXML.onLoad=function(success){
            //create the main array
            var myArray:Array = new Array();
            if(success){
                //this will search through the players
                for(var i:Number = 0; i<this.firstChild.childNodes.length; i++){
                    //create the temporary array to be placed in the main array
                    var tempArray:Array = new Array();
                    tempArray.label =
                        this.firstChild.childNodes[i].attributes.name;
                    tempArray.number =
                this.firstChild.childNodes[i].childNodes[0].childNodes[0].nodeValue;
                        tempArray.position =
        this.firstChild.childNodes[i].childNodes[1].childNodes[0].nodeValue;
                        myArray[i] = tempArray;
                    }
            }else{
                    trace("there was a major error");
            }
            //now set the data provider for the List component
            myList_lb.dataProvider = myArray;
        }
        //now load the content
        myXML.load("team2.xml");
        //now create the object to listen to the List
        var listListen:Object = new Object();
        //now the event for when a user selects an item
        listListen.change=function(){
            number_ta.text = myList_lb.selectedItem.number;
            position_ta.text = myList_lb.selectedItem.position;
        }
        //add the event listener to the List component
        myList_lb.addEventListener("change",listListen);
```

The preceding code creates the XML object to handle the XML data. It creates the callback
for when the XML is completely loaded, and within this callback, it creates an array,
which we use later in the code. It loops through the XML placing information into a
temporary array that is then added to the end of the main array. At the end of the loop,
we set the dataProvider property of the myList_lb List component. After that, it loads the
XML into the XML object.

Then it creates a generic object to listen for the event that is triggered when a user selects a player from the List component. When a user makes a selection, the TextArea components receive the information, and the number and position of the selected player is shown. After that, it sets the event listener to our List component, myList_lb.

Run this code, and you will see that every time you click a player's name, his information is shown in the TextArea components, as shown in Figure 21.6. You can go out and change the XML file to have more players, and this application will still work. That's the benefit of using XML data and Flash; you can build rich, engaging interfaces that will always run with the newest information.

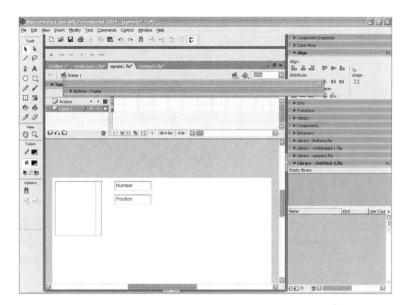

**FIGURE 21.5**  Components are used to speed production of the project.

So far we have covered how to work with XML manually. Now with Flash MX 2004 Professional, you can use the XMLConnector component to help speed up production.

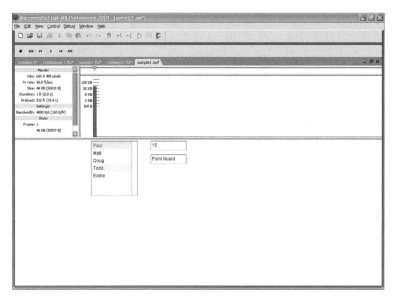

**FIGURE 21.6**    Every time a player's name is selected, his information is displayed in the application.

## The XMLConnector **Component**

The Professional edition of the new Flash MX 2004 comes with a set of data components. These components are meant to help Flash developers and designers to quickly and efficiently hook their applications into external data sources. The one we are focusing on in this chapter is the XMLConnector component.

This component will assist you in connecting to outside XML documents. It has five parameters:

- URL—The path either relative or absolute to the XML document.

- direction—This parameter is for either sending or receiving XML information or both.

- ignoreWhite—This parameter is similar to the ignoreWhite property of the XML object; it will set whether or not Flash should take into account the white space of the XML document when parsing.

- multipleSimultaneousAllowed—This parameter sets whether the connector can make several calls to the XML document at once.

- suppressInvalidCalls—If true, this parameter will halt the trigger() method being called if databound parameters are invalid.

Those are the parameters of the XMLConnector component. The next step is to know how it works.

## The trigger() Method

The trigger() method is called on an instance of the XMLConnector object to go out and either send data to an XML document, or receive data from an XML document. It has no parameters.

Its generic layout is as follows:

```
myConnector.trigger();
```

Now what do we do with the data when it comes back?

## The result Event

The result event is the event we use when data is received by the XMLConnector. This event uses a special component event listener.

Here is the generic layout of how to use the result event:

```
listener.result=function(result){
    trace(result.target.results);
}
```

This event has one parameter, the result parameter. The result parameter is the XML being received, and to use it, use result.target.results, which will be the actual XML that has been returned.

Enough talking about what it does. Let's do an example:

1. Create a new Flash document.

2. Save this document as **xmlConnector.fla** in the same directory as the team1.xml file.

3. Drag an instance of the XMLConnector component onto the stage, give it an instance name of **xmlCon**, and use these settings for the parameters:

   - URL—team1.xml
   - direction—receive
   - ignoreWhite—true
   - multipleSimultaneousAllowed—false
   - suppressInvalidCalls—false

4. Now create a new layer and call it **actions**.

5. In the actions layer, open the Actions panel, and place these actions in it:

```
//create the listener object
var xmlListen:Object=new Object();
//create the event
xmlListen.result=function(result){
    var endXML:XML = result.target.results;
    //this will search through the players
      for(var i:Number = 0; i<endXML.firstChild.childNodes.length; i++){
      //this will search through the players' nodes
        for(var j:Number = 0;
➥          j<endXML.firstChild.childNodes[i].childNodes.length; j++){
            var nodeName:String =
➥            endXML.firstChild.childNodes[i].childNodes[j].nodeName;
            var nodeValue:String =
➥endXML.firstChild.childNodes[i].childNodes[j].childNodes[0].nodeValue;
            trace(nodeName+"="+nodeValue);
        }
      }
}
//add the event listener
xmlCon.addEventListener("result", xmlListen);
//trigger the XML Connector to get the XML
xmlCon.trigger();
```

Some of the preceding code should look familiar. We created a listener for the `result` event, and then created the event. In the event, we create an XML object that will hold the XML data coming back to the connector. We walk the tree the same way we would any other XML object, and send the results to the Output panel. Then we add the event listener to the XMLConnector component, and finally trigger the component to go out and get the XML.

Run this movie, and you should see a screen similar to Figure 21.7. Notice that the information is sent to the Output panel just as it was before, and the component we dragged out onto the stage is now invisible.

**FIGURE 21.7**  Using the XMLConnector can have the same results as the XML object with a faster implementation for the developer.

## Summary

This chapter has taken the idea of dynamic content to a new level. XML is much more than a simple buzzword on the Internet; it is well-formed and structured data that nearly all applications on the Web can run on, including any you build in Flash.

We not only covered how to use it in Flash, but also how to create well-formed XML, a good asset to have. We even covered the new XMLConnector component, the easiest way to connect to your XML documents.

The next few chapters delve deeper into the idea of dynamic content by using middleware, servers, and databases.

CHAPTER **22**

# Integrating Flash with PHP

$P$HP is a server-side scripting language. Some of its syntax was derived from C, Perl, and Java. You will notice many similarities between ActionScript syntax and PHP as well, which makes it easy to use the two languages together. PHP allows embedded Web content to be served to Web site visitors dynamically and quickly, and to both Windows and Unix servers.

PHP was originally conceived by Rasmus Lerdorf in 1994 for use on his personal home page. The name PHP originally derived from the initial letters of the phrase "personal home page." The current version of PHP, weighing in as another recursive acronym, stands for "PHP: Hypertext Preprocessor." PHP has been adopted by the Open Source development community, which has brought PHP to its current, mature form, now in version 5.

The PHP language was written specifically for the Web. This means it has built-in tools for Web developers as well as providing connectivity to powerful databases, including the following:

- dBASE
- DBM
- FilePro
- Hyperwave
- Informix
- InterBase
- Microsoft SQL Server
- mSQL

- MySQL

- ODBC

- Oracle

- Oracle9

- PostgreSQL

- Sybase

PHP is known for its speed and efficiency, causing little overhead on a server's resources. This allows it to run on even the most simple of hardware setups while handling millions of hits per day.

PHP is the scripting tool of choice for many Linux servers on the Web. A common setup uses Apache as the Web-serving software, PHP for scripting, and MySQL for database functions.

Besides Linux, PHP runs on other Unix flavors, such as Mac OS X and IRIX. It is also available on Windows servers running Microsoft Internet Information Services (IIS) or Apache. PHP's design is native to Unix, so some functionality is not fully supported in a Windows environment.

PHP's incredible popularity can be attributed to its efficiency, reliability, ease of learning, connectivity to many databases, and its attractive pricing (pronounced *free*).

It serves over 7.5 million domains as of this writing, and over 1 million IP addresses. (To view the latest PHP statistics, along with other Web facts for geeks, see `www.netcraft.com`.)

PHP scripts are interpreted by the server, not the client, making them compatible with all browsers. This also has the benefit of adding a level of security to your code because the final output is the only thing sent to the browser.

Often, the output of PHP is dynamically created HTML pages; however, it also can support XML, Java, SWF, PDF, and dynamically created JPEG and PNG images.

## Why PHP and Flash?

Flash is a great interactive interface to the end user. Flash allows developers to work in a multimedia format that's presented consistently each time it is viewed, regardless of the visitor's computer or operating system.

Macromedia's ActionScript has become a powerful language that allows complicated functions to be done directly within the Flash Player.

When the time comes to automate your site's updates, to add functionality not available in ActionScript, or to interact with external data on the server, it's time to use PHP.

PHP is analogous to a shoe salesman in a mall store. For example, a visitor puts his foot out, and PHP runs to the back room to open the MySQL database warehouse. PHP then retrieves the size and color of shoe the visitor requested and brings it back to the visitor and crams his foot in. PHP then rings up the sale, verifies the visitor's identification, offers the visitor a chance to sign up for notification of future sales, and hands the visitor a bag filled with colorful shoe paraphernalia.

PHP speaks to the server's securely guarded resources and retrieves information for the end user. These attributes, when coupled with the relational database, MySQL, result in putting you two steps away from world domination (or at least some pretty good dynamic Web sites). Here are some things you can do using PHP and Flash:

- Externalize Flash content such as menu choices, images, and text

- Create PHP scripts to update content on numerous Flash pages

- Read and store information in databases

- Load variables from dynamic sources outside of Flash

- Pass variables from Flash to PHP

- Run server-side scripts using information supplied by visitors

- Create e-commerce sites

- Create shopping carts

- Secure Web transactions

- Allow users to upload or download server files

- Launch email scripts

- Generate dynamic images, PDFs, and SWF files

- Create calendars, time, and date outputs

- Run text-filtering scripts to process large amounts of data, outputting specific parts

- Set cookies

- Allow content to be updated from a browser, without the need to republish the SWF movie

# PHP Scripting for Dynamic Content

Let's start with the opposite of dynamic, which is **static**. Static sites (or Web brochures) are the same each time they are visited. Updates to static pages are done manually.

**Dynamic**, on the other hand, refers to actions that take place at the moment they are needed, rather than in advance. For Web sites, this means that Web pages sent to the visitor's browser are created at the server, when they are needed.

Web sites that use dynamic content might ask the server to retrieve updated information or to run scripts to access other data before delivering the page to the visitor.

This process may take slightly longer than serving a static page, but the payoff for a few milliseconds delay is the ability to offer new, fresh content without constant Webmaster involvement. Therefore, a good PHP scripter is worth ten or twenty thousand static Webmasters (and should be compensated accordingly).

A search function is a good example of a dynamic Web page. The visitor inputs search terms into a form and submits the information to the server. A server-side script processes the input, retrieves information from a database, and serves the results to the visitor.

Figure 22.1 depicts a typical visit to a dynamic Web page using PHP. The developer writes scripts and develops pages ahead of time that take advantage of dynamic content. When these are in place, the server will deliver pages to visitors without the need for time-consuming manual page editing, as in static sites.

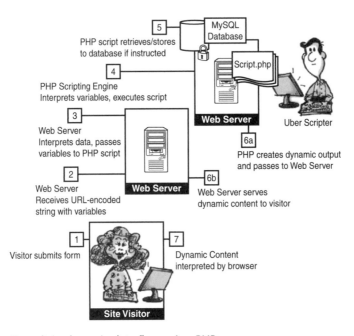

**FIGURE 22.1**    Roundtrip dynamic data flow using PHP.

A dynamic data flow operates as follows:

1. A visitor fills in the entries on a Web form within an HTML or Flash site and submits the form.

2. The information is sent through the Internet by a URL-encoded query string. When the developer uses the GET or POST option in a form, Flash takes care of the details to pass the data correctly. All the scripter has to do is set up the form correctly in Flash.

**3.** When the Web server receives the form data, it interprets the instructions and executes the proper PHP script. The server recognizes the characters, separating the variables and passing them to the PHP script.

**4.** The PHP script is executed.

**5.** At the core of PHP is the Zend engine (`www.zend.com`), which processes the PHP script, substituting variable name pairs with the client-supplied data where they are called in the script.

**6.** The dynamic output of the script is passed back through the Internet and forwarded to the visitor.

**7.** The visitor's browser recognizes the returning data, just like any other Web page, and displays it. This is the magic of dynamic Web pages! On a remote paradise island, a scripter reads the site's visitor stats over his laptop and lets out the trademark PHP roar of victory.

Now that you've followed along the road a Web form takes, you should have a good understanding of what is taking place and what is handling the code throughout the process.

## Your First PHP Script: Testing the Server

As one of the most popular scripting language on the Web, PHP is probably supported by your hosting server. If you are not sure whether your server is running PHP, this test will determine whether you have the power of PHP at your disposal.

If you have access to your own server, you can download the latest files to install PHP at `www.php.net`. And to install PHP on Windows, go to `http://us2.php.net/ install.windows`.

This first test script uses the PHP function `phpinfo`, which has the benefit of letting you look at the PHP server settings and see what modules and options are loaded.

The only requirement is that you have access to a Web server and the ability to upload files, because you will need to upload your PHP scripts in order to run them. PHP scripts are simple text files and don't need to be made executable by the operating system in order for them to work. The server's setup knows what to do when it receives PHP scripts.

> **NOTE**
>
> Be sure your PHP script's filename has the extension needed by your server's configuration. Some servers may be set up to recognize PHP files with the `.php` file extension (the default), whereas some servers may require an extension of `.php3`, `.php4`, `.php5`, or `.phtml`. If your script does not work initially, try renaming the script with one of the other possible extensions. If your server requires a `.php3` extension, that may mean it is only running PHP version 3, in which case it is in desperate need of an upgrade.

## Writing the Script

A PHP script is nothing more than a simple text file. It doesn't need to be compiled or made executable in order to work. Simply saving the script to your PHP-enabled server allows the script to be used immediately. Here are the steps to follow:

1. Using your favorite text editor, create a file with the following lines:

```
<?php
phpinfo();
?>
```

2. Save the file to your Web server and name it `phpinfo.php` (be sure to use the extension specified by your server's administrator). Here's an example:

```
http://www.YourDomain.com/php/phpinfo.php
```

3. Execute the script by launching a browser and pointing it to the file you created. If everything is working correctly on the server, you should see a page like the one shown in Figure 22.2 depending on which version you're running.

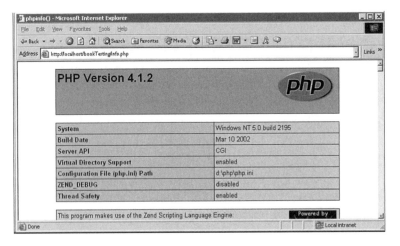

**FIGURE 22.2**    The PHP info screen.

## Troubleshooting the PHP Installation

If you don't get output similar to Figure 22.2, here are some areas to check:

• Check for typing errors. Make sure the semicolon at the end of `phpinfo();` is present.

• Check the path where you loaded the file and try again.

- Your file extension needs to have the extension required by your server's configuration. Try renaming your file using one of the several possible extensions (`.php`, `.php3`, `.php4`, or `.phtml`). Also, if you are using a Windows system, check to make sure that Windows didn't sneak a `.txt` extension onto the end of your file.

- The directory or file permissions are not correct. You need to have "read" access to the files from a browser.

  In Unix, `chmod 644 filename` will give your file read/write access for the owner and read-only access for groups and others.

> **CAUTION**
>
> Be careful when changing permissions on files on your server connected to the Web or on your intranet. Be sure you understand the security implications of granting even read access to files. The ability of maliciously intended evildoers to exploit your code is a serious threat to you and your company's data and systems.

- Your server is not running PHP. In this case, you need to pull whatever strings are required to get it loaded or find a hosting company that supports PHP scripting.

If you get the PHP information screen, congratulations! You are knocking at the door of complete and total control of the world you live in (or at least some pretty snazzy, dynamic Web sites).

Take a few moments to look through the output of the PHP info screen. You should see many directives and settings specific to your server. Most of these will not make much sense at first, but you can easily see what your server is configured to do.

You will also see the command used when the software was compiled, bringing out excitement in any true, card-carrying geek.

Some of the settings will be very important if you want to make a specific database work or to perform image manipulation of certain file types. Some of the values may be baked into the software at compile time; others may be changeable within the server's `php.ini` configuration file, and still others may be set within your scripts. These are advanced topics you can find more information on in resources dedicated to PHP development as mentioned in the section "Further Reading," at the end of this chapter.

## Exploring Optional Modules

PHP allows additional functionality to be specified during compiling. One of these functions is the ability to create dynamic images, such as JPEG, PNG, or WBMP images (not GIFs), from scripts through the GD Graphics Library, in addition to reading, modifying, and re-creating images.

---

> **NOTE**
>
> More information on the GD Library can be found at www.boutell.com/gd.

---

In the past, there have been other modules that increase the functionality of PHP. Development for some modules may come and go because they usually bridge a gap between what is available within PHP and what is desired. Therefore, it is always good to look at what the latest version of PHP is doing, as well as Flash, so you can plan sites that take advantage of your main tools first.

# PHP Fundamentals

After getting the PHP info screen on your server, shown earlier in Figure 22.2, you are ready to start creating dynamic sites.

If you're new to scripting, this is a great way to introduce yourself to a powerful language.

## Personalization

The rest of the examples in this chapter will use personalization and directory structures that have been built for simplicity and tested to run without error.

After going through these examples, you will most probably want to develop your own structures for your sites that work best for you.

Your PHP server may be different, depending on how it is configured. The examples in this chapter make use of the default PHP server settings.

## Case Sensitivity

PHP, like ActionScript, is case sensitive. This is important when you're passing data between Flash, PHP, and the server. MySQL is also case sensitive. Some people like to use all lowercase letters for variables, and other people prefer to use all capital letters. The examples in this chapter use capitalization for the first letter of each word. This lets us string many words together while making them easy to decipher. For example, we'll use variable names such as `MyVariable`.

## Directory Structures

In this chapter's examples, we use the following directory structure:

- Site root—www.YourSiteRoot/
- Flash movies—www.YourSiteRoot/flash/
- PHP scripts—www.YourSiteRoot/php/

Published SWF movies are placed in the `flash` folder along with the HTML files that hold them. The PHP scripts are placed in the `php` directory.

## Relative Paths

The scripts referenced in these examples use relative paths. Because our PHP scripts are in a separate directory from the HTML that launches the movie, we must tell our `LoadVars` objects how to get to that directory. The HTML files are located in the same directory as the Flash SWF movie files they hold.

We want to keep our PHP scripts in their own directory to allow our root directory to remain uncluttered. By doing this, we will make it easy to remember where the scripts are located.

Because our Flash movie will eventually be viewed in a browser from an HTML page (when using PHP scripts within our ActionScript code), we have to tell the Flash Player where to get the script. Using `"../php/"` tells the Flash Player that we are traveling up our directory tree one level, and then down again into the `php` directory.

The term *relative* here refers to where our Flash SWF file is being viewed from, which as far as the browser is concerned, is from the HTML file.

## Why Not Absolute Paths?

You might be thinking, why not just use absolute paths, and not bother with the confusion—just point to our scripts with `http://www.bhhstudio.com/php/simple.php`?

This might work for linking to other Web pages or launching other SWF movies, but for PHP scripts and interacting with the server, our Flash movies and scripts must reside within the same domain; otherwise, the Flash Player will reject them because of its sandbox security measures.

By keeping our scripts relative to the Flash files, we also avoid problems associated with testing on local servers, where a browser may change the path

```
http://your_server/intranet-testing/
```

into this one

```
file://E:/your_server/intranet-testing/.
```

If your ActionScript uses absolute paths, the latter address would reject your script as being from a different domain.

## Domain Criteria for External Scripts

In order to prevent security problems and unauthorized use of data residing on sites outside of the requested URL, the Flash Player will not accept data from outside addresses using `loadVariables`, `LoadVars`, `XML.load`, `XML.sendAndLoad`, or `XMLSocket.connect`.

To ensure that your external data will not get rejected by the Flash Player, your request for external data must meet the following criteria:

- Be a relative URL, such as `../php/MyOwnSweetFile.php`, or an absolute URL such as `http://www.myServer.com/foo.php`.

- The Flash SWF movie and the requested external file must be on the same domain.

When developing dynamic content with PHP and Flash on a local server, you may run into the browser rejecting your external data, even though it is on the same subdomain. Your browser may try to resolve the addresses by using a path such as `file://localhost/E:/intranet/flash/simple.html`, which causes the Flash Player to reject the external data.

Make sure, when viewing your content in your browser, that you use `http://` rather than `file://`, which will keep both your browser and Flash development on the same address as well as allowing the browser to parse it, instead of trying to open it in an HTML editor.

Also, when previewing your Flash movies that use PHP scripts, you will only be able to run the scripts on a server running PHP. Some things may work within the Flash previewer, such as reading PHP scripts as text files. However, the best way to completely test your movies is to test them on the Web server and run them from within a browser.

## Script Syntax for ActionScript and PHP

Both ActionScript and PHP use the semicolon character as the instruction terminator, which tells the script to follow the instructions preceding it. It is a good idea to use a syntax-highlighting text editor when writing scripts. As you edit your ActionScript code, you will see correctly formatted terms change colors in the Actions panel. Flash MX 2004 also has ActionScript code hinting, which helps you properly construct your scripts.

To activate the code hints, put your cursor between parentheses while entering scripts and select the Code Hint icon (see Figure 22.3).

**FIGURE 22.3**    ActionScript syntax highlighting and code hinting.

For editing PHP, using a text editor that offers syntax highlighting makes it easy to avoid mistakes as you develop your scripts. SciTe Flash at www.bomberstudios.com/sciteflash/ has customizable syntax highlighting for PHP, HTML, and other languages including ActionScript, and provides a good way to work when simultaneously switching between PHP and other languages, such as HTML or XML.

## Variables for ActionScript and PHP

PHP variables must begin with a letter or an underscore, not a number. Flash variables can be used directly within PHP by adding a $ symbol to the variable name.

When using the Flash variable called `MyVariable`, you would use the PHP variable `$MyVariable` inside your PHP script (we discuss how to pass variables from Flash to PHP later).

## Commenting Your Code

Both ActionScript and PHP use double-slash commenting. Consider the following examples:

```
//This is a comment in ActionScript.
//This is a comment in PHP (Look familiar?).
```

## Escape Characters

Both ActionScript and PHP use the backslash to escape characters to prevent them from being interpreted as code. For example, the `\"quotes\"` in this line have been escaped by backslashes.

You may also see backslash escape characters in dynamic text output from a server. PHP has built-in functions to handle escape characters with `addslashes` and `stripslashes` commands. This is a security function of the Web server software to prevent malicious visitors from entering code within forms and executing horrible things on your server.

For instance, if a visitor tries to run the Unix `ls` command in order to run a list of the server's files from a form by typing `'ls'`, the Web server escapes the single quotes with backslashes (`\'ls\'`), thus preventing it from being interpreted as a system command.

# Receiving Data from PHP to Flash

The PHP script in this example passes information to Flash's variables. The following files are used from the companion Web site:

- `flash/simple.fla`—The Flash development file
- `flash/simple.swf`—The published Flash movie
- `flash/simple.html`—Holds the `simple.swf` movie
- `php/simple.php`—The external PHP file to be loaded

You will need to copy these files to a Web server running PHP in order to use the PHP scripts.

We are going to use the `LoadVars` object to get information from PHP for a dynamic text field on the main (root) timeline. First, we create the object, and then we set a function to the `onLoad` event, so when data is received, it will put the variables coming from PHP into the dynamic text fields.

```
var simple_lv:LoadVars = new LoadVars();
simple_lv.onLoad=function(success:Boolean){
    if(success){
        name_txt.text=this.Name;
        location_txt.text=this.Location;
    }else{
        trace("error");
    }
}
```

In this example, we aren't sending any variables, so the "method" for transferring data is left out, making the ActionScript for Button A (`buttonA`) like this:

```
buttonA.onRelease=function() {
    simple_lv.load("../php/simple.php");
}
```

## Examining the PHP Script

Looking at the `php/simple.php` file, you can see that the contents are as follows:

```
<?php
echo "
&Name=Brittany&
&Location=Earth&
";
?>
```

First, the open part of the PHP tag `<?php` tells the server that this is a PHP script. This is also the way PHP is embedded within the body of HTML code.

Several options are available for opening and closing your PHP scripts; some require customization on the PHP server to work. Besides the default tags, there are the following types of tags:

- Short tags—`<?` to open and `?>` to close

- ASP tags—`<%` to open and `%>` to close

- Script tags—Similar to JavaScript, which takes the form of `<SCRIPT LANGUAGE='php'>` to open and `</SCRIPT>` to close

For the examples in this chapter, we will use the `<?php` default tags. This is also the method you will need if you plan on integrating XML into your scripts later on.

Next, the variables are written one on each line, giving the variable `Name` a value of `Brittany` and the variable `Location` a value of `Earth`. The variables are placed one on each line in order to make the file easier to read and edit.

Ampersands are placed on both sides of each `Name=Variable` pair. We could call this technique *amper-sandwiching*, but we probably shouldn't.

The `echo` command is ended with double quotes, and the instructions are ended with a semicolon. Finally, we put a bow on it by using the default PHP close tag, `?>`.

The beauty of using external data like this is that by simply editing this PHP script, every Flash file that references this file will be updated automatically the next time someone visits it. Once again, everyone will bow to your greatness as geek-of-wonder, commander of external text files with ampersands.

### Developing the Flash File

Open the file `flash/simple.fla` and select the dynamic text "Name." The first variable coming back from PHP is called `Name`, and will appear in this text field. The other dynamic text field, "Location", will receive the other variable coming back from PHP. All variables within the external file will be passed to Flash at once. Whether we use them all or not is up to us.

Next, we will tell Flash to place the variables received in the `LoadVars` object in their respective text fields. A variable is a container for data. The data put into the variable could be from a user-input box from somewhere else in our script, or from an outside source. In this example, the variables (containers) are `Name` and `Location`. They will be received from our PHP script, and placed into the text fields.

You may want the external data to be available in the main timeline, on a particular level, or from within an embedded movie clip. Once we bring in the data with the `LoadVars` object, it will be available to us for all these methods. We only need to change our ActionScript in order to direct the variable's data to its correct location within our movie.

We have accomplished, with this example, the loading of externally created variables into Flash. This is exactly the same method you would use if the external data were a simple text (TXT) file. However, by using a properly formatted PHP file, you now have a good understanding of how to talk to PHP on the receiving end in Flash.

## Sending Data from Flash to PHP (to Flash)

In this example, a PHP script will read variable data sent from Flash. PHP will read in the variables, use them within its script, and then echo back to Flash using the variables within multiline text.

This example uses the following files from the companion Web site:

- `flash/Flash2PHP.fla`—The Flash development file

- `flash/Flash2PHP.swf`—The published Flash movie

- `flash/Flash2PHP.html`—Holds the `Flash2PHP.swf` movie

- `php/variables.php`—The PHP script

The functionality of this example shows how dynamic content can be used to generate interactive Flash pages. Open the file `Flash2PHP.fla`.

The variables defined in Flash are passed to the PHP script when Button A is released. Here's the ActionScript for Button A:

```
buttonA.onRelease=function() {
    sample2_lv.Name = name_txt.text;
    sample2_lv.sendAndLoad("http://localhost/php/variables.php",
            ➥sample2_lv, "POST");
}
```

This example passes data directly from the main (root) timeline to PHP with the `LoadVars` object using `POST`. Notice that we first set the property `Name` in the `sample2_lv` `LoadVars` object; this is what will be sent to the PHP script. In practice, you will most probably want to limit the data being passed to PHP. You can do this by using the `LoadVars` object. You can have several different `LoadVars` objects for different scripts.

When the data is returned, the `LoadVars` object is triggered with the `onLoad` event that places the info in the text field, as you can see in the following code:

```
//the event for when data is received
sample2_lv.onLoad=function(success:Boolean){
    if(success){
        fromPHP_txt.text = this.FromPHP;
    }else{
        trace("error");
    }
}
```

In our example, we're using the main timeline with the PHP script `php/variables.php`:

```
<?php
echo "
&FromPHP=Hello $Name, This is from the script.
Coming back at you live, all day, all night.
365 days a year, for all your day and night
comin' back at you live stuff, for as long
```

```
as you can stand it. Probably even longer.
And stand it you will, bla bla bla...&";
?>
```

When the variables are passed to the PHP script from Flash, PHP can use them if you simply add the dollar sign ($) symbol to the variable names in your PHP script. This allows you to echo the Name variable back to Flash.

You can see that if you communicate back and forth with a server's scripting engine, the possibilities are many. Developers who already use server-sided scripting but are new to Flash should see Flash as a way to integrate an attractive graphical front end to otherwise boring HTML-only database-driven sites.

Flash developers new to server-sided scripting should see solutions to some of their client-only development problems, such as the inability to store user information or the lack of dynamically created content.

"You can do that with PHP" will become a common phrase in your Web designing stages after learning its many uses. For example, when a client asks for the ability to update his Web pages without the assistance of a dedicated Webmaster, you could say, "You can do that with PHP." When a Flash designer needs to find a way to retrieve information from a database and tell Flash to load a specific frame based on the database's output, you might say, "You can do that with PHP."

By using Flash and PHP together, developers get the client-side power of ActionScript along with integrated server-side PHP tools. The ability to pass variables to and from Flash and PHP allows the two languages to communicate and act on each others' output.

Something else you may want to do with this capability is let Flash check for the script and provide gracious error checking in case the script can't be read. Also, for larger amounts of data, you can give the user a progress bar and signal to Flash when the script has been fully downloaded.

The important thing to remember with interactive, dynamic pages like this is to make the most use of your scripts while keeping them manageable. Some of the scripting may be better left to ActionScript within each movie, whereas for other things, it makes sense to create PHP scripts that update all your Flash movies.

With ActionScript becoming a more and more powerful language of its own with every incarnation, the art of combining the ActionScript and PHP languages, each doing what it does best, is key to great, interactive, and problem-free sites.

## Echo Valley Becomes a Wishing Well

Storing information on the server and the ability to store information in such a way that a visitor can ask questions and retrieve answers from the server are what databases are all about. Information is stored in tables and organized in ways that queries can be sent to the server and the results given back.

A one-on-one interaction with the server, where a developer uses Flash as a front end for database management, is like Echo Valley. The server is pretty much giving back what the developer is putting in. But when you add the communication of the Internet, with people plugged into the same database, each inputting data, and the ability for any subscriber to retrieve data collected from everyone else, PHP at the core, driving this machine is less like Echo Valley and a lot more like a wishing well. You can throw a question to it and receive a new and unique answer based on the data stored within the database.

PHP acts as the middleware between Flash and a database. It translates Flash's queries in the format MySQL needs, and the output of MySQL is translated through PHP back to Flash.

## Using MySQL

MySQL is a database management system. It is available to download through the GNU Public License (GPL) or through commercial licensing at a low cost through MySQL AB. MySQL AB is the company owned by the MySQL founders. More information can be found at `www.mysql.com`.

In a database, information is organized into tables, which are used on the Web to store information to support things such as e-commerce sites, shopping carts, address books, online catalogs, and so on. They all fulfill one common need: the ability to quickly search and retrieve information from a large amount of data.

Large amounts of data can be stored in flat files, which grow larger as more data is entered. Imagine a real-world situation such as printing a phone book for a large city. This single book grows larger and larger as the city grows. By the time the book gets to be about 4 inches thick, it becomes difficult to find information quickly. The book may be broken up into smaller books (by alphabet, for example), making the information within each book manageable.

In database terms, a single phone book could be stored in one flat file, but as it grows, the computer would take more time to sort through it in order to find answers. This is the job of a relational database management system (RDBMS). An RDBMS allows tables to relate to each other through common attributes, thus speeding up the searching and retrieving of data.

MySQL is one of the most widely used relational databases on the Internet today. Like PHP, MySQL runs efficiently, making it very fast. It is easy to learn and is available on both Unix and Windows platforms.

This section explains how to use Flash, PHP, and MySQL together. Along the way, you'll learn some database basics.

Like PHP, MySQL must be run on your server. Depending on your situation, you may be using your own server or relying on a hosting company that supports MySQL databases.

You may have privileges to create an unlimited amount of databases, or you may have a limit on the number of databases you can create.

When you have access to a MySQL database, you're ready to begin using Flash as a front end. In order to allow Flash to talk to MySQL, we will use PHP as the translator (that is, the middleware).

Getting the `mysql>` command prompt will vary from system to system. Rather than discuss MySQL setups, we'll begin after you have made your way through your hosting company or system administrator in order to access the `mysql` command. But to add a user to MySQL, check out this link: `http://www.mysql.com/doc/en/Adding_users.html`.

When you have access to a database, you'll log in with something like the following:

```
mysql -u brian -p
    Enter password:******
Welcome to the MySQL monitor. Commands end with ; or \g.
Your MySQL connection is 258 to server version: 4.0.15
Type 'help' for help.
mysql>
```

## Creating a Database in MySQL

The following command creates the new database called MyDatabase:

```
mysql> CREATE DATABASE MyDatabase;
Query OK, 1 row affected (0.01 sec)
```

## Showing Databases

You can show databases in MySQL with the SHOW DATABASES command. A listing will appear as shown here:

```
mysql> show databases;
+-----------+
| Database  |
+-----------+
| MyDatabase|
| mysql     |
| test      |
+-----------+
5 rows in set (0.00 sec)
```

MyDatabase is the database we have just created, and mysql and test are the MySQL default databases. The mysql database is the administrator's database.

## Creating a New User

Your hosting company may have already set you up to use MySQL or may have granted you access to a database with a login name.

If you are running your own server, you will need to create a user using an administrator login. When the new user is created, log out of the administrator account and log in as the new user.

In this example, we will create the user Nathan. Using an account with access to the administrator mysql database, create a new user:

```
mysql>use mysql
Database changed
```

The privilege system for MySQL allows critical data to be protected, and users may be granted or revoked privileges by administrators. Tables, columns, and databases all have permissions that users must be given access to work with. Understanding the MySQL privilege system will require some study.

We will create a monster of a user, with full privileges on the database. The syntax is GRANT privileges ON database TO username@host IDENTIFIED BY 'password' options. Here's the actual code:

```
mysql>GRANT all
    ->ON MyDatabase.*
    ->TO Nathan@localhost IDENTIFIED BY 'NaS&L';
    ->WITH GRANT OPTION
Query OK, 0 rows affected (0.01 sec)
```

## Granting Database Privileges

The following command will grant permissions to Nathan for the MyDatabase database. Use this to add privileges to existing users. For this example, we are granting all privileges, but in the real world you will need to limit the privileges of users on your database by specifying only the necessary privileges needed by each user. Your methods will depend on the sensitivity of your data. Here's the code for granting the database privilege:

```
mysql> GRANT all
    -> on MyDatabase.*
    -> to Nathan;
Query OK, 0 rows affected (0.01 sec)
mysql> quit
Bye
```

Now, log in using the new user name:

```
    mysql -u Nathan -p
    Enter password: NaS&L
Welcome to the MySQL monitor. Commands end with ; or \g.
Your MySQL connection id is 36 to server version: 3.22.21
Type 'help' for help.
```

## Column Types

Depending on the type of data to be stored within each table, you must define the data type to be used. MySQL supports many data types. The data types are grouped into three categories: numeric, date and time, and string (characters).

Table 22.1 details some of the more common data types used in typical databases. A complete list of types, along with detailed explanations, is available at www.mysql.com/doc/C/o/Column_types.html.

**TABLE 22.1**    Common Database Data Types

| Data Type | Definition |
| --- | --- |
| **Numeric** | |
| INT | Integers |
| FLOAT | Floating-point numbers |
| DOUBLE | Double-precision floating-point numbers |
| **Date and Time** | |
| DEC | Decimals stored as a text string |
| DATE | Any date |
| YEAR | Years between 1900 and 2155 |
| **String** | |
| CHAR | Fixed-length strings from 0 to 255 characters |
| VARCHAR | Variable-length strings from 0 to 255 characters |
| TEXT | Text fields from 0 to 65,535 bytes |

## Creating a Table

To create a new table, issue the CREATE TABLE command, followed by a comma-separated list of the new columns. Here's the syntax for this command:

```
CREATE TABLE TableName(Column1 Type(Length), Column2 Type(Length), etc;
```

Let's create a table for tracking information about the aliens we've captured. First, we need to make sure we are at the correct database:

```
    mysql> USE MyDatabase
    Database changed
```

```
mysql> CREATE TABLE Aliens (
    -> AlienID INT NOT NULL AUTO_INCREMENT PRIMARY KEY,
    -> AlienName CHAR(30),
    -> LocationCaptured CHAR(50)
    -> );
Query OK, 0 rows affected (0.02 sec)
```

## Showing the Tables

To see the tables in our database, issue the SHOW tables command. You should see a display like this one, showing our new Aliens table:

```
mysql> SHOW tables;
+--------------------+
| Tables in MyDatabase |
+--------------------+
| Aliens             |
+--------------------+
1 row in set (0.00 sec)
```

## Describing the Tables

In order to see our columns, use the DESCRIBE command, followed by the name of the table:

```
mysql> DESCRIBE Aliens;
```

You should see a result similar to Figure 22.4.

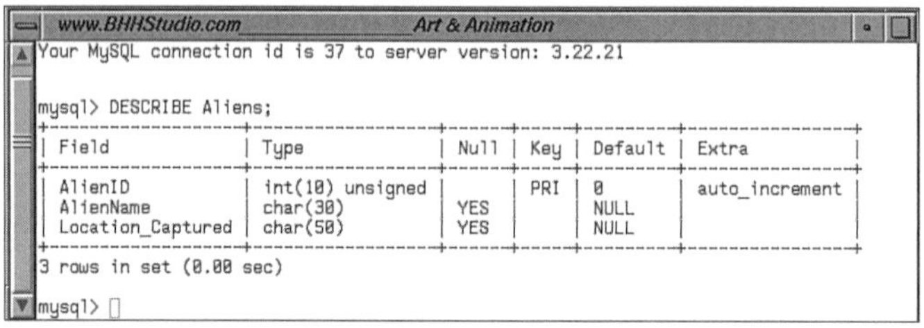

**FIGURE 22.4**    MySQL command-line output.

## Entering Information into Tables

Data can be entered into tables in several ways. Here's a common method:

```
INSERT INTO tablename VALUES(value1, value2);
```

Here's an example using this method:

```
INSERT INTO Aliens VALUES (NULL, "Brittany", "Earth");
```

When entering text strings, wrap the string in single or double quotes. If you want to specify only certain columns within the table or enter data in a different order, you could use the following:

```
INSERT INTO tablename (column1, column2) VALUES ("YourData");
```

For example, enter this into the table to add the new alien named Henry from our last Mars expedition:

```
INSERT INTO Aliens (LocationCaptured, AlienName) VALUES ("Mars", "Henry");
```

## Showing Table Contents

Now that we have a couple of entries in our table, let's see how it looks. Issue the SELECT command to view the table:

```
mysql> SELECT * from Aliens;
+---------+-----------+------------------+
| AlienID | AlienName | LocationCaptured |
+---------+-----------+------------------+
|       1 | Brittany  | Earth            |
|       2 | Henry     | Mars             |
+---------+-----------+------------------+
2 rows in set (0.00 sec)
```

The wildcard character (*) tells SELECT to list everything in the table. Notice that the AlienID column is automatically filled in for us. Remember that when we created the table, we gave the AlienID column the following creation instructions:

```
AlienID INT NOT NULL AUTO_INCREMENT PRIMARY KEY,
```

By creating the AUTO_INCREMENT column called AlienID, we have a running numerical list, which MySQL takes care of without our input.

## Selecting Data from a Table

When the table grows in size, the ability to selectively query the database for just the information that interests us at the time becomes important. It's also important to be able to sort data a certain way based on criteria we provide. We do this by using the SELECT command like this:

```
mysql> SELECT items
    -> FROM tables
    -> WHERE condition;
```

Notice the semicolon on the last line. MySQL waits for the semicolon/instruction termina-tor before executing the command. You could also write the same command in one line, like this:

```
mysql> SELECT items FROM tables WHERE condition;
```

The SELECT command has many more options, allowing for the sorting, grouping, and limiting of information. For our examples, we will be using simple conditions in order to blaze the trail for using Flash and allow you to explore more advanced uses.

Before we ask the database for information, let's ask ourselves a regular question that makes sense to the humanoid in us: Where was Brittany captured?

Now, let's convert this question into a database query using the following syntax:

```
mysql> SELECT column
    -> FROM table
    -> WHERE condition;
```

Here's what we would write, along with the result of our query:

```
mysql> SELECT LocationCaptured
    -> FROM Aliens
    -> WHERE AlienName="Brittany";
+------------------+
| LocationCaptured |
+------------------+
| Earth            |
+------------------+
1 row in set (0.00 sec)
```

We have successfully created a database, added a table, and put data into the table. Now we can ask questions to the database and receive formatted answers based on criteria we provide. Who's kicking sand in whose face now, on this dynamic cyber-beach of muscle? *You* are, and it's all because of the alphabet soup of acronyms known as PHP/MySQL-ville.

## Connecting PHP to MySQL

In order to communicate with the database, we must open the door with a proper user-name and password as well as a host. This is done from PHP using the mysql_connect function. Here's the syntax for mysql_connect:

```
mysql_connect("servername", "user", "password");
```

For this example, we will be using the following files from the companion Web Site:

- flash/Flash2MySQL.html—The HTML file that holds our movie
- flash/Flash2MySQL.fla—The Flash development file

- `flash/Flash2MySQL.swf`—The published movie

- `php/AddAlien.php`—The PHP script

Refer to the PHP script `php/AddAlien.php`.

The `php/AddAlien.php` script allows Flash to communicate to the MySQL database through PHP and add an entry to the Alien table. The backslashes (\) in the following script are inserted for publication purposes; when typing in the code by hand, make sure these lines are continuous.

```php
<?php
//Set common variables
$Host="localhost";
// We'll get $User="Nathan"; from Flash2MySQL.swf
// This is Nathan's password on the MyDatabase Database on MySQL
$Passwd="NaS&L";
$FailMsg="Something's not right...";
$SuccessMsg="&Status=Added new Alien named \
$AlienName, from $LocationCaptured.";
$DBName="MyDatabase";
$TableName="Aliens";
$Column1="LocationCaptured";
$Column2="AlienName";
//Get busy...
//1: Connect to Database
$Connect=mysql_connect($Host, $User, $Passwd);
//2: Select Database
mysql_select_db($DBName, $Connect);
//3: Create MySQL command Query
$Query="INSERT INTO $TableName (LocationCaptured, AlienName) \
VALUES('$LocationCaptured', '$AlienName')";
//4: Send Query to MySQL, Adds new entry to database
mysql_query($Query, $Connect);
echo "$SuccessMsg";
?>
```

The Flash variable `User` is passed from Flash to PHP through the `LoadVars` object. Inside the `AddAlien.php` script, several variables are defined within PHP. By defining these at the beginning of the script, we'll find it easier to modify the script later while maintaining the integrity of the rest of the script.

This script is commented along the way, so it's quite self-explanatory. You can see that we get `User` from Flash and use it in several places. Also, when the user clicks Button A, the new column and value information is sent as well. PHP connects to the MySQL database using `mysql_connect` and selects the database to use with `mysql_select_db`. Also, the Flash dynamic text field Status_txt receives the output from PHP after the database has been updated.

Using these techniques, you can also add, delete, and modify MySQL databases from Flash. The possibilities are limited only by your imagination.

## Further Reading

Integrating Flash with PHP brings about an entirely new dimension to the types of products you can create over using Flash alone.

If the idea of Open Source software appeals to you, PHP is a great start. The generosity and sense of community that exist within the Open Source movement continue to amaze me. The benefits are better tools for everyone and an opportunity to learn and grow in developing valuable career skills in Web and interactive development.

PHP is a well-documented language. You will have no problem finding answers within the Open Source community. In order to complete your PHP training as Uber-Scripter/World Dominator, you should add the following books to your library:

- *PHP and MySQL Web Development, Second Edition*, by Luke Welling and Laura Thomson (ISBN: 0-672-32525-X)

- *Sams Teach Yourself PHP in 24 Hours*, by Matt Zandstra (ISBN: 0-672-32619-1)

Here's a list of online resources:

- An online reference is available along with everything else about PHP at www.php.net.

- PHP uses the Zend scripting language engine by Zend Technologies. More information can be found at www.zend.com.

## Summary

This chapter has gone over some of the basics of creating and using PHP scripts with Flash as the front end. Things to remember about using Flash with PHP include using the LoadVars object to send and collect data. Use the onLoad event to run code when the data is received back from the PHP script.

This chapter also went into more advanced ways of combining PHP with MySQL databases to create truly dynamic content for Flash.

If you are interested in continuing to learn more about combining Flash with PHP and MySQL, review the section "Further Reading" in this chapter.

The next chapter will cover another server-side technology in ColdFusion, a very different language from PHP.

CHAPTER **23**

# Integrating ColdFusion with Flash

In this chapter we're going to briefly cover Flash and ColdFusion integration. This might seem a bit overwhelming at first, but after we've covered the basic principles, you'll be well on your way to developing the next generation of integrated applications. We'll take a brief look at components, some of the previous Flash methods, and Flash Remoting, which consists of ActionScript classes not included with Flash MX 2004 as well as the Flash Gateway. We'll end up walking through a basic application that goes into detail using some of the new versions of components that ship with Flash and ColdFusion MX.

Of course, you could still develop this application using methods available in previous Flash versions, such as loadVariables, getURL, and the XML object. Not that these methods aren't up to the task, but the functionality built into the new products provides for better performance and reliability. You will also see that the integration is tighter, meaning that you don't have to deal with common workarounds to get Flash and ColdFusion to talk to each other. What's more, you'll get a taste of using Flash Remoting to communicate with leading Web application servers. Macromedia has worked hard to achieve tighter integration among its flagship products, which is a strong selling point for ColdFusion. This allows developers and designers to create robust Flash applications that increase useability and efficiency.

With Flash MX 2004 Professional, Macromedia introduces the next generation of Rich Internet applications and Web development. Designers and developers can work together to create robust Flash applications. This goes beyond using Flash as a visual element; instead, it's used to create a unique user experience integrated with a powerful database back end. This allows for the separation of application logic and the Flash user interface. Designers can create the Flash UI while developers concentrate on creating reuseable components. Developers can pass these components on to designers, so that all the designers need to do is specify certain parameters and default values for the components to work. This not only separates application logic from the Flash UI but allows designers and developers to work in conjunction—which gives new meaning to Internet development.

Now with this version of Flash and ColdFusion, Macromedia has brought the client and server closer together. The communication is still done over HTTP but with a new format called the **Action Message Format (AMF)**. AMF is part of Flash Remoting, which Macromedia has introduced in Flash and ColdFusion MX. You're now able to access the client ActionScript classes that will communicate with the Flash Gateway, the server-side component of Flash Remoting. In the past, most integration with application servers such as ColdFusion was accomplished with `getURL`, `loadVariables`, and the `XML` object. These methods are still available in the Flash 7 player, but AMF is preferred when dealing with integers, recordsets, arrays, and structures.

The era of Flash 5, also known as the "Skip Intro" era, left a bad taste in the mouths of many developers that Flash was only good for annoying animations that people had to endure. This chapter aims to go beyond using Flash as an animation tool by integrating unique user experiences with database back ends. Flash provides new meaning to Internet applications via the capability to interact with enterprise application servers and display on devices such as PDAs, game consoles, and smart phones. This will allow designers to create a Flash UI that displays consistently across multiple platforms. Developers can create application logic to interact with the Flash UI and provide dynamic content wherever the Flash movie is being viewed.

## Components

Along with increased useability, the development process is improved because designers and developers can work together to create Flash applications. Flash MX 2004 Professional has a new version of built-in components that are similar to smart clips but offer more functionality. You can access all sorts of properties, parameters, and methods of these components. The components can be found in the Components panel (Window, Development Panels, Components) and can simply be dragged and dropped onto the stage. Figure 23.1 shows the default Components panel that ships with Flash MX 2004 Professional.

These are the default components that ship with Flash MX 2004 Professional, and they allow for more control of forms and maintaining data. But these are not the last of the components; you can download new components at `http://www.macromedia.com/exchange/flash`.

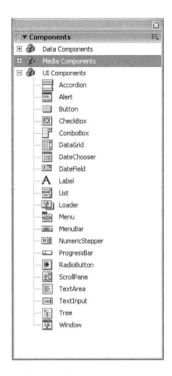

**FIGURE 23.1** Flash MX 2004 Professional Components panel.

You will need the Macromedia Extension Manager to install new components. The Extension Manager and most of these components are free, easy to install, and well worth the time they'll save you in the future. Many components are available on the Macromedia Exchange, and you can even feel free to submit your own. Many components are added daily, making this a great place to start when building your application. Figure 23.2 shows the second component set.

These components contain many methods and properties that add interactivity and functionality to your Flash movies. For more information on components, look in Chapter 16, "Components." You'll see in the examples in this chapter that these components come in very handy when integrating with ColdFusion. For example, at some point you'll need to use a scrollbar in one of your applications. Coding a scrollbar isn't considered anything complex, but it can definitely be time-consuming. The purpose of components is to provide reuseable code so that you don't end up reinventing the wheel.

Not only do components save time, but they also offer a way for designers and developers to work together when creating Flash applications. Components provide a way to separate the code from the display. Developers can create custom components and pass them on to junior-level developers or designers to include in their movies. The designer simply needs to know how to set a few properties or parameters for the clip, and everything else is taken care of. This provides for a rapid application development (RAD) environment for Web teams. Libraries of custom components can be developed and reused in future projects, which can save hours of development and debugging time.

# Older Integration Methods

In previous versions of Flash, Macromedia introduced ways to communicate with application servers over HTTP. These methods included `getURL`, `loadVariables`, `LoadVars`, and the `XML` object. Each method has its pros and cons and is still available in the Flash 7 player. Although we'll cover these older methods briefly, this chapter focuses primarily on new ways of accomplishing these tasks.

### getURL

The `getURL` method was introduced in the Flash 2 player, but the `GET` and `POST` options are only available to the Flash 4 player and above. This has always been a good way to send data to the server, but it calls for the Flash movie to redirect the browser to another page. This usually consists of a Flash movie sending variables to a non-Flash page, which in turn processes the data. This is also a one-way path because you can only send data from Flash but not retrieve it.

### loadVariables

The `loadVariables` method was a great addition to the Flash 4 player, providing the ability to send data via `GET` or `POST`. The advantage of using `loadVariables` is that the Flash movie makes an HTTP request to the server without having to redirect the Flash movie. This is all handled behind the scenes. The problem with `loadVariables` is that the data needs to be URL-encoded and sent in name/value pairs. This prevents sending and receiving complex data such as arrays, objects, and recordsets. There are ways to accomplish sending complex structures to and from Flash, but this requires a good bit of ActionScript knowledge, and these workarounds generally require more overhead from the Flash player.

### LoadVars

The `LoadVars` object was introduced back in Flash MX with the Flash 6 player. It is a full-blown object designed for integrating Flash with server-side technologies. It uses HTTP to send and receive data from the server using both `GET` and `POST`, but the information sent does not have to be URL-encoded; it can be properties of the `LoadVars` object. The `LoadVars` object even has built-in events that will trigger when data is received. You still cannot send arrays or other types of objects with just the `LoadVars` object, but it is a big step up from `loadVariables`. For more on `LoadVars`, see Chapter 20, "Introduction to Data Integration."

## The XML Object

The XML object provides a great way to send and receive complex data structures to and from Flash. This was introduced in Flash 5 and works seamlessly with servers that transfer information using XML packets. Sending data using the XML object provides structure to your data as well as increased speed and reliability. The XML parsing and performance has improved dramatically in the Flash 7 player. In version 5, an XML packet that contained many child nodes ran poorly, and the preferred method was to use XML packets that contained attributes instead of nodes. Now XML packets can contain many child nodes, and the performance gain is substantial. Although performance has increased, you should still exercise caution as to how much data you're loading. It is still recommended that you break your data up into pieces if you're dealing with XML documents with substantial file sizes such as over 100KB. This can reduce strain on the Flash player and improve the end-user experience.

If you need to interact with different application servers that utilize XML, using the XML object is the preferred method. Because performance and reliability have increased, it would be advantageous to become familiar with the XML object and use it in your applications.

As you can see, these methods from previous versions of Flash all have their pros and cons. If you're dealing with simple integration, getURL, loadVariables, and the LoadVars object are all up to the task. If you need to transfer structured data in an efficient manner, consider using the XML object. Make sure you analyze your application before development. Outline a specification document that will help you determine whether you can use these older methods to accomplish your task.

If you're looking to build a robust Flash application where Flash will serve solely as the front end, you should explore Flash Remoting. We'll discuss Flash Remoting and then get our hands dirty with an account management application that expands on Flash and ColdFusion integration.

## Macromedia Flash Remoting

Flash Remoting serves as the layer of communication between Flash and the application server. Developers will now be able to interact with different application servers, such as ColdFusion, Java, and .NET servers. All communication will be handled via the new Action Message Format (AMF), which works over HTTP. The server-side component of Flash Remoting, known as the Flash Gateway, allows developers to make calls from Flash to the application server. Flash Remoting classes are available in ActionScript that allow Flash to communicate with the server through the Flash Gateway. These classes are known as NetServices and offer increased performance and functionality over older methods.

Figure 23.2 shows where Flash remoting fits in with application development.

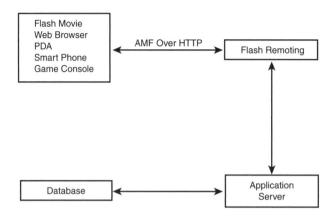

**FIGURE 23.2**    The relationship between Flash, Flash Remoting, and the application server.

You'll become more familiar with Flash Remoting and how it works when we take a look at the sample application for this chapter. The Flash Remoting component, from a user's standpoint, is completely invisible. It was designed to make the developer's life easier by creating a standardized method of developing and debugging entire Flash applications. With it, you can transfer not only strings of information from application servers, but also recordsets and objects.

# A Basic Account Management System

Now that you have a basic grasp of the server-side functionality, we're going to walk through an entire application that utilizes some of the new features. As mentioned earlier, this application could be developed the old way using LoadVars or the XML object. Our goal is to walk through the development of an application that shows the power and capabilities of Flash Remoting. There are so many new server-side components that it's almost like learning an entirely new program. We can't cover everything in this chapter, but this application should be just enough to intrigue you and get you started developing your own Flash/ColdFusion applications.

This example requires that you have ColdFusion MX installed and running. A 30-day trial version can be found at http://www.macromedia.com/cfusion/tdrc/ index.cfm?product=coldfusion. You'll also need the Flash MX 2004 add-ons, which contain the ActionScript classes and components necessary to connect to the Flash Gateway and help you debug your application. The application will be tested and run from localhost, and you can change this to whatever your IP address or hostname is. You'll see this specified in the ActionScript code shortly.

## Getting Started

Copy the file ch23.zip to your Web root C:\Inetpub\wwwroot. Now unzip this file and make sure the files reside in C:\Inetpub\wwwroot\flashexamples\ch23. This directory structure is key to developing the application. Of course, you can change the structure, but this should be reflected within the Flash ActionScript code.

This application will demonstrate a user account management system in which data records can be updated and deleted from the Flash UI. The Flash Gateway, the server-side component of Flash Remoting, will be used to transmit information between itself and the application server. The application server will then query a database and pass information back to the Flash Gateway. Figure 23.3 demonstrates the communication process.

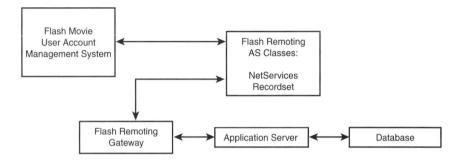

**FIGURE 23.3**    The communication process via Flash Remoting.

Flash Remoting requires the use of ActionScript classes along with server-side creation of Flash Remoting services in ColdFusion MX. As you can see, Flash Remoting serves as the bridge between Flash and the ColdFusion application server. The following account management application will introduce the code and techniques to build dynamic Web applications. Let's get started.

## Files in the Application

First, we're going to take a look through each of the files and get a basic of understanding of what they do. Following is a list of files included with this application that can be found in /wwwroot/flashexamples/ch23/:

- Accountmanagement.fla
- Accountmanagement.html
- Accountmanagement.swf
- Application.cfm
- deleteUser.cfm
- getUserInfo.cfm
- getUserList.cfm
- index.cfm

- `NetConnection.as`

- `NetConnectionAS2.as`

- `NetServiceProxy.as`

- `NetServiceProxyResponder.as`

- `NetServices.as`

- `RecordSet.as`

- `RsDataFetcher.as`

- `RsDataProviderClass.as`

- `updateUser.cfm`

- `users.mdb`

### The Database

The key to any Web application is the database and the way it structures the data. If you take a look at `users.mdb`, you'll see the very basic design of the table for this example, as shown in Figure 23.4.

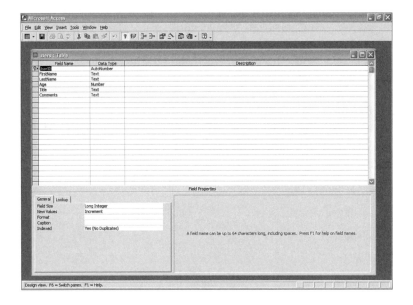

**FIGURE 23.4**    Database structure for the users' table.

The data structure is very straightforward, and you'll see that UserID is the primary key for the users' table. This is what we'll use to pass data between the Flash Gateway and ColdFusion when updating and deleting records. Other information will be passed, but the user ID is unique to each user and lets us know which record to update or delete.

### The ColdFusion Templates

Now we're going to take a look at each of the ColdFusion templates. `Application.cfm` simply serves to store the Data Source Name (DSN), which in this case is `accountmanagement`. This is set as a global request variable and will be called from other templates when making database queries. The DSN will need to be set up through the ColdFusion Administrator, which is shown in Figure 23.5. You can change the DSN to any name you prefer—just make sure this is consistent in the `Application.cfm` template and the ColdFusion administrator and that the driver is set to Microsoft Access.

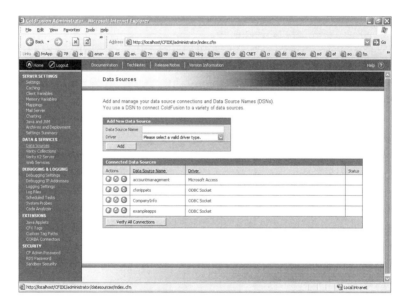

**FIGURE 23.5**    Managing ODBC data sources in ColdFusion Administrator.

We'll take a brief look at the rest of the templates in the order they'll be accessed throughout the application. The `getUserList.cfm` template is used to populate the `List` component within Flash. Figure 23.6 shows the communication process, which grabs information from ColdFusion and populates the `List` component. You'll see that this component has tremendous functionality and can even be controlled using the up and down arrows on your keyboard. When a selection is made, a change event will trigger, and a function will be called (in this case, it calls the `getUserInfo.cfm` template).

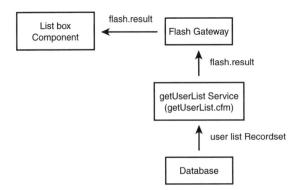

**FIGURE 23.6**    Communication between Flash and the application server to retrieve the user list.

The `getUserInfo.cfm` template is used to query the database and grab the selected user's information, as shown in Figure 23.7. When the user makes a selection from the list box, a unique user ID is passed to the template. The user ID is passed through the Flash Gateway, and the template queries the database via the user ID. The recordset is then passed back to Flash and handled accordingly to display the user's information.

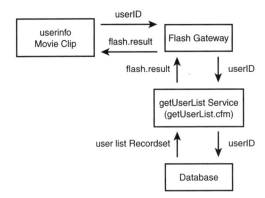

**FIGURE 23.7**    Communication between Flash and the application server to retrieve the user's information.

When the information has been loaded into the Flash UI, the user can then edit the text fields and modify the data. If the Update button is clicked, an event is triggered that will send the user ID along with the other data to the `updateUser.cfm` template through the Flash Gateway. The template will then update the database via the unique user ID. After the database has been updated, another call to the `getUserList.cfm` template is made that will update the list box in case any names have been changed.

Similarly, when the Delete button is clicked, the user ID will be passed to the `deleteUser.cfm` template. The record will be removed from the database via the user ID. When the record has been removed, we'll call the `getUserList.cfm` template again to display the most current list of names.

### The Flash File

The Flash source file, `Accountmanagement.fla`, contains all the ActionScript, components, and graphics that create the front end of the sample application.

The compiled Flash file, `Accountmanagement.swf`, is what will be displayed in the `Accountmanagement.html` file. We'll be accessing this HTML page when we're not testing inside the Flash Integrated Development Environment (IDE).

We're now going to take a detailed look at the source code and how it interacts with the Flash Gateway.

### Movie Structure

Let's open the Flash source file and look at the overall structure of the sample movie. The structure of this movie consists of two main movie clips that handle the display of information. The first clip is actually a `List` component and is assigned an instance name of `myList_lb`. You can view instance names of movie clips in the Properties panel. The next movie clip is given an instance name of `userInfo_mc` and will be used to display the user's information along with the Update and Delete buttons. The `userInfo_mc` clip also contains a couple of subclips that display different response messages, depending on the user's selection. There are a few other graphical elements you can see while looking through the movie structure displayed in Figure 23.8.

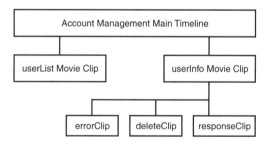

**FIGURE 23.8**   The `Accountmanagement.fla` movie structure.

### Understanding the Code

In frame 1 of the main timeline, you'll see most of the ActionScript code necessary to run the user-management application. For learning purposes, most of the code resides here, because it's easier to follow than having to search for code within different movie clips. It's always good practice to build modular code (that is, code that's broken into components). The code is centralized, but you'll see that it is broken into different components that handle different functions.

As mentioned earlier, you'll need to install the Flash MX add-ons, which include several classes as well as the all-important gateway. The updated class files for remoting reside in the directory with other source files. And because of Flash's new classpath, you do not need to use an #include action as you would have in previous editions.

The first class we call, the NetServices class, is used to create the two-way connection between Flash and the Flash Gateway. Now that you understand how the class files are automatically included, we can start using them by making a connection to the Flash Gateway.

```
// let's make sure we only run this block of code once
 if (initialized == null) {
    // set initialized to true so we don't run this again
    var initialized = true;
    //
    NetServices.setDefaultGatewayUrl("http://localhost/flashservices/gateway");
    var gatewayConnection = NetServices.createGatewayConnection();
    var userService = gatewayConnection.getService("flashExamples.ch23", this);
}
```

> **NOTE**
>
> Depending on which Flash Remoting you have installed, the gateway URL may differ, so check your local documentation to see where your gateway is.

The connection to the gateway only needs to be established once. Therefore, we check for the existence of the variable initialized. If it doesn't exist, the if statement will run and set it to true, meaning it will only run once. After the initial connection is made, we can make as many calls and data transfers as necessary throughout our application. The default gateway URL specifies the gateway we'll be connecting to on the local machine. You can also specify a secure protocol (HTTPS) to be used with the Flash Gateway. The next line of code actually creates the connection to the Flash Gateway and sets it to the gatewayConnection variable. A URL string can also be specified as a parameter for this method, but Macromedia recommends specifying the URL in the setDefaultGatewayURL method. When the connection has been made, we connect to our service directory under flashexamples.ch23 and set this to the userService variable. We will now be able to make calls to our Flash Remoting server-side services via the userService variable.

We'll now be accessing service functions, which correspond to the ColdFusion templates mentioned earlier, to handle our data. The first service function we'll look into is the getUserList function:

```
getUserList = function() {
    userService.getUserList();
}
```

```
//call the function to get all users
getUserList();
```

The order in which this code is specified matters. We must create the function first, and then we can call the function getUserList. The user list service is called several times throughout the application and is used to load or reload data into the List component. Note that when we make a call to a service function, we'll be waiting for the data to be returned from the Flash Gateway. To capture the results, we need to specify a result function that will capture the data. All data returned to service functions will be sent to the function with _Result appended to the name (for example, getUserList_Result):

```
// initialize the array to store our list elements
var valueList:Array = new Array();

getUserList_Result=function(resultRecordset) {
    //clean the array out
    valueList.length=0;
    for (i in resultRecordset.items) {
        // grab the id, first name, and last name to store in tempObj
        var userid:Number = resultRecordset.items[i].userid;
        var firstname:String = resultRecordset.items[i].firstname;
        var lastname:String = resultRecordset.items[i].lastname;
        // create a temporary object that will contain
                //the id, first name, and last name
        // the first name and last name will be labels
                // and the id will be our data
        // then set it in the array which will be used to populate our userlist
        var tempObj:Object = new Object();
        tempObj.label = firstname + " " + lastname;
        tempObj.data = userid;
        valueList[i] = tempObj;
    }
    // set the user list
    myList_lb.dataProvider=valueList;
}
```

When the movie initially plays, we call the getUserList service, and the recordset is sent back to getUserList_Result. This function is used to loop through the items of the recordset, and we set them to local variables in Flash. In this case, we're dealing with the userid, firstname, and lastname of each user. While we're looping through the recordset, we create a temporary object to store the object's label and data. The label for the list box is the user's first name and last name, which will display in the list box. We also set the data for each user in the temporary object, which is userid. The data variable is invisible to the user and is what we'll use to grab the user's information, update it, and delete the record. Through each iteration of the loop, we set the temporary object and then append it to the `valueList` array. When the looping has completed, we take the `valueList` array and place it in the `dataProvider` property of the `myList_lb` list box. Remember that `myList_lb` corresponds to the instance name of the `List` component on the stage. See Figure 23.9 to view the populated `List` component.

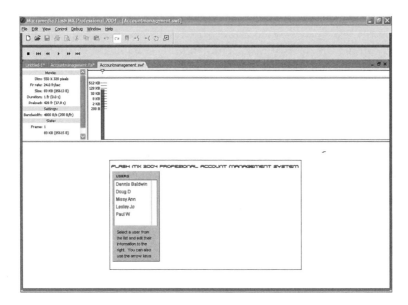

**FIGURE 23.9**    User list displayed in the Flash movie.

The `dataProvider` property of the `List` component is one of many properties we have access to with the new Flash MX 2004 components. To learn more about the methods and properties of components, be sure to view the ActionScript dictionary.

So far, you've seen the code that loops through the user list recordset. Now you need to see what's happening on the server side. If you look at the server-side code in `getUserList.cfm`, here's what you'll see:

```
<cfquery datasource="#request.dsn#" name="getusers" dbtype="odbc">
select userid, firstname, lastname
from users;
</cfquery>
<cfset flash.result=getusers>
```

In this query, we're grabbing a recordset from the database that contains the user's ID, first name, and last name. These results are then assigned to `flash.result`, which will be passed back to the `getUserList_Result` function in Flash.

If you're familiar with ColdFusion, you will notice that the variable scope includes the Flash variable scope, which will pass the result to the Flash Gateway and then to the Flash movie. Here is a list of the variables within the Flash scope:

- `flash.result`—A variable that will be passed to the Flash movie

- `flash.params`—A structure of parameters passed from the Flash movie

- `flash.pagesize`—Specifies the number of records passed to the Flash movie at a time

The `flash.result` variable can pass strings, integers, recordsets, arrays, structures, and Boolean values to the Flash movie. This makes it easier to send structured data, such as recordsets, to Flash movies than it is with other, more primitive methods.

So we've successfully made our initial request to the server and populated the list box with our results—not too shabby! Now the next step is to handle the event of a user clicking one of the list box entries. What we want to do is display the information for the selected user. We first create an object to listen for the `change` event. We then create a function for when the event happens that will get the user's information, and go to the correct spot in the `userInfo_mc` movie. And finally we add the event to the `myList_lb` List component.

```
//this is the listener object for the list box
listEvt=new Object();
//set the event to the object
listEvt.change = function(eventObj){
    var selectedID:Number = eventObj.target.value;
    getUserInfo(selectedID);
    userInfo_mc.gotoAndStop(2);
    //trace("Value changed to " + );
}
//add the listener for the event
myList_lb.addEventListener("change", listEvt);
```

When the event is triggered by the user selecting a name from the list box, the function will initialize the `selectedID` variable and set the user ID to it. The `data` property of the selected item corresponds to the user ID and was set earlier by our `getUserList_Result` function. Once again, UserID serves as the unique key for our users and allows us to retrieve, update, and delete user data.

We now make a call to the `getUserInfo` service, which queries the database and returns the information for the selected user. After the call is made to the server for the user information, we tell the `userInfo_mc` movie clip to go to and stop on frame 2. This all happens instantaneously, and while the `userInfo_mc` clip is sent to frame 2, we wait for the Flash Gateway to return the recordset to getUserInfo_Result:

```
getUserInfo_Result=function(resultRecordset) {
    // grab the values from the recordset
```

```
    var userid:Number = resultRecordset.items[0].userid;
    var firstname:String = resultRecordset.items[0].firstname;
    var lastname:String = resultRecordset.items[0].lastname;
    var age:Number = resultRecordset.items[0].age;
    var title:String = resultRecordset.items[0].title;
    var comments:String = resultRecordset.items[0].comments;
// set the values in the userInfo_mc clip for display
// the userid will be used to update and delete users
    userInfo_mc.userid = userid;
    userInfo_mc.firstName_txt.text = firstname;
    userInfo_mc.lastName_txt.text = lastname;
    userInfo_mc.age_txt.text = age;
    userInfo_mc.title_txt.text = title;
    userInfo_mc.comments_txt.text = comments;
}
```

The function waits for the recordset object that is passed back from the getUserInfo
service. The necessary variables—userid, firstname, lastname, age, title, and comments—
are pulled from the recordset and then placed in the userInfo_mc clip for display. The
output of the userInfo_mc clip is shown in Figure 23.10.

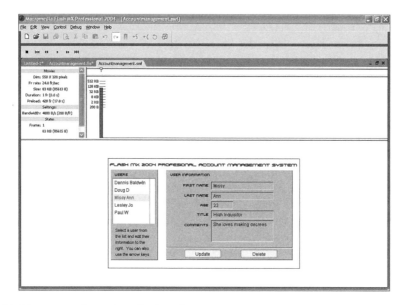

**FIGURE 23.10**    User information displayed in the Flash movie.

Let's take a look at the server-side ColdFusion getUserInfo service and the code that
handles this task:

```
<cfset userid = flash.params[1]>
<cfquery datasource="#request.dsn#" name="getuserinfo">
select userid, firstname, lastname, age, title, comments
from users
where userid = #userid#;
</cfquery>
<cfset flash.result=getuserinfo>
```

The first <cfset> statement grabs the user ID that is passed from the Flash getUserInfo(userid) function and sets it to a local CF variable. Next, we query the database using the user ID and place the results of the recordset in the flash.result variable. This is passed through the Flash Gateway and back to Flash and is handled by the getUserInfo_Result function.

So far, everything we've covered has been read-only type interaction. Now we're going to look into updating and deleting user information and the code that will handle these tasks.

If you look inside the userInfo_mc clip, frame 1 contains the necessary ActionScript functions and objects to handle the update and delete actions. These functions are declared in frame 1 and await a user event after the movie clip is sent to frame 2. In frame 2, you'll see the dynamic text fields along with the Update and Delete buttons, and some ActionScript that sets the events for the buttons.

The Update button's event we are using is the click event. When the button is clicked, the event is called and the function for the event is put to work:

```
//create the object for the update
updateObj=new Object();
updateObj.click=function(evt) {
    // make sure that all fields are filled out
    // simple validation to see if data exists in the text field
    if(firstName_txt.text != '' && lastName_txt.text != '' &&
➥age_txt.text != '' && title_txt.text != '' && comments_txt.text !='') {
        // go to frame 3 which will display the response message
        gotoAndStop(3);
        // call the update user service to update the database contents
        // the result will be returned to updateUser_Result in _root
        _root.userService.updateUser(userid, firstName_txt.text,
➥lastName_txt.text, age_txt.text, title_txt.text, comments_txt.text);
        // refresh the user list in case a firstname or lastname was changed
        _root.userService.getUserList();
    } else {
        // send error message that one or more fields are missing
```

```
            errorClip.gotoAndPlay(2);
    }
}
```

This function performs basic validation, just to see whether the fields actually have any data in them before the service is called. If there is no data in the fields, we target the clip errorClip and tell it to play. This basically prompts the user to fill out these fields. If there is data in the fields, the userInfo_mc clip is sent to frame 3, which displays a subclip called responseClip and displays an "Updating Database" message.

The updateUser service is then called (note that we call it from root because that's where updateUser_Result resides). We pass the userid parameter, and the firstName_txt, lastName_txt, age_txt, title_txt, and comments_txt text properties to the updateUser service. The ColdFusion updateUser.cfm template will take these parameters and update the database with the new information:

```
<cftry>
<cfset userid = flash.params[1]>
<cfset firstname = flash.params[2]>
<cfset lastname = flash.params[3]>
<cfset age = flash.params[4]>
<cfset title = flash.params[5]>
<cfset comments = flash.params[6]>
<cfquery datasource="#request.dsn#" dbtype="odbc">
update users
set firstname='#firstname#', lastname='#lastname#',
➥age=#age#, title='#title#', comments='#comments#'
where userid = #userid#;
</cfquery>
<cfset flash.result=1>
        <cfcatch>
                <cfset flash.result=0>
        </cfcatch>
</cftry>
```

With this template, we're basically setting the parameters passed from Flash, through the gateway, to local CF variables. The query then updates the user's information based on the user ID. You'll see that we've introduced a <cftry>...<cfcatch> statement that will tell us whether the update was successful. If it is successful, we send a value of 1 (true) back to Flash. If it is not successful, we send 0 (false).

With these values, the updateUser_Result function will then determine what response to send to the user through the userInfo.responseClip movie clip:

```
updateUser_Result=function(success) {
    if(success) {
```

```
    // update successful so display the success message
        userInfo_mc.responseClip.gotoAndPlay("success");
    } else {
    // update failed so display the failed message
        userInfo_mc.responseClip.gotoAndPlay("failed");
    }
}
```

If the update is successful, we target responseClip and tell it to go to and play the success frame. This will display a message of "success" to the user. After this message is finished displaying, the *parent* clip of responseClip, which is userInfo_mc, is sent back to frame 2. The new information is displayed, and a call is made to the getUserList service. The reason for the call to getUserList is to refresh the list box with the new firstname and lastname values if the record was updated.

The last piece of the puzzle involves handling the Delete button if it's clicked. You'll see that the sequence of events is very similar to the update action. The click event for the Delete button is the deleteUser function, which resides in frame 1 of the userInfo_mc clip.

Before we let users delete any information, we first need to prompt them to confirm that this is what they want to do:

```
//create the object for the delete
deleteObj=new Object();
deleteObj.click=function(evt){
    // set the current userid in the delete clip
    // the userid will be passed from the delete clip to the deleteUser service
    deleteClip.userid = userid;
    // play the delete clip
    deleteClip.play();
}
```

We set the userid inside deleteClip, which resides in frame 2 of the userInfo movie clip. After we set the userid, we then tell the delete movie clip to play. This will display a prompt and then let the user click a Yes or No button to confirm. The click events for both of these buttons reside in frame 1 of deleteClip:

```
//create the objects for deleting the record, or not
yesObj=new Object();
noObj=new Object();

yesObj.click=function (evt) {
    // call the deleteUser service which will be returned
    // to deleteUser_Result in _root
```

23

```
    _root.userService.deleteUser(userid);
}

noObj.click=function (evt) {
    // return the current clip to frame 1
    gotoAndStop(1);
}
```

If the Yes button is clicked, we call the deleteUser service, pass the userid, and wait for the response in _root. The deleteUser_Result function will wait for the response and, if successful, display a "success" message. If it fails, a "failed" message is displayed:

```
deleteUser_Result=function(success) {
    if(success) {
        // delete successful so display the success message
        userInfo_mc.deleteClip.gotoAndPlay("success");
        // reload the user list since the user has been deleted
        userService.getUserList();
        // reset the userInfo_mc fields until another user has been selected
        userInfo_mc.firstName_txt.text = "";
        userInfo_mc.lastName_txt.text = "";
        userInfo_mc.age_txt.text = "";
        userInfo_mc.title_txt.text = "";
        userInfo_mc.comments_txt.text = "";
    } else {
        // delete failed so display the failed message
        userInfo_mc.deleteClip.gotoAndPlay("failed");
    }
}
```

We also need to reset the fields in the userInfo_mc clip when deleting the user, as you can see in the preceding code snippet. The last thing we'll look into is the code for the ColdFusion deleteUser.cfm template:

```
<cftry>
        <cfset userid = flash.params[1]>
                <cfquery datasource="#request.dsn#" name="getuserinfo">
                delete from users
                where userid = #userid#;
        </cfquery>
        <cfset flash.result=1>
                <cfcatch>
                <cfset flash.result=0>
        </cfcatch>
</cftry>
```

Once again, we set the `userid` passed from Flash to a local CF variable; then we perform a delete query based on the `userid` variable. If the query is successful, we send a value of 1 to Flash; if the query is not successful, we send a value of 0. The `deleteUser_Result` function will take care of the rest and determine what message to display to the user.

## Advancing Your Skills

This application would not be complete without the ability to add new users to the database. That's why we challenge you to use what you've learned in this chapter to apply "Add User" functionality. You will then be able to add users to the database, modify their information, and delete them if necessary.

Also consider using shared objects to store data locally on the user's machine. You could let users log in and have their personal information pulled into Flash from the local machine without having to send a request to the server. This would save you from having to make any unnecessary calls to the server. After the information is updated, you could send the information to the server and also save it locally for the next time the information is displayed.

Another area to explore is ColdFusion components. Components provide a means of reusing code that is stored in a single location. You can invoke methods on components and receive method results. These are similar to Flash components in that they provide for RAD and allow you to separate application logic from the display code. ColdFusion components are stored in files with a `.cfc` extension. You can also use ColdFusion to expose methods as Web services.

## Summary

As mentioned earlier, you have unlimited possibilities with Flash and ColdFusion. With Flash as the front end, ColdFusion as the middleware, and databases to hold the actual content, you can create a truly dynamic Rich Internet application. Using Flash Remoting, you can also create more structured data transfer.

The next chapter continues down the dynamic content road, introducing you to Web Services.

CHAPTER **24**

# Web Services and Flash

So far, we have been moving data with name/value pairs, static XML documents, or with ColdFusion and Flash Remoting. This chapter will change all that by opening your eyes to the world of Web services.

We will go over what Web services are and why to use them, as well as how to create them and how to tie into them using Flash MX 2004. And we will finish up by creating an application to search the Web using the Google API.

## What Is a Web Service?

A Web service is exactly what it says; it's a service on the Web. So what service do Web services provide?

A Web service's goal is to provide raw data in XML format to any application that makes a request to it. That may not make sense by itself, so here is exactly what a Web service does.

A Web service sits on a server much like any server-side page, and when a request is made to it, the Web service will perform a desired task, and return data in the form of XML. XML, as you learned in Chapter 21, "XML and Flash," is a language that nearly any application can read because it is in fact a metalanguage made up of customized tags containing well-formed and structured data.

And that is what a Web service is, and does, but that doesn't explain why anyone should use them.

## Why Use Web Services?

Some time ago, I was working on a sales force application that managed all the retail outlets for a client's sales force. I made all the Flash pieces, and the objects necessary for it to work, but when I started testing it with live data, it wouldn't return all the correct information. I looked through the database itself at the point where it was getting hung up, and lo and behold, there was an ampersand in not only one, but a few of the store names. Remember back in Chapter 20, "Introduction to Data Integration," where you were introduced to data integration with Flash? You learned that name/value pairs are separated by ampersands. This means that when the parser reached the store name with the ampersand, it would think that part of the name was data, and the other part was the beginning of the next name/value pair like this:

The original store name: `A&B Grocery`

Was thought to be: `name=A&B Grocery=`

You can see how frustrated I was after checking everything else first.

This is a very common problem for developers and middleware, having to check individual data pieces to make sure each one fits exactly. And then you have to make sure the data cannot be put back in with an ampersand so that the problem won't happen again. Even worse, what if I could not only see the data, but I couldn't see the middleware page either? I would be stuck with no idea of what is causing the strange error with my data.

This is where Web services really fit in. Because Web services send back XML data, all I have to do is create a parser to parse XML, and then it does not matter what data is coming back because the XML is self-describing with its tags.

Web services can be written in several different languages, but in this chapter, we will use ASP.NET. Each Web service written will have a WSDL (Web Services Description Language) file that will describe our Web service to anyone who intends to use it. More on that later in this chapter.

To use .NET you must have a personal Web server (or a Web server on the Web with .NET installed) and you must install .NET. You can get .NET from this link:

```
http://www.microsoft.com/downloads/details.aspx?
➥familyid=9B3A2CA6-3647-4070-9F41-A333C6B9181D&displaylang=en
```

Not all examples will require you to have .NET or a personal Web server installed, but to re-create some of the Web services from this chapter, you will need it.

## Creating a Web Service

To create a Web service, open your favorite text editor such as Notepad or SciTe. ASP.NET supports several different languages for Web services, but we will be using the C# language as it closely mimics ActionScript.

The first line of a Web service will declare that we are in fact creating a Web service, which language we are using, whether or not to allow debugging, and any Web service classes we will be creating.

Here is a generic template for the first line:

```
<%@ WebService Language="c#" debug="true" class="MyClass" %>
```

In the preceding code, we declare that we are creating a Web service in the C# language, that we will allow debugging (very important in case you make minor errors), and that we will be creating a Web service class called MyClass.

**NOTE**

Notice that the first line of the Web service falls within the <% %> tags. This is because we want the browser to recognize anything between these two tags as a server-side script. The rest of the Web service itself does not require them, but the first line does.

After that, you need to get a few Web service namespaces that we will need to produce the correct results:

```
using System.IO;
using System.Web.Services;
```

In this code, we used the keyword using to signify that we will be using the System.IO and the System.Web.Services namespaces.

After that, we begin to create the Web service methods. These are the methods that will be called from the Web service itself, and describe what the service does.

First, declare the class of Web service:

```
public class MyClass: System.Web.Services.WebService{
```

Notice that this class is public, which means it can be called from outside the service itself. After that, we use the class keyword and name our class MyClass. Then we begin to create the service with the System.Web.Services.WebService class.

The next step is to begin declaring the Web methods. To do this, you use the keyword WebMethod in brackets, along with a description, if desired, that will help anyone looking at the Web service tell what each Web method is doing.

```
[WebMethod(Description="Description of the Web method")]
```

Then create the Web method itself declaring whether it is private or public. Before you name the Web method, you have to declare what data type will be returned. For example, the following will return an integer data type, so we use the keyword int:

```
public  int myMethod(){
      return 15;
   }
}
```

Now that you have seen the basic parts of a Web service, we can begin to create them.

The first Web service will simply return a string saying "hello." So open your favorite text editor and place this code in it:

```
<%@ WebService Language="c#" debug="true" class="Hello" %>
using System.IO;
using System.Web.Services;

public class Hello: System.Web.Services.WebService{

  [WebMethod(Description="Say hello")]
  public  string sayHello() {
      return "hello";
  }
}
```

The preceding code does everything we have discussed so far. It declares that we are creating a Web service in C#. It then gets the classes we need to use. After that, it creates the `Hello` class and then the method `sayHello`, which will send the string literal "hello" back to us.

Now save as `hello.asmx` in either your Web server or PWS (personal Web server). The directory on most Web servers including PWS's is at `c:\inetpub\wwwroot\` or one of its subdirectories. The `.asmx` extension is the extension for the Web services on .NET.

Map to the new file using the browser, using `http://` not `file://`, and you should see a screen similar to Figure 24.1.

> **NOTE**
> You must browse to Web services in order to view them in action. Otherwise, the browser will attempt to open them up in an application.

This screen is created automatically to help test the Web service without an application. You can see all the Web methods listed (in this case, just the `sayHello` method) and their description if it was declared. Select the `sayHello` method, and you will be taken to a screen that looks like Figure 24.2. Here you can invoke (run) the method to see its results. Also, you can see all the information about the method including its return value, and if we had any parameters, they would be shown here as well. Choose the Invoke button, and another browser window will pop up with XML data as shown in Figure 24.3. This is the result of the Web service. Now in this case, it's not all that impressive, but as we move forward it will become so.

**FIGURE 24.1**    You can test your Web methods without an application.

**FIGURE 24.2**    The Web method information.

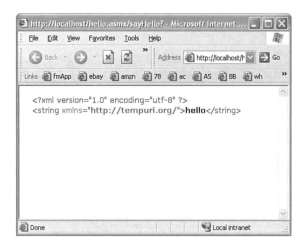

**FIGURE 24.3**    The results from the Web service.

And the final page to look at is the WSDL, so return to the original page, and at the top, choose the Service Description link, and the window will fill with more XML data as shown in Figure 24.4. This tells any user of the Web service everything they need to know to use it. It shows all the methods, their return values, and their parameters.

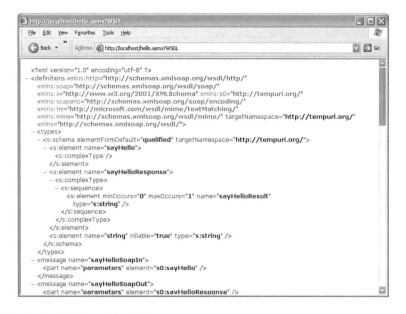

**FIGURE 24.4**    The WSDL of the Web service.

# Consuming Web Services with Flash

Now that you see how to make a basic Web service, and how to test it, let's take it a step further and bring the data into Flash.

We will begin working with the XML object to bring the data in, and finally move over to using Flash Remoting.

## Using the XML Object

We went over the basics of the XML object back in Chapter 21. Now we are going to use it to consume our Web service that we have already created.

To absorb a Web service with the XML object, when you load it in, use the path to the Web service, followed by a slash, then the name of the Web method being called, like this:

```
myXML.load("http://localhost/myWebService.asmx/myWebMethod");
```

And after it is loaded, you will have to parse the data like an XML document.

This example will use the Web service we have already created to bring in the word "hello" and put it in a dynamic text field on the stage.

1. Create a new Flash document.

2. Draw a dynamic text field on the stage, give it an instance name of **myText_txt**, and make sure the border setting is turned on.

3. Create a new layer called **actions**.

4. In the actions layer, open the Actions panel, and place this code in it:

```
//create the XML object
var myXML:XML = new XML();
//ignore white space
myXML.ignoreWhite = true;
//create the event for when data is loaded
myXML.onLoad=function(){
    myText_txt.text = this.firstChild.childNodes[0].nodeValue;
}
//load the web method result
myXML.load("http://localhost/hello.asmx/sayHello");
```

The preceding code first creates an XML object to absorb the Web service. It then sets the ignoreWhite property to true. After that, it creates the event callback for the XML object, so that when it receives data back, it will send the result to the text field. Finally, it loads the Web method.

Test the movie and you will see that the word "hello" has appeared in the text field.

---

**NOTE**

If you are running certain versions of the .NET framework, the preceding code may not work correctly by default. If this is the case, add this to the `web.config` file located on `c:\`:

```
<webServices>
        <protocols>
          <add name="HttpGet"/>
        </protocols>
</webServices>
```

Add the preceding code before the `</system.web>` closing tag, and then restart your computer.

---

That example demonstrated how to absorb a Web service with the XML object, but there is a much better way to do it using Flash Remoting.

# Flash Remoting

As mentioned in Chapter 23, "Integrating ColdFusion with Flash," Flash Remoting is a way of interacting with Web services in a whole new light. Instead of receiving XML back from the Web service, Flash Remoting returns objects that are easier to use and parse.

If you do not have Flash Remoting, you can download the free developer edition here:

```
http://www.macromedia.com/software/flashremoting/downloads/components/
```

Also, for Flash Remoting to work, you will need the .NET Framework Redistributable installed, which can be found here:

```
http://www.microsoft.com/downloads/details.aspx?FamilyId=262D25E3-F589-4842-
8157-034D1E7CF3A3&displaylang=en
```

When you complete the download, a new directory in your local host directory will be created called `flashremoting`. This directory is important because it will hold the gateway we need to go through in order to use Flash Remoting. Now you will be able to absorb Web services with it instead of using the XML object.

When connecting to a Web service with remoting, we use a different path than we do with the XML object. We place the path in a string literal followed by a question mark and `"WSDL"`. This is how Flash Remoting connects to Web services.

Also, when retrieving results, you build a function with the same name as the Web method you want it to collect from followed by `_Result`.

For example, if you had a Web method called `myWebMethod`, you would collect the results like this:

```
myWebMethod_Result = function(result){
    trace(result);
}
```

In the same file we just worked in, change the code in the first frame of the actions layer to this:

```
#include "NetServices.as"
#include "NetDebug.as"

//set the path for the gateway
gateway = "http://localhost/flashremoting/gateway.aspx";
//create the gateway connection
myConn = NetServices.createGatewayConnection(gateway);
//set the path to the service
service = "http://localhost/hello.asmx?WSDL";
//absorb the service
myServiceObject = myConn.getService(service, this);

//call the web method
myServiceObject.sayHello();
//when the web method receives results back
sayHello_Result = function(result){
    myText_txt.text=result;
}
```

This code first includes the necessary remoting files. Then it sets the path for the gateway in a variable and creates the gateway connection. After that, it creates the path to the Web service and connects to it. We then create the function to handle the results from the Web method being returned. Finally, we call the Web method.

Test the movie again, and you will get the same results as the preceding example.

Now that we are interacting successfully with our Web service, let's actually make the Web service useful.

In the following example, we will create a Web service that will accept a parameter, then square it, and return the results.

Open a text editor, create a new file and enter the following code, and then save the file to your Web root directory as squareService.asmx.

```
<%@ WebService Language="c#" debug="true" class="Square" %>
using System.IO;
```

```
using System.Web.Services;

public class Square: System.Web.Services.WebService{

  [WebMethod(Description="Square the number")]
  public  int squareNum(int sentNum) {
        int myReturn = sentNum*sentNum;
        return myReturn;
    }
}
```

Much like our previous Web service, this one starts off by declaring that it is a Web service written in C#. It then grabs the object classes we need. Next, it declares the Web service class. After that, we declare the Web method and set its description. Then we create the Web method. Notice we declare that the result being returned will be an integer. And the parameter being sent will also be an integer.

Save this file, and then browse to it and choose the squareNum Web method. You will see a screen like Figure 24.5. As you can see, the Web service has provided a field where we can place a number to test, so enter the number 2004, and click Invoke. You should then see another browser screen like Figure 24.6 indicating that it worked.

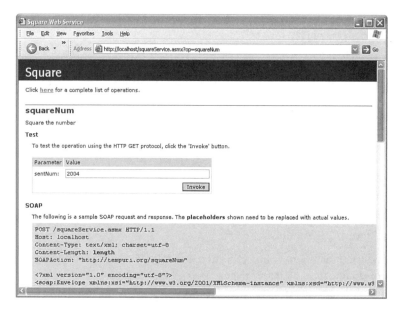

**FIGURE 24.5**   The Web service provides a field to test the Web method.

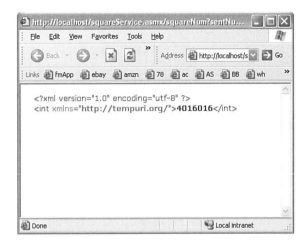

**FIGURE 24.6**   Use parameters in Web methods to make Web services work for you.

Okay, now we have the Web service working, so let's create the Flash application to use it.

1. Create a new Flash document.

2. Drag an instance of the `TextInput` component to the top left of the stage, give it an instance name of **number_ti**, and keep the default parameters.

3. Drag an instance of the `Button` component onto the stage right below the `TextInput` component; give it an instance name of **square_pb** and change its label to square.

4. Copy the instance of the `TextInput` component, and paste it under the `Button` component; change the instance name to **results_ti** and change its editable parameter to `false`.

   Your screen should now look like Figure 24.7.

5. Create a new layer called **actions**.

6. In the actions layer, open the Actions panel and place this code in:

```
#include "NetServices.as"
#include "NetDebug.as"


//set the path for the gateway
gateway = "http://localhost/flashremoting/gateway.aspx";
//create the gateway connection
myConn = NetServices.createGatewayConnection(gateway);
//set the path to the service
service = "http://localhost/squareService.asmx?WSDL";
//absorb the service
```

```
    myServiceObject = myConn.getService(service, this);

    //create the object to listen to the button component
    var clickListen:Object = new Object();
    //create the click event for the listener
    clickListen.click = function(){
        if(number_ti.text.length > 0){
            //call the web method
            myServiceObject.squareNum(Number(number_ti.text));
        }else{
            trace("error");
        }
    }
    //add the listener to the button component
    square_pb.addEventListener("click", clickListen);

    //when the web method receives results back
    squareNum_Result = function(result){
        results_ti.text=result;
    }
```

This code is doing a lot of things, so let's break it up into pieces and review what each
section is doing.

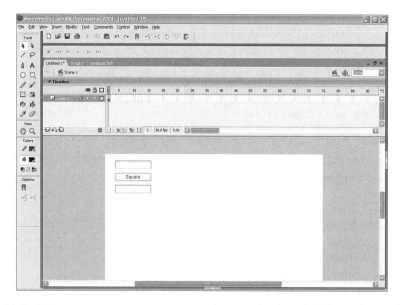

**FIGURE 24.7**   Using components, you can speed up production of Web service applications.

The first part of the code includes the external class files we will need to use remoting.

```
#include "NetServices.as"
#include "NetDebug.as"
```

Next, we create the path to the gateway, make the connection, create the path to the Web service, and finally connect to the Web service through the gateway.

```
//set the path for the gateway
gateway = "http://localhost/flashremoting/gateway.aspx";
//create the gateway connection
myConn = NetServices.createGatewayConnection(gateway);
//set the path to the service
service = "http://localhost/squareService.asmx?WSDL";
//absorb the service
myServiceObject = myConn.getService(service, this);
```

Then we create an object to listen to the button being clicked. We then create the event for the listener that checks to make sure the user has entered something into the input field. If so, it calls the Web method while passing the information from the input text field that is converted to a number because, as you might remember, data coming directly from a TextInput component will automatically be a string. Finally, we add the listener as an event listener to the Button component.

```
//create the object to listen to the button component
var clickListen:Object = new Object();
//create the click event for the listener
clickListen.click = function(){
    if(number_ti.text.length > 0){
        //call the web method
        myServiceObject.squareNum(Number(number_ti.text));
    }else{
        trace("error");
    }
}
//add the listener to the button component
square_pb.addEventListener("click", clickListen);
```

And the last section creates the function that will collect the results from the Web method and display them in the other text field.

```
//when the web method receives results back
squareNum_Result = function(result){
    results_ti.text=result;
}
```

If you are not using remoting, and would prefer to use XML, here is the code to use instead of the preceding:

```
//create the XML object
var myXML:XML = new XML();
//ignore the white space
myXML.ignoreWhite = true;

//create the object to listen to the button component
var clickListen:Object = new Object();
//create the click event for the listener
clickListen.click = function(){
    if(number_ti.text.length > 0){
        //load the XML
        myXML.load("http://localhost/squareService.asmx/squareNum?
➥sentNum="+Number(number_ti.text));
    }else{
        trace("error");
    }
}
//add the listener to the button component
square_pb.addEventListener("click", clickListen);

//when the XML object receives data
myXML.onLoad = function(){
    results_ti.text = this.firstChild.childNodes[0].nodeValue;
}
```

Now test the movie, and you will see that after you put in a number, and click the button to call the Web method, the results will be returned to the other `TextInput` component.

Now that you have seen how to create and consume Web services, let's create an application that will use an outside Web service.

## Consuming Outside Web Services

So far, the only Web services we have worked with are the ones we built ourselves. That's not the idea behind Web services. The idea is that anyone can build them, and anyone can use them as long as they know how to work with them.

There are a couple of great sites on the Web that store references to Web services for people to work with:

```
http://www.webservicex.net/WS/default.aspx
```

```
http://www.xmethods.com/
```

The one we will be using can be found at

`http://www.aspxpressway.com/maincontent/webservices/piglatin.asmx`

This Web service will translate a string of text we send it to pig Latin and return it.

For those not familiar with pig Latin, it's a language that moves the first letter from the front of certain words to the end, and adds an "ay" to it.

So if you have a sentence just like this, it would read like this:

So if you avehay a entencesay ustjay ikelay isthay, it ouldway eadray ikelay isthay.

And the following example will build an application to do just that.

1. Create a new Flash document.

2. Drag the `TextArea` component onto the stage; give it an instance name of **input_ta**, and change its dimensions to 250×130.

3. Now drag an instance of the `Button` component onto the stage under the `TextArea` component; give it an instance name of **translator_pb**, and change its label parameter to "Translate".

4. Create a new layer called **actions**.

5. In the first frame of the actions layer, open the Actions panel and place this code in:

```
#include "NetServices.as"
#include "NetDebug.as"

gateway = "http://localhost/flashremoting/gateway.aspx";
myConn = NetServices.createGatewayConnection(gateway);
service = "http://www.aspxpressway.com/maincontent/webservices/
➥piglatin.asmx?wsdl";
myServiceObject = myConn.getService(service, this);

//create the new object
var clickListen:Object = new Object();
//create the event for the listener
clickListen.click=function(){
    //get the text
    var myString_str:String = input_ta.text;
    //call the web method
    myServiceObject.toPigLatin(myString_str);
    //let the user know something is happening
    input_ta.text="translating . . . ";
    //don't let the user click the button until the method is done
    translator_pb.enabled = false;
```

24

```
    }
    //add the listener to the button
    translator_pb.addEventListener("click", clickListen);
    //collect the results from the web method
    toPigLatin_Result=function(result){
        //display the results
        input_ta.text=result;
        //turn the button back on
        translator_pb.enabled = true;
    }
```

Much like last time, this code does a lot, so let's look at it in sections.

The first section gets the necessary external class files and brings them in:

```
#include "NetServices.as"
#include "NetDebug.as"
```

The next section initializes the gateway and the service connection with the correct paths:

```
gateway = "http://localhost/flashremoting/gateway.aspx";
myConn = NetServices.createGatewayConnection(gateway);
service = "http://www.aspxpressway.com/maincontent/webservices/
➥piglatin.asmx?wsdl";
myServiceObject = myConn.getService(service, this);
```

After that, we create an object to listen to the button-click event. We then add the event callback to the listener. In the event callback, when the button is clicked, a variable is created that holds the information in the TextArea component. We then call the Web method to translate the text while passing the variable with the original text. After that, we place text in the component to show the user something is happening, and then we turn off the ability for the user to click the button again until the results have returned. Next, we add the event listener object to the Button component.

```
//create the new object
var clickListen:Object = new Object();
//create the event for the listener
clickListen.click=function(){
    //get the text
    var myString_str:String = input_ta.text;
    //call the web method
    myServiceObject.toPigLatin(myString_str);
    //let the user know something is happening
    input_ta.text="translating . . . ";
    //don't let the user click the button until the method is done
```

```
        translator_pb.enabled = false;
}
//add the listener to the button
translator_pb.addEventListener("click", clickListen);
```

Finally, we create the `results` function to collect the translated text coming back. It will display the results in the `TextArea` component, and turn the button back on to use again.

```
//collect the results from the web method
toPigLatin_Result=function(result){
    //display the results
    input_ta.text=result;
    //turn the button back on
    translator_pb.enabled = true;
}
```

Now test the movie, place this paragraph in (or one of your own), and click the Translate button. When the results are returned you should see something like Figure 24.8.

And if you are working with XML, replace the preceding code in the actions layer with this:

```
//create the XML object
var myXML:XML = new XML();
//ignore the white space
myXML.ignoreWhite = true;

//create the path to the web service
var thePath:String = "http://www.aspxpressway.com/maincontent/webservices/
➥piglatin.asmx/toPigLatin?textToTranslate=";
//create the new object
var clickListen:Object = new Object();
//create the event for the listener
clickListen.click=function(){
    //get the text
    var myString_str:String = input_ta.text;
    //call the web method
    myXML.load(thePath+myString_str);
    //let the user know something is happening
    input_ta.text="translating . . . ";
    //don't let the user click the button until the method is done
    translator_pb.enabled = false;
}
//add the listener to the button
```

24

```
translator_pb.addEventListener("click", clickListen);
//collect the results from the web method
myXML.onLoad=function(){
    //display the results
    input_ta.text=this.firstChild.childNodes[0].nodeValue;
    //turn the button back on
    translator_pb.enabled = true;
}
```

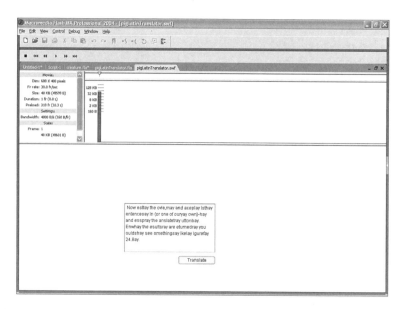

**FIGURE 24.8**   Experiment with other Web services that have been built to create some very interesting applications.

Like most everything in Flash, there is always more than one way to do it. And this next section is going to show you the quick and easy way to tie into Web services.

## The Web Services Panel

The Web Services panel is an easy way to keep track of all of your Web services you are working or experimenting with. To open it, go to Window, Development Panels, Web Services.

The window that opens up will look like Figure 24.9. You will see two buttons at the top, the Define Web Services and the Refresh Web Services buttons. The Refresh Web Services button will refresh all the information with regards to the current Web services in the panel. The Define Web Services button will add Web services.

Click the Define Web Services button to see the Define Web Services dialog box as in Figure 24.10. Add the three Web services we have used so far:

- `http://localhost/hello.asmx?WSDL`

- `http://localhost/squareService.asmx?WSDL`

- `http://www.aspxpressway.com/maincontent/Webservices/piglatin.asmx?WSDL`

**FIGURE 24.9**   The Web Services panel.

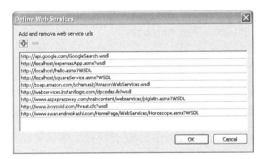

**FIGURE 24.10**   The Define Web Services dialog box.

Now that you have the three Web services in the dialog box, click OK to return to the Web Services panel, and you should see all three listed there. If you click the plus signs beside them, they will expand to show you all Web methods as well as results and parameters for each one.

This panel is an invaluable tool for working with Web services. You can put your Web service in, and instantly see everything you need to know about it. It also ties into the `WebServiceConnector` component.

## The `WebServiceConnector` **Component**

The `WebServiceConnector` component is designed to easily and quickly connect to Web services on the Web. To use it, simply drag it onto the stage, set the URL for the Web service, and trigger it.

Data from the `WebServiceConnector` comes back as an object as you will see in the following example.

1.  Create a new Flash document.

2.  Drag an instance of the `WebServiceConnector` component onto the stage; give it an instance name of `myConnector`, set its WSDLURL parameter to `http://localhost/hello.asmx?WSDL` (because you put it in the Web Services panel, you can actually just use the drop-down menu and choose it), and then set the operation parameter to `sayHello` (it will be the only choice in the drop-down).

3.  Now drag an instance of the `TextInput` component onto the stage; give it an instance name of **results_ti**.

4.  Now create a new layer called **actions**.

5.  In the first frame of the actions layer, open the Actions panel, and place this code in:

    ```
    //create an object to listen for when the WebServiceConnector receives data
    var resultListen:Object = new Object();
    //create the event for the listener
    resultListen.result=function (myResults) {
        results_ti.text = myResults.target.results;
    }
    //add the event listener to the WebServiceConnector
    myConnector.addEventListener("result", resultListen);
    //connect to the web service
    myConnector.trigger();
    ```

The preceding code creates a listener object for the `WebServiceConnector` component. It then creates an event callback passing it one parameter, the `myResults` parameter, which will be the results coming back from the Web service. We then add the event listener to the `WebServiceConnector`, and finally call the `trigger()` method, which will activate the `WebServiceConnector`.

When you test the movie, you will get the same result as before using this Web service. This example just shows how simple it is to connect to Web services using the `WebServiceConnector`.

But what if it were simpler?

1.  Return to the stage, and open up the Actions panel in the first frame of the actions layer. Remove all but the last line, so the code should now read like this:

    ```
    myConnector.trigger();
    ```

2. Now select the `WebServiceConnector` component, go to the Component Inspector panel (Window, Development Panels, Component Inspector), and select the Binding tab.

3. Select the Add Binding button, and the panel should then look like Figure 24.11. Choose `results:String` and click OK.

4. Now you will see the "results" data binding in the Component Inspector panel. Select it, and click in the `bound to` field.

5. When you do this, a magnifying glass will appear at the end of the field. Select it, and the Bound To dialog box appears as shown in Figure 24.12.

6. Select the `TextInput` component in the left window, and click OK.

Now test the movie again.

Again, you get the exact same results as before, but the difference is the only ActionScript in this file is the line that activates the `WebServiceConnector` component.

**FIGURE 24.11**   The Add Binding dialog box used to add data bindings between components for fast development.

Now let's revisit the `squareService` Web service we built a while back, but this time we will use the `WebServiceConnector` component to take out a lot of the hard work. Again, the only code we will need is the code that will activate the connection.

1. Create a new Flash document.

2. Drag an instance of the `WebServiceConnector` component onto the stage, and give it an instance name of `myConnector`; set the `WSDLURL` parameter to `http://localhost/squareService.asmx?WSDL`, and set the operation parameter to `squareNum`.

3. Now drag an instance of the `TextInput` component onto the stage and give it an instance name of `num_ti`.

4. Drag an instance of the `Button` component onto the stage under the `num_ti` `TextInput` component; give it an instance name of `square_pb`, and change its label to `square`.

5. Copy the `TextInput` component, and paste it under the button; change its instance name to `results_ti`.

6. Select the `myConnector` `WebServiceConnector`, and open the Component Inspector panel.

7. As you did before, choose the Binding tab, and select Add Binding; select `sentNum:` `Integer` and click OK.

8. Select the Bound To field, bind it to the `num_ti` `TextInput` component, and click OK.

9. This time, we will be do something a little different. Now select the Formatter field and choose Number Formatter (this will format the information of the `TextInput` component to a number so it can be used with the Web service).

10. Now select Add Binding again, and choose `results:Integer`.

11. Select the Bound To field and bind it to the `results_ti` `TextInput` component.

12. Now create a new layer called **actions**.

13. Place the following code in the first frame of the actions layer:

```
//create the listener object
var clickListen:Object = new Object();
//add the event to the listener
clickListen.click = function(){
    myConnector.trigger();
}
//finally add the event listener to the button
square_pb.addEventListener("click", clickListen);
```

The preceding code is nothing new; we create the event listener object. Then we set the event to the listener that will trigger the `WebServiceConnector` to activate. And finally, we add the event listener to the `Button` component.

Test the movie, and you will see the same results as before, but this time with very little coding at all.

Using the `WebServiceConnector` component makes creating Web-service–ready applications quick and easy. Use it to experiment with other Web services.

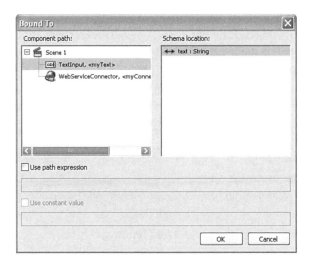

**FIGURE 24.12** The Bound To dialog box.

Now that you have seen how to absorb Web services created by other people, you might want to start working on some of the major Web services on the Web such as the Amazon.com Web service found at:

```
http://www.amazon.com/gp/aws/landing.html/002-9580473-9832806
```

Or possibly you might want to experiment with the Web service API of the mother of all search engines, Google.

## Absorbing the Google Web Service

Google is one of the most well-known search engines on the planet, and they have opened up their search engine to the public for free.

With the Google Web service, you can search the Web for anything, and have the results sent back to an application you design and build.

The first thing you will have to do is get your key from Google by signing up at

```
http://www.google.com/apis/
```

The key lets Google know who is using the search engine, and you are only allowed 1000 requests per day, but that's plenty.

When you have gotten your personal key, you will need to download the sample file for this application from the accompanying Web site. The application itself has everything but the key.

The purpose of this application is to see the power of Web services. This example will allow you to search at will, and it will return 10 results each time. When one of those results is selected, it will display a short description of the link. And if you have selected a link, you can launch it into a browser window using the Launch Link button.

When you have downloaded the sample application and have gotten your key, open the file googleSearch.fla and follow these steps to make it work:

1.  Select the WebServiceConnector component in the top left of the stage.

2.  Open the Component Inspector panel (Window, Development Panels, Component Inspector).

3.  Select the Binding tab where you will see a list of all the bindings that have already been set.

4.  Choose the first binding, the params.key binding.

5.  Select the Bound To field, and click the magnifying glass that appears.

6.  When the Bound To dialog appears, select the bottom check box, Use a Constant Value.

7.  Then in the accompanying field, type in your key.

8.  Click OK, and test the application, which should look like Figure 24.13.

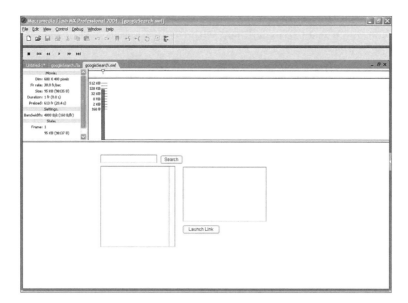

**FIGURE 24.13**    The Google search application using Web services.

Let's go over the code in the first frame of the actions layer.

The first section creates the object to listen to the search button. We then assign the event to it that, when triggered, will activate the WebServiceConnector component. It will also clear the description because there is new data coming back. And finally, we add the event listener to the Search button.

```
//create the search object
var searchListen:Object = new Object();
//create the event for search button listener
searchListen.click=function(){
    //trigger the WebServiceConnector
    myConnector.trigger();
    //clear the description field
    description_ta.text = "";
}
//add the event to the search button
search_pb.addEventListener("click", searchListen);
```

The next section creates another listener object, this time for the List component. When the event is triggered, the description text component will display the information from the actual WebServiceConnector component based on which element was selected. And as before, the event listener is added to the instance of the List component.

```
//create the listener object for the list component
var listListen:Object = new Object();
//add the event to the listener
listListen.change=function(){
    //send a description to the text field
    description_ta.text=myConnector.results.resultElements
➥[list_lb.selectedIndex].snippet;
}
//add the listener for the list component
list_lb.addEventListener("change", listListen);
```

The final section again creates another listener object, this time for the Launch button, that will allow users interested in the search results to view the Web page. Then the event is added that will call the getURL() method and place the content in its own browser window. Finally, the event listener is added to the launch button.

```
//create the object for the launch button
var launchListen:Object = new Object();
//create the event for the listener
launchListen.click=function(){
    getURL(list_lb.value,"_blank");
}
```

24

```
//add the event to the launch button
launch_pb.addEventListener("click", launchListen);
```

This application is not using all the results that are returned. Use the Web Services panel to see what else is available, such as the total number of results as well as the amount of time it took to search for a given topic. The possibilities are endless, and this application is merely a good start.

## Summary

This chapter covered a lot of material pertaining to Web services and their integration into Flash. If Web services are the future in middleware, and Flash is the future of application front ends, it's a perfect match.

Follow the links to other Web services provided earlier in this chapter, and add them to the Web Services panel to see how to use and experiment with them.

This section ends the data integration part of the book, but the next chapter goes in a different direction with dynamic content covering Flash's new streaming technologies.

CHAPTER **25**

# Streaming Media

Earlier in this book, in Chapter 7, "Working with Sound and Video," we covered how Flash can import and work with video. This chapter takes that a step further by showing not only how to import video, but also how to convert it to Flash's proprietary video format Flash Video. We will also go over how to work with this video format, along with other media formats, to create a more media-centric application.

## Why Stream Media?

Flash is not just a Web application tool or a vector animation application; it is also a media creation tool. Even though you can import video and sound into Flash and then use it, that creates large file sizes in most instances. This is where streaming comes in.

**Streaming** is the ability to load a file, and as soon as it begins loading.

So what does this mean? Well, in previous versions of Flash, the only type of media that could have been streamed was MP3 (unless, of course, you were using the Flash Communication server). But now, with the introduction of Flash MX 2004, you can also stream video in the Flash 7 Player without any server software. This means that anyone can take nearly any video they create, and with a few clicks of a button, have it streaming on the Web.

A great benefit of streaming technology is the ability to keep the video outside the main file, thereby making the main file size that much smaller.

But before you can stream video, you need to know how to create video in the format Flash will be able to stream.

# Creating a Flash Video

There are several programs that will allow the conversion of normal video directly to Flash Video format (.flv). There is also a plug-in available that will work with most video editing programs, allowing you to save as Flash Video. And of course, the Flash Communication Server has the ability to record video from Flash directly into Flash Video (FLV). But, if you don't feel like paying for any of these, Flash has a way of converting video to FLV as well.

When you bring video into Flash, you can then export directly from the video's property dialog box to FLV.

Follow these steps to create your first Flash video:

1.  Create a new Flash document.

2.  Choose File, Import, Import to Library, which will pop open the Import to Library dialog box and allow you to choose a video.

    Flash can import most video formats, including

    - .wmv

    - .avi

    - .mov

    - .asf

    - .flv

    - .mpg

    - .mpeg

    - .dv

    - .dvi

    It does not, however, support Real Player video.

3.  After you have chosen your favorite video to import, the Video Import Wizard will open as shown in Figure 25.1. For this example, we will import the entire video, so choose that option and click Next.

4.  The next screen will allow you to choose the quality of the video and make minor adjustments to the coloring and shading of the video, as you can see in Figure 25.2. Keep the default settings for the time being, and choose Finish.

> **NOTE**
>
> When you're choosing the video quality for an imported video, keep in mind what speeds your audience will be using. The higher the quality, the higher the file size, and the longer the video will take to completely stream.

5. When the video has finished importing, open up your library (Window, Library) and you will see the video. Select it and click the info button at the bottom of the library (or right-click it and choose Properties), and you will see the properties dialog box for the video. Here you can update the video by choosing Update. You can also import FLV files directly, and finally, you can export.

6. After you click Export, the Export FLV window will appear allowing you to choose where you want to save this FLV. So give it a name, choose the desktop, and click Save.

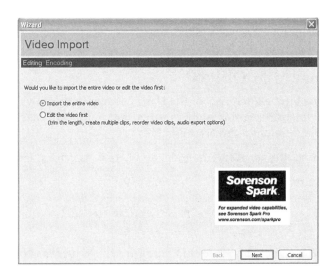

**FIGURE 25.1**    The Video Import Wizard.

That was it; you have now made your first Flash video. And not only was it easy, but it was free (provided you already own Flash, of course). Now that you have the video, let's go over what is necessary to stream into Flash.

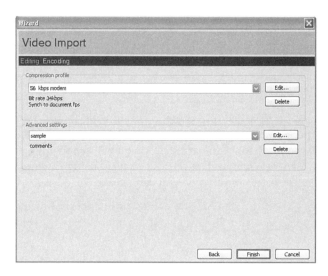

**FIGURE 25.2**    Options for importing external video.

## The NetConnection Object

The NetConnection object allows users of the Flash 7 Player to stream video or audio directly into Flash. If NetConnection is used in the Flash 6 Player, it must be in conjunction with the Flash Communication Server.

It has a single method, the connect() method, and here is its general layout:

```
myConn.connect(null);
```

When you call the connect method, you pass the parameter null so that it will create a local connection.

This object by itself is useless, but in conjunction with the NetStream object, it is very important.

## The NetStream Object

The NetStream object class allows the control of streaming video through the NetConnection object. The NetStream object has several properties, methods, and an event to assist in controlling the playing of video as well as monitoring its progress.

When instantiating a new NetStream object, you pass it the NetConnection object that the video will go through, like this:

```
//first create an instance of the object
var netCon:NetConnection = new NetConnection();
//now call the connect method
netCon.connect(null);
```

```
//Create the NetStream object
var myStream:NetStream = new NetStream(netCon);
```

Notice that we create a `NetConnection` object, call the `connect()` method, and then create an instance of the `NetStream` object, passing it the `NetConnection`.

Here are some of the methods and properties for the `NetStream` object that we will be using throughout this chapter.

### The play() Method

The `play()` method for the `NetStream` object is used to begin the streaming of a certain Flash Video. You pass the string literal path of the FLV as a parameter in this method like this:

```
myNetStream.play("myVideo.flv");
```

When this method is called, if the video is found it will begin to stream. If the video is not found, the `onStatus` event is invoked.

> **NOTE**
>
> Just calling the `NetStream.play()` method will not display the video. The video must be attached to a `Video` object first. However, the audio from the Flash Video will begin to start playing automatically.

### The pause() Method

The `pause()` method can be misleading if used incorrectly. It not only pauses an incoming video, but it can also resume play.

Its generic layout is as follows:

```
myNetStream.pause(pauseResume);
```

The only parameter is the `pauseResume` parameter, which is a Boolean value passed to the method saying whether to pause or resume the video feed:

- `true`—Pauses the video
- `false`—Resumes the video from its current position

If the parameter is left out, the `pause()` method will switch back and forth between resuming and pausing like a toggle switch.

### The close() Method

The `close` method will stop all streaming media coming into the `NetStream` instance and will reset the `NetStream` itself to be used for another video.

Its generic layout looks like this:

```
myNetStream.close();
```

## The `seek()` Method

The `seek()` method will allow users to move to a certain point in the stream. It does this by going to the closest keyframe that matches the number of seconds passed into the `seek()` method. When the stream reaches that point, it will resume playing.

Its generic layout is as follows:

```
myNetStream.seek(seconds);
```

The `seconds` parameter is the number of seconds since the beginning of the video, where playback would preferably begin. You can use this method in several ways:

```
myStream.seek(20);    //moves to the 20 seconds spot
myStream.seek(0);    //moves to the beginning of the stream
myStream.seek(myStream.time - 10);
//moves to the current position minus 10 seconds
```

## The `setBufferTime()` Method

The `setBufferTime()` method is an important one because it controls how many seconds must be in the buffer before the stream can begin playing. Use this method to control playback of the stream especially on slow connections.

Its generic layout is like this:

```
myStream.setBufferTime(seconds);
```

The only parameter is the `seconds` parameter specifying how many seconds to have in the buffer before playing. The default value is 0.1 (one-tenth of a second).

## The `onStatus` Event

The `onStatus` event is the only event for the `NetStream` object, and it is triggered often. Whenever any aspect of a `NetStream` instance changes, the event is triggered and can pass information about what caused the event.

The generic layout for this event is in a callback like this:

```
myStream.onStatus = function(infoObj){
    //code to run
}
```

The one parameter associated with this event is the `infoObj` parameter. This parameter is a reference to an object that will store information about the triggering event.

The `infoObj` parameter has two properties, the `code` property giving information on what caused the status change, and the `level` property showing whether it was a simple status change or an error.

Table 25.1 shows the different values for the `code` property and their meanings.

**TABLE 25.1**   Possible Values for the `Code` Property

| Code | Level | Description |
| --- | --- | --- |
| NetStream.Play.Start | Status | The stream has begun playing. |
| NetStream.Play.Stop | Status | The stream has stopped playing. |
| NetStream.Buffer.Full | Status | The buffer has reached its defined point in seconds, and the stream will begin to play. |
| NetStream.Buffer.Empty | Status | Data from the stream is not filling the buffer fast enough, and playback will stop until the buffer is full again. |
| NetStream.Play.StreamNotFound | Error | Flash cannot find the FLV. |

And all of these properties can be received by being called on the `infoObj` parameter within the `onStatus` event like this:

```
myStream.onStatus = function(infoObj){
    trace(infoObj.code);
    trace(infoObj.level);
}
```

Those were the methods and event for the `NetStream` object, and it also has a few properties.

### Properties of the `NetStream` Object

Here are just a few of the properties of the `NetStream` object that you might use when working with streaming video:

- `bufferLength`—The number of seconds currently in the buffer
- `time`—The position in the stream where the playhead is in seconds
- `currentFps`—The current frames per second the stream is displaying
- `bufferTime`—The number of seconds that must be in the buffer before it is full

Now you know how to get the video in, but before you can see anything, you have to attach the stream coming in to a `Video` object.

## The Video Object

Although you may not have known it, we already created one video object when we imported the video into Flash. Video objects do more than that, though; they allow developers to display video streaming from external sources. To do this, you have to create a blank video object.

Follow these steps to create a new blank video object:

1. Start a new Flash document.

2. Open the library (Window, Library).

3. Select the Options drop-down in the top right of the library and choose New Video.

Now if you want to use it, just drag it out onto the stage, and give it an instance name so that you can refer to it in ActionScript.

And that was it—you now have a blank video object on the stage.

The Video object has a few methods and properties, but the one we will be using is the attachVideo() method.

### The attachVideo() Method

The attachVideo() method allows video being streamed to a NetStream object to be viewed on the stage. You can also set a Camera object to it (more on the Camera object later in this chapter).

The generic layout to attach a NetStream to a Video object is as follows:

```
myVideo.attachVideo(myStream);
```

The only parameter passed is the NetStream object being displayed.

We have covered a lot of code that shows how to create a video stream. Now let's put it all together.

## Streaming Video

This section will bring together all the steps we have gone over so far into a media streaming application.

The first step is to either create your own Flash Video using the steps we went over earlier or download the one from the companion Web site.

When you have the Flash video, follow these steps to build a simple video streaming application:

1. Create a new Flash document.

2. Save it as **videoStream.fla** in the same directory as the Flash Video cats.flv.

3. Create a new blank video object the same way we did earlier.

4. Drag the blank video object out of the library and onto the stage. Give it an instance name of **myVideo**, and change its dimensions to 200×160.

5. Drag an instance of the `Button` component onto the stage and place it under the instance of the `Video` object.

6. Give the button an instance name of **play_pb** and change its label to "Play".

7. Create a dynamic text field, give it an instance name of status_txt, turn the border on, and set it beside the play button.

8. Create a new layer called **actions**.

9. In the first frame of the actions layer, open the Actions panel, and place this code in:

```
//Create the NetConnection object:
var myConn:NetConnection = new NetConnection();
//Create the connection
myConn.connect(null);
//Create the NetStream object
var myStream:NetStream = new NetStream(myConn);
//Set the onStatus event for the NetStream object
myStream.onStatus = function(infoObject){
    status_txt.text=infoObject.code;
}
//Attach the NetStream video to the Video object
myVideo.attachVideo(myStream);
//Set the buffer time
myStream.setBufferTime(5);
//create a variable to see if we have played the video yet
var played:Boolean = false;
//create an object to listen to our play button
var clickListen:Object = new Object();
//create the event for the listener
clickListen.click = function(){
    if(!played){
        myStream.play("cats.flv");
        played = true;
        play_pb.label = "Pause";
    }else{
        if(play_pb.label == "Play"){
            play_pb.label = "Pause";
        }else{
            play_pb.label = "Play";
        }
        myStream.pause();
    }
}
//now add the listener to the button
play_pb.addEventListener("click", clickListen);
```

This code accomplishes several things; let's break it up into sections so that it can be more easily analyzed.

The first section creates a `NetConnection` object and then calls the `connect()` method to make a local connection:

```
    //Create the NetConnection object:
var myConn:NetConnection = new NetConnection();
//Create the connection
myConn.connect(null);
```

The next section creates the `NetStream` object and sets its `onStatus` event to send what caused the event to the text field we created.

```
//Create the NetStream object
var myStream:NetStream = new NetStream(myConn);
//Set the onStatus event for the NetStream object
myStream.onStatus = function(infoObject){
    status_txt.text=infoObject.code;
}
```

The next section attaches the `NetStream` video to the video object. Then it sets the buffer time (but because we are running local, it really doesn't matter). And finally, it creates a variable we will use to see if the video has started streaming yet or not.

```
//Attach the NetStream video to the Video object
myVideo.attachVideo(myStream);
//Set the buffer time
myStream.setBufferTime(5);
//create a variable to see if we have played the video yet
var played:Boolean = false;
```

In the final section, we create a listener to listen to the play button component. We create the event for the listener that checks to see if the user has started streaming the video yet. If the video has not started streaming yet, it will start; set the variable to `true` so it won't try to start it again, and set the label for the play button to "Pause" so that the user will know it is playing. After that, if the user clicks the button again, it checks the label to see what the user is trying to do, and either plays or pauses the movie accordingly. Finally, we add the event listener to the `Button` component.

```
//create an object to listen to our play button
var clickListen:Object = new Object();
//create the event for the listener
clickListen.click = function(){
    if(!played){
        myStream.play("cats.flv");
        played = true;
```

```
            play_pb.label = "Pause";
    }else{
        if(play_pb.label == "Play"){
            play_pb.label = "Pause";
        }else{
            play_pb.label = "Play";
        }
        myStream.pause();
    }
}
//now add the listener to the button
play_pb.addEventListener("click", clickListen);
```

Test the movie and click the play button; you will see something similar to Figure 25.3. You can then pause and resume play, and the text field shows you when the onStatus event fires.

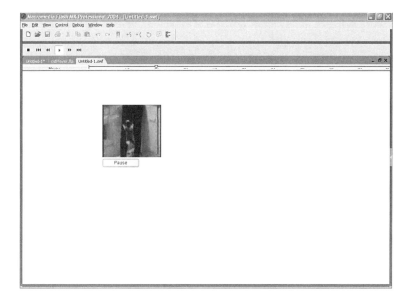

**FIGURE 25.3**    Streaming video is a snap now in Flash MX 2004.

Now that you have coded all of that, and built the video streaming application, we move on to the easy way to do it using the media components.

## The Media Components

With Flash MX 2004 Professional come a lot of components including the set of media components that will help speed application development of streaming media applications.

There are three media components:

- MediaController
- MediaDisplay
- MediaPlayback

The MediaPlayback component is the one we will be working with because it is basically the other two media components rolled into one.

With the MediaPlayback component, you can drag it onto the stage, set a single parameter, and you now have a streaming media application. It is really that easy, as you will see.

Before we build one, we should look at its parameters. Drag an instance of the MediaPlayback onto the stage, select it, and open the Component Inspector (Window, Development Panels, Component Inspector). As you can see in Figure 25.4, this is not your normal parameters panel. With this unique parameters menu, you can select several options including having the ability to stream MP3s instead of video. The parameter we will be setting is the URL parameter, which is the path to the video we are going to load.

**FIGURE 25.4**    The Component Inspector for the MediaPlayback component.

Now let's see how easy it is to create a media streaming application with this media component.

1. Create a new Flash document.

2. Save it in the same directory as the Flash Video as `mediaStreamerComponent.fla`.

3. Drag an instance of the `MediaPlayback` component onto the stage.

4. Set its URL parameter to `cats.flv`.

5. Test the movie.

That's it! That is all it took to build a streaming media application.

That was how to stream video, but there is another object you can send to the `Video` object: the `Camera` object.

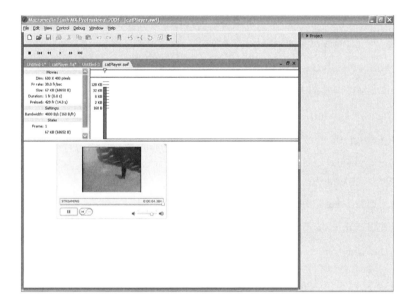

**FIGURE 25.5**    Use the media components to build streaming media applications quickly.

## The `Camera` **Object**

The `Camera` object, which is available in the Flash 6 Player, but is undocumented there, is a way to get to Web cams running on local machines. It isn't really streaming but is a lot of fun to work with, and it can be placed in the `Video` object, so I put it in this chapter.

The `Camera` object has a lot of methods, properties, and events, but the two we are going to focus on are the `get()` method and the `activityLevel` property.

## The `get()` Method

The `get()` method for the `Camera` object is used to get the Web cam. If more than one Web cam is attached to your computer, you can choose which one you want to work with; otherwise, the `get()` method will use the default camera.

The generic layout for the `get()` method is as follows:

```
myCamera.get(index);
```

The parameter `index` is used in case there is more than one camera attached to the computer. It is a numerical value representing each camera, starting at zero.

## The `activityLevel` Property

The `activityLevel` property returns the amount of visual activity the camera is detecting ranging from zero to 100.

This property will only work when you have created an `onActivity` event callback.

Now let's see the `Camera` object at work:

1. Create a new Flash document.

2. Create a blank video object as you did before.

3. Drag the blank video object onto the stage and give it an instance name of **myVideo**.

4. Create a dynamic text field under the blank video object.

5. Give the text field an instance name of **activity_txt** and make sure the `border` property is turned on.

6. Create a new layer called **actions**.

7. In the first frame of the actions layer, open the Actions panel and place this code in:

```
//get the web cam
myCam = Camera.get();
//create the function to monitor the activity
this.onEnterFrame = function(){
    activity_txt.text = myCam.activityLevel;
}
//create a blank event handler to start the activityLevel property
myCam.onActivity=function(){};
//attach the cam to the video object
myVideo.attachVideo(Camera.get());
```

The preceding code creates a reference to the Web cam we are getting. Then it creates a constantly repeating event that will send the `activityLevel` of the Web cam to the text field. After that, we create a blank event callback for the `onActivity` event to initialize the `activityLevel` property. Finally, we attach the video from the Web cam to the `Video` object.

Test the movie, and you will see something like Figure 25.6. If you get a pop-up asking to allow local access to your Web cam or microphone, go ahead and allow it so that it will work.

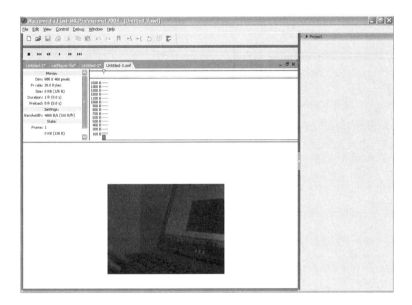

**FIGURE 25.6**   Use a Web cam as another means of sending video to the `Video` object.

## Summary

This chapter covered the basics of streaming media into Flash as well as some of the reasons behind it including smaller file size. We went over all the major objects required to stream media including the `NetConnection`, `NetStream`, and the `Video` objects as well as the components that make building streaming video applications a breeze. We finished up with another approach to putting video into Flash by means of a Web cam using the `Camera` object.

Streaming video in Flash is a major step forward for making Flash a central application development tool for a rich Internet experience.

# CHAPTER 26

# Extending the Flash Authoring Environment

In the new version of Flash, Macromedia was not satisfied with just creating a better authoring environment and more tools to create better content. They have also added the ability for any user to extend the authoring environment using the extensibility layer.

The extensibility layer allows users to create custom tools and panels as well as personalized commands, behaviors, and effects. Most of this is accomplished with either the new JavaScript Flash Language (JSFL) or using XML-driven GUI interfaces.

To go over every individual piece of code the JSFL has and every way to use it is beyond the scope of this chapter. But this chapter covers each item that can be built in the extensibility layer, and goes over some basic uses of JSFL and the XML-to-UI interface.

## Why Extend Flash?

I remember in previous versions of Flash always wanting some tool that didn't exist, or a panel to take care of something that hadn't been made yet. Now, I can do more than just want them—I can create them.

When Macromedia gave the ability to extend the Flash authoring environment to all users, they gave us the power to make the newest version of Flash our own. You can create your own panel sets to do certain things. You can create your own custom tools to draw more shapes than just circles and squares. You can create custom commands to do repetitive tasks and then link them to shortcuts. You can even create your own behaviors, which are small, reuseable pieces of code, and effects, which are reuseable visual controls for objects.

The first extendable item covered in this chapter is the command.

# Commands

JSFL commands are reuseable pieces of JSFL code that control any aspect of the Flash's DOM (Document Object Model). This means that commands can be written to do anything that you do manually in the Flash authoring environment plus a lot more. They can do just about anything ranging from drawing a simple line on the stage all the way to saving the document with custom settings.

Not only can they be written manually in JSFL, but they can also be created directly from the History panel.

## The History Panel

The History panel is new to Flash MX 2004. It records each step taking place in the authoring environment. You can open the History panel by choosing Window, Other Panels, History. Figure 26.1 shows the History panel.

**FIGURE 26.1**   The History panel.

The History panel has several control features including the slide bar, which will allow you to go back to a certain point, or record up to that point into a command. You can also replay a selected step by selecting the step and clicking the Replay button. The two options on the bottom right of the History panel are used in creating commands. The first will copy a selected step or steps in JSFL to the clipboard, and the second button will save those steps as a command.

Before we go over how to create a command, there are also a few options for the History panel; one in particular is the view. The default view for the History panel shows the names of the steps being taken, as you can see in Figure 26.1. To get used to JSFL, you should switch the view to JavaScript in Panel by choosing View, JavaScript in Panel. This will show the JSFL commands being called as shown in Figure 26.2. After this option is changed, you will be able to view the JSFL commands that are being run as well as any parameters being passed to the commands.

**FIGURE 26.2**    The names of the commands are replaced with the actual JSFL commands.

To see the process of replaying a command, follow these steps:

1. Create a new Flash document.

2. Open the History panel by choosing Window, Other Panels, History.

3. Make sure the History panel's view setting is set to JavaScript in Panel.

4. Draw a square on the stage and a command will appear in the History panel similar to this:

```
fl.getDocumentDOM().addNewRectangle(
➥{left:107.0, top:105, right:203.0, bottom:201}, 0);
```

This command creates a rectangle with several parameters showing position and size of the square.

5. Now highlight the entire square, including its stroke, and delete it. Another command should appear in the History panel similar to this:

```
fl.getDocumentDOM().setSelectionRect(
➥{left:1, top:69, right:322.0, bottom:287.9});
fl.getDocumentDOM().deleteSelection();
```

These commands create a selection rectangle to highlight the rectangle shape we created and then delete it.

6. Now that your stage is blank, select the command that created the rectangle, and click the Replay button.

26

You will see the rectangle reappear again. If you moved or deleted the rectangle, and then selected the same command and clicked Replay again, it would still work.

That example demonstrated how to replay a step in the History panel. Now we are going to see how to save a step or groups of steps as commands.

## Saving Commands from the History Panel

Creating commands from the History panel is the quickest and simplest way to create commands. You simply highlight the steps you want to become a command, and click the Save Selected Steps as a Command button.

Follow these steps to do an example of creating your first command in the History panel:

1. Create a new Flash document.

2. Make sure the History panel is open and you can see the JSFL commands in the view.

3. Draw a square on the stage.

4. Choose Edit, Select All, and this command should appear in the History panel.

   ```
   fl.getDocumentDOM().selectAll();
   ```

   This command selects everything on the stage.

5. Now press the Delete key, which will delete the square as well as put the delete command in the History panel again.

6. Highlight the selection command and the delete command in the History panel and click the Save Selected Steps as a Command button, which will pop up the Save As Command dialog box as shown in Figure 26.3.

7. Give the command the name "Delete All" and click OK.

8. Now on the stage, draw several different shapes, lines or curves.

9. Go to Commands in the menu bar, and you will see the new command you just created. Select it and everything on the stage will be deleted.

   That was a good example of a useable command, but you have to go to Commands to get to it every time, which takes two clicks more than necessary. So now let's add a shortcut key combination to this new command.

10. Choose Edit, Keyboard Shortcuts from the menu bar, which will pop up the Keyboard Shortcuts dialog box.

11. In order to create your own shortcut keys, you must make a copy of the default Keyboard Shortcuts by choosing the Duplicate Set button; give the new set the name "Flash Unleashed."

12. Now select Drawing Menu Commands from the Commands drop-down menu as in Figure 26.4. Then select the Add Shortcut button (the plus sign).

13. Now in the Press Key field, press Ctrl+Alt+D at the same time, click Change, and then click OK.

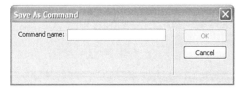

**FIGURE 26.3**    The Save As Command dialog box where you name your commands.

Now you will be able to use that keyboard combination as a shortcut for the command, and if you select Commands from the menu bar, you will see that the command you just created now has a shortcut associated with it.

**FIGURE 26.4**    Create custom shortcut key combinations for your new commands.

That was how to make a command with the History panel. It was quick and easy, but not all that powerful because we could not customize it to the way we want. In the next section, we will cover how to create commands manually using JSFL.

## Creating Commands Manually with JSFL

Building commands from scratch is a little more difficult and requires correct coding of JSFL or errors will appear. However, it's more powerful than creating commands from the History panel because there are more commands available.

To create a JSFL file, select File, New and choose Flash JavaScript File. This will change the entire authoring environment to look like Figure 26.5. The stage will disappear, there will be an actions window filling up most of the authoring environment, and the surrounding area will be grayed out for the most part.

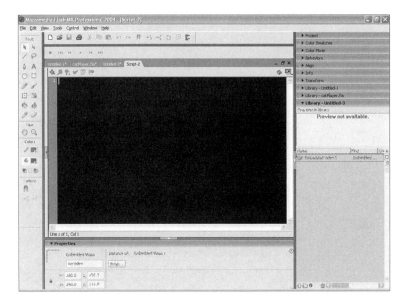

**FIGURE 26.5** The authoring environment for creating JSFL files.

This actions window acts in much the same way the Actions panel does. You can type in code manually, or use the Add New Script button.

Let's jump right in and create a very basic command that will send a string to the Output panel while still in the authoring environment.

1. Create a new Flash JavaScript file.

2. Place this code within the file:

```
fl.trace("my first manual command");
```

3. Now save this command to your desktop as `traceMe.jsfl`.

4. Create a new Flash document.

5. Choose Commands, Run Command, which will open the Open File dialog box. Choose the `traceMe.jsfl` command and the Output panel should then look like Figure 26.6.

**FIGURE 26.6**   Create manual commands to accomplish tasks in the authoring environment.

That was a pretty basic example, and we will return to it in a following section.

In this situation, we use the Run Command option from the Commands menu, but if you wanted it to appear with the other commands, you would have to place the JSFL file in the Commands directory located at `C:\Program Files\Macromedia\Flash MX 2004\en\First Run\Commands` for Windows and `Applications\Macromedia\Flash MX 2004\en\First Run\Commands` for Macs. Then reboot Flash for the new command to be visible in the Commands menu.

Now that you know how to create commands two different ways, we can go over how to manage those commands.

## Managing Commands

Managing commands is pretty easy. Select Commands, Manage Saved Commands for the Manage Saved Commands window to open as shown in Figure 26.7. You can rename or delete each command from there.

**FIGURE 26.7**   Use the Manage Saved Commands window to control all saved commands created manually or with the History panel.

The preceding example did in fact send a string of text to the Output panel in the authoring environment, but every time we ran the command, it kept sending the exact same message, which is not very useful. In the next section we will go over one of the ways to add dynamic content and customization to commands, as well as other extensible objects.

## XML-to-UI Controls

There are two ways to create an interface between extendable JSFL files and Flash. One, which we will discuss later in this chapter, you build directly in Flash itself. The other involves a specific way of coding XML.

Using specific XML tags (elements), we can describe and define a user interface for controlling any of our JSFL files. Listing every single tag is beyond the scope of this chapter, but Tables 26.1 and 26.2 show a few of the major tags. Table 26.1 lists layout tags, and Table 26.2 lists UI element tags.

**TABLE 26.1**    Layout Tags

| Tag | Description | Attributes | Child Tags |
| --- | --- | --- | --- |
| <dialog> | This tag will hold the entire UI. | buttons (Accept, Cancel, Help) title | <hbox>, <vbox>, <grid> |
| <hbox> | Contains horizontally aligned UI elements. | N/A | <hbox>, <vbox>, controls |
| <vbox> | Contains vertically aligned UI elements. | N/A | <hbox>, <vbox>, controls |
| <spacer> | Invisible bumper for arranging UI elements. | N/A | N/A |
| <separator> | Visible bar aligned with parent <vbox> or <hbox>. | N/A | N/A |
| <grid> | Used to lay out tabular elements. | N/A | <columns>,<rows> |
| <columns> | Holds individual <column> tags. | N/A | <column> |
| <column> | Specifies column in grid. | N/A | controls |
| <rows> | Holds individual <row> tags. | N/A | <row> |
| <row> | Controls to be placed within these tags. | align (start, center, end, baseline) | controls |

**TABLE 26.2**    UI Element Tags (Controls)

| Tag | Description | Attributes | Child Tags |
| --- | --- | --- | --- |
| <button> | Clickable buttons | id<br>label<br>accesskey<br>tabindex<br>oncommand | N/A |

**TABLE 26.2**    Continued

| Tag | Description | Attributes | Child Tags |
|-----|-------------|------------|------------|
| `<checkbox>` | Element for selecting Boolean values (true/false, yes/no) | id<br>label<br>accesskey<br>tabindex<br>checked (true, false) | N/A |
| `<colorchip>` | Color grid where a user can choose a certain color | id<br>color (default color) | N/A |
| `<listbox>` | Holds `<listitem>` tags in a list box | id<br>tabindex<br>rows (rows to display) | `<listitem>` |
| `<listitem>` | A single element in a list box | label<br>value | N/A |
| `<menulist>` | A drop-down list or combo box | id<br>tabindex | `<menupop>` |
| `<menupop>` | Part of the `<menulist>` drop-down box | N/A | `<menuitem>` |
| `<menuitem>` | Item in the `<menulist>` drop-down box | label<br>value | N/A |
| `<radiogroup>` | Holds radio button objects | id<br>tabindex | `<radio>`<br>N/A |
| `<radio>` | Individual choice in a `<radiogroup>` | label<br>selected (true, false)<br>accesskey | |
| `<popupslider>` | A slider with a movable slide bar to control the value | id<br>tabindex<br>minvalue<br>maxvalue | N/A<br><br><br>N/A |
| `<textbox>` | Simple text field | id<br>maxlength<br>value (default text)<br>tabindex<br>size (in characters)<br>literal (puts quote marks around text) | <br><br><br><br><br>N/A |
| `<label>` | Text label for UI elements | control (id of control being labeled)<br>accesskey<br>value | N/A |
| `<flash>` | Embedded Flash movie (`.swf`) | id<br>width<br>height<br>src (source file) | N/A |

**TABLE 26.2**    Continued

| Tag | Description | Attributes | Child Tags |
|---|---|---|---|
| `<targetlist>` | Used to sort through and choose instances of objects on the stage | id<br>class<br>tabindex<br>required (true, false) | N/A |

So now that you've seen the basic code being used, let's return to the `myTrace.jsfl` example and make it more dynamic.

1. Open a text editor such as Notepad or SciTe.

2. Save the file on the desktop as `traceMe.xml`.

3. Place the following code within it.

```
<dialog buttons="accept, cancel" title="Trace What?">
    <hbox>
        <label value="String: "/>
        <textbox id="string" value="Sample Text" size="40"/>
    </hbox>
</dialog>
```

The preceding code creates a UI box with the title "Trace What?" and two buttons. It then creates the type of UI box (`<hbox>`) and within that it labels the text field, which is created 40 characters wide with the default text "Sample Text". And as in all XML documents, when a tag is opened, it must be closed.

4. Now return to Flash and open `myTrace.jsfl`.

5. Change the code that is already present to the following:

```
myResult = fl.getDocumentDOM().xmlPanel(fl.configURI +
➥ "/Commands/traceMe.xml");
if(myResult.dismiss == "accept"){
    fl.trace(myResult.string);
}
```

What this code is doing is: First, it maps to the XML file that describes the UI for this command, and sets it to a variable `myResult`. Then, using a conditional statement, we check whether the user has clicked the Accept button or the Cancel button because we only want the command to run if the user clicks Accept. If the Accept (OK) button is clicked, it will send the message that is in the text field to the Output panel.

6. Now save the JSFL file to the desktop.

7. Copy both the JSFL file and the XML document to the Commands folder in the Flash 2004 MX directory and restart Flash.

After you have restarted Flash, you can go to Commands in the menu bar, and you should see traceMe as a listed command. Select it and Figure 26.8 should appear. You can type in anything or keep the default text, and when you click OK (the Accept button), the message will be sent to the Output panel. Also, if you select Cancel, nothing will happen except that the UI box will close.

> **NOTE**
>
> It is not necessary to have buttons in the UI (although you would normally want to). If a user cannot close the dialog box by clicking a button, the Escape key will always close the UI box.

**FIGURE 26.8**    Enter some text to have the traceMe command trace the text.

That was one way to use the XML-to-UI API. Another way is with behaviors.

## Creating Behaviors

Behaviors, as discussed in Chapter 8, "Welcome to ActionScript 2.0," are small blocks of code that can be adjusted to fit individual needs. Some of the behaviors that come with Flash can be used to control movie clips, screens (Flash PRO only), and opening new Web pages. Those are okay, but for more intermediate to advanced developers, you will want more. Building behaviors is a simple process provided you familiarized yourself with the XML-to-UI API. Table 26.3 shows a few other tags for behaviors that you should make yourself aware of.

**TABLE 26.3**    XML Tags for Behaviors

| Tag | Definition | Attributes | Child Tags |
|---|---|---|---|
| <flash_behavior> | Tells Flash that this XML is for a behavior | version | N/A |
| <behavior_definition> | Defines certain aspects of the behavior | dialogID category name class | N/A |

**TABLE 26.3**    Continued

| Tag | Definition | Attributes | Child Tags |
|---|---|---|---|
| `<properties>` | Holds the declared properties `<property>` | N/A | `<property>` |
| `<property>` | Declares a property of the behavior | id<br>default | N/A |
| `<actionscript>` | Holds the ActionScript being placed | N/A | N/A |

Now that you have seen the new tags for behaviors, we can go ahead and begin creating them.

In the following example, we will create a behavior to color components:

1. Open up your favorite text editor.

2. Save the file to the `C:\Program Files\Macromedia\Flash MX 2004\en\First Run\Behaviors` directory of the Flash MX 2004 directory as `componentColor.xml`.

3. Place this code in, and then we can go over each part:

```
<?xml version="1.0"?>
<flash_behavior version="1.0">
<behavior_definition dialogID="Style component"
➥category="Unleashed" name ="Style component" >
<properties>
    <property id="TARGET" default=""/>
    <property id="COLOR" default="#000000"/>
</properties>
  <dialog id="Style-component" title="Style a component"
➥buttons="accept, cancel">
    <vbox>
        <hbox>
            <label value="Select a component:" control="TARGET"
➥required="true"/>
            <targetlist id="TARGET"/>
        </hbox>
        <separator/>
        <hbox>
            <label value="Select a color:" control="COLOR" required="true"/>
            <colorchip id="COLOR" color="#000000"/>
        </hbox>
    </vbox>
  </dialog>
<actionscript>
<![CDATA[
```

```
    // Color a component
    var htmlColor:String = "$COLOR$";
    $TARGET$.setStyle("themeColor", "0x"+htmlColor.slice(1));
    //end of code
    ]]>
    </actionscript>
    </behavior_definition>
    </flash_behavior>
```

This code does a lot of things, so let's break it apart, and talk about each piece.

The first piece declares that it is an XML document, and then that it is a Flash behavior.

```
    <?xml version="1.0"?>
         <flash_behavior version="1.0">
```

The next section sets some of the behavior's attributes and declares a couple of properties.

```
<behavior_definition dialogID="Style component"
➡category="Unleashed" name ="Style component" >
<properties>
    <property id="TARGET" default=""/>
    <property id="COLOR" default="#000000"/>
</properties>
```

After that comes the dialog box construction with all of the elements.

```
  <dialog id="Stylecomponent" title="Style a component" buttons="accept,
➡ cancel">
    <vbox>
        <hbox>
            <label value="Select a component:" control="TARGET" required="true"/>
            <targetlist id="TARGET"/>
        </hbox>
        <separator/>
        <hbox>
            <label value="Select a color:" control="COLOR" required="true"/>
            <colorchip id="COLOR" color="#000000"/>
        </hbox>
    </vbox>
  </dialog>
```

After that the ActionScript is created. Here are some things to know about sending ActionScript out of the behavior: In addition to the fact that it must be between <actionscript> tags, it must also follow <![CDATA[ and end with ]]>. Getting information from the UI elements in the dialog box is as easy as wrapping the *id* attribute of that element in dollar signs (*$id$*).

```
<actionscript>
    <![CDATA[
    // Color a component
    var htmlColor:String = "$COLOR$";
    $TARGET$.setStyle("themeColor", "0x"+htmlColor.slice(1));
    //end of code
    ]]>
</actionscript>
```

And finally, the other open tags are closed as well.

```
</behavior_definition>
</flash_behavior>
```

Now that you understand the fundamentals behind the behavior we just built, let's use it.

1. Make sure the `componentColor.xml` document is in the `behaviors` directory of the Flash MX 2004 directory.

2. Restart Flash.

3. Create a new Flash document.

4. Drag the `Button` component onto the stage.

5. Create another layer called actions.

6. Select the first frame of the actions layer, and open the Behaviors panel by choosing Window, Development Panels, Behaviors.

7. Click the Add Behavior button and choose Unleashed, Style Component, which will pop up the dialog box shown in Figure 26.9.

8. Choose the `Button` component that was placed on the stage, and because it wasn't given an instance name, another dialog box will pop up that is built into the `targetlist` UI element, as you can see in Figure 26.10. Give the `Button` component the instance name of `myButton` and choose your favorite color.

9. Now test the movie, and you will see that the button has taken on the color characteristics of the color you have chosen (sometimes it's hard to see until the button is actually clicked).

And that was how to make a behavior. To see more about behaviors, look at the ones that come with Flash. Because they are made in XML, they are open source, so learn from their creators.

Behaviors can save you development time, and so does the topic of the next section.

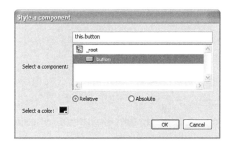

**FIGURE 26.9**   The User Interface for your first custom behavior.

**FIGURE 26.10**   The Instance Name dialog box.

# Creating Your Own Panels

Flash comes with a lot of panels, but you might not need or want every one. No worries—
you can create your panels, which isn't really new, but now you can use the `MMExecute()`
method, which will execute any JSFL command within the authoring environment. When
the Flash file (`.swf`) has been created, you can drop it in the `WindowSWF` directory in the
Flash MX 2004 directory, and restart the Flash authoring environment. Then you can find
it under Windows, Other Panels in the menu bar.

The basic layout of the `MMExecute()` method is as follows:

```
MMExecute(command);
```

The difficult aspect of using the `MMExecute()` method is that the command must be passed
as a string, but the dynamic content cannot. For instance, if you were to send the current
date and time to the Output panel, it would look something like this:

```
MMExecute("fl.trace('" + new Date() + "');");
```

Notice the abundance of quotation marks to make it work right, just something to keep in
mind when using the `MMExecute()` method.

Now that you have seen the basic usage of the method we are going to use to create our
first panel, let's get started.

1. Create a new Flash document.

2. Set its dimensions to 200×100.

3. Drag three components onto the stage and place them as follows:

   `TextInput` component: Set its width to about 180, give it an instance name of `myText`, and place it in the top half of the stage.

   `Button` component: Give it an instance name of `myButton`, set its label parameter to "Send", change its width to about 48, and place it in the bottom left of the stage.

   `ComboBox` component: Give it an instance name of `myCombo`, place it at the bottom right of the stage, and give it two labels:

   "to output"

   "to alert"

   Your stage should now look like Figure 26.11.

4. Create a new layer called **actions**.

5. Open the actions panel in the first frame of the Actions layer and place this code in:

```
//event listener object
var clickListen:Object = new Object();
//create the event
clickListen.click = function(){
    if(myCombo.value == "to output"){
        MMExecute("fl.trace('" + myText.text + "');");
    }else{
        MMExecute("alert('"+myText.text + "');");
    }
}
//add the listener
myButton.addEventListener("click",clickListen);
```

   The preceding code first creates an event listener object. Then it creates an event callback method for that object that checks where the string from the `TextInput` component is supposed to go, either to the Output panel, or to an alert message. Then finally we add the event listener to the `Button` component.

6. Now save the file as `Send Out.fla` and test the movie.

7. Copy the `.swf` file created to the `WindowSWF` directory and restart Flash.

8. When Flash has been restarted, choose Window, Other Panels, Send Out. Now you have the ability to send messages to the Output panel as well as in the form of alert messages as in Figure 26.12.

This example does not have the most practical uses, but it does show what is possible by combining Flash developing, JSFL, and the `MMExecute()` method. As you become more comfortable with JSFL, you will begin to create many of your own panels.

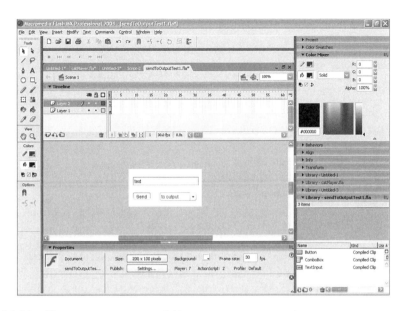

**FIGURE 26.11**   Use components to quickly create custom panels.

**FIGURE 26.12**   You can see that the panel created can send messages both to the Output panel and as an alert message.

But panels are not the end of customizing the authoring environment of Flash. You can also create your own tools with JSFL and place them in the toolbar.

# Creating Custom Tools

Other great objects that you can create on the extensibility layer are custom tools. Custom tools can be used to do a lot of things including drawing shapes, adjusting elements on the stage, and even creating new instances of objects.

There are certain aspects of JSFL that are used specifically for tools, but we will go over them as we build our tool.

The tool being built in the following example will be a drawing tool designed for drawing check marks just as quickly and easily as drawing squares in Flash.

1. Create a new JavaScript Flash file.

2. Save the document in the tools directory of the Flash MX 2004 directory as
   `checkmark.jsfl`.

3. Place this code in:

```
function configureTool(){
    myTool = fl.tools.activeTool;
    myTool.setToolName("Check");
    myTool.setIcon("Check.png");
    myTool.setMenuString("Check Mark Tool");
    myTool.setToolTip("Check Mark Tool");
}
function drawCheck(startX,startY,theWidth,theHeight){
    thePath.addPoint(startX,startY+(theHeight*.6));
    thePath.addPoint(startX+(theWidth*.3), startY+theHeight);
    thePath.addPoint(startX+theWidth, startY);
    thePath.addPoint(startX+(theWidth*.3), startY+(theHeight*.8));
    thePath.addPoint(startX, startY+(theHeight*.6));
}
function activate(){
    myTool = fl.tools.activeTool;
}
function mouseDown(){
    fl.drawingLayer.beginDraw();
}
function mouseMove(){
    if(fl.tools.mouseIsDown){
        var vm = fl.getDocumentDOM().viewMatrix;
        var difX=fl.tools.penLoc.x-fl.tools.penDownLoc.x;
        var difY=fl.tools.penLoc.y-fl.tools.penDownLoc.y;
        fl.drawingLayer.beginFrame();
        drawLayer = fl.drawingLayer;
        thePath = drawLayer.newPath();
        if(fl.tools.shiftIsDown){
            if(difX > difY){
                difY = difX;
            }else if(difY > difX){
                difX = difY;
            }
        }
        drawCheck(fl.tools.penDownLoc.x,fl.tools.penDownLoc.y,difX,difY);
        drawLayer.drawPath(thePath);
        fl.drawingLayer.endFrame();
```

```
        }
    }
    function mouseUp(){
        fl.drawingLayer.endDraw();
        thePath.makeShape();
    }
```

This code may look like a lot, but it isn't as you will see as it is broken apart into sections.

The first section appears to create a function, but in fact, it creates a function specific to tools, the `configureTool()` function. Within this function, we set the active tool to a variable for easy reference. We then set the tool's name along with its icon (which we will build later). After that the menu string is set as well as the tooltip, which will appear when the tool is hovered over in the toolbar.

```
function configureTool(){
    myTool = fl.tools.activeTool;
    myTool.setToolName("Check");
    myTool.setIcon("Check.png");
    myTool.setMenuString("Check Mark Tool");
    myTool.setToolTip("Check Mark Tool");
}
```

After that, we create a function that we use later in the code. The `drawCheck()` function does all the hard work and the math for drawing the actual check mark.

```
function drawCheck(startX,startY,theWidth,theHeight){
    thePath.addPoint(startX,startY+(theHeight*.6));
    thePath.addPoint(startX+(theWidth*.3), startY+theHeight);
    thePath.addPoint(startX+theWidth, startY);
    thePath.addPoint(startX+(theWidth*.3), startY+(theHeight*.8));
    thePath.addPoint(startX, startY+(theHeight*.6));
}
```

After that comes another specific function for the tool object, the `activate()` function, which is called when the specific tool is activated.

```
function activate(){
    myTool = fl.tools.activeTool;
}
```

After that, the `mouseDown()` function is created, which will be called after the tool is selected, and the user presses the mouse button on the stage.

```
function mouseDown(){
    fl.drawingLayer.beginDraw();
}
```

26

After that, the `mouseMove()` function is created. This function first checks to make sure that the user is still clicking the mouse button; otherwise, it will draw a single check mark as long as the mouse moves around on the stage. If the mouse is down (meaning that the user is in fact trying to draw something), it gets the most recent position of when the user clicked the mouse, using the `penDownLoc` property. It then activates the drawing layer and creates a new path in the drawing layer. After that, it checks to see if the Shift key is down. This makes the Check Mark Drawing tool act similar to the Rectangle and Oval tool; when the Shift key is held down while drawing, the check mark will sustain its proportions no matter how large or small it is drawn. After that, the `drawCheck()` function is called, which will draw the check mark on the stage. And after that, we set the drawing path, and end the drawing frame.

```
function mouseMove(){
    if(fl.tools.mouseIsDown){
        var vm = fl.getDocumentDOM().viewMatrix;
        var difX=fl.tools.penLoc.x-fl.tools.penDownLoc.x;
        var difY=fl.tools.penLoc.y-fl.tools.penDownLoc.y;
        fl.drawingLayer.beginFrame();
        drawLayer = fl.drawingLayer;
        thePath = drawLayer.newPath();
        if(fl.tools.shiftIsDown){
            if(difX > difY){
                difY = difX;
            }else if(difY > difX){
                difX = difY;
            }
        }
        drawCheck(fl.tools.penDownLoc.x,fl.tools.penDownLoc.y,difX,difY);
        drawLayer.drawPath(thePath);
        fl.drawingLayer.endFrame();
    }
}
```

And the final function is created for when the user releases the mouse. When this occurs, we stop drawing on the drawing layer, and create the shape with the fill color and stroke already set in the authoring environment.

```
function mouseUp(){
    fl.drawingLayer.endDraw();
    thePath.makeShape();
}
```

Now that you see what the code is doing, the next step is to create the icon for our tool. Still in Flash, or any other drawing program you use such as Fireworks, draw a basic check mark, about 16×16 and save it as `Check.png` in the same directory as the JSFL file.

After that, there is one final step before we have to reboot Flash; we have to add the tool to the toolbar. In the tools directory, open `toolConfig.xml` and change its content (add the line shown in bold):

```
<group name="selection">
    <tool name="arrow" />
    <tool name="bezierSelect" />
    <tool name="line" />
    <tool name="lasso" />
    <tool name="pen" />
    <tool name="text" />
    <tool name="oval" />
    <tool name="rect">
        <tool name="polystar" />
        <tool name="Check"/>
    </tool>
    <tool name="pencil" />
    <tool name="brush" />
    <tool name="freeXform" />
    <tool name="fillXform" />
    <tool name="inkBottle" />
    <tool name="bucket" />
    <tool name="eyeDropper" />
    <tool name="eraser" />
    <tool name="hand" />
    <tool name="magnifier" />
</group>
```

All we did here is add the Check tool after the Polystar tool.

Now restart Flash, create a new Flash document, select the rectangle tool in the toolbar, hold down, and you will see the check mark tool, which makes it easy to draw check marks, as shown in Figure 26.13.

Even after everything we have gone over that can be created with the extensibility layer, JSFL, and the XML-to-UI API, there is one more: effects.

26

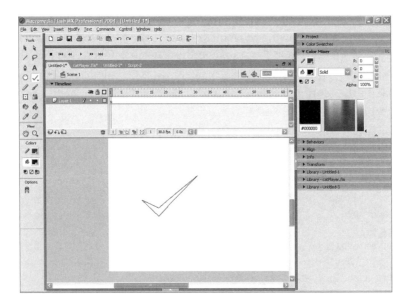

**FIGURE 26.13**    Create custom tools for your own needs and preferences.

## Creating Custom Effects

Effects are reuseable and customizable ways to create visual effects with objects on the stage such as movie clips or static text fields. There are several built-in effects, but it's important to understand how to make your own.

Much like tools, effects have certain functions that are specific for them, and as before, we will go over them as we build our effect.

The effect we are going to create will fade a movie clip to a certain point in a certain number of frames that we will set using XML to UI.

1. Open your favorite text editor and save a file in the effects directory in the Flash MX 2004 directory as fade.xml.

2. Place this code within it:

```
<group name="Unleashed">
    <effect name="Fade">
    <source file="fade.jsfl">
    <allow types="all">
</group>
<properties>
    <property name="Fade To" variable="alpha" defaultValue="0"
➡type="Number"/>
```

```
      <property name="Frame Amount" variable="frameAmount"
➥ defaultValue="10" type="Number"/>
</properties>
```

The preceding code creates the group name and the effect's name. It also declares the source JSFL file for the effect and declares what type of objects can use this. Then we declare the two properties we will use, the fade to point, and the frame amount with some default values.

3. Now create a new JSFL file and save it as `fade.jsfl` in the same directory as the XML file.

4. Place this code within it:

```
function executeEffect(){
    var myEffect = fl.activeEffect;
    var myDoc = fl.getDocumentDOM();
    var myTimeline = myDoc.getTimeline();
    var theFrame = myTimeline.currentFrame;
    myTimeline.insertFrames(myEffect.frameAmount-1);
    myDoc.enterEditMode();
    myTimeline = myDoc.getTimeline();
    myTimeline.insertFrames(myEffect.frameAmount-1);
    myTimeline.createMotionTween(0, myEffect.frameAmount-1);
    myTimeline.convertToKeyframes(myEffect.frameAmount-1);
    myTimeline.currentFrame = myEffect.frameAmount-1;
    myDoc.selectAll();
    myDoc.setInstanceAlpha(myEffect.alpha);
    myDoc.exitEditMode();
    myTimeline = myDoc.getTimeline();
    myTimeline.currentFrame = theFrame;
}
function removeEffect(){
    var myDoc = fl.getDocumentDOM();
    myDoc.enterEditMode();
    var myTimeline = myDoc.getTimeline();
    var totalFrames = myTimeline.layers[0].frameCount;
    myTimeline.removeFrames(1, totalFrames);
    myTimeline.setFrameProperty('tweenType', 'none', 0);
    myTimeline.currentFrame = 0;
    myDoc.selectAll();
      myDoc.exitEditMode();
    myTimeline = myDoc.getTimeline();
    var selFrames = myTimeline.getSelectedFrames();
```

26

```
        myTimeline.removeFrames(selFrames[1]+1, selFrames[2]);
        myTimeline.setSelectedFrames(selFrames[1], selFrames[1]);
    }
```

The preceding code creates two functions, both specific for effects. The first is the executeEffect() function, which will be called when the user creates the effect. The second function is the removeEffect() function for when a user wants to remove an effect.

The first function, executeEffect(), sets the active effect and places it in the myEffect variable. It then gets the Flash DOM and sets that to the myDoc variable. Then it grabs the current timeline and that timeline's currentFrame. Once it has that, it can begin adding the correct number of frames to the timeline, and because it already has a frame, we subtract one from the total frames given by the user and add the new amount to the current timeline. We then enter edit mode, which will allow us to create the tween. We enter the edit mode, create the total frames there, and then we create the motion tween, grab the content in the final frame, and reset its alpha. After that, we exit the edit mode and select the current frame in the current timeline.

```
function executeEffect(){
    var myEffect = fl.activeEffect;
    var myDoc = fl.getDocumentDOM();
    var myTimeline = myDoc.getTimeline();
    var theFrame = myTimeline.currentFrame;
    myTimeline.insertFrames(myEffect.frameAmount-1);
    myDoc.enterEditMode();
    myTimeline = myDoc.getTimeline();
    myTimeline.insertFrames(myEffect.frameAmount-1);
    myTimeline.createMotionTween(0, myEffect.frameAmount-1);
    myTimeline.convertToKeyframes(myEffect.frameAmount-1);
    myTimeline.currentFrame = myEffect.frameAmount-1;
    myDoc.selectAll();
    myDoc.setInstanceAlpha(myEffect.alpha);
    myDoc.exitEditMode();
    myTimeline = myDoc.getTimeline();
    myTimeline.currentFrame = theFrame;
}
```

The second function created will remove the effect if the user wants. It first grabs the DOM and then enters edit mode. Once in edit mode, it removes the frames and the tween setting. Then it goes back to the previous timeline and removes the excess frames there as well.

```
function removeEffect(){
    var myDoc = fl.getDocumentDOM();
```

```
    myDoc.enterEditMode();
    var myTimeline = myDoc.getTimeline();
    var totalFrames = myTimeline.layers[0].frameCount;
    myTimeline.removeFrames(1, totalFrames);
    myTimeline.setFrameProperty('tweenType', 'none', 0);
    myTimeline.currentFrame = 0;
    myDoc.selectAll();
      myDoc.exitEditMode();
    myTimeline = myDoc.getTimeline();
    var selFrames = myTimeline.getSelectedFrames();
    myTimeline.removeFrames(selFrames[1]+1, selFrames[2]);
    myTimeline.setSelectedFrames(selFrames[1], selFrames[1]);
}
```

Make sure both the XML document and the JSFL file are in the `effects` directory in the Flash MX 2004 directory and restart Flash. Then create a square, convert it to a movie clip, select it, and choose Insert, Timeline Effects, Unleashed, Fade. The dialog box shown in Figure 26.14 will pop up. You can use the default settings and then test the movie and watch the square fade out over and over again.

**FIGURE 26.14**  Custom effects make visual eye candy quickly and easily.

Now you have seen the extensibility layer, and some of the things that can be created within it, but you do not necessarily have to create them yourself.

## Online Extensions

For some, the extensibility layer is a great place to show off your development skills, but for others, it's just a waste of time. That doesn't mean that you can't ever extend the Flash authoring environment.

Macromedia has two spots you can go where you can find two types of extensions, free and not-free.

The not-free ones including extensions from Swish and Zoomify can be found at: `http://www.macromedia.com/software/flash/extensions/`.

And the free ones can be found at the Macromedia Exchange at: `http://www.macromedia.com/go/flash_exchange/`.

## Summary

This chapter covered a lot of new technologies in this new version of Flash including JSFL and the XML-to-UI API. With these technologies, you can extend the Flash authoring environment as far as you like to increase efficiency and speed in creating, managing, and organizing Flash content. The most important things to take away from this chapter are the fundamentals and the desire to experiment. Try taking what you have seen in this chapter and combining certain steps into your own panel or tool.

CHAPTER **27**

# Beyond Flash

**IN THIS CHAPTER**

- Flash Alternatives
- Enhancing Flash Files
- Beyond the Web

Throughout this book, we have covered nearly all aspects of Flash and creating Flash content. I say "nearly" because Flash is not the only tool on the block that can create Flash content, but it is the best. There are, however, several alternatives for creating Flash content as well as third-party applications for enriching content.

This chapter covers many other applications that can create the now-famous Swiff (.swf) format. We also go over some applications that can help you with creating and even securing your Flash files.

## Flash Alternatives

There are several alternatives to using Flash to create Flash content quickly; the first is FlashKit.com's FLASHtyper.

### FLASHtyper

FLASHtyper is a free Flash content builder created by FlashKit.com. It can be found at http://www.flashkit.com and again, is free. FlashKit.com is a great developer community and resource site for Flash. It not only hosts FLASHtyper but also has tutorials, sample files, and Flash news.

What FLASHtyper is, is an animated text generator; what it is not is a total replacement for Flash MX 2004. Keep that in mind as we review FLASHtyper.

#### Sign Up and Log In

In order to use the FLASHtyper application, FlashKit requires you to be a member of the site. Underneath the application is what is known as the myFK engine. This allows you to individualize FLASHtyper to your own tastes by storing your selection of favorite fonts and text effects at the Web site. Membership is free. Select Sign Up Here! on the FLASHtyper

Web page to sign up. When you have signed up, you have the choice of taking a short tutorial or proceeding with the application.

### The FLASHtyper Desktop Screen

After you have logged in, you are just six steps away from making your first FLASHtyper animation, but first let's take a tour of the main screen:

- **Text Box Attributes**. Indicates the offset of your text from the upper-left corner of the text box as well as the size of the text box in pixels.

- **Load Movie**. This menu allows you to enter the URL of your SWF file and put it right in the background to view how the text effect you are creating will look when it is imported into your SWF file.

- **High/Low**. This toggle allows you to optimize FLASHtyper for your computer. The Low setting is for older computers, but it is not as much of an issue nowadays.

- **Help**. Provides access to online tutorials for FLASHtyper.

- **Text Editor**. Enter the text you want for your text effect.

- **Color Editor**. Select the color to be used for your text.

- **BackColor Editor**. Select the background color for your text box.

- **FX Editor**. Select the special effect for your text.

- **Text Options Editor**. Select the font, size, kerning, and line spacing for your text.

- **0,0 Corner**. This is a reference point representing the upper-left corner of the text box.

- **Drag Me GENERATE**. This dialog box shows the current text contained in your text box and allows you to change the size of the box, change the offset of the text from the corner of the box, and launch the preview and generation of your SWF file.

- **Text Attributes**. This window is located on the right side of the screen and provides a glance at the current status of your text attributes.

From this main screen, you have a number of panels and menus at your disposal for creating your text animation and providing an at-a-glance view of your progress (see Figure 27.1).

There is another alternative to creating Flash content from scratch, but this one is going to cost a little bit.

## SWiSHmax

Swish has been around for several years starting out as a general text animator that can export in the form of .swf files. It has blossomed into a full-blown Flash content creator while maintaining its roots in text animation with over 200 individual effects. The stage has the same feel as Swish 2.0, as you can see in Figure 27.2, but the effects are now limitless.

SWiSHmax can be found at http://www.swishzone.com and it costs about $100.

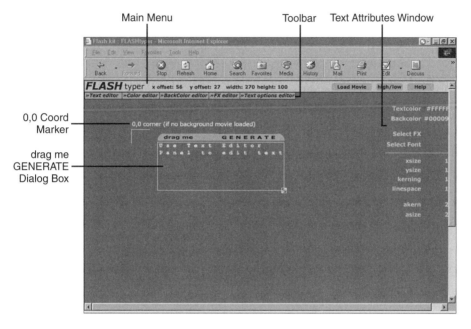

FIGURE 27.1    The FLASHtyper Desktop screen.

Building files in SWiSHmax is fast and easy.

1. After closing the pop-up dialog box that will appear by default, create a new Swish file.

2. Select the Text tool and draw a text field on the stage.

3. Select the Text tab in the options menu on the right of the stage, and in the window, type **Flash MX Unleashed 2004**.

   Notice that when you create a text field, a layer is created automatically in the timeline.

4. Now select the first frame in the new layer and click the Add Effect button.

5. Move down and select Looping Continuously, Flapping Wave.

6. Now the timeline has 20 frames in it. Click the Play Effect button to see the effect at work.

7. You can also customize the effect by selecting the effect and choosing Edit, Properties as you can see in Figure 27.3.

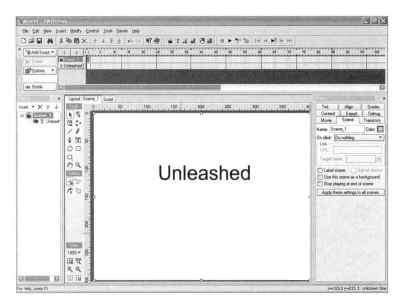

**FIGURE 27.2**    The SWiSHmax stage where you can create elements to be animated.

Play with the different effects and customize them to get your own. From the properties dialog box of the effects, you can even save your own effects to distribute to your friends.

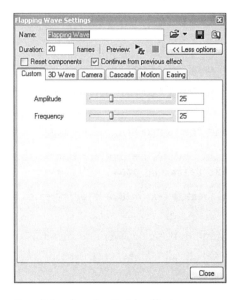

**FIGURE 27.3**    The properties dialog box for Swish effects.

But this time around, Swish did not stop at just creating a new version of their popular software product; they have even created a new program altogether.

## SWiSHpix

At the time of this writing, SWiSHpix was still in beta, but very powerful. It allows users to quickly create digital photo albums, which you can animate and even put to music. After that, you can either burn to a CD or quickly upload to a Web server via FTP.

The program has five simple steps:

1. **Get Pictures**. You gather the pictures and make minor edits to their layout and title.

2. **Edit Pictures**. You crop and adjust brightness and contrast of the images.

3. **Create Album**. You set options for the album such as music, time delays, and theme.

4. **Decorate Pictures**. You add text bubbles or clip art to individual images.

5. **Publish Album**. You make choices for the form that the album will be published in, such as on a CD or published directly to the Web.

SWiSHpix is a great tool to quickly create online content for photo albums, screen savers, or CD albums. It is available at `swishzone.com`.

SWiSH also has a set of Flash extensions available for purchase at `http://www.swishzone.com`.

But SWiSH isn't the only great software for people to quickly and easily create Flash files. PowerCONVERTER from PresentationPro is another one.

## PowerCONVERTER

PowerCONVERTER is great for users who like to build presentations in PowerPoint, but want to move to the Web. PowerCONVERTER will take any and all PowerPoint presentations (`.ppt`) and convert them to either a Swiff file (`.swf`) for the Web, or a projector file (`.exe`) for CD content.

You can get a trial version of PowerCONVERTER from PresentationPro at `http://www.presentationpro.com`. You can also send them a PowerPoint presentation, and they will convert it for you as a service and to show how powerful PowerCONVERTER really is.

Some of the features PresentationPro says PowerCONVERTER has are

- File size reduction up to 97% from PowerPoint to Swiff (`.swf`)

- Retains all sounds, transactions, and graphics

- Secure file conversion free of viruses

27

And it currently retails for about $400.

If you are interested in converting video to Flash, but do not need the entire Flash suite, there are two very good options available.

## Wildform FlixPro

FlixPro is a product that makes turning video into a Swiff file very easy and fast. It also has a great compression ratio and several built-in players.

The software is available at `http://www.wildform.com` and retails for about $150. It does have a trial version.

With FlixPro, you can import and convert the following formats:

- `.avi`
- `.dv`
- `.mov/.qt`
- `.mpeg`
- `.mp4`
- `.3gp`
- `.asf/.wmv`

With the ability to export as a raw Swiff file, or as a Swiff file with a built-in video player, if all you are interested in is converting video to `.swf`, FlixPro is definitely an option, but not the only option.

## Sorenson Squeeze

Sorenson Squeeze is another good choice for converting video to Flash. It has many settings for controlling quality output and has a great compression package.

Sorenson Squeeze can be found at `http://www.sorenson.com` and has a trial version. The retail price on the full suite of Sorenson Squeeze Compression is about $450.

Here are the formats Sorenson Squeeze supports for importing:

- `.aif/.aiff`
- `.asf`
- `.avi`
- DV
- `.mov`

- .wmv

- .wma

- .wav

It supports most of the same video formats, but it can export to some of them as well as .swf and .flv (Flash Video).

But if video is not what you are looking for, there is another product that can produce high-end 3D vector graphics and animations that can be exported into Flash format.

### Swift 3D

Swift 3D, from Electric Rain, is the premier product for creating 3D vector animations. It can export in a variety of popular formats including .swf and .svg. Some of its features include

- Enhanced vector realism

- Full preview system

- Sophisticated cameras and lighting

- High level of object control

- Advanced modeling

Swift 3D can be found at http://www.swift3d.com. Unfortunately, it does not have a free trial version, but it does have a 30-day money-back guarantee for its $169 price tag.

So far, we have talked about the different ways to make Flash content without necessarily using Flash. Next we will go over some third-party applications that will significantly improve certain aspects of what can be accomplished using Flash.

## Enhancing Flash Files

These next few applications will take different approaches in how they help developers to improve aspects of their Flash file and to be able to retrieve lost information.

The first application will help users drastically reduce their file size of their work.

### Optimaze

Optimaze is a vector-crunching machine. It can compress vector graphics up to 60% better than Flash itself can while maintaining the same crisp, tight lines that it was originally created in.

It has a very familiar and Flash-based interface for controlling the compression, and it imports .swf files directly, so the original .fla file is not necessary.

Optimaze can be found at `http://www.optimaze.biz`. It does not have a trial version, but at about $130, if you are into animation in Flash, or you use a lot of vector graphics in your sites or applications, Optimaze is a good tool to keep on hand.

The next software doesn't necessarily help in the design or development stage itself, but if you are like me and constantly accidentally overwriting the newest version of your Flash file with an older one, this next tool is for you.

## Action Script Viewer 4.0

Sometimes, you might lose the original source code, or accidentally overwrite a newer version of the `.fla` file with an older one, and then realize that your last ten hours of coding have been lost. In steps Action Script Viewer.

Now in version 4.0, Action Script Viewer from Manitu Group can decompile compiled `.swf` files into readable format. After you have decompiled the file, you can view any and all ActionScript within the file as well as export certain resources from within the file such as bitmaps, sounds, and movies. The new version of Action Script Viewer has gone even further by allowing the resources and a JSFL command to be created to assist in reconstructing an original FLA file.

At the time of this writing, there was no demo version of version 4 available (but there is a demo for version 3, which has most of the same features). Version 4 is available to purchase for about $60 at `http://www.buraks.com/asv/index.html`.

Also available on their site are many tools, which complement the Action Script Viewer application, and they are free of charge.

Now that you know Flash files can be decompiled, read and in some cases, can even be turned back into an original source file, you might be wondering what you can do to keep someone else from doing this to your files.

## ActionScript Obfuscator

Even though for the most part, Flash is an open-source community, sometimes you might not want prying eyes looking at how your application works. Or worse yet, they could find the server-side pages you are using, and corrupt the data on the back end. Not to worry—ActionScript Obfuscator is here to help.

ActionScript is written in plain English (or whatever other language you choose to write it in) for anyone to be able to read. ActionScript Obfuscator takes ActionScript and changes it to a bunch of numbers in place of words. The computer can still understand exactly what the ActionScript is saying, but it is very difficult for anyone looking at it to see what it says.

Here is an example of what ActionScript Obfuscator might do to your ActionScript.

Before ActionScript Obfuscator, the code looked like this:

```
function randomWord (uppercase, wordlength) {
    var result = "";
    var charbase = uppercase ? 65 : 97;
    var i = 0;
    while (i < wordlength) {
        var randomchar = charbase + random (26);
        result += String.fromCharCode(randomchar);
        i++;
    }
    return result;
}
```

After ActionScript Obfuscator, the code looks like this:

```
function -1 (1, 2) {
    var +1 = "";
    var +4 = 1 ? 65 : 97;
    var +2 = 0;
    while (+2 < 2) {
        var +5 = (+4 + random (26));
        +1 = +1 + String.fromCharCode(+5);
        +2++;
    }
    return (+1);
}
```

You can clearly see the difference in the two blocks of code. Even though this tool is great for keeping prying eyes from looking at your code, it does have its downfalls. You cannot use dynamic variable references because they will cause errors at runtime.

At the time of this writing, ASO was a free download in the Pro version, and can be found at http://www.genable.com/aso.

Now you have seen several ways to create Flash content and to improve Flash content. You have even seen how to decompile Flash content if you want, but what if you want to take the Flash content itself beyond the Web?

# Beyond the Web

Flash does come bundled with the ability to export its content in the form of a projector file, which means it can be placed on a CD and distributed without the need for the player because the projector file has its own built-in player. You can also export in the form of a QuickTime movie (.mov) if you have the required plug-in, which costs about $30. But both of these formats have their shortcomings. Even though projector files can be easily created, they are not very powerful and have difficulty interacting with the user's computer.

This section focuses on three applications that will help take your Flash content to places you might never have imagined, starting with screen savers.

## ScreenTime

ScreenTime is an application built to allow users to quickly build screen savers for both Windows and Macintosh platforms with their Flash movies.

How easy is it to use? These are the directions from their Web site:

1. Drop a SWF on the ScreenTime window.

2. Click Build.

And that is it.

Of course, you can do more steps if you like to further customize your screen saver, and you can even create another Flash file to be the control panel for your screen saver for other users to make adjustments to variables.

ScreenTime can be found at `http://www.screentime.com`; it does have a trial version, and the full version is about $200.

Another format you might want to put your Flash content in is video, and as mentioned before, with the correct plug-in you can export your Flash files in QuickTime (.mov) format. But what if you want to export in another video format?

## SWF2Video

SWF2Video allows Flash designers and developers to convert their SWF files to AVI video files while maintaining ActionScript and interactivity. It can even do batch jobs converting several compiled Flash files to AVI.

You can find SWF2Video at `http://www.flashants.com/root/swf2video.shtml`. It does have a trial version available for download, and to purchase the full version will set you back about $80.

Also available on their site is an SWF2Video plug-in for Adobe Premier. This plug-in will allow Adobe Premier users to import SWF files directly into Premier for editing.

The final third-party application that can help take your Flash content beyond the Web is SWF Studio 2.2.

## SWF Studio 2.2

SWF Studio 2.2 is the last third-party application in this chapter for a reason. It can take your Flash file and convert it to a full-blown desktop application. It accomplishes this by wrapping the compiled SWF file with several plug-ins that can be accessed by using the `fscommand()` method in Flash.

Here is an example that will send a message to a pop-up window when it has been wrapped with SWF Studio:

```
fscommand("Debug","There was an error!");
```

Of course, that is a very generic example of what can be done. Using SWF Studio, you can interact with an FTP server, the user's local computer file system, as well as the registry, and even create your own browser. For an example with all source code, go to the companion site for a simple MP3 player.

SWF Studio has a very easy-to-use interface, as you can see in Figures 27.4 and 27.5.

In addition, you can set custom icons and expiration dates, and it can control external video sources such as Windows media files.

SWF Studio is not limited to creating desktop applications; it can also create screen savers.

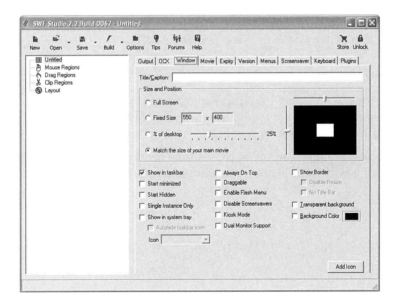

**FIGURE 27.4**    Basic options for the application being created in SWF Studio.

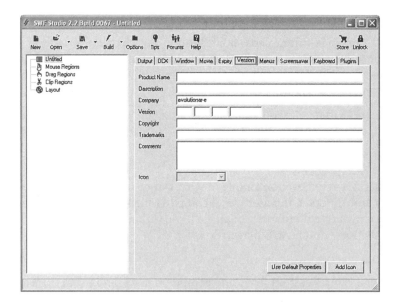

**FIGURE 27.5**    Another screen showing some application information that will be persistent with the application.

SWF Studio can be found at http://www.northcode.com and it does have a free trial download. The purchase price for the full version is about $139.

## Summary

This chapter has covered many third-party applications to help you not only create Flash content without Flash itself, but to also improve your content either by lowering its file size or taking it beyond the Web altogether.

If you are planning to purchase any of these third-party applications, if they have a free trial download, download it, play with it, and then make a decision.

# PART IV

## Appendix

## IN THIS PART

# APPENDIX **A**

# The ActionScript Reference

This appendix covers many different sections of Flash's programming language ActionScript. Because ActionScript has grown since its previous version, and continues to grow, not every single script of ActionScript is in this reference.

This appendix includes all global functions and global properties as well as statements, operators, and constants. It also covers a few select built-in Flash objects.

The order of these scripts follows closely the drop-down menu in the actions panel.

## Global Functions

### Timeline Control

#### gotoAndPlay
**Availability:** Flash Player 2

**Generic Template:** gotoAndPlay(*scene*, *frame*);

**Parameters:**

>   *scene*—The scene where you would like to go. Optional
>
>   *frame*—The frame where you would like to go.

**Description:**

This script sends the playhead to a specific frame in the specified scene and then plays. If there is no scene specified, the playhead moves to the frame in the current scene.

**Example:**

This example moves the playhead to frame 10 and plays when the interpreter reads it:

```
gotoAndPlay(10);
```

## gotoAndStop
**Availability:** Flash Player 2

**Generic Template:** gotoAndStop(*scene*, *frame*);

**Parameters:**

> *scene*—The scene where you would like to go. Optional
>
> *frame*—The frame where you would like to go.

**Description:**

This script sends the playhead to a specific frame in the specified scene and stops there. If no scene is specified, the playhead moves to the frame in the current scene.

**Example:**

This example moves the playhead to the frame labeled myFrame and stops when the interpreter reads it:

```
gotoAndStop("myFrame");
```

## nextFrame
**Availability:** Flash Player 2

**Generic Template:** nextFrame();

**Parameters:** None

**Description:**

Sends the playhead to the next frame and stops. This can also be used as a constraint for gotoAndPlay and gotoAndStop.

**Example:**

The first example moves the playhead to the next frame and stops when a mouse is clicked; the second example uses nextFrame in a gotoAndPlay action:

```
onClipEvent(mouseDown){
    nextFrame();
}
gotoAndPlay(nextFrame());
```

## nextScene

**Availability:** Flash Player 2

**Generic Template:** nextScene();

**Parameters:** None

**Description:**

Sends the playhead to the next scene and stops. This can also be used as a constraint for gotoAndPlay and gotoAndStop.

**Example:**

The first example moves the playhead to the next scene and stops when a mouse is clicked; the second example uses nextScene in a gotoAndPlay action:

```
onClipEvent(mouseDown){
    nextScene();
}
//move to next scene
gotoAndPlay(nextScene());
```

## play

**Availability:** Flash Player 2

**Generic Template:** play();

**Parameters:** None

**Description:**

Moves the playhead forward.

**Example:**

This example moves the timeline forward when a button is pressed.

```
on(press){
    play();
}
```

## prevFrame

**Availability:** Flash Player 2

**Generic Template:** prevFrame();

**Parameters:** None

A

**Description:**

Sends the playhead to the previous frame and stops. This can also be used as a constraint for gotoAndPlay and gotoAndStop.

**Example:**

This example uses an on event handler to move the playhead back one frame:

```
on(press) {
    prevFrame();
}
```

## prevScene

**Availability:** Flash Player 2

**Generic Template:** prevScene();

**Parameters:** None

**Description:**

Sends the playhead to the previous scene and stops. This can also be used as a constraint for gotoAndPlay and gotoAndStop.

**Example:**

The first example moves the playhead to the previous scene and stops when a button is pressed; the second example uses prevScene in a gotoAndPlay action:

```
on(press){
    prevScene();
}
gotoAndPlay(prevScene());
```

## stop

**Availability:** Flash Player 2

**Generic Template:** stop();

**Parameters:** None

**Description:**

Stops the playhead from moving on the timeline.

**Example:**

This example stops the movie when a button is pressed:

```
on(press){
    stop();
}
```

## stopAllSounds

**Availability:** Flash Player 3

**Generic Template:** stopAllSounds();

**Parameters:** None

**Description:**

Stops all sounds that are playing without affecting the playhead. Sounds placed directly on the timeline begin again as the playhead moves past the stopAllSounds action.

**Example:**

The following example stops all sounds when the loop variable reaches 3:

```
if(loop >=3){
    stopAllSounds();
}
```

# Browser/Network

## fscommand

**Availability:** Flash Player 3

**Generic Template:** fscommand(*command*, *parameter*);

**Parameters:**

    *command*—A string passed for any purpose or as a command to the hosting application.

    *parameter*—Another string passed for any purpose or as a value.

**Description:**

This script allows the Flash movie to communicate with its host, including the Flash player. It can also be used to pass variables to other programs that can host ActiveX controls.

A

---

**NOTE**

When passing commands to the Flash Player, you must use the following predefined commands:

- `allowscale`. Allows or disallows the ability to enlarge and shrink the content of the Flash movie. The parameters can be `true` or `false`.

- `fullscreen`. Fills the user's entire screen when parameters are set to `true`. The parameters can be `true` or `false`.

- `showmenu`. Can display or not display the controls in the context menu. The parameters can be `true` or `false`.

- `rapallkeys`. Can allow or disallow the ability to pass keystrokes to the Flash Player. The parameters can be `true` or `false`.

- `exec`. Can execute an application from inside the Flash player. The parameter is the name of the application.

- `quit`. Closes the standalone Flash player (does not close browser). No arguments.

---

**Example:**

These examples show how to use some of the predefined commands:

```
fscommand("fullscreen", "true");
fscommand("trapallkeys", "false");
fscommand("quit");
```

# getURL

**Availability:** Flash Player 2

**Generic Template:** getURL(*url*, *window*, *variable*);

**Parameters:**

*url*—A string representing the exact URL for the document you want to obtain.

*window*—An optional assignment that represents where to load the URL, including _blank, _self, _parent, and _top.

*variable*—Another optional command stating how to send variables associated with the Flash movie, such as GET and POST.

**Description:**

The getURL script can do much more than simply open another Web page; it can also execute code in HTML and initiate events in the Flash movie.

**Example:**

The first example loads a Web page into a new window; the second example triggers a javascript action to pop up an alert:

```
getURL("http://samspublishing.com", "_blank");
getURL("javascript:alert('Flash Unleashed');");
```

## loadMovie

**Availability:** Flash Player 3

**Generic Template:** loadMovie(*url, level/target[, variable]*);

**Parameters:**

> *url*—A direct link to the SWF or JPG file you would like to load into the main Flash movie. When being used in the standalone player or in the testing environment, the loaded movie must be stored in the same folder.

> *level*—A numeric value representing the level in which to load the movie.

> *target*—A target movie clip or level number representing where the movie will be loaded.

> *target movieclip*—A direct path to the movie clip where you would load the movie. When a loaded movie is placed within a movie clip, anything that currently resides in that movie clip is replaced by the loaded movie.

> *variable*—An optional command stating how to send variables associated with the Flash movie. The two options are GET and POST.

**Description:**

This script loads a movie or JPEG into the main Flash movie either by using *target movieclip* or *level number* to represent where the movie is to be loaded. If the movie is loaded into a level, the script changes from loadMovie to loadMovieNum.

If a movie or picture is loaded into a movie clip, that file takes on the characteristics the movie clip already possesses, such as position, size, and alpha.

**Example:**

This example shows how to load a movie into a movie clip called myMovieclip.

```
loadMovie("theMovie.swf", "_root.myMovieclip");
```

**A**

## loadMovieNum

**Availability:** Flash Player 4

**Generic Template:** loadMovieNum(*url, level, variable*);

**Parameters:**

> *url*—A direct link to the SWF or JPG file you would like to load into the main Flash movie. When being used in the standalone player or in the testing environment, the loaded movie must be stored in the same folder.

> *level*—A numeric value representing the level in which to load the movie.
>
> *variable*—An optional command stating how to send variables associated with the Flash movie, such as GET and POST.

### Description:

This script loads a movie or JPEG into the main Flash movie by level number to represent where the movie is to be loaded. If the movie is loaded into a level, the script changes from loadMovie to loadMovieNum.

If you load a movie into a level that already contains content, the loaded file replaces that content.

Levels provide a simple stacking method that Flash uses to separate different parts of the Flash movie. The levels start at 0. After a movie is loaded into a Flash movie, you can refer to it as _level followed by the level you have loaded it into. For example, if you load a movie into the second level, refer to it as _level2.

### Example:

This example loads a JPEG file called myJpeg.jpg into a specified level:

```
loadMovieNum("myJpeg.jpg", 1);
```

## loadVariables

**Availability:** Flash Player 4

**Generic Template:** loadVariables(*url* , *level*/"*target*"[, *variable*]);

### Parameters:

> *url*—A direct link to a file containing the variables you would like to load into the main Flash movie. When being used in the standalone player or in the testing environment, the loaded movie must be stored in the same folder.
>
> *level*—A numeric value representing the level in which to load the variables. In normal mode in the ActionScript panel, when you attempt to put a number in the loadVariables script, the panel converts it to LoadVariablesNum. Just something to remember.
>
> *target*—A target movie clip or level number representing where the movie will be loaded.
>
> *variable*—An optional command stating how to send variables associated with the Flash movie. The two options are GET and POST.

### Description:

This script loads variables from a text file or a file created by another script, such as CGI or ASP. The text must be in MIME format. Also, the file must be in the same folder as the Flash movie that is loading it.

You can only load these variables into a target movie clip or a level number.

**Standard MIME Format:**

```
myVariable=Flash%20Unleashed&myName=David&myAge=23
```

**Example:**

This example loads a text file holding the variables into a movie clip:

```
loadVariables("myVariables.txt", "_root.myMovieclip");
```

# loadVariablesNum

**Availability:** Flash Player 4

**Generic Template:** loadVariables(*url* , *level*, *variable*);

**Parameters:**

*url*—A direct link to a file containing the variables you would like to load into the main Flash movie. When being used in the standalone player or in the testing environment, the loaded movie must be stored in the same folder.

*level*—A numeric value representing the level to load the variables in. When using loadVariablesNum, you must signify the level in the movie in which to load the variables.

*variable*—An optional command stating how to send variables associated with the Flash movie. The two options are GET and POST.

**Description:**

This script loads variables from a text file or a file created by another script, such as CGI or ASP. The text must be in MIME format. Also, the file must be in the same folder as the Flash movie that is loading it.

**Standard MIME Format:**

```
myVariable=Flash%20Unleashed&myName=David&myAge=23
```

**Example:**

This example loads variables into the root of a movie:

```
loadVariablesNum("myData.txt", 0);
```

# unloadMovie

**Availability:** Flash Player 3

**Generic Template:** unloadMovie(*level*/*target*);

**Parameters:**

> *level*—A numeric value representing the level from which to unload the movie.
>
> *target*—A target movie clip or level number representing from where the movie will be loaded.

**Description:**

This script removes a loaded movie from a target movie clip or level (using unloadMovieNum).

**Example:**

This example unloads a movie from a movie clip:

```
unloadMovie("_root.myMovie.myLoadedMovie");
```

## unloadMovieNum

**Availability:** Flash Player 3

**Generic Template:** unloadMovieNum(*level*);

**Parameters:**

> *level*—The level from where you are unloading the loaded movie.

**Description:**

This script removes a loaded movie from a level in the main movie.

**Example:**

This example unloads a loaded movie from the _root level.

```
unloadMovieNum(0);
```

# Movie Clip Control

## duplicateMovieClip

**Availability:** Flash Player 4

**Generic Template:** duplicateMovieClip(*target*, *newName*, *depth*);

**Parameters:**

> *target*—The path to the movie you would like to duplicate.
>
> *newName*—The name given to the duplicated movie clip. This name must be unique.
>
> *depth*—The amount of duplication to take place. This is also used for stacking so that multiple duplicated movies do not replace each other.

**Description:**

This script creates a new instance of the target movie clip. Each duplicated movie clip has its own unique name. The parent movie clip must remain for the duplicated movies to remain.

**Example:**

This example duplicates a movie five times using five unique instances of the original:

```
i = 0;
while(i < 5) {
    duplicateMovieClip(myClip, "myClip"+i, i);
    i++;
}
```

## getProperty

**Availability:** Flash Player 4

**Generic Template:** getProperty(*name*, *property*);

**Parameters:**

> *name*—The name of the instance of a movie clip from which you're trying to access a property.
>
> *property*—The name of the property you're trying to access.

**Description:**

This function retrieves the specific property of the specific instance being referred to.

**Example:**

This example attempts to retrieve the horizontal position of a movie clip:

```
trace(getProperty(myMovie, _x));
```

## on

**Availability:** Flash Player 2

**Generic Template:**

```
on(buttonEvent){
    statement(s);
}
```

**A**

### Parameters:

*buttonEvent*

> press—Occurs when the button is clicked (or pressed).
>
> release—Occurs when the button is released while the mouse is over it.
>
> releaseOutside—Occurs when the button is pressed and then released while the mouse is *not* over it.
>
> rollOut—Occurs when the mouse moves from being over the button to *not* being over the button.
>
> rollOver—Occurs when the mouse moves over the button.
>
> dragOut—Occurs when the button is pressed and the mouse moves outside the button without the button being released.
>
> dragOver—Occurs when the user presses the button, drags outside the button, and drags back over the button, all without releasing the mouse button.
>
> keyPress("*key*")—Unlike the other events, this one takes place when a key is pressed. Here, "*key*" can only be one key.
>
> *statement(s)*—Code to be executed when *buttonEvent* occurs.

### Description:

An event handler that occurs within a button when a mouse event or keystroke occurs.

### Example:

The first example runs a simple trace function when a button is pressed; the second example stops the dragging of a button:

```
//when the mouse clicks on the button, the statement will be traced
on(press) {
    trace("This button has been pressed");
}
//the next event will stop an object from being dragged
on(release, releaseOutside){
    stopDrag();
}
```

## onClipEvent

**Availability:** Flash Player 5

### Generic Template:

```
onClipEvent(movieEvent){
        statements;
}
```

## Parameters:

*movieEvent*—An event that triggers any actions between the curly brackets.

load—The first time the instance of the movie appears on the timeline.

unload—This takes place when a movie clip has been removed from the timeline.

enterFrame—Actions are executed at the frame rate of the movie continuously.

mouseMove—Any time the _x or _y coordinate of the mouse changes within the borders of the root movie, code is executed.

mouseDown—Occurs when the left mouse button is pressed.

mouseUp—Occurs when the left mouse button is released.

keyDown—Occurs when a key on the keyboard is pressed.

keyUp—Occurs when a key on the keyboard is released.

data—When data is received from a loadVariables script, this event activates when the last piece of data is loaded. When a loadMovie script is run, the code runs continuously as each piece of the movie is loaded.

*statements*—The code to be executed when the clipEvent is true.

## Description:

An event handler that focuses on movie events that can happen once or several times.

## Example:

This example continually traces a string while the movie is on the stage:

```
onClipEvent(enterFrame){
    trace("entering");
}
```

# removeMovieClip

**Availability:** Flash Player 4

**Generic Template:** removeMovieClip(*target*);

## Parameters:

*target*—The target path to a movie created by duplicateMovieClip or attachMovie.

## Description:

This script removes a movie clip instance of movies created with either duplicateMovieClip or attachMovie.

**Example:**

This example removes a movie recently created with `duplicateMovieClip`:

```
duplicateMovieClip(myMovie, "myMovie1", 1);
removeMovieClip(myMovie1);
```

## setProperty

**Availability:** Flash Player 4

**Generic Template:** `setProperty(target, property, value/expression);`

**Parameters:**

> `target`—A string literal representing the direct path to the movie for which you want to set the properties.
>
> `property`—The property you want to set.
>
> `value`—The value to which you want to set the property.
>
> `expression`—Any viable expression.

**Description:**

Changes the property of a movie during playback.

**Example:**

This example sets the alpha of a movie clip to 70:

```
setProperty("myMovie", _alpha, "70");
```

## startDrag

**Availability:** Flash Player 4

**Generic Template:** `startDrag(target, lockCenter, left, top, right, bottom);`

**Parameters:**

> `target`—The direct path to the movie clip you would like to drag.
>
> `lockCenter`—Optional parameter, if set to `true`, the mouse locks to the center of the movie clip.
>
> `left, top, right, bottom`—Optional parameter that you can set so that the movie clip cannot drag outside of these boundaries.

**Description:**

This script allows a single movie clip to be draggable until a `stopDrag` script is executed or another movie clip is set to be draggable.

**Example:**

This example starts dragging a button when the button is pressed and stops dragging the button when the button is released:

```
on(press){
    startDrag(this,false);
}
on(release){
    stopDrag();
}
```

## stopDrag

**Availability:** Flash Player 4

**Generic Template:** stopDrag();

**Parameters:** None

**Description:**

When this code is executed, any movie clip that is set to be draggable will be stopped at its current position until it's set to be draggable again.

**Example:**

This example starts dragging a button when the button is pressed and stops dragging the button when the button is released.

```
on(press){
    startDrag(this,false);
}
on(release){
    stopDrag();
}
```

## targetPath

**Availability:** Flash Player 5

**Generic Template:** targetPath(movie);

**Parameters:**

> movie—This is a reference to a movie clip.

**Description:**

This function returns the target path to a movie in dot syntax.

**Example:**

Here is an example of using the `targetPath` function to return a target path to a movie:

```
trace(targetPath(myMovie));
```

## updateAfterEvent

**Availability:** Flash Player 5

**Generic Template:** `updateAfterEvent();`

**Parameters:** None

**Description:**

This script updates a movie and is not dependent on frame rate speed. The `updateAfterEvent` script must be placed within a clip event handler.

**Example:**

This example moves a movie clip each time the user clicks the mouse. If the `updateAfterEvent` method were not present, it would be possible for the user to click faster than the frame rate, but with the `updateAfterEvent` method, it updates instantly.

```
onClipEvent(mouseDown){
    this._x++;
    updateAfterEvent();
}
```

# Printing Functions

## print

**Availability:** Flash Player 4.20

**Generic Template:** `print(target, boundaryBox);`

**Parameters:**

*target*—A path to the movie clip to print. Unless otherwise assigned, the `print` action prints all frames. To specify which frames to print, assign a frame label of #p to them.

*boundaryBox*—A modifier used to crop frames that are to be printed. Special values are used for this, and they are as follows:

bmovie—This sets the printable area of all frames in a movie clip to the printable area of a specific frame labeled #b.

bmax—All the printable frames are pooled to form one printable area for each box. This is useful if each frame changes size.

bframe—This designates each frame's printable area based on the individual frame. This is useful if you want each frame to fill in as much space on a page as possible.

**Description:**

This script prints frames out of a movie clip. It prints all frames unless individual frames are labeled with #p. Boundaries can be set by using some of the keywords listed under *boundaryBox*.

Although the quality is higher with this script, you cannot print transparencies or certain special color effects. For those, you must use `printAsBitmap`.

All images must be loaded before they can be printed.

**Example:**

This example prints frames out of a movie and sets it so that each frame's print area is dependent on its individual area, instead of other frames' areas:

```
print("myMovie", "bframe");
```

## printAsBitmap

**Availability:** Flash Player 4.20

**Generic Template:** printAsBitmap(*target*, *boundaryBox*);

**Parameters:**

*target*—A path to the movie clip to print. Unless otherwise assigned, the `print` action prints all frames. To specify which frames to print, assign a frame label of #p to them.

*boundaryBox*—A modifier used to crop frames that are to be printed. Special values are used for this, and they are as follows:

bmovie—This sets the printable area of all frames in a movie clip to the printable area of a specific frame labeled #b.

bmax—All the printable frames are pooled to form one printable area for each box. This is useful if each frame changes size.

bframe—This designates each frame's printable area based on the individual frame. This is useful if you want each frame to fill in as much space on a page as possible.

**Description:**

This script prints frames out of movies as bitmaps to maintain transparency and special coloring. The image is printed at the highest quality the printer can handle.

If there are no transparencies in your movie, try using the `print` action instead for higher quality. All images must be loaded before they can be printed.

**Example:**

This example prints a specific movie that has frames labeled with #p when a button is pressed:

```
on(press){
    printAsBitmap("myPrint", "bmax");
}
```

## printAsBitmapNum

**Availability:** Flash Player 5

**Generic Template:** printAsBitmapNum(*level*, *boundaryBox*);

**Parameters:**

> *level*—The level of the Flash movie you would like to print.
>
> *boundaryBox*—A modifier used to crop frames that are to be printed. Special values are used for this, and they are as follows:
>
> > bmovie—This sets the printable area of all frames in a movie clip to the printable area of a specific frame labeled #b.
> >
> > bmax—All the printable frames are pooled to form one printable area for each box. This is useful if each frame changes size.
> >
> > bframe—This designates each frame's printable area based on the individual frame. This is useful if you want each frame to fill in as much space on a page as possible.

**Description:**

This script prints frames out of levels as bitmaps to maintain transparency and special coloring. The image is printed at the highest quality the printer can handle.

If there are no transparencies in your level, try using the printNum action instead for higher quality. All images must be loaded before they can be printed.

**Example:**

This example prints a frame labeled with #p when a button is pressed:

```
on(press){
    printAsBitmapNum(1,"bmovie");
}
```

## printNum

**Availability:** Flash Player 5

**Generic Template:** printNum(*level*, *boundaryBox*);

## Parameters:

*level*—The level of the Flash movie you would like to print.

*boundaryBox*—A modifier used to crop frames that are to be printed. Special values are used for this, and they are as follows:

bmovie—This sets the printable area of all frames in a movie clip to the printable area of a specific frame labeled #b.

bmax—All the printable frames are pooled to form one printable area for each box. This is useful if each frame changes size.

bframe—This designates each frame's printable area based on the individual frame. This is useful if you want each frame to fill in as much space on a page as possible.

## Description:

This script prints frames out of a level in the player. It prints all frames unless individual frames are labeled with #p. Boundaries can be set by using some of the keywords listed under *boundaryBox*.

Although the quality is higher with this script, you cannot print transparencies or certain special color effects. For those you must use printAsBitmapNum. All images must be loaded before they can be printed.

## Example:

This example prints frames containing the label #p in a specified label when the playhead reaches the action:

```
printNum(2,"bmax");
```

# Miscellaneous Functions

## clearInterval

**Availability:** Flash Player 6

**Generic Template:** clearInterval(*interval*);

**Parameters:**

*interval*—An object that has been returned using a call and is sent to a setInterval action.

## Description:

This script clears a call and sends it to the setInterval action.

**Example:**

This example sets an interval call and then clears it:

```
function myFunction() {
    trace("initialized interval");
}
var myInterval = setInterval(myFunction, 2000);
clearInterval(myInterval);
```

## escape

**Availability:** Flash Player 5

**Generic Template:** escape(*expression*);

**Parameters:**

    *expression*—Will be converted to a string and encoded into a URL-encoded format.

**Description:**

This function converts the expression to a string and then encodes it in a URL-encoded format.

**Example:**

Here is an example of the escape function:

```
var name = "David 123";
trace(escape(name));
//output: David%20123
```

## eval

**Availability:** Flash Player 4

**Generic Template:** eval(*expression*);

**Parameters:**

    *expression*—A string representing the name of a variable, property, object, or movie clip.

**Description:**

This function is used to access an expression and return a value if the expression is a property or variable. Alternatively, it returns a reference if the expression is an object or movie clip. If the expression cannot be found, this function gives the value of undefined.

**Example:**

Here is an example of the eval function looking for a variable:

```
var myName = "David";
trace(eval("myName"));
//output: David
```

## getTimer

**Availability:** Flash Player 4

**Generic Template:** getTimer();

**Parameters:** None

**Description:**

This function gets the amount of milliseconds that have passed since the movie began playing.

**Example:**

Here is an example of the getTimer function:

```
_root.onEnterFrame=function(){
    if(getTimer() >= 5000){
        trace("5 seconds has passed");
    }
}
```

## getVersion

**Availability:** Flash Player 5

**Generic Template:** getVersion();

**Parameters:** None

**Description:**

This function retrieves the Flash player version on the user's local computer at runtime.

**Example:**

Here is a simple way to use the getVersion function:

```
trace(getVersion());
//output: WIN 7,0,14,0
```

## MMExecute

**Availability:** Flash Player 7

**Generic Template:** MMExecute("JSFL command");

**Parameters:** The only parameter this functions uses is a JSFL (JavaScript Flash Language) command as a string literal.

**Description:**

This function executes any JSFL command when called. It is used often in the building of custom panels.

**Example:**

This example sends a message to the output panel when called from a custom panel:

```
MMExecute("fl.trace('message 123');");
```

## setInterval

**Availability:** Flash Player 6

**Generic Template:**

```
setInterval(function, interval, parameters);
setInterval(object, method, interval, parameters);
```

**Parameters:**

> *function*—The name of a function or a reference to an anonymous function.
>
> *interval*—The time in milliseconds between calls to the function.
>
> *parameters*—These are arguments that can be optionally passed to the function or method.
>
> *object*—Any object.
>
> *method*—A method to call in regard to the object.

**Returns:**

An interval that can be sent to `clearInterval` to cancel the specified `interval` itself.

**Description:**

This script calls a function, method, or object at periodic intervals. It can be used to update information from a remote file while the movie is playing.

The interval is a numeric value that represents how many milliseconds must occur until the script is run again.

> **NOTE**
>
> Use the `updateAfterEvent` action to make sure the screen refreshes fast enough if the interval is much faster than the frame rate.

**Example:**

This example calls a simple function and passes the parameters in the interval statement; the script is run about every second (1,000 milliseconds):

```
function displayName(name){
    trace(name);
}
setInterval(displayName, 1000, "David");
```

This example calls a function that has no parameters every half a second:

```
function displayName(){
    trace("David");
}
setInterval(displayName, 500);
```

## trace

**Availability:** Flash Player 4

**Generic Template:** `trace(expression);`

**Parameters:**

    *expression*—Any viable expression. It is displayed in the output window when the movie is tested.

**Description:**

This script evaluates the expression and displays the result in the output window when the movie is tested. This script does not display anything except in the output window. You can use the Omit Trace option to remove the `trace` actions when exporting for file size.

**Example:**

This example traces a simple string:

```
trace("This was traced");
```

## unescape

**Availability:** Flash Player 5

**Generic Template:** `unescape(hex);`

A

**Parameters:**

> *hex*—A string representing a hexadecimal sequence to escape.

**Description:**

This function evaluates hex, decodes it from the URL-encoded format, and then returns a string.

**Example:**

Here is an example using the unescape function:

```
trace(unescape("David %7b%5bVogeleer%5D%7D"));
//output: David {[Vogeleer]}
```

# Mathematical Functions

## isFinite

**Availability:** Flash Player 5

**Generic Template:** isFinite(*expression*);

**Parameters:**

> *expression*—A Boolean, variable, or other expression that can be evaluated.

**Description:**

This function evaluates an expression to see whether it is finite instead of infinity or negative infinity. If the expression is finite, it evaluates to true; otherwise, it evaluates to false.

**Example:**

Here is an example using the isFinite function:

```
var x = 10;
trace(isFinite(x));
//output: true
```

## isNaN

**Availability:** Flash Player 5

**Generic Template:** isNaN(*expression*);

**Parameters:** None

**Description:**

This function evaluates an expression, checking whether it is not a real number. If the expression is a real number, the function evaluates it to `false`. Otherwise, it evaluates to `true`.

**Example:**

Here are a couple of examples using the `isNaN` function:

```
trace(isNaN("David"));
//output: true

trace(isNaN(5));
//output: false
```

## parseFloat

**Availability:** Flash Player 5

**Generic Template:** parseFloat(*string*);

**Parameters:**

> *string*—The string to convert into a floating-point number.

**Description:**

This function converts a string into a floating-point number if and only if the string starts with an integer. If the string does not start with an integer, the function returns NaN. When the parse reaches a nonnumeric value in the string, it stops converting.

**Example:**

Here are some examples of using the `parseFloat` function:

```
trace(parseFloat("5.5"));
//output: 5.5

trace(parseFloat("T1"));
//output: NaN

trace(parseFloat("1T"));
//output: 1
```

## parseInt

**Availability:** Flash Player 5

**Generic Template:** parseInt(*string*, *radix*);

**Parameters:**

> *string*—The string to convert into a floating-point integer.
>
> *radix*—An optional parameter representing the radix (or base) of the number to parse, which can be between 2 and 26.

**Description:**

This function converts a string to a number. If the string cannot convert to a number, the function returns NaN.

**Example:**

Here are some examples of the `parseInt` function:

```
trace(parseInt("5"));
//output: 5

trace(parseInt("David"));
//output: NaN

trace(parseInt(0x123));
//output: 291
```

# Conversion Functions

**Availability:** Flash Player 4 (with some changes in behavior in the 7 player)

**Generic Template:** `typeOfConversion (value);`

**Parameters:**

> *typeOfConversion*—The different types of conversions, including array, Boolean, number, object, and string.
>
> *value*—Any viable expression.

**Description:**

Each type of conversion function converts the value to its data type.

**Example:**

Here are some basic examples of data-conversion functions:

```
var x = 5;
trace(typeof x);
//output: number
```

```
trace(typeof Array(x));
//output: object

trace(typeof Boolean(x));
//output: boolean

trace(typeof String(x));
//output: string
```

# Global Properties

## _accProps

**Availability:** Flash Player 6 version 65

**Generic Template:** `this._accProps.propertyName = value;`

**Parameters:**

>*propertyName*—The name of the accessibility property you want to change.

>*value*—The value you want to change the property to.

**Description:**

The `_accProps` property enables developers to manipulate Flash elements in regard to accessibility pertaining to screen readers.

**Example:**

This example changes the property name of the _accProps property:

```
this._accProps.name = "Sample";
```

## _focusrect

**Availability:** Flash Player 4

**Generic Template:** `movieClip._focusrect = value;`

**Parameters:**

>*movieClip*—An instance of a movie clip on the timeline.

>*value*—A Boolean value (true/false).

**Description:**

This property returns a Boolean value if the movie clip has a yellow rectangle surrounding it when it has keyboard focus.

**Example:**

This example checks a movie clip to see whether it has keyboard focus. If so, it displays a message in the output window:

```
if(myMovie._focusrect){
    trace(myMovie._name+" has keyboard focus");
}
```

# Identifiers

**Generic Template:** `identifier.member`

**Parameters:**

> *member*—Any function, property, or object that can be referred to in ActionScript.
>
> *identifier*—The type of identifier; the following is a list of the available identifiers.
>
> - `_global`—Allows any associated member to be accessed from anywhere in the Flash movie.
> - `_level`—This identifier is used to retrieve or set the level depth of a movie clip.
> - `_parent`—This identifier represents one level of hierarchy up from the current movie.
> - `_root`—This identifier represents the main timeline.
> - `super`—This identifier is used to perform a superclass initialization.
> - `this`—This identifier refers to the current timeline of object in which it is residing.

**Description:**

Identifiers are used to reference individual members or elements in Flash from different locations.

**Example:**

The following example creates a global property that can be accessed from anywhere in the Flash movie:

```
_global.name = "David";
```

## _quality

**Availability:** Flash Player 5

**Generic Template:** _quality

**Parameters:** None

**Description:**

This global property can be set or retrieved and represents the rendering quality used in the movie.

The different types of quality are as follows:

Low—Graphics are not antialiased; bitmaps are not smooth.

Medium—Graphics are antialiased using a 2×2 grid, in pixels, but bitmaps are still not smooth.

High—Graphics are antialiased using a 4×4 grid, in pixels, and bitmaps are smoothed. Note that this is Flash's default setting.

Best—Graphics are antialiased using a 4×4 grid, in pixels, and bitmaps are smooth.

**Example:**

This example turns the rendering quality to best:

```
_quality = "Best";
```

## _soundbuftime

**Availability:** Flash Player 4

**Generic Template:** _soundbuftime = *number*;

**Parameters:**

*number*—The number of seconds before a movie begins to stream.

**Description:**

This property can be used to set a buffer before a movie or sound, in seconds, that stops the playback until the indicated number of seconds has gone by (five is the default value).

**Example:**

This example sets soundbuftime to 15 seconds so that the sound does not play for 15 seconds:

```
_soundbuftime = 15;
```

# Statements

## Class Constructs

## class

**Availability:** Flash Player 6

**Generic Template:**

```
class ClassName {
    //class members
}
```

A

**Parameters:**

> *ClassName*—The name of the custom class being created.

**Description:**

The keyword `class` can only be used in the Flash Player 6 or greater with ActionScript 2.0 being set and must be within an external ActionScript file. It is used to create an object class to be used within Flash.

**Example:**

This example creates a simple class of object:

```
//create the class
class MyClass {
    public var myVar:String;
    public function myFunction(){
        //do something
    }
}
```

## dynamic

**Availability:** Flash Player 6

**Generic Template:**

```
dynamic class ClassName {
    //class members
}
```

**Parameters:**

> *ClassName*—The name of the class being created.

**Description:**

The keyword `dynamic` can only be used in the Flash Player 6 or later with ActionScript 2.0 set and must be within an external ActionScript file. If an object is instantiated from a dynamic class, methods of the object can be called that were not present at the object's instantiation.

**Example:**

In this example, you create a simple class of object with a function labeled "a". Then in Flash, you set a new instance of this object to a variable while calling a method on the object that does not exist. This is allowed, and does not cause errors.

```
//create the class
dynamic class MyClass {
    public var myVar:String;
    public function a(){
        //do something
    }
}
//back in Flash
var myVar = new MyClass().b;
```

## extends

**Availability:** Flash Player 6

**Generic Template:**

```
class ClassName extends ParentClass{
    //class members
}
```

**Parameters:**

> *ClassName*—The name of the class being created.

> *ParentClass*—The name of the object class that is being extended.

**Description:**

The keyword extends can only be used in the Flash Player 6 or later with ActionScript 2.0 set and must be within an external ActionScript file. It allows a class being created to receive all methods, properties, and events of its parent class.

**Example:**

This example extends the MovieClip class:

```
//create the class
class MyClass extends MovieClip{
    function onEnterFrame(){
        this._x++;
    }
}
```

## get

**Availability:** Flash Player 6

**Generic Template:**

```
function get functionName(){}
```

**Parameters:**

*functionName*—The name of the getter/setter function being created.

**Description:**

The keyword get can only be used in Flash Player 6 or later with ActionScript 2.0 set and must be within an external ActionScript file. It is part of the getter/setter function set that allows access to properties of the object through means of a method that appears like a property to the user.

**Example:**

This example creates a getter/setter function combination, and then uses the getter part in Flash.

```
//create the class
class RaceCar {
    private var speed:Number = 50;
    function get mySpeed():Number{
        return this.speed;
    }
    function set mySpeed(amount:Number):Void{
        this.speed = amount;
    }
}
//back in Flash
myCar = new RaceCar();
myCar.mySpeed = 20;
trace(myCar.mySpeed);
//output: 20
```

## implements

**Availability:** Flash Player 6

**Generic Template:**

```
class ClassName implements Interface {
    //class members
}
```

**Parameters:**

*ClassName*—The name of the class being created.

*Interface*—The interface being implemented.

## Description:

The keyword `implements` can only be used in Flash Player 6 or later with ActionScript 2.0 set and must be within an external ActionScript file. It is used when defining a class that must supply implementations for all methods defined in the interface being used.

## Example:

This example creates an interface, and then creates a class that implements that interface:

```
//create the interface
interface MyInterface{
  function a():String;
  function b(num:Number):Number;
}
//create the class
class MyClass implements MyInterface{
    function a():String {
        return "sample";
    }
    function b(num:Number):Number {
        return 10+num;
    }
}
```

## import
**Availability:** Flash Player 6

### Generic Template:

import.ClassName

### Parameters:

> *ClassName*—The name of the class or package being imported.

### Description:

The keyword `import` can only be used in Flash Player 6 or later with ActionScript 2.0 set. It is used to import other classes or packages so that their methods and properties can be used within the class being constructed.

### Example:

In this example, the `EventDispatcher` class is imported so that the class being constructed can support event listeners:

```
//import the object class needed
import mx.events.EventDispatcher;
```

```
class Bird extends MovieClip {
    //create two methods that will be used in Flash
    public var addEventListener:Function;
    public var removeEventListener:Function;
    //declare the event from the EventDispatcher object
    private var dispatchEvent:Function;
    //declare the constructor function
    function Bird() {
        //initialize the EventDispatcher to work with this object
        EventDispatcher.initialize(this);
    }
}
```

## interface

**Availability:** Flash Player 6

**Generic Template:**

```
interface InterfaceName {
    //interface members
}
```

**Parameters:**

> *InterfaceName*—The name of the interface being created.

**Description:**

The keyword interface can only be used in Flash Player 6 or later with ActionScript 2.0 set and must be within an external ActionScript file. It is used to create an interface in much the same way as creating a class. There are subtle differences, and here they are:

- Interfaces can only declare members; they cannot implement them.
- Interfaces can only declare public members.
- Interfaces cannot use getter/setter functions.

**Example:**

This example creates an interface, and then creates a class that implements that interface:

```
//create the interface
interface MyInterface{
  function a():String;
  function b(num:Number):Number;
}
```

```
//create the class
class MyClass implements MyInterface{
    function a():String {
        return "sample";
    }
    function b(num:Number):Number {
        return 10+num;
    }
}
```

## private
**Availability:** Flash Player 6

**Generic Template:** private *member*

**Parameters:**

> *member*—A method or property of the object class.

### Description:

The keyword private can only be used in Flash Player 6 or later with ActionScript 2.0 set and must be within an external ActionScript file. It is used to declare members that are accessible only from within the object class, and not from an instance of the object.

### Example:

This example creates a private property, and uses it in a public method:

```
//create the class
class MyClass {
    private var speed:Number = 50;
    public function accelerate(amount:Number):Number{
        this.speed += amount;
        return this.speed;
    }
}
```

## public
**Availability:** Flash Player 6

**Generic Template:** public *member*

**Parameters:**

> *member*—A method or property of the object class.

### Description:

The keyword public can only be used in Flash Player 6 or later with ActionScript 2.0 set and must be within an external ActionScript file. It is used to declare members as public so they can be used with instances of the object as well as from within the object class itself.

### Example:

This example creates a `private` property, and uses it in a `public` method:

```
//create the class
class MyClass {
    private var speed:Number = 50;
    public function accelerate(amount:Number):Number{
        this.speed += amount;
        return this.speed;
    }
}
```

## set

**Availability:** Flash Player 6

**Generic Template:** `function set functionName():Void{}`

**Parameters:**

> `functionName`—The name of the getter/setter function being created.

### Description:

The keyword set can only be used in Flash Player 6 or later with ActionScript 2.0 set and must be within an external ActionScript file. It is part of the getter/setter function set that allows access to properties of the object through means of a method that appears like a property to the user. The setter part should have no return value.

### Example:

This example creates a getter/setter function combination, and then uses the getter part in Flash.

```
//create the class
class RaceCar {
    private var speed:Number = 50;
    function get mySpeed():Number{
        return this.speed;
    }
    function set mySpeed(amount:Number):Void{
        this.speed = amount;
```

```
    }
}
//back in Flash
myCar = new RaceCar();
myCar.mySpeed = 20;
trace(myCar.mySpeed);
//output: 20
```

## static
**Availability:** Flash Player 6

**Generic Template:** `static member`

**Parameters:**

    *Class member*—A method or property of the object class.

**Description:**

The keyword `static` can only be used in Flash Player 6 or later with ActionScript 2.0 set and must be within an external ActionScript file. It is used to declare members that can only be accessed through the class name and not with instances of the class.

**Example:**

This example creates a class with a static property, and then goes to Flash and calls that property:

```
//create the class
class MyClass {
    static var sample:String = "sample 1";
}
//back in Flash
trace(MyClass.sample);
//output: sample 1
```

# Conditions/Loops

## break
**Availability:** Flash Player 4

**Generic Template:** `break;`

**Description:**

This script is used for stopping loop statements. When the interpreter reaches a break, it skips the rest of the statement and moves on to the code following the closing brackets.

**Example:**

This script stops an otherwise unstoppable loop:

```
for(var i=0; true; i++){
    if(i >=20){
        break;
    }
}
```

## case

**Availability:** Flash Player 4

**Generic Template:** case *expression*: *statements*

**Parameters:**

> *expression*—Any viable expression.
>
> *statements*—Code to be executed if the expression matches that of the switch action.

**Description:**

This script is a keyword that represents a condition to be used in the switch action. The statements in the case script execute if the expression in case matches the expression in the switch action.

**Example:**

This example checks to see which case matches the switch statement, similar to a conditional statement, and displays the results in the output window:

```
switch (1) {
    case 1:
        trace("It's Case 1");
        break;
    case 2:
        trace("It's Case 2");
        break;
    default:
        trace("None of the cases");
}
//output:  It's Case 1
```

## continue

**Availability:** Flash Player 4

**Generic Template:** continue;

**Description:**

This script is used in many different ways, depending on what type of loop statement it's being placed in.

while/do while—A continue statement skips the rest of the statements and moves back to the condition.

for...continue—Skips the rest of the statements and goes back to the evaluation.

for in...continue—Causes the interpreter to skip the rest of the statements and go back to the top and process the next incremental variable.

**Example:**

This example uses a do while loop with a trace statement that is skipped every time:

```
var i=0;
do {
    i++;
    continue;
    trace("this is skipped");
}while(i <=10);
```

# default

**Availability:** Flash Player 6

**Generic Template:** default: *statements*;

**Parameters:**

*statements*—The script to be executed if all cases in a switch statement evaluate to false.

**Description:**

This code is the default code to be executed if all cases in a switch statement do not evaluate to true.

**Example:**

This example goes through all the cases and uses the default because none of the cases evaluate to true:

```
switch("Flash"){
    case "Unleashed":
        trace("Unleashed");
        break;
    case "2004":
        trace("2004");
        break;
```

A

```
        default:
            trace("Default works");
}
//output: Default works
```

## do while

**Availability:** Flash Player 4

**Generic Template:**

```
do{
    statements;
}while(condition);
```

**Parameters:**

> *statements*—Code to be executed while *condition* is true.
>
> *condition*—The condition that must be evaluated.

**Description:**

This code executes its statements and then evaluates the condition. If the condition is true, the loop reiterates; otherwise, the loop ends.

**Example:**

This example traces the variable i until the condition evaluates to `false`:

```
var i = 0;
do{
    trace(i);
    i++;
}while(i<10);
```

## else

**Availability:** Flash Player 4

**Generic Template:**

```
else{
    statements;
}
```

**Parameters:**

> *statements*—Code to be executed if previous if and else if statements do not evaluate to true.

**Description:**

The `else` statement executes code when the `if` and `else if` statements evaluate to `false`.

**Example:**

This example uses an `else` statement similar to the way a `switch` statement would use a default statement:

```
var name = "David";
userName = "Admin";
if(name == userName){
    trace("Welcome");
}else{
    trace("No Entrance");
}
```

## else if

**Availability:** Flash Player 4

**Generic Template:**

```
else if(condition){
    statements;
}
```

**Parameters:**

> `condition`—The condition that must be evaluated.

> `statements`—Code to be run if `condition` evaluates to `true`.

**Description:**

Another conditional statement that can be stacked if an `if` statement evaluates to `false`.

**Example:**

This example looks at several possibilities and narrows them down with conditional statements, including the `else if` statement:

```
var age = 23;
if(age <= 20){
    trace("20");
}else if(age == 21){
    trace("21");
}else if(age == 22){
    trace("22");
```

```
}else {
    trace("Older than 22");
}
```

## for

**Availability:** Flash Player 5

**Generic Template:**

```
for(variable; condition; change){
    statements;
}
```

**Parameters:**

> *variable*—A variable is created to use in the condition.
>
> *condition*—The condition that must be evaluated.
>
> *change*—The change in the variable that allows the loop to have an end.

**Description:**

A loop statement that uses its user-defined variable to control the amount of times it loops. The *change* constraint is used to eventually stop the loop statement.

**Example:**

This example uses a for loop to count down from 10:

```
for(var i = 11; i > 0; i--){
    trace(i);
}
```

## for in

**Availability:** Flash Player 5

**Generic Template:**

```
for(variable in object){
    statements;
}
```

**Parameters:**

> *variable*—This variable represents a property in an object or element in an array.
>
> *object*—The object associated with the variable.
>
> *statements*—The statements to be run in regard to the object.

**Description:**

A loop statement that cycles through each property of an object or element of an array, iterating a set of statements for each property or element.

Not all properties of an object are used. The built-in objects, such as _alpha and _xscale, are not used.

**Example:**

This example traces every property in the object (note that it traces the property's name, not the value):

```
var myObject = new Object();
myObject.name = "David";
myObject.age = 23;
myObject.location = "Richmond";
for(myProp in myObject){
    trace(myProp);
}
//output: location
//        age
//        name
```

# if
**Availability:** Flash Player 4

**Generic Template:**

```
if(condition){
    statements;
}
```

**Parameters:**

> *condition*—The condition that needs to be evaluated.

> *statements*—The statements to be run when the condition evaluates to true.

**Description:**

A conditional statement that, if it evaluates to true, runs the associated statements contained between the curly brackets. If the condition evaluates to false, all content between the curly brackets is skipped.

**Example:**

This example checks whether a user's age is high enough to enter a site:

```
var requiredAge = 21;
var inputAge;
```

```
if(inputAge >= requiredAge){
    gotoAndPlay("welcome");
}else{
    trace("Come back in " + (requiredAge-inputAge)+" years");
}
```

## switch

**Availability:** Flash Player 4

**Generic Template:**

```
switch(expression){
    standardCase:
        statements;
    defaultCase:
        statements;
}
```

**Parameters:**

> *expression*—The expression that is compared to the cases.
>
> standardCase—This is a case that compares another expression to the switch expression. There can be more than one standardCase.
>
> *statements*—In standardCase the scripts are run if that particular case's expression is the same as the expression of switch; in defaultCase the scripts are run if none of the standardCases evaluate to true.
>
> defaultCase—The last case scenario. All scripts associated with it are run if this case is reached.

**Description:**

This script is a conditional statement similar to the if statement. It identifies an expression and, if any cases evaluate to true, the statements are run. If none of the cases evaluate to true, defaultCase is often used to run scripts automatically.

**Example:**

This example looks for a certain name in some of the cases and runs a script if this name is found:

```
var name = "David";
switch(name){
    case "Kevin":
        trace("Name is Kevin");
        break;
```

```
    case "Tanner":
        trace("Name is Tanner");
        break;
    case "David":
        trace("Name is David");
        break;
    default:
        trace("We don't know name");
}
```

# while

**Availability:** Flash Player 4

**Generic Template:**

```
while(condition){
    statements;
}
```

**Parameters:**

> *condition*—A condition that must be evaluated.
>
> *statements*—The script to be run while the condition is true.

**Description:**

This script is a loop statement that runs its statements as long as the condition continues to evaluate to true. Unlike the do while loop statement, the while loop statement evaluates the condition before executing any code.

Remember when using loop statements to make sure the loop can come to an end to avoid errors.

**Example:**

This example increases a movie clip's horizontal position until it has reached or gone past a designated point:

```
while(myMovie._x<=100){
    myMovie._x+=5;
}
```

A

## Exceptions

### `throw, try, catch, and finally`

**Availability:** Flash Player 7

**Generic Template:**

```
expression(){
    throw new Error();
}
try{
    expression();
}catch{
    //code to run
}finally{
    //code to run
}
```

**Parameters:**

*expression*—An expression that includes the `throw` action to send out an error.

**Description:**

This group of actions is used for advanced error checking of expressions such as functions. Each individual part has a specific job, and they are as follows:

- `throw`—Sends the error message out.

- `try`—Runs the expression within the `try` block, and must contain either a `catch` block of code or a `finally` block of code, or both.

- `catch`—Used to catch the error from the `throw` action if thrown, and run any code within its block.

- `finally`—Runs any code within its block regardless of whether an error has been thrown or not.

**Example:**

This example creates a generic function that automatically throws an error message when the `try` block is run:

```
//create the function
function myFunction(){
    throw new Error(" error 1 ");
}
try{
    //call the function
```

```
    myFunction();
}catch{
    trace;
    break;
}finally{
    trace("finally");
}
//output:  error 1
//         finally
```

# User-Defined Functions

## function
**Availability:** Flash Player 5

**Generic Template:**

```
function functionName(variables){
    statements;
}
```

**Parameters:**

>functionName—Name of the function.

>variables—The parameters to use in the function that can be set when the function is called.

>statements—The script to be run when the function is called.

**Description:**

This script declares functions that can be used to do almost any task inside the Flash player. You set parameters to use in the function, and they can be set to anything when the function is called.

You can do two things with this script: First, you can create a function and use it later by calling it (you can even call it from anywhere in the Flash movie thanks to the new global function). Second, you can use it as an expression to create methods for objects.

**Example:**

This example declares a simple function:

```
function difference(x, y){
    trace(x-y);
}
difference(5,2);
```

A

# return

**Availability:** Flash Player 5

**Generic Template:** `return expression;`

**Constraint:**

> `expression`—Any data type or expression that can be evaluated.

**Description:**

This script is used in a function to evaluate some of its statements. After the `return` action is run, it stops and replaces the function with the value of the expression it ran.

**Example:**

This example uses a simple function and sets a variable to its return value; then the variable is traced:

```
function difference(x,y){
    return x-y;
}
myDif = difference(10,5);
trace(myDif);
```

# Variables

## delete

**Availability:** Flash Player 5

**Generic Template:** `delete object;`

**Parameters:**

> `object`—The variable or object you want to delete.

**Returns:**

Boolean value stating if the object was removed.

**Description:**

This script deletes an object, variable, or even a user-defined property of an object in its entirety.

You cannot, however, delete a predefined object or property of Flash.

**Example:**

This example creates and traces a variable and then deletes the variable and traces again:

```
var myVariable = "Flash";
trace(myVariable);
delete myVariable;
trace(myVariable);
//output: Flash
//        undefined
```

## set variable

**Availability:** Flash Player 4

**Generic Template:** set(*variable*, *value*);

**Parameters:**

> *variable*—The name of the variable you want to set.
>
> *value*—The value of the variable you want to set.

**Description:**

This script assigns a value to a variable. A variable is a storage device that can hold a string, number, or Boolean as well as other data types.

**Example:**

This example sets a variable to the horizontal position of the mouse:

```
set(xMouse, _xmouse);
```

## var

**Availability:** Flash Player 5

**Generic Template:** var *name* = *value*;

**Parameters:**

> *name*—The name of the variable.
>
> *value*—The value that is set to the variable.

**Description:**

This script declares and assigns a value to a variable. It is possible to declare multiple variables on one line by separating the value from the next variable's name by a comma.

**Example:**

The first example declares a single variable and sets it to a string literal; the second example sets multiple variables:

```
//this will create a variable that will hold a string
var myVariable = "Flash";

//this will create multiple variables on a single line
var x = 10, y = 20, z = 30;
```

## with

**Availability:** Flash Player 5

**Generic Template:**

```
with(object){
    statements;
}
```

**Parameters:**

>    *object*—A movie clip or user-defined object.

>    *statements*—The code to be run with the object associated with it.

**Description:**

This script executes code with the given object.

**Example:**

This example sets the horizontal and vertical position of a movie clip:

```
with(myMovie){
    _x = 125;
    _y = 225;
}
```

# Operators

# String Delimiter (" ")

**Availability:** Flash Player 4

**Generic Template:** "*string*"

**Parameters:**

>    *string*—Any character or group of characters.

**Description:**

These quotation marks are used to surround a group of characters, declaring it as a string.

**Example:**

This example sets a variable equal to a string:

```
var title = "Flash Unleashed";
trace(title);
```

# Parentheses [()]
**Availability:** Flash Player 4

**Generic Template:** (*expression*)

**Parameters:**

    *expression*—Any viable expression.

**Description:**

This operator groups expressions together.

**Example:**

This example shows different uses for grouping items together using parentheses:

```
x = 3;
y = 4;
z = (x*2)-y;
trace(z);
//output: 2
function myFunction(myVar){
    trace(myVar);
}
```

## Arithmetic Operators

## Minus (-)
**Availability:** Flash Player 4

**Generic Template:** -

**Parameters:** None

**Description:**

This operator can be used in two ways: First, to turn an integer into a negative integer; second, to subtract an integer from another.

**Example:**

Here are some examples of using the minus operator:

```
x = 2;
y = -3;
z = x - y;
```

## Modulo (%)

**Availability:** Flash Player 4

**Generic Template:** *expression % expression*

**Parameters:**

> *expression*—Any viable number or an expression that can be converted to a number.

**Description:**

This operator calculates the remainder of the first expression divided by the second expression.

**Example:**

This example uses the modulo to determine the remainder of apples when the bundle is split up:

```
bundle = 26;
people = 5;
remainder = bundle % people;
trace(remainder);
//output: 1
```

## Multiplication (*)

**Availability:** Flash Player 4

**Generic Template:** *number * number*

**Parameters:**

> *number*—Any viable number.

**Description:**

This operator multiplies two numbers or expressions that evaluate to numbers.

**Example:**

Here is a simple example of the multiplication operator:

```
var area = 10 * 10;
```

## Division (/)

**Availability:** Flash Player 4

**Generic Template:** *number / number*

**Parameters:**

> *number*—Any viable number.

**Description:**

This operator divides two numbers or expressions that evaluate to numbers.

**Example:**

The following example uses the division operator to divide two variables:

```
var total = 100;
var attempts = 10;
var avg = total / attempts;
trace(avg);
```

## Addition (+)

**Availability:** Flash Player 4

**Generic Template:** *expression + expression*

**Parameters:**

> *expression*—Any string or number.

**Description:**

This operator adds two numbers together. It also combines two strings to form one string. If one of the expressions is a string, all expressions are converted to strings and combined.

**Example:**

This example adds two numbers together:

```
var myVar = 1+2;
```

This next example combines two strings:

```
var fName = "Alex";
var lName = "Behr";
var fullName = fName +" "+ lName;
trace(fullName);
```

Finally, this example combines a string with a number to form a string:

```
var player = "Flash ";
var version = 6;
var fullVersion = player + version;
trace(fullVersion);
```

# Assignment

## Subtraction Assignment (-=)

**Availability:** Flash Player 4

**Generic Template:** *expression -= expression*

**Parameters:**

> *expression*—Any viable number or an expression that can be converted to a number.

**Description:**

This operator subtracts the second expression from the first and then sets the first expression to the new value. It is the same as setting the first expression equal to the value of the first expression minus the second.

**Example:**

This example sets a variable equal to itself minus another variable:

```
var x = 5;
var y = 10;
y-=x;
trace(y);
```

## Modulo Assignment (%=)

**Availability:** Flash Player 4

**Generic Template:** *expression %= expression*

**Parameters:**

> *expression*—Any viable number or an expression that can be converted to a number.

**Description:**

This operator performs a modulo operation with both expressions and then sets the first expression to the new value.

**Example:**

This example performs a modulo operation on two expressions and sets the value of the first expression to the new value:

```
var x = 20;
var y = 3;
x %= y;
trace(x);
```

# Bitwise AND Assignment (&=)

**Availability:** Flash Player 5

**Generic Template:** *expression* &= *expression*

**Parameters:**

> *expression*—Any viable number or an expression that can be converted to a number.

**Description:**

This operator performs a bitwise AND operation on expressions and assign the new value to the first expression.

**Example:**

Here is an example using the bitwise AND assignment operator:

```
var x = 6;
var y = 10;
x &= y;
trace(x);
//output: 2
```

# Multiplication Assignment (*=)

**Availability:** Flash Player 4

**Generic Template:** *expression* *= *expression*

**Parameters:**

> *expression*—Any viable number or an expression that can be converted to a number.

A

**Description:**

This operator multiplies two expressions and sets the first expression to the new value.

**Example:**

This example multiplies two variables and assigns the value equal to the first:

```
var x = 4;
var y = 3;
x *= y;
trace(x);
//output: 12
```

# Bitwise OR Assignment (|=)

**Availability:** Flash Player 5

**Generic Template:** *expression* |= *expression*

**Parameters:**

> *expression*—Any viable number or a variable holding a number.

**Description:**

This operator performs a bitwise OR operation on expressions and sets the value of the first expression to the new value.

**Example:**

This example uses the bitwise OR assignment and sets the first variable equal to the result:

```
var x = 10;
var y = 12;
x |= y;
trace(x);
//output: 14
```

# Division Assignment (/=)

**Availability:** Flash Player 4

**Generic Template:** *expression* |= *expression*

**Parameters:**

> *expression*—Any viable number or an expression that can be converted to a number.

**Description:**

This operator divides the first expression by the second and then assigns the value to the first expression.

**Example:**

This example illustrates the use of the division assignment operator:

```
var x = 10;
var y = 5;
x /= y;
trace(x);
```

# Bitwise XOR Assignment (^=)
**Availability:** Flash Player 5

**Generic Template:** *expression ^= expression*

**Parameters:**

> *expression*—Any viable number or a variable holding a number.

**Description:**

This operator performs a bitwise XOR operation on expressions and assigns the value to the first expression.

**Example:**

This example illustrates the use of the bitwise XOR operator:

```
var x = 10;
var y = 6;
x ^= y;
trace(x);
//output: 12
```

# Addition Assignment (+=)
**Availability:** Flash Player 4

**Generic Template:** *expression += expression*

**Parameters:**

> *expression*—Any number, string, or variable holding either a number or string.

**Description:**

This operator adds numbers together and assigns the value to the first expression. It can also combine strings and assign the new string to the first expression.

**Example:**

This example uses the addition assignment to combine numbers:

```
var x = 10;
var y = 5;
x += y;
trace(x);
```

This example combines strings:

```
var name = "David ";
var lName = "Vogeleer";
name += lName;
trace(name);
//output: David Vogeleer
```

## Bitwise Left Shift and Assignment (<<=)

**Availability:** Flash Player 5

**Generic Template:** *expressionA* <<= *expressionB*

**Parameters:**

> *expressionA*—Any number or expression that can evaluate to a number.
>
> *expressionB*—Any number or expression that can evaluate to an integer between 0 and 31.

**Description:**

This operator performs a bitwise left shift on expressions and assigns the value to the first expression.

**Example:**

This example illustrates the use of the bitwise left shift and assignment operator:

```
var x = 10;
var y = 5;
x <<= y;
trace(x);
//output: 320
```

## Assignment (=)

**Availability:** Flash Player 4

**Generic Template:** *expressionA = expressionB*

**Parameters:**

> *expressionA*—Any variable, property, or element of an array.
>
> *expressionB*—A value or expression that will evaluate to a value being assigned to *expressionA*.

**Description:**

This operator assigns a value (*expressionB*) to a named variable, property, or element (*expressionA*).

**Example:**

This example assigns a value to a variable and traces the variable to make sure it is there:

```
var title = "Flash Unleashed";
trace(title);
```

## Bitwise Right Shift and Assignment (>>=)

**Availability:** Flash Player 5

**Generic Template:** *expressionA >>= expressionB*

**Parameters:**

> *expressionA*—Any number or expression that can evaluate to a number.
>
> *expression*—Any number or expression that can evaluate to an integer between 0 and 31.

**Description:**

This operator performs the bitwise right shift operation on expressions and then assigns the value to the first expression.

**Example:**

This example illustrates the use of the bitwise right shift and assignment operator:

```
var x = 10;
var y = 5;
x >>= y;
trace(x);
//output: 0
```

## Bitwise Unsigned Right Shift and Assignment (>>>=)

**Availability:** Flash Player 5

**Generic Template:** `expressionA >>>= expressionB`

**Parameters:**

> `expressionA`—Any number or expression that can evaluate to a number.

> `expressionB`—Any number or expression that can evaluate to an integer between 0 and 31.

**Description:**

This operator performs the bitwise unsigned right shift operation on expressions and then assigns the value to the first expression.

**Example:**

This example illustrates the use of the bitwise unsigned right shift operator:

```
var x = 10;
var y = 5;
x >>>= y;
trace(x);
//output: 0
```

# Bitwise Operators

## Bitwise AND (&)

**Availability:** Flash Player 5

**Generic Template:** `expression & expression`

**Parameters:**

> `expression`—Any viable value or expression that evaluates to a value.

**Description:**

This operator converts expressions to 32-bit unsigned integers and then runs a Boolean AND operation on each bit of the integer parameters, which returns a new 32-bit number.

**Example:**

This example shows the use of the `bitwise AND` operator:

```
var x = 5;
var y = 1;
var z = y & x;
```

```
trace (z);
//output: 1
```

## Bitwise NOT (~)

**Availability:** Flash Player 5

**Generic Template:** ~ *expression*

**Parameters:**

> *expression*—Any viable number.

**Description:**

This operator changes the positive/negative value of a number and then subtracts it by 1.

**Example:**

This example shows the use of the bitwise NOT operator:

```
var x = 10;
trace(~x);
//output: -11
```

## Bitwise OR (|)

**Availability:** Flash Player 5

**Generic Template:** *expression* | *expression*

**Parameters:**

> *expression*—Any viable number.

**Description:**

This operator converts expressions to 32-bit unsigned integers and sends back the number 1 in each bit position, where the corresponding bits of either expression are equal to 1.

**Example:**

This example shows the use of the bitwise OR operator:

```
var x = 10;
var y = 5;
var z = x | y;
trace(z);
//output: 15
```

## Bitwise XOR (^)

**Availability:** Flash Player 5

**Generic Template:** *expression ^ expression*

**Parameters:**

> *expression*—Any viable number.

**Description:**

This operator converts expressions to 32-bit unsigned integers and sends back the number 1 in each bit position, where the corresponding bits of either expression, but not both, are 1.

**Example:**

This example shows the use of the bitwise XOR operator:

```
var x = 10;
var y = 5;
var z = x ^ y;
trace(z);
//output: 15
```

## Bitwise Left Shift (<<)

**Availability:** Flash Player 5

**Generic Template:** *expressionA << expressionB*

**Parameters:**

> *expressionA*—Any number or expression that can evaluate to a number.

> *expressionB*—Any number or expression that can evaluate to an integer between 0 and 31.

**Description:**

This operator converts the expressions to 32-bit integers and shifts each bit in *expressionA* to the left by the number of places specified by the integer resulting from the conversion of *expressionB*. The empty bits are filled in with zeros. A shift to the left of an integer is equivalent to multiplying that integer by 2. In effect, here is what happens:

```
var i = 0;
while(i < expressionB){
    expressionA*=2;
    i++;
}
trace(expressionA);
```

**Example:**

This example shows the use of the bitwise left shift operator:

```
var x = 10;
var y = 5;
var z = x << y;
trace(z);
//output: 320
```

## Bitwise Right Shift (>>)

**Availability:** Flash Player 5

**Generic Template:** *expressionA* >> *expressionB*

**Parameters:**

> *expressionA*—Any number or expression that can evaluate to a number.
>
> *expressionB*—Any number or expression that can evaluate to an integer between 0 and 31.

**Description:**

This operator converts the expressions to 32-bit integers and then shifts the bits in *expressionA* to the right by the number of places specified by the integer resulting from the conversion of *expressionB*. All bits that are shifted to the right are useless. Extra bits that remain on the left are replaced with zeros. The result of this operator is *expressionA* being divided by 2 the number of times indicated in *expressionB*, and the remainder is left off. If expressionB is equal to 4, expressionA would be divided by the number 2 four times.

Basically, it is equal to this:

```
var i = 0;
while(i<expressionB){
    expressionA = Math.floor(expressionA / 2);
    i++;
}
trace(expressionA);
```

**Example:**

This example shows the use of the bitwise right shift operator:

```
var x = 10;
var y = 2;
var z = x >> y;
trace(z);
//output: 2
```

## Bitwise Unsigned Right Shift (>>>)

**Availability:** Flash Player 5

**Generic Template:** *expressionA >>> expressionB*

**Parameters:**

>*expressionA*—Any number or expression that can evaluate to a number.

>*expressionB*—Any number or expression that can evaluate to an integer between 0 and 31.

**Description:**

This operator acts the same as the bitwise right shift operator. The only difference in the two is that the bitwise unsigned right shift operator does not keep the sign of the original expression because the left-side bits are continuously filled with zeros.

**Example:**

Here's an example of the bitwise unsigned right shift operator:

```
var x = 10;
var y = 2;
var z = x >>> y;
trace(z);
//output: 2
```

## Comparison Operators

## Inequality (!=)

**Availability:** Flash Player 5

**Generic Template:** *value != value*

**Parameters:**

>*value*—Any viable number or string.

**Description:**

This operator evaluates two values, and if they are not equivalent, the expression evaluates to `true`. If the two values are equivalent, the expression evaluates to `false`.

**Example:**

Here are some examples using the inequality operator:

```
trace(10 != 5);
//output: true
```

```
trace(5 != 5);
//output: false

trace("David" != "david");
//output: true

trace("Alex" != "Alex");
//output: false
```

## Strict Inequality (!==)

**Availability:** Flash Player 6

**Generic Template:** *value* !== *value*

**Parameters:**

> *value*—Any viable number or string.

**Description:**

This operator performs the same evaluation as the inequality operator, except that values of different data types are not converted and are automatically not equivalent to each other. If the two values are not equivalent, the expression evaluates to true. If the two values are equivalent, the expression evaluates to false.

**Example:**

This example not only shows the use of the strict inequality operator but also compares its use to the inequality operator:

```
trace(5 !== 10);
//output: true

trace(5 !== 5);
//output: false

trace(5 != "5");
//output: false

trace(5 !== "5");
//output: true
```

## Less Than (<)

**Availability:** Flash Player 4

**Generic Template:** *value* < *value*

**Parameters:**

    *value*—Any viable number or string.

**Description:**

This operator compares two values, and if the first value is less than the second, the expression evaluates to true. If the first value is greater than or equal to the second value, the expression evaluates to false.

**Example:**

Here are a few example of the less than operator:

```
trace(3 < 4);
//output: true

trace(4 < 3);
//output: false

trace(3 < 3);
//output: false

trace("a" < "b");
//output: true
```

## Less Than Equal To (<=)

**Availability:** Flash Player 4

**Generic Template:** *value* <= *value*

**Parameters:**

    *value*—Any viable number or string.

**Description:**

This operator compares two values, and if the first value is less than or equal to the second, the expression evaluates to true. If the first value is greater than the second value, the expression evaluates to false.

**Example:**

Here are a few examples using the less than equal to operator:

```
trace(3 <= 4);
//output: true
```

```
trace(4 <= 3);
//output: false

trace(3 <= 3);
//output: true

trace("a" <= "b");
//output: true
```

## Equality (==)

**Availability:** Flash Player 5

**Generic Template:** *value == value*

**Parameters:**

> *value*—Any viable number, string, Boolean, variable, object, array, or function.

**Description:**

This operator compares two values. If the values are equal to one another, the expression evaluates to true. If the two values are not equal to each other, the expression evaluates to false.

More than one data type can be evaluated, and they each evaluate differently. Let's take a look at them:

> *Number and Boolean.* These two data types are compared by raw value.
>
> *String.* This data type is evaluated by comparing the ASCII values of corresponding characters in the two strings.
>
> *Variable, object, and function.* Variables are considered equal if they refer to the identical object, function, or array.
>
> *Array.* Arrays cannot be compared directly. This always returns a false evaluation. However, the elements in an array can be compared the same way variables are compared.

**Example:**

Here are a few examples using the equality operator:

```
trace(5==5);
//output: true

trace("David" == "david");
//output: false
```

```
var myArray = new Array();
var anotherArray = new Array();
trace(myArray == anotherArray);
//output: false

var myArray = new Array("David");
var anotherArray = new Array("David");
trace(myArray[0] == anotherArray[0]);
//output: true
```

## Strict Equality (===)

**Availability:** Flash Player 6

**Generic Template:** *value* === *value*

**Parameters:**

> *value*—Any viable number, string, Boolean, variable, object, array, or function.

**Description:**

This operator compares two values just like the equality operator. However, unlike the equality operator, values are not converted for comparison. If the two values are of different data types, the expression automatically evaluates to `false`. That aside, if the values are equal to one another, the expression evaluates to `true`. If the two values are not equal to each other, the expression evaluates to `false`.

More than one data type can be evaluated, and they each evaluate differently. Let's take a look at them:

> *Number and Boolean.* These two data types are compared by raw value.
>
> *String.* This data type is evaluated by the number of characters. If the characters match identically, remember when you're comparing strings, the comparison *is case sensitive*.
>
> *Variable, object, and function.* Variables are considered equal if they refer to the identical object, function, or array.
>
> *Array.* Arrays cannot be compared directly. This always returns a false evaluation. However, the elements in an array can be compared the same way variables are compared.

**Example:**

Here are a few examples using the strict equality operator and a comparison to the equality operator:

```
trace(5 === 5);
//output: true
```

```
trace("Alex" === "Alex");
//output: true

trace(10 == "10");
//output: true

trace(10 === "10");
//output: false
```

## Greater Than (>)

**Availability:** Flash Player 4

**Generic Template:** *value* > *value*

**Parameters:**

> *value*—Any viable number or string.

**Description:**

This operator compares two values. If the first value is greater than the second, the expression evaluates to true. If the first value is less than or equivalent to the second value, the expression evaluates to false.

**Example:**

Here are a few examples using the greater than operator:

```
trace(4 > 3);
//output: true

trace(3 > 4);
//output: false

trace(3 > 3);
//output: false

trace("a" > "b");
//output: false
```

## Greater Than Equal To (>=)

**Availability:** Flash Player 4

**Generic Template:** *value* >= *value*

**Parameters:**

> *value*—Any viable number or string.

**Description:**

This operator compares the two values. If the first value is greater than or equal to the second, the expression evaluates to true. If the first value is less than the second value, the expression evaluates to false.

**Example:**

Here are a few examples using the greater than equal to operator:

```
trace(4 >= 3);
//output: true

trace(3 >= 4);
//output: false

trace(3 >= 3);
//output: true

trace("a" >= "a");
//output: true
```

# Logical Operators

## Logical NOT (!)
**Availability:** Flash Player 4

**Generic Template:** *!expression*

**Parameters:** None

**Description:**

This operator inverts the Boolean value of the expression. If the Boolean value equals true, this operator converts it to false, and if the Boolean value is false, the operator converts it to true.

**Example:**

The logical NOT operator is used in this example in an if statement:

```
var myVar = false;
if(!myVar){
    trace("It converted the false to true");
}
```

## Short-circuit AND (&&)

**Availability:** Flash Player 4

**Generic Template:** *expression* && *expression*

**Parameters:** None

**Description:**

This operator connects two conditionals for evaluation. If the first condition evaluates to true, the second condition is evaluated. However, if the first condition evaluates to false, the second condition is never evaluated.

**Example:**

Here is an example using the short-circuit AND operator to link two conditionals in a looping statement:

```
var i = 0;
var j = 1;
while(i <10 && j <10){
    trace("i= " + i);
    trace("j= " + j);
    i++;
    j++;
}
```

## Logical OR (||)

**Availability:** Flash Player 4

**Generic Template:** *condition* || *condition*

**Parameters:** None

**Description:**

This operator connects two conditionals for evaluation. If the first condition evaluates to true, the second condition is skipped. However, if the first condition evaluates to false, the second condition is evaluated.

**Example:**

Here is an example of the logical OR operator in a looping statement:

```
var i = 0;
var j = 1;
while(i <10 || j <10){
    trace("i= " + i);
    trace("j= " + j);
    i++;
```

```
    j++;
}
```

# Miscellaneous Operators

## Decrement (--)
**Availability:** Flash Player 4

**Generic Template:**

*--number*

*number--*

**Parameters:**

      *number*—Any viable number, property of a movie clip, or variable holding a number.

**Description:**

This operator has two uses. The first is the pre-number decrement (*--number*), which subtracts one from the number and returns that value. The second use is the post-number decrement (*number--*), which subtracts one from the number.

The decrement operator is often used in loop statements to end them.

**Example:**

These examples show some uses of the decrement operator:

```
var x = 5;
var y = --x;
trace(y);
//output: 4

var x = 5;
var y = x--;
trace(y);
//output: 5

var i = 5;
while(i > 0){
    trace(i);
    i--;
}
```

# Conditional (?:)

**Availability:** Flash Player 4

**Generic Template:** *condition? expressionA: expressionB*

**Parameters:**

*condition*—A condition to be evaluated.

*expressionA*—The value returned if the condition is `true`.

*expressionB*—The value returned if the condition is `false`.

**Description:**

This operator evaluates the condition; if it evaluates to `true`, *expressionA* is returned. If the condition evaluates to `false`, *expressionB* is returned.

**Example:**

This example uses the conditional operator:

```
var x = 10;
(x > 5)? trace("X is greater"): trace("X is less than");
```

# Increment (++)

**Availability:** Flash Player 4

**Generic Template:**

*++number*

*number++*

**Parameters:**

*number*—Any viable number, property of a movie clip, or variable holding a number.

**Description:**

This operator has two uses: The first is the pre-number increment (*++number*), which adds one to the number and returns the new value. The second use is the post-number increment (*number++*), which adds one to the number and returns the value of the number before one was added to it.

The increment operator is often used in loop statements to end them.

**Example:**

Here is an example of the increment operator:

```
var i = 0;
while(i <=10){
    trace("i = "+i);
    i++;
}
```

## instanceof

**Availability:** Flash Player 6

**Generic Template:** *object* instanceof *class*

**Parameters:**

>   *object*—Any viable ActionScript object.
>
>   *class*—Refers to an ActionScript constructor function.

### Returns:

If object is an instanceof class, the operator returns a value of true; otherwise, it returns a value of false.

### Description:

This operator determines whether the object is part of the class. If it is, the value returned is true; otherwise, the value returned is false.

### Example:

Here is an example using the instanceof operator:

```
trace(new Array (myArray) instanceof Array);
//output: true
```

## typeof

**Availability:** Flash Player 5

**Generic Template:** typeof *value*

**Parameters:**

>   *value*—Any viable type of string, movie clip, button, object, Boolean, number, variable, or function.

### Description:

This operator, when placed before a value, evaluates the type of value.

### Example:

This example uses the typeof operator to evaluate a variable to indicate what type it is:

```
var name = "David";
trace(typeof name);
//output: string
```

## void

**Availability:** Flash Player 5

**Generic Template:** void (*expression*);

**Parameters:**

>  *expression*—Any viable expression.

**Description:**

This operator evaluates an expression, disregards it, and returns a value of undefined.

**Example:**

This example shows the use of the void operator by using it on a simple expression of two variables:

```
var x = 10;
var y = 5;
var z = void(x+y);
trace(z);
//output: undefined
```

# Constants

## -Infinity

**Availability:** Flash Player 5

**Generic Template:** -Infinity

**Parameters:** None

**Description:**

This constant represents the IEEE-754 value of negative infinity. This constant is the same as Number.NEGATIVE_INFINITY.

**Example:**

This example checks a number to see if it is greater than -Infinity:

```
if(-4000 > -Infinity){
    trace("-4000 is greater than -Infinity");
}
//output: -4000 is greater than -Infinity
```

A

## false

**Availability:** Flash Player 5

**Generic Template:** `false`

**Parameters:** None

**Description:**

A Boolean value representing the opposite of `true`.

**Example:**

This example sets the visibility of a movie clip to `false`, thus making it invisible:

```
myMovie._visible = false;
```

## Infinity

**Availability:** Flash Player 5

**Generic Template:** `Infinity`

**Parameters:** None

**Description:**

This constant represents the IEEE-754 value of infinity. This constant is the same as `Number.POSITIVE_INFINITY`.

**Example:**

This example checks a number to see if it is less than `Infinity`:

```
if(4000 < Infinity){
    trace("4000 is less than Infinity");
}
//output: 4000 is less than Infinity
```

## newline

**Availability:** Flash Player 4

**Generic Template:** `newline`

**Parameters:** None

**Description:**

This constant inserts a carriage return character (\n) that will create a new line in any output text.

## null

**Availability:** Flash Player 5

**Generic Template:** null

**Parameters:** None

**Description:**

This constant is a keyword for representing the lack of data in variables.

**Example:**

This example sets a variable equal to null:

```
var myVariable = null;
```

## true

**Availability:** Flash Player 5

**Generic Template:** true

**Parameters:** None

**Description:**

A Boolean value representing the opposite of false.

**Example:**

This example sets the multiline property of a text field to true:

```
//First create the text field
_root.createTextField("myText",0,0,0,100,100);
myText.multiline = true;
```

## undefined

**Availability:** Flash Player 5

**Generic Template:** undefined

**Parameters:** None

**Description:**

This constant is usually returned when you're looking for a variable that isn't identified yet.

Null and undefined are said to be equal to each other.

**Example:**

This example shows how undefined is used by setting one variable, but tracing another variable that has not been created instead. This returns undefined because the variable being looked for has not been created.

```
var x = 10;
trace(y);
//output: undefined
```

# Built-in Classes

## Core

**arguments**

**callee**  **Availability:** Flash Player 5

**Generic Layout:** arguments.callee

**Parameters:** None

**Description:**

A property of the arguments class that refers to the function in which it currently resides in.

**Example:**

This example cycles from the number you pass it down to 1, and adds each number, and finally returns the total value:

```
function cycle(num:Number):Number {
  if (num <= 1) {
    return 1;
  } else {
    return  num+arguments.callee(num-1);
  }
};
trace(cycle(4));
```

**caller**  **Availability:** Flash Player 6

**Generic Layout:** arguments.caller

**Parameters:** None

**Description:**

A property of the arguments class that refers to the calling function.

**length    Availability:** Flash Player 5

**Generic Layout:** `arguments.length`

**Parameters:** None

**Description:**

A property of the arguments class that refers to the amount of arguments being passed to the function in which it is currently residing.

**Example:**

This example creates a function that always returns the amount of parameters passed to it:

```
function howMany(){
    return arguments.length;
}
trace(howMany(1,2,3,4));
```

## Array

### new Array Constructor
**Availability:** Flash Player 5

**Generic Template:** `new Array(elements);`

**Parameters:**

> *elements*—This optional constraint can be either elements that reside in an array, or a single number giving the array that many blank elements.

**Description:**

This constructor creates a `new Array` instance with elements in it if they are defined.

**Example:**

This example shows a `new Array` object being created and filled:

```
var myArray:Array = new Array(1,2,3,4);
```

### Methods
**concat    Availability:** Flash Player 5

**Generic Template:** `array.concat(anotherArray);`

**Parameters:**

> *anotherArray*—An array that is added to the array the method is being called on; it can also be multiple arrays separated by commas.

**Returns:**

A new array.

**Description:**

This method creates a new array based on the array it is being called on and the array(s) being passed to it without affecting the original array.

**Example:**

This example creates an array, and then adds an anonymous array to it to be included in yet another array:

```
var myArray:Array = new Array(1,2,3);
anotherArray=myArray.concat([4,5,6]);
trace(anotherArray);
//output: 1,2,3,4,5,6
```

**join    Availability:** Flash Player 5

**Generic Template:** `array.join(separator);`

**Parameters:**

> *separator*—This optional parameter is a string holding the charater that is placed between each element when they are joined.

**Returns:**

A string.

**Description:**

This method combines every element in the array into a single string with the *separator* residing between each element

**Example:**

This example creates an array, and then joins it together in a single string:

```
var myArray:Array = new Array(1,2,3);
trace(myArray.join("~"));
//output: 1~2~3
```

**pop    Availability:** Flash Player 5

**Generic Template:** `array.pop();`

**Parameters:** None

**Returns:**

Last element in the array.

**Description:**

This method removes the last element from an array and returns its value.

**Example:**

This example removes and traces the last element in an array:

```
var myArray:Array = new Array(1,2,3);
trace(myArray.pop());
//output: 3
```

**push**   **Availability:** Flash Player 5

**Generic Template:** `array.push(value);`

**Parameters:**

> *value*—One or more elements to be placed at the end of the array.

**Returns:**

The array's length as a number.

**Description:**

This method adds an element(s) to the end of an array and returns the new length of that array.

**Example:**

This example adds a number to the end of the array, and traces the entire array:

```
var myArray:Array = new Array(1,2,3);
myArray.push(4);
trace(myArray);
//output: 1,2,3,4
```

**reverse**   **Availability:** Flash Player 5

**Generic Template:** `array.reverse();`

**Parameters:** None

**Returns:**

Nothing.

**Description:**

This method reverses the order of all the elements in the array.

**Example:**

This example reverses the elements in the array, and sends it to the output panel:

```
var myArray:Array = new Array(1,2,3);
myArray.reverse();
trace(myArray);
//output:3,2,1
```

**shift**   **Availability:** Flash Player 5

**Generic Template:** `array.shift();`

**Parameters:** None

**Returns:**

The first element in the array.

**Description:**

This method removes the first element (array[0]) and returns its value.

**Example:**

This example removes the first element in the array, and traces the new array:

```
var myArray:Array = new Array(1,2,3);
myArray.shift();
trace(myArray);
//output:2,3
```

**slice**   **Availability:** Flash Player 5

**Generic Template:** `array.slice(start, end);`

**Parameters:**

> *start*—A number representing the starting point in the array.
>
> *end*—A number representing the end point of the array; if omitted, it goes to the end automatically.

**Returns:**

A new array.

**Description:**

This method removes a section of an array, and returns it as another array.

**Example:**

This example removes the middle two elements in an array and sends them to the output panel:

```
var myArray:Array = new Array(1,2,3,4);
trace(myArray.slice(1,3));
//output: 2,3
```

**sort**   **Availability:** Flash Player 5

**Generic Template:** `array.sort(option);`

**Parameters:**

> *option*—An optional parameter declaring how the array should be sorted; here is a list of numbers to use that can be be separated with (|) to use multiple options:
>
> - 1—Case insensitive or Array.CASEINSENSITIVE
> - 2—Descending or Array.DESCENDING
> - 4—Unique or Array.UNIQUE
> - 8—Return indexed array or Array.RETURNINDEXEDARRAY
> - 16—Numeric or Array.NUMERIC

**Returns:**

- If 4 is used as an option: If two elements are identical, the number zero is returned.
- If 8 is used an option: An array is returned without modifying the original.
- If neither of those are used, nothing is returned, and the array is sorted.

**Description:**

This method is used to sort an array based on certain options.

**Example:**

This example sorts an array of numbers, and then sends the new array to the output panel:

```
var myArray:Array = new Array(4,2,1,3);
trace(myArray.sort());
//output: 1,2,3,4
```

**sortOn**   **Availability:** Flash Player 5

**Generic Template:** `array.sortOn(fieldname, option);`

**Parameters:**

> *fieldname*—The name of the element to sort on.
>
> *option*—An optional parameter declaring how the array should be sorted; here is a list of numbers to use which can be be separated with (|) to use multiple options:

- 1—Case insensitive
- 2—Descending
- 4—Unique
- 8—Return indexed—fixed array
- 16—Numeric

**Returns:**

- If 4 is used as an option: If two elements are identical, the number zero is returned.
- If 8 is used an option: An array is returned without modifying the original.
- If neither of those are used, nothing is returned, and the array is sorted.

**Description:**

This method is used to sort an array containing nested arrays based on certain options.

**Example:**

This example sorts an array of nested arrays, and sends the sorted array to the output panel:

```
var myArray:Array = new Array();
//add some elements
myArray.push({name:"David", age: 23});
myArray.push({name:"Todd", age: 28});
myArray.push({name:"Paul", age: 20});
myArray.push({name:"Independence", age: 227});
//send the newly sorted array to the output
myArray.sortOn(name,2);
for(var i=0;i<myArray.length;i++){
    trace(myArray[i].name);
}
```

**splice    Availability:** Flash Player 5

**Generic Template:** array.splice(start, deleteCount, values);

**Parameters:**

*start*—A number representing the starting point in the array.

*deleteCount*—The number of elements to be removed; if it is left blank, all elements after the *start* are removed.

*values*—Optional parameter containing the values to be inserted into the array at the *start*; each value must be separated by a comma.

**Returns:**

An array of the removed elements.

**Description:**

This method can remove elements from an array, as well as place elements within an array.

**Example:**

This example removes the middle two elements in an array and adds in a new one; then it sends the new array to the output panel:

```
var myArray:Array = new Array(1,2,3,4);
myArray.splice(1,2,7);
trace(myArray);
//output: 1,7,4
```

**toString    Availability:** Flash Player 5

**Generic Template:** `array.toString();`

**Parameters:** None

**Returns:**

A string.

**Description:**

This method converts the contents of an array to a string.

**Example:**

This example converts an array of numbers to a string and sends the string to the output panel:

```
var myArray:Array = new Array(1,2,3,4);
trace(myArray.toString());
//output: 1,2,3,4
```

**unshift    Availability:** Flash Player 5

**Generic Template:** `array.unshift(values);`

**Parameters:**

> `values`—The values to be inserted into the array at the beginning; each value must be separated by a comma.

A

**Returns:**

Length of the new array.

**Description:**

This method adds elements to the beginning of an array.

**Example:**

This example removes the middle two elements in an array and adds in a new one; then it sends the new array to the output panel:

```
var myArray:Array = new Array(1,2,3,4);
myArray.unshift(5,6,7);
trace(myArray);
//output: 5,6,7,1,2,3,4
```

Properties
**length**    **Availability:** Flash Player 5

**Generic Template:** `array.length`

**Parameters:** None

**Description:**

This property represents the number of elements in an array.

**Example:**

This example sends the number of elements to the output panel:

```
var myArray:Array = new Array(1,2,3,4);
trace(myArray.length);
//output:   4
```

## Boolean

### new Boolean Constructor
**Availability:** Flash Player 5

**Generic Template:** `new Boolean(expression);`

**Parameters:**

> *expression*—Any viable expression that is translated to a Boolean value.

**Description:**

This constructor creates a new `Boolean` instance with an expression to decide what value it has. If no expression is declared, the default value is false.

**Example:**

This example shows a new `Boolean` object being created:

```
var myBool:Boolean = new Boolean(true);
```

Methods

**toString    Availability:** Flash Player 5

**Generic Template:** `boolean.toString();`

**Parameters:** None

**Returns:**

A string.

**Description:**

This method converts the value of the Boolean instance to a string representation of either "true" or "false".

**Example:**

This example sends the string output of the `toString()` method to the output panel:

```
var myBool:Boolean = new Boolean(true);
trace(myBool.toString());
//output: true
```

**valueOf    Availability:** Flash Player 5

**Generic Template:** `boolean.valueOf();`

**Parameters:** None

**Returns:**

A Boolean.

**Description:**

This method returns the Boolean data type of the Boolean instance.

**Example:**

This example sends the string output of the `valueOf()` method to the output panel:

```
var myBool:Boolean = new Boolean();
trace(myBool.valueOf());
//output: false
```

# Date

## new Date Constructor

**Availability:** Flash Player 5

**Generic Template:** new Date(*plus*);

**Parameters:**

> *plus*—In the new Date object, you can specify several pieces of information, separated by commas.
>
> > *year*—If you want the year to be between 1900 and 1999, you can specify a number between 0 and 99; otherwise, you must place the entire four digits.
> >
> > *month*—A numerical value between 0 and 11, with 0 being January and 11 being December.
> >
> > *date*—A number between 1 and 31 for specifying the day of the month.
> >
> > *hour*—A number between 0 and 23, where 0 is midnight and 23 is 11 p.m.
> >
> > *minute*—A number between 0 and 59.
> >
> > *second*—A number between 0 and 59.
> >
> > *millisecond*—A number between 0 and 999.

**Description:**

This constructor object creates a new Date object.

**Example:**

This example creates a Date object and then gets the time:

```
myDate = new Date();
myHour = myDate.getHours();
myMin = myDate.getMinutes();
myTime = (myHour+":"+myMin);
trace(myTime);
```

### Methods

Three types of methods are associated with the Date object: general methods, get methods, and set methods. This section describes the methods in these groupings.

### General Methods

*toString*    **Availability:** Flash Player 5

**Generic Template:** myDate.toString();

**Parameters:** None

**Returns:**

This method returns a string.

**Description:**

This method converts the Date object to a string literal.

**Example:**

This example specifies a date and converts it to a string:

```
var bDay = new Date(80, 0, 9, 17, 30);
trace(bDay.toString());
//output: Wed Jan 9 17:30:00 UTC-0500 1980
```

*UTC*    **Availability:** Flash Player 5

**Generic Template:** Date.UTC(*year, month, date, hour, minute, second, millisecond*)

**Parameters:**

> *year*—A four-digit number representing the year.
>
> *month*—A numerical value between 0 and 11, with 0 being January and 11 being December.
>
> *date*—A number between 1 and 31 for specifying the day of the month.
>
> *hour*—A number between 0 and 23, where 0 is midnight and 23 is 11 p.m.
>
> *minute*—A number between 0 and 59.
>
> *second*—A number between 0 and 59.
>
> *millisecond*—A number between 0 and 999.

**Example:**

This example sets the Date object to a specific date:

```
merryChristmas = new Date(Date.UTC(2002, 11, 25));
```

**get Methods**    Because all get methods for the Date object have the same generic template, each one does not have its own section; rather, they all are covered in this section.

*getDate( )*    **Availability:** Flash Player 5

**Generic Template:** Date.getDate();

**Parameters:**

> *Date*—A user-defined Date object.

**Description:**

This method gets the day of the month in a numeric form (1–31).

**Example:**

This example retrieves the current date from the user's system:

```
//Create the date object
myDate = new Date();
//Retrieve the information
theDate = myDate.getDate();
//Display the date
trace(theDate);
```

### *getDay()*    **Availability:** Flash Player 5

**Generic Template:** *Date*.getDay();

**Parameters:**

> *Date*—A user-defined Date object.

**Description:**

This method returns a numerical value representing the day of the week (0–6, where 0 is Sunday and 6 is Saturday).

**Example:**

This example retrieves the current day from the user's system:

```
//Create the date object
myDate = new Date();
//Retrieve the information
theDay = myDate.getDay();
//Display the day
trace(theDay);
```

### *getFullYear()*    **Availability:** Flash Player 5

**Generic Template:** *Date*.getFullYear();

**Parameters:**

> *Date*—A user-defined Date object.

**Description:**

This method returns the four-digit value of the current year.

**Example:**

This example retrieves the current full year from the user's system:

```
//Create the date object
myDate = new Date();
//Retrieve the full year
theFullYear = myDate.getFullYear();
//Display the full year
trace(theFullYear);
```

***getHours()***    **Availability:** Flash Player 5

**Generic Template:** *Date*.getHours();

**Parameters:**

> *Date*—A user-defined Date object.

**Description:**

This method returns the current hour in a numeric form (between 0 and 23; 0 being midnight and 23 being 11:00 p.m.).

**Example:**

This example retrieves the current hour from the user's system:

```
//Create the date object
myDate = new Date();
//Retrieve the hour
theHour = myDate.getHours();
//Display the hour
trace(theHour);
```

***getMilliseconds()***    **Availability:** Flash Player 5

**Generic Template:** *Date*.getMilliseconds();

**Parameters:**

> *Date*—A user-defined Date object.

**Description:**

This method returns the current milliseconds in a numeric form (between 0 and 999).

**Example:**

This example retrieves the current millisecond from the user's system:

```
//Create the date object
myDate = new Date();
//Retrieve the milliseconds
```

A

```
theMillisecond = myDate.getMilliseconds();
//Display the milliseconds
trace(theMillisecond);
```

### getMinutes( )    **Availability:** Flash Player 5

**Generic Template:** `Date.getMinutes();`

**Parameters:**

> `Date`—A user-defined `Date` object.

### Description:

This method returns the current minutes in numerical form (between 0 and 59).

### Example:

This example retrieves the current minute from the user's system:

```
//Create the date object
myDate = new Date();
//Retrieve the minutes
theMinute = myDate.getMinutes();
//Display the minutes
trace(theMinute);
```

### getMonth( )    **Availability:** Flash Player 5

**Generic Template:** `Date.getMonth();`

**Parameters:**

> `Date`—A user-defined `Date` object.

### Description:

This method returns a numerical value representing the current month (0–11, where 0 is January and 11 is December).

### Example:

This example retrieves the current month from the user's system:

```
//Create the date object
myDate = new Date();
//Retrieve the month
theMonth = myDate.getMonth();
//Display the month
trace(theMonth);
```

***getSeconds()*** **Availability:** Flash Player 5

**Generic Template:** *Date*.getSeconds();

**Parameters:**

> *Date*—A user-defined Date object.

**Description:**

This method returns the current seconds in numerical form (between 0 and 59).

**Example:**

This example retrieves the current second from the user's system:

```
//Create the date object
myDate = new Date();
//Retrieve the seconds
theSecond = myDate.getSeconds();
//Display the seconds
trace(theSecond);
```

***getTime()*** **Availability:** Flash Player 5

**Generic Template:** *Date*.getTime();

**Parameters:**

> *Date*—A user-defined Date object.

**Description:**

This method returns the number of milliseconds that have elapsed in universal time, from midnight January 1, 1970.

**Example:**

This example retrieves the current number of milliseconds since midnight UTC on January 1, 1970, from the user's system:

```
//Create the date object
myDate = new Date();
//Retrieve the information
theTime = myDate.getTime();
//Display the information
trace(theTime);
```

*getTimezoneOffset( )*    **Availability:** Flash Player 5

**Generic Template:** *Date*.getTimezoneOffset();

**Parameters:**

> *Date*—A user-defined Date object.

**Description:**

This method returns the difference, in minutes, between the operating system's local time and universal time.

**Example:**

This example retrieves the current time zone offset from the user's system:

```
//Create the date object
myDate = new Date();
//Retrieve the information
theTimeOffset = myDate.getTimezoneOffset();
//Display the information
trace(theTimeOffset);
```

*getUTCDate( )*    **Availability:** Flash Player 5

**Generic Template:** *Date*.getUTCDate();

**Parameters:**

> *Date*—A user-defined Date object.

**Description:**

This method returns a specific day in the month, according to universal time in the form of an integer ranging from 1 to 31.

**Example:**

This example retrieves the current UTC date from the user's system:

```
//Create the date object
myDate = new Date();
//Retrieve the information
theUTCDate = myDate.getUTCDate();
//Display the information
trace(theUTCDate);
```

***getUTCDay( )***     **Availability:** Flash Player 5

**Generic Template:** *Date*.getUTCDay();

**Parameters:**

>   *Date*—A user-defined Date object.

**Description:**

This method returns the day of the week, according to universal time in the form of an integer ranging from 0 to 6.

**Example:**

This example retrieves the current UTC day from the user's system:

```
//Create the date object
myDate = new Date();
//Retrieve the information
theUTCDay = myDate.getUTCDay();
//Display the information
trace(theUTCDay);
```

***getUTCFullYear( )***     **Availability:** Flash Player 5

**Generic Template:** *Date*.getUTCFullYear();

**Parameters:**

>   *Date*—A user-defined Date object.

**Description:**

This method returns the four-digit year, according to universal time.

**Example:**

This example retrieves the current UTC full year from the user's system:

```
//Create the date object
myDate = new Date();
//Retrieve the information
theUTCFullYear = myDate.getUTCFullYear();
//Display the information
trace(theUTCFullYear);
```

A

*getUTCHours()*    **Availability:** Flash Player 5

**Generic Template:** *Date*.getUTCHours();

**Parameters:**

> *Date*—A user-defined Date object.

## Description:

This method returns the hours, according to universal time in the form of an integer ranging from 0 to 23.

**Example:**

This example retrieves the current UTC hour from the user's system:

```
//Create the date object
myDate = new Date();
//Retrieve the information
theUTCHour = myDate.getUTCHours() ;
//Display the information
trace(theUTCHour);
```

*getUTCMilliseconds()*    **Availability:** Flash Player 5

**Generic Template:** *Date*.getUTCMilliseconds();

**Parameters:**

> *Date*—A user-defined Date object.

## Description:

This method returns the milliseconds, according to universal time in the form of an integer ranging from 0 to 999.

**Example:**

This example retrieves the current UTC milliseconds from the user's system:

```
//Create the date object
myDate = new Date();
//Retrieve the information
theUTCMillisecond = myDate.getUTCMilliseconds();
//Display the information
trace(theUTCMillisecond);
```

***getUTCMinutes( )***    **Availability:** Flash Player 5

**Generic Template:** `Date.getUTCMinutes();`

**Parameters:**

> `Date`—A user-defined `Date` object.

**Description:**

This method returns the minutes, according to universal time in the form of an integer ranging from 0 to 59.

**Example:**

This example retrieves the current UTC minute from the user's system:

```
//Create the date object
myDate = new Date();
//Retrieve the information
theUTCMinute = myDate.getUTCMinutes();
//Display the information
trace(theUTCMinute);
```

***getUTCMonth( )***    **Availability:** Flash Player 5

**Generic Template:** `Date.getUTCMonth();`

**Parameters:**

> `Date`—A user-defined `Date` object.

**Description:**

This method returns the month, according to universal time in the form of an integer ranging from 0 to 11.

**Example:**

This example retrieves the current UTC month from the user's system:

```
//Create the date object
myDate = new Date();
//Retrieve the information
theUTCMonth  = myDate.getUTCMonth();
//Display the information
trace(theUTCMonth );
```

*getUTCSeconds( )*    **Availability:** Flash Player 5

**Generic Template:** `Date.getUTCSeconds();`

**Parameters:**

> `Date`—A user-defined `Date` object.

**Description:**

This method gets the seconds from a Date object in the form of an integer ranging from 0 to 59.

**Example:**

This example retrieves the current UTC second from the user's system:

```
//Create the date object
myDate = new Date();
//Retrieve the information
theUTCSeconds  = myDate.getUTCSeconds();
//Display the information
trace(theUTCSeconds );
```

*getYear( )*    **Availability:** Flash Player 5

**Generic Template:** `Date.getYear()   ;`

**Parameters:**

> `Date`—A user-defined `Date` object.

**Description:**

This method returns the full local year minus 1900 (in other words, the year 1998 would appear as 98).

**Example:**

This example retrieves the current year from the user's system:

```
//Create the date object
myDate = new Date();
//Retrieve the information
theYear  = myDate.getYear();
//Display the information
trace(theYear);
```

## set Methods
### *setDate( )*    **Availability:** Flash Player 5

**Generic Template:** *Date.* setDate *(value)* ;

**Parameters:**

> *Date*—A user-defined Date object.

> *value*—A number between 1 and 31 for specifying the day of the month.

**Description:**

This method sets the date of a Date object.

**Example:**

This example sets the date of the Date object:

```
myDate = new Date();
mySetDate = myDate.setDate(12);
```

### *setFullYear( )*    **Availability:** Flash Player 5

**Generic Template:** *Date.* setFullYear *(year [, month [, date]])* ;

**Parameters:**

> *Date*—A user-defined Date object.

> *year*—The year you would like to set.

> *month*—The month you would like to set (0–11).

> *date*—The date you would like to set.

**Description:**

This method sets the full year of a Date object.

**Example:**

This example sets the year of a Date object:

```
myDate = new Date();
mySetFullYear = myDate.setFullYear(2002);
```

### *setHours( )*    **Availability:** Flash Player 5

**Generic Template:** *Date.* setHours *(value)* ;

**Parameters:**

> *Date*—A user-defined Date object.

> *value*—The hour to which you want to set the Date object.

**Returns:**

An integer representing the new time in milliseconds.

**Description:**

This method sets the hour of a Date object.

**Example:**

This example sets the hour of a Date object:

```
myDate = new Date();
mySetHour = myDate.setHours(10);
```

*setMilliseconds()*    **Availability:** Flash Player 5

**Generic Template:** *Date*.setMilliseconds*(value)*;

**Parameters:**

> *Date*—A user-defined Date object.
>
> *value*—The millisecond to which you want to set the Date object.

**Returns:**

An integer representing the new time in milliseconds.

**Description:**

This method sets the millisecond of a Date object.

**Example:**

This example sets the millisecond of a Date object:

```
myDate = new Date();
mySetMilliseconds = myDate.setMilliseconds(30);
```

*setMinutes()*    **Availability:** Flash Player 5

**Generic Template:** *Date*.setMinutes*(value)*;

**Parameters:**

> *Date*—A user-defined Date object.
>
> *value*—The minute to which you want to set the Date object.

**Returns:**

An integer representing the new time in milliseconds.

**Description:**

This method sets the minute of a Date object.

**Example:**

This example sets the minute of a Date object:

```
myDate = new Date();
mySetMinutes = myDate.setMinutes(30);
```

***setMonth( )***    **Availability:** Flash Player 5

**Generic Template:** *Date*.setMonth*(value)*;

**Parameters:**

>    *Date*—A user-defined Date object.

>    *value*—The month you want to set the Date object to (0–11).

**Returns:**

An integer representing the new time in milliseconds.

**Description:**

This method sets the month of a Date object.

**Example:**

This example sets the month of a Date object to January:

```
myDate = new Date();
mySetMonth = myDate.setMonth(0);
```

***setSeconds( )***    **Availability:** Flash Player 5

**Generic Template:** *Date*.setSeconds*(value)*;

**Parameters:**

>    *Date*—A user-defined Date object.

>    *value*—The second to which you want to set the Date object.

**Returns:**

An integer representing the new time in milliseconds.

**Description:**

This method sets the second of a Date object.

A

**Example:**

This example sets the second of a Date object:

```
myDate = new Date();
mySetSeconds = myDate.setSeconds(30);
```

***setTime( )***    **Availability:** Flash Player 5

**Generic Template:** *Date.*setTime*(value)*;

**Parameters:**

> *Date*—A user-defined Date object.
>
> *value*—The time, in milliseconds, to which you want to set the Date object (0 is midnight January 1, 1970).

**Returns:**

An integer representing the new time in milliseconds.

**Description:**

This method sets the time, in milliseconds, of a Date object.

**Example:**

This example sets the time of a Date object:

```
myDate = new Date();
mySetTime = myDate.setTime(45);
```

***setUTCDate( )***    **Availability:** Flash Player 5

**Generic Template:** *Date.*setUTCDate*(value)*;

**Parameters:**

> *Date*—A user-defined Date object.
>
> *value*—The date to which you want to set the Date object (1–31).

**Returns:**

An integer representing the new time in milliseconds.

**Description:**

This method sets the UTC date of a Date object.

**Example:**

This example sets the UTC date of a Date object:

```
myDate = new Date();
mySetUTCDate = myDate.setUTCDate(2);
```

### *setUTCFullYear()*    **Availability:** Flash Player 5

**Generic Template:** *Date.*setFullYear*(year [, month [, date]])*;

**Parameters:**

> *Date*—A user-defined Date object.
>
> *year*—The year you would like to set.
>
> *month*—The month you would like to set (0–11).
>
> *date*—The date you would like to set.

**Returns:**

An integer representing the new time in milliseconds.

**Description:**

This method sets the UTC date of a Date object.

**Example:**

This example sets the UTC date of a Date object:

```
myDate = new Date();
mySetUTCFullYear = myDate.setUTCFullYear(2002);
```

### *setUTCHours()*    **Availability:** Flash Player 5

**Generic Template:** *Date.*setUTCHours *(hour[, minute [, second [, millisecond]]])*

**Parameters:**

> *Date*—A user-defined Date object.
>
> *hour*—The hour to which you want to set the Date object.
>
> *minute*—The minute to which you want to set the Date object.
>
> *second*—The second to which you want to set the Date object.
>
> *millisecond*—The millisecond to which you want to set the Date object.

**Returns:**

An integer representing the new time in milliseconds.

**Description:**

This method sets the UTC hour of a Date object.

**Example:**

This example sets the UTC hour of a `Date` object:

```
myDate = new Date();
mySetUTCHours = myDate.setUTCHours(2);
```

### *setUTCMilliseconds( )*    **Availability:** Flash Player 5

**Generic Template:** `Date.setUTCMilliseconds(value);`

**Parameters:**

> *Date*—A user-defined `Date` object.
>
> *Value*—The number of milliseconds to which you want to set the `Date` object.

**Returns:**

An integer representing the new time in milliseconds.

**Description:**

This method sets the UTC milliseconds of a `Date` object.

**Example:**

This example sets the UTC millisecond of a `Date` object:

```
myDate = new Date();
mySetUTCMilliseconds = myDate.setUTCMilliseconds(12);
```

### *setUTCMinutes( )*    **Availability:** Flash Player 5

**Generic Template:** `Date.setUTCMinutes(minute [, second [, millisecond]])`

**Parameters:**

> *Date*—A user-defined `Date` object.
>
> *minute*—The minute to which you want to set the `Date` object.
>
> *second*—The second to which you want to set the `Date` object.
>
> *millisecond*—The millisecond to which you want to set the `Date` object.

**Returns:**

An integer representing the new time in milliseconds.

**Description:**

This method sets the UTC minute of a `Date` object.

**Example:**

This example sets the UTC minute of the Date object:

```
myDate = new Date();
mySetUTCMinutes = myDate.setUTCMinutes(12);
```

***setUTCMonth( )***    **Availability:** Flash Player 5

**Generic Template:** *Date.*setUTCMonth*(month [, date])*

**Parameters:**

> *Date*—A user-defined Date object.
>
> *month*—The month to which you want to set the Date object.
>
> *date*—The date to which you want to set the Date object.

**Returns:**

An integer representing the new time in milliseconds.

**Description:**

This method sets the UTC month of a Date object.

**Example:**

This example sets the UTC month of a Date object:

```
myDate = new Date();
mySetUTCMonth = myDate.setUTCMonth(10);
```

***setUTCSeconds( )***    **Availability:** Flash Player 5

**Generic Template:** *Date.*setUTCSeconds*(second [, millisecond])*

**Parameters:**

> *Date*—A user-defined Date object.
>
> *second*—The second to which you want to set the Date object.
>
> *millisecond*—The millisecond to which you want to set the Date object.

**Returns:**

An integer representing the new time in milliseconds.

**Description:**

This method sets the UTC second of a Date object.

A

**Example:**

This example sets the UTC second of a Date object:

```
myDate = new Date();
mySetUTCSeconds = myDate.setUTCSeconds(12);
```

*setYear()*   **Availability:** Flash Player 5

**Generic Template:** *Date.setYear(value)*

**Parameters:**

> *Date*—A user-defined Date object.
>
> *value*—The year to which you would like to set your Date object. Note that if this is a number between 0 and 99, the interpreter sets the date with the prefix "19" for 1900 instead of "20" for 2000.

**Returns:**

An integer representing the new time in milliseconds.

**Description:**

This method sets the year of a Date object.

**Example:**

This example sets the year of a Date object:

```
myDate = new Date();
mySetYear = myDate.setYear(2002);
```

## Error

## new Error Constructor
**Availability:** Flash Player 7

**Generic Template:** new Error(*message*);

**Parameters:**

> *message*—A string literal declaring the error message to be sent.

**Description:**

This constructor creates an Error object with or without a message.

**Example:**

This example creates a new Error object instance:

```
var myError:Error = new Error();
```

## Methods

**toString**    **Availability:** Flash Player 7

**Generic Template:** `error.toString();`

**Parameters:** None

**Returns:**

A string.

**Description:**

This method converts the message property of the Error object to a string. The default value is "Error".

**Example:**

This example sends the string output of the `toString()` method to the output panel:

```
var myError:Error = new Error("error 1");
trace(myError.toString());
//output: error 1
```

## Properties

**message**    **Availability:** Flash Player 7

**Generic Template:** `error.message;`

**Parameters:** None

**Description:**

This property declares the message to be sent out either to a `catch` block or to the output panel.

**Example:**

This example uses the `throw` action to send the error to the output panel:

```
var myError:Error = new Error();
myError.message = "error 1";
throw myError;
//output: error 1
```

A

**name    Availability:** Flash Player 7

**Generic Template:** `error.name;`

**Parameters:** None

**Description:**

This property declares the name of the Error object instance.  By default, the value is "Error".

**Example:**

This example creates a new Error object instance, and sends its default name to the output panel:

```
var myError:Error = new Error("error 1");
trace(myError.name);
//output: Error
```

## Function

**Methods**
**apply    Availability:** Flash Player 6

**Generic Template:** `function.apply(object, arguments);`

**Parameters:**

> *object*—The object to which the function is being applied.

> *arguments*—An array of elements that are used as parameters.

**Returns:**

Any value specified by the function itself.

**Description:**

This method allows any function or method in ActionScript to be called.

**Example:**

This example creates a function, and then calls it using the `apply` method:

```
function addNums(num1:Number, num2:Number):Void{
    trace(num1+num2);
}
//call the function using apply
addNums.apply(null,[4,5]);
//output: 9
```

**call**   **Availability:** Flash Player 6

**Generic Template:** `function.call(object, arguments);`

**Parameters:**

*object*—The object to which the function is being applied.

*arguments*—An array of elements that are used as parameters.

**Returns:**

Nothing.

**Description:**

This method allows any methods to be called on objects that do not have the method implicitly associated with them.

**Example:**

This example shows two different ways of calling the same method:

```
trace(Math.floor(Math.PI + 7));
trace(Math.floor.call(null, Math.PI + 7));
//output: 10
//        10
```

Properties
**prototype**   **Availability:** Flash Player 5

**Generic Template:** `function.prototype;`

**Parameters:** None

**Description:**

This property allows the addition of properties and methods to an already constructed object by adding them to the prototype chain.

**Example:**

This example creates a class, and then adds a property to it after it has been created:

```
function MyClass(){
    //nothing
}
//add a property to the class
MyClass.prototype.myVar = 10;
//create an instance of the object
sample = new MyClass();
trace(sample.myVar);
//output: 10
```

## Math

### Methods
All methods of the Math object have the same generic template. Therefore, they all are discussed in this section.

**Availability:** Flash Player 5

**Generic Template:** `Math.method(number);`

**Returns:**

These methods return a number.

**Parameters:**

> *number*—Any viable numeric value.
>
> *method*—Each method in the Math object performs its own unique mathematical calculation. Here are the methods and the calculations they perform:
>
> > abs(*num*)—Evaluates and returns an absolute value of *num*. Here's an example:
> >
> > ```
> > trace(Math.abs(-10));
> > //output: 10
> > ```
> >
> > acos(*num*)—Evaluates and returns the arccosine of *num* in radians. Here's an example:
> >
> > ```
> > trace(Math.acos(1));
> > //output: 0
> > ```
> >
> > asin(*num*)—Evaluates and returns the arcsine of *num* in radians. Here's an example:
> >
> > ```
> > trace(Math.asin(1));
> > //output: 1.5707963267949
> > ```
> >
> > atan(*num*)—Evaluates and returns the arctangent of *num* (the value returned is between negative pi divided by two and pi divided by two). Here's an example:
> >
> > ```
> > trace(Math.atan(1));
> > //output: 0.785398163397448
> > ```
> >
> > atan2(*numA,numB*)—Evaluates and returns the arctangent of *numA/numB*, where *numA* is the opposite side of a right triangle and *numB* is the adjacent side. Here's an example:
> >
> > ```
> > trace(Math.atan2(1,2));
> > //output: 0.463647609000806
> > ```
> >
> > ceil(*num*)—Evaluates and returns the greatest whole number greater than or equal to *num*. Here's an example:
> >
> > ```
> > trace(Math.ceil(5.2));
> > //output: 6
> > ```

cos*(num)*—Evaluates and returns the cosine of angle *num*, where *num* is specified in radians and the result is a floating-point number between –1 and 1. Here's an example:

```
trace(Math.cos(1));
//output: 0.54030230586814
```

exp*(num)*—Evaluates and returns the value of the base of the natural logarithm to the power of *num*. Here's an example:

```
trace(Math.exp(1));
//output: 2.71828182845905
```

floor*(num)*—Evaluates and returns the nearest whole number that is less than or equal to *num*. Here's an example:

```
trace(Math.floor(2.4));
//output: 2
```

log*(num)*—Evaluates and returns the natural logarithm of *num*. Here's an example:

```
trace(Math.log(10));
//output: 2.30258509299405
```

max*(numA, numB)*—Evaluates and returns the larger number between *numA* and *numB*. Here's an example:

```
trace(Math.max(10,15));
//output: 15
```

min*(numA, numB)*—Evaluates and returns the smaller number between *numA* and *numb*. Here's an example:

```
trace(Math.min(10,15));
//output: 10
```

pow*(numA, numB)*—Evaluates and returns *numA* to the power of *numB*. Here's an example:

```
trace(Math.pow(2,4));
//output: 16
```

random*()*—Evaluates and returns any floating point number between (0 and 1). Here's an example:

```
trace(Math.random());
//output: a random number between 0 and 1
```

round*(num)*—Evaluates and returns *num* rounded up or down to the nearest whole number. Here's an example:

```
trace(Math.round(2.4));
//output: 2
```

sin*(num)*—Evaluates and returns the sine of *num* in radians. Here's an example:

```
trace(Math.sin(1));
//output: 0.841470984807897
```

sqrt*(num)*—Evaluates and returns the square root of *num*. Here's an example:

```
trace(Math.sqrt(16));
//output: 4
```

tan*(num)*—Evaluates and returns the tangent of *num* in radians. Here's an example:

```
trace(Math.tan(1));
//output: 1.5574077246549
```

## Constants

All Math constants have the same generic template and are discussed in this section.

**Availability:** Flash Player 5

**Generic Template:** Math.*constant*

**Parameters:**

*constant*—A numerical value that remains constant and can be called by using the Math object. Here are the Math constants:

Math.E—This constant is the base of natural logarithms, expressed as e, and is approximately equal to 2.71828.

Math.LN2—This constant is the natural logarithm of 2, expressed as log2, and is approximately equal to 0.69314718055994528623.

Math.LN10—This constant is the natural logarithm of 10, expressed as log10, and is approximately equal to 2.3025850929940459011.

Math.LOG2E—This constant is the base-2 logarithm of Math.E, expressed as log2, and is approximately equal to 1.442695040888963387.

Math.LOG10E—This constant is the base-10 logarithm of Math.E, expressed as log10, and is approximately equal to 0.43429448190325181667.

Math.PI—This constant is the ratio of the circumference of a circle to its diameter (or half of its radius), expressed as pi. It's approximately equal to 3.14159265358979.

Math.SQRT1_2—This constant is the reciprocal of the square root of one half and is approximately equal to 0.707106781186.

Math.SQRT2—This constant is the square root of 2 and is approximately equal to 1.414213562373.

## Number

### new Number Constructor
**Availability:** Flash Player 5

**Generic Template:** new Object(*value*);

**Parameters:**

> *value*—Any numerical value.

**Description:**

This constructor creates a Number instance.

**Example:**

This example creates a new Number:

```
myNum = new Number(15);
```

### Methods
**toString    Availability:** Flash Player 5

**Generic Template:** number.toString();

**Parameters:** None

**Returns:**

A string.

**Description:**

This method converts the value of the Number instance to a string.

**Example:**

This example sends the string output of the toString() method to the output panel:

```
var myNum:Number = new Number(15);
trace(myNum.toString());
//output: 15
```

**valueOf    Availability:** Flash Player 5

**Generic Template:** number.valueOf();

**Parameters:** None

A

**Returns:**

A number.

**Description:**

This method returns the numerical value of the Number instance it is being called on.

**Example:**

This example sends the output of the valueOf() method to the output panel:

```
var myNum:Number = new Number(15);
trace(myNum.valueOf());
//output: 15
```

### Properties
All the Number properties have the same layout so they are combined into this section.

**Availability:** Flash Player 5

**Generic Layout:** number.constant

**Parameters:**

*constant*—There are five different values for this parameter:

- MAX_VALUE—The largest possible number (IEEE-754), which is approximately 1.79E+308.

- MIN_VALUE—The smallest possible positive number (IEEE-754), which is approximately 5e-324.

- NaN—Not a number.

- NEGATIVE_INFINITY—A constant representation of negative infinity.

- POSITIVE_INFINITY—A constant representation of positive infinity.

## Object

### new Object Constructor
**Availability:** Flash Player 5

**Generic Template:** new Object(*value*);

**Parameters:**

> *value*—Any viable expression that is converted to an object. If this is left blank, an empty object is created.

**Description:**

This constructor creates an Object object.

**Example:**

This example creates a new object:

```
myObj = new Object();
```

## Methods
**AddProperty    Availability:** Flash Player 6

**Generic Template:** myObject.addProperty(*prop*, *get*, *set*);

**Parameters:**

> *prop*—A reference to the property being created.
>
> *get*—This is a function that gets the value of *prop*.
>
> *set*—This is a function that sets the value of *prop*. If it is set to null, *prop* is considered read-only.

**Returns:**

This method returns true if *prop* was created; otherwise, it returns false.

**Description:**

This method creates a GnS property (get and set). When the interpreter reaches a GnS property, it calls the get function, and the function's return value becomes a value of *prop*. When the interpreter writes a GnS property, it calls the set function and passes it the new value as a constraint. When the property is written, it overwrites any prior version of itself.

When the get function is called, it retrieves any type of data, even if the data does not match that of the previous *prop*.

The set function takes the data from the get function and sets it to prop, even if it means overwriting the existing data.

**Example:**

This example shows the Object.addProperty method in use:

```
scrollBox.addProperty("scroll", scrollBox.getScroll, scrollBox.setScroll);
scrollBox.addProperty("maxscroll", scrollBox.getMaxScroll, null);
```

**registerClass    Availability:** Flash Player 6

**Generic Template:** Object.registerClass(*symbol*, *class*);

**Parameters:**

> *symbol*—A reference to the identifier of the movie clip or ActionScript class.
>
> *class*—This is a reference to a constructor. To unregister the symbol, use `null`.

**Returns:**

This method returns `true` if the class registration was successful; it returns `false` otherwise.

**Description:**

This method associates an ActionScript class with a movie clip symbol. If the symbol is nonexistent, the interpreter creates a string identifier instead and links it to the class.

If the movie is on the timeline, it is registered to the new class instead of the `MovieClip` class. This happens to the movie clip if it is placed manually on the stage or with the `attachMovie` action. Also, if the movie clip identified uses the `duplicateMovieClip` action, this movie clip is placed in the class instead of the `MovieClip` class.

If the class is set to `null`, the `registerClass` method removes any remaining ActionScript definitions of the class, but the movies within the class remain intact.

Finally, if a movie clip is already in a class when it is invoked, the previous class is overwritten.

**Example:**

This example registers the `ballClass` class with the ball symbol:

```
Object.registerClass("ball" ,ballClass);
```

**toString    Availability:** Flash Player 5

**Generic Template:** *myObject*.toString();

**Parameters:**

> *myObject*—A user-defined object.

**Description:**

This method converts an object to a string, and then returns that string.

**Example:**

This example tests the `toString` method:

```
var myObj = new Object;
trace (typeof myObj);
//output: object
trace(typeof myObj.toString());
//output: string
```

**unwatch**  **Availability:** Flash Player 6

**Generic Template:** *myObject*.unwatch(*prop*);

**Parameters:**

> *myObject*—A user-defined object.
>
> *prop*—Refers to the property of the object that should no longer be watched.

**Returns:**

This method returns `true` if the watch was successfully removed; it returns `false` otherwise.

**Description:**

This method removes a watchpoint created by a `watch` method from an object.

**Example:**

This example will `unwatch` the property "value" in the `CheckBox` component:

```
myObj.unwatch("myProp");
```

**valueOf**  **Availability:** Flash Player 5
**Generic Template:** *myObject*.valueOf();

**Parameters:**

> *myObject*—A user-defined object.

**Description:**

This method returns a primitive value of an object unless the object does not contain one, in which case it returns the object itself.

**Example:**

This example sets the value of an object to the number 4 and traces the value of that new object:

```
var myObj = new Object(4);
trace (myObj.valueOf());
//output: 4
```

**watch**  **Availability:** Flash Player 6
**Generic Template:** *myObject*.watch(*prop*, *callback*, *data*);

**Returns:**

This method returns `true` if the watchpoint was created successfully; it returns `false` otherwise.

**Parameters:**

> *myObject*—A user-defined object.
>
> *prop*—A reference to the object property to watch.
>
> *callback*—This constraint is a function that is invoked when the watched property changes. The callback form is callback(*prop*, *oldValue*, *newValue*, *data*).
>
> *data*—An optional piece of ActionScript data that is sent to the callback method. If the data parameter is not present, callback receives an undefined value.

**Description:**

This method defines a callback function that is invoked when a property of an ActionScript object has changed.

Watchpoints are assigned to properties to "keep an eye on them" if *oldValue* and *newValue* do not match. If the property is removed, the watchpoint is not. The watchpoint must be cleared with an unwatch method. Only one watchpoint per property can be assigned.

Most ActionScript properties cannot be watched, including _x, _alpha, _height, and so on. This is because they are GnS properties already.

**Example:**

This example uses the RadioButton component to set and watch a defined property:

```
//Now make a constructor for and define the RadioButton class
function RadioButton() {
//then set the watch method
    this.watch ('value', function (id, oldval, newval)){
    }
}
```

**Properties**
**__proto__    Availability:** Flash Player 5

**Generic Template:** myObject.__proto__

**Parameters:** None

**Description:**

This property is a reference to the prototype property of the constructor function that creates an Object object. The __proto__ property is assigned automatically to all objects when they are created. The interpreter uses __proto__ to access the prototype property to find out what properties and methods can be inherited from the class.

**Example:**

In this example, the __proto__ property is used to declare the property "name":

```
//Create the class
function myObj (){
    this.__proto__.name="Ball";
}
//Now create a new object from the myObj
theObj = new myObj();
//Now trace the name of the new object you just created
trace(theObj.name);
```

## String

### new String Constructor

**Availability:** Flash Player 5

**Generic Template:** new String(*value*);

**Parameters:**

    *value*—A string literal representing the value of the instance of the String being created.

**Description:**

This constructor creates a String object instance.

**Example:**

This example creates a new String instance:

```
myString = new String("my string");
```

**Methods**
**charAt**  **Availability:** Flash Player 5

**Generic Template:** *string*.charAt(index);

**Parameters:**

    *index*—A number representing which character to choose.

**Returns:**

This method returns the character at the index point.

**Description:**

This method returns the character at any given position within a string including spaces. Keep in mind, the first letter of a string is at index zero, not one.

**Example:**

This example creates a string, and then grabs the fourth character in the string:

```
var myString:String = new String("sample");
trace(myString.charAt(3));
//output: p
```

**charCodeAt**    **Availability:** Flash Player 5
**Generic Template:** *string*.charCodeAt(index);

**Parameters:**

> *index*—A number representing which character to choose.

**Returns:**

This is an integer representing the character at point *index*.

**Description:**

This method returns the 16-bit equivalent to the character at point index. Keep in mind, the first letter of a string is at index zero, not one.

**Example:**

This example creates a string, and then grabs code for the fourth character in the string:

```
var myString:String = new String("sample");
trace(myString.charCodeAt(3));
//output: 112
```

**concat**    **Availability:** Flash Player 5

**Generic Template:** *string*.concat(values);

**Parameters:**

> *values*—The string elements to be added to the original string, separated by commas.

**Returns:**

A string comprised of the original string and the values passed through the method.

**Description:**

This method returns the original string plus the values passed to it without affecting the original string.

**Example:**

This example adds a string to another string, and sends the combination to the output panel:

```
var myString:String = new String("sample");
trace(myString.concat(" test"));
//output: sample test
```

**fromCharCode    Availability:** Flash Player 5

**Generic Template:** *String*.fromCharCode(code);

**Parameters:**

    *code*—A decimal integer representing an ASCII character.

**Returns:**

A character or group of characters as a string.

**Description:**

This method returns a character or group of characters based on numbers passed to it. It must called on the object class, and not an instance of the object.

**Example:**

This example sends a flower made of characters to the output panel:

```
trace(String.fromCharCode(64,45,45,62,45,45,45,45));
//output: @-->----
```

**indexOf    Availability:** Flash Player 5

**Generic Template:** *string*.indexOf(search, startIndex);

**Parameters:**

    *search*—A string literal that is being searched for within the string.

    *startIndex*—An optional starting point for the search.

**Returns:**

A number representing the first character that matches the string.

**Description:**

This method returns a number representing the index point of the first match in the string.

**Example:**

This example looks for the first letter s in a word:

```
var myString:String = new String("Mississippi");
trace(myString.indexOf("s"));
//output: 2
```

**lastIndexOf**    **Availability:** Flash Player 5

**Generic Template:** *string*.lastIndexOf(search, startIndex);

**Parameters:**

  *search*—A string literal that is being searched for within the string.

  *startIndex*—An optional starting point for the search.

**Returns:**

A number representing the last character that matches the string.

**Description:**

This method returns a number representing the index point of the last match in the string.

**Example:**

This example looks for the last letter s in a word:

```
var myString:String = new String("Mississippi");
trace(myString.lastIndexOf("s"));
//output: 6
```

**slice**    **Availability:** Flash Player 5

**Generic Template:** *string*.slice(start, end);

**Parameters:**

  *start*—A starting index point.

  *end*—An ending index point; if not included, it defaults to string.length.

**Returns:**

A string of what was captured.

**Description:**

This method returns a substring of text starting at the start index, and ending with the end point -1; the original string is not affected.

**Example:**

This example extracts a section of a string:

```
var myString:String = new String("Mississippi");
trace(myString.slice(6,9));
//output: sip
```

**split    Availability:** Flash Player 5

**Generic Template:** *string*.split(character, limit);

**Parameters:**

> *character*—A string literal declaring what to separate the string by.
>
> *limit*—An optional constraint declaring the maximum allowable amount of elements that can placed in the array.

**Returns:**

An array of strings.

**Description:**

This method returns an array of strings that have been pulled out individually based on the *character* constraint.

**Example:**

This example extracts all the words out of a sentence using the space as a separator:

```
var myString:String = new String("See John run");
trace(myString.split(" "));
//output: See,John,run
```

**substr    Availability:** Flash Player 5

**Generic Template:** *string*.substr(start, length);

**Parameters:**

> *start*—A number representing the starting index.
>
> *length*—An optional parameter declaring the amount of characters to remove; if left blank, it goes to the end of the string.

**Returns:**

A string.

**Description:**

This method returns a substring of characters ranging from *start* to *start* + *length*; it does not alter the original string.

**Example:**

This example captures the first three characters in a string, and sends them to the output panel:

```
var myString:String = new String("sample");
trace(myString.substr(0,3));
//output: sam
```

*substring*    **Availability:** Flash Player 5

**Generic Template:** *string*.substr(start, end);

**Parameters:**

>    *start*—A number representing the starting index.

>    *end*—An optional parameter declaring the end index; if left blank, it goes to the end of the string.

**Returns:**

A string.

**Description:**

This method returns a substring of characters ranging from *start* to *end*; it does not alter the original string.

**Example:**

This example captures the second character all the way to the end of the string and sends it to the output panel:

```
var myString:String = new String("sample");
trace(myString.substring(1));
//output: ample
```

**toLowerCase**    **Availability:** Flash Player 5

**Generic Template:** *string*.toLowerCase();

**Parameters:** None

**Returns:**

A string.

**Description:**

This method returns the string with all lowercase characters without altering the original string.

**Example:**

This example sends a string to the output panel in all lowercase characters:

```
var myString:String = new String("SaMpLe");
trace(myString.toLowerCase());
//output: sample
```

**toUpperCase    Availability:** Flash Player 5

**Generic Template:** *string*.toUpperCase();

**Parameters:** None

**Returns:**

A string.

**Description:**

This method returns the string with all uppercase characters without altering the original string.

**Example:**

This example sends a string to the output panel in all uppercase characters:

```
var myString:String = new String("SaMpLe");
trace(myString.toUpperCase());
//output: SAMPLE
```

Properties
**length    Availability:** Flash Player 5

**Generic Template:** *string*.length;

**Parameters:** None

**Description:**

This property returns the number of characters in a string.

**Example:**

This example sends the number of characters in a string to the output panel:

```
var myString:String = new String("sample");
trace(myString.length);
//output: 6
```

A

# Index

## Symbols

## A

*How can we make this index more useful? Email us at indexes@samspublishing.com*

*How can we make this index more useful? Email us at indexes@sampspublishing.com*

*How can we make this index more useful? Email us at indexes@samspublishing.com*

# Your Guide
# to Computer
# Technology

## www.informit.com